A New Buddhist Movement 1

THE COMPLETE WORKS OF SANGHARAKSHITA
include all his previously published work, as well as talks,
seminars, and writings published here for the first time. The
collection represents the definitive edition of his life's work as
Buddhist writer and teacher. For further details, including the
contents of each volume, please turn to the 'Guide' on pp. 799–807.

COMPLETE WORKS II **THE WEST**

Sangharakshita
A New Buddhist
Movement 1

EDITED BY PABODHANA

Windhorse Publications
38 Newmarket Road
Cambridge CB5 8DT

info@windhorsepublications.com
www.windhorsepublications.com

Cover design by Dhammarati
Cover images: Front: Aloka sculpting the Buddha rupa,
London Buddhist Centre, 1976. Photo: Vajradipa
Back flap: *Liberated Zone*, Golgonooza Community,
London Buddhist Centre, 1978. Photo: Siddhiratna
Both images courtesy of Urgyen Sangharakshita Trust

Typesetting and layout Tarajyoti
Printed by Bell & Bain Ltd, Glasgow

British Library Cataloguing in Publication Data:
A catalogue record for this book is
available from the British Library.

ISBN 978-1-915342-16-4 (paperback)
ISBN 978-1-915342-15-7 (hardback)

CONTENTS

LIST OF IMAGES

EDITORIAL NOTE

This is the first of two volumes of Sangharakshita's *Complete Works* entitled 'A New Buddhist Movement'. It contains talks, interviews, and articles written or spoken by Sangharakshita between 1965 and 2009. Most of the material has been published previously either in the form of books and pamphlets or as magazine and journal articles, and this has provided the basis for the way the volume is organized. Books occupy part 1, interviews and magazine articles make up part 2, and previously unpublished talks are presented in part 3.

As far as possible, we have set out the material chronologically, following the approach adopted also for *Complete Works* volume 12. The aim has been to allow the material to 'tell a story' in its own way, as Vidyadevi puts it in her preface to that volume, and for this reason the items have been arranged here according to their date of delivery, rather than their date of publication. *Buddhism for Today – and Tomorrow*, for example, consists of talks given in 1976 but not published for another twenty years.

Like any plan, the implementation has sometimes thrown up inconsistencies. Some of the books in Part 1 are themselves collections from different sources and different dates, and this means that our chronological sequence is not quite as smooth as could be wished. The same is true of the magazine articles in Part 2 and the talks in Part 3, where the decision to group all the pieces from a given source under a single heading sometimes interrupts our arrangement.

Ritual and Devotion in Buddhism, an early product of the Spoken Word Project,[1] takes its place in this volume based on the year in which the majority of its content was delivered, namely between 1967 and 1978. The biggest single source is a seminar on the Sevenfold Puja given in 1978, providing most of chapters 5 and 7–12 and some of chapters 3 and 4, while chapters 1 and 2 of the book are drawn mainly from lectures given in 1967 and 1968 respectively. A large part of chapter 13 comes from a lecture given in 1972 and the remainder of the material in *Ritual and Devotion* comprises short extracts from other seminars, mostly from the 1980s. The seminar material was rendered into continuous prose from the original dialogue format and rearranged to make it more easily readable.

Apart from the talks in Part 3, which were transcribed posthumously, the edited versions of everything in this volume of the *Complete Works* were approved by Sangharakshita. In some cases, Sangharakshita has also written short introductions, such as to the pieces when they were published in an anthology of writings entitled *The Priceless Jewel* in 1993, and some extraneous information has also been relocated from the main text into endnotes. In both cases, Sangharakshita's notes and comments have been appended with (S).

All the books and articles in this volume trace the development of Sangharakshita's thinking during the years when the Movement he founded was starting to put down roots, especially in Britain. During this period, Sangharakshita was the head of what was known as the Western Buddhist Order (WBO) and in the original texts, references to the WBO, the Trailokya Bauddha Mahasangha Sahayak Gana (TBMSG), and the Friends of the Western Buddhist Order (FWBO) remain unchanged. Since 2010, the Order has been known as the Triratna Buddhist Order, while the Friends of the Western Buddhist Order (FWBO) is now known as the Triratna Buddhist Community. The Order's Indian wing, the Trailokya Bauddha Mahasangha Sahayak Gana (TBMSG) became the Triratna Bauddha Mahasangha Sahayak Gana at the same time. The endnotes therefore refer only to the Triratna Buddhist Order, the Triratna Bauddha Mahasangha Sahayak Gana, and the Triratna Buddhist Community.

Another change during this period was to the titles by which members of the Order are known. The titles *upāsaka* (masc.) and *upāsikā* (fem.) are no longer used, having been replaced by the terms *dhammacāri* (masc.) and *dhammacārinī* (fem.).

ACKNOWLEDGEMENTS

We gratefully acknowledge the work done by the editorial team at Windhorse Publications, namely, Michelle Bernard, Pasadanita, Dhammamegha, Walter Monticelli, and Utpalavajri. We are also grateful to Shantavira in his role as *Complete Works* copy editor and researcher, unearthing the dates and locations of the various talks in this volume. Thanks are also due to Kalyanasri for her proofreading, to Satyalila for indexing, to Tarajyoti and Dhammarati for their inspirational design, to Aloka for the use of his image of the *ḍākinī*, and to Śraddhāpa and Dhivan for help with the Sanskrit and Pāli references. We are grateful to the Triratna Picture Library for the use of the photographs, and to the editors of the original imprints of the books and articles that make up the volume, including Nagabodhi, Vidyadevi, Jnanasiddhi, Vishvapani, Simon Carruth, and others. Finally, we are indebted to the many transcribers of Sangharakshita's talks and seminars over the years, initially under the direction of Silabhadra, to whom this and many other volumes in the *Complete Works* series owe their existence.

Pabodhana
Loughborough
August 2023

FOREWORD

> A Buddhist does not 'represent' Buddhism. If you represent
> Buddhism, you are not a Buddhist. A Buddhist *is* Buddhism – in
> miniature.[2]

On 22 April 1908 the first English *bhikkhu* to return to England from
what was then Ceylon arrived in London on the steamship *Ava*. His
name was Ananda Metteyya and he was accompanied by what has
been called the earliest Buddhist mission to England.[3] Sangharakshita
was therefore not among the first generation of Europeans to journey
overseas in search of the Dharma, but if his generation is the second,
then I was among the third, making the journey not from England but
from my native Finland to join the order Sangharakshita founded. My
involvement with Sangharakshita's teaching has now lasted almost
fifty years and the books and articles in this volume of his *Complete
Works* span roughly the same period. They are drawn from the period
in Sangharakshita's life when, between 1965 and 2009, Buddhism was
brought more fully into contact with the non-Buddhist cultures of the
twentieth century.

Eight years after my ordination, I took part in a retreat at Il
Convento, a former Augustinian monastery in Tuscany. During those
three months Sangharakshita spoke on St Jerome, a fifth-century
translator of the Bible, hinting at his own role in translating Buddhism
into something appropriate for the twentieth century. It struck a chord

because some years earlier I had chosen to study translation. Not being much of a scholar in the classical sense, I was motivated to find out what Buddhism was all about by translating Sangharakshita's writings. I went on to translate a number of his books into my native Finnish, including one or two that appear in this volume. For me, translation and study are virtually the same thing and if, in the process, I have made Sangharakshita's work available to a Finnish readership, then so much the better.

People new to translation might consider it quite straightforward, like turning on a tap to get water, but translation also involves understanding. When you turn on your tap there can be no mistaking what comes out. Translation, on the other hand, always involves inaccuracies, often inadequacies, and sometimes mistakes, and it is far from instant. Translation is more like a journey. It starts where you are, at what's known to translators as the 'target language', and from there one travels all the way to where the text exists in its original form. This is known as the 'source' language, and it's important not to stop before you get there. In translation you need to go right to the end of your journey, and only when you have really understood the full weight of meaning are you ready to return with it. Then the whole meaning has to come all the way back to the target language with you if the translation is to be faithful to the original. When it comes to the translation not of a single book but of Buddhism itself, the journey is on a very different scale. It is the journey of a lifetime and longer. The translation of the Dharma into another culture is the work of many generations, because the true Dharma does not exist in books and cannot be translated as if it were.

But if the Dharma is not in books, then where is it? *The Taste of Freedom* gives a hint. The Dharma is vast, unfathomable, and not at all easy to know. Like the ocean, says Sangharakshita,

the Unconditioned is strange to us; the Transcendental is strange to us. It is something of which we have only heard. It is foreign to us; it is not our native element. Indeed, the Buddha himself is strange to us. He is a stranger in an ultimate sense. He comes from another world, another dimension, as it were. He stands at our door, perhaps, but we do not recognize him. Even the spiritual community is strange to us if we are not ourselves true individuals, or not spiritually committed. Thus the mighty ocean of the *Dharma-Vinaya* is strange to us.[4]

We need translation because we do not understand. We need it to turn the unfamiliar into something we can relate to. Yet faced with such strangeness, it is hardly surprising that people want to hold onto something for safety. It might be an institution or a fixed idea, but very often it's language that we cling to, grasping at the superficial, even literal, meanings with which we are already familiar. In the Finland sangha's early days, newcomers were often puzzled by the idea that things could be true, but not literally so. Practising the Sevenfold Puja, for example, did not come easily to them. The puja's 'confession' section includes the line 'standing before them with hands raised in reverence' and when Vajrabodhi, one of Finland's very first Order members, was asked in all innocence why this was recited sitting down, he decided it was time to ask Sangharakshita to produce a more straightforward version. The result was the Threefold Puja still in use today.

'It is as though the human mind has an inbuilt tendency to slip into literalism', writes Sangharakshita, 'however many warnings are given against it.' The puja is a simple example, but the problem of literalism can be present at any level of practice. To repeat words that others have given you is not in itself a problem, but to start using Buddhist words and think that makes us Buddhists is to miss the entire point of what we have set out to do on our 'translation journey'. Our goal is Awakening and, to quote Sangharakshita, 'This is not a merely theoretical or intellectual understanding, but actual insight into that to which the teaching of the truths refers. It is a liberating spiritual experience.'[5]

In recent years, the language of Buddhism has increasingly become part of the western vernacular, cropping up time and again in self-help books, on social media, and even as aphorisms on calendars. But it's often clear that precious little spiritual weight lies behind what is being said. Listening to Sangharakshita all those years ago at Il Convento was quite another matter. His teaching had weight. And not just weight, there was something beautiful and something alive behind it. It was more than mere words.

In *The Taste of Freedom* Sangharakshita approaches the idea of literalism or superficiality through what are traditionally known as the *saṃyojanas* or 'fetters'. Departing from the traditional Pāli formulation to use what he calls, 'basic – or down-to-earth – terms', he discusses 'firstly, the fetter of *habit*; secondly, the fetter of *vagueness*; and thirdly, the fetter of *superficiality*.' The 'true individual' overcomes habit by being creative, dispels vagueness with clarity, and avoids superficiality through commitment, so that when the first three fetters are broken 'one becomes a "Stream Entrant", or – to use another traditional term – an *ārya-pudgala* or "true individual."'[6] This is Sangharakshita's lesson in how to get to the heart of the theories and concepts that have come down to us in the Buddhist tradition and to make the words our own. In one way or another we need to become translators ourselves. The work of translation needs to take place within each and every one of us. In fact, the only way you can really translate Dharma is to *become* Dharma.

Sangharakshita's aphorism that 'A Buddhist *is* Buddhism in miniature' is a realistic way of describing the emergence of true individuality as against the mentality of the group, even though all these terms, individuality, true individuality, are so easy to take literally and when taken literally they become useless. Sangharakshita's aphorism bypasses all those literal interpretations and gets to the heart of the matter. Individuality must come from one's own direct spiritual experience; otherwise you are not speaking as an individual, only as a mouthpiece for something else. Your statements are then no longer spiritual statements but worldly ones. To make a spiritual statement, we need to rely upon the spirit of the teaching rather than its outward form. To do that, we need direct experience of something deeper than mere words. How can we achieve such depth? Often it comes without warning, when things go badly wrong.

Sangharakshita describes one such critical situation in a talk given on his first visit to a Buddhafield festival. He recalls the year 1956, when many hundreds of thousands of ex-Untouchable Buddhists were left without leadership following the sudden death of Dr B. R. Ambedkar. From the point of view of the Dharma it was a potentially disastrous situation, and Sangharakshita, who was at that time still in India, decided, in partnership with others, that something had to be done quickly. 'In the course of four days', says Sangharakshita, 'I addressed nearly thirty mass meetings, and I think I can say without vanity that I created a tremendous impression.' In a letter to a friend, Sangharakshita describes his spiritual experience during this period as 'most peculiar. I felt that I was not a person but an impersonal force. At one stage I was working quite literally without any thought, just as one is in *samādhi*. Also, I felt hardly any tiredness – certainly not at all what one would have expected from such a tremendous strain'.[7] In subsequent months and years, much of Sangharakshita's time was spent teaching the Dharma to these new Buddhists, moving about different parts of India to give talks and lectures to different groups and individuals. 'I am reminded of that very much today' says Sangharakshita to his Buddhafield listeners, 'because they were sitting on the floor just as you are sitting now.'[8]

In 1964, Sangharakshita took the decision to move to England at the invitation of the English Sangha Trust. His aim was to bring together the contending factions of British Buddhism and guide them forward. After two years in London he returned to India for a brief 'farewell visit', and whilst there he received a letter from the English Sangha Trust informing him that his services were no longer required and that he would be better off staying where he was. It must have come as a bitter blow, yet Sangharakshita had made up his mind; he returned to England to begin the long and uncharted journey towards a genuinely new Buddhist movement, building it from the ground up. In his biography, Subhuti describes how 'in many ways, Sangharakshita was very much alone at this time.... He would sometimes wander by himself through the streets, calling in rough working men's pubs for a pint of Guinness, enjoying his aloneness in the midst of others.'[9] Sangharakshita's plan to work for the good of Buddhism in the West had exploded overnight, or so it seemed. Yet it was a productive explosion because, without it, Sangharakshita would never have formulated the teaching in the way that he went on to do.

His response was characteristically positive.

When some of those who considered themselves the leaders of British Buddhism decided that they did not want me back ... I was delighted. Despite the fact that, owing to their machinations, the situation was for a time rather unpleasant, it did make it possible for me to start up something completely new, which is what I wanted to do anyway.[10]

In adversity, even catastrophe, our cherished plans come up against objective reality. We suddenly catch sight of the world not as we thought it was but as it actually is, and in that way transformation becomes possible. One door closes and another opens. This was also my experience in Finland. It was only when I met a catastrophe not unlike Sangharakshita's 'letter' that my eyes were opened to the situation I myself had unwittingly helped to bring about. People were not the problem. Our blindness to what we were actually doing was the problem. In fact, we were so unaware of our mistakes that even if the Buddha himself had come to point them out, we would have told him he was wrong. In other words, despite our disagreements, we all had one thing in common. We were driven by what Sangharakshita calls 'group' mentality, the opposite of true individuality.

Our response to adversity is a measure of our willingness to admit change and to work with it. Sangharakshita recognized the need to make a sustained effort to rebuild connections with those who wanted to eject him from the closed world of English Buddhism, notably Christmas Humphreys, the founder and president of London's Buddhist Society.

> After my return to England in 1967 and the establishment of the FWBO, there followed several years during which we did not see each other at all, but gradually contact was re-established. During the last seven or eight years of his life we met at least once or twice a year.[11]

It would therefore not be correct to speak of Sangharakshita's detractors as bad or unskilful. In hindsight, they achieved something that perhaps no one else could have done. Their actions resulted in what we now have in the Triratna Buddhist Order and Community. These 'adversaries' actually made our movement happen, and in that sense did so much for Buddhism that we can consider them the very best of people.

After our difficulties in Finland, I also knew I needed somehow to restore relationships that had been badly broken. After all, what's done is done and we had to move on. What concerned me was that if there was animosity between us, these same people would be reborn together to continue our arguments in future lives. Who in their right mind would wish for that? That's also why, in my own case, and on a good day, I feel thankful to my detractors.

The relationship, sometimes even conflict, between the would-be individual and the group is a recurrent theme in this volume. In the West, where you cannot be 'born into' Buddhism, the question of personal choice gains in importance, in both a positive and a negative sense. Newcomers to Buddhism often go through a period of 'shopping around' between different spiritual traditions before settling on their chosen path of practice. This is a good thing, but when the choice has been made, that is when the real work begins. Amaradakini, the first Estonian *dhammacārinī*, realized this when reflecting on what she thought our movement has to offer. 'Work', she said, 'only hard work.' I was impressed. However, the word 'work' alone doesn't quite convey what she meant, it needs 'responsibility' added to it.

One sometimes sees people who have committed themselves to a guru or spiritual teaching turning away, saying the teachings turned out to be false, or at least not pure enough. This is not so much 'shopping around' as an abdication of responsibility. It's the responsibility of the person coming along to make use of whatever he or she can, be it teachings, friendships, or the opportunity to work in pursuit of a definite aim. One needs to give oneself to that tradition or teaching, although never blindly. And while we are not in the business of 'shopping around' for teachings, the principle of *caveat emptor* applies even here. Responsibility lies with the individual. If we decide to commit ourselves to a path of practice, we have to do it in the full awareness of what we are doing and not claim after the event that we had been tricked into something against our will.

By developing that kind of awareness, says Sangharakshita, 'we not only resolve unawareness, thus eventually achieving self-consciousness or true individuality, but also effect a switch-over of energy from the cyclical to the spiral type of conditionality, that is to say, from the reactive and repetitive to the free and creative type of mental functioning.'[12] This is the mental functioning of the responsible 'true individual' who cannot be content either to go along with the group, or react against it when things go wrong.

Sangharakshita's account of the spiral or progressive order of conditionality has been a significant teaching for me. I have often learned that if I try to start something new, hoping to push things forward, it simply doesn't work. I come up against incomprehensible, silly difficulties, or I just get ill. Whatever I have achieved – and I suppose

I have achieved a lot – it has happened by my being ready when the right circumstances arose. When you are trying to build something – a business, a community, a spiritual movement – the next stage grows out of the fullness of the present stage, and there is no use in trying to reach out for it.

Sangharakshita's *Buddhism for Today – and Tomorrow*, delivered as a series of talks in 1976, includes a section with the title 'A Blueprint for a New World'. But Sangharakshita makes clear from the outset that this is not to be taken literally. 'If it exists at all', he says, 'it exists only in the imagination, only as a dream,'[13] and to speak of a blueprint at all is only a figure of speech. The process is organic and will not unfold according to some imaginary master plan, however promising it may seem.

Any naive celebration of Sangharakshita as a heroic figure underestimates his true achievement. Sangharakshita is a translator and an interpreter of Buddhism, but the best translators strive to make themselves invisible. Sangharakshita's uniqueness lay in his ability to understand and foster what is actually an organic process. We are not 'building' a movement so much as cultivating the conditions in which it can grow quite naturally of itself. Sangharakshita had the inspired vision of the truly creative individual, able to see the potential in the world about him and to seize the day. This is how, at the age of seventy, he could reflect that

> things have grown, things have developed. I think that I – or we – have been reasonably successful, certainly not unsuccessful, but there is so much still to be done, so many possibilities of further expansion, that I feel no inclination either to sit on my own laurels, such as they are, or to encourage others to sit on their laurels, those that have them. I hope that everybody will carry on doing more and more – not in a superficial activist way, but in a very genuine way, on the basis of their own understanding and experience, and in cooperation and harmony with each other.[14]

This 'very genuine way' is our work, and this is also our responsibility. We, ourselves, the new sangha, are responsible for what twenty-first-century Buddhism will become, and how it will turn out. These writings by Sangharakshita offer an inspiring view of what was only ever a beginning. We cannot afford simply to copy or even consolidate what has gone before, if that is all we do, because to do so would be to stop our journey only halfway. This is what 'A New Buddhist Movement', the title of this volume, really amounts to. The book is published, the texts are once more available, but the work of translation still continues. Now the real work must be done by us.

Sarvamitra
Tampere, Finland
August 2023

PART I
PUBLISHED WORKS, 1967–1992

Sangharakshita at Padmaloka, Norfolk, England. 1980s

BUDDHA MIND

Experiences are preceded by mind, led by mind, and produced by mind. If one speaks or acts with an impure mind, suffering follows even as the cart-wheel follows the hoof of the ox.

Experiences are preceded by mind, led by mind, and produced by mind. If one speaks or acts with a pure mind, happiness follows like a shadow that never departs.[15]

BREAKING THROUGH INTO
BUDDHAHOOD

Western Buddhist Order first anniversary celebration, Centre House, London, 27 April 1969.

We usually think of the spiritual life in terms of growth, in terms of progress, development, and evolution. Something slow, steady, proceeding by regular continuous steps. This concept of gradual evolution is a perfectly valid one, and a very good and helpful way of thinking and speaking of the spiritual life. But we can think of the spiritual life and the spiritual experience in another way, in terms of breaking through, and there are certain advantages in thinking of it in this way. If we think in terms of breaking through – or, if you like, of bursting through – it becomes clear that spiritual life consists, in part at least, or from one point of view at least, in an abrupt transition from one level or dimension of experience, or one mode of being, to another. It draws attention to the fact that the spiritual life involves not just effort, but even violence. The idea that the spiritual life involves violence is not a very popular one, but involve violence it does. Not, of course, violence to others, but violence to oneself, or to certain aspects of oneself that constitute obstacles which need to be overcome. We all come up against these obstacles, these very difficult, obstinate aspects of ourselves, which stand in the way of our higher development and evolution. Sometimes they are very intractable indeed, and we find that they cannot be charmed away by any sort of siren song, nor does it seem possible to remove them or dismantle them bit by bit. There they are in all their intractable tangibility, like great rocks and boulders, blocking our path. Sometimes we just have to break through, to burst through, with the help of a sort of charge of spiritual dynamite, regardless of consequences. It cannot always be easy, gradual, or smooth; sometimes it has to be violent and abrupt, even dramatic. We may say that the average spiritual life consists of periods of fairly steady progress, perhaps even apparent stagnation, separated by more or less violent and dramatic breakthroughs. This is the picture, the graph as it were, of the average spiritual life. There is a period of very slow progress followed by a breakthrough to another, higher level, then another period of slow steady progress and then another breakthrough.

So we are concerned here with the aspect of breakthrough, and we are going to discuss it under three main headings, which are not mutually exclusive: (1) what one breaks through; (2) how one breaks through; and (3) when and where one breaks through.

WHAT ONE BREAKS THROUGH

In principle, one has to break through everything that is mundane, everything that is conditioned, that is 'of this world', that is part and parcel of *saṃsāra*; everything that represents a segment or a spoke or an aspect of the wheel of life. But this statement, though true, is too general. The mundane, the conditioned, the *saṃsāra*, has so many different aspects, which are like so many thick impenetrable veils – like so many barriers or road blocks, so many great boulders piled high in our path, all of which have to be broken through. I am going to discuss just four of the more important blockages, or important aspects of the conditioned, of the mundane, that have to be broken through if Buddhahood is to be attained. First of all, negative emotions; secondly, psychological conditionings; thirdly, rational thinking; and fourthly, time sense.

Negative Emotions

In their primary form, negative emotions are three in number. There is craving, in the sense of neurotic desire, there is hatred, and there is fear. There are also many secondary and tertiary forms, for example anxiety, insecurity, jealousy, self-pity, guilt, remorse, contempt, conceit, envy, depression, pessimism, gloom, alarm, despondency, despair, suspicion, and resentment.[16] I'm not going to say much about them, as preoccupation with negative emotions is itself very likely to generate negative emotion.

All the negative emotions represent leakages or drainings away of emotional energy. When we indulge in negative emotions, whether in their primary, secondary, or tertiary forms, energy – psychical energy, even spiritual energy – is draining away from us in all directions, all the time. Therefore, indulgence in the negative emotions weakens us and this causes us to withdraw into ourselves, to contract. The effect of indulging constantly and persistently in the negative emotions is that we contract into what we may describe as a cold, hard, tight knot of separate selfhood. Unfortunately, we may say that the negative emotions are extremely widespread, practically all-pervasive, and it seems to be the special function of several ubiquitous agencies to intensify these negative emotions as much as possible.

Take, for example, the daily newspapers, many of which specialize in the sensational, the shocking, and the horrible. In this way negative emotions are stimulated. Then there is the advertising industry, a very large, important, and powerful industry, whose special function seems to be to stimulate neurotic craving, to multiply people's wants rather than to meet their needs. Then again, we find that most people we meet are negative rather than positive in their emotional attitudes and responses. So we have to be very careful not to allow ourselves to be influenced by, to be tinged with, this grey emotional state. We have to break through, to burst through, into a positive emotional state of love, of faith and devotion, of compassion and joy, and we should do our best to encourage positive emotions and attitudes in others.

Psychological Conditionings

These may be defined as factors that influence, even determine, our mental attitudes and behaviour without our being fully aware of it or perhaps without our being aware of it at all. Suppose, for instance, we are born in England. We naturally grow up speaking the English language. We are educated in an English school, exposed to all the rigours of the English climate. All this will affect or influence our outlook very deeply without our being aware of it. It will result in an English psychological conditioning rather than, say, a French or Chinese psychological conditioning. The natural result will be that we shall look out upon the world as an Englishman and see things from that special point of view. We may be rather surprised when one day we perhaps wake up to the fact that other people in the world see things rather differently.

This is just one example, but psychological conditioning is of very many different kinds. We are psychologically conditioned by our race, by our class, and by the work we do. Just think of it: you do the same kind of work, in many cases, so many hours of the day, days of the week, weeks of the year, years of your life, so that you start seeing things in a special way, from the standpoint of your employment, your profession, your occupation, your vocation. Moreover, we are psychologically conditioned by the social and economic system of which we are a part and by the religion into which we are born or in which we have been brought up. All this goes to show that we are just a mass of psychological conditioning: a class conditioning, plus an economic conditioning, plus a religious conditioning, plus a national conditioning, plus a linguistic conditioning. There is very little, in fact, that is really ours, really our own. There is very little in our lives and experience that is really free and spontaneous, that is really, in a word, us. For the most part we think, even feel, and certainly act in certain ways because we have been conditioned to do so. For the most part we are no better than Pavlov's dogs. A bell rings: we react, we respond. And bells are ringing all the time – religious bells, economic bells, social bells, political bells. The bells go on ringing and ringing, and we respond like mad and call this our freedom. We may say that, really and truly, we are machines rather than human beings.

So we have to break through all these conditionings, we have to shatter, to smash, our own mechanicalness, otherwise there is no Buddhahood – not even, in fact, any real spiritual life.

This breaking through the barriers and obstacles of psychological conditioning means a sort of de-identification of ourselves, a sort of dissociation from that part of ourselves which is machine-like. Spiritual people, we may say, will not think of themselves as being English, or working-class, or middle-class, or any class. They won't think of themselves as townspeople if they live in the town, or as country folk if they live in the country. The spiritual person won't think of themselves as essentially being a doctor, or a bus driver, or a housewife, and therefore will not think or feel or act out of any such conditioning. He or she will act freely and spontaneously out of the 'depths' of pure, clear awareness. Such a person eventually won't think of themselves as being even a human being. If such a person, such a spiritual person – or, one might even say, transcendental person – thinks at all, which is doubtful, they will think of themself as a Buddha, and will act as a Buddha, because he or she will have broken through all psychological conditioning, will have broken through into Buddhahood.

Rational Thinking

This kind of breaking through is indeed difficult to imagine. We can well understand the need for breaking through our negative emotions, which are obviously undesirable. We can understand, with a bit of effort, at least theoretically, the need for breaking through psychological conditioning. But though we understand, it is, after all, our rational mind that is understanding, and now our mind is being asked to contemplate, to agree to, its own dissolution. It's terrifying to experience this even as an idea, even as a thought, even as a concept. The rational mind, we know, is an extremely important faculty. It has been developed over hundreds of thousands of years of evolution, and is the chief instrument of human survival. It is, therefore, natural that it should be valued very highly, but it should not be overvalued. It is invaluable for practical purposes. After all, it was the rational mind that discovered fire, that invented the wheel, that domesticated animals at the dawn of history, that forged tools and implements, that established cities and systems of government, that built roads and bridges. More recently, the rational mind, the rational intelligence, has created the aeroplane and radio and television. It is the rational mind that split the atom, and it is the rational mind that is at present dreaming, if you can speak of it as dreaming, of interplanetary and intergalactic travel. But though the rational mind may achieve all this, and even more that we cannot even imagine, the rational mind cannot know reality. In the Buddha's words, or rather word, reality – truth itself, the absolute, the unconditioned, the ultimate – is *atakkāvacara*. *Takka* means rational thinking, rational thought, even logic, and the Buddha says clearly, emphatically, unmistakably, that in order to experience reality, one must go beyond this, one must break through the rational mind, even break down the rational mind, and only then can one break through into Buddhahood.

For most people, this is very difficult to accept. The rational mind has achieved so much. We like to think that with it we can understand

Buddhism, the nature of Enlightenment, and Zen. In the West, very many books have been written by all sorts of people about Zen – all written with the rational mind – whereas Zen is in fact nothing but a gigantic, overwhelming protest against the assumption, the blasphemous assumption even, that the rational mind can know reality. Zen, we may say, most rudely gives the rational mind a violent slap in the face. Usually, people like to think that the rational mind is omnipotent – that it can do everything, know everything. They don't like to be asked to contemplate the weakness of the rational mind, or to be reminded of the power of the non-rational. For this reason they react, sometimes rather strongly, to things that remind them of the non-rational, or that make them feel the presence – even the pulling, or the pushing – of the non-rational. This is why some people react rather strongly to things like insanity. It is perhaps rather significant that in this country we lock up the insane, or at least put them away – even the quite harmless ones. In India, by contrast, the insane are allowed to roam freely in the streets of the cities and villages. The Indians are not afraid of the insane, and this is because they are not afraid of the non-rational.

Similarly, we tend to be afraid of our violent emotions, which might carry us away out of ourselves, force us to lose control. We tend to like nice, gentle, soft, tame, manageable emotions. We don't like violent emotions; we react rather strongly to drugs, or to surrealist art, or even to people who are a bit different from us. It is rather significant that gypsies are harassed so much by urban district councils and the like. It is because they represent the unharnessable, the unmanageable, the untameable. They all represent for us the power of the non-rational, they all represent the possibility, and also the danger, of breaking through the rational mind.

Time Sense

One could say that time is security, that is, insecurity; but perhaps this is too cryptic. There are two kinds of time – some people say three or four, but let us say two today: organic time and mechanical or clock time. By organic time we mean our own total experience of pure continuous duration, with no thought of before or after, just a direct immediate present. Here there is no splitting up of the time flow into past, present, and future. Mechanical or clock time is the experience of travelling as though along a straight line. This is also sometimes called linear time. It is divided into past, present, and future; it is chopped up into hours, minutes, seconds. Organic time, we may say, expands and contracts, according to the intensity of one's experience. If one's experience is more intense, then organic time expands; if it is less intense, one's organic time contracts. But clock time is relatively uniform, it is the same all the time. So clock time does not correspond to organic time and cannot measure organic time, or one's experience within clock time. When one speaks of breaking through the time sense, or breaking through time, one means mechanical time or clock time.

Most of us, sad to say, especially those of us who live in cities, are slaves of clock time. We live our lives according to the clock. For example, at one o'clock, we say it is time to eat, whether or not we feel hungry. In the same way we work when it is time to work, sleep when it is time to sleep, and even meditate when it is time to meditate – often for no other reason. Our lives are geared to the clock, and in this way the natural self-regulating rhythm of the organism is disrupted, and one's experience of organic time, of pure duration, is lost. Our life's experiences don't emerge and flower from the depths of the eternal now. We see them strung out, like washing on a line, and therefore we mentally anticipate our experiences, we mentally pre-arrange them. We draw up programmes and diaries and so on because, basically, we don't trust ourselves to the experience of organic time, of pure continuous duration – we feel insecure. (This is why I said that time is security, and therefore insecurity.) We like to think within this context of clock time, 'Well, tomorrow is Monday, I'll be doing such-and-such; next week I'll be doing this, next year I'll be doing that.' So some people plan and organize their whole lives in this way, right up to the day of retirement, and after that, of course, there is just a blank, a sort of dreary miserable space before death, and this is a really frightening thought. I suppose it is not altogether our own individual fault, because pressure is brought upon us all the time to live in this way, to regulate our lives and gear our existence to the clock – which of course means not really living at all. So we have to break through the time sense, break through mechanical time. We have, as it were, to smash the clock, or at least allow it to run down.

A Vision of Freedom

So we must break through negative emotions, through psychological conditioning, through rational thinking, and through the time sense. In this way, from all these four angles and directions simultaneously, we can break through into, or converge upon, Buddhahood.

Now Buddhahood has various aspects which correspond to different aspects of the conditioned, the mundane, the *saṃsāra*. If we break through the conditioned at a certain point, we shall break through into the corresponding aspect of Buddhahood. If, for instance, we break through the suffering of conditioned existence, we shall break through into the bliss, the happiness, the everlasting joy, of Buddhahood. Similarly with regard to the four aspects of the conditioned with which we have been dealing. Breaking through the negative emotions means breaking through into the positive emotions of love and compassion. Breaking through psychological conditioning means breaking through into a state of complete freedom, spontaneity, and unconditioned creativity. Breaking through the rational mind means breaking through into a state of what we may describe as transcendental non-rationality. Finally, breaking through the time sense means breaking through into the experience of the eternal everlasting now.

What Would a Buddha be Like?

Love and compassion, freedom and spontaneity, transcendental non-rationality, and living in the eternal now are all aspects of Buddhahood, and are also characteristics of the Enlightened person. The Enlightened person will manifest, will radiate, positive emotions, will be completely unconditioned and spontaneous in behaviour and will therefore be unpredictable. He may be liable to do anything at any moment, will not be bound by rational thinking, and will be quite devoid of any sense of mechanical time, living from moment to moment and enjoying, as it were, the bliss of pure duration. From all this we can see that the Enlightened person cuts a rather unconventional figure.

Some Hindu texts raise the question: How would the liberated, Enlightened person appear to others? Within himself he would know reality, would know God or Brahman, but what would he look like to others? Some of the texts give a threefold reply. They say that the

Enlightened person will appear like a child, like a madman, and like a ghost. Like a child because the child is spontaneous and uninhibited, like a madman because the Enlightened person in a sense is just mad, and like a ghost because the ghost just comes and goes, you don't know where from or where to. The Enlightened person is like that. You cannot tie him down or corner him. You cannot keep track of him: he slips through your fingers. There is also something a little uncanny about him. The Enlightened person, one may say, will certainly not appear to other people like a respectable and law-abiding citizen.

HOW ONE BREAKS THROUGH

The Way of Mindfulness

Breaking through any aspect of conditioned existence, any aspect of the wheel of life, is accomplished mainly through the cultivation of awareness, mindfulness, and recollection. Awareness, we may say, is the great dissolver of negative emotions, of psychological conditionings, in fact every aspect of the conditioned within ourselves. There is no spiritual life without awareness. An action, thought, or feeling is spiritual to the extent that it is accompanied by awareness. If there is anything negative in the thought, feeling, or action, anything that smacks of the conditioned, then the awareness with which it is done, if that awareness is maintained, will sooner or later eat away at all the conditioning and negativity, so awareness is of paramount importance in the spiritual life. There is no spiritual life, no breakthrough, without awareness.

A Path of Regular Steps

Breaking through is also accompanied by means of regular spiritual practice of one kind or another: puja, making offerings, meditation, giving *dāna*. Every time one practises, an effect is produced. The practice may be very little, very limited, but there is an effect. If you keep up the limited practice, and if it is regular – daily, even hourly – then the effect accumulates within the form of what the Yogācāra calls the 'good seeds'.[17] If we keep up the regular practice long enough, these 'good seeds' within us, these wholesome effects, will accumulate to the point of bursting and there will be a breakthrough. But of course, if we do things in this way, we must have patience. An example often given is that of the rock which is split by the twentieth blow. The first nineteen were not useless, though they did not appear to have any effect. Without them the twentieth blow could not have done its work. So this is another way of breaking through: keeping up these strokes, i.e. the regular practice, month after month, year after year: ten, twenty, thirty years. The effects accumulate, tensions accumulate, and then one breaks through. Breakthrough is also achieved by the introduction into one's life of a new factor, especially of a new person – something or someone who jolts us out of our accustomed routine, who breaks up our accustomed routine, who gets us to some extent out of our conditioning. How does one break through the four aspects of the conditioned already mentioned?

Breaking Through Negative Emotions

One breaks through negative emotions principally by cultivating the positive emotions. Here, practices like the *mettā bhāvanā*, the development of universal loving-kindness, though rather difficult, help very much. One can also break through negative emotions by associating more with people who are emotionally positive, who are either full of love and compassion, of joy and confidence, or even just ordinary cheerfulness. Also, eating the right kind of food can help – not the kind that clogs the system and weighs you down, making you feel heavy and stiff and lethargic. One can also break through into the positive emotions, to some extent, by living more in the open air, by staying in the sunshine as much as possible, looking at green grass and blue sky, and by surrounding oneself with bright colours. Perhaps one should dress more brightly, more colourfully, because this too has a positive emotional effect.

Breaking Through Psychological Conditionings

One breaks through psychological conditionings mainly, of course, through awareness: awareness that one is conditioned, is mechanical, is not free. But how does one develop this sort of awareness? How does one extend and amplify it? One can sometimes do this by subjecting oneself, quite deliberately, to an unfamiliar type of conditioning. If, for instance, one's psychological conditioning is English, then one could go and live for a time in Italy, or India, or Japan. In this way one will become aware of one's own conditioning, because one will have become aware of the unfamiliar conditioning of the people in the midst of whom one is living. Their conditioning will impinge, sometimes rather uncomfortably, on your conditioning. For instance, people in India eat with their fingers. At first English people are often shocked by this and think it terribly unhygienic. After a time, however, you get used to it, and you realize that it was because of your own conditioning that you were shocked. So to the extent that you become aware of your conditioning, to that extent you become free from it. For this reason it is very good to travel and see new countries, meet new people of different races, religions, colours, and cultures. As we get older – and we're getting older every day – the general tendency is to visit only the old familiar places. We say, 'Ah well, I'll go back there. I went there ten years ago, fifteen years ago. I have been there maybe every year for ten, fifteen, twenty years. Let's have another holiday there. It's the same old hotel keeper, the same old beach; it hasn't changed a bit.' In this way we travel in the same old rut over and over again.

Breaking Through Rational Thinking

This is rather more difficult to do. Traditionally there are several ways. The Perfection of Wisdom literature employs the method of paradox.[18] A paradox has been defined or described as a truth standing on its head to attract attention, but it's really much more than that. The paradox is a using of conceptual thought to transcend conceptual thought. In the Perfection of Wisdom texts, for instance, the Buddha says that the bodhisattva, the one who wants to gain Enlightenment for the sake of all, must vow to save all beings. He must vow, 'I'll deliver, I'll save, I'll help all beings in the universe.' And then, the Buddha goes on to say, he must at the same time realize that no beings exist, otherwise he is not a bodhisattva. In the same way, the texts say that the bodhisattva must go all out for Enlightenment, practise the perfections, the *pāramitās*, sacrifice life and limb, shed his blood; at the same time he must realize that there is no such thing as Enlightenment, and no one attains it. This is the paradoxical approach to the Perfection of Wisdom literature, which really brings the intellect right up against it.

This sort of method or approach is exemplified, is crystallized, in the koan of Zen. I am not going to try to define a koan, but those of you who have studied the literature on Zen – admittedly literature written mainly with the rational mind – know that the koan is very much used in Zen, especially in the Rinzai school, and that it is a sort of apparently contradictory, or even nonsensical, statement. For instance, when you clap your two hands together, you produce a clapping sound, so the koan says 'What is the sound of one hand clapping?' Or the master says to the disciple, 'What are you carrying?' The disciple replies, 'I'm not carrying anything.' And the master says, 'Well, drop it then.' There are hundreds of such koan, and in the traditional system the disciple sits in the meditation hall, meditating on one or another of them, hour after hour for days and weeks on end. We are told that sometimes he breaks out in a sweat. He doesn't know whether it is snowing or raining, whether it is spring or autumn, day or night. He is just stuck with this koan, which sometimes becomes like a great lump of ice, or like a red-hot iron ball that he has swallowed: he cannot get it up and he cannot get it down. But eventually he breaks through – he bursts through – the rational mind. This method presupposes a great faith in the master and a strong traditional system of discipline, and is therefore rather difficult to transplant to the West.

But there are other ways of breaking through the rational mind, not perhaps so drastic as the koan method, but certainly still effective. We can, for instance, have more recourse to non-conceptual modes of communication. We can have more recourse to things like myths, legends, and symbols, all of which are nowadays coming more and more into their own. Formerly when people translated the Buddhist scriptures they just cut out all the 'mythical bits',[19] saying that the monks had inserted those much later, and that only the rational bits were the real bits and what the Buddha had actually said. Fortunately for us, Jung has rather altered all that, and has taught us to appreciate and to evaluate these things rather differently. So we have put all the mythological bits back and when we read them we find that they speak to us, that they have a meaning – though not a conceptual meaning. They have a message, they have an impact. There is something that carries over from them above and beyond, or even round about and underneath, the rational mind. These myths, these symbols – whether the ladder down which the Buddha came from heaven to earth; or his seven steps; or his encounter with the earth goddess under the bodhi tree; or Mucalinda – all help to communicate the non-conceptual, trans-conceptual truth of Buddhism, of the Buddha's Enlightenment.[20] So we shouldn't think that communication is only conceptual, only verbal, only a matter of ideas and thoughts and philosophies. We must try to emphasize the importance of the non-conceptual, the mythical, the symbolical – if you like, of the archetypal, the direct, the experiential.

Breaking Through the Time Sense

We can make a very good beginning by doing without a watch. One can also, to some extent, break through mechanical time by having a job which does not oblige one to live according to the clock, where one will not have regular hours, if that is possible. This, I appreciate, is rather difficult to do, except of course for people like artists who can work, we are told, just when they feel like it, without having to stick to any deadline or programme or to keep their eye on the clock.

WHERE AND WHEN ONE BREAKS THROUGH

One may say that the most favourable conditions for breaking through are the unfavourable ones. Usually one does not break through when things are going well, when it is all plain sailing, when everything is going according to plan. One is more likely to break through in times of crisis. The Buddha sweated and struggled and starved himself for six years, and he seemed, to himself at least, to be no nearer his goal. So, according to legend, he sat down under the bodhi tree, and clenched his teeth, and said, 'Flesh may wither away, blood may dry up, but until I have gained Enlightenment I am not getting up from this seat.'[21] So for him it was Enlightenment or death. This was the crisis for him, the crisis which, in a sense, he created for himself.

Some people have been known to break through at a time of physical deprivation. It is as though the weakening of the body strengthens the spirit. Some people have been known to break through when undergoing a prolonged fast. Sometimes, strange to say, one can break through when one is ill. This would seem to be a very unfavourable time: you cannot meditate, sometimes you cannot read; but many people have had important breakthroughs, in fact crucial breakthroughs, at such times. For instance, when you get a high fever – especially in the East this is the case – though you have got the fever, though in a sense you are sick, even suffering, you are sort of strangely exhilarated, and awareness can be intensified, and you can have a breakthrough at that time. You can also have a breakthrough when you have had a shock of some kind: when you have suffered a great bereavement; or when you have lost an enormous sum of money: or your plans have been laid in ruins; or everything has gone hopelessly astray, contrary to your expectations; when you seem to have no hope and no prospects: sometimes in conditions like this you will have a breakthrough.

Death – The Crucial Situation

According to *The Tibetan Book of the Dead*, one can break through even at the time of death. Death, in a sense, is the greatest crisis, the most crucial situation of all – it also therefore represents the greatest opportunity. According to the tradition which is embodied in *The Tibetan Book of the Dead*, at the time of death, and just after death, one experiences, at least momentarily, what is known as the clear light of the Void,[22] the light of reality shining, as it were, upon one. Transcendental though it is, awe-inspiring though it is, this is not anything that comes from outside: it is the light, the great white light, of one's own true mind, which is identical, ultimately, in its absolute depths, with reality itself. If one can only recognize this, at that moment, either during the time of death, or just after death, then one is liberated, and there may be for one no more rebirth.

Freedom is Frightening

In these pages we have tried to understand what we break through, how we break through, and when and where we break through. Our approach has inevitably been rather conceptual, even though, at the same time, the limitations of the conceptual have been indicated. I would like to end with a picture of breaking through – a picture from Tibetan Buddhism, from the Tantric tradition. It is a picture, an image, a form, of what is known as a wrathful deity, or even a wrathful Buddha. What does this wrathful figure look like? How does he appear? First of all, he is a dark-blue male figure, very powerfully built, with a massive torso, enormous legs, and enormous arms. Sometimes naked, sometimes draped in a tiger skin, he wears a garland of human skulls.

He has a third eye in the middle of his forehead. All three eyes glare with an expression of terrible, terrific anger. From the mouth there stick out fangs and a red blood-dripping tongue. This fearful dark-blue figure tramples on enemies – upon ignorance, upon craving – and his hands – sometimes two, sometimes four, sometimes eight, sometimes sixteen, sometimes thirty-two – grasp various weapons. What does this figure, this form, represent? This is the image of breaking through. This fearful, or this wrathful, or this terrific form, represents the forces of Enlightenment breaking, even bursting, through the thick dense darkness of ignorance and unawareness. This form, this image, represents transcendental consciousness at the point of, at the moment of, breaking through into Buddhahood. The whole figure is surrounded by an aureole of flames. And what does the aureole of flames represent? Breaking through on any level, with regard to any medium, entails friction, just as, when a spacecraft re-enters the Earth's atmosphere, there is tremendous friction. Friction generates heat, and heat, when it reaches a certain point, a certain pitch of intensity, results in a conflagration, in a bursting into flames.

So the wrathful Buddha bursting through the conditioned is therefore surrounded by this aureole of flames, and these flames consume and burn up the darkness, burn up everything conditioned. And when everything conditioned is burned up, is consumed, is broken through, then breaking through into Buddhahood is complete, is accomplished. Then there is no more darkness, no more friction, no more flames, but only the shining figure of the Buddha, a Buddha, *another* Buddha, seated beneath the bodhi tree.

MIND – REACTIVE AND CREATIVE

Reading University Buddhist Society, 19 March 1967. First published in the Middle Way, *August 1971.*

Taking a bird's-eye view of human culture, we see that there exist in the world numerous spiritual traditions. Some of these are of great antiquity, coming down from the remote past with all the authority and prestige of that which has been long established; others are of more recent origin. While some have crystallized, in the course of centuries, into religious cults with enormous followings, others have remained more of the nature of philosophies, making few concessions to popular tastes and needs. Each one of these traditions has its own system, that is to say, its own special concatenation – its own network – of ideas and ideals, of beliefs and practices, as well as its own particular starting-point in thought or experience out of which the whole system evolves. This starting-point is the 'golden string' which, when wound into the ball of the total system, will lead one in at 'heaven's gate, built in Jerusalem's wall'[23] of the tradition concerned.

Among the spiritual traditions of the world one of the oldest and most important is that known to us as Buddhism, the tradition deriving from the life and teaching of Gautama the Buddha, an Indian master the vibrations of whose extraordinary spiritual dynamism not only electrified north-eastern India in the sixth century BCE but subsequently propagated themselves all over Asia and beyond. Like other traditions Buddhism possesses its own special system and its own distinctive starting point. The system of Buddhism is what is known as the 'Dharma', a Sanskrit word meaning, in this context, the doctrine or the teaching, and connoting the sum total of the insights and experiences conducive to the attainment of Enlightenment or Buddhahood. Its starting-point is the mind.

A SHARED TRADITION

That this, and no other, is the starting-point, is illustrated by two quotations from what are sometimes regarded as the two most highly antithetical, not to say mutually exclusive, developments within the whole field of Buddhism: Theravāda and Zen. According to the first two verses of the *Dhammapada*, an ancient collection of metrical aphorisms included in the Pāli canon of the Theravādins,

> Experiences are preceded by mind, led by mind, and produced by mind. If one speaks or acts with an impure mind, suffering follows even as the cart-wheel follows the hoof of the ox.

> Experiences are preceded by mind, led by mind, and produced by mind. If one speaks or acts with a pure mind, happiness follows like a shadow that never departs.[24]

The Zen quotation is, if anything, more emphatic. In a verse which made its appearance in China during the Tang dynasty, Zen itself, which claims to convey from generation to generation of disciples the very heart of the Buddha's spiritual experience, is briefly characterized as:

> A special transmission outside the Scriptures.
> No dependence on words and letters.
> Direct pointing to the mind.
> Seeing into one's own nature and realizing Buddhahood.[25]

From these quotations, representative of many others which could be made, it is clear that the starting-point of Buddhism is not anything outside us. In the language of Western thought, it is not objective but subjective. The starting-point is the mind.

But what do we mean by mind? In the *Dhammapada* verses the original Pāli word is *mano*; in the Chinese Zen stanza it is *xīn*, corresponding to the Sanskrit and Pāli *citta*. As both these terms can be quite adequately rendered by the English 'mind' there is no need to explore etymologies and we can plunge at once into the heart of our subject.

To begin with, mind is twofold. On the one hand there is absolute mind; on the other, relative mind. By absolute mind is meant that infinite cosmic or transcendental awareness within whose pure timeless flow the subject–object polarity as we ordinarily experience it is forever dissolved. For mind in this exalted sense Buddhism employs, according to context, a number of expressions, each with its own distinctive shade of meaning. Prominent among these expressions are the One Mind, the Unconditioned, Buddha-nature, the Void. In the more neutral language of philosophy, absolute mind is Reality. It is the realization of absolute mind through the dissolution of the subject–object polarity – the waking up to Reality out of the dream of mundane existence – which constitutes Enlightenment, the attainment of Enlightenment being, of course, the ultimate aim of Buddhism.

By relative mind is meant the individual mind or consciousness, functioning within the framework of the subject–object polarity, and it is with this mind that we are now concerned. Like mind in general, relative mind or consciousness is of two kinds: reactive and creative.

MIND REACTIVE, MIND CREATIVE

While these are not traditional Buddhist expressions, neither of them rendering any one technical term in any of the canonical languages, they seem to express very well the import of the Buddha's teaching. In any case, the distinction which they represent is of fundamental importance not only in the 'system' of Buddhism but in the spiritual life generally and even in the entire scheme of human evolution. The transition from 'reactive' to 'creative' marks, indeed, the beginning of spiritual life. It is conversion in the true sense of the term. What, then, do we mean by speaking of 'reactive mind' and 'creative mind'?

In the first place, we should not imagine that there are literally two relative minds, one reactive, the other creative. Rather should we understand that there are two ways in which relative mind or the individual consciousness is capable of functioning. It is capable of functioning reactively and it is capable of functioning creatively. When it functions in a reactive manner, it is known as the reactive mind; when it functions in a creative manner, it is known as the creative mind – but there is only one relative mind.

REACTIVE MIND

By the reactive mind is meant our ordinary, everyday mind, the mind that most people use most of the time, or, rather, it is the mind that uses them. In extreme cases, indeed, the reactive mind functions all the time, the creative mind remaining in complete abeyance. People of this type are born, live, and die animals; though possessing the human form they are in fact not human beings at all. Rather than attempt an abstract definition of the reactive mind let us try to grasp its nature by examining some of its actual characteristics.

The Reactive Mind

In the first place, the reactive mind is a *re*-active mind. It does not really act, but only *re*-acts. Instead of acting spontaneously, out of its own inner fullness and abundance, it requires an external stimulus to set it in motion. This stimulus usually comes through the five senses. We are walking along the street, an advertisement catches our eye, its bright colours and bold lettering making an instant appeal. Perhaps it is an advertisement for a certain brand of cigarette, or for a certain make of car, or for summer holidays on the sun-drenched beaches of some distant pleasure resort. Whatever the goods or services depicted, our attention is attracted, arrested. We go and do what the advertisement is designed to make us do, or make a mental note to do it, or are left with an unconscious disposition to do it as and when circumstances permit. We have not acted, but have been activated. We have *re*-acted.

The reactive mind is, therefore, the conditioned mind. It is conditioned by its object (e.g. the advertisement) in the sense of being not merely dependent upon it but actually determined by it. The reactive mind is not free.

The Mechanical Mind

Since it is conditioned the reactive mind is, moreover, purely mechanical. As such it can be appropriately described as the 'penny-in-the-slot' mind. Insert the coin, and out comes the packet. In much the same way, let the reactive mind be confronted with a certain situation or experience and it will react automatically, in an entirely mechanical, hence predictable, fashion. Not only our behaviour but even much of our 'thinking' conforms to this pattern. Whether in the field of politics, or literature, or religion, or whether in the affairs of everyday life, the opinions we so firmly hold and so confidently profess are very rarely the outcome of conscious reflection, of our individual effort to arrive at the truth. Our ideas are hardly ever our own. Only too often have they been fed into us from external sources, from books, newspapers, and conversations, and we have accepted them, or rather received them, in a passive and unreflecting manner. When the appropriate stimulus occurs we automatically reproduce whatever has been fed into our system, and it is this purely mechanical reaction that passes for expression of opinion. Truly original thought on any subject is, indeed, extremely rare, though 'original' does not necessarily mean 'different', but rather whatever one creates out of one's own inner resources regardless of whether or not this coincides with something previously created by somebody else. Some, of course, *try* to be different. This can, however, be a subtle form of conditionedness, for in trying to be different such people are still being determined by an object, by whatever or whoever it is they are trying to be different from. They are still *re*-acting, instead of really acting.

The Repetitive Mind

Besides being conditioned and mechanical, the reactive mind is repetitive. Being 'programmed' as it were by needs of which it is largely unconscious, it reacts to the same stimuli in much the same way, and like a machine therefore goes on performing the same operation over and over again. It is owing to this characteristic of the reactive mind that 'human' life as a whole becomes so much a matter of fixed and settled habit, in a world of routine. As we grow older, especially, we develop a passive resistance to change, preferring to deepen the old ruts rather than strike out in a new direction. Even our religious life, if we are not careful, can become incorporated into the routine, can become part of the pattern, part of the machinery of existence. The Sunday service or the mid-week meditation become fixed as reference points in our lives, buoys charting a way through the dangerous waters of freedom, along with the weekly visit to the cinema and the launderette, the annual holiday at the seaside, and the seasonal spree.

The Unaware Mind

Above all, however, the reactive mind is the unaware mind. Whatever it does, it does without any real knowledge of what it is doing. Metaphorically speaking, the reactive mind is asleep. Those in whom it predominates can, therefore, be described as asleep rather than awake. In a state of sleep they live out their lives; in a state of sleep they eat, drink, talk, work, play, vote, make love; in a state of sleep, even, they read books on Buddhism and try to meditate. Like somnambulists who walk with eyes wide open, they only appear to be awake. Some people, indeed, are so fast asleep that for all their apparent activity they can more adequately be described as dead. Their movements are those of a zombie, or a robot with all its controls switched on, rather than those of a truly aware human being. It is with this realization – when we become aware of our own unawareness, when we wake up to the fact that we are asleep – that spiritual life begins. One might, indeed, go so far as to say that it marks the beginning of truly human existence, though this would imply, indeed, a far higher conception of human existence than the word usually conveys – a conception nearer to what is usually termed spiritual. This brings us to the second kind of relative mind, to what we have termed the creative mind.

CREATIVE MIND

The characteristics of the creative mind are the opposite of those of the reactive mind. The creative mind does not *re*-act. It is not dependent on, or determined by, the stimuli with which it comes into contact. On the contrary, it is active on its own account, functioning spontaneously, out of the depths of its own intrinsic nature. Even when initially prompted by something external to itself it quickly transcends its original point of departure and starts functioning independently. The creative mind can therefore be said to *respond* rather than to react. Indeed, it is capable of transcending conditions altogether. Hence it can also be said that whereas the reactive mind is essentially pessimistic, being confined to what is given in immediate experience, the creative mind is profoundly and radically optimistic. Its optimism is not, however, the superficial optimism of the streets, no mere unthinking reaction to, or rationalization of, pleasurable stimuli. By virtue of the very nature of the creative mind such a reaction would be impossible. On the contrary, the optimism of the creative mind persists despite unpleasant stimuli, despite conditions unfavourable for optimism, or even when there are no conditions for it at all. The creative mind loves where there is no reason to love, is happy where there is no reason for happiness, creates where there is no possibility of creativity, and in this way 'builds a heaven in hell's despair'.[26]

The Independent Mind

Not being dependent on any object, the creative mind is essentially non-conditioned. It is independent by nature, and functions, therefore, in a perfectly spontaneous manner. When functioning on the highest possible level, at its highest pitch of intensity, the creative mind is identical with the Unconditioned; that is to say, it coincides with absolute mind. Being non-conditioned the creative mind is free; indeed, it is Freedom itself. It is also original in the true sense of the term, being characterized by ceaseless productivity. This productivity is not necessarily artistic, literary, or musical, even though the painting, the poem, and the symphony are admittedly among its most typical, even as among its most strikingly adequate, manifestations. Moreover, just as the creative mind does not necessarily find expression in 'works of art', so what are conventionally regarded as 'works of art' are not necessarily all expressions of the creative mind. Imitative and lacking true originality, some of them are more likely to be the mechanical products of the reactive mind.

The Responsive Mind

Outside the sphere of the fine arts the creative mind finds expression in productive personal relations, as when through our own emotional positivity others become more emotionally positive, or as when through the intensity of their mutual awareness two or more people reach out towards, and together experience, a dimension of being greater and more inclusive than their separate individualities. In these and similar cases the creative mind is productive in the sense of contributing to the increase, in the world, of the sum total of positive emotion, of higher states of being and consciousness.

The Aware Mind

Finally, as just indicated the creative mind is above all the aware mind. Being aware, or rather, being Awareness itself, the creative mind is also intensely and radiantly alive. The creative person, as one in whom the creative mind manifests may be termed, is not only more aware than the reactive person but possessed of far greater vitality. This vitality is not just animal high spirits or emotional exuberance, much less still mere intellectual energy or the compulsive urgency of egoistic volition. Were such expressions permissible, one might say it is the Spirit of Life itself rising like a fountain from the infinite depths of existence, and vivifying, through the creative person, all with whom it comes into contact.

SYMBOLS OF MIND

One picture being worth a thousand words, the reactive mind and the creative mind are illustrated by two important Buddhist symbols. These are the symbols of the wheel of life and the path (or way), otherwise known – more abstractly and geometrically – as the circle and the spiral.

The Wheel of Life

The wheel of life, or wheel of becoming, occupies an important place in Tibetan popular religious art, being depicted in gigantic size on the walls of temples, usually in the vestibule, as well as on a reduced scale in painted scrolls. It consists of four concentric circles.

The Three Poisons

In the first circle, or hub of the wheel, are depicted a cock, a snake, and a pig, each biting the tail of the one in front. These three animals represent the three 'unskilful roots' or 'poisons' of craving, aversion, and delusion, which are, of course, the three mainsprings of the reactive mind, the first and second being the two principal negative emotions and the third the darkness of spiritual unawareness out of which they arise. Their biting one another's tails signifies their interdependence, or the fact that the circle is a vicious circle.

Around and Around

The second circle is divided vertically into two segments, a black one on the right-hand side and a white one on the left. In the black segment the figures of naked human beings, chained together, are seen plunging headlong downwards with expressions of anguish and terror. In the white segment modestly clad figures, carrying *mani*-cylinders (what in the West are erroneously termed 'prayer wheels') and religious offerings move gently upwards with serene and happy countenances. These two segments represent two opposite movements or tendencies within the wheel itself, one centripetal and the other centrifugal. In other words, while the black segment represents a movement in the direction of the hub of the wheel the white segment represents a movement away from the hub and towards the circumference – towards freedom, ultimately, from the reactive mind. Though in a sense constituting a stage of the path, or a section of the spiral, it is still part of the wheel inasmuch as regression from it, in the form of a transition from the white to the black segment, is liable to occur at any time. The white segment can therefore be regarded as representing states of consciousness intermediate between the reactive mind and the creative mind from which one can either slide back into the former or rise up into the latter. As the presence of the *mani*-cylinders and the religious offerings suggests, the white segment also represents conventional piety, which being part of the process of the reactive mind is not in itself a sufficient means to Enlightenment and from which, therefore, a reaction to a life of vice and impiety – to the black segment – is always possible.

The Six Realms

The third circle of the wheel of life is divided as though by spokes into five or six segments. These are the five or six 'spheres', or planes, of conditioned existence into which sentient beings are reborn in accordance with their skilful and unskilful bodily, verbal, and mental actions, in other words, as the result of their past 'good' and 'bad' karma. These spheres, depicted in Tibetan religious art with great richness of detail, are (proceeding clockwise from the top) those of the gods, the titans, the hungry ghosts, beings in hell, animals, and human beings. The total number of segments is either five or six depending on whether the gods and the titans, who are engaged in perpetual warfare with each other, are enumerated separately or together. In all the segments the presence of a differently coloured Buddha figure represents the persistence of the possibility of Enlightenment even under the most adverse conditions.

Although the five or six spheres of conditioned existence are usually interpreted cosmologically – as objectively existing worlds which are just as real, for the beings inhabiting them, as our own world is for human beings – it is nevertheless also possible to interpret them psychologically, as representing different states of human life and consciousness – an interpretation which has some sanction in tradition. Looked at in this way the sphere of the gods represents a life of security and contentment, that of the titans one of jealousy, competition, and aggressiveness, that of the hungry ghosts one of neurotic dependence and craving, that of the beings in hell one of physical and mental suffering, that of the animals one of barbarism and ignorance, while the human sphere represents a mixed state of existence with neither pleasure nor pain predominating. In the course of a single lifetime one may experience all six states, living now as it were in 'heaven', now as it were in 'hell', and so on.

'This Being, That Becomes'

The fourth and last circle, or rim of the wheel, is divided into twelve segments, each containing a picture. The twelve pictures (again proceeding clockwise) depict a blind man with a stick, a potter with a wheel and pots, a monkey climbing a flowering tree, a boat with four passengers, one of whom is steering, an empty house, a man and woman embracing, a man with an arrow in his eye, a woman offering a drink to a seated man, a man gathering fruit from a tree, a pregnant woman, a woman in childbirth, and a man carrying a corpse to the cremation ground. These pictures illustrate the twelve 'links' in the chain of cyclical conditionality, each of which arises in dependence on, or is conditioned by, the one immediately preceding.

- In dependence upon ignorance, the 'first' link of the chain, arise
- the volitional factors which determine the nature of the next rebirth.
- These give rise to consciousness, in the sense of the karmically neutral 'resultant' consciousness, which begins functioning at the moment of conception.
- In dependence on consciousness arises the psychophysical organism.
- In dependence on the psychophysical organism arise the six sense-organs (mind being reckoned as a sixth sense).
- In dependence on these there arises contact with the external world,
- which gives rise to sensation,
- which gives rise to craving,
- which gives rise to grasping,
- which gives rise to 'coming-to-be'.
- In dependence on 'coming-to-be', by which is meant the renewed process of conditioned existence, arises birth, in the sense of rebirth, from which sooner or later there inevitably follows
- death.

As even a bare enumeration of them is sufficient to make clear, the twelve links are primarily regarded as being distributed over three successive lives, the first two belonging to the previous life, the middle eight to the present life, and the last two to the future life. However, just as the five or six spheres of sentient existence can be interpreted psychologically as well as cosmologically, so the whole twelve-linked chain of cyclical conditionality is also to be regarded as operating within the limits of a single experience of the reactive mind.

Completing the symbolism, Tibetan religious art depicts the whole wheel of life, with its four circles and its innumerable sentient creatures, as being gripped from behind by a monstrous demon, the head, tail, and claws of whom are visible. This is the demon of Impermanence, or the great principle of Change, which though dreadful to the majority nevertheless contains the promise and potentiality of development, of evolution.

The Wheel as Symbol

From the description just given it is clear that the Tibetan wheel of life is able to symbolize the workings of the reactive mind because the reactive mind is itself a wheel. Like a wheel, it simply goes round and round. Prompted by negative emotions springing from the depths of unawareness, it again and again reacts to stimuli impinging on it from the outside world, and again and again precipitates itself into one or another sphere or mode of conditioned existence. Moreover, the wheel is a machine, perhaps the most primitive of all machines, and as such the wheel of life represents the mechanical and repetitive nature of the reactive mind.

Some paintings of the wheel of life depict in their top right-hand corner the Buddha, clad in the saffron robes of a wanderer, pointing with the fingers of his right hand. He is indicating the path or way. To this symbol, second of the two great symbols with which we are concerned, we must now turn.

THE SPIRAL PATH

As previously explained, just as the wheel of life symbolizes the reactive mind, so the path or way symbolizes the creative mind, or the whole process of cumulative, as distinct from reactive, conditionality. It works on the principle not of *round and round*, but of *up and up*. In the case of the wheel of life, as depicted in Tibetan religious art, practically all the different aspects of the reactive mind coalesce into a single composite symbol of marvellous richness and complexity. For the path or way there seems to be no corresponding picture. Instead, there are a number of relatively independent representations, some of them in the form of images, others in the form of conceptual formulations of the various successive stages of the path. Among the former are the images of the tree of Enlightenment, or cosmic tree, at the foot of which the Buddha seated himself on the eve of his great attainment, and the ladder of jewels on which, after instructing his deceased mother in the higher truths of Buddhism, he descended to earth from the Heaven of the Thirty-three.[27] Among the conceptual formulations of the path are the three trainings (i.e. ethics, meditation, and wisdom), the Noble Eightfold Path, the series of twelve positive 'links' beginning with suffering and ending with knowledge of the destruction of the biases, the seven stages of purification, and the seven 'limbs' of Enlightenment. All these concrete images and conceptual formulations of the path represent one or another aspect of the total process of the creative mind, a process of such multi-faceted splendour that tradition has been unable, apparently, to combine them all into one composite representation of their common object. For the purpose of our present exposition we shall select one of the conceptual formulations of the path, that of the seven 'limbs' of Enlightenment, as this exhibits in a particularly clear and striking manner the cumulative and truly progressive nature of the creative mind.

The Seven Factors of Enlightenment

The seven 'limbs' or 'factors' (*aṅga*) of Enlightenment (*bodhi*) are: recollection or awareness, investigation of mental states, energy or vigour, rapture, 'tension release', concentration, and tranquillity. Each of these limbs or factors arises in dependence on the one immediately preceding – out of its fullness, as it were – and as we shall now see in detail, each one, as it arises, constitutes a still higher development of the creative mind as it spirals towards the final – and everlasting – explosion of creativity that constitutes Enlightenment.[28]

1. Recollection or Awareness (*smṛti*)

As insisted once already, spiritual life begins with awareness, when one becomes aware that one is unaware, or when one wakes up to the fact that one is asleep. Within the context of the total evolutionary process this 'limb' or 'factor', the emergence of which constitutes one a human being, occupies a middle place, being intermediate between the total unawareness, or unconsciousness, of the stone, and the Perfect Awareness of Buddhahood. Within the comparatively narrow but still aeonic context of purely human development, awareness occupies a middle position between the simple sense consciousness of the animal and the higher spiritual awareness of the person who has begun to confront the transcendental. Thus we arrive at a hierarchy which, excluding unconsciousness and the vegetative sensitivity of the plant, consists of the four principal degrees of (1) sense consciousness, (2) human consciousness or awareness proper, (3) transcendental awareness, and (4) Perfect Awareness. As one of the limbs of Enlightenment or

Enlightenment factors, recollection or awareness corresponds to the second of these degrees, that of human consciousness or awareness proper. Awareness in this sense is synonymous with self-consciousness, a term that draws attention to one of the most important characteristics of awareness. Whereas sense consciousness is simply consciousness of external things and of one's own experience, awareness consists in being conscious that one is conscious, in knowing that one knows, or, in a word, of *realizing*. Though the traditional vocabulary of Buddhism does not contain any term strictly correspondent with self-consciousness, the explanation that is given makes it clear that this is what, in fact, it is. Awareness consists, according to the texts, of awareness of one's bodily posture and movements, of one's sensations, whether pleasurable or painful, and of the presence within oneself of skilful and unskilful mental states. More will be said about each of these later on.

2. Investigation of Mental States (*dharma-vicaya*)

From awareness in general we pass to awareness, particularly, of the psychical as distinct from the physical side of our being. This psychical side is not static but dynamic. It is made up of an endless stream of mental states. These states are of two kinds, skilful and unskilful. Unskilful mental states are those rooted in craving, hatred, and delusion. Skilful mental states are those rooted in non-craving, non-hatred, and non-delusion, in other words in contentment, love, and wisdom. The investigation of mental states is a kind of sorting-out operation whereby one distinguishes between the skilful and the unskilful states and separates them into two different categories. In terms of our present discussion one distinguishes between what in the mind is reactive and what is creative. It is, however, awareness that releases creativity. By becoming more aware we not only resolve unawareness, thus eventually achieving self-consciousness or true individuality, but also effect a switch-over of energy from the cyclical to the spiral type of conditionality, that is to say, from the reactive and repetitive to the free and creative type of mental functioning.

3. Energy or Vigour (*vīrya*)

Although often defined as the effort to cultivate skilful and eradicate unskilful mental states, the third Enlightenment factor is much more in the nature of a spontaneous upsurge of energy coming about with the birth of awareness and the growing capacity to discriminate between the reactive and the creative mind. Most people live far below the level of their optimum vitality. Their energies are either expended in ways that are ultimately frustrating or simply blocked. With increased awareness, however, through meditation, and through improved communication with other people – perhaps with the help of a freer lifestyle and more truly fulfilling means of livelihood – a change takes place. Blockages are removed, tensions relaxed. More and more energy is released. Eventually, like a great dynamo humming into activity as soon as the current is switched on, or a tree bursting into bloom as the spring rain flushes up through its branches, the whole being is recharged, revitalized, and one expends oneself in intense creative activity.

4. Rapture (*prīti*)

Release of blocked and frustrated energy is accompanied by an overwhelming feeling of delight and ecstasy which is not confined to the mind but in which the senses and the emotions both participate. This is rapture, the fourth Enlightenment factor, of which there are five degrees. These five degrees produce physical innervations of corresponding degrees of intensity. The lesser thrill is only able to raise the hairs of the body; momentary rapture is like repeated flashes of lightning; flooding rapture descends on the body like waves breaking on the seashore; in all-pervading rapture the whole body is completely surcharged, blown like a full bladder or like a mountain cavern pouring forth a mighty flood of water; while transporting rapture is so strong that it lifts the body up to the extent of launching it in the air. Under ordinary circumstances only prolonged meditation enables one to experience Rapture in its fullness, from the lowest to the highest degree, but this is not to say that it cannot be experienced to a great extent in other ways as well. The creation and enjoyment of works of art, appreciation of the beauties of nature, solving problems in mathematics, authentic human communication – these and similar activities all involve release of energy and all are, therefore, experienced as intensely pleasurable.

5. Tension Release (*praśrabdhi*)

Blocked and frustrated energy having been fully released, the physical innervations by which the release was accompanied gradually subside and the mind experiences a state of non-hedonic spiritual happiness unmixed with any bodily sensation. Subsidence of the physical innervations of rapture, as well as of the perceptions and motivations derived therefrom, is known as tension release. This Enlightenment factor, the fifth in the series, thus represents the stage of transition from the psychosomatic to the mental-spiritual level of experience. Awareness of one's physical body and one's surroundings becomes minimal, or disappears entirely, and one becomes more and more deeply absorbed in a state of 'changeless, timeless bliss' quite impossible to describe.

6. Concentration (*samādhi*)

Impelled by the inherent momentum of one's experience, absorption in this state gradually becomes complete. Such total absorption is known as *samādhi*. Though untranslatable by any one English word, this term is usually rendered as concentration, a meaning which it admittedly does bear in many contexts. As the sixth of the Enlightenment factors, *samādhi* stands for very much more than simple fixation of the mind on a single object, especially if this fixation is understood as something that is achieved forcibly, by sheer exercise of will, or despite strong resistance from other parts of the psyche. Rather is it the spontaneous merging of all the energies of the psyche in an experience so intensely pleasurable that thought and volition are suspended, space vanishes, and time stands still. It is in fact a state of total integration and absorption rather than of 'concentration' in the more limited and artificial sense of the term, and as such can be compared best, though still inadequately, to the experience of the musician rapt in the enjoyment of a piece of music or of the lover immersed in the joys of love.

7. Tranquillity (*upekṣā*)

When perfectly concentrated the mind attains a state of poise and equilibrium free from the slightest trace of wavering or unsteadiness. This equilibrium is not only psychological as between contrary emotional states but spiritual as between such pairs of opposites as enjoyment and suffering, acquisition and deprivation, self and not-self, finite and infinite, existence and non-existence, life and death. As a spiritual state or experience it is known as tranquillity, the seventh and last of the Enlightenment factors and the culmination, so far as this formulation is concerned, of the whole process of the creative mind. Though sometimes connoting simply a psychological state of security and rest it is here synonymous with Nirvāṇa or Enlightenment itself. It is that state of absolute metaphysical axiality – of complete equilibrium of *being* – to which the Buddha refers in the *Maṅgala Sutta*, or 'Discourse on Auspicious Signs', saying:

He whose firm mind, untroubled by the touch
Of all terrestrial happenings whatsoe'er,
Is void of sorrow, stainless, and secure –
This is the most auspicious sign of all.[29]

THE CRUCIAL POINT

In this manner, each member of the series arising out of the abundance – even the exuberance – of the one by which it was immediately preceded, the seven Enlightenment factors collectively illustrate the way in which the creative mind functions, how it progresses from perfection to ever greater perfection, until the fullness of creativity is attained. But having arrived at this point, thus completing our brief study of the two principal symbols of Buddhism, we cannot help asking what the connection is between them. At what point, if any, do the wheel and the path, the circle and the spiral, intersect?

In order to answer this question we shall have to refer back to the twelve links in the chain of cyclical conditionality. Besides being distributed over three successive lifetimes, these are regarded as being either volitions or the results of volitions, and as belonging, therefore, either to what is known as the cause-process or to what is known as the effect-process. Ignorance and the karma-formations, the first two links, constitute the cause-process of the past. They represent the sum total of karmic factors responsible for the present birth, or rather rebirth, of the individual concerned. Consciousness, the psychophysical organism, the six sense-organs, contact, and feeling make up the effect-process of the present life. Craving, grasping, and coming-to-be are the cause-process of the present life, while birth together with old age, disease, and death constitute the effect-process of the future. From this account it is clear that feeling, the last link of the effect-process of the present life, is immediately followed by craving, the first link of the cause-process of the present life. This is the crucial point. This is the point at which the wheel either stops, or begins to make a fresh revolution. It is also the point of intersection between the wheel and the path.

Mindfulness Clear and Radiant

As we have seen, the first of the seven Enlightenment factors is recollection or awareness. If we remain simply aware of the pleasurable and painful feelings that arise within us as a result of our contact with the external world, instead of reacting to them with craving and aversion, then craving, the first link of the cause-process of the present life, will be unable to come into existence. Awareness puts, as it were, a brake on the wheel. For this reason the cultivation of awareness occupies a central place in the Buddhist scheme of spiritual self-discipline. It is the principal means of transition from the reactive mind to the creative mind, from the wheel to the path, from the circle to the spiral – ultimately, from *saṃsāra* to *nirvāṇa*.

Tradition distinguishes four different kinds of awareness, or four different levels on which it is to be cultivated.[30]

- In the first place, one is aware of one's bodily posture and movements. This consists in the awareness that one is, for example, standing, or sitting, or walking, or lying down, as well as in the mindful performance of all bodily actions, from the vigorous use of the morning toothbrush to the delicate wielding, the almost imperceptible manipulation, of the surgeon's scalpel or the artist's brush.
- Secondly, one is aware of one's feelings, pleasant, painful, and neutral, as well as of the emotions arising in direct or indirect dependence upon them. One knows whether one feels elated or depressed, whether one's emotional state is one of love or hatred, hope or fear, frustration or fulfilment, and so on. One is also aware of more complex and ambivalent emotions. In order to be aware of one's feelings and emotional reactions one must of course allow oneself to experience

them, one must recognize and acknowledge them as one's own. This is not to recommend emotional self-indulgence, but only to emphasize the fact that repression and awareness are incompatible.

- Thirdly, one is aware of one's thoughts. This consists not only of the vigilant observation of images and ideas, mental associations, trains of reflection, and conceptual systems, but also in seeing to what extent these are rooted in the unskilful states of neurotic craving, aversion, and spiritual ignorance, and to what extent they are rooted in the opposite states, that is to say in states of contentment, love, and wisdom. Practising these three kinds of awareness, or cultivating awareness on these three different levels, we begin to see how conditioned we are, how machine-like in our functioning, how dead.

- Fourthly and lastly, one is aware of the difference between one's past dead state of mental conditionedness and mechanicalness and one's (potential) more alive future state of freedom and spontaneity. Awareness of the wheel and of the fact that one is bound on the wheel generates awareness of the path, as well as of the fact that one has the capacity to follow it.

Awareness is therefore of crucial importance in human existence. As the bud presages the flower, so the development of awareness heralds the dawn of the still higher development that we term the spiritual life. Such being the case it is not surprising that in Buddhism there are a number of practices designed to promote the growth of this all-important quality, but it must be emphasized that unless we exercise the utmost caution these practices will themselves tend to become mechanical and, therefore, bricks in the prison-house of our conditionedness rather than the implements of its destruction. The same warning applies to all 'religious' beliefs and practices without exception. If eternal vigilance is the price of mundane liberty how much more is it the price of spiritual freedom! Whether studying mystical theology or making votive offerings, engaging in spiritual discussion with friends or reading about 'Mind – Reactive and Creative', unless we remember the Buddha's 'Parable of the Raft'[31] and constantly remind ourselves what the true function of all these activities is, there is the danger that we shall find ourselves not midstream on the raft, not bound for the further shore, but on the contrary taking refuge in a structure which, while apparently constructed out of the same materials as the raft, nevertheless remains firmly stuck in the mudflats of this shore. Only by remaining constantly on our guard shall we succeed in making the difficult transition from the reactive mind to the creative mind, thus inheriting the spirit of the Buddha's teaching and realizing the true purpose of human life.

THE TASTE OF FREEDOM

Brighton, England, 1979.

What is Buddhism? Over the years there have been quite a number of attempts to answer this question, or to define this protean term. Buddhism has been defined as a code or system of ethics, as an Eastern philosophy, and even as a form of Eastern mysticism. It has been described as a spiritual path and as a tradition. By some people, on at least some occasions, it has even been described as a religion. Worse still, for the last hundred or so years it has been described as 'Buddhism'. Until that time what we nowadays call Buddhism was known simply as the Dharma or, more precisely, as the *Dharma-Vinaya*: the principle and the practice.

But going back to the beginning, we find that it was the Buddha himself who gave us the best definition – or at least the best description – of Buddhism, and he gave it in the form of an image rather than in terms of concepts or abstract ideas. The Buddha simply said that Buddhism, or the *Dharma-Vinaya*, was an ocean, a great and mighty ocean.

This description occurs in a Pāli text: the *Udāna* or 'Verses of Uplift'. The *Udāna* tells us that one full moon night the Buddha was seated surrounded by a great number of what the text calls *bhikkhus*.[32] This word is usually translated, in its singular form, as 'monk' or 'brother', but is perhaps better translated as 'partaker', the *bhikkhu* being one who partakes of, or shares in, the food of the land in the form of his daily alms, as well as one who partakes of, or shares in, the spiritual life along with the Buddha and his fellow disciples. Thus the Buddha was seated surrounded by a great number of partakers. According to the *Udāna*, they all sat there together, in complete silence, not just for one or two hours, but for the whole night. They didn't say a word. They didn't fidget. They didn't even blow their noses. One could say they meditated together, but perhaps they were all at a stage where you don't even need to meditate. You simply sit there – all night.

Then, just as dawn was about to break, something happened. I won't go into the full story, but it transpired that one of those present, though professing to be committed to the spiritual life, was in fact 'unvirtuous, wicked, unclean, of suspect habits, secretive of his acts, no monk but claiming to be one'. Mahā-Moggallāna, who among all the Buddha's disciples was known for the accuracy of his intuition, became aware of this man's true nature, and prevailed upon him to leave. And it was with reference to this incident that the Buddha described the *Dharma-Vinaya* in terms of the 'mighty ocean'. There were eight strange and wonderful things about the mighty ocean, he said, and similarly there were eight strange and wonderful things about the *Dharma-Vinaya*.

THE EIGHT STRANGE AND WONDERFUL THINGS

Firstly, the mighty ocean gets deeper little by little. We are to imagine, it seems, a gradually sloping shore, not a coastline of sheer cliffs dropping suddenly into the sea. Similarly, the training, the course, the path, of the *Dharma-Vinaya* is gradual. There is no abrupt penetration of knowledge. The path is – as we shall see in the next chapter – a path of regular steps.

Secondly, the Buddha said, the mighty ocean is 'of a stable nature, not overpassing its boundary'. Just so, the Buddha's disciples do not transgress, even for the sake of life itself, the training he has enjoined on them. In more familiar terms, the commitment of the Buddha's disciples to the *Dharma-Vinaya* is absolute.

Thirdly, the mighty ocean 'does not associate with a dead body but casts it up on to the shore'. In the same way, the sangha or spiritual community of the Buddha's disciples rejects one who is not, in fact, leading a spiritual life, though outwardly professing to do so. Even though seated in the midst of the sangha such a person is far from the sangha, and the sangha is far from him. This, of course, is a reference to what has just happened. In other words, there is no such thing as nominal membership of the spiritual community. There is no such thing as honorary membership. Sooner or later, therefore, a nominal member will have to 'leave', or rather, as the bogus 'partaker' did, simply find himself or herself outside.

Fourthly, when great rivers reach the mighty ocean they abandon their former names and lineage, and instead of being known as the Ganges, the Jumna, and so on, are reckoned simply as 'mighty ocean'. In the same way those who 'go forth' from home into the homeless life in response to the *Dharma-Vinaya* proclaimed by the Buddha lose their former names and lineage and are reckoned simply as 'ascetics who are sons of the Śākyan', that is to say, ascetics who are disciples or followers of the Buddha. In other words, they become part of the spiritual community – or, to put it more precisely, they are 'merged' with the spiritual community without losing their individual spiritual identity.

The Buddha himself spoke in terms of abandoning one's *caste* identity as a noble, a Brahmin, a merchant, or a serf – those being the four main hereditary castes of his day. But we in the West must think in rather different terms. We can speak, for example, of abandoning our national identity. Within the spiritual community there is no question of being English or Irish or Scottish or Welsh, no question of being American or Indian or Australian or Finnish or Dutch. Within the spiritual community one is simply a spiritually committed human being, relating as such to other spiritually committed human beings.

Fifthly, whatever streams flow into the mighty ocean, or whatever rains fall from the sky, the mighty ocean neither increases nor decreases. This is not strictly true, of course: in the Buddha's day people did not, it seems, know anything about the polar ice caps. However, that does not really matter. The important thing is not the scientific accuracy of the comparison, but the point it is meant to illustrate. If we can imagine that the mighty ocean neither increases nor decreases, then we can say that, similarly, though many people pass finally away into that condition of Nirvāṇa which 'leaves nothing behind', yet that condition of Nirvāṇa neither increases nor decreases.

Sixthly, the mighty ocean has one taste, the taste of salt. Just so, the *Dharma-Vinaya* has one taste, the taste of freedom.

Seventhly, the mighty ocean contains many kinds of gems. As the poet Gray puts it in his 'Elegy in a Country Churchyard',

Full many a gem of purest ray serene
The dark unfathom'd caves of ocean bear.

Similarly, the *Dharma-Vinaya* contains many kinds of spiritual teachings, such as the four foundations of mindfulness, the five spiritual faculties, the seven factors of Enlightenment, the Noble Eightfold Path, and so on.

Eighthly and lastly, the mighty ocean is the abode of monsters such as the leviathan, the fisheater, and so on. Here the *Udāna* seems to be a little uncertain about its marine biology, but evidently creatures like whales and sharks are meant, besides creatures of a more fabulous kind. Whatever they are, the mighty ocean is their abode. In the same way, the *Dharma-Vinaya* is the abode of great beings such as Stream Entrants, once-returners, non-returners, and *arhants*. It is also the abode, we could add (though the *Udāna* does not actually say so), of bodhisattvas and *mahāsiddhas*, gurus and *devas*, *ḍākas* and *ḍākinīs* and *dharmapālas*.

Thus there are these eight strange and wonderful things about the mighty ocean, and these eight strange and wonderful things about the *Dharma-Vinaya*. And of these eight things we are here going to be focusing on the sixth, on the fact that the *Dharma-Vinaya*, or what we have got into the habit – unfortunately – of calling Buddhism, has 'the taste of freedom'. But before doing so, let us pause for a moment over something that we might easily overlook in the Buddha's description of the *Dharma-Vinaya* as being like the mighty ocean. We need to allow these two epithets – 'strange' and 'wonderful' – to have their full effect on us.

In what sense is the mighty ocean strange? Here we must remember that the Buddha lived and taught in the valley of the Ganges, many hundreds of miles from the sea. So far as we know, he had never seen the mighty ocean, and the vast majority of his disciples had never seen it either. They had probably simply heard a rumour to the effect that far beyond their own land there existed a great body of water far greater than any river, greater even than the Ganges itself. So to them the mighty ocean was a foreign, an unfamiliar, element.

It was the same – it *is* the same – in the case of the *Dharma-Vinaya*. The *Dharma-Vinaya* is strange to us. We can in fact go further and say that the spiritual life is strange to us; the Unconditioned is strange to us; the Transcendental is strange to us. It is something of which we have only heard. It is foreign to us; it is not our native element. Indeed, the

Buddha himself is strange to us. He is a stranger in an ultimate sense. He comes from another world, another dimension, as it were. He stands at our door, perhaps, but we do not recognize him. Even the spiritual community is strange to us if we are not ourselves true individuals, or are not spiritually committed. Thus the mighty ocean of the *Dharma-Vinaya* is strange to us.

But in what sense is the mighty ocean wonderful? It is wonderful in its vast extent. It is wonderful in its perpetual movement: it never rests, not even for a moment, not even the tiniest particle of it. It is wonderful in its uninterrupted music: 'the sound of the ocean tide'. It is wonderful in its ever-changing lights and colours: the blue and the green and the mauve; the purple, the gold. It is wonderful in its unfathomable depths. It is particularly wonderful when we see it, and come into contact with it, and perhaps swim in it, when we plunge in, move our arms and legs about and, perhaps for the first time in our lives, find that we are swimming in the mighty ocean. Or at least, if we haven't summoned up the nerve to take the plunge, we can at least paddle, feeling the force of the waves, looking in wonder towards the horizon where sea meets sky.

It is the same with the *Dharma-Vinaya*, except that the *Dharma-Vinaya* is not simply vast; it is infinite. The *Dharma-Vinaya* – the principle and the practice of the Dharma – is a shoreless ocean. We can see no end to it. And it is not fixed, rigid, static, unmoving, unchanging, but full of life, full of movement. It is continually adapting itself to the needs of living beings, continually speaking to us, singing to us, playing its own inimitable music to us, in its own indescribably appealing and fascinating way. It is no dull religious monument; it is alive with all sorts of brilliant and tender lights, all sorts of vivid and delicate colours. It is alive with the radiantly colourful forms of Buddhas and bodhisattvas, *ḍākas* and *ḍākinīs*. And it is so deep, this mighty ocean of the *Dharma-Vinaya*, that we can never hope to fathom it. The *Dharma-Vinaya* is wonderful in all these ways.

Perhaps we don't usually think of the *Dharma-Vinaya* in this manner; but this is what it is really like. It is wonderful. The Buddha is wonderful. As Mātṛceṭa says in his 'Five Hundred Verses of Worship':

What steadfastness! What conduct! What form! What virtues!
In a Buddha's dharmas [attributes] there is nothing that is not
wonderful.[33]

The spiritual community is wonderful. Spiritual life is wonderful. It is wonderful that we can sit and meditate together. It is wonderful that we can live in residential spiritual communities. It is wonderful that we can work in right livelihood projects. It is wonderful that I am able to speak to you in this way. It is wonderful that what I am communicating in the form of a talk can be metamorphosed by editors into the chapter of a book. It is wonderful that you are reading this book now. Thus the *Dharma-Vinaya* is indeed wonderful: strange and wonderful.

Perhaps this is how we experience the *Dharma-Vinaya* when we first come across it, and we might think that we will never forget how wonderful it is. But after a while, I'm sorry to say, we are only too likely to start experiencing Buddhism – or spiritual life – as 'old hat': a stage we went through when we were young and naive, but which we have long since outgrown. It is said that familiarity breeds contempt, but it is probably more true to say that familiarity breeds indifference.

Of course, in the case of the *Dharma-Vinaya*, the familiarity that breeds contempt is usually with the words, concepts, and external forms in which it finds expression. But the *Dharma-Vinaya* is not to be identified with its external forms. And if we become familiar with the *spirit* of the *Dharma-Vinaya*, or even have a tongue-tip taste of it, we will see the *Dharma-Vinaya* as more and more wonderful. It is important to keep alive this sense that the *Dharma-Vinaya* is a wonderful thing; and thus at the same time keep alive a sense of the spirit of the *Dharma-Vinaya*. According to Plato, philosophy begins with a sense of wonder; and certainly there is no spiritual life without an ever-continuing sense of wonder.[34]

But we can go further than that – and in the *Udāna* the Buddha does so. The *Udāna* goes further than that. After describing the eight strange and wonderful qualities of the *Dharma-Vinaya*, the Buddha says 'These, then, partakers, are the eight strange and wonderful things in this *Dharma-Vinaya*, beholding which again and again partakers take delight in this *Dharma-Vinaya*.'

Here again we find a couple of very significant expressions. Firstly, just as some people see a film again and again without ever becoming tired of it, so the partakers – that is, the followers of the Buddha – see the *Dharma-Vinaya*, look at the *Dharma-Vinaya*, hear the *Dharma-Vinaya*, without ever becoming tired of it. In fact the more they see and hear of the *Dharma-Vinaya* the more wonderful it appears.

Secondly, the partakers take delight in the *Dharma-Vinaya*. The *Dharma-Vinaya* is not only wonderful but also enjoyable. It is enjoyable because it is wonderful. It is wonderful because it is enjoyable. Spiritual life is enjoyable. Meditation is enjoyable. Living in a residential spiritual community is enjoyable. Working in a right livelihood project is enjoyable. Being 'thrown in at the deep end' is enjoyable. Not being allowed to rationalize away our slips and failings is enjoyable. It is important to remember this: that in every way the *Dharma-Vinaya* is enjoyable. Buddhism is enjoyable. It is something in which, seeing it again and again, we take delight. It is hardly necessary to point out how greatly this differs from the usual conception of religion and religious life.

And of all the strange and wonderful qualities of the *Dharma-Vinaya*, I want now to focus on one in particular: that it has the taste of freedom.

WHAT IS FREEDOM?

This is perhaps a question that we ask ourselves even more often than we ask 'What is Buddhism?' and the answer for most of us will have, probably, something to do with civil and political liberties. However, the concept we are dealing with here is expressed by another word altogether, of which 'freedom' is just a translation. In Sanskrit this is *vimukti* (the Pāli is *vimutti*), which translates as 'release', 'emancipation', or 'freedom'. Thus we are concerned not with the meaning of the English word, as such, but only with its meaning as a provisional equivalent of the original Pāli term. We are concerned with freedom in the sense of *vimukti*, not with *vimukti* in the sense of freedom.

What, then, is *vimukti*? In order to begin to understand this we shall have to see what place *vimukti* occupies in the complete scheme of spiritual self-development; and we can do this by looking at where it comes in the series of the 'positive' *nidānas*, as I have called them.

These *nidānas* represent stages of spiritual development. They are called *nidānas* or 'links' because each one arises in dependence on the one preceding or, we may say, out of the fullness of the one preceding. Thus in dependence on suffering arises faith and devotion; in dependence on faith and devotion arises satisfaction and delight; in dependence on satisfaction and delight arises rapture; in dependence on rapture arises tranquillity; in dependence on tranquillity arises bliss;

in dependence on bliss arises *samādhi* or 'concentration' – in the sense not of mere mental concentration, but of the complete integration of all the psychophysical energies of one's being; in dependence on *samādhi* arises knowledge and vision of things as they really are; in dependence on knowledge and vision of things as they really are arises disengagement, or disentanglement; in dependence on disengagement, or disentanglement, arises dispassion; in dependence on dispassion arises *vimukti*; in dependence on *vimukti* arises knowledge of the destruction of the 'biases' (craving, wrong views, and ignorance).

And this is the last of the twelve positive *nidānas*, for knowledge of the destruction of the biases is equivalent to Enlightenment, representing the goal and consummation of the entire spiritual life, as well as the complete overcoming of mundane existence, and, by implication, the complete realization of the Unconditioned and Transcendental.

This is not the place for a detailed account of this progressive series. Simply listing them, however, makes clear one thing at least: that *vimukti* occupies a very high place indeed in the whole series, and thus in the complete scheme of spiritual self-development. It is, in fact, the penultimate stage. *Vimukti* is not, therefore, what we ordinarily understand by freedom: it goes far, far beyond that. It goes far beyond any question of political and civil liberties, and far beyond freedom in the ordinary psychological sense. But if this is so, then what are we to make of the term? Let us see if we can work our way towards a clearer impression of the nature of freedom in the sense of *vimukti*.

The fourth to the seventh *nidānas* – rapture, tranquillity, bliss, and *samādhi* – represent the process of what is usually called meditation, that is to say, meditation in the sense of an actual experience of higher states of consciousness, not meditation simply in the sense of preliminary concentration. They constitute meditation in the sense of what is technically called *śamatha* or 'calm', and they are very considerable attainments indeed. But it is the next stage, 'knowledge and vision of things as they really are', that is the important one. In fact, the transition from *samādhi* to knowledge and vision of reality is absolutely crucial. It represents the great turning point in the spiritual life. It is the point at which our most refined, most blissful, most beatific experience of the conditioned, or of the mundane, is succeeded by the first 'experience' – there is no other word for us to use here – of the unconditioned, the transcendental. 'Knowledge and vision of things as they really are' thus constitutes a form of what is technically called *vipaśyanā* or insight.

The fact that *vimukti* occurs subsequent to knowledge and vision of things as they really are (with two other stages in between) means that there is no *vimukti* – no real freedom – without insight. Moreover, when 'knowledge and vision of things as they really are' arises, and one makes that crucial transition from calm to insight, one is said – in traditional Buddhist language – to 'enter the stream': one becomes a 'Stream Entrant', or – to use another traditional term – an *ārya-pudgala* or 'true individual'. So freedom in the sense of *vimukti* is accessible only to one who has become a Stream Entrant, a true individual.

All this should establish unequivocally the scale of experience denoted by the term *vimukti*, or freedom. However, it may still leave us little the wiser as to the actual nature of *vimukti*. To begin to estimate this we need to look at that crucial point when we 'enter the stream'. What in fact happens as we do that, or as that happens to us – both these expressions here have the same meaning – is that we break free from (or there are broken) the first three 'fetters' binding us to the lower, grosser levels of mundane existence. It is the breaking of these fetters that will give us a real 'taste of freedom'.

These three fetters are usually described as: firstly, the fetter of belief in an essential, unchanging self; secondly, the fetter of doubt and indecision with regard to the Dharma; and thirdly, the fetter of attachment to religious observances as ends in themselves. Here, however, we are going to approach them in very general, even basic – or down-to-earth – terms, as: firstly, the fetter of *habit*; secondly, the fetter of *vagueness*; and thirdly, the fetter of *superficiality*.[35]

THE FETTER OF HABIT

A habit is something we are said to *have*. We have 'the tendency or disposition to act in a particular way'. However, as this dictionary definition makes clear, a habit consists of actions, and action is an essential part of us, not just something added on, something we have. In fact according to the *Dharma-Vinaya* we *are* our actions. And this is the way we usually think of, and refer to, a person: someone is the sum total of his or her actions of body, speech, and mind, and doesn't exist apart from these.

The fact that we have a 'tendency or disposition to *act* in a particular way' means, therefore, that we have a tendency or disposition to *be* in a particular way. We are not just the sum total of our actions: we are the sum total of our habits. We *are* our habits. We could even say that each one of us is simply a habit – probably a bad habit. The person we think of as George or Mary, and recognize as acting in a particular way, is simply a habit that a certain stream of consciousness has got into.

But since it has got into it, it can get out of it. It is like a knot tied in a piece of string: it can be untied. Breaking the fetter of habit means, essentially, getting out of the habit of being a particular kind of person. It is only a habit you have got into. You don't *have* to be the way you are. There is no necessity about it. Breaking the fetter of habit means, therefore, getting rid of the old self, the past self. It means becoming a true individual; that is, becoming continually aware and emotionally positive, continually responsible, sensitive, and creative – continually creative of one's own self.

This is the meaning of the Buddhist doctrine of *anātman* (Pāli *anattā*) or 'no-self'. It is not so much that we never have a self as that we always have a *new* self. And if each new self is a better one than the last, then we can say that spiritual progress is taking place.

It is not easy to get out of the habit of being the kind of person that we are. It is not easy to get rid of the old self and become a true individual. One of the reasons for this is other people. Not only have we ourselves got into the habit of being in a particular way, but other people have got into the habit of experiencing us as being in the habit of being in a particular way.

The people who experience us as what we *were* rather than as what we *are* – or what we are in process of becoming – represent a collective way of thinking, feeling, and acting. They represent the group as opposed to the individual. The group is the enemy of the individual – of the true individual – inasmuch as it will not allow the true individual to emerge from its ranks. It insists on dealing with you not as you are but as you were, and to this extent it tries to deal with someone who no longer exists. This tends to happen, for example, when one visits one's family after some time.

Becoming free of the group does not, of course, necessarily mean actually breaking off relations with the group. What it means is breaking away from the influence – the habit-reinforcing influence – of the group.

'Vague' means 'indistinct, not clearly expressed or identified, of uncertain or ill-defined meaning or character'. So why should anyone *be* vague? The fact is, we are vague when we are undecided, vague when we don't *want* to decide, and, above all, vague when we don't want to commit ourselves. Our vagueness is, therefore, a dishonest vagueness.

After all, spiritual life is very difficult. Growth and development is often a painful process (even though it is always enjoyable). Therefore we tend to shrink back. We keep our options open. We keep a number of different interests, or a number of different aims, on which we can fall back, and allow ourselves to oscillate between them, even to drift between them. At all costs we remain vague: woolly, foggy, shapeless, indistinct, unclear.

Breaking the fetter of vagueness means being willing to think clearly. It means giving time to thinking things out, having the determination to think things through. It means being prepared to look at what the alternatives really are, and to sort out one's priorities. It means being ready to make up one's mind. It means making a decision to choose the best and then to act wholeheartedly upon that choice. It means not postponing the moment of decision.

THE FETTER OF SUPERFICIALITY

To be superficial means to act from the surface of ourselves and, in consequence, to act without thoroughness or care; it is about acting in outward appearance rather than genuinely or actually. Now why should we do this? Why should we act superficially?

The reason is that we are divided. More often than not, the conscious rational surface is divided from the unconscious emotional depths. We act out of intellectual conviction but do not succeed in carrying the emotions with us. Sometimes, of course, we do act out of the fullness of our emotions but then, only too often, the rational mind holds back, and even, perhaps, does not approve. In neither case do we act totally, wholeheartedly. We do not act with the whole of ourselves and, therefore, in a sense, do not really act at all.

This state of affairs is very general. Superficiality is one of the curses of the modern age. Matthew Arnold, more than a hundred years ago, spoke of our 'sick hurry', our 'divided aims' – and that just about describes the situation.[36] We are neurotically busy, without any real focus, any singleness of purpose. We don't truly, authentically, do anything. We don't do anything with the whole force of our being. When we love we don't really love, and when we hate we don't really hate. We don't even really think. We half do all these things.

It is the same, only too often, when we take up the spiritual life and try to follow the *Dharma-Vinaya*. When we meditate, it is only with part of ourselves. When we communicate, or when we work, again it is only with part of ourselves. Consequently we don't get very far: we don't really grow; we don't really develop. We don't carry the whole of our being along with us, so to speak. A small part of us is prospecting ahead, but the greater part is lagging far behind.

Breaking the fetter of superficiality therefore means acting with the whole of oneself: acting with thoroughness and care; acting genuinely and actually. It means, in a word, commitment. It means committing oneself to the spiritual life, committing oneself to being a true individual.

TASTING THE TEACHINGS

The three fetters – of habit, of vagueness, and of superficiality – are broken by means of insight, that is, by means of knowledge and vision of things as they really are. In less traditional terms, they are broken by our becoming creative (in the sense of self-creative or creative of our own new self), by becoming clear, and by becoming committed. When insight arises, one enters the Stream, the Stream that leads directly to Enlightenment: one becomes a Stream Entrant and, being a Stream Entrant, one becomes a true individual. And as a true individual, one can experience *vimukti*, one can enjoy the taste of freedom.

Two key points emerge from all this. The first is that only the true individual is really free; the second, that one becomes a true individual only by developing insight: that is, by breaking the three fetters and thereby becoming creative, clear, and committed. This is freedom.

So what does the Buddha mean by the *taste* of freedom? When the Buddha says 'Just as the mighty ocean has one taste, the taste of salt, so the *Dharma-Vinaya* has one taste, the taste of freedom' – what does this mean? It means, of course, what it says – that the *Dharma-Vinaya* is wholly pervaded by the taste of freedom. Every part of it has that taste.

The *Dharma-Vinaya* consists of a great many things – perhaps more now than in the Buddha's own day. It consists of all sorts of teachings, all sorts of practices, all sorts of institutions. It consists of philosophies, concentration techniques, ethical systems, rituals, arts – entire cultures, in fact. But the one question that must be asked about all these things is: do they have the taste of freedom? That is, do they help us, directly or indirectly, to become free in the sense of *vimukti*? Do they help us to develop insight – i.e. to break the three fetters and 'enter the Stream' – and thus become true individuals? Because if they do not, then they form no part of the Buddha's teaching, no part of the *Dharma-Vinaya*.

It must be admitted that there are many things in the traditional practice of Buddhism in the East with regard to which we cannot answer these questions in the affirmative. Whether it is the Theravāda, or Tibetan Buddhism, or Zen, there are many elements within these rich and important traditions that do not have this 'taste of freedom'. This is why we do not, in the Friends of the Western Buddhist Order, identify ourselves exclusively with any one form of traditional Buddhism. Instead, we follow the Buddha's own advice and accept as his teaching only what helps us to grow, or what actually has the taste of freedom.

One issue raised by the title of this essay remains unaddressed. How is it that the Buddha speaks not of the *idea* or *concept* of freedom but of its *taste*? One could, of course, argue that he does this only because he has already spoken of the mighty ocean as having the taste of salt: that the word 'taste' is used literally when referring to the ocean, and only metaphorically with regard to freedom. However, it is in fact the ocean that is the metaphor, not the *Dharma-Vinaya*. He speaks of the taste of salt in order to emphasize a corresponding quality of the *Dharma-Vinaya*: that the *Dharma-Vinaya* likewise has its characteristic taste – the taste of freedom. He wants to emphasize that freedom is something to be tasted. So what is this really about?

The Pāli term translated as 'taste' is *rasa*, which means 'juice, special quality, flavour, taste, relish, pleasure, essential property, extract, or essence'. So *rasa* in the first place means 'juice', and juice is liquid, flowing, has no fixed form. And freedom or *vimukti* is like that. It is not fixed or definite, not conditioned. On the contrary, it is absolute and unconditioned. And the *Dharma-Vinaya*, being pervaded by the taste of freedom, is likewise an uninterrupted flow of spiritual and transcendental states. It may crystallize into different teachings, practices, and so on, but it is not to be identified with them; it remains an uninterrupted flow.

Rasa means not only 'juice', but also 'taste'; and taste is a matter of direct experience. So the taste of freedom as an all-pervading quality of the *Dharma-Vinaya* is a direct, personal experience of freedom. If you practise the *Dharma-Vinaya* you will yourself become free.

Another expression offered to translate *rasa* is 'special quality'. The direct experience of freedom is the special quality of the *Dharma-Vinaya*, i.e. the quality by which you can recognize it. If it doesn't have this quality it isn't the *Dharma-Vinaya*, just as if something doesn't taste sweet it can't be sugar.

This brings us to yet another aspect of the meaning of *rasa*. That special quality of the *Dharma-Vinaya* gives it its distinctive 'flavour'. With practice we begin to appreciate this flavour, even to relish it: we begin to take pleasure in it, and to enjoy it. And so we find that *rasa* means also 'relish' and 'pleasure'.

Furthermore, *rasa* means 'essential property'. The experience of freedom is an essential property of the *Dharma-Vinaya*, and there is no *Dharma-Vinaya* without it. Whatever else you may have, if you don't have the experience of freedom you don't have the *Dharma-Vinaya*. Finally, *rasa* means 'extract' or 'essence'. If you were able to take the mighty ocean of the *Dharma-Vinaya* and distil it, if you were able to boil it down and condense it into a single drop, that drop would be freedom, or *vimukti*.

If we were then to visualize an image of that quintessential spirit, we would begin with the image of space or the image of the usual way we perceive space: the sky, infinite in extent, deep blue in colour, and perfectly pure. In the midst of this image there would be another image: a figure flying through the sky. It is a naked, red figure, a female figure. Her long black hair is streaming out behind her, her face is uplifted in ecstasy, and there is a smile on her lips. She is what is known in Buddhist tradition as the *ḍākinī* or 'lady of space', the embodiment of the spiritual energy of the Buddha. She is absolutely free: free to fly in any direction – north, south, east, west, the zenith, and the nadir. She is free, even, to remain still. Hers is the liberty of infinite space. She enjoys the Taste of Freedom.

THE PATH OF REGULAR STEPS AND
THE PATH OF IRREGULAR STEPS

Caxton Hall, Westminster, under the auspices of the London Buddhist Society, 23 October 1974.

In recent years the whole character of Buddhism in the West has radically and crucially changed. Buddhists today are likely to be much more deeply and wholeheartedly involved in the actual practice of Buddhism than they would have been before. They are much more concerned with the application of the Dharma – the teaching of the Buddha – to all aspects of their lives. Thus this radical and crucial change is essentially a change on the level of the individual Buddhist.

As you put an ever greater effort into following the path, changes take place in your being and consciousness, and because of these changes you begin to see things differently. What was formerly important becomes unimportant, and vice versa. Such radical change may bring problems to be confronted; but as your Buddhist life simultaneously broadens and deepens, a sublime range of opportunities opens up before you. Not only that: as you actually follow the path taught by the Buddha – as you *become* that path – you begin to understand its nature more and more deeply and clearly.

You begin to see that within the one great central path there are a number of alternative pathways to follow, or rather, that there are different ways of following the path – some, perhaps, more helpful than others. In particular, you begin to appreciate the importance for your whole future spiritual development of the absolutely basic distinction between the path of regular steps and the path of irregular steps.

This distinction is a very ancient one. It goes back to sixth-century China, to the great Chinese teacher Zhiyi, who was the virtual founder of one of the greatest of all Buddhist schools – though so far rather neglected by Western Buddhists – the Tiantai school.[37] Besides producing important works of scholarship, Zhiyi founded monasteries and preached the Dharma widely. By reason of his profound spiritual attainments he was able to attract an extraordinarily large number of disciples, and these he addressed from time to time, commenting upon the scriptures, speaking about the spiritual life, and especially, it seems, giving instruction on meditation. In the course of his discourses on meditation, many of which have come down to us, Zhiyi spoke of meditation by regular steps, of meditation by irregular steps, and also of meditation without any steps at all.

When one mentions the third kind of meditation people usually become rather interested. They are not at all interested in meditation by regular steps, which sounds rather dull and prosaic. Meditation by irregular steps appeals to them quite a bit. But what really captivates and fascinates them is the idea of 'meditation without any steps at all', which means that one attains Enlightenment instantaneously by means of one phrase or even one word.

Unfortunately, people are usually attracted to this kind of meditation for entirely the wrong reasons; and at the risk of disappointing some readers we shall not give it any further consideration here. However, this still leaves us with more than enough to chew over, because Zhiyi's distinction between meditation by regular steps and meditation by irregular steps is applicable not only to the practice of meditation but to the practice and experience of the whole spiritual path, in all its stages and all its aspects.

The fact that one can approach the path, or the spiritual life, either by way of regular steps or by way of irregular steps is well understood in the Buddhist East, even though the two ways are not always differentiated in these terms. However, in Western Buddhist circles it is only recently that people have begun to appreciate the importance of the distinction between them – or even mention it. Perhaps the reason for this is that we have only recently reached the point where such a distinction becomes meaningful and helpful and even, I may say, necessary if we are to make further progress.

What then is the path of regular steps? What is the path of irregular steps? In attempting to answer these questions I propose to be a little irregular myself and deal with the second path first.

THE PATH OF IRREGULAR STEPS

When we look at Buddhism in the West today, the first thing that we see is books – hundreds of books – about Buddhism. This is the most conspicuous feature of Buddhism in the West. We see big books and small books, little pamphlets from the East and lavishly illustrated volumes from leading publishing houses in London and New York. We see simple, popular introductions to Buddhism, even books for children, and we see works of pure and daunting scholarship. We see books on Theravāda, books on Mahāyāna, and of course books on Zen and the Tantra. We see books written by Buddhists of various persuasions, books written by non-Buddhists, books written by anti-Buddhists, and books written by all sorts of people who do not know *what* they are. Some of these books are original works, the product of much independent thought and study, while others are translations from Sanskrit, Pāli, Chinese, Japanese, and so on. Altogether, there are thousands upon thousands of books with a connection of one sort or another with Buddhism.

If we are young and enthusiastic, and have lots of time, we start trying to read them all – or at least as many as we can of the better-known ones. Some of us may even get around to reading the Buddhist scriptures as well. And as we start to get an impression of Buddhism through our miscellaneous reading we also start forming ideas about it. These ideas tend to be very confused. If one approaches Buddhism through books one is almost bound to start off with confused ideas, so much so that we do not even begin to realize how confused we are until perhaps years afterwards – if indeed we ever do. But meanwhile, if we do enough reading, it is possible to make the big mistake of thinking that we understand Buddhism.

Then if we are not careful we may be tempted, after a few years, to share our understanding – in other words, our confusion – with other people. We start writing and speaking on Buddhism and in this way become quite well known: we may even have people sitting at our feet and drinking in our words of wisdom. We may be asked to speak on the radio, or appear on television, and with a little luck we may even be invited to 'represent Buddhism' – whatever that may mean – at some interreligious gathering. But, all this time, what is really the position?

The position is that, quite literally, we do not understand Buddhism at all. It is not that we have a limited or partial grasp of Buddhism. The position is that if we think we understand Buddhism, we do not understand it at all.

When we understand a thing – whether we really understand it or just think we do – we become in some sense superior to that thing. Understanding means appropriating; it means taking the subject of one's knowledge into oneself, making it part of oneself, making it one's own. Thus we speak in terms of 'mastering' a subject: mastering accountancy, or mastering mathematics. And so we speak, or at least think – or even half-think – of mastering Buddhism. In this way the idea we have that we might understand or master Buddhism precludes the possibility of looking up to it, of feeling towards Buddhism, towards the Dharma, any real devotion or reverence. In 'mastering' the subject we have completely misunderstood it.

This kind of attitude is not new, and it is by no means confined to modern Western Buddhists. It has been widespread in the Western world for quite a long time. We find Samuel Taylor Coleridge, the great poet and thinker, complaining about it 150 years ago (of course, within a Christian context) in the following terms:

There is now no reverence for any thing; and the reason is that men possess conceptions only, and all their knowledge is conceptional only. Now as to conceive is a work of the mere understanding, and as all that can be conceived may be comprehended, it is impossible that a man should reverence that to which he must always feel something in himself superior. If it were possible to conceive God in a strict sense, that is, as we conceive of a horse or a tree, even God himself could not excite any reverence.

And reverence, Coleridge goes on to say,

is only due from man, and, indeed, only excitable in man, towards ideal truths, which are always mysteries to the understanding, for the same reason that the motion of my finger behind my back is a mystery to you now – your eyes not being made for seeing through my body.[38]

At about the same time as Coleridge was delivering himself of these sentiments, an even greater poet and thinker was saying much the same thing, though rather more briefly. In his *Maxims and Reflections* Goethe writes:

The finest achievement for men of thought is to have fathomed the fathomable, and quietly to revere the unfathomable.[39]

It is this quiet revering of the unfathomable, of that which, in Buddhist terminology, is *atakkāvacara* or beyond the reach of thought – beyond the reach of understanding and conception – that until recently has been so lacking among Western Buddhists. We have been much too quick to 'understand', much too ready to speak, even about the unfathomable – in fact, *especially* about the unfathomable.

This is not altogether our fault. To a great extent it is the result of the situation in which we find ourselves. Amongst the mass of published material available to us – amongst so many translations of ancient Buddhist texts – there is much that is extremely advanced. Some of the great Mahāyāna *sūtras*, for example, are addressed to disciples of a high degree of spiritual development, as is made evident in their opening scenes. They begin with the Buddha seated in the midst of a great concourse of disciples, perhaps in some heaven or archetypal realm. All around him are *arhants* and great bodhisattvas, even irreversible bodhisattvas, that is, bodhisattvas who cannot regress from the ideal of supreme Buddhahood and who have, as it were, Nirvāṇa in the palm of their hand. The sublime teachings that the Buddha proceeds to give are addressed to such beings as these – beings who exist on a level of spirituality beyond all that we can conceive or imagine.

Being able to possess paperback translations of such *sūtras*, it is perhaps easy for us to imagine that we can master their contents just as we can master the contents of any other paperback. We may tend then to adopt a cool, knowledgeable, even patronizing attitude towards Buddhism. Some of us may even think it unnecessary to call ourselves Buddhists at all – after all, we have 'gone beyond' all that. We may even look down somewhat on those simple-minded folk in the West who actually choose to call themselves Buddhists, who actually pay their respects to images of the Buddha, who actually offer flowers and light candles, and who actually try to observe the precepts.

We may think our lofty, detached attitude more advanced, but the truth is that it is simply superficial – a theoretical approach without any roots in genuine reverence, faith, and devotion. This shallow, purely mental approach, devoid of all devotion, of all 'quiet revering of the unfathomable', has generally characterized Buddhism in the West until comparatively recently. Indeed, there is still a strong tendency among Western Buddhists to pick and choose from the teachings 'on offer', not according to their own real spiritual needs but according to subjective and superficial whims and fancies. We like this bit, but not that bit. We are happy with the idea of karma, say, but we don't like the idea of rebirth. Or you find people being very much drawn by the doctrine of *anātman* (for some reason or other, the idea that they do not have a soul or a self seems rather to attract some people) but at the same time finding the thought of Nirvāṇa rather depressing.

Then, of course, likes and dislikes often change. For a while one may be very much into Zen, because one rather likes the idea that one is already a Buddha, already 'there', and that there is nothing to do. It seems to make life a lot easier: one does not have to practise anything, apparently, or give up anything. But eventually one gets rather bored with being a Buddha, so one starts getting into the Tantra; and Tantra, of course, immediately conjures up visions of sex, and one starts getting into the yoga of sex (theoretically, of course). In this sort of way one can browse and dabble for years.

Every one of us has experienced these difficulties in some degree or another, but still, a number of Western Buddhists do get around, in the end, to practising Buddhism. At a liberal estimate – based simply on personal experience – perhaps one in twenty Western Buddhists moves on and actually tries to practise Buddhism. Eventually the realization dawns that Buddhism is not just a collection of interesting ideas – not just a philosophy, not just something to think about. One tumbles to the fact that Buddhism is something to be applied, even something to be experienced.

Unfortunately, so strong is the force of conditioning and habit that even when one starts trying to practise Buddhism the same old pattern of picking and choosing, the same shallow, appropriative theorizing, persists. To see how this happens, we could take the case of an imaginary Buddhist called, say, John. He is 24, and has been interested in Buddhism since he was twelve. Let us say that John is a bookish young man and has read all the standard authors on all aspects of Buddhism. You name a book on Buddhism and the chances are that John has read it. At last, after all that reading, it occurs to him that there might be more to Buddhism than reading about it, and he finds his way to a meditation class, where he learns, week by week, a technique of concentrating the mind. He gets on quite well, so much so that he can maintain a pleasurable experience of integrated concentration for ten minutes or so at a time, quite regularly.

But after two or three months he starts finding the whole thing rather pointless and boring. Nothing much seems to be happening. He just gets into a nice, concentrated state. There are no wonderful visions, no revelations, no divine voices speaking to him. He is beginning to lose interest altogether when he is lucky enough to hear about a wonderful new meditation teacher whom not many people know about because he has only recently arrived in the West. John finds that this teacher has all the unmistakable hallmarks of an authentic guru: a compassionate smile, a mellifluous voice, a penetrating gaze, and a wonderful beard. The first thing the teacher tells John is that he should forget whatever he has previously learned about meditation. It was all wrong. His previous teachers did not know the first thing about meditation. This naturally comes as a bit of a shock, and John feels rather disoriented; but anyway, he starts practising the new method of meditation with the new teacher and gets on quite well. In fact, he gets on about as well as he had done before, with the old method: neither better nor worse.

Unfortunately, after two months a rather serious setback occurs. The wonderful new teacher disappears. Not in the magical sense; John just goes along to the class one evening and finds that he is not there. Some people say he has gone back to India. Others say he has gone to America. There are different reports. Poor John is left high and dry, and doesn't know what to do.

However, he meets someone who introduces him to a kind of Sufi group. He finds the people there quite sociable, quite friendly; but he does not get anything out of the teaching. In fact there isn't any teaching as such, because as far as this particular group is concerned, everything is one. So back he goes to Buddhism: or rather, back to reading books about Buddhism.

One day he happens to read a book about Buddhism and vegetarianism. 'That's very interesting,' he thinks, 'Buddhists go some way to avoid causing harm to living beings by the simple expedient of not eating meat. I never realized that before. Also, I see that they preserve their mindfulness by not indulging in alcohol. I had not thought of that either. In fact, Buddhists try to avoid doing quite a number of things.' This aspect of Buddhism had not struck him before. He has been so preoccupied with Buddhist philosophy, so preoccupied with the meaning of Emptiness and the One Mind, that it has not occurred to him until now that there might be quite simple, practical things to do, or precepts to observe.

In other words, John begins to see that there is an ethical side to Buddhism. Formerly he had not had time for anything so elementary as that, but now he starts thinking about it quite seriously, and actually starts trying, rather gingerly, to observe at least a few of the precepts. He gives up meat, stops drinking and smoking, and tries very hard not to tell lies or even to exaggerate. In his growing enthusiasm he starts becoming a bit puritanical. He starts carrying these things too far. But he is sincere, and as a result of his observance of the precepts he starts feeling like practising meditation again. Unfortunately, there are no wonderful new teachers around, so back he goes to his old class, which is still carrying on. Again he gets into regular practice, does quite well, and after some months is able to sit for over an hour without too much difficulty.

One day a rather strange thing happens. John arrives for the weekly class late and exhausted after a heavy day. He is not at all in the mood for meditation: he thinks that since he is tired it is going to be rather a waste of time. But he goes anyway and he sits. Without any warning, after he has sat for a few minutes, he finds himself in a completely different state of consciousness. How he got into it he does not know. He is hardly aware of his body. Everything seems very bright and luminous, very buoyant. He feels fresh, without any trace of tiredness, as though some inexhaustible spring was welling up within him. It is as though his whole being is expanding, and he begins to glimpse things he has never glimpsed before, despite all his reading of books and his intellectual understanding. A great wave of bliss descends upon him. He feels as he has never felt before, and never thought to feel. How long he remains in this completely different state of consciousness he does not know. It may be ten minutes, or even half an hour.

Whatever it is, the experience has a very profound effect on John. He *knows* now that there is some higher state of consciousness, of being. It is not just words, not just theory, any more. It is not just something he has read in a book. He feels that at last some progress has been made; and he is so impressed, so elated, that he starts thinking of becoming a monk, going to the East, leading an ascetic life, and so on. He even feels he can gain Enlightenment quite soon.

Elated and pleased with himself, he becomes a little more expansive, a little more outward-going than before – and at this point Māra starts taking an interest in John. Māra is the demonic being who symbolizes all forces inimical to the Truth, to the Dharma, and he has not bothered about John before. After all, it has not been necessary, since some of the books John has been reading have been doing Māra's work for him.

Now there is a girl who has been coming to the meditation class for a few weeks. She is a well-meaning girl, but she is destined to be the innocent instrument of John's downfall. Being rather shy, John has never spoken to her, but in his present elated, expansive mood he loses his shyness. He speaks to her that week, the following week they become friends, and to cut a not very long story short John falls violently in love with her. But the girl, perverse creature that she is, does not fall in love with him. She is in love with somebody else. Poor John! He cannot eat, he cannot sleep, and of course he cannot meditate. He forgets all about his wonderful experience. It is as though it has never been.

We all experience something like this from time to time. You get into a wonderful, exalted state, and think that you are going to have no more trouble, no more problems. 'Now I really know what it's all about,' you say, 'I shall never be such a fool again.' But a few days – even a few hours – later, you are back where you were before, apparently. It is like that with John. It is as though he has never had that experience of a higher state of consciousness in the first place. He forgets all about Buddhism. He does not go to the meditation class any more because he cannot bear to meet the girl. In fact, he feels like committing suicide.

But one day someone invites him to a party. Now John does not usually go to parties. As I said, he has become a bit puritanical. But he is feeling so miserable that he accepts, goes to the party, and gets drunk.

Bang goes a precept, of course, and he wakes up the next morning with a terrible headache. But John is young, and youth is resilient. Eventually he gets over his disappointment. Our latest news of him is that he is no longer trying to observe the precepts, and has given up meditation, but he is busy reading books on Tantric Buddhism, and thinking of taking up the study of Tibetan.

It is very easy to smile and shake one's head at John's confusion, to feel a bit superior. But of course he has just been following the path of irregular steps; and this is what we all do, and perhaps have to do, at least for a time. We practise now this meditation and now that, and then maybe we do not meditate at all for a while. We go through a period of observing the precepts quite strictly, we are even quite puritanical; but then we do not bother about them for a while. One day we feel like giving everything up, going off to the East and becoming a monk; but the next day we start wondering whether Buddhism is really the thing for us at all. Thus we follow the path of irregular steps – and sometimes our steps are very irregular indeed.

Not so long ago there was very little Buddhism in the West, in any form, whether books or otherwise. Now, one might say that there is almost too much. There are so many books, so many practices, so many teachers, so many schools to choose from. There is such a bewildering confusion and profusion of forms in which Buddhism is presented. In our excitement and greed we snatch first at this and then at that, sampling a bit here and a bit there, like a greedy child in a sweet shop. We are in the transcendental sweet shop of Buddhism, with all these beautiful spiritual goodies around us. And so we reach for this and scoop up a handful of that: Zen, Tantra, Theravāda; ethics strict and ethics liberal; meditation plain and meditation colourful. We just grab – that, it has to be said, is what our approach to Buddhism amounts to at times. But all the same we do make some progress in this way. The path of irregular steps is still a path, and it does give us some experience of Buddhism.

But only up to a point. As we follow the path of irregular steps we find, sooner or later, that we are slowing down. We seem to be up against an invisible obstacle. Apparently in a sort of spiritual doldrums, we are going through the motions, but nothing is happening: we don't seem to be getting anywhere. At this point a radical change is called for. We need to make not just another change of direction within the path of irregular steps, but a more fundamental transition: a transition from the path of irregular steps to the path of regular steps.

Now why is this? And what, anyway, is the distinction between these two 'paths'? To answer these questions we must first understand the nature of the path in general, the path which leads from the *saṃsāra*, the round of mundane, conditioned existence, to Nirvāṇa, the 'realm' of unconditioned being, the path from unenlightened humanity to the Enlightened humanity of the Buddha.

THE THREEFOLD PATH

The Buddhist path is traditionally divided into three successive stages: the stage of *śīla* or morality, the stage of *samādhi* or meditation, and the stage of *prajñā* or wisdom. Though there are other ways of dividing – and even subdividing – the path, this threefold division remains the most important and the most fundamental.

Śīla, morality, is simply skilful action: action which benefits oneself, which helps one to grow and develop; and action which benefits others too, which helps them also to grow and develop. Not that *śīla* is a matter of external action divorced from mental attitude; it is both the mental attitude and the mode of behaviour in which that attitude naturally expresses itself. Thus *śīla* is skilful action in the sense that it is action arising from certain skilful mental states, especially states of love, generosity, peace, and contentment. It is, indeed, everything one does out of these skilful mental states. That, essentially, is what morality or ethics in Buddhism comprises: actions expressive of skilful mental states.

Samādhi, usually translated 'meditation', is a word with many different meanings on a number of different levels. First of all it consists in the gathering together of all one's scattered energies into a single focus. Most of the time our energies are divided; they take different directions; they are unintegrated. So first of all we have to integrate them. This does not mean forcibly concentrating on a particular point; it means bringing together all our energies, both conscious and unconscious, and harmonizing them in a natural and spontaneous manner. Thus concentration, in the sense of the complete unification of one's psychospiritual energies, is the first grade or level of *samādhi*.

Next, *samādhi* consists in the experience of progressively higher states of consciousness – states extending into what are called the *dhyānas* or superconscious states. In these states we transcend the body (in the sense of physical awareness) and also, eventually, the mind (in the sense of discursive mental activity). We also experience bliss, peace, joy, and ecstasy (but not transcendental insight, since we are still within *saṃsāra*, still within the realm of the mundane).

Finally, *samādhi* includes the development of such supernormal powers of the mind as telepathy, clairvoyance, clairaudience, and the recollection of one's previous existences. However, 'supernormal' does not mean 'supernatural': when these powers arise in the course of meditation, they do so quite naturally and spontaneously.

The last stage of the threefold path is *prajñā* or wisdom. This consists in direct insight into, or personal contact with, the truth or reality. At first it occurs only momentarily, like a sudden flash of lightning that, on a dark night, lights up the landscape just for an instant. As the flashes of insight become more frequent, however, and more continuous, they eventually become a steady beam of light that is capable of penetrating as it were into the very depths of reality.

When fully developed, this wisdom or insight is what we call *bodhi* or Enlightenment – though at that level it is not to be spoken of in exclusively cognitive terms. At that level we also have to speak of it in terms of love and compassion or, rather, in terms of the transcendental counterpart of the emotions which we usually designate by those names.

THE PATH OF REGULAR STEPS

Thus the path, which constitutes the main theme of Buddhism on the practical side, is divided into these three great stages of morality, meditation, and wisdom. The division is not an arbitrary one: the stages are no mere chalk marks, but are inherent in the path itself, and represent natural stages in the spiritual and transcendental growth of the individual. As such they resemble stages in the growth of a plant: from the seed comes forth a little shoot, which grows into a stem, from which leaves and finally buds and flowers are produced.

Of course we must not push an analogy of this sort too far. The whole process of the flower's growth is unconscious. The flower does not have to decide whether to grow or not; nature 'decides' for it. But in the case of a human being spiritual development is conscious and deliberate, and by its very nature must be so. We are dependent for our further growth on our own individual, personal effort – though this is not a one-sided, egoistic, straining wilfulness, but the growth and development, in awareness, of the whole being.

A more satisfactory analogy for spiritual development from this point of view (though it doesn't work so well as an illustration of a development from within) is that of the construction of a house or any multistorey building. First you lay the foundation, then build the first storey, then the second, and so on, and finally you put on the roof. You cannot reverse the sequence, because it is determined by the nature of the structure itself.

The stages of the path of regular steps correspond to various Buddhist teachings; and different teachings pertain to different stages of the path, that is, to different stages of spiritual and transcendental development. When we practise the Dharma we should therefore practise those teachings that correspond to the stage of development we have actually reached – and reached not mentally or theoretically but with our whole being. This is the traditional method, or at least the predominant traditional method.

So first you practise morality: you observe the precepts. In doing so, you gradually become a thoroughly ethical individual, both inwardly and outwardly; this may take several years. Then, when your ethical individuality has been established relatively firmly, you take up the practice of concentration: you learn to tame the unruly wandering mind, and to concentrate at will on any object for any length of time – which may take several more years. Then, very slowly, you start raising your level of consciousness. You experience the first *dhyāna*, the second *dhyāna*, and so on, gradually training yourself not just to touch them but even to dwell in these superconscious states. Finally, perhaps after many years of endeavour, you direct your purified, elevated, and sublimely concentrated mind, together with the integrated energies of your whole being, to the contemplation of reality itself. This is the path of regular steps. Progress is systematic; you consolidate each stage of the path before proceeding to the next one.

By contrast, in treading the path of irregular steps one starts practising on the basis of a more or less mental or theoretical grasp of the Dharma (and a confused and incomplete grasp at that). Usually, I am afraid, in the West, one begins without a teacher; and one does not start practising those teachings which correspond to the stage of development one has actually reached, because one does not know what stage one is at anyway. One starts practising in a way that is immediately and superficially appealing – one starts practising, perhaps, what appeals to one's vanity. One might, for instance, start practising the Perfection of Wisdom.

Now it is not absolutely impossible, even for an absolute beginner – even on the basis of a purely theoretical understanding of the subject – to practise the Perfection of Wisdom. After all, the seed of Buddhahood is there, however deeply hidden. Deep down, an affinity with the Perfection of Wisdom is there. One may succeed, to a very slight extent, by sheer force of the egoistic will, in holding oneself, just for an instant, at a level of concentration where one gets just a glimpse of the Perfection of Wisdom, an experience, however fleeting, of the Void.

However, one will not be able to keep it up. One will sink back from it, and there will even be a reaction – a reaction from one's whole being or consciousness, which is, as a whole, simply not at that level and not ready to practise the Perfection of Wisdom. So one has to go back. One has to practise ethics and meditation, develop higher states of consciousness, and, in this way, create a firm basis from which to practise the Perfection of Wisdom effectively.

So following the path of irregular steps usually involves forcing the process of spiritual development. It is like trying to make a plant grow by forcibly opening the buds with one's fingers, or like building a house without foundations. Sooner or later we discover that it cannot be done. Instead of pulling open the buds one has to water the roots. One doesn't start building anything until one has dug the foundations. As Buddhists, the flower that we want to see blooming is the thousand-petalled lotus itself, so plenty of water is needed. The tower we want to build is the tower that reaches up into the very heavens, so a very firm foundation is required.

To state the matter axiomatically, we may say that a higher stage of the path cannot be developed even to a moderate extent before a lower stage of the path has been developed in its fullness. This is the basic principle. If we want to experience the higher stage, or higher level, with any intensity or any permanence, we must first perfect the lower stage. There is no other way. This is why, sooner or later, we have to make the transition from the path of irregular steps to the path of regular steps. And this transition means, basically, going back in order to go forward.

We have already noted that the character of Western Buddhism has recently undergone a radical change. We can now begin to see in what that change consists. It consists, essentially, in a transition from the path of irregular steps to the path of regular steps. More and more Western Buddhists are beginning to realize that a shallow, superficial approach to the Dharma – an irregular, unsystematic, improperly based practice of the path – is not enough. They have begun to realize that we have to go back to the beginning, back, one might almost say, to the spiritual kindergarten, to start learning our spiritual ABC.

But how far back does this mean? One could say: back to morality – back to basics. Or one could say: back to the Hīnayāna, back to basic Buddhism; put aside Tibetan Buddhism, put aside the Tantra and Zen, and get back to the Theravāda. But in fact we have to go back to something even more fundamental than morality, even more basic than the Hīnayāna. We have to go back to the Three Jewels.

We have to sit or kneel with hands together, and go for Refuge, saying 'Buddhaṃ saraṇaṃ gacchāmi, Dhammaṃ saraṇaṃ gacchāmi, Saṅghaṃ saraṇaṃ gacchāmi. To the Buddha for Refuge I go, to the Dharma for Refuge I go, to the Sangha for Refuge I go.' This is where Buddhism really begins. This is the root, the foundation, the absolute bedrock of our spiritual life. This is how we really start practising the path – by Going for Refuge.

Thus we make – or begin to make – the transition from the path of irregular steps to the path of regular steps. We go for Refuge to the Buddha: we commit ourselves to the ideal of human Enlightenment, and we make it the aim and object of our lives to become Enlightened even as the Buddha was Enlightened. We go for Refuge to the Dharma: we commit ourselves to the systematic, wholehearted practice of the path to Enlightenment. And we go for Refuge to the Sangha: we commit ourselves to cultivating the spiritual friendship of those who are treading, or who have trodden, the path to Enlightenment.

Going for Refuge is the basic declaration of commitment to the Buddhist path. It is the quintessential act of the path of regular steps, an act of commitment by the whole person. It is, therefore, at once basic and momentous. In fact, if one goes for Refuge to the Three Jewels, and if, as an expression of one's determination to follow the path of regular steps, one also undertakes to observe a greater or smaller number of moral precepts, and if one moreover does all this openly and publicly, in the traditional manner, then this Going for Refuge, or commitment, is what we call ordination.

Usually it is assumed that ordination means monastic ordination, that is, we think it means becoming a *bhikkhu* or *gelong*. But this is a great misconception and it is high time we sorted it out. Monastic ordination is only one kind of ordination. The Pāli and Sanskrit word for ordination is *saṃvara* – literally a 'binding' – and we therefore speak of *upāsaka-saṃvara*, *bhikkhu-saṃvara*, and even *bodhisattva-saṃvara*, as well as the feminine equivalents of the first two – *upāsikā-saṃvara* and *bhikkhunī-saṃvara*. In other words we speak of lay ordination, monastic ordination, and even bodhisattva ordination. But all three are ordinations, the same word, *saṃvara*, being applied to each of them.

Upāsaka/upāsikā, *bhikkhu/bhikkhunī*, and bodhisattva all equally go for Refuge – the bodhisattva, perhaps, in a deeper sense than the other two. All three commit themselves to the Three Jewels. Any difference between them is simply as regards the number and, in the case of the bodhisattva, the kind of precepts observed. So what the monk and the layman, the *bhikkhu* and the *upāsaka*, have in common is far more important than what they do not have in common. What they have in common is the Three Jewels, or the Three Refuges, and for the Buddhist nothing can be more important than that. Thus the real line of demarcation is not between monks and laymen but, properly speaking, between those who have gone for Refuge and those who have not.

The sangha or spiritual community in the ordinary sense of the term (as distinct from the Sangha in the sense of all the bodhisattvas, *arhants*, and other great saints), is simply and straightforwardly made up of all those who have gone for Refuge. The distinction between the monk and layman is, therefore, a distinction *within* the sangha. We may even go so far as to say that so far as the sangha is concerned the distinction between the monk and layman probably owes more to the social and cultural condition of India at the time of the Buddha than to the intrinsic nature of the Dharma itself; in which case, it is a distinction that may or may not be relevant to the development of Buddhism in the West.

Unfortunately, the supreme, overriding importance of Going for Refuge is not always appreciated. Only too often it is regarded as a rather ordinary thing. For example, one afternoon a good many years ago now, a young man came to see me and said, 'I am quite interested in Buddhism: I have read a few books, and done a little meditation. But I don't want to commit myself to Buddhism; I think I am more interested in worldly life. So would you please just give me the Refuges and Precepts?' I had to explain that his request was self-contradictory. Commitment is what Going for Refuge means. There is no point in 'taking' the Refuges if one is not prepared to commit oneself; one would be merely repeating the words. The young man could not understand this and went away disappointed and dissatisfied. Subsequently I heard that he had 'gone for Refuge' with a more accommodating teacher and then continued with his worldly life.

This sort of misunderstanding is not, it should be said, peculiar to the West. In fact it has spread to the West from the East. In the East Buddhism has had a very long and a very glorious history, of which we can be justly proud. During the 2,500 years of its existence, Buddhism has produced great art and great literature, great systems of thought and, above all, great lives. But it would be idle to pretend that serious degeneration has not taken place in some areas, and we can see instances of this in the matter of the 'Going for Refuge'. Originally, Going for Refuge represented a profound spiritual experience: you were moved to the very depths of your being, as we know was the case with the people who went for Refuge to the Buddha himself when he was alive. It was a matter of wholehearted commitment – wholehearted surrender – to the Three Jewels and to the spiritual life. Nowadays, unfortunately, in many parts of the Buddhist East, the whole concept and experience of Going for Refuge has been devalued. The absolute bedrock of Buddhism appears as just something that you recite, in a dead language, on festive occasions.

It is easy to see how this has come about. After all, if the term 'Buddhist' means anything it means 'one who goes for Refuge'; and yet in some parts of the East the whole population considers itself Buddhist, just as until recently the whole population of Britain considered itself Christian. For such people the term 'Buddhist' does not necessarily imply a vigorous commitment to genuine spiritual values. So Going for Refuge – or 'taking the Refuges' – has become something one does in order simply to accord oneself the denominational label of 'Buddhist'.

In some Buddhist countries, therefore, we have a rather curious situation. When one does want to commit oneself to the spiritual life and take Buddhism seriously – when really one wants to go for Refuge – one thinks not in terms of going for Refuge, but in terms of becoming a monk (or nun, though that is largely impossible these days). Even though one's commitment to the Three Jewels may not include a heartfelt desire to express that commitment through taking the step of monastic ordination, one still thinks in terms of joining a monastery and putting on the yellow robe. Meanwhile, the vast majority of the population formally 'go for Refuge' to signify only a nominal loyalty to the Three Jewels. The result is that the most fundamental act of a Buddhist is drained of significance, while the committed spiritual life comes to be more or less identified with a monastic life that is itself, all too often, only nominally monastic.

One can understand how this situation has come about in the East; there are all sorts of historical reasons for it. But in the West there is no excuse whatsoever for perpetuating what is in fact a very serious distortion of Buddhism. Unfortunately, visiting Buddhist teachers from the East have rarely perceived this distortion or understood what ordination and Going for Refuge really mean. If you show any sign of genuine interest in Buddhism they want to make you a monk – sometimes on the spot – because to them ordination means monastic ordination. But as we have already seen, ordination essentially means Going for Refuge, and Going for Refuge means ordination, or commitment.

As Western Buddhists make the great transition from the path of irregular steps to the path of regular steps – as they start becoming ordained – we don't have to imagine people rushing off to the East and donning robes. What we can expect to see is a form of ordination for men and women in the West that reflects the true meaning of Buddhist ordination. And one situation at least where this can be found at present is in the Friends of the Western Buddhist Order. The heart of this organization is the Western Buddhist Order, founded in 1968, which is a community of people who have committed themselves to the spiritual life, to the Three Jewels, who have, individually and in fellowship with one another, gone for Refuge.

The Order was originally called 'Western' because it arose in the West, under the conditions of a secularized and industrialized society. It is called 'Buddhist' because it derives its inspiration ultimately from the teachings and the example of Gautama the Buddha and all the great Enlightened saints and sages and spiritual masters who are his spiritual descendants. It is an 'Order' because it recognizes – in the midst of a world which is in many ways difficult and destructive – the great value of spiritual fellowship in treading the Path; and because it seeks to create a reservoir of spiritual energy on which all may draw and from which all can benefit; and because, above all, it realizes the importance of the distinction between the path of regular steps and the path of irregular steps.

ENLIGHTENMENT AS EXPERIENCE
AND AS NON-EXPERIENCE

Caxton Hall, Westminster, under the auspices of the London Buddhist Society, 1975.

Buddhism consists of two things: a path, or way; and a goal, or objective.

The Path has been described in various ways, according to context. It is delineated as the Noble (or Holy) Eightfold Path – a path of eight stages, or more accurately, eight members or factors. It is outlined as the path of the six (or ten) *pāramitās* or perfections. It is also defined as the middle way, the path between and above extremes. These are only some of the ways in which it is described.

As for the goal, this is described – very provisionally – as Buddhahood, in the sense of Supreme Perfect Enlightenment. This goal can also be conceptualized in various ways. It can be seen as supreme wisdom, or absolute gnosis, or insight into things 'as they really are', as the plenitude of compassion pouring out on all sentient beings simultaneously, and as infinite spiritual – even transcendental – energy radiating in all directions. It can also be conceived in terms of complete and utter purity, a purity that is not only clear of the stain of evil but beyond the polarity of good and evil. Enlightenment can be cognized in these and many other ways. In particular we can think of it as an experience, as *the* experience, even the culminating experience or, if you like, the experience to end all experiences.

But what is an 'experience' anyway? We use the term often enough, but what do we mean by it? In a sense any and every object of perception, whether physical or mental, whether sense-based or abstract, is an experience of some kind. But usually we like to distinguish experience from thought – or at least from abstract or conceptual thought. Basically, experience is a matter of perception and feeling; it means the actual living through of an event, the actual – as we say – *experiencing* of it, not just the experience of looking at it or contemplating it. 'Experience' also suggests real life as distinct from ideal or imaginary life or existence.

Enlightenment as experience means, therefore, Enlightenment as something you actually perceive, actually feel. It is, in the words of Wordsworth in his poem 'Tintern Abbey', 'felt in the blood, and felt along the heart'.[40] It is felt in the nerves, felt in the bone. It is not just abstractly thought and speculated about, or imagined and fantasized about; it is something that you live through. However, if you do live through the experience of Enlightenment, you do so in a way that marks it uniquely apart from any other experience.

With any other experience you come out at the other end, so to speak, whether intact or (to some extent) not intact. But you do not come out at the other end of the experience of Enlightenment. There is no other end. Maybe there is an end of 'you', but that is another matter. 'You' do not come out at the other end. What we can say is that your life continues, after you have experienced Enlightenment, not as you but as Enlightenment; or, rather, that your life becomes a continuing part of Enlightenment itself.

But how did we come to think of Enlightenment in this way – as experience? For we must not think, just because we have become used to it, that this is the natural, the inevitable, and the only way of thinking about it. Indeed, it is a rather odd way of thinking; and there are alternative ways.

Indian Buddhism does not refer to Enlightenment as experience. In the Pāli scriptures of the Theravāda school, some portions of which evidently come close to describing the way the Buddha originally taught, there is no reference to Enlightenment as an experience. The very early Buddhists did not, so far as we know, think of Enlightenment in that way at all. Experience was implied, but it was not stated in so many words: indeed, there was no equivalent expression in Pāli.

In a later text, one of the greatest of the Mahāyāna *sūtras*, the *Laṅkāvatāra*, we find an expression that its translator into English, D. T. Suzuki, renders as the experience of 'noble wisdom'.[41] So it would seem that there was a change of emphasis between the earliest Pāli texts and this relatively late *sūtra*, compiled in its present form probably not less than 800 years after the time of the Buddha. One might even say that its emphasis on experience, or on something corresponding to what we now call experience, reflects developments taking place in India analogous to certain developments that took place in the West very much later.

However, the word 'experience' in Suzuki's English version of the *Laṅkāvatāra* is actually a very approximate, not to say loose, translation of the Sanskrit term *gatigocara*. Also from the *Laṅkāvatāra* we have the term *pratyātmagocara*, which Suzuki renders as 'inner realization'.[42] Again, this term resembles, in its meaning, something close to what we understand by the idea of experience without doing so closely enough to call it such. Thus even if we accept that the *Laṅkāvatāra* does, in a way, speak of Enlightenment in terms of experience, it does so in a rather indirect and equivocal manner (as neither *gatigocara* or *pratyātmagocara* can be translated with any real precision by the word 'experience').

In Pāli and Sanskrit it is as difficult to speak of Enlightenment as experience (in the current sense of the term) as it is to express another notion current amongst Western Buddhists but apparently unknown to ancient Buddhists, which is that 'all life is one'. To say that all life is one may be a justifiable interpretation or reinterpretation of Buddhist teaching, but you can't put it back into either Pāli or Sanskrit. It represents a quite different mode of expression – a mode of expression that is the product of a modern, Western way of thinking.

If you do translate 'Enlightenment is an experience' or 'all life is one' back into Pāli or Sanskrit you then become involved not in translating but in reinterpreting the *sūtras*, in rethinking and, if you like, in re-experiencing them or making them new – which according to some schools of Buddhism is one of the things you must not do. *Navakata*, as they call it, or making new, is for them equivalent to heresy.

So speaking of Enlightenment as experience is a mode of expression peculiar to our own particular mode of experience – to use the very word we are discussing. Seeing things in terms of experience is part of the way in which we have come generally to regard religion – and, indeed, life itself.

RELIGION SEEN AS EXPERIENCE

Now how is this? This is no place for a detailed historical analysis but in brief we can say that up to the time of the sixteenth-century

Reformation European religion was a very much richer and more complex phenomenon than it subsequently became. Up to that time religion – consisting almost entirely of a single strand of Christianity which had superseded earlier beliefs – presented quite a number of different aspects. There was doctrine, especially in the form of theology and scholastic philosophy; there was ethics; there was ritual, sacrament, and liturgy; there were festivals, celebrations, and pageants; there were social institutions, folk customs, law (i.e. canon law), myth, legend, mysticism, asceticism – even marvels and miracles. Up to the time of the Reformation, all these things went to make up religion. We can even include art – painting, sculpture, architecture, and music – all of which, in their most ambitious and refined forms, were mainly or at least ostensibly concerned with, and celebrated, religion as the dominant system of values. So in religion we had, at one time, a many-splendoured thing indeed, something very rich, very complex, and very inspiring.

But the great synthesis broke down. With the Reformation came a change, especially in the Protestant parts of Europe. There wasn't any one Christian doctrine any more, and as the number of conflicting and competing versions of the 'one true faith' proliferated, doctrine became much more rigid. Myth and legend and all the more colourful elements – in the Protestant countries especially – gradually disappeared, while ritual dwindled to a ghost of its former splendid self. In some areas, ritual was banished altogether. The fine arts became more and more secularized. The church was separated from the state. Religion was divorced from secular life and became more and more a matter of private morality and personal feeling.

In England this trend was intensified during the Victorian period, when the traditional religious doctrine of the origin of the universe and of mankind was very much undermined by discoveries in the fields of geology and biology – particularly by Darwin's theory of evolution. For many good, serious-minded, and sincere people the Christian religion became more and more intellectually untenable. For some, like Matthew Arnold, religion became simply 'morality touched by emotion',[43] as he calls it. The morality was often little more than social conformity, and the emotion little more than a feeling of nostalgia for a lost faith. For others, religion became not morality touched by emotion but emotion touched by morality and, as the decades went by, that emotion became less and less touched by morality.

It was at this point, roughly one hundred years ago, that Buddhism first made a real impact in the West. If we wanted a date, we could fix upon 1879, the year of the publication of Sir Edwin Arnold's beautiful and justly celebrated poem on the life of the Buddha, *The Light of Asia*.[44] And as was inevitable, Buddhism came to be regarded in much the same way that Christianity was, either as a system of ethics, or as a particular kind of religious sentiment or feeling, that is, as an experience.

Thus one could have predicted that Buddhism would not, at that stage, be taken very seriously as a 'doctrine' or 'philosophy' (for want of a better term) – and nor was it. The depths of Buddhist thought were not plumbed at that time. They did not even begin to be plumbed, and we are far from doing so even today, a hundred years later.

Nor should it have been difficult to foresee how people would take to Buddhist myth and legend. The long and hopeless struggle of Christian myth or legend to dress up as historical fact had put people in no mood for what they would naturally imagine might be more of the same from Buddhism. As for rituals, festivals, and social institutions, and all the more popular and colourful developments of Buddhism, these would have been regarded as being simply out of the question even by the very, very few in Europe who, in those days, thought of themselves as Buddhists. After all (they might have argued) had not the Buddha, good Protestant that he was, condemned rites and ceremonies as a fetter?

On the basis of this initial reception of Buddhism in the West as a religion of ethics or of 'experience', one should also have been able to forecast, at the end of the nineteenth century, which forms of Buddhism would be the most popular in the West during the first half of the twentieth century. These were, of course, Theravāda and Zen – Theravāda as representing a code of ethics, and Zen as representing experience. Thus it was that the way we in the West have come to regard Buddhism is the result of the way in which we have come, almost insensibly, and over hundreds of years, to regard religion in general.

LIFE SEEN AS EXPERIENCE

The way we regard religion – even unconsciously – ties in closely with the way we regard life itself, that is, the organized life of the human community, or social life in the widest sense, along with its various aspects, political, economic, cultural, and domestic. The question we need to ask, however, is perhaps not so much how we feel about Life – Life with a capital L – as whether many of us feel very much about life at all. Do most of us, to be honest, feel anything more than simply confused and bewildered?

Life has indeed become so complicated that sometimes it seems as though we have become caught up in a vast machine, too big and complex for us to understand or do anything about. We are so well-informed about whatever is happening all over the world, all the time, and yet even when these events affect our own lives deeply and intimately, we are apparently powerless to do anything about them. The juggernaut of world events rolls on. Even if the wheels are crushing the life out of us, it seems that we can do nothing. It is easy to feel helpless, impotent, frustrated.

At the same time, life can often seem to be a very dull and routine affair. We rumble or creep along tracks which were laid down for us even before we were born – perhaps before even our parents were born. One hardly needs to describe where the familiar journey takes us. First comes school and, of course, nobody asks to be sent to school. After school comes some combination of work and marriage, mortgage and children, promotion (which means more work), redundancy and retirement, followed inevitably by death. This is what life means for most people, and apparently there is no alternative. The wheel has trapped us, and rolls on and on.

This predicament is vividly illustrated in a very striking painting by Burne-Jones, called 'The Wheel of Fortune'[45] (though 'The Wheel of Misfortune' would have been a better title). It depicts an enormous wheel turned by a rather stern-looking woman, and on this inexorably turning wheel are strapped a variety of helpless (male) figures. It presents a pattern of meaning that many, perhaps, would identify as being applicable to their own lives.

Crucial to the perception that we have of the meaning of our lives is, usually, work – work in the sense of gainful employment. We devote more time and energy to work in this sense than to any other single activity – perhaps with the exception of sleep. Yet work is generally perceived as something dull, repetitive, exhausting, and boring. Few find any joy or sense of fulfilment in it; few find a feeling of creativity or any real outlet for their energies. People may be bursting with energy, but they can rarely put it into their work even if they have work; it is not needed there. And if there is no creative outlet for these energies, such people feel frustrated, impotent, and, deep down, very resentful. But again, only too often, they have not the resources to express that resentment. The expression of resentment is a luxury that very few workers can afford. In any case, if they work for a multinational conglomerate, who is there to vent it on? Understandably, some of those who have little to lose express their resentment in criminal activities, even in criminal violence.

Without an outlet for our energies, we gradually lose contact with our feelings; when we lose contact with our feelings we lose contact with ourselves; and when we lose contact with ourselves we lose contact with life. We become dull, tired, mechanical, dead. We become walking corpses. We all know, more or less, what this is like; from time to time we have seen it in ourselves, to some extent, and we have seen it in others. The great poet and visionary, William Blake, saw it nearly 200 years ago, at the time of the grimy dawn of the Industrial Revolution. He says:

> I wander thro' each charter'd street,
> Near where the charter'd Thames does flow,
> And mark in every face I meet
> Marks of weakness, marks of woe.[46]

We can see these same 'marks of weakness, marks of woe' on the faces of people in the streets, in cars, on buses and trains, today. The only difference, 200 years after Blake, is that those marks are now, if anything, more deeply scored.

But of course human beings are very resilient; the energy is still there, however distorted or deeply buried. We don't always take things lying down – and quite rightly so. We look about us for something to relieve the sense of frustration, of numbness. We look for some excitement, for something that will give us a bit of a thrill: something that will make us feel more alive; something that will take us out of ourselves; something that will make us forget everything – for a while anyway.

So we turn to food, to sex, to alcohol and other drugs, to the television, and to the passive consumption of music and art and literature – with an occasional surrender to the ever-present lure of a more expensive dress, a faster car, a more powerful motorbike, or a smaller computer.

For an extra boost of stimulation, we plug in to the tribal excitement of a crowd at a football match, or even the bloodlust of the foxhounds on the hunting field. In its extreme form this tendency will seek fulfilment in violence and sadism. In our search for relief from boredom we turn to all sorts of things, from the sublime to the sordid, from Beethoven to bingo.

Not all the above examples are, of course, bad things in themselves. It is the use we make of them that is questionable – that can be neurotic or, in the more traditional Buddhist terminology, 'unskilful'. In fact anything we undertake simply to relieve boredom and frustration will, in the long run, make us feel more empty, more frustrated, more drained, more exhausted, than ever. Unfortunately, this self-defeating exercise is, as we know, a universal phenomenon of modern life.

So we tend to feel rather ambivalent about life. On the one hand we find it oppressive, frustrating, burdensome, stultifying. But on the other we expect from it something that will alleviate that frustration, something compensatory: an *experience*.

We can now begin to see how the way we regard religion links up with the way we regard life. There is a common emphasis, eventually, on experience (in the wider sense of the term). This is why it is almost inevitable that we should think of Enlightenment too in terms of experience. For purely historical reasons we are predisposed to think of religion, and of Enlightenment, in terms of experience. And on account of the general nature of modern life we are on the lookout for experience anyway; we are on the lookout for *the* experience that will transport us beyond that life, even beyond ourselves.

So not only are we in a position of quite naturally thinking in terms of religion as experience; we also have a neurotic need for experience to alleviate our mundane boredom and frustration. Hence we come to place a great emphasis on experience, and crave experience; and that emphasis is unhealthy because we are, very often, alienated from experience.

ENLIGHTENMENT SEEN AS EXPERIENCE

Many of those who turn for their favourite brand of experience to the various spiritual traditions of the world are very tightly locked in to this neurotic craving for – and at the same time alienation from – experience.

They have already tired of at least some of the more usual forms of distraction. In some cases they may even have dropped out of ordinary social and economic life altogether, possibly because they were too weak or sensitive to cope. With nowhere and nothing to turn to – with even, perhaps, no one to turn to – they are willing to try anything to relieve this dull, aching inner void.

So they start haunting spiritual groups and workshops, religious and occult bookshops, meditation classes and initiations. They take up astrology, magic, and witchcraft – white witchcraft, black witchcraft, and probably a sort of grey witchcraft too. They take up occultism, the Cabbala, the Vedānta, Sufism, Taoism, Buddhism. They take up anything that might take them out of themselves, anything that might give some shadow of meaning to their lives; anything that might give them an experience.

Not long after I returned to England in the 1960s, having spent twenty years or so in India, I happened to visit a well-known occult and oriental bookshop in London. Rather to my surprise it was full of people, even though it was a weekday, and I saw that all these people were absolutely oblivious to one another. They all had their eyes glued – not to say riveted – to the bookshelves. As I entered the shop I also noticed that the whole place was pervaded by a heavy, oppressive atmosphere which I felt I had encountered before – though where and on what occasion eluded me.

And then it came to me. Two years earlier I had been in a large department store in an English seaside town, and in the food section, standing around just like waxworks, were a number of elderly women with shopping baskets. They all stood quite motionless gazing fixedly at the food, and they gazed at it with what can only be described as dull, reptilian greed. It was this same greed that I saw and felt there in the bookshop. It was the same greed for pabulum, for something to feed on, the same neurotic craving for experience.

There is, however, a crucial distinction to be drawn between the neurotic craving for higher spiritual experience, and a genuine *aspiration* for such experience. The distinction is essentially between wanting to acquire and wanting to attain. Attainment is the result of a gradual growth, an extension of our own being and consciousness into higher levels and new dimensions, an extension which is, in a sense, a natural process. By contrast, acquisition in this context is the attempted appropriation of the higher level, or of the new dimension, by and for ourselves *as we are now*, an unnatural and unrealistic process – unrealistic, because it cannot possibly succeed.

Attainment is like the growth, the gradual unfoldment and flowering, of a healthy plant. But acquisition is taking to ourselves something which we ourselves haven't produced, like a neglected plant with a stolen bloom – or even a plastic flower – tied on to its sapless stem. It is as if we were to tie a lifeless simulacrum of the Buddha's own golden flower, the flower of Enlightenment, on to the barren branches of our own lives. So attainment is a matter of growing, acquisition a matter of grabbing – a sort of smash-and-grab raid on the Absolute.

Nor is this grabbing attitude towards spiritual experiences the worst kind of acquisitive attitude. There is, after all, something to be said for people who seize what they want with both hands. One can't help grudgingly admiring the boldness of the bank robber, for instance, in one's weaker moments. Much more unhealthy, much more hopeless, is an attitude of passive expectancy: lying back, mouth wide open, waiting for the experience to be fed to one, claiming transcendental experience as if one had some kind of inalienable right to it, and resenting the idea that anyone, let alone oneself, should be excluded from this experience simply because they do not measure up to it. This idea that the universe owes us not just a living, but an experience – even *the* experience – is a particularly disabling example of the false positions we can get into when we project the notion of Enlightenment as experience.

I have taken an extreme, even exaggerated, look at these false positions in order to throw into stark relief what we are really looking for when we turn for guidance to Eastern spiritual traditions – particularly to Buddhism. The purpose of the exercise is a very practical one. After all, the cultural conditioning that emphasizes feeling and experience is a hard fact of all our lives. So is the modern world with its high-speed travel, mass information, and controls and regulations. We cannot avoid being affected to a greater or a lesser extent by the world in which we live. We *are* the modern world, each of us to a certain extent, so that each of us is alienated to a certain extent – alienated from ourselves, and alienated from life – and we are all therefore, whether we want to or not, looking for compensations.

So we approach Buddhism with very mixed motives, partly healthy and partly unhealthy. No doubt in principle each and every one of us would wish to think in terms of attainment, of growth, but only too often we behave in terms of acquisition – we grab. We need to be aware of the whole underlying tendency to think of the goal as an experience, because the consequences of thinking in this way are potentially disastrous for the spiritual life. Before moving on to consider Enlightenment in terms of non-experience, then, let us first be clear about what these dangers are.

If our attitude is one of neurotic craving, if we are passive and demanding, and if we expect to be *given* a spiritual experience, then our expectation will take one or more of three specific forms. We will expect the experience to come from some*where*, or from some*one*, or from some*thing*. On account of this threefold expectation we may fall victim to three different syndromes which we can describe as pseudo-spiritual exoticism, pseudo-spiritual projection, and pseudo-spiritual technism.

PSEUDO-SPIRITUAL EXOTICISM

Pseudo-spiritual exoticism means that we expect the great experience to come from far away – the further away the better. Ideally, it should come from outer space, but if that is not possible then it should at least come from the East – if, that is, if we live in the West. If we live in the East and suffer from this same syndrome, we expect the great experience to come from the West. It seems that young Japanese Buddhists, for example, have been known to sing Protestant Christian hymns in their temple because they sounded so exotic.

This is more or less what we do in the West. Buddhism, for instance, is of oriental origin, historically speaking, and it generally comes to us dressed in oriental garb, not to say oriental ornaments. It comes to us wearing an Indian, or a Japanese, or a Tibetan style of dress, and we are naturally fascinated by this strange, beautiful, and glamorous apparel. The problem is that we may well be more interested in the outfit than in what is inside – than in Buddhism itself as a universally valid spiritual teaching which is in its essence neither of the East nor of the West. We even think that Buddhism *is* the costume it comes in. We may even think that if only we could get hold of a little scrap of this dress – a little relic, as it were – then we would have something essentially Buddhist, something authentically spiritual that will magically transform our lives.

The basic assumption that supports this idea is that the East is good and the West is bad. Some people even talk about 'the Eastern mind' as if it were constitutionally different from 'the Western mind' – the Eastern mind being a highly spiritual mind, and the Western mind a grossly materialistic mind. But this is, of course, a complete travesty of the facts.

Sad to say, some Eastern teachers, or perhaps I should say certain persons coming from the East and purporting to teach, encourage this sort of attitude. It makes them feel good and sometimes, to put it bluntly, even flatters their nationalistic prejudices. They too, in the course of centuries, have come to think that the dress is Buddhism, or that the dress is the Vedānta, or that the dress is Sufism, as the case may be.

Of course there are highly spiritual teachings in the East, and of course we can learn from those teachings, and should be immensely grateful that we have been brought into contact with them. But our concern with them should be a concern with the truth, not a concern with the exotic.

PSEUDO-SPIRITUAL PROJECTION

In the case of pseudo-spiritual projection we expect the experience to come not just from somewhere else but from some*one* else. Personal relationships are, as we know, much more intense – much more 'loaded' – than non-personal ones, and hence this particular syndrome is much more dangerous than the last. The person from whom we expect the experience is, of course, the great guru. We ourselves have to do nothing. All we have to do, miserable wretches that we are, is to believe in him, believe that he can give us the experience.

Naturally, the experience can't be given by just an ordinary man, not even by an ordinary, run-of-the-mill guru. It can be given only by a very great guru indeed – a living Buddha, a fully realized master, the embodiment or incarnation of God, or at least the personal representative of God on earth. Unless we believe in him in this way we don't get our experience. Not only that, but because we so much need to believe in this particular person, we cannot entertain a doubt, we cannot tolerate criticism of him. And criticism is here understood as including any disinclination to accept him as God or as a fully Enlightened master. Everybody has got to believe in him just as we

THE TASTE OF FREEDOM / 83

do. If necessary they must be made to believe. It's all for their own good, anyway.

But how do you know that the great guru is God, or a Buddha, or Enlightened? Well, it's quite simple. You know because he says so. In this way a very dangerous situation develops. The bigger the claims made by the great guru, the more likely it is that the kind of vulnerable people who *need* to believe him *will* believe him. Since there is no shortage of such people nowadays, this kind of self-inflated guru quickly rakes together quite a large following.

A different case is when an ordinary guru is turned into a great guru by his own followers. They see more in him than is actually there. He may be a good man, even a spiritual man, but they project onto him qualities that he does not objectively possess, and sometimes he succumbs to their projections. Should he not succumb the followers are often very disappointed. They feel rather let down. They may even become angry if he refuses to accept their projections, or to allow them to build him up into a great guru. So they leave him. They continue their search for the great guru, for someone who will give them the experience they want – or at least promise to give it.

All these things have happened – they do happen – and it is all very sad. One cannot help feeling, it must be said, deeply ashamed sometimes of what has been done and is being done in the name of Eastern religions, even in the name of Buddhism – ashamed of the way in which the weak-minded and the credulous have been exploited by the globe-trotting gurus of the twentieth century. One can even find in fringe newspapers, alternative lifestyle magazines, and the like, all kinds of such gurus advertising themselves like so many brands of soap powder, all making tremendous claims, all asking for support, for belief.

If we are going to be on our guard against this sort of thing, we have to see where the source of the trouble lies. It is not so much in the great guru: it is in ourselves, in our own weakness and passivity, our own wish to have things done for us, our own neurotic craving for experience – an experience that someone else must give us as a free gift. And we need to see as well where our real solutions are going to come from: again, they lie within us, in our own potential to grow into the experience ourselves, as a result of our own individual, responsible effort and exertion.

Pseudo-spiritual technism consists in attaching exaggerated importance to particular methods of practice, especially methods of meditation, or concentration techniques. We think that if we can only find the one right, infallible method or technique, it will automatically give us the experience. Or else we believe that we have actually found such a method or technique, and then of course we become very dogmatic and intolerant about it. All other methods are dismissed as worthless. Only our own technique, only the method to which we ourselves have recourse, is the right and efficacious one.

Such pseudo-spiritual technism may be encountered within almost any school, but for myself I have in the past encountered it particularly among followers of what used to be called vipassanā meditation – i.e. the New Burman Satipaṭṭhāna method[47] – and also in connection with Zen. Some practitioners of these methods have tended, sad to say, to be rather contemptuous of other forms of meditation practice, thinking that if one is not practising *their* favoured method then one is not meditating at all.

This neurotic overvaluing of one particular technique is to forget that in Buddhism, especially, there are many different methods of meditation, many different concentration techniques, every single one of which has been tested for centuries and every single one of which works – provided one practises it. One method may be more suited to a particular temperament, or a particular stage of development, than another, but we can never say that any one method is intrinsically better than any other.

ENLIGHTENMENT AS NON-EXPERIENCE

These three syndromes are the unwholesome consequences of thinking of religion, and thinking of Enlightenment, too literally and exclusively in terms of experience. But what is the alternative? What may be prescribed to relieve us of them? To begin with, we can try a simple but radical experiment: just to stop thinking in terms of experience for a while and instead to start thinking in terms of *non*-experience; to start thinking of Enlightenment itself, even, as non-experience.

This way of thinking can be traced in the Pāli scriptures. In the *Dhammapada*, for instance, we encounter the saying '*Nibbānaṃ paramaṃ sukhaṃ*: Nirvāṇa is the supreme bliss.'[48] The implication is that there is a difference between worldly bliss, including the highest heavenly bliss, and supreme or nirvāṇic bliss. So where does this difference lie?

The essential characteristic of worldly bliss is that it depends on contact between the sense-organs and the mind on the one hand, and their respective physical and mental objects on the other. It depends on some kind of contact between a subject and an object. Worldly bliss depends, in short, on experience; it is a form of experience. But nirvāṇic bliss is not so dependent; it does not arise in dependence upon any sort of contact, and is not the product of contact. When all contacts cease, that is Nirvāṇa, that is the bliss of Nirvāṇa. Hence Nirvāṇa is not an experience, and we can only describe it as a non-experience. Nirvāṇa is the experience you have when you've stopped experiencing.

Nirvāṇa as non-experience is also described in terms of cessation (*nirodha*), that is, in terms of the entire, complete, remainderless cessation of the conditioned. What this means so far as we are concerned is the cessation of experience – because all our experience is conditioned. The cessation of the conditioned means the cessation of all our experience because conditioned experience is the only kind of experience we know. We do not know any other kind of experience. We do not know unconditioned experience. For us, unconditioned experience is a contradiction in terms, a logical impossibility. Therefore, to the extent that we think of Nirvāṇa, or of Enlightenment, as cessation, we must think of it as non-experience.

But here we stand on the Everest of Buddhism, where the air is very clear but very cold. Perhaps we had better go a little lower down, and try to find a more positive, more concrete way of approaching Enlightenment as non-experience – a way that is more helpful to the genuine fulfilment of our real human needs. We need, in short, to think not only of Enlightenment as non-experience, but also of religion, of spiritual development, of the Buddhist path or way, as non-experience. I am going to suggest three ways of approaching the Buddhist path as non-experience – all very closely linked. These are: seeing it in terms of *growth*; seeing it in terms of *work*; and seeing it in terms of *duty*.

The primary image of growth or growing is that of the plant, an image that figures very prominently in traditional Buddhism. To take a central instance, the Buddha's vision of humanity as he sat under the bodhi tree after the Enlightenment (if Enlightenment has an 'after') was as a great bed of lotuses in various stages of development.[49] Looking out over the world he saw that some people were sunk in the mud, so to speak, some were halfway to the surface, while others had risen above the water and stood drinking in the sunlight with open petals. The Buddha saw all living beings in this way: as plants – as lotuses – at different stages of development.

This great vision has stayed with Buddhism throughout its 2,500 years of history. There have been many great philosophical developments, some of them, in all conscience, dry and abstract enough. There has been a good deal of scholasticism and, later on, plenty of formalism. But Buddhism has never forgotten the Buddha's great vision of that bed of lotuses standing there in the early morning sunlight. It has never forgotten that image of growth, of growing; and the image has assumed many different forms.

It has become, for instance, the Lotus Throne, that many-petalled throne on which innumerable Buddhas and transcendental bodhisattvas sit and meditate, teach, and radiate light.[50] It has become the great lotus-like Refuge Tree,[51] with its central trunk and four great branches, each terminating in an enormous many-petalled lotus flower on which sit Buddhas, bodhisattvas, *arhants*, gurus, *yidams*, and *ḍākinīs*. Perhaps above all, we think of its appearance in the *White Lotus Sūtra*'s parable of the herbs and plants, also known as the Parable of the Rain Cloud.[52] In this parable the Buddha sees humanity not just as lotuses but as plants of many different kinds: trees, shrubs, creepers, grasses, herbs. When the rain of the Dharma falls the 'plants' all grow, but they grow – and here is the parable's distinctive teaching – in their own way, each according to its own individual nature.

There is no need to multiply examples, suffice it to say that they all bear witness to the advantages in thinking of Buddhism not so much in terms of experience as in terms of growth, seeing ourselves drinking in the Dharma as a plant drinks in the rain. Growth is a total thing: the whole of us is – or should be – growing all the time. There is no question of our working our way up to growth. The process is absolutely continuous. Growth doesn't lie only at the end of the process; if we are working our way up we are growing. All such effort is growth.

We may say that the spiritual life, the Path, is like the plant, and Enlightenment, the goal, is like the flower. In one sense, of course, the flower is separate from the plant. However, in another sense the flower is part of the plant, the natural product of the plant, the culmination of its growth. It cannot be stuck onto the plant from outside. It cannot appear before the plant has reached the stage of development when the flower *naturally* comes forth. Whether it seems to us premature or late, the flower always appears at the appropriate time.

So likewise with the flower of Enlightenment. You can reach the goal of Enlightenment only by following the Path. You cannot grab Enlightenment as if it existed apart from the following of the Path. Enlightenment is no more separate from the Path than the flower is separate from the plant.

The image of the plant and the flower is a beautiful and appropriate one, but like all images it has its limitations. A flower, after all, fades and loses its petals, which is hardly the case with the culmination of the spiritual life. Therefore, if we want the image to carry its meaning further, we have to stretch our imagination in order to expand and develop the image.

So firstly, we have to imagine a flower that does not fade, whose petals do not fall. We have to imagine a flower that remains when all the rest of the plant, the stalk and the leaves, have dropped away. Or else, perhaps, we should imagine that the whole plant has become the flower, which seems to float, suspended, in the sky. Moreover, like other flowers, this flower seeds new plants, which produce flowers in their turn which also remain floating in the sky. And as this process has no end we have to imagine it continuing to eternity, and then we must imagine the whole of space becoming filled with flowers. This meditative vision of the whole of space filled with a vast network of great golden lotus flowers – a network expanding to infinity in all directions – is what the Buddhist life is really like.

But it is time we came down to earth, and back to a sense of space and time. It is time we came down from the flower to the plant, back to the individual struggling to grow, back to ourselves. As the parable of the herbs and plants reminds us, the plant needs rain – but it needs quite a number of other things too, if it is to grow. It needs sunshine, it needs, perhaps, wind; it needs soil, with everything soil contains; it needs even so humble a thing as manure; and maybe a little pruning from time to time, or protection from pests or wild animals. It may even need – if it is not so proud as to disdain the aid – a stick to support it for a while. In other words, growth depends on a whole complex of favourable conditions. All of which brings us to a very important point indeed: that we need to establish the process of growth within a wider and ever wider context. And this implies a fuller and richer conception of Buddhism itself.

Buddhism is not just ethics, not just meditation. It is a lot more than these two things, great and important as they are. Buddhism is a doctrine, a teaching, even a philosophy. It is a whole series of great myths. It is a body of legends. It is a complex of social institutions. It is a regular pattern of festivals and celebrations. It is a treasure-house of the arts. It is ritual. It is work. As Buddhists we need to be nourished by all these things, though we may need more of some than of others, depending on the kind of plant we are.

Buddhism is also a whole range of different schools and movements and traditions, and we need the nourishment of all of them. We don't need them in the rather mutually exclusive, occasionally sectarian form in which they exist in at least some parts of the East. We need what is essential in them all – what is fundamental, living, and nourishing in them all – as we try to grow in the light of Buddhism here in the West.

Perhaps the *triyāna* Buddhism of Tibet offers a model in this respect.[53] There is probably a hopeful sign for Western Buddhism in the fact that the dry bones of contemporary Theravāda and the cold tea-leaves of modern Zen have now been replaced in popular favour by the rich symbolism of Tibetan Buddhism (leaving aside the element of pseudo-spiritual exoticism in that appeal). However, the Tiantai Buddhism of China (continued in Japan as the Tendai school) perhaps offers us an even better model than does Tibetan Buddhism, being not *triyāna* but *ekayāna*: not three ways but, in principle, one.[54]

SEEING BUDDHISM IN TERMS OF WORK

Let us begin by making it clear that work, here, is not to be confused with gainful employment, with wage-slavery. Work is the productive expenditure of energy. This is the true, noble meaning of the word 'work'. Work in this sense is the exact opposite of passively waiting for an experience. It is the direct opposite of the neurotic craving for experience. It is a joyful and creative thing. Work is productive in the sense of helping us to grow.

The most productive kind of work, the most productive expenditure of energy, is work for the Dharma – if possible, full-time work. And work for the Dharma does not just mean giving lectures and taking classes on Buddhism. Not everybody is equipped to do that. There is also bricklaying for the Dharma, cooking and cleaning for the Dharma, painting ceilings for the Dharma: a productive expenditure of energy through which we grow, and grow rapidly. For work of this sort, the more of us there are, the wider the context we need.

That wider context is the sangha, or spiritual community, in the widest sense; that is, the sangha as consisting not just of those who are technically and officially monks, but of all those who are treading the Path of the Buddha. We began by reminding ourselves that Buddhism consisted of two things: the Goal and the Path – the Buddha and the Dharma. But in fact Buddhism consists also of this third thing: the sangha or spiritual community of all those who are seeking to attain the Goal, who are treading the Path, who are growing, and who are working together for the Dharma.

SEEING BUDDHISM IN TERMS OF DUTY

Duty is not a word that goes down very well with many people. It lost its popular appeal somewhere in the mud of Flanders in the First World War. However, any adult learns to accept duties of one kind or another, even at the basic level of, say, having a duty to one's children. So how do we define duty? What is one's duty?

To this question the great German poet and thinker Goethe answered: 'The demands of the day.' There is just one modification one would wish to make to this magisterial definition. If one said 'the demands of the *larger* day,' one would bring out the necessary distinction between lesser claims on us and greater claims. Goethe goes on: 'How can we learn self-knowledge? Never by taking thought but rather by action. Try to do your duty and you'll soon discover what you're like.'[55]

What then is the duty of a Buddhist – of one who has gone for Refuge? What is our duty as members of the spiritual community? It is simply to work – productively, joyfully, creatively. It is to do whatever can reasonably – or even in some circumstances unreasonably – be expected of us in the situation in which we find ourselves. If we do our duty as Buddhists – if we work as Buddhists, work for the Dharma – we shall know ourselves as Buddhists. In fact we shall eventually know ourselves as Buddhas. We will gain Enlightenment: gain Enlightenment as experience and as non-experience – and both, and neither.

HUMAN ENLIGHTENMENT
An Encounter with the Ideals and Methods of Buddhism

Auckland, New Zealand, February 1975.

PREFACE

The ideal of human Enlightenment is the highest ideal conceivable by man. The way *par excellence* to the realization of that ideal is meditation, understood as comprising all those methods that raise the level of consciousness and transform human life by acting directly on the mind itself. Like all other methods of raising the level of consciousness – all other ways of realizing the ideal of human Enlightenment – meditation is best practised within the context of the spiritual community, that is to say, within the context of a free association of true individuals who are united in their common commitment to a common goal and who relate to one another primarily on that basis. It is with these related themes of Enlightenment, meditation, and spiritual community that the three lectures that make up the present work are concerned.

The lectures were given in the Town Hall, Auckland, on 6, 13, and 20 February 1975, under the auspices of the Friends of the Western Buddhist Order (FWBO). I had arrived in New Zealand three months earlier, and in the course of that time had conducted meditation classes at the FWBO centres in Auckland and Christchurch, besides leading retreats in various places. FWBO activities had started in New Zealand as long ago as 1970, when Upāsaka Akshobhya started holding meditation classes in Auckland and Lim Poi Cheng began playing tapes of my lectures in Christchurch. Now, four or five years later, the Movement had gathered sufficient momentum for nine or ten people to want to commit themselves to the Three Jewels – to the Buddha, the Dharma, and the Sangha – as members of the Western Buddhist Order, and it was largely in response to their request that I had decided to visit New Zealand. The first batch of ordinations had, in fact, been held two months earlier, so that when I gave my lectures there was already a presence of the Order in New Zealand and thus, it was hoped, a firm basis for the future development of the Movement in that country.

During the time I was giving the lectures I stayed outside Auckland, in the Waitakere Hills. All around me were slopes covered with the vivid green of what I had come to recognize as typical New Zealand bush. It was bush that was resonant with the chirring of cicadas and with unfamiliar bird calls, and from which the opossums came out at night. Shortly before the lectures began, a friend brought me a copy of the poster that had been printed. Looking at it, I noticed that the lectures had been announced not as lectures on Buddhism but as *Buddhist* lectures. Whether intentional or not, the emphasis was significant. Buddhism is not a 'subject', not a body of facts on which one can talk without being involved in the meaning of those facts, and my lectures were therefore not lectures on Buddhism in the same sense that one might have lectures on botany or biology. The lectures that I gave in Auckland were *Buddhist* lectures, and as such they were meant not merely to convey facts about Buddhism, whether historical or doctrinal, but rather to communicate the results of one individual Buddhist's personal experience of Buddhism, in both East and West, over a period of more than thirty years.

Although my involvement with classes, retreats, and lectures did not allow me to see as much of New Zealand as I would have liked, I saw enough of it to convince me that conditions there were as favourable to the leading of the spiritual life as they were anywhere in the world – perhaps even more favourable. New Zealand had an agreeable climate and great natural beauty. Life under its blue skies was comparatively relaxed, and it was not difficult to make a living. Even in a place like Auckland there was not much hurry and bustle, not much pressure. There was plenty of space – plenty of fresh air – for everybody. Indeed, in a country somewhat bigger than Great Britain there were only three million people, nearly two thirds of them concentrated in the three major cities. Moreover, the country as a whole was relatively free from internal tensions, and people were not particularly weighed down by social convention and religious tradition. I therefore felt that the path of the Higher Evolution, as I had outlined it in my three Buddhist lectures, had a great future in New Zealand, *if only people made the effort to practise it* – if only they took full advantage of the facilities for spiritual self-development that were being increasingly offered by the FWBO. This feeling was confirmed on my second visit, which took place in 1979. Even in those parts of the world where conditions were *not* so favourable to the spiritual life as they are in New Zealand, it is of course still possible to follow the path of the Higher Evolution – still possible to realize the ideal of human Enlightenment – and it is for this reason that these lectures are now being brought out in book form, in the hope that in this form they will be able to reach a wider audience than the one to which the 'Ideal of Human Enlightenment' was originally presented.

I would like to thank Nagabodhi and Nigel Seller for their work in editing the verbatim transcript of these lectures for publication.

Sangharakshita
Padmaloka
Surlingham
Norfolk
28 May 1980

To all the *upāsakas, upāsikās*, Mitras, and Friends with whom I shared the experience of spiritual community on my two visits to the Land of the Long White Cloud.

THE IDEAL OF HUMAN ENLIGHTENMENT

When a Buddhist thinks about Buddhism – about what Buddhists call the Dharma – usually the first thing of which he thinks is the Buddha, the 'Enlightened One'. Strangely enough, the first thing of which the non-Buddhist too usually thinks is the Buddha. We may not know anything at all about the teachings of Buddhism, but we will at least have seen an image or picture of the Buddha, and may even be quite familiar with it, even have a definite feeling for it. What, then, does that image or picture show? It shows a man in the prime of life, well built and handsome. He is seated cross-legged beneath a tree. His eyes are half closed and there is a smile on his lips. Looking at the figure we feel that, as a whole, it conveys an impression of solidity and stability, as well as of strength. It conveys an impression of absolute calm, absolute repose. But what attracts us most of all, more even than the total figure itself, is the face, because this conveys something which it is very difficult indeed to put into words. As we look at it, perhaps even concentrate on it, we see that the face is alive, that it is *alight,* and in that light we see reflected an unfathomable knowledge, a boundless compassion, and an ineffable joy. This, then, is the figure, this the image or the picture, of the Buddha, the Enlightened One. Usually it represents the historical Gautama the Buddha, the 'founder' of Buddhism – represents, that is to say, the great Indian teacher who lived approximately 500 years before Christ. But the figure also possesses a wider significance. It represents the subject of this lecture. In other words, it represents the ideal of human Enlightenment.

Human Enlightenment is the central theme, the central preoccupation, of Buddhism. It is what Buddhism is basically concerned with, both theoretically and practically. Indeed, it is what the Buddhist himself is basically concerned with. In the course of this lecture, therefore, we shall be trying to understand what is meant by Enlightenment in general and, in particular, by 'human Enlightenment'.

Before going into this subject, however, I want to say a few words about the third item in our title. I want to examine the word 'ideal'. We speak of the *ideal* of human Enlightenment, but what does the word mean? I do not want to go into the dictionary definitions, much less still into what are really philosophical questions. For the purpose of our present discussion we shall confine ourselves to the ordinary, everyday usage of the word.

In the first place, the word means 'the best imaginable of its kind'. For instance, in London, every summer, there is a famous exhibition known as the Ideal Home Exhibition.[56] Every year thousands, even hundreds of thousands, of people visit it and look around the different sections. There they see ideal kitchens, ideal bathrooms, ideal garages, ideal shaving mirrors, ideal bread knives, ideal refrigerators, ideal lawnmowers, ideal armchairs, and even ideal egg-whisks. They see hundreds of different items, each of them claiming to be 'ideal', the best imaginable of its kind (though, of course, different manufacturers may have different ideas as to what actually is the best). Each of them, it is claimed, fulfils its function in the best possible way, and all of these things add up to the ideal home, add up, in other words, to the best imaginable home, the home that perfectly fulfils the function of a home, the home that everybody would like to live in – if only they could afford it.

In the same way we speak of various other things. We speak of the ideal wife, which is to say the wife who is a good cook and manager, who keeps the ideal home in perfect order, who drives her husband to work every morning, who never asks him for extra housekeeping money, and who laughs at all his jokes. We even speak of the ideal husband, though he is of course much rarer. Similarly we speak of the ideal couple, the ideal holiday, ideal weather, ideal arrangements, the ideal job, the ideal employer, the ideal employee, and so on. In other words we speak of something as being the best imaginable of its kind, as best fulfilling its natural function or what is believed to be its natural function. This is the first usage of the term.

In the second place, the word 'ideal' means a model or pattern: something that can be taken as an example and imitated or copied. Nowadays this usage is less common than the first, although it overlaps it to some extent. According to this usage, we see that the ideal home is not merely the best imaginable home but also the model, or pattern, for all homes. It is what you should try to make your own home look like, at least to some extent. Thus this usage would suggest that the ideal is a model. It implies a sort of comparison between the ideal, on the one hand, and the actual on the other, in this case between the real home that we actually have and the ideal home that we would like to have if we could afford it.

There is, however, a third usage of the term. For example, suppose you ask a friend what he would like to do when he retires. He might say that what he would really like to do is to go away to some beautiful tropical island with a marvellous climate, with beautiful sunshine, beautiful beaches, beautiful sea, beautiful surf, and just live there for the rest of his life, just to get away from it all. But then perhaps he says, 'Ah well, I don't suppose I ever shall. It's just an ideal.' In this instance the word 'ideal' represents a state of affairs that is regarded as highly desirable, which is certainly imaginable – which you can certainly conceive, even quite clearly – but which is regarded, for some reason or other, as impossible of attainment. These, then, are the three different ways in which we use the word 'ideal'.

Having gained some understanding of how we use the word 'ideal', we come on to a very important question, and with this question we start to approach the heart of our present subject. We have spoken of the ideal home, and we can all understand what that might be. We have mentioned the ideal wife, the ideal husband, the ideal job – even the ideal egg-whisk. But we have forgotten perhaps one thing. What about the person who uses all these articles, who enters into all these relationships? What about the individual human being? We seem to have lost sight of him, or her, as so easily happens in the midst of the complexities of modern life. The question that we are really asking is, 'What is the ideal man?' We all think we know what is meant by the ideal home, the ideal wife, or the ideal husband, but have we ever considered the question, 'What is the best imaginable kind of human being?' Not just the best kind of employee, or the best kind of citizen, or the best kind of member of a particular social group, or a particular age group, but the best kind of man *per se,* the best kind of man *as man.* Because we *are* men, and this question very seriously concerns us. What *is* the ideal for our lives? The Buddhist answer to this question comes clearly, categorically, and unambiguously. The ideal man is the Enlightened man. The ideal man is the Buddha. That is to say, the ideal for humanity – the ideal for individual human beings – is Enlightenment. The ideal is Buddhahood.

Now this raises three questions, and with each question we have to deal in turn. The three questions are, firstly, 'What is Enlightenment, or Buddhahood?' Secondly, 'How do we know that this state which we call Enlightenment is the ideal for man?' Thirdly, 'Where does this ideal of Enlightenment come from? Whence do we derive it? Whence does it originate?' Once these three questions are answered we shall have, perhaps, quite a good idea – or at least a general idea – of what is meant by the ideal of human Enlightenment.

WHAT IS ENLIGHTENMENT?

Buddhist tradition, of all schools, speaks of Enlightenment as comprising mainly three things. To begin with, Enlightenment is spoken of as a state of pure, clear – even radiant – awareness. Some schools go so far as to say that in this state of awareness the subject–object duality is no longer experienced. There is no 'out there', no 'in here'. That distinction, that subject–object distinction as we usually call it, is entirely transcended. There is only one continuous, pure, clear awareness, extending as it were in all directions, pure and homogeneous. It is, moreover, an awareness of things *as they really are,* which is, of course, not things in the sense of objects, but things as, so to speak, transcending the duality of subject and object. Hence this pure, clear awareness is also spoken of as an awareness of reality, and therefore also as a state of knowledge. This knowledge is not knowledge in the ordinary sense – not the knowledge which functions within the framework of the subject–object duality – but rather a state of direct, unmediated spiritual vision that sees all things directly, clearly, vividly, and truly. It is a spiritual vision – even a transcendental vision – which is free from all delusion, all misconception, all wrong, crooked thinking, all vagueness, all obscurity, all mental conditioning, all prejudice. First of all, then, Enlightenment is this state of pure, clear awareness, this state of knowledge or vision. Secondly, and no less importantly, Enlightenment is spoken of as a state of intense, profound, overflowing love and compassion. Sometimes this love is compared to the love of a mother for her only child. This comparison occurs, for instance, in a very famous Buddhist text called the *Karaṇīyamettā Sutta*, the 'Discourse on Loving-Kindness'. In this discourse the Buddha says, 'Just as a mother would protect her only child at the risk of her own life, even so let him cultivate a boundless heart towards all beings.'[57] This is the sort of feeling, the sort of attitude, that we must cultivate. You notice that the Buddha does not just talk about all human beings, but all beings: all that lives, all that breathes, all that moves, all that is sentient. This is how the Enlightened mind feels. And that love and compassion consists, we are further told, in a heartfelt desire – a deep, burning desire – for their well-being, for their happiness: a desire that all beings should be set free from suffering, from all difficulties, that they should grow and develop, and that ultimately they should gain Enlightenment. Love and compassion of this kind – love infinite, overflowing, boundless, directed towards all living beings – this too is part of Enlightenment.

Thirdly, Enlightenment consists in a state, or experience, of inexhaustible mental and spiritual energy. We see this very well exemplified by an incident in the life of the Buddha himself. As you may know, he gained Enlightenment at the age of 35, and he continued teaching and communicating with others until the ripe old age of 80, although his physical body eventually became very frail. On one occasion he said, 'My body is just like an old, broken-down cart, which has been repaired many times. It has been kept going with bits of string, as it were. But my mind is as vigorous as ever. Even if I had to be carried from place to place on a litter, if anyone came to me, I would still be able to answer his questions, I would still be able to teach him. My intellectual and spiritual vigour is undiminished, despite the enfeebled state of my body.'[58] So energy is characteristic of the state of Enlightenment. We could say that the state of Enlightenment is one of tremendous energy, of absolute spontaneity, continually bubbling forth: a state of uninterrupted creativity. In a nutshell, we may say that the state of Enlightenment is a state of perfect, unconditioned freedom from all subjective limitations.

This, then, is what is meant by Enlightenment, as it is understood in the Buddhist tradition – so far, at least, as Enlightenment can be described, so far as its different aspects can be tabulated in this way.

What really happens is that knowledge passes into love and compassion, love and compassion into energy, energy into knowledge, and so on. We cannot really split any one aspect off from the others. Nonetheless, we are traditionally given this 'tabulated' account of Enlightenment, just to convey some hint of the experience, just to give some little idea, or feeling, of what it is like. If we want to have a better idea than this, then we shall have to read, perhaps, some more extended, poetic account, preferably one found in the Buddhist scriptures;[59] or we shall have to take up the practice of meditation, and try to get at least a glimpse of the state of Enlightenment as we meditate. So when Buddhism speaks of Enlightenment, of Buddhahood or Nirvāṇa, this is what it means: it means a state of supreme knowledge, love and compassion, and energy.

HOW DO WE KNOW THAT THIS STATE OF ENLIGHTENMENT IS THE IDEAL FOR MAN?

Before attempting to answer this question, we shall have to distinguish between two kinds of ideal. There are no actual terms for them in circulation, but we can call them 'natural ideals' and 'artificial ideals'. A natural ideal, we may say, is an ideal which takes into consideration the nature of the thing or the person for which it is an ideal. The artificial ideal, on the other hand, does not do this. The artificial ideal imposes itself from the outside, in an artificial manner. For instance, if we go back to our ideal home, then however beautiful, however luxurious, however convenient it may be in many ways, it would not be an ideal home for a disabled person if it contained several flights of stairs. In the same way the life of a Henry Ford would not be an ideal for someone who was, by temperament, an artist.[60]

Using this distinction, we may say that Enlightenment is not an artificial ideal. It is not something imposed on man from outside, something that does not belong to him or accord with his nature. Enlightenment is a natural ideal for man, or even, we may say, *the* natural ideal. There is nothing artificial about it, nothing arbitrary. It is an ideal that corresponds to man's nature, and to his needs. We know this in two ways. I have spoken about the nature of Enlightenment, and obviously it has seemed, though intelligible, something very, very rarefied indeed, something very remote, even, from our present experience. But the qualities that constitute Enlightenment are, in fact, already found in man, in germinal form; they are not completely foreign to him. They are, in a sense, natural to man. In every man, in every woman, and even in every child, there is *some* knowledge – *some* experience – of reality, however remote and far removed, *some* feeling of love and compassion, however limited and exclusive, and *some* energy, however gross and unrefined – however conditioned and unspontaneous. All these qualities are already there, to some extent. It is, in fact, these qualities that distinguish man from the animal. But in the state of Enlightenment these qualities are fully and perfectly developed, to a degree that we can hardly imagine. It is for this reason – because the qualities of knowledge, love, and energy are already present within him, in however embryonic a form – that man has, as it were, a natural affinity with Enlightenment, and can respond to the ideal of Enlightenment when he encounters it. Thus even when someone speaks in terms of absolute knowledge, of the vision of reality, or in terms of boundless, unlimited love and compassion for all living beings, it is not something completely foreign to us, it is not just so many words. We *can* feel something. And this is because the germ, the seed, is already there, in our own experience, and we can respond to the ideal of Enlightenment whenever and however we encounter it – even when we encounter it in comparatively weak, limited, or distorted forms.

We also know that Enlightenment is the natural ideal for man because, in the long run, man is never really satisfied by anything else. We can have all sorts of pleasures, all sorts of achievements, but eventually we still feel within ourselves something dissatisfied, something non-satisfied. This is what in Buddhism is called *duḥkha:* unsatisfactoriness, or even suffering. Tradition speaks of three forms of *duḥkha,* three kinds of suffering. The first is called simply, 'the suffering which is suffering'. It is obviously suffering if we cut our finger, or when someone upsets us or disappoints us, for instance. This is the kind of suffering that is, simply, suffering. Then there is what is called 'suffering by way of transformation'. We have something, we enjoy it – we get a great deal of pleasure from it – but by its very nature that thing cannot last, or our relationship with it cannot last. Eventually the thing goes, the relationship with it breaks up, and because we have enjoyed it, because we have become very attached to it, suffering results. This is the suffering that comes about as a result of transformation, of change, of time. Then there is 'the suffering of conditioned existence itself': the suffering, ultimately, of everything which is not Enlightenment. Even if we do acquire things, and even if we go on possessing them and enjoying them, there is still some corner of our heart which is not satisfied, which wants something more, something further, something greater. And this something is what we call Enlightenment. So from this too we know that Enlightenment is the natural ideal for man, because man, the true man, the real human being, the true individual, is ultimately not satisfied with anything less. Personifying the ideal of Enlightenment, and borrowing the somewhat theistic language of St Augustine, we may say, 'Thou hast made us for thyself, and restless is our heart until it comes to rest in thee.'[61]

WHERE DOES THE IDEAL OF ENLIGHTENMENT COME FROM?

The ideal comes from human life itself; it comes from human history. It could not come from any other source. The ideal for man, we may say, can only come from man himself, can only come from a human being. And if we look back into history we can see various people who have actually achieved Enlightenment, who have closed the gap between the real and the ideal. We can see people who have fully actualized all those spiritual qualities which in most men and women are only germinal. If we look back in history we can see individuals who are living embodiments of the ideal. In particular, as we look back into the history of the East, of India, we see the figure of the Buddha. We see the figure of the young Indian patrician who, some 2,500 years ago, gained Enlightenment or, as the Buddhist scriptures call it, *bodhi,* which is 'knowledge' or 'awakening'. He it was who, after gaining that state of Enlightenment, inaugurated the great spiritual revolution – the great spiritual tradition – that we now call Buddhism.

At this point I would like to clear up certain misunderstandings that exist with regard to the Buddha and Buddhism. At the beginning of this lecture I said that even the non-Buddhist has at least seen an image or picture of the Buddha, and that he might even be quite familiar with it. However, although he might have seen it many times, he may not have a very clear idea of what it represents; he may not know who, or what, the Buddha is. There are, in fact, on the part of many people, some quite serious misunderstandings about him. There are in particular two major misunderstandings: firstly, that the Buddha was an ordinary man, and secondly, that the Buddha was God. Both of these misunderstandings are the result of thinking, consciously or unconsciously, in Christian terms, or at least in theistic terms, which is to say, in terms of a personal God, a supreme being who has created the universe, and who governs it by his providence.

For orthodox Christianity, as most of us know, God and man are entirely different beings. God is 'up there', man is 'down here', and there is a great gulf between them. God is the creator. He has called man into existence out of the dust. Man is the created. He has been created, according to some accounts, much as a potter creates a pot. Moreover, God is pure, God is holy, God is sinless; but man is sinful, and man can never become God: such an idea would be meaningless according to orthodox Christian, theistic tradition. Not only that. With only one exception, God can never become man. The exception is, of course, Jesus Christ, who for orthodox Christianity is God incarnate. Thus the Christian has, we may say, three categories with which to operate: God, man, which is to say 'sinful man', and God incarnate, or Christ. So where does the Buddha fit in? How does the orthodox Christian apply his categories when confronted by the figure of the Buddha? Obviously for the orthodox Christian the Buddha is not God. (There is only one God anyway.) Equally obviously, he is not God incarnate, since according to orthodox Christian teaching God incarnated only once, as Jesus Christ. That leaves only man. Orthodox Christians, therefore, when confronted by the figure of the Buddha, classify him as a man – as an ordinary man, essentially just like everyone else – even as a sinful man albeit perhaps better than most people. But however much better he might be, he is still seen as immeasurably inferior to God, and immeasurably inferior to Christ.

So much, then, for the first misunderstanding. The second arises out of the first. It is said, even by Christian scholars working in the field of Buddhist studies, that although the Buddha was only an ordinary man his followers made him into a God. You often read in books, even now, that after his death the Buddha's followers 'deified' him.[62] This is indicated, we are told, by the fact that Buddhists *worship* the Buddha, and of course worship is due only to God. If you worship someone or something, a Christian will inevitably think you are treating it, or him, as God.

Now both these misunderstandings can be cleared up quite easily. All we have to do is to free ourselves from our Christian conditioning, a conditioning which affects – at least unconsciously – even those who no longer think of themselves as Christians. We have to stop trying to think of the Buddha in what are really non-Buddhistic terms. We have to remember that Buddhism is a non-theistic tradition – which is to say that it does not believe in the existence of a supreme being who created the universe. Buddhism, in fact, distinctly denies the existence of such a being. The Buddha even went so far as to treat the belief in a personal God, a creator figure, as a hindrance to the living of the spiritual life.[63]

So who, or what, was the Buddha? How do *Buddhists* think of him? How did he think of himself? In the first place, the Buddha was a man, a human being. But he was not an ordinary man; he was an Enlightened man: a man who was the living embodiment of perfect knowledge, unbounded love and compassion, and inexhaustible energy. But he was not *born* an extraordinary man. He *became* an extraordinary man, became an Enlightened One, as a result of his own human effort to make actual what was potential in himself, to develop to the full what was only germinal in himself. So Buddhism recognizes two great categories: the category of the ordinary man, and the category of the Enlightened man. Now although the gulf between these two is not unbridgeable, as is the gulf between God and man in Christianity, the distance between them is very, very great, and it takes a tremendous effort to traverse this gap. Many Buddhists, in fact, believe that this effort has to be maintained through a whole succession of lives, whether here on earth or in higher realms. For this reason, the Enlightened man is regarded as constituting an independent category of existence. According to Buddhism, the Enlightened man is regarded as the highest being in the universe, higher even than the gods. For this reason the Enlightened man is worshipped. He is worshipped out of gratitude for setting an example, for showing the way, for showing us what we too are capable of becoming. In other words, the Buddha is worshipped not as God, but as teacher, as exemplar, as guide.

In this connection, Gautama the Buddha is often referred to as *lokajyeṣṭha*. In the West Gautama the Buddha is best known simply as the Buddha, but in the East there are quite a few well-known titles for him. He is known as *Tathāgata*, as *Bhagavan*, as *arhant,* and also as *lokajyeṣṭha*. The term *lokajyeṣṭha* means 'elder brother of the world', or 'elder brother of mankind', and the Buddha is so called because he has been born, spiritually, first, as we are born, spiritually, afterwards. The Buddha is often represented as saying to his disciples, 'You are my own true sons, born of my mouth, born of the Teaching: the heirs to spiritual things, not heirs to worldly things.' Sometimes, as in the Vinaya Piṭaka, the Buddha is compared to the first chick to emerge from a clutch of eggs.[64] The first-born chick starts to tap on the shells of the other eggs with his little beak, helping the other chicks to emerge. And so, we are told, the Buddha is like that first chick. He is the first to emerge from the shell of ignorance, the shell of spiritual darkness and blindness, and then he taps on our shells, he wakes us up with his teaching – he helps us to *emerge*.

From all this we can see that the Buddhist conception of the Enlightened man, the Buddha, represents a category for which we have no equivalent in Western thought or Western religious tradition. He is neither God nor man in the Christian sense. He is not even man-without-God – man left on his own without God, as it were. He is something in between and above.

Perhaps we can best think of Enlightened man in evolutionary terms. Man is an animal, but he is no ordinary animal. For want of a better term, he is a rational animal. He represents a new mutation, a new species, a new category: an animal but, at the same time, infinitely more than an animal. He is a human being, a man. In the same way, a Buddha is a man, but he is not an ordinary man. He is an Enlightened man. He too represents a new mutation, a new species, a new category of existence: a human being but, at the same time, infinitely more than a human being: an *Enlightened* human being, a *Buddha*.

We can now move on to the misunderstandings about Buddhism. These are, as one might expect, closely connected with the misunderstandings about the Buddha. Inasmuch as Buddhism is non-theistic, it is not really a religion in the ordinary Western sense of the term. People sometimes find this hard to understand because they have always regarded Buddhism as a religion. Perhaps they have seen it classified in this way in encyclopaedias, or on television, or of course they have a vague idea that 'religion' means belief in God anyway. They therefore think that Buddhism *must* teach belief in God. But this is just muddled thinking. Some people even think there must be a God in Buddhism *somewhere* – and do their best to find him. They even accuse Buddhists of mislaying him, or losing him, or even trying to hide him!

If Buddhism is not a religion in the Christian sense, then what is it? We can best answer this question by going back to our distinction between the real and the ideal, between the Enlightened man and the unenlightened man. Buddhism, or what is traditionally known as the Dharma, is whatever helps us transform the real into the ideal. It is whatever helps us to bridge the gap between the state of ignorance and the state of Enlightenment. In other words, Buddhism is whatever helps us to develop, whatever helps us to grow. For this reason we find the Buddha saying to his aunt and foster-mother, Mahāprajāpatī Gautami,

> Whatsoever teachings conduce to dispassion, to detachment, to decrease of worldly gains, to frugality, to content, to solitude, to energy, to delight in good, of these teachings you can be certain that they are the teaching of the Buddha.[65]

The criterion is, then, not theoretical but practical. In the course of its long history, Buddhism has developed many different philosophies, as we may call them, many different methods, many different institutions, but they all have one sole purpose, and that purpose is to assist the individual human being to develop from the state of an ordinary human being to the state of an Enlightened human being, a Buddha.

Let us conclude, then, as we began: with the figure of Gautama the Buddha. He is seated under the bodhi tree, just a few weeks after his great awakening. According to one of the oldest accounts, at that time he looked out over the world, over the whole of humanity – not with the eye of the flesh but with his spiritual vision, or what is called his 'divine eye'. And as he looked out in this way, he saw mankind as like a great bed of lotus flowers. He saw, moreover, that some of the flowers were deeply immersed in the mud, while others rose half out of the water. Some were even standing completely clear of the water.[66] In other words, he saw all these 'flowers' – all human beings – as being at different stages of growth, different stages of development. And that, we could say, is how Buddhism has seen humanity ever since: as a bed of plants capable of producing shoots, as shoots capable of producing buds, as buds capable of opening into flowers, into lotus flowers, even into the thousand-petalled lotus itself. But in order to grow, in order to develop, human beings must have something to grow *into*. They cannot grow unconsciously, as the plant does: they must grow consciously.

We may say, in fact, that for human beings growth *means* growth in consciousness, growth in awareness. This is why man needs an ideal – not just an ideal for this or that aspect of his being only, not an ideal for himself simply in terms of this or that relationship of life, but an ideal for himself as a human being. It must be an ideal, moreover, which is not artificial but natural, not imposed upon him from without but implicit in his own nature, his own being: an ideal which represents, indeed, the fulfilment of his nature in the deepest possible sense. It is this ideal, the ideal of human Enlightenment, that I have tried to communicate to you in this lecture.

Nowadays we have to recognize that many people are sceptical about ideals, and especially so, perhaps, about spiritual ideals – about the possibility of transforming the real into the ideal. Buddhism, however, is not sceptical. It has faith in the ideal – faith in the spiritual ideal, faith in the ideal of human Enlightenment – and it has faith in the ideal because it has faith in man, in the creative potential of man. Because it has faith in man, it asks man to have faith in himself. It does not ask him to 'believe', least of all to 'believe' in Buddhism. Instead, it asks him to take the ideal of human Enlightenment as a practical, working hypothesis. It asks him to *make the experiment*. It asks him to *try*.

WHAT MEDITATION REALLY IS

In the course of the last few decades quite a number of changes have taken place in different parts of the world, particularly, perhaps, in the Western world. Political changes have taken place, as well as social changes, cultural changes, and also great technological changes. We might even go so far as to say that in the course of the last few decades more changes have taken place in the world, and in the Western world in particular, than during any comparable period in human history.

So far as human affairs, at least, are concerned, in the course of the last decade or more we have seen a constantly accelerating rate of change. More and more changes seem to be taking place, within shorter and ever shorter periods of time. Formerly, when the pace was slower, and you had time to 'grow up', several generations might elapse before a change in some particular department of life started becoming noticeable. But this is no longer the case. Now these changes are noticeable in the course of a single lifetime, even in the space of a single decade – or half a decade. And we see this constantly accelerating rate of change in practically all fields of human life and human endeavour, whether political, social, economic, or cultural.

But in this lecture we are concerned with just one of those fields, which I shall call – to use a good, neutral, general term – the cultural field. In this particular field, one of the biggest, one of the greatest, and also potentially one of the most important changes to have taken place in recent years is with regard to the subject of meditation.

Fifteen or twenty years ago, meditation had hardly been heard of in the West. Whatever knowledge or interest there was, so far as meditation was concerned, was for the most part confined to obscure groups and eccentric individuals. But now we may say that the term meditation is almost a household word. Nevertheless, though the word is widely current, this does not mean that what the word represents – what meditation *means* – is at all well understood.

So many times I have heard people say, 'Meditation means making the mind a blank – making the mind empty.' Others seem to think that meditation simply means sitting and doing nothing. Sitting and doing nothing may be a fine thing to do, or not to do, but it is not meditation. Again, sometimes you hear people say, or you even read, that meditation means sitting and gazing at your navel, possibly squinting as you do so, or that it means going into some kind of trance. (Unfortunately, one well-known and generally reliable writer on Buddhism has, to some extent, popularized this word 'trance' as a synonym for meditation.)[67] Other people think that meditation means just sitting quietly and thinking about things, 'turning things over in one's mind'. Others again think that meditation means getting yourself into a sort of self-induced hypnotic state. These are just a few of the more popular and more widespread misunderstandings about meditation.

Why there should be these misunderstandings seems fairly obvious. Meditation is comparatively new in the West: at least it is new in the modern West. There has not been, at least in recent history, anything quite like it within the range of our experience. We do not even have the proper words, the proper specialized terms, to describe meditation states and meditation processes. It is only natural, therefore, that at first there should be some misunderstanding.

Again, we must remember that meditation is essentially something to be practised – that it is something which one does, or which one comes to experience. But most people still know about meditation only from hearsay. They do not know about it from their own personal practice and experience. They therefore rely on second-hand, third-hand, and even fourth-hand information. Some even rely – perhaps have to rely – for their information about meditation on books. Nowadays there are quite a few books on the market dealing, or purporting to deal, with meditation. Unfortunately these books themselves are only too often based on hearsay rather than on personal knowledge and experience. In some cases they may be based on pure imagination, not to say speculation. Already in this field there are quite a number of self-appointed experts. When something becomes popular, as meditation is becoming, only too many people are ready to cash in on the boom. I remember, in this connection, my own experience during the Buddha Jayanti year, the year in which the Buddhist world celebrated the 2500th anniversary of the *parinirvāṇa*, or passing away, of the Buddha – celebrated 2,500 years of Buddhism. The Government of India sponsored the celebrations in India, while the different South-east Asian governments sponsored the celebrations in their own respective countries. A great deal of interest was aroused, and since there was a great demand for literature all sorts of people set to work writing books, pamphlets, and articles on Buddhism, in many cases without the slightest qualification. There they were, all collecting material from here and there – sometimes from reliable, sometimes from unreliable sources – and by this means all producing another 'work' on Buddhism.

In the West today there is a boom in spiritual things in general, and at least a modest boom in meditation. Quite a number of people are dissatisfied with their ordinary, everyday lives, their conventional way of living and doing things. People cannot accept a purely scientific explanation of life, despite the great practical success of science in dealing with the material world, while at the same time they find themselves unable to accept the traditional, mainly Judaeo-Christian, explanation of things either. They therefore begin looking for something which will satisfy them more deeply, more permanently, more creatively, and more constructively. Some people look in the direction of the Eastern spiritual traditions, and especially in the direction of meditation. They want to know about meditation, want to practise meditation – want to go along to meditation classes, attend meditation weekends – and in this way a demand for meditation is created.

Of course, only too many people are ready to fulfil that demand – in some cases for a consideration. Some of these people may be quite well qualified to meet the demand – quite well qualified to teach meditation – and others may not. In this way, too, all sorts of misunderstandings arise. Quite often meditation is identified with a particular *kind* of meditation, or with a particular concentration technique. It is not, perhaps, generally understood that there are many kinds of meditation – many methods, and many concentration techniques. Sometimes people who just know about one of these, or who practise just one, tend to identify the whole practice of meditation exclusively with that particular method, that particular technique. They may claim that their method is the best one, or even that it is the only one, and that you are not actually meditating at all unless you meditate in that particular way, using that particular technique. The other techniques, the other practices, the other traditions are, they claim, of no value. This is the sort of claim that is made. It becomes all the more important, therefore, to clear up the confusion, to resolve the misunderstandings. It becomes important to understand *what meditation really is.* In order to do this we shall have to bear in mind the gap between the ideal and the real, between the Enlightened man, or Buddha, and the unenlightened, ordinary man. We shall have to bear in mind the nature of Buddhism itself.

As we saw in the previous lecture, the Buddha, or Enlightened man, represents a state, an attainment – a mode of being and consciousness – for which we have really no equivalent in Western thought, and for which we have, therefore, no equivalent word or term. 'Buddha' does not mean God, the supreme being, the creator of the universe, nor does 'Buddha' mean God incarnate. Neither does 'Buddha' mean man, in the ordinary sense. Rather, we can best think of the Buddha, the Enlightened One, in evolutionary terms. The Buddha, the Enlightened One, is a man, but he is a very special kind of man, a more developed man. In fact he is an infinitely developed man. That is to say, he is a man who has reached, and realized fully, the state of spiritual perfection that we call Enlightenment. This is what 'Buddha' means. And Buddhism is whatever helps close the gap between the ideal and the real; whatever helps transform the unenlightened man into the Enlightened man; whatever helps us to grow, to evolve, to develop. When the real man becomes the ideal man – when the unenlightened man is transformed into the Enlightened man – a tremendous change takes place – perhaps the greatest human change and development that *can* take place. And it is this kind of development that we call the spiritual life, or the process of what is sometimes called the Higher Evolution. But what is it that changes? In what does this development consist?

Obviously it is not the physical body that changes, because physically the Enlightened man and the unenlightened man look very much alike. The change that takes place is a purely mental one – using the word mental in its widest sense. It is *consciousness* that develops, and this is the great difference, we may say, between the Higher Evolution, on the one hand, and the lower evolution on the other. What we call the lower evolution corresponds to the whole process of development from amoeba up to ordinary man, or unenlightened man. This is a predominantly biological process, a process that becomes psychological only towards the end. The Higher Evolution corresponds to the whole process – the whole course – of development which leads from unenlightened man up to Enlightened man, and this is purely a psychological and spiritual process, a process which may, eventually, become entirely dissociated from the physical body.

Now traditional Buddhism speaks in terms of four grades, or four levels, of consciousness, each one higher than the one preceding. First of all, there is consciousness associated with the plane, or 'world', of sensuous experience. Secondly, there is consciousness associated with the plane, or 'world', of mental and spiritual form – the plane or world of archetypes. Then there is consciousness associated with the formless plane or 'world', and finally, consciousness associated with the transcendental path, which is to say, with the path leading directly to Nirvāna, Enlightenment, or Buddhahood, as well as with Nirvāna, Enlightenment, or Buddhahood itself.

There is another classification we sometimes use which may be more helpful. Here too there are four stages, or four levels, of consciousness, although they do not correspond very exactly to the four already enumerated. Here, first of all, comes what we call sense-consciousness, which is to say, consciousness associated with objects experienced through the physical senses. This is sometimes called simple consciousness, also animal consciousness. It is the consciousness we share with members of the animal kingdom. Secondly, there is self-consciousness: not self-consciousness in the more colloquial sense of the term, but self-consciousness in the sense of *awareness of being aware,* knowing that we know. This is sometimes called reflexive consciousness because, here, consciousness so to speak bends back upon itself, knows itself, experiences itself, is aware of itself. We may say, perhaps, that this self-consciousness, or reflexive consciousness, is human consciousness in the full sense of the term. Thirdly, there is what we call transcendental consciousness. This means consciousness of, or even direct personal contact with, reality – ultimate reality – experienced as an object 'out there'. Finally, there is absolute consciousness, in which the subject–object relation is entirely dissolved, and in which there is a full realization of ultimate reality, as transcending altogether the subject–object duality.

In both these classifications, the first consciousness enumerated is that, predominantly, of the ordinary unenlightened man, the man who is not even trying to develop spiritually. And the fourth consciousness, in both cases, is that of the Enlightened man.

We can now begin to see in what the spiritual life – in what the Higher Evolution – essentially consists. We may say that it consists in a continual progression from lower to higher, and ever higher, states of being and consciousness: from the world of sensuous experience to the world of mental and spiritual form, from the world of mental and spiritual form to the formless world, and from the formless world to Nirvāṇa, or Enlightenment; or, from sense-consciousness to self-consciousness, self-consciousness to transcendental consciousness, transcendental consciousness to absolute consciousness.

We can now begin to see what meditation really is. Indeed, we shall see it all the more clearly for having gone a little way into these fundamentals first. There is, however, just one more point to be made. Spiritual life, as we have said, consists in the development of consciousness. And Buddhism, the Dharma, the teaching of the Buddha, is whatever helps in that development. But there are two different ways in which consciousness can be developed, or at least two different methods of approach. We call these methods the subjective and the objective, or the direct and the indirect. Having recognized this distinction, we are at last in a position to see what meditation really is. Meditation is the subjective or direct way of raising the level of consciousness. In meditation we raise the level of consciousness by working directly on the mind itself.

First of all, however, I must say something about 'objective' or indirect methods of raising the level of consciousness. Some people appear to think that meditation is the only way there is to raise the level of consciousness, as if to say that consciousness must be raised directly by working on the mind itself or not at all. Such people therefore identify meditation with the spiritual life, and the spiritual life exclusively with meditation. They therefore claim that if you are not meditating you cannot possibly be leading a spiritual life. Sometimes they even identify the spiritual life with a particular kind of meditation, or a particular concentration technique. But this is far too narrow a view. It makes us forget what the spiritual life really is – which is to say that it consists in the raising of the level of consciousness – and it makes us forget, sometimes, what meditation itself really is. It is true, of course, that the raising of the level of consciousness by direct methods is at least as important as raising it by indirect methods; we might even say that it is perhaps more important. But we should not forget that other methods do exist; if we did forget this our approach would be too one-sided; and if we acted upon this, we would tend to make the spiritual life itself one-sided and even to exclude certain kinds of people – people of certain temperaments, for example – who were not, perhaps, particularly interested in meditation. So let us very briefly look at some of these indirect, non-meditative methods of raising the level of consciousness.

First of all, there is change of environment. This is quite consciously employed as an indirect means of changing, and hopefully raising, our level of consciousness when we go away on retreat – perhaps into the country, to a retreat centre. There we spend a few days, or even a few weeks, simply in more pleasant, more congenial surroundings, perhaps not even doing anything in particular. This is often more helpful than people realize, and it suggests that the environment in which we normally have to live and work is not particularly good for us – does not help in the raising of the level of awareness. It really does seem as if, for most people, a positive change of environment leads quite naturally to a raising of their level of consciousness – even without any further effort.

Another quite practical and simple indirect method of raising the level of consciousness is what we call, in Buddhism, right livelihood. Practically everybody has to work for a living. Quite a lot of us do the same kind of work every day, five days a week, fifty weeks of the year. We may do it for five, ten, fifteen, twenty, twenty-five, or thirty years, until we come to the age of retirement. All this has a continuous effect on our state of mind. If our work is unhealthy in the mental, moral, and spiritual sense, the effect on our minds will also be unhealthy. So therefore, in Buddhism, in the Buddha's teaching, we are advised very strongly to look at our means of livelihood and to practise right livelihood, which means earning our living in a way that does not lower our state of consciousness, that does not prevent us raising it, even, and that does no harm to other living beings. In Buddhist tradition there is a list of occupations that are seen not to be very helpful: the work of a butcher, of a trader in arms, of a dealer in liquor, and so on. By changing our means of livelihood (assuming that at present it is not quite right), then just that change of work, change of place, change of environment – that change in the sort of people we work with, the sort of thing that we have to do every day – will have a positive and helpful effect on our level of consciousness – or at least it will not prevent it from rising.

Then again, to become more specific and concrete, there is the leading of a regular and disciplined life: something which apparently is becoming less and less popular. This may consist in the observance and practice of certain moral precepts and principles, in having regular hours for meals, for work, for recreation, and for study, or in observing moderation in such things as eating, sleeping, and talking – perhaps even in fasting occasionally, or observing silence for a few days or weeks. In its fully developed form this more regular, disciplined life is what we call the monastic life. Among those who are leading such a regular, disciplined life, even without any meditation, over a period of years, one can see quite clearly a change taking place in their state, their level, of consciousness.

There are other indirect methods, such as hatha yoga or yoga in the more physical sense. Especially there are what are called yogic *āsanas*, which affect not only the body, but the mind as well. They affect the mind *through* the body, and even people who meditate regularly sometimes find these *āsanas* very helpful. Sometimes even the experienced meditator may be a bit too tired at the end of a day's work, or a bit too worried, to meditate properly. At such times he may practise a few *āsanas* until his mind becomes calmer and more concentrated. Thus he loses his tiredness and becomes more refreshed, almost as though he had meditated.

Then again there are the various Japanese *dō* or 'ways' – like *ikebana,* flower arrangement. It might seem a very simple and ordinary thing just to arrange a few flowers in a vase in a traditional way, but people who have engaged in this over a period of years are definitely changed in their minds, changed in their consciousness. One can also think of things like t'ai chi ch'uan and so on. These all have an effect upon the mind. They are all indirect ways of raising the level of consciousness. Likewise, the enjoyment of great works of art – of great poetry, music, and painting – often helps to raise the level of consciousness. Such enjoyment raises it if the works in question are truly great – if they really do issue from a higher state of consciousness in the artist himself – if they actually are an expression of a higher state of consciousness than we usually experience.

On a more practical level, there is simply helping other people. We might devote ourselves to helping the sick, the destitute, and the mentally disturbed, as well as to visiting those in prison. We might do these things very willingly and cheerfully, disregarding our own comfort and convenience – might do them without any personal, selfish motive. This is what in the Hindu tradition is called *Niṣkāmakarma Yoga,* or the yoga of disinterested action. This too is an indirect means of raising our state of consciousness.

Then there is association with spiritually-minded people, especially those who are more spiritually advanced than ourselves – if we are able to find them. Such association is regarded in some traditions, or by some teachers, as the most important of all the indirect methods. It is what is referred to again and again in Indian religious and spiritual literature as *satsaṅgh. Sat* means true, real, authentic, genuine, spiritual – even transcendental – while *saṅgh* means association, or communion, or fellowship. *Satsaṅgh* is simply a getting together – often in a very happy, carefree spirit – with people who are on the spiritual path and whose predominant interest is in spiritual things. This rubs off on oneself, almost without any effort on one's own part. Thus *satsaṅgh* too is an indirect means of raising the level of consciousness. It is what in Buddhism we call *kalyāṇa mitratā.*

Then again, there is chanting and ritual worship. Ritual is very much looked down upon today, especially by the more intelligent, or perhaps I should say 'intellectual'. But it is a time-honoured method of raising the level of consciousness. Even if we simply offer a few flowers, or light a candle and place it in front of an image or picture, all this has an effect upon the mind, and sometimes we are surprised to find how much effect it does have. We might read lots of books about the spiritual life, we might even have tried to meditate – might even have succeeded in meditating – but sometimes we find that the performance of a simple, but meaningful, symbolic ritual action helps us far more.

There are many more indirect methods that could be mentioned, and these methods can of course be combined with each other. Some of them can be combined with the direct method, with the practice of meditation. However, good though these indirect methods are, some of them at least cannot carry us very far. They cannot carry us up through all the levels of consciousness. But since in most cases it will be quite a while before we do pass on to the higher levels of consciousness, the indirect methods will be useful to us for a long time. However, if by means of such methods we do succeed in getting anywhere near those higher levels then, in order to progress further, we shall have to have greater and greater recourse to meditation. We shall have to start working directly on the mind itself.

Now how do we do this? In what does this direct working on the mind consist? So far I have been using only the very general term, 'meditation', because this is the one that has gained currency in the West, or at least in the English-speaking countries. But this English word 'meditation' does not correspond to any one Indian or Buddhist term. What we call meditation in English corresponds to at least three rather different things, covers in fact three different ways of working directly on the mind – three different stages, even, in the development of consciousness – and for all these three things, Buddhism, like other Indian spiritual traditions, has quite separate terms. In plain English 'meditation' comprises concentration, absorption, and insight.

THE STAGE OF CONCENTRATION

Concentration is of a twofold nature, involving both a narrowing of the focus of attention and a unification of energy. As such, concentration can be spoken of as integration, which is of two kinds, the 'horizontal' and the 'vertical' as I shall call them. Horizontal integration means the integration of the ordinary waking consciousness within itself, or on its own level, while vertical integration means the integration of the conscious mind with the subconscious mind, a process which involves the freeing of blocked somatic energy as well as the tapping of deeper and ever deeper energies within the psyche.

Horizontal integration corresponds to what is generally known as mindfulness and recollection. This English word 'recollection' is rather a good one, because it means just what it says – re-collection. It is a collecting together of what has been scattered, and what has been scattered is *ourselves,* our conscious selves, or so-called conscious selves. We have become divided into a number of selves, or part-selves, each with its own interests, its own desires, and so on, each trying to go its own way. At one time one self is uppermost, at another time another, so that sometimes we hardly know who we are. There is a dutiful self and there is a disobedient self. There is a self that would like to run away from it all, and there is a self that would like to stay at home and be a good boy or a good girl, and so on. We hardly know, very often, which of these selves we really and truly are. Each of them is our self, and yet none of them is our self. The truth is that we do not really have a self at all. It has not yet come into existence. It has not yet been born. The self – the overall self, as it were – comes into existence only with the practice of mindfulness and recollection, when we 'collect' all these selves together.

Mindfulness, or recollection, in Buddhist tradition is of three kinds. Firstly, there is mindfulness of the body and its movements: knowing exactly where the body is and what it is doing. Here we make no unmindful movements, no movements of which we are unaware. When we speak, too, we are mindful, knowing what we are saying and why we are saying it. We are fully alert, composed, aware. Secondly, there is mindfulness of feelings and emotions. We become quite clearly conscious of our passing, changing moods, of whether we are sad or happy, pleased or displeased, anxious, afraid, joyful, or excited. We watch, we see it all, we know exactly how we are. Of course this does not mean standing back from our feelings and emotions like a sort of spectator, looking at them in a very external, alienated way. It means experiencing our feelings and emotions – being 'with' them, not cut off from them – but at the same time being always mindful of them and observing them. Thirdly and lastly, there is mindfulness of thoughts: knowing just what we are thinking, just where our mind actually is from instant to instant. As we know, the mind wanders very easily. We are usually in an *un*concentrated, *un*recollected state as regards our thoughts. For this reason we have to practise being mindful of our thoughts, aware of what we are thinking from moment to moment.

If we practise in this way, then horizontal integration is achieved. We are brought together, and a self is created. When this is properly and perfectly done, we develop complete self-consciousness: we become truly human. But concentration is not only horizontal; it is also vertical. The conscious mind must now be integrated with the subconscious mind. This is achieved by having recourse to an object of concentration – an object on which one learns to concentrate one's whole attention, and into which the energies of the subconscious are allowed to be gradually absorbed.

At this point, the meditator, or the would-be meditator, having achieved horizontal integration, has reached a very crucial stage. He is about to make a very important transition, from the plane or world of sensuous experience to the plane or world of mental and spiritual form. But he is held back by what are known as the five mental hindrances, which have to be suppressed before the stage of absorption can be entered upon. (This suppression is temporary. The five mental hindrances are permanently eradicated only when insight has been attained.) First of all, there is the hindrance of desire for sensuous experience through the five physical senses, desire, that is, for agreeable visual, auditory, olfactory, gustatory, and tactile sensations – especially those connected with food and with sex. So long as desires of this sort are present in the mind, no transition to the stage of absorption is possible, since while they are present the meditator cannot really occupy himself with the concentration object. Secondly, there is the hindrance of hatred, which is the feeling of ill will and resentment that arises when the desire for sensuous experience is frustrated – a feeling that is sometimes directed towards the object of the desire itself. Thirdly, comes the hindrance of sloth and torpor, which keeps one on the plane of sensuous desire, on the ordinary, everyday level of consciousness. It is a sort of animal-like stagnation, both mental and physical. Fourthly, there is the opposite hindrance to sloth and torpor, the hindrance of restlessness and worry. This is the inability to settle down to anything for very long. It is a state of continual fussing and bothering, never really getting anything done. Fifthly and lastly, there is the hindrance of doubt – not a sort of honest intellectual doubt, but something more like indecision, or even unwillingness to make up one's mind, to commit oneself. Basically, it is a lack of faith, a lack of trust: a reluctance to acknowledge that there is a higher state of consciousness for man to achieve. These, then, are the five mental hindrances that must be allowed to subside, or must even be suppressed, before we take up the concentration object and prepare to enter upon the stage of absorption.

For a mind obscured by the five mental hindrances, as our minds so often are, there are five traditional similes, in each of which the mind itself is likened to water. The mind which is contaminated by desire for sensuous experience is likened to water in which various bright colours have been mixed. It is pretty, perhaps, but the purity and translucency of the water has been lost. The mind which is contaminated by hatred is, we are told, like water that has been brought to the boil, which is hissing and bubbling and seething. The mind contaminated by sloth and torpor is said to be like water choked with a thick growth of weeds, so that nothing can get through it. The mind contaminated by restlessness and worry is like water which has been whipped up into waves by the wind, even by a great storm. Lastly, the mind which is contaminated by doubt, by uncertainty, is like water full of mud. When the five hindrances are suppressed, the conscious mind becomes like pure water. It becomes cool, it becomes calm and clear. It is now ready to take up an object of concentration.[68]

These objects of concentration, even in the Buddhist tradition alone, are of very many kinds. Some are rather ordinary and everyday, while others are rather extraordinary. First of all there is the breath, our own breath, as it comes in and goes out. There are various forms of this practice, several different techniques. Another object of concentration, a very important one, is sound, especially the sacred sound that we call mantra. Or we can take as an object of concentration a disc of very pure, bright colour, red or blue or green, etc. according to temperament. Again, we can make our object of concentration a piece of human bone, preferably a sizeable piece to provide a good solid object of concentration. Alternatively we can take an idea, take a concept of a particular virtue to be cultivated, such as generosity. And again – to take something quite ordinary and mundane – we can concentrate on the flame of a lamp, or on a candle. We can also concentrate on the various psychic centres within our own body, or on a mental image or picture of the Buddha, or of a great bodhisattva or teacher. In all of these objects, whether the breath, the sound, the mantra, the flame, the image or picture of the Buddha, etc. the mind can become absorbed, even deeply absorbed.

We do not have to practise concentration with each and every one of these objects, though it is possible for several different concentration objects to be combined in sequence in one particular system or tradition of meditation practice. The different objects of concentration can also be combined with some of the indirect methods of raising the level of consciousness, particularly, for example, with chanting and with ritual.

Now if we proceed in this manner, that is to say, if we integrate the conscious mind with itself, if we integrate the conscious mind with the subconscious mind, if we suppress the five mental hindrances, if we take up an object or objects of concentration, and if our deeper energies start flowing more and more powerfully into the object of concentration, then a great change will take place: our level of consciousness will definitely start rising, from the plane or world of sensuous experience to the plane or world of mental and spiritual form. In other words, we begin to pass from the first to the second stage of meditation, from meditation in the sense of concentration, to meditation in the sense of absorption.

THE STAGE OF ABSORPTION

Absorption, the second level of meditation, is generally divided into four levels, and throughout these four levels the process of vertical integration, begun at the stage of concentration, continues. Here, it has to be noted, there is no question of integrating the conscious and the subconscious mind, for that has already been done. Here the purified, integrated conscious mind is itself integrated with the *superconscious.* And the energies of the superconscious – energies, that is to say, that are purely spiritual – begin to be tapped. Absorption represents, therefore, the unification of the mind on higher and ever higher levels of consciousness and being. As this process continues, our cruder mental states and cruder mental functions are progressively refined and our energies are absorbed into higher states and higher functions.

In what we call the first level of absorption there is a certain amount of mental activity present. We are still thinking about this and that, thinking, perhaps, subtle thoughts about worldly matters, or even thinking about our meditation practice itself. From the second level of absorption onwards, mental activity of this kind is entirely absent. Thinking as we know it entirely disappears. One might expect that because we are not thinking we should become dead and inert, but this would be a great mistake. We might even say that because we are *not* thinking, consciousness becomes clearer, brighter, more intense, more radiant than ever. But since thinking does not occur at the second and higher levels, it is important not to *think* about these levels of absorption too much, or preferably not at all. Instead, we should try to get some *feeling* of what they are like, proceeding not analytically, not intellectually, but with the help of images, symbols, and similes. We can best do this with the help of the four traditional similes for the four states of absorption – similes which go back to the Buddha's own personal teaching.[69]

The simile for the first level of absorption is that of the soap powder and the water. The Buddha asks us to imagine that a bath attendant takes some soap powder in one hand – apparently they had soap powder in ancient India – and some water in the other. He mixes the two together on a platter in such a way that all the water is fully absorbed by the soap powder, and all the soap powder thoroughly saturated by the water. There is not a single speck of soap powder unsaturated, and not a single drop of water left over. The first stage of absorption, the Buddha says, is just like that. In it, the entire psychophysical organism is completely saturated with feelings of bliss, of ecstasy, of supreme happiness, and these feelings are all *contained*. At the same time, the whole being is *saturated* – there is no part of the being, physical or mental, unsaturated – and yet there is nothing left over. Thus there is no inequality, no imbalance. It is all calm, and steady, and stable, and firm: all naturally concentrated.

Describing the second level of absorption, the Buddha asks us to imagine a great lake of water, very pure, very calm and still. This lake is fed by a subterranean spring, so that all the time in the very heart of the lake there is a bubbling up of pure water from a very great depth. The second level of absorption is like this. It is calm and it is clear, it is peaceful, pure, translucent, but from an even greater depth there is something even *more* pure, even *more* bright, even *more* wonderful, bubbling up all the time. This 'something' is the higher spiritual element, the higher spiritual consciousness, by which we are now as it were infiltrated – by which we are inspired.

The third level of absorption, the Buddha says, is like the same lake, the same body of water, only with lotus blossoms growing in it. These lotus blossoms are standing right in the water, are soaked and pervaded by it. They are thoroughly enjoying the water, you could say. Similarly, in the third level of absorption, we are, so to speak, bathing in that higher spiritual element, that higher spiritual consciousness – bathing in it and soaking in it – permeated by it within and surrounded by it without. This, the Buddha said, is what the third level of absorption is like.

In the case of the fourth and last level of absorption, the Buddha asks us to imagine a man who, on a very hot day, has a bath in a beautiful great lake. Having washed himself clean, he comes out, and then wraps his whole body in a sparkling white, clean, new sheet – what Indians call a dhoti – so that he is swathed in it, and it completely covers and cloaks him. The fourth level of absorption, the Buddha says, is like that. We are insulated by that higher spiritual consciousness from the contact, and from the influence, of those states and levels which are lower. It is as though we were surrounded by a powerful aura. It is not that we immerse ourselves in that state, but rather that the state has descended into us, permeated us. Furthermore, it has started radiating outwards from us so that we have a sort of aura of meditation extending from us in all directions. In this state we cannot be easily influenced or easily affected, although we can easily influence and affect other people.

These, then, are the four levels of absorption. If we want to recall them, and get the *feeling* of them, perhaps we should just recollect the four beautiful similes given by the Buddha to illustrate them. Having traversed, at least in imagination, these four levels of absorption, we can now come on to the third and last stage of meditation.

THE STAGE OF INSIGHT

By insight we mean the clear vision, the clear perception, of the true nature of things – of what in traditional Buddhist terminology is called things 'as they really are'. In other words, to use more abstract, more philosophical phraseology, it is a direct perception of reality itself. This is what meditation at its height is – this is what insight, or *sight,* really is. Such perception is twofold. It is insight into the conditioned, which is to say, the 'world', or whatever is mundane, transitory, and so on; and it is insight into the Unconditioned, that which transcends the world: the Absolute, the Ultimate.

The former, which is to say insight into the conditioned, consists in three things, or has three aspects. We see, first of all, that conditioned things, worldly things, by their very nature cannot give permanent and lasting satisfaction. For that we have to look elsewhere. Secondly, we see that all conditioned things are impermanent. We cannot possess any of them for ever. And thirdly and lastly, we see that all conditioned things are only relatively existent. They are not absolutely existent. They do not possess permanent, ultimate reality.

Now insight into the Unconditioned consists, in one formulation, of what are known as the five knowledges, or the five wisdoms. This is not knowledge in the ordinary sense, but something far beyond that. First of all, there is what we can only describe as the knowledge of the totality of things, not so much in their aggregated particularity, but in and through their ultimate depths and spiritual essence – in the light of their common unifying principle. Then there is the knowledge of all things, conditioned and unconditioned, without the slightest trace of subjective distortion. This knowledge is sometimes called the mirror-like knowledge. It is so called because it is like a great mirror that reflects everything just as it is – without subjectivity, or prejudice, or dimming, or clouding, or obscuration. In it everything is seen just as it is. Thirdly, there is the knowledge of things in their absolute sameness and identity – seeing everywhere one mind, one reality, one *śūnyatā*. Fourthly, there is the knowledge of things in their difference. The absolute unity does not wipe out the absolute difference. There is no one-sidedness. We see things in their absolute unity, but we also see them in their absolute multiplicity – their absolute uniqueness. We see them in both ways at once. And then, finally, there is the knowledge of what is to be done for the spiritual welfare of other living beings.

These five knowledges, or five wisdoms, are symbolized in Buddhist iconography by what we call the mandala of the five Buddhas. Visualizing this mandala, we see first of all a vast expanse of blue sky, very deep and very brilliant. At the centre of this expanse we see appearing a pure white Buddha figure, holding in his hand a brilliant golden wheel. Then in the east we see a deep, dark-blue Buddha holding in his hand a 'diamond sceptre'. In the south we see a golden-yellow Buddha holding in his hand a brilliantly shining jewel. In the west we see a deep-red Buddha holding in his hand a red lotus. And in the north we see a green Buddha, holding two 'diamond sceptres' crossed.

When all the five knowledges dawn, Enlightenment has been attained. We become, ourself, the embodiment of all five Buddhas. At this stage insight has been fully developed, meditation has been practised to the very limit, and we have understood for ourselves what meditation really is.

THE MEANING OF SPIRITUAL COMMUNITY

In the first of these three lectures I dealt with a very lofty subject, with nothing less than the ideal of human Enlightenment itself. In the second lecture I dealt, in part at least, with quite advanced, quite sublime, spiritual experiences, such as might not come to everybody – at least not for a while. But in this lecture I'm going to deal with something very down-to-earth, something that could be of personal and practical significance for anyone: the meaning of spiritual community. I shall deal with the subject under three main headings. Who are the members of the spiritual community? Where is the spiritual community to be found? And what do the members of the spiritual community do – for themselves, for one another, and even for the world?

However, before taking up the first of these questions, I would like to resolve a possible misunderstanding about the word 'spiritual'. We speak of the *spiritual* community, the *spiritual* life, the *spiritual* ideal, and *spiritual* practice; but the question arises, what do we mean by the word 'spiritual'? It is a word that we very often use, perhaps in quite a number of different senses. Sometimes people use the word rather loosely, and sometimes, I am afraid, people use it in no sense at all, but rather to disguise general poverty of thought, or to convey a vague sense of uplift. It is therefore important that we clarify the meaning of this word.

In my own use of the term, as you will have seen from these lectures, the 'spiritual' is to be contrasted with the 'psychological', as well as with what I call the 'worldly'. By 'psychological' I mean consisting of, or pertaining to, mental states, including mental processes or functions, *in general*; and by 'spiritual' I mean consisting of, or pertaining to, what are called *skilful* mental states.

Now this in turn raises the question of what is meant by the word 'skilful'. After all, this is a term that we come across again and again in Buddhist literature. In fact, this word 'skilful', with its antonym 'unskilful', is one of the most important terms in the whole range of Buddhist psychology and ethics. Unskilful means consisting of, or associated with, craving, aversion, and delusion, while skilful, on the contrary, means consisting of, or associated with, the absence of these states, that is to say, with the absence of craving, aversion, and delusion. Putting it more positively, skilful mental states are those associated with content (one might almost say peace of mind), friendliness, and knowledge – in the sense of wisdom.

You may have noticed that Buddhist literature does not speak in terms of good and evil. It does not use terms like sin, or vice, or virtue – at least not in their Christian sense. When it is speaking precisely and accurately – speaking as it were philosophically – in its own distinctive language, it speaks in terms of what is skilful and what is unskilful. Such usage suggests quite a number of things. It suggests, for instance, that good intentions or good feelings are not enough. It suggests that what we call the 'good' life must include an element of knowledge, of *understanding*. We therefore find that, in Buddhist literature, there is no such thing as the 'holy fool', which is to say, someone who is good, even very good, but stupid. For Buddhism this would be a contradiction in terms. The Buddhist usage of the term skilful also suggests that by being *un*skilful we get ourselves into difficulties – even incur inconvenience, not to say suffering – just as if we handle a knife or chisel clumsily, then sooner or later we are bound to cut ourselves.

The three English words craving, aversion, and delusion, do render quite faithfully and accurately, indeed almost literally, the three corresponding terms in the original languages, Sanskrit and Pāli, but perhaps they do not give us much real insight into the meaning of those terms. A Tibetan source, however, gives a more extended and detailed account. According to this source, craving is longing desire to possess objects of sensuous cognition which you like, and to include them in your ego-identity, in the hope of getting a sense of security from having them as part of you. Aversion is defined as fearful and angered repulsion to get rid of objects of sensuous cognition which you dislike, and to exclude them from your ego-identity, in the hope of getting a sense of security from *not* having them as part of you. As you can see from these definitions, one is the opposite of the other. Finally, delusion, which is defined as a stubborn closed-mindedness about learning anything which you feel might threaten your ego-identity, and upset the sense of security you wish to get from it, but which you are unaware of, and therefore feel you must protect. Even though comparatively short, these three definitions are quite profound and far-reaching.

With the help of these three definitions we can begin to see what is meant by spiritual community. By spiritual community we mean a community which encourages the development in its members of skilful, rather than unskilful, mental states as being the best ideal for human beings. In the same way, the spiritual life is a life devoted to the elimination of unskilful, and to the development of skilful, mental states. In a higher sense, it is a life that is entirely based upon, and expressive of, the skilful mental states of contentment or peace of mind, friendliness, and wisdom. Spiritual practice, it follows, is therefore any observance, any method or exercise, which is conducive to the eradication of unskilful, and to the development of skilful, mental states.

The distinction between skilful and unskilful mental states can serve as a basis for distinguishing between different levels of experience. Firstly, there is a level of consciousness on which only unskilful mental states are present; secondly, there is a level of consciousness on which only skilful mental states are present; and thirdly, there is a level of consciousness which is just mixed. Further, these three levels of consciousness can be seen to correspond with three planes of existence. Arranging them in a slightly different way, in an ascending order, we get, first of all, what we may call the worldly plane. This is a plane of existence on which people are motivated entirely, or almost entirely, by the unskilful thoughts of craving, aversion, and delusion. It is a 'state' in which they perform unskilful acts, which is to say they harm other living beings, take what has not been given, and indulge in sexual misconduct. They also speak unskilful words: words that are untrue or false, harsh and malicious, which create dissension, and which are idle, frivolous, and useless. This, then, is the worldly plane, or plane of worldly life. We could simply call it *the world*.

Secondly, the mixed plane is a plane of struggle, of effort and contest. It is a plane on which skilful and unskilful states are fairly evenly balanced. It is the plane where we find those who have just started to lead a spiritual life, who have just started trying to evolve. Just as an amphibian is a creature that lives partly in the water and partly on dry land, so the person dwelling on this mixed plane is spiritually amphibious. Sometimes such a person is very worldly, but at other times they might be quite spiritual.

Thirdly, there is the spiritual plane. This is the plane on which people are motivated entirely, or almost entirely, by skilful mental states: motivated by contentment, love, and knowledge; motivated by mindfulness, energy, faith, joy, compassion, and so on. It is the plane on which they perform actions that are helpful, generous, and pure, where they speak words that are true, that are affectionate, that promote concord and harmony, and that conduce to the good of the hearer.

As you will have seen in the previous lecture, Buddhism speaks in terms of four levels of consciousness: consciousness associated with the plane of sensuous experience, consciousness associated with the plane of mental and spiritual form, consciousness associated with the formless plane, and, finally, consciousness associated with the transcendental path and with Nirvāna. What I am here calling the world therefore corresponds with the plane of sensuous experience, and what I am here calling the spiritual plane corresponds with the plane of mental and spiritual form, together with the formless plane. Sometimes the word 'spiritual' is used in such a way as to include the Transcendental as well, but my own preference is to make quite a sharp distinction between the spiritual and the Transcendental.

It is perhaps worth noting here that the spiritual plane corresponds to meditation in the sense of absorption. It therefore follows that the meditation experience is best seen as an uninterrupted flow of skilful mental states, without any unskilful thought intruding. This is what meditation essentially is, and this is quite a useful way of looking at it, since it makes it clear that meditation does not necessarily mean *sitting* in meditation. Meditation, essentially, is simply this flow of spiritual thoughts – whether we are sitting, walking, standing, or doing anything else.

If living in the world means being motivated by unskilful thoughts, speaking unskilful words, and performing unskilful actions, and if the spiritual life consists in the progressive eradication of unskilful, and the development of skilful, mental states – consists eventually in being entirely motivated by such states – then the more we lead a spiritual life the less we will tend to live in the world. This separation, this leaving the world behind, may be only mental, but it may be physical as well. People sometimes say that it is enough to give something up mentally, and that to do it physically and verbally is not so important. Usually, however, we do not really know whether or not we have given something up unless we try to do it literally. In Buddhism the literal giving up of the world is traditionally known as 'the going forth from home into the homeless life'. Essentially, it consists in giving up worldly attitudes, giving up unskilful mental states. But it is not easy to do this, especially if the people all around you are freely indulging in such states and giving expression to them in the form of unskilful words and unskilful deeds, and even expecting *you* to join in. In this way a great deal of strain and tension arises, even a great deal of conflict. *You* are trying to do one thing, *they* are trying to do another. *You* are trying to develop skilful thoughts, *they* are giving way to unskilful thoughts. One day – or one night – you decide that you cannot stand the strain any longer. You just want to be free: free from that struggle, that conflict. You want to be free to stand on your own feet, free to develop in your own way, *skilfully*. So you just give up everything. You just walk out. You *go forth*.

We have, in the Buddhist tradition, a classic example of this going forth in the story of the Buddha himself – or rather of the future Buddha, the Buddha-to-be. If you know, at least in outline, the story of the Buddha, you will know that Siddhārtha, as he then was, was born into the proud and warlike Śākya tribe. Coming from a wealthy and aristocratic family, he was in the position of being able to satisfy whatever desires he had. Whether health, youth, strength, riches, social position, or education, he had everything the world could offer. He had plenty of leisure, plenty of friends and relations; he had a wife and a child. But although he had all these things, they could not give him what he really wanted. For even though he may not have known it at this stage, what he really wanted was something spiritual, something transcendental. He consequently felt worldly life to be increasingly oppressive, increasingly stuffy, and, one day, he decided to leave it all.

He waited until nightfall, until everybody was asleep, and then rode out into the night on his favourite horse, leaving behind his palace, leaving his home, accompanied, we are told, by a single faithful servant, who ran along at the heels of the horse. He rode until dawn broke, when he found himself on the bank of a river which marked the boundary of his father's territory. He then dismounted, cut off his hair and beard with his sword, and then changed clothes with a beggar who happened to be passing by. Finally, he sent the horse and the servant home, and went on his way alone. This is known as the 'going forth' of Siddhārtha, who became the Buddha. It is also known as the 'Great Renunciation', and for Buddhists it is the classic example of going forth – of going forth not just mentally but literally, with body, speech, and mind. One could even say that the Buddha's going forth is the archetypal going forth. After all, it is not only Siddhārtha who has gone forth. Many people have gone forth, not just in the Buddha's day but in all ages of history; not just in the past, but also in the present. Perhaps, by virtue of the fact that you are listening to this lecture, you too have gone forth – not literally perhaps, but certainly mentally to some extent: gone forth from at least some worldly attitudes, from conventional ways of thinking, and from collective attitudes of various kinds.

But what happens when we have gone forth? Very often, of course, nothing happens. Very often we just continue to go forth, indefinitely as it were, and remain on our own. If we are 'lucky', however, something does happen: we start to meet others who have gone forth in the same sort of way as ourselves. Moreover, we meet not only people who have 'gone forth' *from* but people who have 'gone forth' *to*: people who are committed to the spiritual, committed, even, to the Transcendental. In other words, we have come in contact with the spiritual community.

You may be thinking by now that it has taken us a long time to get around to the spiritual community! But this is, in fact, what very often happens. Siddhārtha himself, the future Buddha, never came in contact with the spiritual community – not, at least, during his period of going forth. He had to establish one after his Enlightenment. But we are much more fortunate. We do have the opportunity of coming into contact with the spiritual community. What is it, then, that we come into contact with?

In brief, we may say that the members of the spiritual community are individuals who have gone for Refuge. They are individuals who have committed themselves to what are known as the Three Jewels. Before saying more about the Three Jewels, however, I would like, first of all, to draw attention to this word 'individual'. In consisting of individuals, the spiritual community consists of people who have made an individual choice and an individual decision. They have accepted responsibility for their own lives, and have decided that they want to develop as human beings, they want to grow. The spiritual community is not, therefore, a group in the ordinary sense. It is not something collective, with a collective mind or soul. It has no collective identity in which you lose your own, or in which you become submerged. The spiritual community is a voluntary association of free individuals who have come together on account of a common commitment to a common ideal: a commitment to what we call the Three Jewels.

The Three Jewels are, firstly, the ideal of human Enlightenment, secondly, the path of the Higher Evolution – which is to say, the path of successively higher levels of consciousness, from self-consciousness to absolute consciousness – and thirdly, the spiritual community itself. The spiritual community consists, therefore, of all those who, with the object of attaining Enlightenment, are devoting themselves to the development of skilful, rather than unskilful, mental states. In the highest sense, the third Jewel is what we call the transcendental community: it is that part of the spiritual community which has not only gone for Refuge, not only developed skilful mental states – not only become *absorbed* – but which has developed insight: which sees, at least for a moment, reality – face to face. Members of this 'community' have broken the first three fetters, as they are called, that bind man to conditioned existence. They are prepared to die in order that they may be spiritually reborn. Their practice of the Path is wholehearted, and not merely conventional. Their commitment is absolute, without any reservations whatsoever.

In more traditional Buddhist language, the Three Jewels are known as the Buddha-Jewel, the Dharma-Jewel, and the Sangha-Jewel. They are called jewels because, until modern times, jewels were the most precious of all material things. So the Three Jewels represent, in the same way, what is spiritually most precious, spiritually most valuable, and spiritually most worthwhile. In short they represent the highest values of, and for, human existence.

In more concrete terms, the members of the spiritual community are all those who have been 'ordained' – to use the English word in a very provisional sense. They have committed themselves to the Three Jewels not just mentally, but fully and openly, with body and speech as well: they have committed themselves with their whole being. Further, that commitment has been acknowledged by existing members of the spiritual community, in particular by a senior member of the community. They have also pledged themselves to the observance of certain moral precepts. Members of the spiritual community, in this sense, may be young or old, male or female, 'educated' or uneducated. They may be living at home with their family – living, that is to say, outwardly in the world – or they may have 'gone forth' in the literal sense. They may be lay brothers or lay sisters, as they are sometimes called, or they may be monks or nuns – to use rather un-Buddhistic expressions. They may be more, or less, spiritually advanced. But *all* have gone for Refuge, all are committed to the Three Jewels, and are therefore all, equally, members of the spiritual community.

WHERE IS THE SPIRITUAL COMMUNITY TO BE FOUND?

The spiritual community is to be found wherever there are individuals who have gone for Refuge. Especially, it is found wherever such individuals are in personal contact, where they meet regularly. Of course, that contact is not simply social: it is spiritual, one might even say existential. Where members of the spiritual community live under the same roof they are known as a residential spiritual community. Residential spiritual communities can be of various kinds. For instance, they can be monastic – or semi-monastic – in character. (I do not particularly like the word 'monastic', which is not a very Buddhistic expression, but we do not seem to have a better one in the English language.) The monastic – or semi-monastic – residential spiritual community can be a community of men or a community of women. In either case, the members of the community live together under comparatively ideal conditions, often in a quiet, secluded place, and they devote themselves mainly to study, to meditation, and to productive work – the last usually taking a 'cooperative' form.

In some parts of the Buddhist world, the spiritual community has come to be identified exclusively with the monastic community, even with the monastic community in a rather formalistic sense. This, however, is a great mistake. The spiritual community consists of all those who have gone for Refuge.

WHAT DO THE MEMBERS OF THE SPIRITUAL COMMUNITY DO – FOR THEMSELVES, FOR ONE ANOTHER, AND FOR THE WORLD?

Firstly, what do they do for themselves? Clearly, they carry on with their individual spiritual practice. They continue to study, they meditate, they practise right livelihood, they observe the precepts, and so on. But this is rather general. To explain, however, what members of the spiritual community do for themselves *as* members of the spiritual community, is very difficult, since it means describing, to some extent at least, what it is like to *be* a member of the spiritual community. It is possible to say one thing, however. A member of the spiritual community puts himself or herself in a position of being able to relate to others on a purely spiritual basis, or at least on a predominantly spiritual basis: on the basis of a common spiritual ideal, a common spiritual commitment.

Now what does this mean? We meet people all the time, whether at home, at a club, in a coffee bar, or wherever, and we relate to these people that we meet in a number of different ways. Usually, we relate on the basis of our own need – though the need may, of course, be mutual. Sometimes it is a sexual need, sometimes it is an economic need or a social need, but it is a need, and the relationship is therefore very often exploitive, even mutually exploitive. Of course, we do not usually care to admit this – do not care to say what it is that we really want from other people. Sometimes we do not even fully and consciously know what we are really looking for ourselves. This means that only too often our relationships are dishonest or, at best, confused. It means that they are accompanied by a certain amount of mutual misunderstanding, and a certain amount of rationalization.

Within the spiritual community, however, we do not relate to others in this kind of way. Within the spiritual community the situation is that we all want to develop spiritually. After all, we have all gone for Refuge! We therefore relate on the basis of our common commitment and our common ideal – relate on the basis of our highest common interest, our highest common concern. If, moreover, we relate to others on this basis, then we experience others in a way in which we do not usually experience them. We experience them as spiritual beings. And because we experience *others* as spiritual beings – because we are *relating* to them as spiritual beings – we experience *ourselves* as spiritual beings too. In this way the pace of spiritual development is accelerated. We experience ourselves more and more truly, more and more intensely. Within the spiritual community, then, we can be ourselves as we are at our best and at our highest. Very often, when we speak of 'being ourselves', we mean being ourselves at our worst, letting out that part of ourselves that we do not usually like to acknowledge. But there is another way in which we can be ourselves, for, very often, it is the best in us, rather than the worst, that has no opportunity to express itself. So, within the context of the spiritual community, we can be ourselves at our best. If necessary, we can be ourselves at our 'worst' occasionally, but the important thing is that we can *be ourselves* fully, wholly, and perfectly.

To be ourselves in this way is rarely possible within the context of ordinary life, even with our 'nearest and dearest', whether parents, husbands or wives, or our closest friends. Only too often, on certain occasions, or in connection with certain topics, we cannot be fully ourselves – not even with one person. Indeed, quite a few people go through their lives without being able to be themselves completely and continuously with anyone. They consequently find it very difficult even to *experience* themselves as they are, even to experience themselves at their best.

Within the spiritual community, on the other hand, we can be ourselves, and not just with one person, but even with two or three people – even with many people. This sort of experience is, perhaps, unprecedented in the lives of the majority of people. Just imagine, for a moment, what it would be like if you were to have five or six – or even fifty or sixty – people present, but all of you *being yourselves*. This should be quite possible within the spiritual community, because here we are relating on the basis of the shared spiritual commitment, the shared spiritual ideal – relating on the basis of what is best and highest in each and every one of us. We therefore experience, within the spiritual community, a great relief and a great joy. There is no need to put up any psychological defences, no need to pretend, no need to guard against misunderstanding. With complete transparency we can be ourselves with others who are also being themselves.

In a situation like this, we naturally develop more rapidly than would otherwise be possible. We do a great deal for ourselves simply by being members of the spiritual community – that is to say, *active* members, though really there is no other kind.

What do members of the spiritual community also do for one another? Obviously they help one another in all possible ways – *not* just spiritually. They help one another psychologically, economically, and even in quite simple, everyday matters. However, I am going to mention two ways in which members of the spiritual community help one another which are particularly relevant. As I have said, within the spiritual community we relate on the basis of the common spiritual commitment, the common spiritual ideal. But this is not always easy. After all, many people 'join' the spiritual community: many people commit themselves. Among them there are people of many different kinds, having different backgrounds, different outlooks, different temperaments. We may find some of them quite easy to get on with, and others not so easy. We may find some of them impossible to get on with! So what are we to do? We do not want to leave the spiritual community, and we can hardly ask *them* to leave. There is only one thing for us to do: to work hard on it together. We have to recognize that what we have in common is much more important than what we do not have in common. We have to learn to relate – even painfully learn – on the basis of that which we do have in common. This certainly is not easy, but with patience we can gradually succeed. In this way, members of the spiritual community help one another – help one another to overcome purely subjective, purely personal limitations and learn how to relate on the basis of what is higher.

Again, spiritual life is not easy. It is not easy to eradicate unskilful thoughts, not easy to develop skilful ones. Sometimes we may feel like giving up altogether. 'It's too much for us, it goes too much against the grain, there are too many difficulties,' we may protest. We may even think of leaving the spiritual community. At times like these, members of the spiritual community help one another: support one another, encourage one another, inspire one another. This is the most important thing that they can do for one another, perhaps, this bearing one another up when they get into a difficult and disturbed condition, or when they get depressed, as any member of the spiritual community may until such time as he has his feet firmly on the path. When going through this kind of crisis, it is a great comfort, a great consolation, to have around us others who sincerely wish us well, who desire our spiritual welfare, and who can help us through this quite difficult period.

Finally, what do members of the spiritual community do for the world? You might expect me to say here something about the role of the spiritual community in world history, or its significance for the total evolutionary process, but such considerations would take us beyond the scope of this brief exposition. I shall confine myself, instead, to a few practical points, and then conclude.

First of all, there is one thing that needs to be made clear. Members of the spiritual community are not obliged to do anything at all for the world. The operative word here being *obliged*. Whatever they do, they do quite freely: they do it because they want to, because they like doing it. There is no obligation involved. They do it, even, as part of the process of their own spiritual development, their own spiritual life. To put this in a slightly different way, the spiritual community does not have to justify its existence to the world. It does not have to show that it brings about social and economic improvements, that it is helpful to the government or the administration. It does not have to show that it benefits the world *in a worldly sense*.

However, in general, the members of the spiritual community do two things for the world. First of all, they keep the spiritual community itself in existence. One might say that it is good for the world that such a thing as the spiritual community should simply be there, good that there should be people around who are dedicated to the spiritual life, dedicated to the development of skilful states of mind. This is good because it helps to develop a more wholesome atmosphere in the world.

Secondly, members of the spiritual community help the world by building a bridge between the world and the spiritual community – or at least laying down a few stepping-stones. They do this by getting together, in teams of four, or five, or more, and conducting various activities conducive to the development of skilful mental states. These activities help people to evolve from the worldly plane to the mixed plane, perhaps even from the mixed plane to the spiritual plane. These activities might be meditation classes, retreats, lectures, yoga classes, courses in human communication, and so on. They are open to anyone who cares to take advantage of them: one does not even have to join anything or pay a subscription!

In this way members of the spiritual community, or those individuals who are committed to the ideal of human Enlightenment – committed to the attainment of higher levels of consciousness and insight – help people in the world to develop more and more skilful thoughts, to grow in contentment, in love, and in understanding, and to know indeed, for themselves, the meaning of spiritual community.

BUDDHISM FOR TODAY – AND TOMORROW

The Royal Pavilion, Brighton, England, 1976.

INTRODUCTION

Buddhism has been known now in Europe and North America for considerably more than a hundred years, and one might have thought that, at least in some quarters, it would have become fairly well known. Unfortunately this is by no means the case. Even after all this time and so much scholarship, it is still relatively unknown and often misunderstood. Some people, for example, still classify Buddhism as one of the various 'religions' of the world – which it is not, if the word 'religion' is taken to mean (as it almost always is) 'religion as revelation' or 'revealed religion'. For other people Buddhism is some sort of exotic oriental cult. For others again, Buddhism is a system of abstract philosophical ideas, quite remote from ordinary life, something in fact that does not impinge on life at any point. Another misunderstanding that used to be very widespread is the view of Buddhism as simply a code of ethics that tells you what you should or should not do – merely a system of rules and prohibitions. Yet others see Buddhism as a form of asceticism – at least, this was the case when I returned to England from India in 1964. In those days, when people came to visit me in the vihara, or small monastery, where I was staying, they were surprised to find that there were no high walls or barbed wire surrounding the building and that everybody could enter freely and talk to whomever they chose. They seemed to expect that we would be completely secluded from the world, and living in perpetual solemn silence (despite the fact that the vihara was in the middle of Hampstead). This used to be quite a prevalent impression of Buddhism then, that it was something negative, repressive, and life-denying.

In addition to these general misunderstandings, many people identify Buddhism with one or another of its specific forms. For example, they encounter the Buddhism of Thailand or the Buddhism of Sri Lanka and think that this, and only this, is Buddhism. Or they come into contact with the colourful and rich tradition of Tibetan Buddhism, and they are carried away by their feelings for lamas, thigh-bone trumpets, thangkas, and all the rest of the Tantric tradition, and think that this is Buddhism – just this and nothing more. Others read books by Japanese masters, start trying to solve koan, and think, 'Zen! Zen is Buddhism. All the other schools, all the other teachings, are not Buddhism at all. Zen is the real thing!' Perhaps the most damaging identification of this kind is to confuse Buddhism with Nichiren Buddhism, a sect that is so far from the central Buddhist tradition as to exhibit some of the characteristics of a 'revealed religion', including an infallible book (the *White Lotus Sūtra*), a prophet (Nichiren), and an intolerant and dismissive attitude towards other forms of Buddhism. Confusing Buddhism with any one of its specific forms in this way is like identifying an entire oak tree with a single branch or even a single acorn.

In view of such misunderstandings – and I've just touched upon some of the more prominent, popular ones – it is reasonable to say that Buddhism is not really known in the West. Sometimes it is actually dangerous to be slightly acquainted with something, because we tend to overlook the fact that we do not really know it. As Pope puts it, 'A little learning is a dangerous thing.'[70] In some cases, it might be better to have no knowledge at all, better to wipe the slate clean of all our misunderstandings and misinterpretations and make a completely fresh start. And this is the purpose for which the Friends of the Western Buddhist Order (FWBO) was founded in 1967 – to make a completely fresh start at Buddhism.

The FWBO exists, we may say, to identify the absolute essentials of the Buddha's teaching, and to make those essential principles known and relevant to people's lives in the West. Since its founding in 1967, the FWBO has grown steadily. Not only has it become better known, but more and more individuals have committed themselves to the realization of the ideal for which it stands. It is not that when I founded it I had a detailed or precise idea of what we were setting out to do. However, over the years, the FWBO has gradually come to understand its own nature, so to speak. And this may be said to consist in four things the FWBO has to offer, four things that are of the deepest and truest importance to developing individuals in today's world. These are: a method of personal development, a vision of human existence, the nucleus of a new society, and a blueprint for a new world. Here I want to focus on these four things, and through them I will try to present the concentrated essence of Buddhism in a highly practical form especially suited to the needs of Western men and women – needs that, for better or worse, are fast becoming the needs of the whole world.

I

A METHOD OF PERSONAL DEVELOPMENT

This title raises a couple of questions that have to be answered before we consider what this method actually comprises. For a start, what do we mean by personal development; and why should people need it? Why indeed should they need a *method* of personal development?

If we look at the dictionary, we find that 'to develop' means to unfold gradually, just as a flower unfolds, stage by stage, petal by petal, from the bud. To develop means to evolve; it means to pass through a succession of states or stages, each of which is preparatory to the next; it means to expand by a process of growth; it means to change gradually from a lower to a higher state of being. Development is in fact a law of life. In biological terms, for example, it is the principle of evolution. The unicellular organism develops into the multicellular organism, the invertebrate into the vertebrate. Fish develops into reptile, reptile into mammal, and finally the human-like ape becomes the ape-like human. However, this evolutionary process is simply biological and what develops is simply the bodily structure. Only in later stages of the process do we find any signs of self-consciousness, any signs of psychological, as distinct from biological, development.

The whole of this vast, briefly sketched process of development from amoeba to man represents from a bird's-eye perspective the distance that life has travelled so far. Life has certainly come a long way, and it's a fascinating story. But it doesn't end here, with human beings as we at present know them. From here the process can go on – not that it must or it will, but it can. What we may term the 'lower evolution' can be succeeded by a 'higher evolution', which is the process by which human beings as they are become what they can be; the process by which 'natural man' becomes 'spiritual man', the process by which unenlightened humanity becomes 'Enlightened man', or Buddha. It is the process by which man becomes that which, in a sense – in a deeply metaphysical sense – he (and of course she) always was.

Although the process of the higher evolution coexists with the process of the lower evolution, it is not simply a continuation of it. There are several important differences between the two. In the first place, as already indicated, the higher evolution constitutes not a biological but a psychological, even a spiritual, process. It concerns not the physical structure of the organism, but the mind; and it refers not simply to the processes of reason or the rational faculty, but rather to a whole cluster of mental activities – intelligence, the more refined emotions, creative imagination, and spiritual intuition. The growth of all these mental activities constitutes the Higher Evolution, which is thus a truly human development.

Essentially the Higher Evolution is the development of consciousness, but this should not be understood in some abstract, general sense. It is rather the development of the individual consciousness – the development of your consciousness and mine. Human development is a personal development. It is *our* development – not 'our' in the sense of a corporate, collective development, but our development as individuals, or potential individuals, together. We can no longer rely on being carried forward by the surge of the general evolutionary process as on the crest of an enormous wave. In human beings, at least human beings at their best, reflexive consciousness – consciousness of self – has emerged, and henceforth we can evolve only as individuals. This means individually wanting, and not just wanting but deciding, to evolve, and acting appropriately on that volition.

An author who used to be famous but is little read these days, G. Lowes Dickinson, stated the matter clearly and forcibly in his dialogue *A Modern Symposium*:

> Man is in the making, but henceforth he must make himself. To
> that point Nature has led him out of the primeval slime. She has
> given him limbs, she has given him brains, she has given him the

rudiment of a soul. Now it is for him to make or mar that splendid torso. Let him look no more to her for aid, for it is her will to create one who has the power to create himself. If he fails, she fails: back goes the metal to the pot and the great process begins anew. If he succeeds, he succeeds alone; his fate is in his own hands.[71]

'His fate is in his own hands': these – if we accept their force – are momentous words indeed, and they challenge us to acknowledge a tremendous responsibility. We have a responsibility for our own life, our own growth, our own happiness. Sometimes that responsibility seems very heavy, even too heavy to bear, and we may be tempted to try to rid ourselves of the weight of it. We may think how comfortable it would be if only we could hand over that responsibility for ourselves to somebody else – maybe to 'God' or Jesus, or else to some fashionable guru figure, or even to some political leader. There are so many figures and agencies and groups who seem willing to relieve us of this intolerable burden. Sometimes we may even try to forget the whole troublesome question. 'Why bother with all this effort?' we may ask ourselves. Why bother with all these methods and practices? Why not just sit back and enjoy life like an ordinary human being and forget about this notion of a 'Higher Evolution' and personal development?

But, fortunately or unfortunately, once we have reached a certain point, once self-consciousness has begun to emerge, we cannot do that. We cannot set it all aside and forget about it. We want to grow, and we want to grow simply because we are living beings. Every living being wants to fulfil the law of its own nature, which is to develop. We want to actualize our own deepest potential, to become what we really are, to achieve in time what we are in eternity. If we are prevented from doing this, whether by others or by ourselves, we inevitably suffer, because we are going against the law of our own nature. Think how terrible it would be if in a year's time, or five or ten years' time, we were the same people that we are today. Think how terrible it would be if we never changed or grew in any way.

So we want to grow and develop, but we do not always know how. Many of us find ourselves in this situation today. All sorts of factors, external and internal, impede our growth. We are not satisfied with our progress, but we cannot forget all about the idea of growth and change.

Caught in the doldrums, we are dissatisfied with ourselves as we are. We would like to be something greater, nobler, more highly developed, but we do not know how to proceed.

At this point we need a method of development. This is the first thing that Buddhism offers, the first thing that the FWBO offers. And this method is meditation. As we have seen, human development is essentially a change from a lower to a higher level of consciousness, and meditation helps us to make this transition. Not that meditation is the only method of developing a higher level of consciousness. Other methods, such as leading an ethical life, participating in symbolic rituals like those found in Tantric practice, and engaging in devotional practices, social service, or the arts, also affect one's level of consciousness. However, these methods work indirectly, in the sense that they have an effect through the physical body and senses – the mind being included as a sense according to Buddhism. Meditation, on the other hand, acts on consciousness directly, and for this reason it can be regarded as the primary method of personal development.

I have referred to the development of consciousness and levels of consciousness. But how do lower and higher states of consciousness differ, and how can we tell them apart? In what way does meditative consciousness differ from ordinary consciousness? The first important difference to mention is that meditative consciousness depends less on the physical senses. Much of the time ordinary human consciousness is sense-oriented. Sense impressions constantly seep in through the eye, ear, and senses of touch, smell, and taste, and these impressions trigger various sensations. Our minds become preoccupied with these sensations, and we do not try to reduce this preoccupation. In meditative consciousness, however, although sense impressions may be present, the mind does not react to them. Sense impressions recede to the periphery of consciousness; in deep meditation they may disappear altogether, as our consciousness is absorbed in the object of concentration and in the experience of the higher state. Sense-consciousness, or awareness of the world of sense objects, fades: sense objects are either perceived dimly or, in very deep states of meditation, not perceived at all.

The second way in which the higher consciousness differs from the lower is that it is more concentrated. This does not involve a forcible fixation of attention but rather a natural flowing together of all one's energies. Usually our energies are divided; they are in conflict. Sometimes they are not available to us at all. This is often why we have very little energy; it is blocked or suppressed. However, in meditation, especially when we have been practising for a while and have attained some degree of success, these blocked or suppressed energies gradually become liberated and are gently guided in the same direction. Thus the higher state of consciousness is a more integrated state. There is no conflict or division, and consequently we experience tremendous energy. This is not merely physical energy, although physical vitality may be enhanced; it is psychic and emotional energy liberated in the course of the practice of meditation. This experience of liberated energy is intensely pleasurable, and a higher state of consciousness is therefore a state of joy, rapture, bliss – in other words, a state of intense emotional positivity that we hardly, if ever, experience at other times.

We may notice here an interesting fact – that when we are truly happy, we tend not to think more than is necessary. In fact much of our thinking is unnecessary, and amounts very often to no more than needless anxiety. In the higher, meditative consciousness there is no thought of this kind at all. So long as we are thinking discursively, we are not meditating very seriously. To say that there is no thought is not, however, to say that there is no consciousness or awareness; in fact, in the absence of thought, consciousness is clearer, brighter, and more powerful than ever.

So meditative consciousness differs from ordinary human consciousness in that it depends less on the physical senses, it is more concentrated and integrated, it is more alive and blissful, and it is free from discursive thought. In Buddhism this state of higher meditative consciousness is called *dhyāna*, sometimes described as a superconscious state, inasmuch as it is a state of intensified consciousness or awareness made up of intensified concentration, energy, and joy.

Furthermore, there is not just one *dhyāna* state accessible to us, but a whole series of such states. Buddhist tradition commonly distinguishes four *dhyānas*, or four successively higher states; and these can be described in either psychological or metaphorical terms. Psychologically speaking, in the first *dhyāna* we experience a subtle mental activity, concentration, happiness, and joy. In the second *dhyāna* discursive thought dies away, and we experience only concentration, happiness, and joy. In the third there is a further simplification, and we experience concentration and happiness. In the fourth *dhyāna* the comparatively gross experience of happiness gives way to equanimity, so that we simply experience concentration and equanimity.

This psychological description gives us a good idea of what the four *dhyānas* are like, but there is a traditional metaphorical account of them which may provide a more vivid sense of their nature.[72] Thus the experience of the first *dhyāna* is said to be like mixing soap powder with water, blending the two until every speck of soap powder is saturated with water and no drop of water is left over. Then, the second *dhyāna* is likened to a lake fed by a subterranean spring; fresh, clear, cool water constantly bubbles up from deep within. The image for the third *dhyāna* is of lotus flowers that grow in the water and remain completely immersed in and permeated by it. And the fourth *dhyāna* is like the experience of a man who takes a cool bath on a very hot day and then, emerging from the bath, wraps himself in a pure white sheet.

These descriptions of the four *dhyānas*, both psychological and metaphorical, are traditional; there are other ways to describe them. The most useful terms I have come up with out of my own personal experience and reflection are these: integration, inspiration, permeation, and radiation. In the context of personal development and meditation, the integration is primarily psychological; we are integrating the different aspects and functions of the mind itself. And the nature of integration is such that it is achieved not by force or by means of some external bond, but by bringing these aspects and functions into harmony with a common principle or arranging them around a common centre of interest. Meditation works very much in this way. In the preliminary stages of the practice, it involves focusing attention on a particular sense object, either mental or material, such as a mantra or a coloured disc or our own breath.

This psychological integration is twofold. It is, we may say, both horizontal and vertical. Horizontal integration involves the bringing together of the various aspects of our conscious experience. The process of vertical integration, on the other hand, means integrating consciousness with the unconscious, and it is much more difficult to achieve than horizontal integration because the conscious and the unconscious often pull in opposite directions. However, given a common direction and purpose, they may be brought together. Energy begins to flow from the unconscious into the conscious mind, and concentration then becomes easier. We find that we can meditate: that is, we experience a sense of harmony and repose and an absence of conflict.

Next comes the stage of inspiration. This term derives from a word meaning 'to breathe' – hence, inspiration is what is 'breathed' into us from outside our ordinary, conscious, everyday self. It comes from the heights or, if you prefer, from the depths. It comes, anyway, from some other level of consciousness. Usually we experience this inspiration as an impersonal force or energy – but we may sometimes experience it as a person. The poets, for example, speak of being 'visited by the muse' – a personification of the forces of poetic inspiration – and in ancient times, the poet regularly invoked the muse or goddess of poetry at the beginning of a poem, thus symbolically opening himself to the spiritual energies the muse represented. It is true that in later times the invocation of the muse became a lifeless literary convention, but originally it was an overwhelming emotional and spiritual experience.

This inspirational power is experienced not only by poets. Prophets, for example, find in it a specifically religious force when it arrives in the guise of 'the voice of God', directing their actions and endeavours. As for Buddhists, it may be said to come to them in the form of *nāgas*. These are depicted, in the literature and art of the Mahāyāna tradition, as serpent-like beings with human heads or as human figures with serpentine hoods. They are said to live in rivers, streams, and oceans.

If the *nāgas* represent the forces of inspiration welling up from the depths, the figure of the *ḍākinī* from the Tantric Buddhist tradition represents a corresponding force of inspiration from the heights. *Ḍākinī* is sometimes translated as 'space traveller' or 'sky walker'. Buddhist art and temple paintings depict *ḍākinīs* as beautiful young women flying through the air, trailing rainbow scarves. They symbolize the active forces of higher inspiration moving freely in the vast expanse of reality.

When experienced as rising from the depths, the forces of inspiration seem to bring us up with them; when experienced as descending from the heights, they seem to bend down and catch us up to their exalted level. In either case the experience is the same – we are lifted to a higher level. We are borne on the crest of a wave, or carried on the back of a winged horse; we are taken over by something more powerful than ourselves. Or rather, this is the way it *seems*, for this something is still of course part of ourselves; it is, if you like, another dimension of ourselves. So inspiration is an important stage of personal development. It is intensely pleasurable, even ecstatic. We feel energetic and do everything effortlessly and spontaneously. In fact we may not feel as if we are doing anything at all – things just seem to happen of themselves, in their own beautiful way.

These stages of integration and inspiration can be experienced fairly easily. Most people will experience them after only a few months of meditation, which is why I have gone into them in detail. Since the remaining stages are more difficult to achieve, I will deal with them more briefly.

We can describe the next stage, the stage of permeation, by contrasting it with the previous stage. In the stage of inspiration we experience on the one hand horizontal and vertical integration from the previous stage, and on the other hand a higher level of consciousness which flows into that lower level and is experienced as inspiration. The higher consciousness gradually penetrates the lower consciousness and in the end permeates it completely. The higher level of consciousness also permeates the actual world. We experience that higher level of consciousness not only within ourselves but also as outside ourselves, completely filling the world. The higher state of consciousness is in us, but also we are in it. We are like a balloon that is both filled with air and floating *in* the air. The same element, the same consciousness, is both inside and out, and there is just a thin transparent layer – which represents one's particular sense of self – between the two.

The fourth and last stage – the stage of radiation – is radically different from the three previous stages. The first three *dhyānas* are self-contained and inward-looking; they represent the mind's own experience of itself. In the fourth *dhyāna*, the stage of radiation, however, the mind is directed outwards. It is not affected by the world of external reality but instead acts upon the world. In this stage consciousness is highly integrated, positive, and powerful. We could say it is surrounded by an aura that protects it from external influences. At the same time this aura acts as the medium for influencing the outside world. It is rather like an electric bulb: the bulb's glass protects the filament but at the same time the bulb radiates light.

The quality of this radiation is said to be the basis for developing psychic or supernormal powers. In Sanskrit, the word for psychic powers is *ṛddhi*, which originally referred to the idea of potency, the power to affect one's surroundings. The *ṛddhi* of the king, for example, resided in his power of life and death over thousands of people. The *ṛddhi* arising out of one's state of consciousness in the stage of radiation works in a completely different way from that of a king, but it too is so powerful that one can affect things without being affected oneself. Some of these effects may well seem miraculous: one can give strength to the weak, overcome hatred with love, and even awaken those who are spiritually dead.

Having defined these four successively higher levels of consciousness, let us look briefly at how we can achieve them. Simply to say that they can be achieved through meditation is not enough. You can't just meditate; in a sense, there is no such thing as meditation. There are only *methods* of meditation, of which Buddhism teaches a rich variety, some common to all schools of Buddhism and others special to particular traditions. Some are especially effective for people of a specific temperament; others work best for people wishing to develop certain qualities or to overcome particular weaknesses.

Take, for example, the method of meditation called in the ancient language of Pāli the *mettā bhāvanā*. *Mettā* means 'friendliness' – though in a much more positive, powerful sense than the word possesses in English – while *bhāvanā* means 'making to be', thus 'bringing into existence' or 'development'. Put together, the two terms translate as 'the development of universal friendliness'. The *mettā bhāvanā* is therefore meant especially for those who wish to attain higher levels of consciousness by overcoming hatred and developing friendliness. It is undoubtedly one of the most important and effective methods of personal development. At the same time it shares something fundamental in common with all other methods of meditation, in that it works on the basis of one supremely important fact – that we can change. Consciousness can be restructured; negative states like hatred can be converted to positive states like love. And this is one of the strengths of Buddhism; it does not merely exhort you to change, but shows you exactly *how* to change. It doesn't merely urge you to love your neighbour – such exhortation is easy – but it shows you further exactly how to go about this. Moral exhortations are not enough; we need practical help. Unless we are given some idea of how to go about changing ourselves, we simply feel frustrated and resentful. We may even wonder if personal development is possible at all.

Usually the *mettā bhāvanā* is practised in five successive stages. First of all, you develop friendliness towards yourself, because that's where friendliness starts. If you are unhappy with yourself or do not like yourself, you can't really like other people. Love must begin with self-love. Charity really does begin at home, and home begins with you. Then, once you have developed goodwill towards yourself, you extend it outwards, starting with a near and dear friend – someone you know well and care about deeply. The person should preferably be around your own age, and should be someone to whom you are not sexually attracted, since this feeling of friendliness is not erotic. The friend should also be alive, otherwise the feeling of *mettā* may be tinged with sadness or regret. Next, you bring to mind a 'neutral person' – someone you know quite well by sight and have perhaps met a few times but for whom you have no particular feeling, neither liking them nor disliking them. You then try to extend the same feeling that you have cultivated towards yourself and your close friend to this neutral person. Fourthly, you extend this goodwill to someone whom you positively dislike, or even hate. With a little practice, by the time you come to this fourth stage, you may have developed such a momentum of goodwill that it is quite easy to feel warm towards that person. Feelings of hatred, antagonism, and enmity begin to dissolve; you may feel like letting bygones be bygones and starting afresh. The next time you meet that person you may even be able to feel and behave completely differently, and so begin a new chapter in your relationship.

In the last stage of the *mettā bhāvanā* you think of all four people – self, friend, neutral person, and enemy – simultaneously, and cultivate the same love, the same goodwill, the same friendliness, towards all four. Then you extend that goodwill in ever-widening circles to everybody in the building where you are sitting, then to all the people in the neighbourhood, then to all the people in the town, and all the inhabitants of the whole country. Moving on, you include all the populations of your continent, and finally you extend your *mettā* to the entire world. One way of doing this is to think of anyone you know in different countries throughout the world, and develop this stage of the practice from there.

Of course, you don't have to think of just human beings. You can think of animals, birds, and fish; you may even follow the ubiquitous Buddhist tradition of cultivating *mettā* towards beings of whatever kind throughout the furthest corners of the universe. In this way the practice concludes. By this point one should feel, at least for a time, a sense of expansiveness, a sense of warmth, goodwill, friendliness, and love that has displaced, or even transformed, other more negative and destructive feelings. This has certainly been the experience of the millions of people over the centuries who have practised this meditation. It has been found to work, and it still works today.

The *mettā bhāvanā* does not, as a practice, stand alone. It is one of four practices known as the 'four limitless states',[73] so called because you try to develop the appropriate emotion with no limit whatsoever. The other three practices comprise the development, respectively, of compassion, sympathetic joy, and equanimity. But although there are specific practices for their development, these positive emotions cannot really be separated from the *mettā bhāvanā*. *Mettā* is in fact the basis for them all. When our friendliness comes into contact with suffering, compassion arises. When it comes into contact with other people's happiness, sympathetic joy develops. And when we establish friendliness, compassion, and sympathetic joy equally towards all, then equanimity, or peace, arises. Furthermore, we may add a fifth 'limitless state' to the traditional four: when our friendliness is directed upwards towards a spiritual ideal, we experience reverence or devotion.

These five emotions – friendliness, compassion, sympathetic joy, equanimity, and devotion – are the principal positive emotions that Buddhism encourages us to develop. These emotions occupy a central place in the spiritual life, and when fully developed they constitute what is known as the 'liberation of the heart'. In today's world the development of positive emotion is more important than ever before; without positivity there is no spiritual life. Unfortunately many people in the West fail to realize this. They think religion is dull and gloomy – well, perhaps it is, but Buddhism isn't, and personal development certainly isn't. I would go so far as to say that without strong positive emotion no spiritual progress is possible at all. This means that many people's first duty, to themselves and to others, is simply to be happy: to develop friendliness, compassion, sympathetic joy, equanimity, and devotion.

All this is not, however, enough. There are essentially two different kinds of Buddhist meditation, and up to this point we have touched on only one of them. Meditation as I have described it so far is to do with development of calm – with the calming down of negative, 'unskilful' mental states, and the development of skilful states to the highest possible degree. Although this represents a very high attainment indeed, it has definite limitations. It can be gained, yes, but it can also be lost – and regained, and again lost. For this attainment to be permanent we need to have recourse to the second and, in a sense, higher kind of meditation: the development of 'insight'.

By insight is meant here a direct vision, direct experience, of the true nature of existence. Here one sees the world as it is. One sees also what is beyond the world – one sees *that* as it is too. One sees the world, the conditioned, the phenomenal, as unsatisfactory, impermanent, unreal, and not ultimately beautiful; and one sees what is beyond the world – the unconditioned – as blissful, permanent, real, and beautiful. Seeing in this way, one finally turns away from the world, away from the conditioned, and turns irrevocably towards the Unconditioned. One turns right round. One experiences what is termed in the *Laṅkāvatāra Sūtra* a 'turning about in the deepest seat of consciousness'.[74] Thus insight goes beyond 'calm'. It is not, however, independent of it. It is only on the basis of 'calm' that insight is properly developed. It is because it has behind it the purified and refined energy of the whole being that insight can penetrate into the depths of existence. Insight is therefore not just intellectual understanding, although the content of insight can often be expressed in intellectual terms, at least up to a point. Insight is direct spiritual vision, direct experience of ultimate reality. And when it is fully developed, one achieves what is called 'liberation by wisdom'. Together, liberation of the heart and liberation by wisdom constitute Perfect Enlightenment.[75]

Calm and insight are both necessary. The purified heart must be united with the illumined mind; love and compassion must be united with wisdom. And when we succeed in this union, our personal development will be complete. When, through this method of personal development, we have achieved this unity, we shall begin to see the world and human existence very differently. Indeed, we shall begin to see as a Buddha sees. It is this vision that I now want to consider.

2

A VISION OF HUMAN EXISTENCE

Up to this point we have been concerned with the most practical means of self-development available to us. I want now to consider things from a more theoretical point of view. The theoretical, however, can be practical in its own way. There are always going to be people for whom the practical on its own is not, 'practically' speaking, ever going to be enough.

There are several Buddhist classifications of temperament or psychological type. One of the oldest and most basic of these is the simple classification of the followers of the Buddha as being either 'faith-followers' or 'doctrine-followers'.[76] As the name suggests, faith-followers are guided primarily by their emotions, and they usually respond quickly to what moves them. When faith-followers hear about meditation, they may well take up the practice without further ado simply because it appeals to them. They don't ask a lot of questions, they don't want to know the whys and wherefores of it all. Often faith-followers are also attracted to meditation by the person teaching the meditation, because they attach great importance not only to feelings but also to people, to whom they are drawn by an instinctive positive regard.

Doctrine-followers, on the other hand, are guided more by thought, reflection, even prolonged and detailed consideration. They are unlikely to take up a particular practice until they have understood quite thoroughly what it is all about – how it works, and even why it works. In the case of meditation, they will want to know the philosophy behind the practice before they begin, and they will want this philosophy to give them a reason for practising.

The consideration of meditation is perhaps of special interest to the faith-follower. What follows will appeal more to the doctrine-follower. But inasmuch as most of us are more or less a mixture of the two temperaments, sometimes one predominating, sometimes the other, all of us will find its approach useful at times. At any event, the second great thing that the FWBO has to offer is concerned in some sense – a provisional sense – with philosophy. In the end our subject is not really to do with philosophy at all. It is not a philosophy of existence but a *vision* of existence.

In fact – surprising as it may seem – in the Buddhist tradition there is no such thing as philosophy. In the languages of the Indian Buddhist scriptures, there is no word corresponding to philosophy, either literally or metaphorically. The Sanskrit word *darśana* is sometimes translated 'philosophy', but it actually means 'that which is seen' – a sight, view, perspective, or vision. The word 'philosophy' may literally mean 'love of wisdom', but it is more generally understood to mean a system of abstract ideas; it suggests something thought rather than seen. But *darśana* refers to direct experience and perception – that is, something not mediated by concepts at all.

For example, the *ṣaḍdarśana* of Hinduism, usually and erroneously rendered as 'the six systems of Hindu philosophy',[77] represent not six systems of abstract ideas, but six ways of looking at existence. The *ṣaḍdarśana* are, we may say, six sights, six views, perspectives, or even visions. The mode of expression in both Hinduism and Buddhism may be conceptual – it very often is – but the content of the expression is not conceptual at all. The content is a direct perception of things, a vision. But in fact, the Buddhist term is a different one, though it comes from the same root, meaning 'to see'. In Buddhism we use the term *dṛṣṭi*, which also means a sight, perspective, vision, or view.

Traditionally Buddhism distinguishes two kinds of view: wrong view and right view. We may understand in general terms the difference between the two kinds of 'philosophical' view or vision by making a simple analogy with ordinary physical vision. With good vision we see clearly and for a great distance. Good vision is unblinkered: we can see all around us. Good vision is also undistorted; nothing clouds or colours or refracts it. Conversely, poor vision may be weak in that we do not see very far or distinctly; it may be blinkered, restricted to a narrow field so that we see only what is straight in front of us; or it may be distorted, as when we look through a thick fog or through coloured glass or bottle-glass.

Wrong view is very much like poor vision. First of all, it is weak. Our mental vision is weak when it lacks the concentrated energy to be derived from meditation. It is this energy that transforms a purely conceptual understanding of the truth into direct experience. If this energy is not there, then we do not see deeply into the true nature of things. We do not see things clearly or distinctly; we do not see them as they truly are.

Secondly, wrong view is blinkered. It is limited to a narrow range of experience, to what can be experienced through the five physical senses and the rational mind. It is to have just this narrow viewpoint from which to draw conclusions, to be simply unaware of other possibilities of perception or experience. On a very basic level this kind of wrong view is exemplified by the poverty of outlook of someone who is interested only in their job, their family, football scores, and television programmes. Having no interest in world affairs, the arts and sciences, or personal development, they see life simply in terms of their own limited existence.

Thirdly, wrong view is distorted. Vision can be distorted by our mood – whether we are feeling happy or gloomy. It can be distorted by our likes and dislikes. If we dislike someone we see all sorts of faults, whereas if we like someone we may see in them all sorts of perfections that they do not really possess. Our vision may be distorted, too, by prejudices regarding race, class, religion, or nationality. Thus wrong view is weak, limited to a narrow range of experience, and distorted by personal feelings and prejudices.

Right view, obviously, is the opposite of this. Right view is powerful. Based on the concentrated energy of meditation, it gives rise not just to conceptual understanding but also to direct experience of the truth. For this reason, it does not remain on the surface, but penetrates deep into the heart of things, and sees everything clearly and distinctly. Secondly, right view is unlimited. It ranges over the whole field of human experience; it is not confined to what can be experienced through the physical senses or the rational mind. If it generalizes at all, those generalizations are made from the entire range of human experience in all fields, at all levels. Lastly, right view is not distorted by emotion or prejudice; it sees things as they are.

The distinction between wrong view and right view is of supreme importance in Buddhism. A view does not, after all, exist in the abstract, somehow apart from people. It belongs to someone. So if we can identify two kinds of view, we may also identify two kinds of people. People whose view of existence is limited, restricted, and distorted are known in Buddhism as *pṛthagjanas* – the 'many-folk' – and as the name implies, they constitute the majority of people. Most people have not worked to develop themselves at all and consequently are just as nature made them, so to speak. On the other hand, there are those whose view is unlimited in extent, unrestricted in scope, and without any distortion whatsoever. These are known as *āryas*, the 'spiritually noble'. Such individuals, having worked to attain some degree of personal development, have remodelled themselves, at least to some extent. Of course, the crucial point about these categories is that it is possible to move from the one to the other – by developing awareness, by cultivating positive emotions, by raising the level of consciousness, and, above all, by discarding wrong views and developing right ones.

So these two – wrong view and right view – are what we have to work with, practically speaking. However, there is actually a third kind of view – Perfect View, or rather Perfect Vision. Perfect Vision is right view developed to the fullest possible extent. It is the total vision of the total human being at the highest conceivable level of development. It is the unconditioned vision of the unconditioned reality. It is the vision that does not just look beyond space and time but is totally unconditioned by it, that totally transcends the ordinary framework of perception. Perfect Vision is the vision of the Enlightened One, the Buddha, the one who sees with wisdom and compassion.

For the most part, our own view is wrong view. Moreover, we tend to rationalize our wrong views, presenting them in systematic conceptual form. These rationalizations are the worldly philosophies, the various isms and ologies. Only occasionally do we have a flash of right view – and such sparks of right view derive ultimately from Perfect Vision. They become available to us through the Perfect Vision of the Buddha. If we can attend to what the Buddha has communicated of his vision of existence, we can momentarily rise to that level, at least in imagination, and see exactly where we stand. We will have a true philosophy that will enable us to understand the general principles that underlie the whole process of personal development, and that will give meaning and purpose to our lives.

When we look for the source of the Buddha's vision we naturally arrive at a very familiar image – that of the Buddha beneath the bodhi tree 2,500 years ago. He has just attained Enlightenment. He has seen his great vision of human existence, which is in a sense identical with the experience of Enlightenment itself, and which he is afterwards never to lose. But no sooner has he seen this great vision than a problem arises. How is he to communicate that vision? According to tradition – and here we touch upon something very profound and mysterious indeed – the Buddha feels at first that the vision he has seen, the Enlightenment he has attained, cannot be communicated. Sitting under the bodhi tree, he reflects that Enlightenment is, of its very nature, incommunicable. And seeing this – that what he has experienced is very deep, very subtle, very sublime – he sees also how much people are enmeshed in sensual pleasures, how weak, restricted, and distorted is their view, and he feels it will be impossible for them to understand his vision.

At this point – again according to the tradition, or, if you like, the legend – the god Brahmā, the Lord of a Thousand Worlds, intervenes in dramatic fashion. He points out that for want of the Buddha's vision, the world will perish: 'Let my Lord the Exalted One teach the Truth. For there are some beings whose sight is but little clouded with dust. They are perishing through not hearing the Truth.' (The expression finds an interesting echo in the Old Testament: 'Where there is no vision the people perish.')[78] The Buddha then looks out over the world with his spiritual eye. He sees that people are in different stages of development and that some are indeed sufficiently free of the dust of the world to be able to understand.[79]

Having decided to teach and communicate his vision, the Buddha goes about it in various ways. First of all, he communicates through concepts – that is, by means of abstract ideas, which is perhaps the commonest means of communication, especially today. Secondly, he communicates in terms of myths and parables, metaphors and similes – that is, he communicates through the imagination. Thirdly, he communicates through his actions. There is the kind of action that forms the basis of a whole *sutta*, as when he tends a sick monk who has been neglected by the rest of the Order, or when he remains totally unruffled in the face of a rogue elephant deliberately released into his path; or when, to take an example from the Zen tradition, he goes to address the whole Order of monks and simply holds up a flower.[80] There is also the example of the ordinary day-to-day actions through which he communicates. Even when he does nothing but walk along the road, he communicates to anyone who is ready for the communication, just by the way he walks.

Such non-verbal teaching is not confined to Buddhism. There is, for example, a story from the eighteenth century about a certain spiritual seeker who went to see a great rabbi. Afterwards he was asked why. Was he in search of some great truth or teaching, some explanation of the Cabbala perhaps? 'No,' the spiritual seeker said, 'I went to see the rabbi to see how he tied his shoelaces.'[81] Similarly one might go to see how the Buddha wore his robe or how he ate his food. Everything he did would communicate his vision in some way to the receptive aspirant.

Fourthly, the Buddha communicates by silence – by doing and saying nothing at all. He just is. He communicates by his mere presence – which is, of course, a non-presence. Or rather, we should say that he communicates (so to speak) neither his presence, nor his non-presence, nor both his presence and non-presence, nor neither his presence nor non-presence. And if there is one thing that this language of the Perfection of Wisdom tradition makes crystal clear, it is that this type of communication is intensely difficult to receive – if only because we won't simply listen. Before we can receive that silent communication, we have to stop speaking and thinking, even stop, in a sense, being ourselves. As we go on to examine the substance of the Buddha's more accessible communication – through concepts and through symbols – we need to bear in mind his communication through action and through silence. We should not forget that the Buddha's vision is necessarily expressed in action, and that it is a *vision*, a direct, essentially incommunicable experience.

Let's go back now to the figure of the Buddha seated beneath the bodhi tree. As he sat there, he saw that everything was constantly changing, on all levels, on the mental plane as well as on the material plane. It was true of all forms of life. Nothing remained the same, everything was pure process, everything flowed. In terms of Indian thought, the Buddha saw that in reality there was no such thing as 'being' or 'non-being', only a vast 'becoming'. But he saw more than this. He saw not only the truth of change – that things arise and then pass away. He also saw that this change was not accidental. Things do not arise and pass away by chance. Whatever arises, arises in dependence on conditions; whatever ceases, ceases because those conditions cease; and the conditions are, as we would say, purely natural conditions. They do not depend on anything like, say, the 'will of God'. Thus the Buddha saw not only the truth of change but also the law of conditionality. Though this law is the fundamental principle of Buddhist thought, it can be stated very simply as follows: 'A being present, B arises. In the absence of A, B does not arise.'

On a certain occasion, Aśvajit, who was one of the Buddha's first five disciples, proclaimed this law to Śāriputra, then a wandering ascetic, with immediate results. At the time Śāriputra was looking for a teacher, and in his wanderings he met Aśvajit, who was also a wanderer. Impressed by Aśvajit's calm, happy, radiant demeanour, Śāriputra asked the standard questions that wanderers used to address to each other: 'Who is your teacher?' and 'What teaching does your teacher profess?' Aśvajit said, 'I am only a beginner. I don't know very much. But what I do know, I shall tell you,' and he thereupon recited the following verse:

Of those things which proceed from a cause
The Tathāgata has explained the origin.
Their cessation too, he has explained.
This is the doctrine of the great ascetic.[82]

With one possible exception, this verse is the most famous in all the Buddhist scriptures. Often regarded as a summary of the Dharma (or teaching of the Buddha), it is to be found engraved on ancient monuments and seals throughout the Buddhist world. On hearing this verse, Śāriputra grasped and accepted the concept of conditionality sufficiently deeply to set him at once on an irreversible course towards Enlightenment.

Having seen this universal law of conditionality, the Buddha went on to discover something crucial to human development. Conditionality is not all of the same kind. There are two main orders of conditionality at work in the universe and in human life: cyclical conditionality and spiral conditionality. In the cyclical order of conditionality there is a process of action and reaction between pairs of opposites. Pleasure and pain, happiness and misery, loss and gain – and, within the wider context of a series of lifetimes, birth and death – endlessly succeed one another, as if our experience of the world were a kind of pendulum. In the spiral order, on the other hand, factors progressively augment rather than counteract each other. For example, in dependence upon pleasure arises not pain but happiness; in dependence upon happiness arises not unhappiness but joy. It goes on: in dependence upon joy arises delight, then bliss, then rapture, then ecstasy.

In the life of the individual human being, these two orders of conditionality are reflected in two different ways in which the mind may function. We may function from the reactive mind or from the creative mind. If we function reactively, we are not *acting* at all, only *re*-acting. When we react, we are essentially passive; we are responding automatically to stimuli. To function creatively, on the other hand, means to originate, to bring into existence something that was not there before, whether what we create is a work of art or a higher state of consciousness. It means to act in the full sense of the word. To function reactively is to function mechanically, whereas the creative mind is both spontaneous and aware. When we are reactive we go on repeating ourselves, going over the same old patterns, doing today what we did yesterday, doing this year what we did last year, doing this decade what we did last decade, and even – to extend the context – doing in this life exactly what we did in all our previous lives. However, when we are creative, we change: we move on, we become aware of our old habits of mind and our fixed patterns of feeling and behaviour, and we become free of them.

Personal development is therefore based on conditionality: we cease to live reactively and learn to live creatively. This is by no means easy. It requires, above all, awareness, and awareness in particular of the two kinds of conditionality, not simply as abstract principles but as concrete alternatives actually confronting us virtually every minute of the day. Suppose, for example, that someone speaks unkindly to us. We can either react by becoming angry and feeling hurt, or we can try to sympathize, to understand what has happened and why, or at least to be patient. If we react, we will be going nowhere except in the direction of reinforcing negative patterns of behaviour; but if we are creative, we at once begin to break down that cycle, and in doing so, we take a step forward in our personal development.

There is of course much more one could say about the Buddha's vision as communicated in conceptual terms, but my intention here is to offer just a glimpse – a partial glimpse – of that vision. We must now move on to do the same with respect to the language of myth and imagery and symbolism – a mode of communication that reached its fullest expression within the Tibetan tradition, from which the following imagery is taken.

If we go back to the figure seated beneath the bodhi tree and ask again 'What did the Buddha see?' we may say that he saw two things. The first thing he saw was a great wheel, embracing the whole of conditioned existence. This wheel contains all living things and is constantly turning. It turns by day and by night, it turns through life after life, it turns with age after age. It is coterminous with the cosmos. We cannot see when it first began turning and as yet we cannot see when it will cease to turn.

This great wheel revolves on a hub made up of three creatures that form a circle by each biting the tail of the one in front. A red cock, greedily scratching the earth, bites the tail of a green serpent, its red eyes glaring with anger. The serpent in turn bites the tail of a black pig wallowing in its own ignorance. Surrounding the hub, which forms the first circle of the wheel, is a second, larger circle divided vertically into two halves and containing figures of men and women. On the left half, which is white, figures are ascending, almost floating upwards, as though to the sound of music. Some are holding hands and all are gazing upwards to the zenith with rapt, blissful expressions. On the right the figures are descending – or rather, they are plunging headlong. Some are naked and deformed, others are chained together, and still others are holding their hands to their heads. All are anguished and terrified.

The next circle of the wheel is by far the largest. It is divided by spokes into six segments, each of which depicts what can be seen as a whole realm of existence – although these segments may alternatively be seen as representing a state of mind or plane of consciousness. The order varies, but always right at the top are the gods, who live in luxurious, elegant palaces and are surrounded by all manner of delights. For them existence is like a pleasant dream. Some of the gods have bodies made entirely of light, and they communicate by pure thought. Next, going round this circle in clockwise order, we see the *asuras* or 'jealous gods'. Clad in armour and wielding weapons, *asuras* live in a state of constant hostility and jealousy. They continually fight and compete for possession of the fruits of the 'wish-fulfilling tree'. In the next segment we see various species of animals: fish, insects, birds, reptiles, mammals. Some are large, some small, some are peaceful, some predatory, but all are searching for food. The bottom segment is a hellish realm full of tormented beings. Some are freezing in blocks of ice, others are burning in the flames, still others are being devoured by monsters. In the next segment up, on the left, we see the hungry ghosts. They have enormous swollen bellies but thin necks and mouths no larger than the eyes of tiny needles. All are ravenously hungry, but whatever food they touch turns either to fire or to filth. In the last segment, we see human beings among houses, fields, and gardens. Some people are cultivating the earth, while others are buying and selling, giving alms, or meditating.

These are the vividly contrasting six worlds, the six planes of consciousness, the six kinds of mental state depicted within the Tibetan wheel of life. It should be said, however, that the inhabitants of these worlds do not remain in them indefinitely. They disappear from one segment and reappear in another. Even the gods, although they stay a very long time in their world, eventually disappear and reappear somewhere else.

The outermost circle, the rim of the wheel, details the precise stages of the process by which living beings either pass from segment to segment of the previous circle, or else reappear in the same segment. Twelve stages are depicted, each arising in dependence on the previous one. In clockwise order these are:

1. a blind man with a stick – representing ignorance;
2. a potter with a wheel and pots – representing volitional activities;
3. a monkey climbing a flowering tree – representing sentience;
4. a boat with four passengers, one of whom is steering – representing the psychophysical organism;
5. an empty house with five windows and a door – representing the six senses;
6. a man and a woman embracing – representing contact;
7. a man with an arrow in his eye – representing feeling;
8. a woman offering a drink to a seated man – representing craving;
9. a man gathering fruit from a tree – representing grasping;
10. a pregnant woman – representing becoming, or life;
11. a woman giving birth to a child – representing birth;
12. a corpse being carried to the cremation ground – representing death and decay.

The wheel upon which all these images are ever revolving is clutched from behind by a fearful monster, half demon, half beast. His head, with its three eyes, long fangs, and crown of skulls, peers over the top, his clawed feet stick out either side, and his tail hangs down below.

But there is something more. Above the wheel to the right stands a figure in a yellow robe. This figure points to the space between the seventh and eighth segments of the outermost circle of the wheel, between the man with the arrow in his eye and the woman who is offering a drink to a man. Here, rising out of this space, we see the second thing the Buddha saw in his vision of human existence. Again, it is not so much a symbol as a group of symbols, and it seems to change its form as we look at it.

At first there appears to be a path that stretches far away into the distance, winding now through cultivated fields, now through dense forest. It traverses swamps and deserts, broad rivers and deep ravines; it winds around the feet of mighty, cloud-capped mountains. Eventually, the path disappears over the horizon. But now the symbol changes. The path seems to straighten out, to stand up; it becomes a great ladder stretching from heaven to earth and from earth to heaven. It's a ladder of gold, a ladder of silver, a ladder of crystal. But again the symbol changes. The ladder becomes slender and solid and turns green; it becomes the stem of a gigantic tree with enormous blossoms, blossoms that are bigger the higher up they are. At the very top of the tree, shining like a sun, is the biggest blossom of all. In the centre of each of these blossoms sit all kinds of beautiful and radiant figures: Buddhas and bodhisattvas, *arhants*, *ḍākas*, and *ḍākinīs*.

Such was the Buddha's vision of human existence as he sat beneath the bodhi tree – his vision as communicated in concept and symbol. The significance of the vision is quite clear. It is a vision of possibilities, of alternatives. On the one hand, we have cyclical conditionality, on the other, spiral conditionality. On the one hand, we have the reactive mind, on the other, the creative mind. We can either stagnate or grow. We can either continue to revolve passively and helplessly on the wheel, or we can follow the path, climb the ladder, become the plant, become the blossoms. Our fate is in our own hands.

Today the world is full of woolly thinking. Wrong views abound. They all in one way or another represent rationalizations of a limited range of experience. What we need today, perhaps more than anything else, is right view – vision that is penetrating, unblinkered, and undistorted. We need the Perfect Vision communicated by the Buddha. If we have this vision, we can grow and develop. Without it, we may well perish. This is indeed a challenge that the Buddha lays before us, a challenge that has great implications for the way we live our lives. And those of us who take up this challenge will find ourselves forming the nucleus of a new society – the subject we will now move on to consider.

3

THE NUCLEUS OF A NEW SOCIETY

Here my purpose is to make clear what Buddhism, and in particular the FWBO, has to offer, what it has to give – and this is only fitting since giving, or generosity, is of the very essence of the Dharma. We may even say that where there is no giving, there is no Buddhism. However, so far as the FWBO is concerned, the gifts offered so far are, to some extent at least, external to the FWBO itself. The gift and the giver are distinct. After all, other Buddhist organizations also offer these gifts – a method of personal development and a vision of human existence – albeit in different forms.

In the case of the third gift, by contrast, there is no distinction between the gift and the giver. I want to focus on the nucleus of a new society, and to explore the ways in which the FWBO *is* such a nucleus. In other words, one of the things the FWBO has to offer is itself. In his poem 'Song of Myself' Walt Whitman says, 'When I give, I give myself,'[83] and this, we may say, is real giving. One can give many things – time, energy, money, ideas, work – and yet still not give the greatest of all gifts, oneself.

Since this third gift is of a different nature from the previous two, I want to present it differently. I want to start, in a way that some people would consider rather 'unBuddhistic', by saying something about myself, and how and why I came to start the Friends of the Western Buddhist Order and the Western Buddhist Order. I will then go on to outline what they are and in what way they form the nucleus of a new society.

Altogether I spent some twenty years in the East, including a year in Sri Lanka (which was then Ceylon), a year in Singapore, and eighteen years in India, as well as making visits to Nepal and Sikkim. During all that time I studied and practised Buddhism. However, I discovered Buddhism not in the East but in London, at the age of 16 – or rather I should say that at 16 I realized that I was already a Buddhist and had always been one. I made this discovery when I read two remarkable Buddhist texts: the *Diamond Sūtra* and the *Sūtra of Huineng*.

The *Diamond Sūtra*, one of the shorter Perfection of Wisdom texts, is recited, meditated upon, and studied throughout the whole Buddhist world, particularly in countries that follow the Mahāyāna tradition, like China, Japan, and Tibet. Its content is too profound to be summed up in a few words. Suffice it to say that it deals with *śūnyatā*, with ultimate reality or, literally, the 'Void', and with the wisdom that intuits the Void. The *Sūtra of Huineng*, or *Platform Sūtra*, is in a sense the basic text of the Chan, or Zen, tradition. It is a collection of discourses by – and dialogues and exchanges with – the great master Huineng (formerly rendered Wei Lang), the first Chinese patriarch of the Chan tradition. And again, it is pointless, indeed impossible, to offer any brief idea of its contents, if only because it goes beyond ideas – being, as it is, also concerned with fundamental reality. All I can say is that these two works gave me my first glimpse of the transcendental. Buddhist terminology refers to the transcendental as the *lokuttara*, which means 'beyond the world, the mundane, the conditioned'. In other words, these texts gave me my first glimpse of Perfect Vision. From then on I had no doubts about Buddhism, or about the spiritual path.

I did not meet any other Buddhists until I was 18. Consequently, for two years I was a Buddhist entirely on my own in a non-Buddhist world – in South London, to be precise – and when I say it was non-Buddhist I mean that Buddhism had virtually never been heard of in that world. In my nineteenth year I was conscripted into the Royal Corps of Signals and sent to India. That was in 1944. After the war ended I spent two years wandering mainly in South India, often on foot. For several years I lived like an Indian sadhu or ascetic. I wore saffron robes, carried a begging-bowl, and wandered barefoot from place to place, finding shelter under a tree, in a cave, or at some hospitable temple or ashram. And of course I met all sorts of people.

Eventually I settled in Kalimpong, a small town 4,000 feet above sea level in the eastern Himalayas. From where I lived there were stunning views of the snowy ranges, including the second highest peak in the Himalayas, Kanchenjunga, whose name means 'the Five Treasures of the Snow'. Except during the rainy season, one could see Kanchenjunga almost every day, its crest – wearing, very often, white plumes of snow blown off it by the wind – standing out against the blue sky with the clouds far below. The atmosphere was so clear that you could see for vast distances, and everything stood out with a strange, almost hypnotic, vividness of colour. Sometimes, especially just after the rains, the colours were so bright that everything seemed to be made of jewels – the brilliant white mountains, the intensely blue sky, the vivid green vegetation, the scarlet, yellow, and blue mountain flowers, and the bright, multicoloured costumes of the Tibetans, Bhutanese, Sikkimese, and Indian people.

I lived in this world of jewels for fourteen years. After seven years, I founded a small vihara, where people stayed with me from time to time. During this period I delved more and more deeply into the study and practice of Buddhism. Fortunately I made contact with quite a number of great teachers, especially some Tibetan teachers who were among those just beginning to come to India, and from them I received various ordinations and initiations. I also travelled to the cities of Calcutta, Bombay, and Delhi, as well as to Buddhist holy places like Bodh Gaya, Sarnath, Lumbini, Rajgir, and Nalanda. And during the second half of those fourteen years I also became involved in the mass conversion of ex-Untouchable Hindus to Buddhism.

In addition to studying and meditating, I spent a lot of time writing, especially during the rainy season, which in Kalimpong is a beautiful time of the year. The days are still warm, but the rain comes down all day and every day. You hear it falling peacefully on the roofs, on the leaves of the trees, and on the crops in the fields. Everything becomes quiet and hushed. Since there are no visitors, one can work, meditate, or write in peace. For a number of years the rainy season was my favourite time for writing.

While I lived in Kalimpong, I kept in touch with Buddhists in London through letters and Buddhist magazines, and it came to my notice towards the end of my time there (1962–3) that all was not well with the Buddhist movement in England, especially in London. Although it was a tiny movement, it had already divided into two opposing camps between which, to put it mildly, feelings ran high. Some of my friends felt that my presence in England, at least for a while, might help to restore harmony, so towards the end of 1963 the English Sangha Trust invited me to England for a visit.

The invitation came as quite a surprise. Happily buried in my books and my meditation in Kalimpong, I took it for granted that I would continue my life in India and would die there. I never expected to see England again. But when the invitation arrived, I considered it long and deeply, and discussed it with my friends and teachers, and they all recommended that I should go. Some even felt it was my duty to go inasmuch as I might be able to restore harmony.

So in August 1964, after an absence of twenty years, I returned to England. I did not stay for the four months I originally planned, but for more than two years. I could not seem to get away. During that time I held meditation classes and gave many lectures, mainly at the Hampstead Buddhist Vihara in London, as well as at the premises of the Buddhist Society in Eccleston Square. In addition I visited a number of little – in many cases, tiny – Buddhist groups up and down the country.

Gradually it became clear that the Buddhist movement in England at that time left much to be desired. At the same time I saw that there were people in England who were greatly interested in the Dharma. After again deeply considering the situation and consulting with friends, I decided that I would stay and work for Buddhism in England and the West indefinitely. But first I needed to return to India for a few months and say goodbye to my teachers and friends, and hand over my responsibilities – especially for the vihara in Kalimpong.

I had not been back in India for more than a month when there came a bolt from the blue. I received a letter from the English Sangha Trust stating that it did not propose to renew its invitation and that I would no longer be welcome at the Hampstead Buddhist Vihara. The letter suggested that I should write a statement saying that I had changed my mind and would be staying in India after all; they offered to publish this letter for me in England.

When I read that letter I was standing in the Maha Bodhi Society's headquarters in Calcutta, about to make my way up to Kalimpong in the company of a friend. I remember that I passed the letter over to my friend to read, and said, 'Do you know what this means?' He said, 'No, what does it mean?' And I said, 'It means a new Buddhist movement.' Unbidden, in a flash, the idea for the FWBO had come upon me – as though I actually saw it looming, as it were, in the future.

Evidently during my two years in England I had unintentionally offended several people. Among other things I had succeeded in bringing together the two camps into which, at the time of my arrival, most English Buddhists were divided. This sudden unity had upset extremists on both sides, and they had joined forces to stop me from returning. I was warned – ludicrous as it may sound – that they were prepared to go to any lengths to stop me returning, and from the tone of alarm in some of my correspondence it seemed that I risked being murdered if I went back. Clearly I had trodden on some people's toes very heavily.

However, I did not hesitate. Only rarely in one's life does one find oneself in a position to make a completely free, uncomplicated choice, and I felt at that time that I was in that position. The alternatives were clear. On the one hand, I could remain in India, where I had been for eighteen years. I had founded a vihara in Kalimpong, I had many friends and teachers, I liked India very much, and I was quite happy there. It was a deeply, richly satisfying life. On the other hand, I could return to England, where I had nowhere to stay, no money, and no support from existing Buddhist organizations.

I made my choice, and I never doubted for a moment that it was the right one. Towards the end of March 1967 I returned to England for good. I wasn't murdered, and although I had been warned that I should find every door closed against me, this did not turn out to be the case – at least not entirely. I even found I had some friends left. A few weeks after my return, in April 1967, I started the FWBO.

It is perhaps still not completely clear from the foregoing history precisely why a new movement was needed. Before going on to outline the principal features of the FWBO I must first attempt to characterize the gap – or rather the gaping hole – in English Buddhism that needed to be filled. To begin with, many people who belonged to and controlled Buddhist organizations in England, including some of the people whom I had upset and who tried to prevent my return, were not actually Buddhists. Indeed, they did not even profess to be Buddhists. They had become members of Buddhist organizations simply by paying a subscription. Having joined in this fashion, they could be elected to office and thereby determine policy, even though they knew little or nothing about Buddhism and might even have had no real sympathy with it. This may sound strange, but it is by no means uncommon; indeed, the same thing went on in India. For example, the Maha Bodhi Society, with which I was associated, was virtually taken over by orthodox Hindus, whose ideas were quite opposed to those of Buddhism. It was therefore clear that we needed a new kind of Buddhist organization, one that could not be joined simply by paying a subscription. We needed an organization that one could join – if that is the word – only by committing oneself to the ideals for which it stood. In other words, we needed an order and a spiritual community, or sangha.

Other considerations also led me to this conclusion. As I have mentioned, the Buddhist movement in England at that time was barely alive. There were Buddhist societies and people who were interested in Buddhism, but only a few people were actually *practising* Buddhism. For example, most English Buddhists were not vegetarians, and few practised right livelihood or even thought of doing so. English Buddhists in those days lived the same kind of life – usually quite a middle-class life – as everybody else. Indeed, in those days many English Buddhists prided themselves on being just like everybody else. Personally I found this frustrating because I felt that people were not taking Buddhism seriously. They came to classes and lectures and came up to me afterwards to say how much they had enjoyed them, but then they carried on just as before. Nothing I said seemed to have any discernible effect on their lives. They did not change in any way – they did not even want to change. Clearly this state of affairs could not continue.

On my return to England in 1967, therefore, I decided to found an order: a Western Buddhist Order. First, however, I founded the FWBO, the Friends of the Western Buddhist Order, and under its auspices I held meditation classes, gave lectures, organized retreats in the country, and so on. Gradually I gathered together two or three dozen people who took Buddhism seriously and wanted to change their lives. Some of these people I had known before, during my two-year preliminary visit; others were new. In April 1968 twelve of those people became the first members of the WBO, and the new Buddhist movement came into existence. From those modest beginnings that movement has grown until it now consists of many hundreds of Order members, of both sexes and all adult age groups, who live and work in many different countries in the West and, since the 1980s, in India (where the Movement is not, for obvious reasons, called the FWBO, but TBMSG – Trailokya Bauddha Mahasangha Sahayak Gana).[84]

So how does one join the Western Buddhist Order, if not by paying a subscription? And what is the relation between the WBO and the FWBO? To answer the first question first, one joins the Western Buddhist Order by Going for Refuge to the Three Jewels: the Buddha, the Enlightened teacher; the Dharma, the teaching he gave; and the Sangha, all those who have attained transcendental insight through following the Buddha's path. The Buddha represents the ideal of human Enlightenment, and Going for Refuge to the Buddha means committing oneself to the realization of that ideal, reorienting one's whole life in that direction. The Dharma represents the path leading to the realization of this ideal. It is in principle the sum total of all the methods and practices that help in one's personal development, in one's realization of the ideal. Thus Going for Refuge to the Dharma means actually practising the Dharma. The Sangha represents the spiritual community, the community of those who have gone for Refuge, who have committed themselves to the ideal of Enlightenment and who are practising the Dharma in order to reach that ideal. Going for Refuge to the Sangha means associating with such people, being in communication with them, learning from them, being inspired by them.

Going for Refuge is the central act of the Buddhist life. Going for Refuge to the Buddha, the Dharma, and the Sangha is what makes one a Buddhist. One could even go so far as to say that one's whole Buddhist life is, in a way, a progressive deepening of the Going for Refuge. And one goes for Refuge with one's entire self – with body, speech, and mind. It is not enough to think and feel that you are Going for Refuge. It is not enough even to *say* that you are. You must also *enact* the Going for Refuge; and when one joins the Western Buddhist Order this enactment takes place in a twofold ordination ceremony.

First there is a private ordination which one undertakes alone with a private preceptor – that is, one of a number of senior Order members designated to ordain people. One repeats after him or her the words of the Three Refuges: 'To the Buddha for Refuge I go; to the Dharma for Refuge I go; to the Sangha for Refuge I go.' At the same time one undertakes to observe the ten precepts of ethical behaviour. Three of these precepts refer to bodily actions, four to speech, and three to the mind. Together they represent the purification and transformation of one's entire being. At this private ordination ceremony one is also given a new name to signify that one is now spiritually reborn, having committed oneself with body, speech, and mind to the Three Jewels.

The private ordination signifies your individual commitment to the Three Jewels – that is why it is a private ceremony. It signifies the fact that you have made up your mind to go for Refuge quite independently of any pressure or influence. You have made up your mind as an individual. You are in a state of mind in which you don't, in a sense, care if nobody else in the world is Going for Refuge. This is what *you* have made up your mind to do, and so you are going to do it. The private ordination signifies that sort of resolution – your determination, if it should ever be necessary, to go it alone.

Usually within a few days of the private ordination, the public ordination takes place, in the presence of other Order members (ideally at least five). Here too the words of the Going for Refuge are repeated, this time after a public preceptor, and the ordinand again undertakes to observe the ten precepts. On this occasion the new Order member is invested with a white *kesa*, a simple strip of material embroidered with an emblem of the Three Jewels and worn around the neck. The public ordination represents the fact that, although you are prepared to lead the spiritual life alone, you are not alone. You have become a member of a community of spiritually committed individuals, a member of the Order.

Originally the Western Buddhist Order was conceived of as a lay order rather than a monastic order, an order in which people would commit themselves to the Three Jewels and work on their personal development within the framework of ordinary family life and a full-time job (one in accordance with right livelihood, of course). However, as time went on more and more Order members wanted to give a fuller expression to their commitment. They wanted to give as much as possible of their time and energy to the spiritual life and the work of the FWBO, and they found it difficult to do so within the framework of family life and a regular job. Consequently different roles developed for Order members. Today some Order members are married, some are unmarried, and some have taken a precept of celibacy. Some have full-time jobs, some have part-time jobs, and some have no regular jobs at all. The last usually work full time for the Dharma, and may receive living expenses from the FWBO. Some Order members live at home with their families, others live in communities of various kinds, and a few live on their own. Regardless of these differences, all these Order members are united by a common commitment to the Three Jewels. Thus it is no longer possible to call the Western Buddhist Order a lay order, any more than it can be called a monastic order. Perhaps it represents a new kind of development, one more in line with the original spirit of the Dharma.

As for the relation between the Order and the FWBO, we should be clear first of all that strictly speaking there is no such thing as the FWBO as a whole. There are only FWBOs: the FWBO, West London; the FWBO, Auckland; the FWBO, San Francisco; TBMSG, Bombay; and so on. All these FWBOs are autonomous; all run their own affairs. There is no centralization, no headquarters, and no organizational pyramid to hold them together. But spiritually they are held together by the Order inasmuch as each FWBO is run by Order members working cooperatively. Each FWBO has its own premises and plans its own particular programme of activities, such as meditation classes, yoga classes, lectures, study classes, retreats, arts events, and so on. Since the single purpose of all these activities is to help people in their personal development, they are variously designed to serve the spiritual needs of all who care to come along.

The various FWBOs represent, therefore, the means through which Order members offer their services, offer themselves, to society at large. Each FWBO is an autonomous registered charity (depending, that is, on the legal situation that obtains in any particular country). But the Order itself is a purely spiritual body. It is not a legal entity and therefore has no legal existence.

Not all Order members are occupied in running FWBOs, however. Some may for a long time devote themselves mainly to meditation, some may occupy themselves with literary work, or art or music, or study, while others may spend their time principally in raising their children, and still others may give themselves to travelling from place to place, visiting different FWBOs and making fresh contacts. But whatever they may be doing, the essential thing is that Order members keep in regular contact with one another by means of weekly and monthly meetings and biennial Order conventions, as well as in other ways and on other occasions.

Not all the FWBOs are urban centres running a regular programme of activities. Some function as country retreat centres. Others are residential communities of one kind or another. In certain cases groups of Order members may not function through an FWBO at all but rather through a different kind of organizational set-up, like a publishing house, a school, a restaurant, a housing association, or a business run in accordance with the principles of right livelihood, a topic we will explore in the next chapter.

As we have seen, people join the Order by Going for Refuge to the Three Jewels, by making a spiritual commitment to their personal development, alone as well as in spiritual fellowship with others who are also committed spiritually. However, except in very rare cases, this commitment does not happen the minute a person comes into contact with the Dharma and the FWBO. Usually people decide to commit themselves gradually, step by step. There may even be quite a struggle. Part of you wants to develop, part of you doesn't. For a while you may not even know whether you want to or not.

But suppose you come into contact with the FWBO – perhaps you see a poster, or perhaps a friend takes you – or drags you – to a talk or a meditation class. If you like it and you start coming regularly, you are considered a Friend with a capital F. You have not joined anything – you are simply participating regularly. You don't have to believe or disbelieve in anything either. You can be a Christian, Jew, humanist, agnostic, free-thinker, spiritualist, occultist, Theosophist, Rosicrucian, Sufi, Vedantist – anything you like. This stage of being a Friend can last as long as you like. Many people, in fact, will not want to go any further than this.

If, however, you feel the need for a more definite link with Buddhism, with the Dharma, with the Order, you can ask to become a Mitra (the term is Sanskrit and means 'friend'). You become a Mitra – when you are considered to be ready by Order members who know you – by offering a flower, a candle, and a stick of incense in front of an image of the Buddha in the devotional context of a Sevenfold Puja, in the presence of Order members, Mitras, and Friends.

As is true for Order members, some Mitras live in communities, usually with Order members or other Mitras, while others live at home with their families or on their own. Some Mitras and Friends have jobs, whereas others work full- or part-time for the FWBO. There are special activities – study groups, retreats, and so on – commensurate in intensity with their level of commitment. But again, you can stay a Mitra for as long as you like. If you do want to deepen your involvement, the next step is to ask for ordination. There are special retreats for those preparing themselves to make this full commitment to the Three Jewels. The time it takes for each person to become ready for ordination varies very much because for each person it is a very individual process.

As I have explained how one may become more deeply involved with the FWBO, and how one may avail oneself of what it has to offer, I hope that the way in which the FWBO is the nucleus of a new society has become clear. As you become first a Friend, then a Mitra, then an Order member, you become more of an individual. That is, you become more aware, more sensitive, more responsible, more emotionally positive, more at home in higher states of consciousness, and you have an increasingly clearer and deeper vision of human existence. In other words, you develop spiritually. Furthermore, the more you become an individual yourself, the more you relate to others as an individual, and on the basis of common spiritual ideals. Within the context of the Order this means relating to other Order members more and more on the basis of a common spiritual commitment to the Three Jewels.

Usually, unfortunately, we do not relate to other people as individuals. We tend to relate to people as members of a particular group, profession, nationality, race, sex, age group, income bracket, political party, trade union, and so on. We relate to others on the basis of competition or conflict, or else common need, whether this be economic, political, psychological, or sexual. There is thus the possibility of two kinds of society: on the one hand, a society of individuals based on common spiritual ideals and a common commitment to personal development; and on the other, a society of non-individuals who are simply members of various groups. The first I would term a spiritual community, and the second a 'group'. The first type of society is what I am choosing to call the new society; the second is the old society. The first is based on the spiral type of conditionality, the second on the cyclical type. The first is the achievement of the creative mind, the second the product of the reactive mind. Finally, of course, the first is very small, the second very large. But although it is a daunting task, we must try nevertheless to turn the second into the first, to transform the group into the spiritual community, the old society into the new. I want to move on to discuss some of the ways in which this transformation can be achieved.

It is as the nucleus of a new society that the FWBO offers itself, a nucleus of which the Order is the central and most essential part. The

FWBO offers itself not as an organization but as a spiritual community that is willing to welcome into spiritual fellowship all those who want to grow and develop.

4
A BLUEPRINT FOR A NEW WORLD

Thus far, we have dealt with things that are immediately available, things that are laid out all ready for us to experience. We have them here and now. Not just one method of personal development but a whole range of methods already exist, and people are actually using them and benefiting from them. Similarly there is a vision of human existence, the vision seen by the Buddha and his Enlightened disciples, which we can all glimpse, at least occasionally. And the nucleus of a new society exists quite concretely in the form of the FWBO.

Looked at in this way, a blueprint for a new world is a quite different subject inasmuch as that new world does not yet exist. If it exists at all it exists only in the imagination, only as a dream, but it is no less worthy of our attention for that. The imagination, after all, has its uses. What we imagine today we may do tomorrow; the dream of the night may become the reality of the morning. Let us imagine, let us dream, and we may find that we are closer to reality than we had thought.

Whether a new world seems to us like a distant dream or an approaching reality, most of us will probably think that a 'blueprint for a new world' sounds like a good idea. As any advertising copywriter will tell you, we all respond with approval to the word 'new'. There are of course other words we find attractive. I had a friend once who specialized in publishing popular books on 'the wisdom of the East' and he used to say that if he wasn't very sure of the quality of a book he was bringing out, he would insist that the word 'secret' should be inserted in the title – as in *The Secret Teachings of....* The blueprint I am referring to makes no such claims as this. It is not a *secret* blueprint, but it *is* a blueprint for something new – for a new world – and we may find the idea attractive.

If we do find the idea of a new world attractive, this is presumably for the same reason that we find the idea of anything new attractive: because we are not really satisfied with the old model. However, when we say that we are dissatisfied with the old world, what exactly do we mean? Are we dissatisfied with the earth, with the flowers or the trees? Well, no. When we say that we are dissatisfied with the world, we generally mean that we are dissatisfied with certain aspects of corporate human existence, with certain social, economic, and political arrangements, even with the quality of human life. We are, all of us, in one way or another, dissatisfied with the world in this sense. The real question to ask ourselves is: are we dissatisfied enough? Does our dissatisfaction go deep enough? Or is it like the motorist's dissatisfaction with their car? Yes, one would like a quieter and more powerful engine, power-assisted steering, air bags, more leg-room in the back, and so on. But to what extent is one dissatisfied with that mode of transport as such? To what extent is one really dissatisfied with polluting the air with exhaust fumes or with a way of life that obliges one to spend hours hunched over the wheel instead of walking?

We may be dissatisfied with the amount of money we earn, but our dissatisfaction does not extend so readily to the very idea of working for a wage. We may be dissatisfied with our personal relationships, but do we ever get round to being dissatisfied with the emotional dependence on which those relationships are usually based? We tend to be more dissatisfied with the economic and political status of the country we belong to than we are with nationalism and the whole concept of the sovereign national state. We may be dissatisfied with wars and conflicts all over the globe, but not with those things for which people go to war.

What I'm suggesting is that we do not really want a new world at all; we only want an improved version, perhaps merely a slightly improved version, of the old world. The world that I have in mind, however, is an entirely new world, a world radically different from the old one. This new world will be a world in which we relate to one another as individuals, a world in which we are free to develop to the utmost of our potential, and in which the social, economic, and political structures will help us to do that. The new world will be, in short, a spiritual community – a spiritual community writ large. Our aim, therefore, must be to transform the present world into a spiritual community. This is the only new world that is worth having, the only new world worth working for.

But how are we to bring about this transformation? How are we even to begin? First of all, we must reconcile two apparently divergent views as to how best to go about instituting the kind of radical change I am envisaging. The first view says we must change the system. People are basically all right as they are; they are simply unlucky enough to live under the wrong system. All we need to do, therefore, is replace the wrong system with the right one, and we shall then have a new world in which everybody will be happy. The second view says that change must come from the bottom up; that it is simply up to the individual, as the basic unit of society, to change. Those who hold this view may go so far as to think that the individual human being is greedy, selfish, and stupid, and that all the world's troubles are due to this simple fact. Wars occur because people feel hatred, economic crises occur because people are greedy. It follows that to change the world we must change ourselves: we must become contented, unselfish, generous, and wise. The first view, that we must change the system, is generally regarded as the secular view, and the second, which is a sort of moral appeal – sometimes a vehement moral appeal – to the ordinary individual, is generally regarded as the spiritual view.

In fact these views are not mutually exclusive. Spiritual movements, especially those that trace their descent from 'the wisdom of the East', are generally expected to adopt the spiritual view, but if this is so, the FWBO is an exception. Yes, the development of the individual is fundamental in transforming the world; but at the same time it is important to recognize that external conditions can help or hinder us in our development. Whatever the external conditions, we have to want to develop and we will always have to exert ourselves. But we must also acknowledge that if we live under the right system, it is easier to develop, and if we live under the wrong system, it is more difficult.

Having said that, some people depend less on external conditions than others; in other words, some are more truly individual than others. There are those who will develop no matter how unfavourable the external conditions may be; they will somehow find a way through despite all obstacles. Others, by contrast, will find it almost impossible to develop even if conditions are highly favourable, while still others, of course, simply won't be interested in development at all. But for most people external conditions are important. With the right conditions they will develop, and with the wrong conditions they will not. It's as simple as that.

This becomes clear on a retreat. A retreat involves a number of people going to a beautiful, quiet place in the country for a weekend, or a week, or a month. (Retreats come in all shapes and sizes.) Except for taking turns at cooking, washing dishes, or perhaps some gardening, the participants do not work. Instead they meditate perhaps three or four times a day, they chant together, they take part in pujas, they listen to talks, and they have discussions or study Buddhist texts. In other words, for a time the conditions under which people live are changed; they are provided with conditions that are more conducive to personal development. And in these improved conditions, people change. One can see this happening literally before one's eyes. Sometimes people change dramatically, even after just a few days. They might arrive on the retreat feeling worried, harried, anxious, tired, and irritable – but gradually they become more relaxed, they cheer up, they begin to smile and laugh and seem glad to be alive. They become more aware of themselves, of one another, of their surroundings, of nature, more aware that they are living and breathing on this earth. They also become more free and spontaneous, more themselves. Although I have seen this happen many times, each time the change occurs it seems almost magical.

Unfortunately, however, the retreat must end, and everyone has to go back to wherever they came from. And it is noticeable that people who have experienced a retreat for the first time can be quite reluctant to leave. They can even become tearful at the prospect of going back to less helpful conditions. Indeed, because we generally have to return to a boring or otherwise stressful job, to a noisy crowded city, or to a difficult domestic situation, the change in us does not always last. Nevertheless there is one lasting benefit: we have seen that it is possible to change, that – given the right conditions – we can develop.

It is, therefore, not altogether true after all to say that to offer a blueprint for a new world is to dream of something that does not exist. On retreat we experience, at least to a small extent and for a short time, what the new world could be like. We can even say that on a small scale a retreat *is* a new world. It shows us that the idea of transforming the world into a spiritual community is more than a mere hypothesis. It shows us that the new world need not exist only in the imagination; it is not just a dream.

So, to come back to our original question, how do we go about transforming the world into a spiritual community? How do we begin? Usually people who want to change the world do two things. First they draw up a detailed, comprehensive plan, and then they try to get everybody to adopt it – by force if necessary. Of course some people choose to do only one of these two things. Either they think it is enough to create the plan and leave others to accept it or reject it as they wish, or else they try to seize power in the conviction that once they attain it they will know what to do with it.

From the Buddhist point of view neither of these two courses of action is satisfactory. To begin with, Buddhists distrust abstract theories, theories not directly related to the needs of the concrete human situation. Buddhism delineates general principles but leaves the specific application of those principles to the individual. Take ethics, for example. Buddhism teaches the principle of non-violence, or love, and says that we should do no harm to other living beings. It teaches the principle of generosity and says that we should not take what is not given. In both cases Buddhist tradition indicates some of the more obvious applications of these principles, but it leaves us to understand and enact the principles within the context of our own lives. It is the same in connection with the projection of an ideal world. Buddhist texts describe such a world, but the descriptions are general and inspirational rather than specific; again, we are left to work out the details for ourselves.

As for changing the world by first seizing power and only then developing a plan for an ideal society, this sort of scheme, pragmatic as it may be, is even less suited to Buddhist principles. The spiritual community is not a power structure. It is not based on coercion, or on the authority of one person over another. The spiritual community cannot be created by the exercise of power; only persuasion, through words or through personal example, can bring it into existence. Otherwise, the new world would only be a variant of the old one, with all the old problems.

So what are we to do? The answer is really quite simple. If we want to build a new world, we must expand the nucleus of a new society into the old world. This expansion represents the activity of the spiritual community; it is not just the individual actions of individual committed Buddhists, but rather the actions of *teams* of committed Buddhists. Such teamwork can radically transform two fundamental aspects of our lives: what we do to earn a living, and where we live.

Almost all of us have to work. Right livelihood, therefore, is an integral part of spiritual life and personal development, so integral that it is the fifth element of the Buddha's Noble Eightfold Path. Right livelihood consists in earning a living without doing harm – whether physical, psychological, ethical, or spiritual – to any living being, including yourself. Ideally, the way in which you earn a living should help you and others to grow, directly or indirectly. Even in the world as it is, under existing conditions, we should be able to practise right livelihood, especially if we are not trying to earn as much money as possible as quickly as possible, if we are prepared to live simply. This will certainly help the individual to grow and develop, especially if he or she is determined and self-sufficient. However, it will not necessarily help to bring a new world into existence. For this, we need teams of committed Buddhists – in the case of the FWBO, teams of Order members, Mitras, and Friends – practising right livelihood collectively.

It is possible to set up business organizations in much the same way that FWBO centres are founded: a team of people decide to pool their talents, energy, and resources, and work together to create a new venture. What type of business a team sets up is determined by the principles of right livelihood; profits are ploughed back into the business or used to subsidize other FWBO activities.

This type of arrangement has many advantages. First of all, the team members involved are provided with a means of right livelihood. They do not receive a salary, but are given whatever they need to cover their living expenses. This might mean that the work would in some circumstances be shared among a larger number of people than would be usual in the outside world, in order that team members might devote sufficient time to meditation, study, or the arts.

Secondly, Order members, Mitras, and Friends work together on the basis of a common spiritual commitment. One of the best ways of learning to communicate with and relate to people is by working with them. In a team-based right livelihood business the team members not only practise right livelihood, which is in itself a spiritual practice; they work with other spiritually committed people, which is also a spiritual practice.

Thirdly, the business aims to produce something that is of positive value to society at large. It may be something quite basic like food or clothing, or something of cultural value like books and magazines, or else a service like the repair and decoration of houses, or catering, or even schools or nursing homes.

Fourthly, the business should ideally earn money to support and extend Buddhist activities and facilities that produce little or no income. Right livelihood businesses may finance special events or the establishment of Buddhist centres. In a society in which the general public is largely indifferent to Buddhist ideals, right livelihood enterprises represent one way of raising the necessary funds. Here again, with right livelihood, the blueprint has got well beyond the drawing board and is embodied in a wide range of thriving businesses, which are all realizing the aims and ideals of team-based right livelihood with greater or lesser success.

There is just one more thing that should be mentioned with respect to right livelihood businesses. As we have seen, the Western Buddhist Order is not a monastic community in the traditional sense. It is not a community of monks, or *bhikkhus* – a term that literally means 'those who live on alms'. According to the old tradition, the *bhikkhu* goes once a day from door to door and collects cooked food. He does not need even to cook it, let alone grow it or earn the money to pay for it. He accepts clothing and shelter wherever he can find them. This means that he can lead a very simple life. He has no need to work. Since he depends directly on the lay public for food, clothing, and shelter, he is free to devote all his time to meditation, study, teaching, or writing. As I related in the last chapter, I have myself had some experience of this way of life. Such a life is possible in India because most people believe in the spiritual values according to which the monk lives, even though they do not themselves attempt to live up to those values to anything like the same extent. People are therefore happy to support the monk, believing that they also benefit by doing this.

Needless to say, it is not possible to be a *bhikkhu* in most Western countries; it is not possible to depend directly on the general public for alms. In fact, if you tried to beg for food from door to door, you might even be arrested. In the West most people set little store by spiritual values, and the law reflects this fact. Unfortunately, the same state of affairs is beginning to develop in India. Notices are now appearing outside villages in northern India saying that sadhus – that is ascetics, holy men, or monks – who beg will be prosecuted. In some modern, 'progressive' quarters in India, monks are simply considered to be economically non-productive.

So what is the Buddhist monk in the West to do? Although I have translated the term *bhikkhu* as 'one who depends on alms', it can also be interpreted to mean 'one who shares' – that is, one who shares in the common wealth, who is supported out of the surplus that society produces. This, in the FWBO, is where right livelihood businesses come in. If businesses produce a profit, they are then able not only to provide right livelihood for the team members involved but also to support those Order members who are devoting the whole of their time to meditation, study, and so on. Such Order members will in effect be monks, at least from the economic point of view. They will not depend on the general public but rather on the FWBO, on other individuals who share the same spiritual ideals. This arrangement is already operating on a small scale. A good many Order members are supported by the FWBO and devote all their time and energy to the work of the FWBO and to their own spiritual practice. Such Order members form the heart of the Movement. They may not be wearing yellow robes, but in certain important respects they live like monks. The fact that such monks depend not on the general public but on the Movement suggests that the FWBO is itself a society, a society within the larger society, a small world within the greater world.

Whether or not it is the case that we all have to work, it is certainly the case that we all have to live somewhere. Of course, the most usual living situation has always been, and continues to be, the family – although what this means in Western society today is very different from what it used to mean. The family used to include not only parents and children but unmarried aunts, grandparents, distant cousins, plus various dependants – what we would call an 'extended family'. Although people still live like this in some parts of the world, especially in the East, in modern Western countries families tend to be much smaller – so small, in fact, as to be almost claustrophobic. The scope for personal relations within this tiny family group is limited, and the relationships that do exist tend to be emotionally overloaded, and so tend to produce psychological tensions that can explode with destructive and disintegrating effects.

As an alternative to these small, overloaded, claustrophobic groups, many people practising Buddhism in the context of the FWBO are choosing to live in residential communities based on devotion to a common spiritual ideal. In these communities, Order members, Mitras, and Friends live together on the basis of a common commitment to the Three Jewels and to spiritual development. Today there are many such residential communities throughout the world, and they represent a particular kind of collective presence in the world – indeed, a particular aspect of the new world.

Residential spiritual communities are as varied as the individuals who live in them. Some are in towns, some in cities, and some in the countryside. In the early days of the FWBO some communities included both men and women, with or without children, but these days by far the majority of communities consist of either men or women. Experience has shown that single-sex communities are the most effective and supportive context for spiritual practice.

The advantages of living in a community are quite clear. You can enjoy the regular companionship of other spiritually committed people. You are free to relate at the deepest level of your being, which is very stimulating and inspiring – and also challenging and demanding. You can live economically, since community members can pool resources and buy food in bulk, share the use of things like refrigerators, cars, and washing machines, and also share household chores and child care, if there are children in the community. And spiritual communities also function as a kind of informal Buddhist centre: members can give friends and visitors a glimpse of a new way of life.

Through right livelihood businesses and communities, as well as in many other ways, the Western Buddhist Order is expanding into the world. The new world starts with individuals, but not just with individuals on their own. It starts with spiritually committed teams of individuals. These teams create situations that help people grow, situations that correspond to people's needs, whether economic, artistic, or social. Together, indeed, the various structures created constitute, on a small scale, a new world. So we already have a detailed blueprint for a new world, or something that is perhaps even better: the living, growing seed of a new world. The acorn is the real blueprint for the oak tree.

Although I have covered a lot of ground very briefly, I hope I have managed at least to convey these four things: a method of personal development to be practised, a vision of human existence to provide inspiration, the nucleus of a new society to be enjoyed, and a blueprint of a new world to be worked for. These four things are what the FWBO has to offer the modern man and woman – a Buddhism for today and tomorrow.

RITUAL AND DEVOTION IN BUDDHISM
85

RITUAL AND DEVOTION IN BUDDHISM[85]

I

EMOTIONAL ENERGY AND
SPIRITUAL ASPIRATION

Socrates used to say that to know the good was sufficient. Doing the good, he said, would automatically follow from knowing it.[86] This may have been true for Socrates, but it is certainly not true for the vast majority of us. For us, virtuous action by no means follows automatically upon knowledge of what is right. And why this should be so can be glimpsed in a criticism Aristotle levelled against Socrates. Socrates, he said, left altogether out of account what Aristotle called the 'irrational parts of the soul'.[87]

The point at issue between these two philosophers of ancient Greece raises what is one of the basic problems of the spiritual life: the problem of how to translate knowing into being. To know and understand the truth, to gain an intuitive glimpse of the truth, is difficult enough, but to embody it in one's life and being is a hundred times more difficult. However much we may have understood, and however bright and clear that understanding may be, it is still very difficult indeed to put it into practice, to embody it in our day-to-day activities and behaviour. Any Buddhist will know this from experience.

Buddhism as a whole is very much concerned with this fundamental problem, and awareness of it underlies the distinction made in Buddhism between the Path of Vision and the Path of Transformation. The Path of Vision represents the initial spiritual insight or experience which starts a person off on the spiritual quest. For quite a number of people, this insight or experience comes spontaneously. It suddenly strikes them, even overwhelms them: an unaccountable glimpse of the truth, or at least of some higher and wider dimension of being and consciousness. For others the initial insight or experience may come as a result of study, perhaps while reading a book or musing upon some particular passage. It may come while trying to concentrate the mind during meditation. Indeed, it may come at any time and place, in any way, either spontaneously or in connection with some specific activity, whether religious in the formal sense or otherwise. However it comes, it is what is known in Buddhism as the Path of Vision.

The Path of Transformation represents the gradual transformation of one's whole life in accordance with that initial vision. This second path is therefore very much longer and more difficult than the first. In the famous formulation of the Buddha's teaching known as the Noble Eightfold Path, the Path of Vision is represented as the first step, which is best understood as 'Perfect Vision', although it is often translated, less helpfully, as 'right view' or 'right understanding'. The Path of Transformation is represented by all the other seven steps of the Eightfold Path: Perfect Emotion, Perfect Speech, Perfect Action, Perfect Livelihood, Perfect Effort, Perfect Awareness, and Perfect *Samādhi*. These steps all represent the working out of the initial insight in different aspects of our life and activities.

But why should it be so difficult to translate knowing into being? Why are we not all like Socrates, able to know the good and immediately to do it without any hiatus between the two? What is it in us that prevents us from making the transition immediately from the Path of Vision to the Path of Transformation in its fullness? It is not difficult to answer this question. The answer is implicit in one of those popular figures of speech which sometimes embody a great deal of traditional wisdom. Suppose somebody is engaged in an undertaking which he knows he ought to be doing, but he does not apply himself to it very well and makes a poor job of it. In those circumstances we usually say 'His heart is not in it.'

His heart is not in it. In other words, he is not emotionally involved. Energy depends on emotion. If there is no emotion, there is no energy, no drive, and for that reason the work is not very well done. We can verify this point for ourselves from everyday experience. And if this is true of everyday life, it is perhaps even more true of the spiritual life. We may have a certain amount of spiritual insight, a certain amount of understanding, even a certain amount of experience. But if there is no emotional equivalent, as it were, of that understanding, it does not become embodied in our lives. A useful way of elucidating this situation is to think in terms of three different 'centres' from which we function: a thinking centre, an emotional centre, and a moving centre.[88] And what we find is that the thinking centre can only influence the moving centre through the emotional centre.

Understanding must pass through the emotions before it can influence the way we lead our lives. This is made clear by the structure of the Noble Eightfold Path. The first step is Perfect Vision. The second step, or aspect, is Perfect Emotion (traditionally translated 'right resolve'). Thus Perfect Emotion is the first of the seven steps which between them make up the Path of Transformation. Perfect Vision has to pass through, or be translated into, Perfect Emotion, before it can manifest as Perfect Speech, Perfect Action, and all the other successive steps of the Path. The vital question is how to bring about this positive chain of causation. How do we involve our emotions in spiritual endeavour? And this in turn raises further questions. Why, one might ask, are the emotional energies not involved? Emotion is surely there in us somewhere – so what has happened to it? Why is it not readily available to us?

These questions can be answered both broadly and in more specific terms. Taking the broader issues first, we could say that if there is a general lack of free-flowing emotion in our society, it might be partly the result of necessary socialization. In civilized human society you can't just express your crude feelings and emotions. You might feel like murdering someone, but you can't just go and do it. You might feel like stealing something, but that doesn't mean you're at liberty to do so. A certain amount of socialization – a suppression of the cruder emotions – is necessary. Some of the emotions at work in, say, the behaviour of a football crowd, just need to be suppressed in everyday society. The trouble is that this suppression may be carried to such an extreme that the greater part of people's emotional life is stifled – all the more so if their emotions are generally rather crude and unrefined. There may be nothing that can be allowed to get through.

In order to forestall the destructive expression of crude emotion, society conditions us to develop self-control. It is not an individual who is being crushed in most cases; individuality is not really there yet. Ultimately as Buddhists we aim to be individuals – that is, to go beyond more or less unconsidered adherence to group values. But people need to be positive group members before they can develop individuality. Someone whose emotions are very crude and unruly can start refining them by becoming a positively functioning member of society, assuming that the society is a relatively positive one. If you are lucky with the sort of family you are born into and the sort of school you go to, you can emerge as a healthy group member and a potential individual, ready for the next step. But so many people are just like maimed animals, not even maimed human beings. A rampaging rebel is not necessarily a proto-individual.

So we must beware of romanticizing the situation. The football hooligan is not someone who is trying to be an individual. Very often he is just rejecting the necessary constraints even of the positive group, as if wanting to relapse into a state of animal anarchy and barbarism. It is not the case that, if the restrictions of society were removed, such a person would be revealed as a healthy individual. That would be the Rousseauist view: that the organization of society is wicked and oppresses the individual.[89] There is indeed oppression, but what is being oppressed is not the individual. You need the socialization, the discipline, of the group to some extent before you can begin to be an individual. However, it is as though society insists on self-control to such a point that we get into the unconscious habit of it. It ceases to be conscious and becomes just an automatic process. We then cannot let go, even when occasionally society permits it, or when letting go feels a perfectly justifiable and positive thing to do. What happens only too often is that the incipient individual is crushed by too much control. As individuality starts to blossom, we need to move progressively from discipline, especially unconscious discipline, to genuine refinement of the emotions. An individual of high emotional development does not need external or even much internal discipline in order to behave in positive, helpful ways.

Refinement of the emotions – as opposed to control – can start to happen even in childhood, sometimes in connection with nature or maybe more often in connection with the arts. The child may experience something more refined and start enjoying, say, music or literature, though here obviously it depends on the kind of literature, the kind of music.

Some types of music are palpably more refined than others. Young people dancing to loud music often appear to be in a daze, almost like robots – not lifted by any refinement of emotional experience, but immersed in a crude experience of movement and rhythm. There seems to be hardly any element of feeling in it at all, though it probably represents an advance on totally chaotic energy, inasmuch as it is rhythmical, which implies a measure of control. It is no doubt better to go to a rock concert or club than to throw beer bottles around and smash windows.

It is often assumed that living in large towns and cities makes it very difficult for us to stay in touch with our emotions. Certainly it can feel as though there is a lot of repression in cities, but there is also a lot of freedom. It can seem that people are 'out of touch with nature', but we have to be careful about jumping to conclusions. In the city you are after all still breathing air; you see the sky; there are at least some trees around. Does the average villager necessarily bother much about nature? I remember that once some Lepchas, up from the forest, passed my gate in Kalimpong. They looked up at the mountains and one of them said to the other, 'I can't understand why these foreign visitors keep looking at these mountains. What is there to see? Just some mountains.' They would have preferred Calcutta any day. So although city life may hold disadvantages for our emotional development, we must be very careful not to fall into 'back to the land' romanticism and bucolic cliché. Many people who live in the country regard the city as a place of liberation, away from the restrictions and narrowness, the pettiness and dogmatism, of the village.

The quality of one's contacts with people – the presence or absence of personal communication – is a major factor in this. As a rule, one's emotions are more likely to be blocked, and one's unblocked emotions are more likely to be negative, if one does not have satisfactory communication with other people. That is the basic criterion. And you can find opportunities for genuine communication whether you live in the village or in the city. Indeed, in the city you can always find like-minded people, whatever you are interested in. If you are interested in, say, painting, you can potentially find hundreds of other painters in the city, whereas in a village you might not find a single person to talk to about what matters most to you. But if you live in the city and you can't find any community of like-minded spirits, you can feel very lonely and isolated. The sort of human contact you have may not be at all satisfactory, and you may be conscious of this vast anonymous mass of people all around you, exerting a kind of psychic pressure – which is not a healthy situation. However, in the city there is at least the possibility of more intensive human contact than you would be likely to get in a small town or a village.

So we must beware of a generalized romantic Rousseauism or old-fashioned communism: the notion that people would be really good and happy and healthy and positive and friendly if you only removed the social restrictions, if you only changed the political system, if you only took them out of the big evil cities and settled them down in some Utopia or some Eden.[90] This view is simply not justified. Although Buddhism suggests that the right conditions will help people develop in a positive way, changes in external conditions are not always enough. You can meet some very negative people in what seem to be very positive surroundings. This is because, biologically speaking, we have an animal ancestry, we have animal instincts which are still very strong, indeed still stronger than anything else in us, in most cases. Civilization and culture form a very frail structure superimposed on what is virtually barbarism. We must be careful that in our attack on what is wrong in society, we do not move towards wanting to wipe out civilization and culture altogether, under the impression that there is a sort of primitive innocence underneath. In other words, the importance of the positive group should not be underestimated, however highly we value the spiritual community and however much the social group in which we find ourselves fails to live up to the ideals of a positive group. You can't go straight from primitive savagery into a spiritual community. The positive group is needed to socialize people's energies positively and constructively.

So this is a glimpse of the social background to the difficulty we sometimes experience in feeling and expressing our emotions – a difficulty that can stop us from putting our hearts into the spiritual life. Let us now move on to look more specifically at what happens to stop our emotions being fully involved, and what we can do to change the situation. In my view there are three main reasons why our emotions may not be available to us. They may be blocked; they may be wasted; or they may be too coarse.

Buddhist devotional ritual, or puja, is only one of many methods of spiritual practice which address the problem of how to engage our emotions with the spiritual life. Puja is concerned particularly with the third of the areas I have mentioned, that of refining emotional energies, although on occasions it may also have the effect of removing emotional blocks and preventing the waste of emotional energy, at least for the period that we are engaged in the puja. But an investigation of all three of these areas will help us to understand the special role of ritual in the spiritual life. After all, we can only refine energy that is available to us. If our emotions are blocked, if we habitually waste our emotional energies, we will have precious little energy upon which the puja can work its refining magic.

With regard to emotional energy that is blocked, Ouspensky, Gurdjieff's chief disciple, makes a rather striking point. In his book *In Search of the Miraculous*,[91] he says that people are not nearly emotional enough. What he means by this is that our emotional centres are not functioning freely. The emotions do not flow readily; they have somehow got jammed. It is as though someone has thrown a spanner into the works, as perhaps they did when we were young. The English in particular are often said by people of other nationalities to be very reserved, and on the whole rather emotionally blocked. As a Russian, Ouspensky would probably have agreed with this view.

Whether or not it is true of the English that they are emotionally blocked as compared with other peoples, it is certainly true of adults as compared with the young. In children the emotional centre usually functions very freely indeed. Children are emotionally quite spontaneous, until their parents start conditioning them. Of course a child's emotional centre functions mostly in its lower aspects, but at least it functions freely and spontaneously. In adults this is usually not the case. Very often, the older people grow, the more they are emotionally blocked and unable to express themselves from the heart.

There are various reasons for this blockage. One is that for years on end we may be engaged in routine mechanical work, work into which we are unable to put our emotional energies, work in which we are simply not interested. The effort we have to put into this kind of work induces strain and difficulty, tension and worry. It causes unpleasant reactions and after-effects in us. Inasmuch as we cannot put our emotional energies into work, we get into the habit, as it were, of keeping them in reserve, until eventually those emotional energies become congealed. First they get sticky and gluey, then they harden within us more and more, and ultimately they even petrify, so that we are unable to put any vitality or enthusiasm at all into work or anything else.

Sometimes emotional blockage comes about through plain frustration and disappointment. Many people never really find any positive or creative outlet for their emotions in the course of their lives, whether through work or friendships or whatever. Some people again are very afraid of being wounded through their emotions, so they do not take the risk of letting their emotional energies flow out. They keep them to themselves.

The absence of any real communication with other people is another important cause of blocked emotions. It is quite possible to know many people, have many acquaintances, but never really to communicate with anybody. If we rarely get the opportunity for real communication, on occasions when we do chance to communicate fully with somebody, one result is a feeling of emotional liberation, as though energy has flowed out of us. But, paradoxically, we do not feel depleted by energy flowing out in this way – we feel all the more full of energy. Many people, however, never get the opportunity for this sort of communication. They may try to communicate but they come up against a sort of blank wall – there is no response – so again their emotional energy gets blocked, and they feel impoverished by the whole experience.

The wrong type of conditioning, especially the wrong type of religious conditioning, is also responsible for a great deal of stunted emotion. The orthodox Christian teaching about morals and particularly about sex is a prime example. Most Westerners have been subject to this at some time or other, usually when they were young.

The net effect of all these factors is that a great many people in the West today can be described as emotionally blocked. There is no free outward flow of emotional energy and so their lives are impoverished not only spiritually but even on the psychological level, the everyday human level.

Fortunately these emotional blockages can be removed. As a first step, we can develop greater self-knowledge. Of course, none of us like to think of ourselves as being emotionally blocked. We like to think that we are kind and friendly and outward-going and spontaneous. But in all likelihood the only way we are going to be these things is by first recognizing that we are nowhere near being them, that in fact we are – almost all of us – chronically blocked, so that we do not fully express the emotional drives within us. Uncomfortable though it may be, we have to face up to this fact. Furthermore, we need to try to understand why it is so – not in an intellectual way by reading books on psychology, but just by trying to see how it comes about in practice that our feelings do not find expression, that they go unrecognized, sometimes even by ourselves.

Sometimes emotional blockages are removed 'automatically' in the course of meditation. Even without our knowing anything about it, a release quite often happens in this way. That is why sometimes in the midst of a meditation someone will start crying, perhaps weeping bitterly: it is the relaxation, the resolution at least to some extent, of an emotional blockage. It is a very positive thing when it happens.

Some people find communication exercises very helpful. As practised in the FWBO, communication exercises involve two people sitting opposite each other. After just looking at each other for a few minutes, one of them repeats some predetermined phrase (e.g. 'The sky is blue today') while the other responds with 'Yes', 'Okay', or 'All right'. They then exchange roles and repeat this exercise, and finish with a further period of just looking. The aim is to overcome social inhibitions to communication. At the end of such exercises, people often feel emotionally liberated, as though energy were pouring out of them. They feel greatly stimulated, much more vital and alive than before, because a portion of that blocked energy has been liberated. In these and many other ways previously blocked energy is made available to the whole of the conscious psyche.

Even if the emotions are not blocked, emotional energy may not be available because it is being wasted. We waste it all the time, by indulging in negative emotions such as fear, hatred, jealousy, self-pity, irrational guilt, anxiety, and so on. There is not a scrap of good in any of these negative emotions. They are completely useless and indeed positively harmful. But they fester in most people's minds most of the time. Not only do they fester; they frequently find outward verbal expressions which constantly drain away our emotional energy. No wonder we often feel so weak and depleted.

For example, some people grumble all the time. In Britain it is traditional to grumble about the weather. If it is raining, well, it ought not to be raining, regardless of how good the rain is for the farmer's crops. If it is hot, then of course it is too hot; but if it is cold, it is sure to be too cold. Making the weather into a whipping-boy for our unconscious negative emotions, we persist in grumbling about it. Some people grumble not only about the weather but about almost everything. Satisfied with nothing, they are in a state of constant disgruntlement. This is simply negative emotion finding an outlet.

Another common example of the kind of emotionally draining expression I am referring to is carping criticism. There are people who have a positive genius for finding fault. However good something may be, however successfully something has turned out, they always manage to discover something wrong with it. Nothing is quite satisfactory. Everything is somehow inadequate. Needless to say, I am not speaking here of objective, detached criticism, which is quite a different thing – and unfortunately very rare. Someone who habitually criticizes is inevitably expressing negative emotion.

The next 'verbal leak' I want to mention has no proper name in English, so I have taken the liberty of coining one: 'dismal-jimmyism'. During the Second World War this was officially known as 'spreading alarm and despondency', and in those days it was a punishable offence. A dismal jimmy could be hauled up in front of the magistrate for spreading alarm and despondency. Perhaps it would be a good idea if it were still an offence. The dismal jimmy is always predicting disaster and exaggerating difficulties. He or she thinks that nothing is going to go right, assures you that you cannot possibly succeed, pours cold water on all your cherished schemes and plans. Even if you do succeed, such a person will usually shake his head gloomily and remark, 'It would have been much better if you had failed.'

And there is a form of verbal expression which is even more harmful: gossip. Gossip is one of the most common expressions of negative emotion and also one of the most dangerous. It is very rarely innocent. It may start off innocently enough: 'What do you think about old so-and-so – how is he getting on?' But within half a minute we are up to our necks in tale-telling and insinuations of the worst possible kind. Spreading malicious gossip is really spreading poison within society. It is something that should be avoided at all costs.

Lastly, another all-too-familiar variety of negativity is nagging. This almost invariably happens between husband and wife, and there is a reason for that. If the nagger tried it on anybody else, that person would just leave straightaway, but husband and wife are tied to each other and cannot escape. Traditionally, of course, it is the wife who is cast in the role of the nagger but I rather suspect that the nagging husband is no less common. Nagging kept up – and some people keep it up for hours on end, day after day, week after week – is psychologically very damaging. To be a little provocative, I would go so far as to say that habitual nagging is much worse than occasional adultery.

So these are some of the commonest verbal expressions of negative emotion: grumbling, carping criticism, dismal-jimmyism, gossip, and nagging – a horrible collection. And the only thing to do about them is just to stop. If you start making excuses for them you are already giving in to them. So don't beat about the bush. One of the French poets is reported to have said: 'Take rhetoric and wring its neck.'[92] We might say the same thing about these verbal excrescences: just take them and wring their necks. To do this of course means maintaining constant watchfulness over ourselves so that we do not involuntarily, out of sheer force of habit, start grumbling or gossiping or any of the rest. If we can just cut them off at the roots, a great deal of energy will be saved. And sometimes we will find that the best thing we can do is to say nothing at all.

Something which a lot of people notice on meditation retreats during which there are extended periods of silence is that they experience an access of energy. They feel more alive. This is partly because talking in itself takes effort but perhaps mainly because what we say is so often an expression of negative emotions which waste and drain away energy. For this reason silence is an extremely important spiritual discipline, whether in Buddhism, Hinduism, or Christianity. In all these great spiritual traditions silence is considered important, if not imperative, for the person who seeks to lead a spiritual life. In Pāli and Sanskrit there is one word, *muni*, for both the man who is silent and the wise man. Of course, the 'wise man' who is silent is not silent because he is stupid or incommunicative. Nor does he experience discomfort when nothing is being said. He is never the person who feels the need to announce 'Isn't everybody quiet today!' So the silent person is very often the wise person, not least because he or she avoids wasting energy on negative verbiage.

The third reason that emotional energy is not available for the spiritual life is because it is too coarse. Higher thought, intuition, spiritual vision, can only act through the higher emotions. The ordinary positive emotions have therefore to be refined, sublimated. There are three principal ways to do this: first, through faith and devotion; second, through the fine arts; and third, perhaps most effectively, through a combination of these two.

Just allowing ourselves fully to experience and express whatever feelings we have of faith and devotion towards our spiritual ideal can be very beneficial. By faith and devotion I mean what in Buddhism is generally called *śraddhā*. This term is usually translated as 'faith' although it does not really mean that. The word *śraddhā* comes from a Sanskrit root meaning 'to place the heart on', and it represents our full emotional response to higher reality, to spiritual truth. It is important to understand the difference between *śraddhā* in the Buddhist sense and the kind of religious faith which has become discredited in the eyes of so many Westerners.

Faith occupies an important place in all traditional religions. The majority of the followers of these religions do not understand their religion in an intellectual sense, but nonetheless they have faith, they have devotion, and such faith gives the traditional religions their organizational – as distinct from their spiritual – strength. But unfortunately this faith is often not acted upon by the higher thinking centre, which remains more or less inactive. In other words popular faith and devotion are not generally linked to any higher spiritual vision or insight. They function under their own steam and decide their own course. More than that, it very often happens that the emotional centre itself tries to do the work of the higher thinking centre. The result is that instead of knowledge, there is merely belief. Belief eventually, inevitably, hardens into dogma; and dogma in time becomes quite irreconcilable with the intellect.

This has happened in the modern world, especially – in the case of religion in the West – with Christianity. That is why modern Western people usually react rather strongly against anything that smacks of faith or devotion. They are really reacting against the illegitimate functioning of faith and devotion, against the usurpation by the emotional centre of the function of the higher thinking centre. So it comes about that people may take to Buddhism, practise meditation, study the Dharma, and consider themselves Buddhists, but still have a resistance to faith and devotion, and everything connected with them. This theme will be explored further in chapter 2.

The second way of refining the emotional energies is through the fine arts: the enjoyment of poetry, music, especially classical music, painting, and so on. For many people nowadays this is the easiest, as well as the most natural and enjoyable, way of refining the emotional energies. I would go as far as to say that for many intelligent people one or another of the fine arts functions almost as a substitute for religion itself. People who would not dream of going to church may have no objection to going to hear, say, a concert performance of a mass by Bach or Mozart. The musical expression of devotional feelings appeals to them and they respond to it in a way they would find impossible within a formal religious framework.

Finally, the emotional energies can be refined by a combination of faith and devotion with one or more of the fine arts. Such a combination of devotion and poetry is what we encounter in such practices as the Sevenfold Puja. The Sevenfold Puja is a devotional ritual in which we collectively evoke various spiritual emotions. And these emotions arise in response to our common ideals and shared vision of reality as represented by the Three Jewels – the Buddha, the Dharma, and the Sangha. In the case of the Sevenfold Puja we practise in the FWBO, this evocation is through verses selected from the very beautiful devotional poetry of the great sage Śāntideva.

The origins, meaning, and practice of the Sevenfold Puja are fully discussed, section by section, in chapters 3 to 13, but although those chapters seek to explain what can be explained, I would emphasize that it is only participation in the puja that can give us a real appreciation of its significance and its effects. When we ourselves celebrate the Sevenfold Puja, which combines faith and devotion with poetry and sometimes an element of visual beauty – and music in some Buddhist traditions – we find that our emotional energies are to some extent refined. When this happens, it becomes possible for the vision and insight of the higher thinking centre to act through these refined, sublimated emotional energies directly on the moving centre. In this way, the whole of life is completely transformed.

2

THE PSYCHOLOGY OF RITUAL

Before looking at the ritual of the Sevenfold Puja itself in detail, I want to say something more about ritual in general. As I suggested in the last chapter, there has been in recent times a considerable reaction against anything that smacks of faith and devotion. This has been in part caused by the fact that popular faith has been divorced from what I have termed the 'higher thinking faculty'[93] and so become unacceptable to the intellect, bringing the whole notion of faith and devotion into disrepute, and along with it the practice of ritual. But unfortunately it has to be said that the rejection of faith, devotion, and ritual is for most people not the result of their own earnest and searching intellectual endeavour. More often than not it is just a received view, a part of their conditioning which has no more intellectual legitimacy than the 'blind faith' that they look down upon.

Before we reject ritual we should really think about what is meant by it. What does ritual really signify? What is it really trying to achieve? It tends to be taken for granted that ritual is a sort of outgrowth upon religion. Some people have a very simplified picture of the history of religion, imagining a pristine, simple, purely spiritual teaching at the outset which in the course of a few centuries has degenerated and become loaded down with a lot of unnecessary ritual and dogma, so that periodically it must be purified of these things. People who think in this way see ritual not as really belonging to the essence of religion, but as something added on afterwards, something that they can very well do without – even something harmful.

Other people again regard ritual as a kind of socio-cultural habit surviving from primitive times. Vaguely imagining tribal communities dancing around a bonfire at night, perhaps waving their spears, they think that something of this kind represents the basic, primal form of ritual, and that remnants of this sort of thing survive even in modern life and in the higher religions. According to this view, dancing around the maypole and taking part in a mass are the same sort of thing.

These rather dismissive views of ritual are beginning to shift in some radical circles, but they remain prevalent even among Buddhists, especially in the West. Some Western Buddhists have even been under the strange impression that there is no ritual in Buddhism. Indeed this is one reason why some of them are attracted to Buddhism, or at least to what they think is Buddhism.

It is true that there are elevated states of consciousness in which the need for ritual is transcended, in which our spiritual aspiration is so intrinsic to our being and so refined that it expresses itself purely spiritually and mentally, leaving the physical plane behind. If those who avoid taking part in ritual have attained to such states, that is fine. But we must not confuse that sort of highly positive development with the far more common case of someone who is inhibited about ritual expression because of all sorts of fears and misunderstandings.

The traditional Eastern Buddhist approach starts with devotion. Buddhists who are unable even to observe the precepts, let alone meditate or reflect on the Dharma, are at least able to attend a puja and offer flowers to the Buddha. However, in the West we tend to have to work our way towards devotional practices through meditation and study. The Protestant religion in particular has involved, from its beginnings, a devaluation of ritual, and in its more extreme forms, like Quakerism, has allowed people to profess the Christian faith without any expression of devotion whatsoever. It is of course necessary to resist easy emotional tricks. It may even be necessary sometimes to withdraw from devotional ritual for a while if one has problems with it. But it is unfortunate that in the West we like to think we have gone beyond ritual altogether.

I believe there are two main historical sources of our current devaluation of ritual. The first is to be found in classical rationalism and the second in early psychoanalysis. Rationalism, which goes back to the eighteenth century, tried to reduce religion to a matter of personal and social morality, abolishing anything supernatural, anything metaphysical, in fact anything very spiritual.[94] In its early days, rationalism, as its very name suggests, was hostile to all non-rational elements. In the eighteenth and nineteenth centuries people knew nothing about the subconscious or the unconscious, so it was quite easy for the rationalists and the great thinkers of the Enlightenment period in France, England, and Germany to discount all the non-rational aspects of religion. They were especially opposed to such colourful elements as ritual and to any kind of religious dogma. We are still living to some extent with this heritage of rationalism and reductionism from the eighteenth century.

A much more recent influence on our thinking, dating from early in the twentieth century, has been psychoanalysis. It may seem a little odd that psychoanalysis should be concerned with ritual. In fact this interest arose from early psychoanalysts' studies of the behaviour of neurotic patients. It was discovered that some kinds of neurotics performed private rituals which in many cases had no connection with the patient's own religious beliefs and practices, but which nonetheless did seem to be in many ways similar to religious rituals. One very common example of this is the personal ritual of compulsive washing. Some neurotics have a compulsion to wash their hands every ten minutes – indeed they can be obsessive about all aspects of cleanliness and hygiene. The early psychoanalysts quickly saw that this patently neurotic personal ritual was similar to certain religious rituals, in particular those of purification which feature in nearly all religions. Having noticed the similarity, they concluded that religious ritual and neurotic ritual were very closely related.

Thus it was that the pioneers of psychoanalysis tended to dismiss all religious ritual whatsoever as compulsive and neurotic. Psychoanalysis in its early days was a very self-confident movement. In the first flush of early success it made some sweeping statements and drew some rash conclusions which later on it had to retract or modify, and this was one of them. As psychoanalytic thinking developed, luminaries such as Jung and Fromm came to be much more sympathetic to religious ritual than Freud had been.

There is another factor that has led to confusion about the Buddhist attitude towards ritual, especially in Britain. The first English translations of Buddhist texts from the Pāli canon were made in the late nineteenth century by scholars from the Protestant tradition of Christianity. At that time religious circles in England were ringing with what was known as the 'ritualist controversy' between the high church Anglicans of the Oxford Movement, who sought to revive ritual in the Church of England, and the more extreme members of the evangelical wing of the church. Evangelical associations even went so far as to launch prosecutions against Romanizing clergy who tried to introduce rituals which were not, strictly speaking, authorized by *The Book of Common Prayer* (and thus by Parliament).

The Protestant Pāli scholars of the time could not help being influenced by prevailing religious attitudes, and we find them reading into the Pāli texts attitudes that are not actually there, and embodying those readings in their translations. For instance, the third of the ten fetters which chain us down to *saṃsāra* and prevent us from realizing Nirvāṇa is what is known as *śīlavrata-parāmarśa*, and this was translated as 'dependence on rites and ceremonies'. In other words, the impression was given that, as regards rites and ceremonies, the Buddha adopted a Protestant, as distinct from a Catholic, attitude. However, if we look a little more closely at the original term, we find it does not really mean 'rites and ceremonies' at all. *Śīla* is simply ethical rules, as in *pañcaśīla*, meaning the five ethical precepts. *Vrata* literally means 'vow' and it is a word that was applied to various Vedic religious observances in the days of the Buddha. *Parāmarśa* means dependence in the sense of clinging and attachment, and treating something as an end in itself rather than as a means to an end. So *śīlavrata-parāmarśa* means attachment to ethical rules and religious observances of whatever kind, considered as ends in themselves. It is treating these things as ends rather than as means to an end that constitutes the fetter. We may conclude that what the Buddha had in mind when he spoke of this third fetter was what we today would call irrational dependence on ritual and religious practice in general.

Ritual is an integral part of Buddhism, as it is of all other religions, and an integral part of every school of Buddhism, whether Tibetan, Zen, or Theravāda. Some people like to contrast Theravādin Buddhism with, say, Tibetan Buddhism in this respect, implying that there is no ritual in Theravāda whereas Tibetan Buddhism is full of it (with the assumption that ritual represents a degeneration), but this view is quite wrong. The Theravāda, like any other form of Buddhism, is highly ritualistic. I remember, for instance, that when I visited the Tooth Relic Temple at

Kandy in Sri Lanka many years ago, there were elaborate rituals going on all morning in front of what is believed to be the Buddha's tooth. Zen, in China and Japan, is also highly ritualistic. In a Zen monastery they don't spend all their time meditating. There are all sorts of rituals to engage in: recitation of *sūtras*, chanting of mantras, and a good deal of bowing down. This might come as rather a shock to some Western Zen addicts.

This is not of course to say that there are no differences between the schools as regards the significance accorded to ritual. I would say that, in Tibetan Buddhism especially, the ritual is much more symbolically and spiritually significant. In Theravādin countries it tends to be more of the nature of ceremony than ritual proper; it is not so well integrated into the doctrinal tradition.

My main point is that we cannot get away from ritual in Buddhism, nor should we try to do so. Instead we should try to understand ritual and see what it really is. Erich Fromm, who first introduced the psychoanalytical distinction between rational and irrational ritual, gives an excellent definition of rational ritual as 'shared action, expressive of common strivings, rooted in common values'.[95] Every word of this definition is of import, and worth discussing in some detail.

First of all, ritual is 'shared action'. The fact that ritual is a kind of action is indicated by the traditional Buddhist word for ritual, *kriyā*, which in fact means 'action' – being etymologically connected with the word *karma*, which means action in a more ethical and psychological sense. So *kriyā* or ritual is something done, it is an action, and this fact should, if nothing else, remind us that religion, the spiritual life, is not just a matter of thought and feeling, but also of action: both moral action and ritual action. According to Buddhist tradition, human nature is threefold: body, speech, and mind together make up our total personality. Religion, which is concerned with our total personality, must cater for all three – and in order to involve the body, it must entail action.

Only too often in the West our approach to Buddhism is too one-sided. We pick and choose what we feel suits us, and the result is that part of us is simply never engaged in our practice. We may meditate and study, but if we miss out devotion and ritual, part of us is not involved. We need a Buddhist tradition in the West which provides not only for the head, not only for the heart, but even for the body and speech.

Ritual is not only action, but action that is shared, done together with other people. Here we come to an important difference between irrational, obsessive-compulsive ritual, and rational ritual. Neurotic ritual tends to isolate people. Like washing your hands every ten minutes, it is something done alone which does not bring the person doing it closer to others – quite the reverse. Rational ritual, however, tends to bring people together, and not just physically so. The sense of togetherness can also be, indeed should also be, spiritual. The performance of ritual action in company with others should celebrate a common spiritual attitude. For this reason a feeling of fellowship is essential, which means that ritual implies a spirit of *mettā* (loving-kindness) and solidarity. If this is present, a very powerful spiritual atmosphere can be created.

Fromm's definition goes on to say that rational ritual is 'expressive of common strivings'. Ritual expresses a striving. It is something we make the effort – certainly in Buddhism – to do ourselves. It is not something which is done for us, say by a priest. We don't just sit back and watch someone else conduct it for us. Ritual of that kind is a degeneration. Meaningful ritual is a matter of striving and exertion. It is part of the Buddhist practitioner's *sādhana*, or spiritual practice, or spiritual *exertion*. Ritual is not for the lazy person. Anyone who believes that ritual is a comfortable substitute for the more demanding methods of spiritual practice has not experienced it as it should be performed.

To be a good ritualist is at least as difficult as, say, giving a lecture, or meditating, if not more so. A good ritualist has to be very mindful. You have to say each phrase and do each action in the correct order, in the correct manner, and with the right emphasis, often doing several things at the same time. You need to have your wits about you.

Ritual also requires attention to detail – you need to see that there is water in the offering bowls, that there are incense sticks, that the candles are alight, that the flowers are properly arranged. For a complex ritual, an expert may be required. Once when I lived in Kalimpong, I invited Dhardo Rimpoche, my friend and teacher, to perform a rather complex ritual and, as the custom is, all the offerings were to be placed ready on the shrine before his arrival.[96] Usually my own Tibetan students and disciples made the preparations themselves, but on this occasion they were not satisfied with that. They did set up the elaborate offerings – lots of little lamps, torma,[97] and so on – on lots of little tables, but they then called in a lama to check it all before the Rimpoche arrived. The lama came and cast his eye over the arrangements. 'No. This should be there, that should be over here, these should be the other way round....' In about five minutes he had made the necessary adjustments and satisfied himself that everything was in order. This is the kind of attention to detail required of a good ritualist.

Good ritual must not only be correctly done, it must also be beautiful. If it is not beautiful, it is not inspiring. So an aesthetic sense is essential. Hindus don't generally mind any amount of disorder and dirt in their temples, even while rituals are being conducted. I have seen temples littered with old bits of newspaper (used for wrapping offerings), remnants of coconuts (coconuts being a common offering), and heaps of long-deceased flowers trodden into the floor. But in a Buddhist temple or shrine-room everything is beautifully arranged, clean, and bright. This is true in Tibet, in Sri Lanka, indeed in all Buddhist countries. And Hindus themselves are the first to be impressed by it.

Perhaps most importantly, a good ritualist must understand the meaning of it all. It is no use being able to do the ritual mechanically, to go through all the right actions, without understanding what is really going on. That would be empty ritual.

Finally, I would say a good ritualist needs plenty of physical stamina. You may have to sit chanting for long periods, from time to time performing various ritual actions, and always maintaining graceful composure and appropriate hand gestures or *mudrās*. This takes considerable physical vigour.

Sometimes we in the West like to think that ritual is a sort of kindergarten stage of religion, something for beginners, but the Tibetans do not think like that. Tibetan tradition permits only the spiritually advanced to do lengthy and complex rituals. Certainly every Tibetan Buddhist has a form of ritual which he or she does. But it is only the Rimpoches and the more highly developed people in general who are sanctioned to enact very long and complicated rituals, because ordinary folk do not have the necessary mindfulness, understanding, and stamina.

Dhardo Rimpoche, who was well versed in Buddhist philosophy, an excellent organizer, and highly knowledgeable about Buddhist yoga, was also a very good ritualist. I often watched him for hours on end going through certain rituals, and I sometimes wondered how he was able to correlate it all. He would be chanting maybe for half an hour or an hour, ringing his bell and making offerings. Sometimes as he was chanting and got towards the end of his text, he would start folding the silken cover in which the book was wrapped in a very elaborate way, to make a particular pattern. And I noticed that as the last tinkle of the bell died away, and the last word of the ritual was recited, the last flower thrown – at that very moment, the last fold of the cloth would be put in place. It was all synchronized, effortlessly, so it seemed. It was harmonized like a piece of music and all the elements ended together, just at the right moment, like a closing cadence. His gestures or *mudrās*, like those of many lamas, were very beautiful to watch. He had been trained in these skills for many years and was a perfect master of them.

Most of us will not develop our capacity for ritual to that degree, but nonetheless the ritual we perform at our own level should be something which we work at, and make as harmonious and expressive as we possibly can. It should involve striving – and not only our own striving, but a common striving. The implication of this important point is that the practice of ritual is possible only within a spiritual community. If you are just doing it on your own, it will not be ritual in the full sense. It may be a striving, but it will not be a common striving.

Ritual in the full sense does not just presuppose a common striving; it also *expresses* that common striving. This is the most important point of all: that ritual is an expression. To quote a further definition of Fromm's, ritual is 'a symbolic expression of thoughts and feelings by action'.[98] So what exactly is meant by 'expression'? Essentially expression means bringing something out from within, even from the depths within. It is in order to express our depths that symbolic expression is necessary. Conceptual expression isn't enough. Conceptual expression brings something out only from the conscious level of our minds – and we have got to do more than that. We have got to plumb the depths beneath the conscious level, to contact the parts of our being to which myth and symbol speak. We could say, in fact, that ritual is like an acting out of symbol or myth. By expressing what is deep within our being, we externalize it, see it, make it something we can know. We can then begin to understand it and incorporate it into our conscious attitude. In this way our whole being will be enriched and integrated. Tension between the conscious and the unconscious will be reduced. We will become more whole.

Through ritual expression, not only do we externalize and make conscious our deep spiritual feelings; we also strengthen and intensify them. This touches on another reason why quite a lot of people feel hesitant about expressing themselves through ritual speech and action. They are simply not sure about the feelings themselves. Perhaps in the case of many of us our devotional feelings are still quite underdeveloped. It is a big step to put our trust in these feelings, to give them space to grow and to exert their influence on our conscious lives.

All of this is a matter of experience. By participating in ritual to any degree, we come to know it. It happens even within very simple devotional meetings when we recite the Sevenfold Puja – as long as we do it properly, with concentration. In ritual we create a very specific atmosphere. Just as meditation has its own atmosphere, which is very beautiful, just as a talk on the Dharma has its own very positive and happy ambience, so the Sevenfold Puja also has a distinctive atmosphere of its own which derives from what is brought up from the depths, externalized, and made conscious.

This atmosphere can have a distinct and noticeable effect. At a Buddhist Society summer school which I attended shortly after my return to England in 1964, I remember being rather surprised that, although there were many lectures on the programme – and also a little meditation – there was no provision for any sort of puja. So one day I suggested that we might try out a little ritual in the evening. At first this suggestion was not very well received. I was told that English Buddhists were right off ritual; they preferred the rational approach. So I said, 'Well, never mind. Even if only five or six people want it, let's try it.' It was announced, therefore, that there would be a short and simple puja conducted by myself at nine o'clock that evening. In the event, instead of having five or six people, we had practically the whole summer school, about 140 people. It was difficult to get them all into the room. They continued to come every night after that and seemed thoroughly to enjoy it. Many people remarked that a special atmosphere was created. Something special manifested, they knew not how, they knew not why. But it came from the depths and it created an altogether more meaningful and harmonious atmosphere.[99]

Sometimes people are starved of this sort of thing. They get just the intellectual, conceptual approach: books, talks, ideas, philosophy, theory. It is an imbalance which is even encouraged in some places in the East. I've known Theravādin *bhikkhus* apologize for pujas and say that they were only for lay people, unintellectual people. Intellectuals – and of course Westerners were supposed to be honorary intellectuals – didn't need them at all. What was important was the intellectual understanding of the Dharma. I've even heard Buddhist *bhikkhus* say, 'Well, we *bhikkhus* don't do pujas ourselves.' But although the intellectual approach is no less necessary than the devotional or the imaginal approaches, sooner or later we must begin to engage the depths, the vast resources of energy which lie in the unconscious mind. We must begin to speak the language of myth, symbol, and image, and in this way integrate the unconscious with the conscious. And this is what ritual, among other things, helps us to do.

Lastly, in terms of Fromm's definition, ritual is 'rooted in common values'. Ritual is never just ritual. It is not self-contained. It issues from a whole religious philosophy, a system of beliefs and values. And broadly speaking, the more highly developed the religion is, the richer its ritual expression. The two most highly developed religions of the world are probably Buddhism and Christianity, and these two are, at least in their dominant forms, highly ritualistic. In Christianity, the main forms, the Eastern Orthodox Church and the Roman Catholic Church, are both very ritualistic. And in the case of Buddhism the Tibetan schools, Chan, Zen, and even the Theravāda all give an important place to ritual.

Having studied Fromm's definition of ritual, let us apply it to a simple example drawn from Buddhism: the ritual of Going for Refuge, which is very basic but also very important. First of all, it is an action. We say, '*Buddhaṃ saraṇaṃ gacchāmi*', *gacchāmi* meaning 'I go.' In the Pāli and the Sanskrit, the verb comes out very powerfully because it comes at the end. It is often translated as 'I go for refuge to the Buddha', but a far more powerful translation is 'To the Buddha for refuge I go'. This stresses the fact that Going for Refuge is an action, an action of the whole being. We go for Refuge with body, speech, and mind. In the Tantric tradition it is not felt to be enough to go for Refuge mentally and verbally. You also go for Refuge physically, literally prostrating in front of the image. It is a threefold practice which involves the whole being.

Not only is it an action; it is a shared action, because we repeat the verses of Refuge together, in unison. In traditional Buddhist countries, the *bhikkhu*, or monk, recites first and the others recite after him. What emerges is almost a dialogue; an almost dramatic element is introduced. This emphasizes the fact that we are not just doing something in the same way as other individuals who happen to be there. We do it *with* them, with heart and mind and body.

Next, the Going for Refuge expresses a common striving, which is that we aspire to realize the common goal of Nirvāṇa or Enlightenment. We all want to become like the Buddha. We all want to follow the path of the Dharma. We all want to help, and to receive help from, other members of the Sangha.

Finally, our strivings are rooted in common values, the values which permeate the whole body of the Buddha's teaching. The Going for Refuge is not something isolated in itself. It grows out of the whole teaching and tradition. If one were to expound the meaning of the Three Jewels to which we go for Refuge in full detail, such an exposition would incorporate the whole of Buddhism.

So Fromm's definition of ritual is readily applicable to the fundamental Buddhist practice of Going for Refuge, and it helps to give us some understanding of the psychology of ritual and some appreciation of its value. But the real way to appreciate the value of ritual is to practise it. Some people, as I have indicated, do find this difficult at first.

When I was in Kalimpong, an Englishman came to stay with me who was like this. He had come to me to study Buddhism, and he was very interested in Buddhist philosophy, but he had been brought up as a Protestant and was strongly against ritual. He would say to me, 'I like Buddhism, I love the philosophy, I like the *sūtras* and all the rest of it, but I just can't stand all this bowing and scraping to the shrine.' I would put the Buddhist view on ritual to him and we had several discussions and arguments about it, but whenever I mentioned actually doing a ritual he would go very quiet. He would join in our morning and evening meditations, but he would not take part in the accompanying pujas. He wouldn't even put his hands together. Nonetheless, he was evidently thinking it over, and one day he came dashing into my room and said, 'Bhante, I've done it!' So I asked, 'What do you mean? What have you done?' He said, 'Believe it or not, I went into the shrine-room just now and I bowed down.' I replied, 'Well, that's very good. How do you feel?' And he said, 'I feel quite different. I wouldn't have thought it would make such a difference as that, but I feel quite different for having done it.'

3

ORIGINS OF THE SEVENFOLD PUJA

Speaking very broadly, we could say that the essence of puja is thinking about the Buddha, occupying one's mind with the thought of the Buddha. This thought is not just cold and intellectual, but embraces the heartfelt ideal of Buddhahood. The Buddha is very vividly present in front of us, either in the form of a *rūpa*, or Buddha image, or else visualized, imagined. All the devotional exercises, such as the offerings which take place within the puja, are forms of thinking about the Buddha. Through them, we open ourselves to the ideal of Buddhahood, become more sensitive to it, and are inspired by it. And this paves the way for our eventually breaking through into that higher spiritual dimension that we refer to as the *bodhicitta*.[100]

The Sevenfold Puja is a sequence of seven different devotional moods or aspirations, each of which is evoked by a few verses of traditional text. The verses in the particular version of the Sevenfold Puja used within the FWBO come from a much longer set of over a thousand verses called the *Bodhicaryāvatāra*, the 'Entry into the Path of Enlightenment'.[101] This is a highly poetic and devotional work giving guidance on the attitudes and ways of life that a bodhisattva should adopt. It was written by the great Buddhist master Śāntideva, who lived in India in the eighth century CE. Śāntideva was remarkable in many ways: as a great thinker and metaphysician; as an ardent devotee of the Three Jewels, strong in faith and veneration; and as an outstanding poet. His extraordinary range of qualities make the *Bodhicaryāvatāra* a singularly inspiring and important work.

The tradition of the Sevenfold Puja has its origins in what I believe to be the highest ideal known to humankind: the bodhisattva ideal. I have explained the origin of this sevenfold form of devotional practice in chapter 4 of *A Survey of Buddhism*, as follows:

Strictly speaking, the path of the bodhisattva consists primarily in the practice of the six (or ten) perfections (*pāramitās*), the successful accomplishment of which carries him through ten successive stages (*bhūmis*) of spiritual attainment. So great, however, is the discrepancy between our ability to understand a spiritual teaching and our power to practise it, that most of those who give theoretical assent to the superiority of the Secret Path are unprepared for the practice even of the first *pāramitā*. Between the life of worldly or of 'spiritual' individualism, on the one hand, and the transcendental path of the bodhisattva on the other, the Mahāyāna therefore interpolates a number of observances, the purpose of which is to prepare the mind of the bodhisattva – or rather, of the bodhisattva-to-be – for the practice of the six or ten perfections. Taking the bodhisattva path in its very widest sense, we find that, including these observances, it can be divided into three great stages.... (1) The preliminary devotional practices known collectively as *anuttara-pūjā* or supreme worship; (2) the arising of the Thought of Enlightenment (*bodhicittotpāda*), the making of a great vow (*pranidhāna*), and the receiving of an assurance of Enlightenment (*vyākarana*) from a living Buddha; (3) the four *caryās* or courses of conduct, the third and most important of which is the practice of the perfections (*pāramitā-caryā*)....

By supreme worship is meant not only the adoption of a reverential attitude of mind, but the celebration by the aspirant to bodhisattvahood of a sort of daily office. Our chief literary source for the details of this practice is the second chapter of Śāntideva's sublime canticle the *Bodhicaryāvatāra*, a work of the eighth century. The practice itself, however, was an ancient one. In fact, like many other observances, it was part of the enormous body of doctrines and methods which the Mahāyāna had inherited from the Hīnayāna and assimilated to its own tradition. Flowers, lights, and incense had been offered to the Buddha even during his lifetime; sins had been confessed to him; Brahmā Sahāmpati had implored him to turn the wheel of the Dharma. On the basis of occurrences of this kind the Hīnayāna framed a simple daily office which is still recited, in its Pāli form, by both monks and laymen in Theravādin lands. Some of the formulas used are as old as Buddhism itself. The use of the term *anuttara*, unsurpassed or supreme, for the Mahāyāna office, was perhaps intended to suggest a comparison with its more rudimentary Hīnayāna original. As described by Śāntideva, supreme worship comprises: (1) obeisance (*vandanā*) and worship (*pūjā*); (2) Going for Refuge (*śaraṇa-gamana*); (3) confession of sins (*pāpadeśanā*); (4) rejoicing in merit (*puṇyānumodana*); (5) prayer (*adhyeṣā*) and supplication (*yācanā*); and (6) transference of merits (*pariṇāmanā*) and self-surrender (*atmabhāvādi-parityāga*).[102]

The Sevenfold Puja is thus essentially a sort of lead-up to the arising of the *bodhicitta* incorporating all the main Buddhist observances in a progressive sequence. In the quotation above I spoke of a sixfold puja, the *pūjā* and *vandanā* sections sometimes being joined together as one. I have since thought it better to bring out the significant difference between them by separating them. Also, we now use slightly different translations of some of the terms.

I should explain how we come to have the verses in the particular form that we use. In the early 1960s I wanted to make a version of the Sevenfold Puja that I had described in *A Survey of Buddhism* – just a very short, simple Sevenfold Puja to introduce at the Hampstead Buddhist Vihara. Knowing that the *Bodhicaryāvatāra* was used for this purpose in Tibet, I considered the available translations. There was then only one (incomplete) English translation of it in print, by L. D. Barnett. I was aware, however, that another English translation had been made some years later but never printed in full. It was made by a friend of mine in London, Adrienne Bennett, with whom I was in correspondence while I was in India. Using Adrienne Bennett's version, I took the framework of the Sevenfold Puja, then extracted from chapters 2 and 3 of the *Bodhicaryāvatāra* a few verses under each of the seven headings (the *pūjā*, the *vandanā*, and so on), and in this way arrived at our present version, which has since been published in *The FWBO Puja Book*.[103]

In chapters 5 to 12, I shall give the relevant verses in both Adrienne Bennett's translation and Marion L. Matics' 1971 translation,[104] to facilitate a clear understanding of each verse. Adrienne Bennett's translation certainly conveys the spirit of Śāntideva much better, and is far more poetic and rhythmical. In some cases Matics' translation makes the literal meaning a little clearer but when it comes to reading aloud, it does not flow nearly so well. In recent years, further translations of the *Bodhicaryāvatāra* have been made, notably that by Stephen Batchelor from the Tibetan,[105] which is quite widely used.

It is quite possible to compile a different Sevenfold Puja by selecting appropriate verses from other traditional texts. I have myself arranged verses from the *Sūtra of Golden Light* under the same seven headings, for use on special occasions. This compilation includes a very ample set of verses on confession – a major theme of the *sūtra* – so it can be used when one wishes to stress that particular practice.[106]

The origins of the puja we use – who wrote it, who translated it, how, when, and why it was compiled, and so on – are of historical interest. But it is important to remember that these historical origins are not of any liturgical relevance. When we take part in the puja we should regard it as primordial, something that has always been like that, rather than something associated with particular names and dates. Ideally we should relate to the puja as a timeless process which is going on throughout the universe, practised by countless beings.

4

HOW TO APPROACH THE
SEVENFOLD PUJA

We saw in the last chapter that this form of puja originated as a specific practice to help give rise to the *bodhicitta*, the will to Enlightenment, and this is clearly the way to look at it if we have got as far in our spiritual lives as to be thinking about the *bodhicitta*. The puja is centred on the Buddha who embodies Enlightenment. If you have a very strong feeling for Enlightenment, or the embodiment of Enlightenment, this suggests that ultimately you would like to be like the Buddha yourself. And if you have a very strong urge to be like that, this urge will in time become tantamount to the arising of the *bodhicitta*. The puja can function as an aid to this process. To put it in slightly different terms, the puja can aid the gradual process whereby one eventually commits oneself wholeheartedly to the Buddha, Dharma, and Sangha – or, as we say, one goes for Refuge.

If you have not reached this stage yet, you may see the puja just as a practice that is more colourful, more emotionally engaging, than, say, doctrinal study. For you it may be a practice that helps you to restore your enthusiasm for Buddhism when you have become a bit dull or dry. This too is quite valid – to use puja as a sort of emotional sweetener.

People have sometimes asked me why we should bother with puja at all. Why not just stick with the other practices that Buddhism has to offer? I have already suggested some of the reasons, but my immediate personal response to such a question is, well, I like puja. I love the flowers, the lighted candles, and the chanting. I think it is wonderful. I don't think it will take me all the way to Enlightenment, but it is something helpful along the way which I really enjoy and I would rather not do without it.

So perhaps this is the first thing to say about how to approach the puja: just enjoy it. Enjoy the colour, the poetry, the fragrance of the incense. Don't do it out of a sense of obligation, as though there were some rule that said you have to attend the puja whether you like it or not. Those who do not take to it can opt out of it. On the other hand, one can take the attitude that as other people seem to be enjoying it, it might be worth attending a few times to see what happens – but in a spirit of interest and experimentation, not one of duty.

If you have a developing interest in Buddhism but you are not drawn to puja, even having tried it a number of times, this is not something to be worried about. You can practise meditation or engage in study. We are not all attracted to the same forms of practice. This is why within the FWBO we don't prescribe just one particular spiritual practice – just mantra chanting or just meditation – as some Buddhist schools do. We make available a whole range of Buddhist activities, anything that will help at least some people to grow and develop. It is important, especially in the early stages of following the Buddhist path, to latch on to whichever form of practice seems most inspiring and helpful to you. Other aspects will develop later.

Having said that, if you have decided to make puja a part of your spiritual practice, it is important to take part in it regularly. It may be tempting to skip doing pujas at times when you are not feeling very bright or inspired, but you could adopt just the opposite attitude. If you really feel like doing the puja, it probably doesn't matter too much if you happen to miss it. But if you don't feel like doing it, it can be really beneficial to do it anyway. And sometimes when you don't feel in the mood and may think you are just going through the motions, you may be surprised to find you end up having a very positive experience. Regular practice is important, as long as it comes out of your own sense of commitment, not because you feel some sort of pressure from others.

For most people the Sevenfold Puja does take some getting used to. It is a bit like eating wholesome food, or changing to tea without sugar. When your palate has become vitiated by spicy, salty, or sugary flavours, wholesome food can seem bland and uninviting until you get used to it; but then food becomes much more satisfying. Likewise, once you have made the transition to a regular practice of the puja, it is a source of delight.

The puja is very much rooted in Indian tradition and it can take quite a long time to get a feel for the language and the cultural references. We may well need to find out something of the traditional background. Some years ago someone did try to get round this need by composing an English equivalent to the traditional verses, bringing in roses and daffodils and making it poetic in the English way, but, perhaps surprisingly, people felt quite uncomfortable with it, and it didn't really come off – though I am not suggesting that it could never be done. In any case, once we have overcome the initial unfamiliarity, there is a value in feeling connected with Buddhist tradition through the puja.

Some people have difficulty with the poetry of the puja because they take the words too literally. They forget that it is poetry, and Indian poetry to boot; the Indians do go in for very flowery language. I have known people who objected strongly to the words 'I offer them lamps encrusted with jewels' because the lamps on their shrine did not happen to have any jewels on them. They considered that referring to jewelled lamps in these circumstances was a breach of the precept against false speech and they were therefore quite unable to recite the words. They could not understand that it was an imaginative offering, an offering in spirit. We must try to get in touch with the spirit of the words and not take it all too literally. Of course, to say that the language is poetical does not mean that the puja is some kind of fantasy. It is no fantasy, but a poetical invocation of real spiritual forces.

Even without taking the words literally, the lavishness and exuberance of some of the language in the puja can be hard to take for those who prefer more of a Zen approach. Both the austere approach and the lavish approach to spiritual beauty have their merits and we can learn to appreciate them both. But English people particularly tend to shy away from exuberance; maybe this is just something we have to get over. A middle path is probably needed. One can aim to give the shrine-room a rich but simple beauty, with extra decorations on festival days. The verses of the puja contain some quite lavish turns of phrase, but we recite them in a straightforward way, which also adds an element of simplicity.

During the Sevenfold Puja we refer to spiritual beings, the Buddhas and bodhisattvas. How we should understand these references can be another cause of difficulty. Do we view such beings as having an objective existence or not? Up to a certain point it needn't matter too much. We can view the Buddha as representing our own innate potential, if we wish, and view the protectors as aspects of our own better self and so on – that is quite valid. But even when thinking in this way, we cannot exclude the objective altogether. Suppose we were to actualize our potential. What would happen? We would then be Buddhas, objectively. In which case it is reasonable to suppose that others have actualized their potential before us and become Buddhas – objectively existing Buddhas who can help us spiritually. But it is important to be clear that they are not helpers in the mundane sense. There is no value in praying to them for wealth and riches. That has no place in the puja. The Buddhas and bodhisattvas can help us only if we open ourselves to their influence. So there is a subjective and an objective aspect to the puja. If it were all subjective – just comforting feelings and well-meaning thoughts in our own minds – without anything really objective, without Buddhas – it would not get us very far.

Ideally, the carrying out of the Sevenfold Puja should recapitulate, in a very concentrated, intense form, attitudes and moods which we are trying to cultivate all the time. This overall purpose should become clearer as we study these attitudes and moods one by one in subsequent chapters. It means that we should not leave our worship, salutation, Going for Refuge, and so on until we get round to reciting them in the Sevenfold Puja. We should be working on them all the time so that when we come together with other members of the spiritual community to recite the puja, we are simply experiencing them in a more intense form and in unison. The puja is a statement and enactment of what we are concerned with, devoted to, committed to, all the time. We are trying to direct all our energies, all our activities, towards Enlightenment, and the puja is a sort of microcosm of that, with the Buddha image representing the ideal that we are seeking to realize and towards which all our energies are directed. For people coming along to a puja who do not normally try to direct their thoughts and feelings in this way, obviously the Sevenfold Puja will not and cannot mean so much.

In making this kind of effort to direct our thoughts and feelings, we are giving ourselves to the Buddha. So the puja is essentially an act of giving, not of receiving – or at least we only receive from it to the extent that we are able to give ourselves to it. It is primarily an action and only incidentally an experience. To go along expecting a great emotional experience from the puja without being committed to the ideal of Enlightenment is to miss the point. We just have to offer ourselves. If there is feedback in the form of some emotional experience, so much the better, but we should not see that as the purpose of the puja. If it does not come – if our experience of the puja is even quite dry – that is still all right. It is enough that we go into the shrine-room and express our devotion and reverence to the Buddha.

During the puja our orientation should always be towards the Buddha. If we are sincere and receptive, we know that it is all for the sake of the Buddha, even if that awareness is as yet only germinal. If we should feel that our appreciation of the puja may be merely aesthetic, if we seem to be in danger of enjoying it as no more than a rather pleasant and colourful event, the answer is simply to think more about the Buddha.

The Sevenfold Puja is the act not of a single person or of a group of people, but of the spiritual community. Now you might think that a spiritual community is necessarily a kind of group – and indeed, grammatically, it has to be treated as such. But in fact it is not any kind of collectivity at all. It is a number of individuals whose complete individuality is in no way diluted or compromised by their acting in harmony with one another, by their being in sympathy with one another, and – in the context of the puja – by their speaking in unison with one another. So when the spiritual community refers to itself, neither of the terms 'we' or 'I' answers adequately to the purpose. In the Sevenfold Puja within the FWBO we use the singular throughout, as Śāntideva does. As a balance to this, however, in another puja which is much used in the FWBO, the 'Short Puja',[107] we employ the first person plural.

It is not that the puja cannot ever be done on one's own. Indeed you have got to feel devotion as an individual before you can really meaningfully join in with others. You can even practise 'mental puja', going through the puja silently as a form of meditation, visualizing the Buddha, the offerings, and so on. This is regarded as a higher level of practice which is possible only for those who have the necessary power of concentration and experience. Certain yogis and lamas have an absolute minimum of shrine equipment – perhaps just a picture hanging on the wall – because they create everything else mentally. In fact if you do the puja mentally it is possible to do it all on a much grander scale. You can visualize a thousand lamps and imagine yourself offering the whole universe, which you can hardly do concretely, however devoted you may be. Indeed, you can be completely carried away by devotional feeling in a way that is hardly possible when your sense consciousness is involved.

But mental puja is only possible for someone with a lot of experience of vocally and physically performed puja – and this primarily means 'communal' puja. Individual puja performed vocally and physically is a very different experience from doing it together with others. It is still of value, but it cannot be so full and rich an experience. For those who do sometimes perform the puja alone, it may be helpful at least to imagine the presence of the whole spiritual community, to feel a sense of connectedness with others who are Going for Refuge.

Given that the puja is essentially an expression of the devotion of the whole community, it is almost part of the definition of puja that everybody present on a particular occasion should join in. If there are new people present who do not want to join in, then of course they need not do so, but those who consider themselves Buddhists definitely should take part; otherwise a division within the spiritual community is created between those who are participating and those who are not.

It is quite reasonable to think of the puja as a devotional exercise, a means of strengthening our devotional 'muscles', a means of furthering our own spiritual development, but this is a slightly limited way of looking at it. There is a much greater dimension to the practice of performing the puja together, as a spiritual community. In some of the Mahāyāna *sūtras* there are vivid accounts of the bodhisattvas all assembled around the Buddha and praising him with all sorts of beautiful hymns. Some bodhisattvas even take a vow, we are told, that they will worship all the Buddhas in the universe.[108] They spend millions of years, as it were, going from one part of the universe to another, worshipping all the Buddhas that exist. This is a typically Mahāyāna way of stressing the importance of devotion and worship, even for the most advanced bodhisattvas. And we can regard the Sevenfold Puja as a reflection of that kind of bodhisattva activity on a much lower level. Just as on the level of the *sambhogakāya* (i.e. reality as perceived by bodhisattvas on an archetypal or celestial level) there is the archetypal

Buddha surrounded by all the great bodhisattvas who are singing his praises, so in our own imperfect world there is the Buddha image surrounded by a much more lowly sangha, also praising the Buddha to the best of its abilities. The puja we perform at our Buddhist centre or during our retreat is a reflection of that cosmic puja that is eternally in progress. It is, if you like, a *nirmāṇakāya* puja, i.e. reality perceived and worshipped from a mundane level.

Incidentally, we may, if we wish, bring this larger perspective on our practice of the puja to greater prominence by placing symbols of the *trikāya*, the three 'bodies' of the Buddha, on the shrine. The traditional symbol for the *dharmakāya* is either a crystal sphere (like a divinatory 'crystal ball') or a model of a stupa; for the *sambhogakāya* it is a volume of scripture; and for the *nirmāṇakāya*, a small Buddha image.

The verses of the puja are recited in call and response, which means that somebody present leads the puja. The person who does this should be whoever has the greatest depth of experience in the spiritual life. The leader shows the way, in a sense, and therefore the person who takes this role should be the one whose Going for Refuge is the most effective. This gives greater depth to the proceedings. When the leader says 'To the Buddha for Refuge I go', this statement will mean something different from what it means when the less experienced of those present say it. But they can be conscious of the leader Going for Refuge in a deeper sense than they are yet able to do, and may aspire to go for Refuge in that deeper way. The point is that if you lead a puja, you don't 'officiate', you don't 'guide', you don't stand to one side and lead people through their devotions. Nor are you 'the leader' in any fixed sense. You are simply doing the puja yourself, and others are simply following your lead.

Since the aim is to experience fully the distinctive spiritual mood of each section, we should be careful not to go through it too quickly. That is one reason why a bell or gong is struck at the end of each section. As well as marking the transition from one section to another, it also creates something of a pause.

All times of day are good for pujas. A puja is a good way of closing the day as long as you are not too tired to engage with it – and it is probably fair to say that if you're not too tired to engage with a late-night party, you shouldn't be too tired to engage with a puja. The morning, say after breakfast, is an excellent time for a puja. It will tend to be more vigorous than a late evening puja, just because you are more rested and fresh. Another good time is just as it gets dark, especially if you are in the country. In the city, of course, this may be the rush hour, so it may be too noisy. If you are a 'night person', or at least are not too tired and sleepy, a midnight puja or even a very early morning puja, just before dawn, can be wonderful. There is a very good atmosphere for a puja at around midnight and, say, between three and four o'clock. It is quite a different experience then, as long as you are awake enough and rested enough to be able to appreciate it.

The puja naturally leads into a meditative mood. One can meditate either before or after a puja; both have their merits. Puja is a good preparation for meditation because it gets your energy moving in the right direction, as it were. It enables you to let go of wandering thoughts, to be more integrated and ready to settle down into the meditation. Also, if you have the puja first, everyone can sit on to meditate for as long as they like. On the other hand, some people prefer to do the meditation first because then they will be more fully present for the puja.

Sound – both chanting and the accompanying music, if there is any – is a very important aspect of the Sevenfold Puja. In the next chapter we shall look in some detail at the role the senses play in the puja. Suffice it to say for now that whatever kind of chanting or music is used, it should be uplifting and should convey as far as possible a sense of supramundane beauty. There are certain kinds of music that just would not be suitable for use in the context of a puja, and even certain styles of chanting that would be quite inappropriate. We must be aware of the way in which we are chanting, being careful to avoid a forced or harsh tone. People sometimes chant in a harsh, forced way not because they do not have very good voices but simply because they are not in a positive frame of mind.

Some people with musical talents may want to make personal 'musical offerings' during the puja. However, it is difficult to do this in a way that fits well with the overall spirit of the puja. This is partly because the piece of music has usually been composed for some other reason and partly because, even though it may be intended as an offering, it is difficult to avoid the element of performance being introduced. These considerations apply regardless of the quality of the music or the feeling imparted by it.

There are of course appropriate religious uses of music. In a Christian context, in churches and cathedrals, the traditional music does not seem to detract from the overall effect intended, because it is meant for that purpose and because it is very rarely an individual performance. Even if only one person is performing, the performer is anonymous, so there is no element of theatricality. However, in a smaller gathering such as is usual in a Western Buddhist context at the present time, where everybody knows exactly who is playing or singing, it can become a bit of a performance by that person. This goes against the mood because the puja, by its very nature, is the act of the spiritual community as a whole.

A further difficulty is that in the West the musical offering is not likely to be truly oriented to the Buddha, as it might be in India. A musical rendering during a Hindu temple service is not meant for the audience. It is meant for the god and it is played in front of him, for him to 'hear'. The congregation only *over*hears it. However, since that is not the Western tradition, a Westerner probably cannot genuinely feel that he is performing for the Buddha, ignoring everybody else. He is most likely to feel that he is doing it for the other people present. Thus while the rest of the puja is oriented from the assembled company to the Buddha, the performance in the middle is oriented in the opposite direction, from the performer to the audience, which strikes rather a jarring note.

Admittedly the Tibetans have successfully incorporated music into their pujas, but it is a quite different kind of music from that normally heard in the West. Tibetan musical accompaniment to the puja has a primordial, archetypal power to it which we in the West are hardly likely to be able to develop in the foreseeable future. Russian Orthodox and some early Catholic church music have something of that archetypal power, but it would be no good ending up with anything like Protestant hymns or nineteenth-century choral works. The Christian liturgy was originally something that went on, as it were, on its own account; ideally it was a reflection of a heavenly liturgy being conducted by the angels and archangels. It didn't require either an audience or audience participation. But gradually the Christian churches – including even the Roman Catholic Church – have become secularized. We Buddhists have to be careful not to go the same way. Just because the music of, say, Bach is very refined and profound and stirring doesn't mean that it is necessarily appropriate in a strictly devotional context.

Basically, it is a matter of distinguishing between the sort of personal emotional experience we have when we go to the opera, say, and the essentially sober, dry-eyed, and not impersonal but supra-personal emotions associated with devotion proper. Perhaps devotional feeling can only develop when surface emotions have subsided. You may even have to go through a period when you don't experience anything very much at all in the puja but just do it anyway.

If we use music at all in the puja we should think only in terms of a little discreet musical accompaniment to the chanting – an occasional thump on a drum or a sounding of cymbals. We need, particularly in the case of music, to be on our guard against trying to get out of the puja some kind of emotional experience that it is not designed to give. No doubt there is something very thrilling about a traditional Tibetan puja but we have to remember that it has been developed over several hundred years. There is little point for us in trying to reproduce what for the Tibetans is authentic but to us must necessarily be a lot of exotic effects. Better a dull puja that is authentic in the sense of expressing a genuine offering of ourselves to the Three Jewels than a jazzed-up puja in which we offer 'spiritual entertainment' *to* ourselves. No doubt in time we will develop all sorts of different pujas in association with specific Buddhas and bodhisattvas. But any experimentation, musical or otherwise, should be an expression of devotion rather than boredom. In a way, there's no room for experimentation at all. There's just doing it better. That said, a more substantial musical item might fit in very well in the course of a festival, either before or after the puja.

Another notable aspect of traditional Tibetan puja is its length. The Sevenfold Puja is really just a basic framework, and it is certainly a good idea to hold really big pujas from time to time. But you will notice, if you do ever attend a traditional Tibetan puja, that it is broken up not only with all sorts of mantras and readings and verses and banging of drums and ringing of bells, but also with *light refreshments*. Tea is served every forty-five minutes – it's all part of the puja. In this spirit, if a really long puja is organized in a Western context, the organizer needs to be realistic about just how long everyone can keep going with any real enthusiasm.

On the other hand, even with a twenty-minute puja (with just the usual short reading after the sixth section), it is all too easy for the attention to wander – unless you are practising it with quite a small group. It is, that is to say, easy to forget that the puja is something *you* are doing, that however many people are present, you are not just part of a crowd.

As we have seen, when reciting and chanting the puja, we should primarily be entering into the spiritual mood, the spiritual emotion, represented by each section. When we take part in the puja, it works very much on an emotional and devotional level, rather than an intellectual one. But it is important at other times for us to study the text of the puja so that we can increase our understanding of what lies behind it and reflect on how we can bring the motivations expressed in the puja into play in our daily lives. The text is eminently worthy of study; indeed, study of the whole *Bodhicaryāvatāra* will help to enrich our understanding and experience of the puja. In the following chapters I shall be focusing on each of the seven sections of the puja in turn, looking both at the verses from the *Bodhicaryāvatāra* we recite and at Matics' translation of them. We will begin, as the Sevenfold Puja begins, with worship.

5
WORSHIP

With mandārava, blue lotus, and jasmine,
With all flowers pleasing and fragrant,
And with garlands skilfully woven,
I pay honour to the princes of the Sages,
So worthy of veneration.

I envelop them in clouds of incense,
Sweet and penetrating;
I make them offerings of food, hard and soft,
And pleasing kinds of liquids to drink.

I offer them lamps, encrusted with jewels,
Festooned with golden lotus.
On the paving, sprinkled with perfume,
I scatter handfuls of beautiful flowers.

(Bennett)

With the blossoms of the coral tree, the blue lotus, jasmine, and
the like; with all perfumed and delightful flowers, I praise the
most praiseworthy best of sages with beautifully formed garlands.
I envelop them with clouds of incense, delighting the mind with
dense, expanding aromas; and I offer to them an offering of

various moist and dry foods and libations. I offer them jewel
lamps placed in rows on golden lotuses; and on mosaic pavements
anointed with perfume I scatter many pleasing flowers.

(Matics)[109]

The most obvious and perhaps the most important impression we get from these opening verses is one of beauty – spiritual beauty. Even if we knew nothing at all about the Dharma or about the Sevenfold Puja, just hearing these verses in an open-minded, receptive way would convey that particular kind of beauty to us. Mundane, sensuous things are mentioned – flowers, lamps, and jewels – but the overall impression is surely one of spiritual, rather than worldly, beauty. And if that higher beauty is the object, the corresponding subjective feeling, the natural response to it, is one of faith and devotion.

We set the scene by evoking this sense of refined sensuous beauty. And what we set the scene for is faith and devotion. The words of the puja and everything connected with it should convey that sort of mood, that sort of emotion, that sort of atmosphere. The shrine-room where the puja takes place should always be kept looking beautiful, down to the last detail. Throughout the Buddhist world, great importance is attached to the shrine and the shrine-room: it must be clean, light, bright, and beautiful. The focal point of the shrine, the Buddha image or *rūpa*, greatly affects the overall impression. It is important to choose an image that does not merely remind us of the Buddha – because after all we know it is the Buddha – but which actually conveys something of the Buddha nature, of Enlightenment, by its sheer aesthetic presence. A Buddha image is not just a means of sparking off some mechanical devotional reflex. It must be a work of art, an object of refined spiritual beauty – and all the accessories likewise. For example, we must be sensitive to the colour of the cloth we are using on the shrine. In Buddhist countries they tend to use a lot of yellow and red in association with anything religious or spiritual, but there is no rule about colour as long as the overall effect is one of spiritual beauty.

Incidentally, the table or pedestal upon which the Buddha image is placed should not really be referred to as a shrine. A shrine is simply a place where a sacred image, or in some cases a sacred relic, is kept. Nor should the raised focal point of a Buddhist shrine be called an altar. An altar, strictly speaking, is a place or a table where sacrifice takes place. Originally an animal, or in some early societies even a human being, would be slaughtered, and in later times fruits and flowers would be burned in offering. The focal point of a church is quite properly said to be an altar because Christ is regarded as a sacrifice, an innocent victim being offered up to God as an atonement for the sins of humanity. But in Buddhism there is no such sacrifice. The object of devotion, the Buddha image, is placed on a table or a stand purely for convenience. It is not an altar but merely an image table. If you prepare, or help to prepare, the shrine yourself this will help to put you in a proper devotional mood for the puja. And if you are involved in shrine preparation, it is good to spend as long as possible doing it. You can make it a real labour of love.

And just as the beauty and cleanliness of the shrine create the right physical setting for the puja, the words of this first section of the puja also set the scene by conveying an impression of spiritual beauty. In the presence of such beauty we readily feel uplifted, devotional. The opening verses strike a note of spiritual delight awakened by the experience of beauty and we enter a calm, happy, delighted state. It is not devotion in the strong, ardent sense – which perhaps comes later. The keynote of the first stage, when entering the shrine, seeing the image, the flowers, and the lamps, is just to think 'How beautiful!' and to feel uplifted.

As well as responding to the beauty of the shrine, we also respond to the atmosphere created by those present, so we must not leave ourselves out of the picture; we too are part of the decorations, as it were. And it is not only a question of our disposition or attitude. Turning up for a puja in a beautifully kept shrine-room looking dirty and scruffy does not add to the devotional atmosphere of the occasion. In the matter of dress, at least, *bhikkhus* automatically look decorative because they are in beautiful coloured robes. Usually on Buddhist occasions in South-east Asia there are *bhikkhus* in their yellows, oranges, and saffrons, laymen more often than not in white, and lay women in all sorts of brightly coloured saris. The overall effect is very colourful and enlivening. I would encourage people in the West also to take some care over their appearance for pujas. Perhaps one could keep aside a particular outfit, dress, or robe for pujas, especially for pujas on festive occasions.

How we sit is also important. It is best from an aesthetic point of view if those who are participating in a puja sit in regular parallel rows, not just wherever they happen to find themselves. When we come together for the puja, we are more than a random collection of people. We are not just an audience. We are in fact part of the Three Jewels, at least symbolically. Just as the Buddha image made out of wood or stone or metal symbolizes the Buddha jewel, Enlightenment itself, and just as beautifully bound Buddhist texts placed on the shrine symbolize the Dharma jewel, so we, sitting there in flesh and blood, symbolize the Sangha jewel, the Āryasaṅgha. Even if we are not ourselves *āryas*, even if we have not ourselves attained to the noble company of those moving inexorably towards Enlightenment, we should still seek to symbolize this Āryasaṅgha in the context of the puja.

Let us now consider the verses individually.

With mandārava, blue lotus, and jasmine.

For some reason Matics has rendered '*mandārava*' as 'blossoms of the coral tree'. The *mandārava* is a flower which occurs in various *sūtras* and it is usually explained as a heavenly flower, one that does not grow on Earth. It is enormous, as big as a cart wheel, and bright golden in colour – a sort of celestial marigold of gigantic size that comes floating down from the heavens when the Buddha happens to give a particularly good discourse. So by saying '*mandārava*' right at the beginning of the puja, you immediately create a sort of archetypal atmosphere. You are offering not just earthly flowers, but heavenly flowers. You also offer blue lotus and jasmine, both of which have a special kind of fragrance.

With all flowers pleasing and fragrant,
And with garlands skilfully woven,
I pay honour to the princes of the Sages,
So worthy of veneration.

Flowers are the most characteristic Buddhist offering of all, mainly because they are so beautiful, pleasing, as Śāntideva says, to both the eye and the sense of smell. Flowers common in India, such as the lotus, jasmine, and tuberose, are spectacularly beautiful and have very sweet scents. A quite extraordinary atmosphere of beauty and purity can be created by massed flower offerings.

Śāntideva also mentions garlands, which the Indians are very fond of offering to distinguished visitors and guests. Hindus also place garlands around the necks of images, though Buddhists do not usually do this with Buddha images. The words 'skilfully woven' (or even 'beautifully formed' as Matics has it) convey care and devotion. Someone has given a lot of time and attention to stringing these garlands.

Offering flowers and garlands of one kind or another is, however, just the beginning. Śāntideva mentions many other things to be offered: fruits, herbs, jewels, waters, mountains of jewels, forest-places, vines, trees, fragrant incenses, wish-fulfilling trees, trees of jewels, lakes adorned with lotuses, the endlessly fascinating cry of wild geese, harvests, crops of grain. He offers all these things and then he prepares a bath for the Buddhas and their sons. He offers songs, water-jars encrusted with jewels and filled with flowers, fragrant waters, garments, and ornaments. It is all rather lavish. When I was composing the FWBO's Sevenfold Puja, I trimmed it down so as not to overwhelm the Western Buddhist with too many offerings. The verses I selected mention just flowers, incense, lamps, food, drink, and perfume. Flowers, incense, and lamps are the three main offerings from the earliest days which occur in all forms of Buddhism. All the others seem to have been added later on.

> I envelop them in clouds of incense,
> Sweet and penetrating.

Or according to Matics:

> I envelop them with clouds of incense, delighting the mind with
> dense, expanding aromas.

Incense, which is described here variously as 'delighting the mind' and as 'sweet and penetrating', is very widely used in puja, with the obvious purpose of involving one of our most influential senses to a calming and uplifting effect. We breathe in something beautiful which affects the mind through the senses. But how exactly does it work? The sense of smell is a rather strange thing. If, for instance, we are surrounded by unpleasant, even disgusting smells, that puts us into a mood of withdrawal. We want to get away from them, and if we cannot do so we may become angry. This may have biological roots, based on the need to keep people away from things that would have a bad effect on them. Most bad smells have got some connection with decay or death, with something rotten that would not be good to eat.

On the other hand, a delightful, pleasant, fragrant smell tends to put us into a mental state characterized by welcoming, openness, happiness, satisfaction, and joy. It is as if the fragrant smell is the olfactory equivalent of what we call beauty when referring to visual objects, though the sense of sight is more subtle than the sense of smell, which is relatively gross. Less conscious than sight, more direct, more bodily, more sensuous, it can produce an almost hormonal reaction. So when the sense of smell is aroused, it is as though the body as well as the mind is participating in the puja, thus helping to close one of the main routes by which we are distracted.

It is noticeable that if you burn a lot of incense it seems to set up a sort of vibration in the atmosphere after a while. Traditionally, in the East, incense-like fragrances are associated with the presence of the gods or *devas*. A Burmese friend I stayed with for six months in Kalimpong (he would probably have been the king of Burma had Burma still been a monarchy and not a republic) took this idea quite literally. When I knew him he was about 60 or so. He and his wife had a bungalow and I stayed in a second, smaller guest bungalow a little lower down the hill than theirs. They were great believers in the *devas* and he told me that his wife could see them. He could not see them himself, but whenever they appeared there was a distinctly perceptible fragrance, as avowed by traditional lore. He believed that the *devas* were particularly connected with the Burmese royal family and were at their service, as it were. According to him, they used to supply him and the Princess with money. The Princess used to do her puja and in the morning, when they lifted up the Buddha image, they would find banknotes underneath. (Their friends had rather more mundane explanations for this.)[110]

My Burmese friend was very keen indeed that I should have some experience of the *devas*, which his wife told him were tiny in appearance and very bright, almost like fireflies. One evening he was talking about *devas* in his usual rather excitable way, and he said, 'I'll get the Princess to send one down to you.' So I sat there and he was gone for about half an hour. While he was gone the strange thing was that I perceived a very strong scent of roses. I was quite sure of this – it was a very marked scent – and I was still thinking about it when he came rushing down and said, 'Did you see the *devas*?' I replied 'No, I didn't see any *devas*, but I smelt a very strong rose-like scent.' He was delighted with this and said, 'Yes, the *devas* have visited you. That is a sure sign.'

Make of this story what you please, but one quite persuasive interpretation of this sort of experience is to take the *devas* as representing highly skilful states of mind. The medieval expression 'the odour of sanctity'[111] may mean, as some commentators have irreverently suggested, that Christian saints didn't wash; but alternatively it perhaps derives from the fact that skilful mental states tend to produce positive physical manifestations, some of which can be perceived in the form of fragrant scents. Conversely it does appear that certain fragrances, or combinations of fragrances, can help you into a meditative state. Particular incenses produce particular effects. For instance, when I was in India I used to favour Tibetan incense in the morning. It seemed very fresh and breezy, a sort of pine-like scent. In the evening I used the sweeter Indian varieties of incense. Instead of automatically burning any old joss-stick, it is worth noticing the particular effects that different kinds of incense have and using them accordingly. When you are feeling rather sluggish and dull, use an incense that has a stimulating, open-air effect – I would suggest a good rose incense. On the other hand, when feeling restless and excitable, use one that has a calming effect – but even then it should be refined, clear, and clean: a plain, inexpensive sandalwood, say, rather than a cheap benzene-based product. Through such awareness we can make the most effective use of these devotional accessories.

> I make them offerings of food, hard and soft,
> And pleasing kinds of liquids to drink.

'Hard and soft' – which may also be rendered as 'dry and moist' – is a common Indian classification of food, nothing especially Buddhistic. 'Moist' or 'soft' means rice, dhal, and curries, and 'hard' means baked things like chapattis and sweets. So it simply means food in general, all kinds of food. Offering food and drink to the Buddha image suggests you are treating it like a guest, as though it were a live human being. It is worth examining the background to this.

The puja – whether Buddhist or Hindu – has its cultural roots in the tradition of Indian hospitality, the observance of which is seen as a great virtue. Guests who turn up at someone's house, especially when they arrive unexpectedly, are supposed to be welcomed in a spirit of heartfelt generosity and attention to their needs. They have probably come on foot and their feet are dusty, so first you give them water for washing the feet. Then you give them water to drink, to quench their thirst. Next you greet them by putting beautiful garlands of flowers around their necks to refresh them with the sweet fragrance. You may light incense to keep away the mosquitoes, and you may also light a lamp if it is getting dark. Sometimes lamps are waved in front of guests as a sign of welcome. This waving of lamps, called *ārati*, occupies quite an important place in modern Hindu puja and can be seen in any Hindu temple in the evening. They have a 'tree', as it is called, of lamps which is rotated in front of the image. Indian Buddhists do not usually do this – they simply offer lights – but in either case the origin is in the lamp which is lit when guests arrive – because for poor people this is something of a luxury. After lighting, or even waving, a lamp, the Indian host may sprinkle guests with perfume, and then of course will give them something to eat. If any of the women or girls in the house are skilled at music, they will be called upon to play, to entertain the guests.

In the West we do not really have this sort of tradition, although perhaps we used to, at least in Christian monasteries. The monks were instructed that they should regard a guest as Christ himself come to take shelter among them, but nowadays a guest is someone whom you invite and who turns up at the appointed hour for a meal. Some people just do not like guests, because they get in the way, especially if they turn up uninvited. The word for 'guest' in Sanskrit is *atithi*. *Tithi* is a division of time, like the hour, so *atithi* is one who doesn't come at any particular time. So a guest is not someone you invite for an appointed hour; the *atithi* is the untimely guest, the stranger who just turns up and to whom you are bound to give hospitality simply because he is a stranger and needs food, drink, and shelter. Because life is not so leisurely, not so spacious, as it was a few centuries ago, unexpected guests are now regarded as a disruption to our tightly-organized schedule. This is very different from the Indian tradition of feeling honoured to receive an uninvited guest. In fact in ancient India, in Hinduism, they carried this so far as to say that the only justification for the household life was that you were thereby enabled to give entertainment to guests. As Western Buddhists we have to start from scratch and build up our sense of hospitality. We may, for example, have to work a bit harder at welcoming newcomers – not just to our homes, but to our Buddhist centres as well.

And it is from the Indian style of hospitality that the seven or eight traditional offerings have arisen. They may all literally be placed on the shrine: water for washing the feet, water for drinking, flowers, incense, perfume, lamps, and food. The optional eighth offering, music, may be represented on the shrine by a little pair of cymbals. More usually the seven or eight offerings are represented by seven or eight bowls of water.

The making of these offerings, which were originally made in the context of Indian social life to an honoured guest, signifies an attitude of welcoming the Buddha into the world. The Buddha is the guest, the untimely one who comes unexpectedly into the world from some other dimension – the dimension of Enlightenment. So in a way this practice involves treating the image as a living person. But as this doesn't come easily to Westerners, it is probably best to keep the offerings simple. Indeed, if we have been brought up in the Christian tradition, our only experience of making offerings at all may be in the context of a 'harvest festival', when the first fruits – bunches of grapes, apples, sheaves of corn or loaves of bread – are offered.

In some forms of Buddhism (and also in Hinduism) the image is bathed, dressed, and decorated, then fed and taken on outings – even taken to meet other images. The Hindus are particularly keen on this: they take their images to meet other gods and goddesses who then return their visits, each time processing ceremoniously through the streets. The images are put to bed at night and woken up in the morning with music. In fact Hindus almost play with their images as children play with dolls. Some Japanese Buddhists go so far as to bathe an image of the infant Buddha in warm, weak tea. While this might not strike a very devotional note for us, and might even seem rather absurd, it does help people to relate to the image directly, on a human level.

Some people draw the line at offering food and drink. In India I personally did not like such offerings because of the smells: in the midst of all the fragrant odours of flowers and incense, a spicy curry smell seemed quite out of place. This is not just cultural conditioning – it is because the grosser senses are stimulated in the wrong way, for instance causing the mouth to water, which is clearly not desirable. The Nepalese, I'm afraid, sometimes offer raw meat, which is even less appropriate. In my view nothing more gross than perfume should be brought into a puja; but for those who do want to give food, it is best to offer fruit. If, on the other hand, food and drink seem inappropriate, you can simply offer flowers, lights, and incense; or you can just think of the flowers as being the offering, the lights being there to illuminate, and the incense to create a pleasant atmosphere.

There is another Hindu tradition – also practised in some Mahāyāna Buddhist countries – of eating the food offerings afterwards, which means that the puja becomes an indirect way of producing a feast. Sometimes people say that out of devotion they want to offer the Buddha whatever they are going to eat themselves, but this can easily confuse things. People put more and more offerings in front of the image because then they get more and more afterwards in the form of what the Hindus call *prasad*. But the significance of the offerings is symbolical, and their symbolic value should not be compromised by their also having a mundane consumer value for the worshipper. Eating and devotion should be kept strictly separate. They are not traditionally associated in Buddhism, at least not in early Buddhism.

> I offer them lamps, encrusted with jewels,
> Festooned with golden lotus.

There are several reasons why we offer lamps, or light. Before electric lighting, if you had a puja in the evening, you would need lamps anyway. But more importantly light has a very profound and universal symbolical significance. Light is knowledge; light is wisdom; light is Enlightenment. Furthermore, although we may have forgotten the fact in these days of electricity, candlelight is very beautiful. Traditionally the light offered was usually either candlelight or oil-lamp light: very soft, and golden-glowing. It has its own aesthetic value, as part of the beautiful scene. So to explain the presence of light in the puja, I think we need look no further than the archetypal significance of light and its intrinsic beauty, especially in its more natural forms. Personally I don't like to see modern temples lit up with harsh electric bulbs and fluorescent lighting, sometimes even with naked bulbs around the Buddha's halo. Perhaps they are an expression of devotion, but it is devotion of a rather vulgar and garish kind with no refinement, no spiritual sensibility.

The main offerings, then, are flowers, light, and incense. The flowers can be seen as representing the whole of nature, even the whole of life in a way; and because their lives are so short, they are a gentle reminder of impermanence. The light reminds us not only of the light of the sun in the sky, but also of the 'light' of Enlightenment. And the sweet smell of incense suggests the integration into the puja of even the more gross, physical aspects of our being. With the aid of these offerings the scene of the puja represents a heightened mode of existence – almost like a miniature Pure Land. Indeed, the impression of the Pure Land you get from descriptions in the Mahāyāna *sutras* is as if a great puja were going on all the time. There is the Buddha, not just an image but the Buddha himself on a real lotus throne. Flowers are falling continuously from the sky, and garlands of flowers are being offered. People are seated all around and incense is burning. Chants are being raised and the Dharma is being preached. Life there is just one long puja, and what could be more delightful than that? So when we are engaged in puja, sitting in the shrine-room in front of the image, it should be a foretaste of the Pure Land, of Sukhāvatī itself. That is the spirit in which we should approach puja.

6
OFFERINGS

Having imagined the making of offerings during the verses of worship, we usually make physical offerings to the shrine in between the worship section and the salutation section, while a mantra is chanted in unison by everybody present. On most occasions the Avalokiteśvara mantra is chanted at this stage, but a different mantra can be used for specific occasions – for instance, the Śākyamuni mantra if the puja is to be dedicated especially to the Buddha Śākyamuni. There is a discussion of mantras in chapter 13.

If there are a lot of people at the puja, offerings may not be made at this point in the proceedings but at the end of the puja. This is simply because of the time it takes. In most shrine-rooms only two or three people can make offerings at once, so it can take a very long time with large numbers. The custom has grown in the FWBO that the person leading the puja makes his or her offering last. There is no fixed rule about this, but it does have the advantage of signalling the end of that particular stage of the proceedings.

You need not feel that you have to make an offering just because you are present at a puja. It is understood and accepted that you will make an offering if you feel like it and you need not do so otherwise. Nobody should do it for the sake of appearances. On the other hand, someone may take an individual decision to go up and make an offering even though he or she does not feel like doing so, in the hope that this ritual action will help to generate the corresponding feeling. This would not be going through the motions so much as acting out of a sense of spiritual discipline and allowing this to take precedence over one's present state of mind. In any case, there is no rule about whether one should make an offering on a particular occasion, nor about what one should offer. In the FWBO people usually offer incense, but there are many other traditional kinds of offerings that can be made as well or instead. Flowers are the most usual, after incense.

Sometimes people write down confessions of some unskilful act they have done or resolutions to change their behaviour in a particular way and offer these to the shrine, perhaps on a little paper scroll. This can be a good way to emphasize that the confession or resolution is being made not just to aid one's personal development but as a means of giving oneself to the Three Jewels. We do need to take care that our offerings are not too idiosyncratic and subjective. We may feel an urge to offer something which is of special symbolic – not to say psychotherapeutic – significance to us, but we need to consider the effect it will have on the overall atmosphere of the puja, which is an act of the spiritual community in unison. I would say that, in general, originality of offerings is quite out of place in communal pujas.

For example, someone might feel like offering some bones to the shrine, but that might be simply inappropriate. It is true that in the Vajrayāna tradition of practice there are occasions when representations of parts of the body are offered, to symbolize the dedication of the five senses to the task of attaining Enlightenment. The Tibetans like to do this in as concrete a way as possible: they have a little bowl – perhaps a skull cup – with a pair of ears, a tongue, a nose, and so on all modelled very realistically out of barley flour. If a puja is dedicated to a wrathful deity you may even have pieces of meat – real or modelled – as offerings. By contrast, in the case of a White Tārā puja or Avalokiteśvara puja, you are traditionally supposed to make predominantly white offerings. Something along these lines might be appropriate in a context where all those present had some understanding of the Vajrayāna approach and had been going into the significance of such offerings. But practices of this kind have to be taken seriously, not followed on the basis of a personal whim.

People have been known to make an offering to the shrine that was particularly meaningful to them, and then take the item away again after the puja, but this waters down the whole idea of offerings, which are a form of *dāna* or giving. The Buddhist tradition is quite unambiguous that an offering, once made, should not be taken back. Otherwise it would be like giving someone a box of chocolates and then taking it back to eat the chocolates yourself. Of course things can be *lent* to the shrine to beautify it, but that is not the same as making an offering, and you would not place the object on the shrine during the offerings section of the puja. A clear distinction should be drawn between these two actions.

We usually have incense available in front of the shrine for people to make use of, although this is not really an offering in the strict sense because it has not been provided by the person who offers it. It would perhaps be better for people to bring their own offerings, so that they are truly and clearly giving. Some people do bring flowers, at least on special occasions, but in general people in the West seem rather reluctant to do this. Eastern Buddhists would not dream of offering something that had been provided for them. They remember to bring their own offerings, and if by chance they find themselves without one, they buy an offering from the monks. They may even buy something – in Tibet it is very often a scarf – that has been offered previously by someone else. We in the West should perhaps reflect on this, but equally we need not be too rigid about it. The offering is a symbolic act and the most important thing is that we should have the feeling of giving, whether or not we are literally doing so.

7
SALUTATION

As many atoms as there are
In the thousand million worlds,
So many times I make reverent salutation
To all the Buddhas of the Three Eras,
To the Saddharma,
And to the excellent Community.

I pay homage to all the shrines,
And places in which the Bodhisattvas have been.
I make profound obeisance to the Teachers,
And those to whom respectful salutation is due.

(Bennett)

With salutations as numerous as the atoms in all Buddha-fields, I
salute the Buddhas of all three worlds (of past, present, and future)
and the Dharma, and the great congregations. Likewise, I praise
all shrines and places associated with Bodhisattvas; and I make
obeisance to praiseworthy teachers and ascetics.

(Matics)

The salutation section represents the paying of outward physical respect. It is not enough to keep our feelings of reverence in our minds. Whenever we have any strong inner feeling, we will naturally want to express it outwardly, because we have bodies as well as minds and hearts. To feel something totally means also to feel it physically. Obeisance, the bowing down alluded to in the verses, is the physical expression of the respect we feel for the ideal of Enlightenment.

There is little difference in meaning between the two translations. Notice at the beginning a bit of characteristically Indian exuberance: 'As many atoms as there are in the thousand million worlds, so many times I make reverent salutation.' Clearly it is not to be taken literally. It really means that your life should be one continuous salutation.

First of all, it is the Three Jewels – the Buddha, the Dharma, and the Sangha – that are saluted. More specifically, reverent salutation is made to the Buddhas of the three eras – that is, of past, present, and future – together with the Dharma and the spiritual community. The three Buddhas who usually represent the Buddhas of the past, present, and future are Dīpaṅkara, Śākyamuni, and Maitreya respectively. Śāntideva introduces all three, rather than just Śākyamuni, to give the salutation a more cosmic perspective. Śāntideva is a Mahāyānist, and one of the features which distinguish the Mahāyāna from the Hīnayāna is its wider, more universal vision. Lama Govinda makes the important point that the Mahāyāna's recognition of the plurality of Buddhas throughout time and space represents the fact that Enlightenment can be obtained whenever and wherever circumstances and conditions permit.[112] It suggests the universality of Enlightenment and the universality of the Buddha's teaching. It is therefore implicit in the words of the salutation that we are saluting the Three Jewels not only as our ideal, but as a universal ideal.

The word 'saddharma' in the penultimate line of the first verse simply means the true, the real, the good Dharma. This term also appears in the title of a very important Mahāyāna sūtra, the Saddharma Puṇḍarīka, which means the 'White Lotus of the True Dharma'.

Since the objects of our reverent salutation are the Three Jewels, which are also the objects to which we go for Refuge, in what way does the salutation differ from the Going for Refuge that succeeds it? In what way, indeed, does the salutation differ from the worship that precedes it? In fact each of these sections does represent a distinct response to the ideal, and each builds upon the one before it. During the worship we are confronted by the spiritual ideal. We take delight in it and express that delight, but we don't really do anything about it. We have not started thinking about our own relationship to it. The verses in the worship section don't say anything about the Dharma or the Sangha, only about the Buddha. But when we come to make our salutation, we are recognizing that the ideal is something very much higher than we are. We see the gulf that exists between us and it, a gulf which we will have to cross if we want to realize that ideal. Then in the Going for Refuge it is as though we begin to close the gap. In the worship we are not really conscious of the gap, in the salutation we become conscious of it, and in the Going for Refuge we are determined to close it by treading the path leading from where we are to where the Buddha is. Broadly speaking, this would seem to be the main factor distinguishing between these three phases, and linking them in a series.

Suppose you are travelling and you see a beautiful mountain peak in the distance. You admire it for its beauty; you look up to it, enjoy it, and delight in it. This corresponds to worship. It does not occur to you at this stage that you could possibly climb that peak. Then you start to think, 'That mountain is so much higher than I am; to climb it would be very difficult.' Becoming aware of where you are in relation to the mountain in this way corresponds to the salutation. And having absorbed that situation you decide: 'All right, nonetheless I am going to climb that mountain,' and you start walking towards it. That is Going for Refuge.

Another aspect of the distinction between worship and Going for Refuge in Buddhism is that it may be considered quite appropriate to worship things other than the Three Jewels, but it is always misguided to go for refuge to anything other than the Three Jewels. For example, people throughout history have worshipped certain natural objects. In the presence of, say, a particular tree or rock which seems, at least materially speaking, superior to them in some respect, they have not only empathized with that tree, but also looked up to it. Some have taken it further, imagining that there is a spirit living in the tree. The tree is the house of the tree spirit, and it is the tree spirit that is worshipped, and to which even offerings are made. This sort of thing is a feature of all animistic and pagan religions.

Buddhism does not reject this kind of response to natural phenomena. This used to confuse many early Western visitors to, say, Burma. The

Burmese appeared to follow two different religions. One minute they would be worshipping various gods, and the next they would be worshipping the Buddha. So it was said that Burmese Buddhism was adulterated with animism, or that the Burmese were simply inconsistent – but this was completely to misunderstand the situation. There is no incompatibility between Buddhism and animism. They really go together, just as paganism and Buddhism do. Animism is considered quite healthy. I sometimes wish that in Britain we had more sacred rocks, trees, and groves. Unfortunately there are not many of these sacred sites left.[113]

Nonetheless, while Buddhism has nothing to say against worshipping hills, trees, or rocks, it does take exception to 'going for refuge' to them. If we do that, we are taking nature as our highest value, expecting something from nature which it cannot give. The Buddhist path is a search for the Unconditioned and nature cannot give us that, even though it can manifest qualities which are worthy of reverence.

In a similar vein, Buddhists do not believe that it is wrong to worship the 'gods of the round'. These gods are more powerful beings than humans, existing on higher, subtler (though still mundane) planes, and they can perhaps help us in worldly matters, but they cannot help us on the path to Enlightenment, so we should not go for refuge to them. It is also quite normal for Buddhists (at least in the East) to worship their parents in the sense of paying them honour, respect, and gratitude. Again, however, we would not go for refuge to them, unless of course they happened to be Enlightened.

In this sense we *merely* worship them. The Buddha himself clearly distinguished those of his followers who worshipped him and went for Refuge to him as their teacher from those who *merely* worshipped him in the same way they would worship anyone charismatic, powerful, influential, and to be propitiated – as, in short, they would worship a cult figure. There is nothing wrong in worshipping cult figures either, as long as you don't go for refuge to them. The problem is that cult figures almost always call for an absolute commitment from their followers, incorporating them into a power structure and then exploiting them.

Incidentally the words '*pūjā*' (worship) and '*vandanā*' (salutation) are not always sharply distinguished from each other in the way that I have distinguished them, and this can be a source of confusion. The two terms are more or less interchangeable in Sanskrit, depending on context and usage. '*Vandanā*' can mean no more than a distant, almost social salutation, and '*pūjā*' is then the more heartfelt expression. However, within the FWBO we have adopted the usage outlined above.

> I pay homage to all the shrines,
> And places in which the Bodhisattvas have been.

We pay homage to the shrines – the *caityas* or stupas – because of their associations with the Buddha's life and even with his physical body. The same applies to 'places in which the Bodhisattvas have been'. In medieval India there were all sorts of stupas and *caityas* erected in places that were traditionally identified as where the Buddha, as a bodhisattva in his previous lives, had performed various noble actions and practised the *pāramitās*. There was one, for example, on the spot where the future Buddha was supposed to have sacrificed his body to a starving tigress.

Next we 'make profound obeisance to the Teachers', because they help us to practise the Dharma. They take the place of the Buddha, as it were, in our day-to-day lives. 'Those to whom respectful salutation is due' means any worthy persons who are following the spiritual path. Our salutation overflows to them too.

The salutation is expressed not just in words, but also in the act of bowing down. In the case of the worship section, we are making offerings, or giving gifts, which does not necessarily imply that we regard the person to whom we give the gifts as superior to us. Gifts can be exchanged between equals. (*Pūjā* can also mean bowing down, but in this case it definitely means making offerings.) But when we bow down to someone, we are consciously recognizing that person as superior. This bowing down is referred to explicitly in the line 'I make profound obeisance to the Teachers'. Sometimes in more ceremonial pujas people make full prostrations at this point. More commonly, people bow down when making offerings between the worship and salutation sections.

In the East actual prostration before the image, or before monks or teachers, is very common. In the West we may need to experiment to see how far we can go in our own cultural context. It is not really a sufficient expression of devotion just to recite the words – there should be some appropriate action – but there are different ways of bowing down: the full-length prostration, the kneeling prostration, the semi-kneeling prostration, and the *añjali* salutation, the salutation with folded hands. Whilst the appropriate action depends partly on cultural context – what is natural in India may not seem suitable in the West – it depends more importantly on the feelings of the person doing it. Some Westerners may feel self-conscious about prostrating but in the East there are people who approach it with too little conscious feeling. They often do it in a mechanical way, without even thinking about it, just because it is the custom. I knew a French Buddhist nun who used to go through all the motions, but even as she was getting up from her knees she would be starting to tell her teachers what to do or complaining to them about this and that.[114]

Sometimes there are constraints of space in the shrine-room. There may only be room for people to do ordinary salutations, or for one person to make prostrations on behalf of everybody present. But it is good to keep up the connection with tradition as far as possible. Where there is space, it can be left to people's individual feelings what kind of salutation they make. This is what happened in the Buddha's time. In some of the *sūtras* we find the Buddha seated, about to give a talk, and people are gradually arriving. It is mentioned that some prostrate themselves full-length before the Buddha, others salute him from a distance, and others simply sit down without saluting. The Buddha is never reported as saying anything about this. He never said that people should salute him in any particular way; he just left it to them. So perhaps that is what we should do.

Some people (especially people experiencing a puja ceremony for the first time) react quite strongly to the practice of prostrations. They may think it expresses a slavish mentality. Indeed, people can be outraged by what seems to them to be excessive respect paid either to images or to other human beings. This is an attitude that has deep roots in Western civilization, as is illustrated by the respective attitudes of the ancient Greeks and the ancient Persians. Apparently, when the two cultures came into contact with each other, one of the things that really shocked and displeased the Greeks was the Persians' custom of prostrating in front of their kings. The Greeks thought this most unbefitting a human being: humans should salute only the gods, and even the gods they should salute in quite a moderate fashion. After Alexander the Great became king of Persia, he upset some of his Greek followers by insisting they pay him respect in the manner of the Persians. The bluff, hearty Macedonians did not like that at all and thought that Alexander was getting a bit above himself. So this suspicion of prostration is not only found in the modern West. It goes right back to the ancient Greeks and is connected with their humanism, their respect for the individual – beginning with themselves.

I recall that during the first few weeks of my time in Kalimpong, when I was staying at the Dharmodaya Vihara, a visiting Christian priest stayed there for a few days. He was shocked and horrified by the respect which the Newar Buddhists paid to me as a novice monk, and said, 'In the Catholic Church we don't even pay that sort of respect to the Pope.' Which may well be the case today, but as late as the nineteenth century it was still the custom to kiss the Pope's toe when one had an audience with him. He used to stick out his toe for the purpose.

So in view of the associations it has, we should be a little careful about prostration, and give consideration not only to our own devotional feelings but also to the susceptibilities of others who may be present. Nonetheless, some form of physical salutation is important if we are to engage our emotions fully with this section and move forward from the stage of worship.

8

GOING FOR REFUGE

This very day
I go for my refuge
To the powerful protectors,
Whose purpose is to guard the universe;
The mighty conquerors who overcome suffering everywhere.

Wholeheartedly also I take my refuge
In the Dharma they have ascertained,
Which is the abode of security against the rounds of rebirth.
Likewise in the host of Bodhisattvas
I take my refuge.

(Bennett)

Therefore, I go now for refuge to the Lords of the earth, the ones
labouring for the sake of the earth's protection, the Conquerors
who dispel all fear; and likewise I go for refuge to the Dharma
that is mastered by them, which consumes the fear of rebirth: and
I go to the company of Bodhisattvas.

(Matics)

First we go for Refuge to 'the powerful protectors whose purpose is to guard the universe'. There is a possibility of misunderstanding in connection with this phrase, in that it might seem to suggest something like a creator deity. In fact the sense in which the Buddhas are said to be 'protectors' is not that they 'guard the universe' in the way that Christians would tell us God is supposed to, or protect us from worldly disasters in the way that God might, if he so wished. It is that they keep open the way to Enlightenment. The clue is perhaps to be found in the next two lines, in the fact that the Buddhas are called *jinas*, or 'conquerors'. They overcome suffering everywhere by overcoming their own unskilful states, and inspiring and teaching others to overcome *their* unskilful mental states through their own efforts. We do not go for Refuge to the Buddha for protection from worldly calamities.

The Buddha, in other words, is not a god, though it would probably be impossible to erase this notion completely from the popular mind. The Hindus, especially the Bengalis, often call him 'Buddhadeva', and even some Buddhists worship him as though he were a god. I met with a striking example of this kind of confusion when I was on tour in Assam and staying with some Bengali Buddhists. There was to be a little puja, as is the custom, and they put a small Buddha image on the table and next to that an image of the Hindu goddess Lakshmi. I was quite surprised to find them worshipping this figure, but clearly they were expecting me to do some Buddha puja and some Lakshmi puja before I had my meal. Initially I was unsure what to do – it was not a situation I had run into before – but in the end I resolved it by quietly putting the Lakshmi image to one side so that she was not in the way of the puja. I didn't say anything, but I dare say they understood.

Moving on to the Dharma refuge, Matics' translation, 'the Dharma that is mastered by them', is probably more literal than Adrienne Bennett's 'the Dharma they have ascertained'. Nonetheless 'ascertained' is a very suitable term here. It means 'to find out or to assure oneself of the truth by experiencing it', and it avoids any inappropriate suggestion of power and control which may be implied by the term 'mastered'.

The Dharma – here meaning the transcendental Dharma – is described as 'the abode of security against the rounds of rebirth'. Someone who is on the transcendental path (i.e. someone who has gained some real insight into the nature of reality) is secure against the rounds of rebirth and cannot fall into them any more, or at least not more than a certain number of times. This is what is meant by being secure.

In the case of the third refuge, the Sangha, notice that refuge is taken in 'the host of Bodhisattvas' – not just in a particular bodhisattva but in the Āryasaṅgha as a whole. Here 'bodhisattvas' should be understood in the wider sense to include Stream Entrants (those whose future spiritual progress is assured) and *arhants* (in Hīnayāna terms those who are fully Enlightened and will not be reborn again). These are sometimes called 'Hīnayāna bodhisattvas'. We could call them 'incipient bodhisattvas' in the sense that they could become bodhisattvas if they woke up to that possibility.

There can be considerable confusion over the idea that there are two paths, one for the bodhisattva and one for the *arhant*. There was even a difference of opinion among Buddhists themselves in medieval times.[115] Some would say that once people are on the Hīnayāna path, they can't retrace their steps: they go along that path, as it were, to the bitter end. Having become a Stream Entrant, the only way forward is to become a once-returner, a non-returner, and finally an *arhant*. But other authorities would say that it is possible to change paths. Someone following the Hīnayāna, having come on to the transcendental path as, say, a Stream Entrant, could, having become aware of the greater Mahāyāna ideal, decide thereafter to follow the bodhisattva path. It seems to me that the root of the confusion is that the *arhant* path, and perhaps also the bodhisattva path, have been defined too narrowly and rigidly, making it difficult to bring the two together. The mistake – if one can speak in these terms – lay in separating them in that mutually exclusive way in the first place, rather than recognizing that the so-called 'arhant path' and 'bodhisattva path' represented different dimensions of what is essentially one and the same path.

Historically speaking, it is quite incorrect to represent the Buddha as teaching the 'Hīnayāna path'. The Buddha just taught the path or the way, and that was narrowed down by some of his followers into what became the Hīnayāna or *arhant* path. The Mahāyānists then had to broaden it out, but unfortunately the broadened version remained in contradistinction to the earlier, narrower version, and therefore it too had a certain limitation. I don't feel happy to talk in terms of separate *arhant* and bodhisattva paths at all, even though a lot of the surviving Buddhist canonical literature does just that. Such a separation does not seem to be borne out by the spiritual facts of the situation. It may well be that at certain stages of your spiritual career you are more aware of the individual aspect of the spiritual life while at other times you are more aware of the altruistic aspect, and you act accordingly. But eventually you must come to a state in which your mental constructions of subject and object, self and other, in their mutually exclusive sense, lose their significance. And surely from such a standpoint you will no longer distinguish between the *arhant* ideal and the bodhisattva ideal. Taking this view, we can adopt the position of the *Saddharma Puṇḍarīka Sūtra* and say that all three *yānas* or 'ways' merge into one *yāna*.[116] The *sūtra* teaches that the *śrāvakayāna* (the way of the disciple), the *pratyekabuddhayāna* (the way of private or merely personal Enlightenment) and the *bodhisattvayāna* (the way of the bodhisattva) all merge into the *Buddhayāna* (the way of the Buddha). We can go even further and envisage the Hīnayāna, the Mahāyāna, and the Vajrayāna merging into one *yāna*, one path, one Dharma.

So questions such as whether an *arhant* can wake up to the bodhisattva ideal are quite artificial from a spiritual point of view. It is just a matter of reconciling different scholastic formulations. Sometimes this can be difficult, because the formulations themselves are one-sided, even mutually exclusive, but we should try to see ourselves simply as on the path of being a Buddhist, on the path to Enlightenment. The teachings found under the label 'Hīnayāna' certainly help us, and so do those found under the label 'Mahāyāna'. We can't afford to neglect either of them; they are not mutually exclusive paths between which we have to make a choice, but represent different emphases on different aspects of the spiritual life. A particular emphasis may be more relevant to our needs at one stage of our spiritual career than at another.

When we go for Refuge to the Dharma and to the Sangha, therefore, we should acknowledge them as being manifested in all three traditional *yānas* of Buddhism, rather than taking a narrow, sectarian view. In a similar way, when we go for Refuge to the Buddha-jewel, we should acknowledge it as being manifested in the Buddha's historical life, in his archetypal forms, and ultimately in his absolute nature, about which words are powerless to inform us.

Immediately after the Going for Refuge verses we recite the five precepts or, if only Order members, i.e. *dhammacāris* or *dhammacārinīs* (literally 'Dharma-farers'), are present, the ten precepts. The recitation of the precepts at this stage underlines the fact that by virtue of our Going for Refuge we are committed to transforming our lives. Each precept has a negative form, in which we undertake to abstain from a particular kind of unskilful act, and also a positive form, in which we undertake to practise the corresponding skilful form of action. We normally recite the negative formulation of the precepts in Pāli and the positive formulation in English. For the sake of clarity I shall give them all in English, but with the Pāli terms for the various activities to be abstained from in brackets at the end of the negative precepts. The negative formulations of the five precepts may be rendered as follows:

> I undertake to abstain from taking life (*pāṇātipātā*).
> I undertake to abstain from taking the not-given (*adinnādānā*).
> I undertake to abstain from sexual misconduct (*kāmesu micchācārā*).
> I undertake to abstain from false speech (*musāvādā*).
> I undertake to abstain from taking intoxicants (*surāmeraya majja pamādaṭṭhānā*).

The positive formulations are:

> With deeds of loving-kindness, I purify my body.
> With open-handed generosity, I purify my body.
> With stillness, simplicity, and contentment, I purify my body.
> With truthful communication, I purify my speech.
> With mindfulness clear and radiant, I purify my mind.

The negative formulations of the Ten Precepts are:

> I undertake to abstain from taking life (*pāṇatipātā*).
> I undertake to abstain from taking the not-given (*adinnādānā*).
> I undertake to abstain from sexual misconduct (*kāmesu micchācārā*).
> I undertake to abstain from false speech (*musāvādā*).
> I undertake to abstain from harsh speech (*pharusavācāya*).
> I undertake to abstain from useless speech (*samphappalāpā*).
> I undertake to abstain from slanderous speech (*pisuṇavācāya*).
> I undertake to abstain from covetousness (*abhijjhāya*).
> I undertake to abstain from animosity (*byāpādā*).
> I undertake to abstain from false views (*micchāddiṭṭhiyā*).

Their positive formulations are:

> With deeds of loving-kindness, I purify my body.
> With open-handed generosity, I purify my body.
> With stillness, simplicity, and contentment, I purify my body.
> With truthful communication, I purify my speech.
> With kindly communication, I purify my speech.
> With helpful communication, I purify my speech.
> With harmonious communication, I purify my speech.
> Abandoning covetousness for tranquillity, I purify my mind.
> Changing hatred into compassion, I purify my mind.
> Transforming ignorance into wisdom, I purify my mind.

The difference between the five precepts and the ten precepts is not a matter of more or less of the same sort of thing. It is quite fundamental. For instance, if you were really to give up *micchā-diṭṭhis*, or false views (the tenth precept), you would have attained at least Stream Entry – i.e. you would have achieved transcendental insight. Undertaking to eradicate *micchā-diṭṭhis* suggests a commitment to the Path of Vision. Abstention from *abhijjhā* (covetousness) and *byāpāda* (hatred) means a commitment to the Path of Transformation. So these three precepts are not just precepts in the ethical sense like the others; they have a transcendental significance. They are oriented in the direction of insight and wisdom, so their significance goes far beyond the social and cultural level represented by the five precepts. This is why the ten precepts are taken by the *dhammacāri* or *dhammacārinī*. To go for Refuge effectively, you must intend, consciously and deliberately, to aim for the transcendental. Observing just the five precepts will only get you as far as a good rebirth. If you are seriously Going for Refuge, you want something much more than a good rebirth – you want Enlightenment – so you will need to take the last three of the ten precepts, which indicate purification of mind. It is not enough to purify your actions. It is not enough to purify your speech. You have got to purify your mind of ignorance, because only by doing so can you gain Enlightenment. Even though it is traditional in Buddhist countries for people to take the three Refuges and five precepts and to consider themselves Buddhists because they do so, that is not really enough. It does not bring out the full significance of Going for Refuge in a Buddhist's personal life, practice, and experience.

Another major feature of the ten precepts is that the precept of *musāvāda*, false speech, is expanded into four precepts. This is highly significant. One could just as well have expanded some of the other precepts in this way, but speech has been singled out, emphasizing the tremendous importance of communication in the spiritual life. If you truly observe these precepts, you do not just speak *about* Going for Refuge; your speech *is* Going for Refuge. The medium is the message.

There is one more significant point to notice about the ten precepts. The fifth of the five precepts is missed out. There is a spiritual reason for this. The positive quality corresponding to this precept is awareness; one could say that the state of intoxication, partial or complete, represents a very gross form of unawareness. The mental states refrained from in the ten precepts – *abhijjhā*, *byāpāda*, and *micchā-diṭṭhi* – represent the more subtle, inner, mental, or spiritual forms of intoxication which it becomes much more important to overcome. In the case of the person who is just beginning to be interested in the spiritual life, to avoid just the grosser forms of *moha* or mental intoxication is fair enough. But someone who is really on the path has to avoid the subtle mental intoxications as well. If you are doing this you are very unlikely to get drunk or use intoxicants such as alcohol in an unmindful way; that precept is really implicit in the other three, only raised to a higher and subtler level.

This particular formulation of ten precepts is not normally taken either by monks or by lay people in Buddhist countries in any formal, ceremonial way. There is another set of ten precepts, those taken by the *śrāmaṇera*, which are quite different from these.[117] The ten precepts taken by members of the Western Buddhist Order are, however, traditional, indeed canonical, in origin. They are found as a list of ten skilful actions or *kusala dhammas* in the scriptures,[118] and people are referred to as repeating and practising them, but in modern Buddhist practice (outside the WBO) they are not administered or taken ceremonially. From that point of view, although they are rooted in tradition, their formal use and practice within the WBO represents a new departure.[119]

9

CONFESSION OF FAULTS

The evil that I have heaped up
Through my ignorance and foolishness –
Evil in the world of everyday experience
As well as evil in understanding and intelligence –
All that I acknowledge to the Protectors.

Standing before them
With hands raised in reverence,
And terrified of suffering,
I pay salutations again and again.

May the Leaders receive this kindly,
Just as it is, with its many faults!
What is not good, O Protectors,
I shall not do again.

(Bennett)

Whatever the evil that has been accumulated by my foolishness
and ignorance, and whatever of my speaking and teaching is
objectionable, and whatever is evil by nature: I confess it all,
standing in the presence of the Lords, fearing sorrow, and with
folded hands prostrating myself again and again. May the Leaders

accept my sin and transgression! That which was not good, Lords, will not be done again by me.

(Matics)

Essentially the confession of faults, or *pāpadeśanā*, is a recognition of the darker side of ourselves. It is not a question of breast-beating and bewailing our sins, but rather of a realistic appraisal of our shortcomings and weaknesses so that they may be overcome. It also entails a resolution that we *will* overcome that darker side of ourselves.

In order to understand more fully what the *pāpadeśanā* represents in the context of the Sevenfold Puja, we have to recall the sequence of devotional states represented by the three previous sections. In the worship section we just take delight in the beauty of the spiritual ideal. In the salutation we bow down before that ideal, thereby recognizing the great distance that separates us, as we are at present, from it. When we come to the Going for Refuge, we take courage and determine to close the gap. We *go* for Refuge. We start actively progressing in the direction of the spiritual goal. But once we have started making that effort we soon find that there are all sorts of things holding us back – all sorts of bad habits that we have formed and all kinds of unskilful actions that we have committed. We discover that we are in a bad way in certain respects. So the next stage is to acknowledge that, to confess it – not only in the depths of our own hearts but also in front of the spiritual community. We thus begin to shed some of the baggage that is hindering us from climbing towards the mountain peak of Enlightenment. This is confession in the Buddhist sense, and it follows on naturally from Going for Refuge.

Of course people with a Christian, especially a Catholic, background may have quite a different idea of confession. It conjures up images of people creeping into a little box and whispering through a grille to someone on the other side who listens to all the sordid details and then absolves them so they can go away all clean and pure to do it all over again. In this case the person confessing is terrified not of suffering, the natural consequence of evil, but of punishment, inflicted by an external authority. These connotations of the word 'confession' have nothing to do with the Buddhist practice of *pāpadeśanā*.

'The evil that I have heaped up' arises from the unskilful states of mind that hold us back from Going for Refuge. At root these are all based in greed, hatred, and delusion, even though sometimes they can take very subtle forms. Bennett's translation, 'heaped up', works best here. Matics's 'accumulated' evil suggests something passive like dividends accumulating in the bank without our having to do anything about it. But 'heaped up' evil emphasizes the active part we play, heaping up evil almost like earth or sand. It even seems to emphasize the utter ridiculousness of what we are doing much of the time. We may think that we are doing all sorts of different things, but actually much of it amounts simply to heaping up evil, strengthening the bonds which hold us back on the spiritual path. This is how we pass much of our time, busily heaping up evil.

The next phrase, 'through my ignorance and foolishness', suggests the basic causes of all this unwholesome activity: ignorance in relation to fundamental principles and foolishness in relation to their application in everyday life. When we get our basic principles wrong, when we are unaware of those principles, that is ignorance. And if, despite having some awareness of the principles, we do not manage to apply them properly in everyday life, that is foolishness. Ignorance is more theoretical, foolishness more practical.

Matics' translation follows Śāntideva quite strictly in focusing on the evil actions arising out of the 'everyday experience' of a monk – i.e. out of 'speaking and teaching'. Adrienne Bennett avoids this apparently narrow application of the verse, and this makes her translation more helpful.

All that I acknowledge to the Protectors.

The operative word here is 'all'. It is not easy to confess everything. Usually we fudge, we rationalize, we hold back. And we do this out of fear: fear of change; fear that we will have to give up the activity that is confessed. Very often we are willing to confess only those things that we do not care about very much, or do not really think are sins or offences. We may even confess things of which we are secretly rather proud. Confession then becomes almost a form of boasting. But the things of which we are truly ashamed, the things we really do think are wrong or evil, we find very difficult to confess. We hardly dare even to think about them. We should always be aware of this tendency and try to see what we are holding back: whether, indeed, we are truly confessing at all. There is a difference between merely telling people about something and confessing it, and sometimes it is difficult to distinguish between the two, even to ourselves.

When we really confess, we acknowledge that what we confess is evil. We feel a degree of shame on account of it, and we are also aware that those to whom we are confessing will regard it as evil. They will not brush it aside as something insignificant, something that does not matter. Conversely, there are actions which are only conventionally considered to be wrong. We might feel quite bad about such actions and confess them in all sincerity, only to find out – with the help of our spiritual friends – that they are not in fact unskilful, but only actions conventionally regarded as wrong. We must be careful to distinguish between natural morality – the ethical behaviour suggested by the precepts – and conventional morality, which amounts to no more than what society at large thinks we ought to do.

The hallmark of confession, then, is a feeling of shame, though even 'shame' is not the ideal word for it. 'Guilt' is certainly not the right word. Guilt is the sense of having offended some greater power on which you are emotionally dependent; if you feel guilty when you confess, you are probably suffering from the Christian idea of sin which still lingers on in our society. The feeling that accompanies genuine confession is more like intense regret, especially if the misdeed has involved harm to another person. If you realize that your foolish action has harmed someone, perhaps even irreparably, you will truly wish that you had not done it. You really will see it as evil. So confession is not just a cool, objective recognition, ticking off our actions against the precepts, but something really heartfelt. It should be an emotional experience. Most of us have had that experience at some time in our lives – the realization of having done something wrong which has resulted in pain, suffering, and inconvenience for others – and have felt very sorry and regretful on that account. We can never undo what has been done, and in some cases we cannot even make it up to the person we have wronged. It is not only irreparable but irredeemable.

There are also occasions when we know we could do something – and feel that we should do it – but for some reason we don't do it. That too can be a cause of bitter regret. We could have helped, but we did not. Acts of omission as well as acts of commission have to be confessed. In a broader sense, then, this concept of confession implies responsibility. We are responsible for our actions and our failures to act, whether skilful or unskilful, good or evil. We are the heirs of our own actions, as the Buddha says.[120]

In these verses of confession we acknowledge our evil to the 'Protectors' or Buddhas. If we really have a sense that a Buddha or bodhisattva is present when we say these verses, then to confess in this manner will be effective and sufficient. However, most people do not have a sufficiently vivid sense of the Buddhas as actually present, so for most of us it is necessary also to confess to other people, to spiritual friends whom we trust and respect, and who are perhaps a bit more spiritually developed than we are. If all we do is go into the shrine-room and, as it were, address the Buddha, even though we might feel quite sincere about it, it will probably not be a sufficiently concrete and vivid experience to help us change our behaviour. For one thing, we are unlikely to experience the Buddha as saying anything back to us in the way that our spiritual friends will.

Standing before them
With hands raised in reverence
And terrified of suffering,
I pay salutations again and again.

Some people are very uncomfortable with the phrase 'terrified of suffering'. They are perhaps reminded of 'hellfire' sermons designed to put the fear of God into them. However, it is not the Buddhas who inflict suffering on us, but our own evil deeds operating through the law of karma. The Buddhas are not the administrators of karma. Karma functions, as it were, automatically. There is no notion of judgement, retribution, or punishment here. The Buddhas' attitude towards us will always be one of *mettā* and compassion. They may not approve of some of the things we have done, but they are absolutely unwavering in their compassion, so there is no need to approach them with any sort of fear or apprehension. Nonetheless, even a Buddha cannot take away the effects of your actions. According to the Buddhist view of the universe, karma is a simple fact of life. Just as, under the laws of physics, action and reaction are equal and opposite, so under the law of karma evil actions will sooner or later bring suffering on their perpetrator. So you should indeed feel terrified when you have committed evil actions, because you are going to suffer. By reciting the verse you are not threatening yourself with suffering or trying to bully yourself into doing things which you do not want to do. You are simply reminding yourself in a down-to-earth way that unethical actions have unpleasant consequences.[121]

People who react against such a reminder perhaps do not like to admit that they have committed evil actions, or to think that they are going to suffer. In fact they *are* terrified of suffering, but would prefer not to acknowledge that this is a result of what they themselves have done. Sometimes people have said to me that they simply are not terrified of suffering. If this is really so, it can only be due to a lack of imagination on their part.

> May the leaders receive this kindly,
> Just as it is, with its many faults!
> What is not good, O Protectors,
> I shall not do again.

There is a difference in meaning between Bennett's translation and that of Matics with regard to what the leaders are asked to accept – 'my sin and transgression' (Matics) or the confession itself (Bennett). Adrienne Bennett seems to reflect the Buddhist spirit better here; it is the confession which you are asking the Buddhas to accept. If your confession is effective, there should be a definite step forward. You have come across things in yourself that you have got to overcome. When you say, 'What is not good I shall not do again,' it is as if you have gone beyond your unskilful actions. You are freed from them. Once you have recognized something as evil, once you have confessed it, once the members of the spiritual community have accepted that confession and perhaps given advice, and once you have really made up your mind not to do that thing again – then you should put it behind you. In a sense you should forget all about it. As a result you will feel a freedom and lightness that will lead quite naturally into the rejoicing in merit, which is the next section. It is much easier to rejoice in other people's merits when you can also rejoice in your own. So there is a natural transition here, via this last line of the confession of faults, to the rejoicing in merit.

IO

REJOICING IN MERIT

I rejoice with delight
In the good done by all beings,
Through which they obtain rest
With the end of suffering.
May those who have suffered be happy!

I rejoice in the release of beings
From the sufferings of the rounds of existence;
I rejoice in the nature of the Bodhisattva
And the Buddha,
Who are Protectors.

I rejoice in the arising of the Will to Enlightenment,
And the Teaching:
Those Oceans that bring happiness to all beings,
And are the abode of welfare of all beings.

(Bennett)

I rejoice in exultation at the goodness, and at the cessation
and destruction of sorrow, wrought by all beings. May those
who sorrow achieve joy! I rejoice at the release of embodied
beings from the sorrowful wheel of rebirth. I rejoice at the

Bodhisattvahood and at the Buddhahood of those who have attained salvation. I rejoice at the Oceans of Determination, the Bearers of Happiness to all beings, the Vehicles of Advantage for all beings, and those who teach.

(Matics)

The two translations sound quite different, especially the third verse. Sanskrit is a difficult language with very complex grammar; clauses can be arranged and interpreted in many different ways, especially in a piece of Sanskrit poetry. Adrienne Bennett's rendering seems clearer and more straightforward, but both are probably justified.

During the *puṇyānumodana*, the rejoicing in merit – or virtue as it might also be translated – we recollect the noble lives of others. We think of the Buddhas and bodhisattvas and great spiritual teachers – people like Milarepa, Huineng, and Hakuin. We bring to mind renowned helpers of humanity and even ordinary people whom we know personally to have acted in noble, generous, and kindly ways. The example of all these people provides us with enthusiasm and inspiration. Like us they are human, and reflecting on this fact encourages us to believe that we can become as worthy and noble as they have shown themselves to be. We feel happy on account of their attainments and draw strength from recollecting them.

The practice of rejoicing in merit counteracts unskilful mental states such as jealousy, envy, pride, and egotism. It is part of the definition of a skilful action that there should be no interest in deriving personal recognition from it. You rejoice in good deeds, but you are just as glad if somebody else has done them as if you had done them yourself. You don't feel inferior because somebody else has shown such good qualities, or imagine that that person may look down on you. This kind of over-sensitivity and over-preoccupation with oneself is unfortunately quite common and prevents people from appreciating the good in others. We should, then, rejoice in merits quite impersonally, just as we feel happy that the sun is shining. We don't feel jealous that the sun sheds light when we do not. We just rejoice that there is sunshine around making the world a brighter and better place.

In the context of the Sevenfold Puja, rejoicing in merits represents the converse of the confession of faults. You have freed yourself from faults, so you feel happy and delighted; and being happy and delighted with yourself, you can feel happy and delighted with others. This is an important psychological fact: you cannot be happy with others unless you are first of all happy with yourself. Rejoicing in merit requires a basis of *mettā* and you cannot really feel *mettā* for others unless you feel *mettā* for yourself. Your feelings about yourself and your feelings about others are very intimately connected. It is noticeable, for instance, that people who are feeling guilty because they are out of touch with their own spiritual practice find it very difficult to appreciate what others are doing. They even sometimes adopt a resentful or highly critical attitude towards other people's efforts, and find it quite impossible to rejoice in their merits. By contrast, if you see people who genuinely, freely, and regularly rejoice in the merits of others, you can be sure that they are very much at peace with themselves.

You may of course be doing what you ought to be doing and still not feel any sense of joy. In this case you may be doing the right things in an external sense only, going through the motions without the appropriate mental and emotional attitude. You are just 'being good' – and that can make you all the more resentful because you think, 'Here I am being good, but I don't seem to be getting any results from it. I'm not even *feeling* good.' But sometimes, going through the motions, if you do it consciously and mindfully, helps you to develop the corresponding mental and emotional attitude, and probably an element of that 'disciplinary' approach is necessary for most people. We can't always have skilful mental states before we do skilful actions. Sometimes our unskilful mental states are so powerful that we just have to perform skilful actions anyway, and then gradually try to bring our mental states into line with our actions.

It is an aspect both of ritual and of ethical observance to perform actions which will only subsequently enable you to develop appropriate mental states. Of course, if you adopt this approach, you must understand what you are doing and why – otherwise you can end up losing touch with what you are doing and feeling. A person who is naturally in touch with his or her own feelings should be able to do this quite safely, but a person with a tendency to 'be good' without experiencing their true feelings should have recourse to this approach only with extreme caution.

But although we should observe caution in acting at variance with our feelings, it is not, as some would suggest, hypocritical to do so. If you feel like murdering somebody but you don't actually do it you are not thereby being a hypocrite. You would only be a hypocrite if, when asked about your feelings towards that person, you said 'Oh, I absolutely love them.' Hypocrisy is consciously and deliberately trying to give an impression that your mental state or behaviour is other than it really is, for purely selfish reasons.

Within the spiritual community you should be able to own up to all your unskilful thoughts and feelings. It is also very important when you are practising the *mettā bhāvanā*, the cultivation of loving-kindness, to keep in touch with how you really feel rather than feigning feelings of *mettā* because that is what you 'should' be feeling. Even if what you feel is crude and negative, as long as you are experiencing it consciously, you can begin to work on it and gradually refine it, sublimate it, and make it more positive. But if you are out of touch with how you feel to begin with, what can you possibly do?

The factors in society that lead to people's emotions becoming repressed are quite complex. But whatever the causes may be, when this happens people become unable to rejoice in the merits of others. Clearly it is something that goes very deep. Without strongly developed positive emotions you can't have much individual development. And being emotionally positive has two aspects: feeling happy with yourself and feeling happy with others, or in other words rejoicing in their merits.

> I rejoice with delight
> In the good done by all beings,
> Through which they obtain rest
> With the end of suffering.
> May those who have suffered be happy!

> I rejoice in the release of beings
> From the sufferings of the rounds of existence.

We rejoice in the merits of all those who have gained Enlightenment. Even though this is a Mahāyāna work, these lines express very much the standpoint of the Hīnayāna 'doctrine-follower' (as opposed to the 'faith-follower')[122] until we come to:

> I rejoice in the nature of the Bodhisattva
> And the Buddha,
> Who are Protectors.

You rejoice in their nature. It is as though you are saying, 'Even apart from their functions – teaching, helping, and guiding me – I rejoice in their very nature as Enlightened Ones.' It is intrinsically delightful and you rejoice in it quite disinterestedly. This is like the worship section raised to a much higher level, because your understanding has deepened.

> I rejoice in the arising of the Will to Enlightenment,
> And the Teaching:
> Those Oceans that bring happiness to all beings,
> And are the abode of welfare of all beings.

You rejoice in the arising of the will to Enlightenment wherever it occurs – both in yourself and in others. The *bodhicitta* and the Dharma are 'Oceans' in the sense that they are unlimited just as the ocean is unlimited – poetically speaking, if not literally. These verses convey the attitude of rejoicing in whatever is good in the past, present, and future; rejoicing in the good deeds that people do, their skilful actions, their observance of the precepts, their Going for Refuge, and their practice of the *pāramitās*; and also rejoicing in the transcendental nature of the Buddhas and bodhisattvas and the will to Enlightenment.

If you have this attitude of rejoicing, you are in a very positive mental and emotional state. Your delight in people's good deeds can be seen as a delight in the reflection of the Buddha nature in other people. If you rejoice in the Buddha, you cannot but rejoice in the meritorious actions even of an unenlightened being, because those good deeds reflect or anticipate, however faintly and distantly, Enlightenment itself. Conversely, if as a Buddhist you fail to rejoice in the merits of those who are clearly progressing on the spiritual path, you are practising a form of dishonesty, keeping silent about what in your heart you know to be worthy of recognition. It's a sort of passive lie.

We should rejoice in the merits not just of individuals but of the spiritual community as a whole. We don't always realize just how precarious the whole structure of the spiritual community is in our world. In the first place, society itself is somewhat precarious. Then superimposed on society is a structure of civilization and culture that is even more precarious. And superimposed on that is a spiritual community which is very precarious indeed. It would be quite easy for someone in power who wanted to do so to wipe out the entire Western Buddhist Order, at least within a particular country. In some states this could be done without anyone knowing or noticing that those few hundred people had been rounded up and eliminated. It is not very difficult to dispose of, say, a hundred people, eliminating a spiritual community in a particular region at a stroke. It is not even all that difficult to wipe out an entire civilization and culture. Think of the libraries that have been burned down, the monuments that have been destroyed, the scholars who have been killed, the religions that have been wiped out. Look, for instance, at the destruction of Buddhism in India by Islam; or, in our own day, what has happened to Buddhist culture in parts of South-east Asia, in China, and in Tibet. The destruction of cultures is bad enough, but in some areas like Tibet, a spiritual community has almost been wiped out, with what remains having been driven either underground or beyond the borders.

The events of the twentieth century have shattered Western political optimism for most thinking people. The Second World War and especially the extermination of the Jews shocked anybody who could think seriously because it showed the fragility of civilization and culture. The Germans were one of the most civilized and cultured peoples in Europe – maybe not *en masse*, but they have produced the greatest philosophers and musicians as well as many great scientists and statesmen. They have made a major contribution to Western culture for centuries, yet virtually the whole German population apparently connived at the murder, as one can only call it, of six million people. What a sobering reminder of the barbarism that underlies civilization and culture! And it could happen in other countries too. We may like to think it could not happen in dear old Britain, but under certain circumstances it could. This realization has destroyed the idea that things can be permanently changed and improved almost by Act of Parliament. We can no longer think – if we ever did – that we have only to change social institutions and we will have heaven on earth.

All this is not so surprising if we take a longer-term view. After all, civilization as we know it is only 10,000 or 12,000 years old, and the great religions have had only 2,000 to 2,500 years to influence us – even assuming that all of them were positive to begin with. But humanity has been around for 350,000 years in the form of *homo sapiens*, and 2,000,000 years if we go back to *homo erectus* and *homo habilis*. Humanity was not completely uncivilized during all that period because it developed tribal organization which represents a degree of culture, but we can look even further back to our semi-human ancestry, which existed over 4,000,000 years ago. Many scientists believe that we are descended from carnivorous apes (the smaller variety of *australopithecus*). So we must not be too complacent. We must not think that the upward movement is an easy task. Civilization can break down; it can decline and fall. The Buddhist view is that civilization and culture go through cycles. We climb up to higher civilization, then we sink down to barbarism, and this cycle repeats itself. Progress is not necessarily going to carry on indefinitely. There is only one context – an individual context – in which progress is assured, and that is the transcendental part of the spiral path – beyond Stream Entry. All mundane things are governed by cyclical movement, human society included.

An Enlightened humanity or Enlightened society is therefore an impossibility, a contradiction in terms, even though Enlightened individuals may be emerging all the time. This is because the factors that are required to keep humanity – in the ordinary sense – going are the opposite of the factors that constitute Enlightenment. If one were able somehow to organize society so that it was conducive to spiritual development, would one even, to take a very ordinary example, choose to propagate the race? If one could somehow halt the growth of the population and only encourage the existing individuals until they gradually all became Enlightened – one would have to arrange for them to live for a very long time too – we would end up with an Enlightened society. But new beings are constantly being born. In a karmic sense, we don't even know where they have come from. For all we know, they may have come straight out of some hell realm – and you are unlikely to come out of that in a very positive frame of mind.

We will always have 'little devils' being born into the world as well as 'little angels', and even one devil can spoil it for all the angels just by being a nuisance. If one person shouts during the meditation, that spoils it for everybody else. One country that wants to fight can upset the peace of the whole world. If you like you can work to improve things, but the danger of putting all your energy into improving the world outside instead of balancing that with working on yourself so that you reach a higher level of awareness is that you get dragged down by other people's negativity and destructive behaviour.

We must be quite realistic about these things. Maintaining a positive society in which the spiritual community can flourish is not easy. At the same time we must not be despondent or feel that we are living in a 'dark age' in some sense. Looking back over history, it is hard to identify any age that is clearly better than any other. In some ways ours is a very good age. Since the Second World War there has not been a really big war anywhere in the world, nothing on the scale of the first two world wars. We have kept relatively peaceable over the last forty-five years, compared to previous ages. There is the terrible possibility of a nuclear war, but apart from that the human race has never lived, materially speaking, so comfortably or happily as at present, at least in the Western world. The standard of living has never been so high for so many people. The things that we enjoy now were enjoyed in the past only by members of aristocracies and not always even by them. Many diseases have been more or less brought under control. Yet still there can be no complete end to suffering for humanity or indeed for beings in general. There may be the end of suffering for certain individuals but so long as *saṃsāra* exists – and so far as we know *saṃsāra* always has existed and always will – suffering is inherent in it. However great the number of individuals gaining Enlightenment, *saṃsāra* is beginningless and always producing, as it were, unenlightened individuals. So the bodhisattva's work is never done.

The spiritual community will always exist within a wider community which contains both positive and negative elements. It is important, therefore, for those leading the spiritual life not to lose contact with the wider community, because that is where our energies come from. We must keep in touch with society, but we must not allow those energies to get out of control, and this is a difficult balance to preserve. The most positive sort of community in the broadest sense would be one that gave scope to all those cruder energies and forces, but was at the same time open-ended with regard to the possibility of higher development. We need a spiritual community which is uncompromising in its pursuit of the highest ideals, but which remains in contact with a wider positive group. If the spiritual community were out of touch with everyone else, where would new members come from? There is a sort of hierarchy or gradation of spiritual development and commitment, with many intermediate levels.

In practice, a Buddhist experiences life in terms of a dualism between skilful and unskilful activity, even though Buddhism teaches that ultimately such dualisms can be transcended. In practical terms, life is a constant struggle. And even when the struggle is over for us individually, if we look at society we find there is still a lot to be done. Even if you have finished your own task, attained your own Enlightenment, you still have an infinite number of tasks to do for those around you. You will never be able to settle down and rest, nor would you want to. If you are a bodhisattva, it is your nature to help beings. You are inherently compassionate. Light cannot help being light any more than darkness can help being darkness. When we rejoice in merits, we are rejoicing in this light, in this principle of bodhisattvahood at work in the world. We are recalling just how greatly precious it is, especially when we reflect on what life would be like without it.

11

ENTREATY AND SUPPLICATION

Saluting them with folded hands
I entreat the Buddhas in all the quarters:
May they make shine the lamp of the Dharma
For those wandering in the suffering of delusion!

With hands folded in reverence
I implore the Conquerors desiring to enter Nirvāṇa:
May they remain here for endless ages,
So that life in this world does not grow dark.

(Bennett)

With folded hands, I beseech the perfect Buddhas in all places:
may they cause the light of the Dharma to shine upon those who,
because of confusion, have fallen into sorrow. With folded hands, I
beseech the Conquerors who are desirous of experiencing cessation:
may they pause for countless aeons, lest this world become blind.

(Matics)

There is no significant difference between these two translations.

What essentially is happening in the sixth section, the *adhyeṣā*
and *yācanā*, entreaty and supplication, is that we are developing

receptivity, expressing our readiness to be taught. Very often people, even religious people, are not really ready to be taught – so we have to make ourselves ready. We have, after all, been rejoicing in the good qualities of the Buddhas and bodhisattvas, as well as the arising of the will to Enlightenment and the teaching. Now we make ourselves receptive to all those things, and especially of course to the Buddha and the Dharma. But before we go further into the subject of receptivity, let us have a look at the components of this section of the Sevenfold Puja.

The first verse recalls a particular episode from the scriptures, the famous request of Brahmā Sahāmpati, the 'lord of a thousand worlds'. Shortly after the Buddha's Enlightenment Brahmā Sahāmpati appeared before him and pleaded with him to teach others the way to gain Enlightenment.[123] Through this appeal he overcame the Buddha's initial inclination to think that the Dharma was just too difficult and subtle to be communicated. So here we adopt the attitude of respectful entreaty of Brahmā Sahāmpati. We ask the Buddha to teach. This does not mean that the Buddhas do not teach unless they are asked to; they are always ready, but they cannot teach us unless we are open to their teaching. In this section we express our openness. Indeed, the expression is in a way part of the openness. If we really want something, we ask for it; the asking is a natural extension of the wanting.

Suppose you want something from someone but you are somehow reluctant to make this clear to them. Perhaps you want to borrow some money from a friend; you just need a couple of pounds quickly. You know that they have it and that they would be quite willing to lend it to you, but somehow you hesitate to ask, to make your need known. This sort of situation suggests reserve, holding back, lack of confidence. It may arise from feelings of guilt, or it may be that you are reluctant to put yourself in the position of possibly being refused. This is analogous to a reluctance sometimes to ask for spiritual teaching. Perhaps you feel you are not worthy of it – or perhaps you fear that you might get more than you bargained for. You might indeed *get* some spiritual teaching, not just a little pat on the head. This is especially the case with approaching Zen masters. If you ask them for a teaching you really take your life in your hands. People say they want to be taught, but it is not all that easy to find those who really do want to learn in a truly spiritual sense. So it is good to express your willingness and readiness to learn, to make it absolutely clear that you are open, that you want to be receptive. Incidentally, the same principle applies to asking for ordination. Sometimes people adopt the attitude 'I won't actually ask because when I am ready, people will know and they will just tell me.' This also suggests a certain lack of openness which needs to be overcome.

In the first verse you 'entreat the Buddhas in all the quarters' – not just the Buddhas in your own immediate environment. You are thinking of others as well as yourself. You are requesting not only that you yourself may have teaching, but also that the 'lamp of the Dharma' should be made to shine on all living beings. You want to keep the channels of communication open between the mundane and the transcendental for all beings, for the whole world.

I remember a friend once strongly objecting to the line: 'For those wandering in the suffering of delusion'. He said that he did not feel that he *was* wandering in the suffering of delusion. But of course those who are deluded may not be aware that they are deluded. And while you might not be suffering at present, if you are deluded, the suffering will come sooner or later.

In the second verse we:

… implore the Conquerors desiring to enter Nirvāṇa:
May they remain here for endless ages,
So that life in this world does not grow dark.

This too is based on an episode from the Buddha's life in the scriptures. How genuine it is we do not know, but in the *Mahāparinibbāna Sutta* the Buddha gives Ānanda a broad hint that, if he was asked, he would stay on in the world until the end of the *kalpa*.[124] Commentators differ in their interpretation of this. Some say that '*kalpa*' here means the full term of natural life, i.e. a hundred years; others say it means until the end of the world period. In any case, Ānanda failed to take the hint, due to the intervention of Māra, and the Buddha therefore passed away. It is rather an odd episode and there is no general agreement on what it really means, even supposing it did actually happen. Did the Buddha need to be asked to stay on for the remainder of his hundred years, or until the end of the aeon? Is it a warning that we, like Ānanda in this incident, are ceasing to be receptive? I believe we may take it to mean that there is no end to the need for entreaty. You must not think that once you have asked a bodhisattva to stay and teach, that is that. You have to go on asking and wanting and being receptive. In other words, don't take a Buddha or bodhisattva for granted – even when he has been preaching for forty-five years. Be aware that he might disappear at any minute, because *saṃsāra* is so painful and the pull of Nirvāṇa, which is within his reach, is so strong. Unless you constantly keep your need before him and are really open to him, he might just disappear into Nirvāṇa. So don't let your attention waver for an instant.

However, there is another way of looking at this incident. It shows that spiritual teaching depends upon you. If you are not listening to the Buddhas and bodhisattvas, how can they be said to teach? And if they are not teaching, they might as well be in Nirvāṇa. Indeed you put them into Nirvāṇa, you make them inoperative. How could it be otherwise? The minute your attention slackens or you turn away, they are unable to teach because there is no one there to teach, no resonance. Teaching does not mean emitting words; it means communicating with beings who are listening. The Teachers can break through your inattentiveness, but if you really don't want to be receptive, there is nothing even they can do about it. If you want, you can silence all the Buddhas and bodhisattvas. It is a terrible thought. You can put out the lamp, certainly for yourself, perhaps even for others. To change the metaphor, you've slammed the door in the Buddha's face, so what can he do? He must just sit quietly on the other side until you open it again. You might even forget there was a door there at all, and then you wouldn't be able to tell other people who might not know about it, until finally no one would know that there was a door there to be opened, and it would remain shut for a very long time. So you must keep up your entreaty to keep the Buddhas teaching.

In other words, there is no absolute distinction between a Buddha's activity, if I may call it that, and other beings' receptivity. They go together. If you are receptive, he will be active. If he is active, it means you have at least started to be receptive. You could say that if other beings do not allow him to teach, it is as though the Buddha's own Enlightenment, even, is not complete. This is putting it rather strongly but it gives us something to think about. Perhaps there is no such thing as absolute self-sufficiency, even for a Buddha. It is not easy to describe what the Buddha's experience is like in terms of unenlightened experience, so let us take an ordinary human analogy. Suppose you like somebody in a normal, healthy way. If they are aware of that and like you back, doesn't that give an extra dimension to the fact of your liking them? Or is your liking exactly the same whether they like you or not? Or take the case of ordinary teaching. Without the stimulus of the students' curiosity and interest and alertness and receptivity, no teaching can take place.

This notion of interdependence is expressed in another way in the bodhisattva ideal, in accordance with which the bodhisattva vows not to enter Nirvāṇa until all beings have crossed over the ocean of suffering. If people really want to stay in that ocean of suffering, it follows that they are holding the bodhisattva back. In a sense his Enlightenment is not complete until they too become Enlightened. So it's as though the Buddha is begging sentient beings to let him teach.

It is significant that the entreaty and supplication comes after the rejoicing in merits, which is a very bright, almost radiant state in which you are intensely aware of the merits of other beings, especially the merits of the Buddhas and bodhisattvas. Out of this awareness you rejoice, and in that rejoicing, positive state you become receptive. You open yourself to the influence of the Buddhas and bodhisattvas, to the Dharma itself, as it were, there being no Dharma apart from the Buddhas or bodhisattvas who communicate it.

Very often, however, we are not positive enough to be receptive in this way. We may be afraid of the change that receptivity might initiate, unable to cope, almost. Or we may think we know it all already. There is a little story about a Zen master which concerns this sort of attitude. According to this tale, a university professor went to call on a Zen master to ask the master to teach him. The Zen master received him very politely and, as is the custom, offered him tea. The master then placed two cups on a low table and started pouring tea from the pot into one of the cups. He continued pouring until the cup was full and then went on pouring. The professor watched the tea overflow into the saucer, but the Zen master just went on pouring. Soon the saucer was full to overflowing, so that tea streamed across the tablecloth, and still the Zen master went on pouring. By the time a little rivulet was flowing right on to the floor, the professor could contain himself no longer. He knew that Zen masters were reputed to be pretty strange, but this one was the most eccentric he had ever come across. 'Why are you still pouring?' he asked. 'The cup is full.' The Zen master now looked up from his pouring. 'Why do you come here?' he replied. 'Your cup is full.' And he continued: 'Unless you empty your cup, you cannot receive anything. It's no use expecting me to pour into a full cup.'[125] So we have to make ourselves empty in order to receive – not literally, because we cannot forget everything we know, but we can put it to one side, as it were, so that it will not get in the way.

Even if you are initially receptive to spiritual experience, it can still be difficult to cope with the consequences of that experience. When you 'open up' and receive spiritual teaching or spiritual experience, the initial experience needs to be followed up by a process of assimilation. This is analogous to the Path of Vision being followed by the Path of Transformation. But in order to assimilate the experience, to transform your being in accordance with that experience, you may need to spend time in suitably supportive conditions. Otherwise you can be like the snake in the Indian saying who is trying to swallow a frog that is too big. It is so big he can't get it down but because of the way his fangs curve, he cannot vomit it up either. Through being genuinely open it can sometimes happen that you go through a period of 'spiritual indigestion' when you can be quite unbalanced. There are stories about Zen masters – that is, stories about them before they became Zen masters – where they appear to other people to be quite mad.

It would be wrong to say that you could have too much receptivity, any more than you could have too much awareness or too much mindfulness. However, it may be that sometimes when you have been receptive you are unable, for the time being at least, to handle that experience. You are, as it were, midway between the Path of Vision and the Path of Transformation, and that can be quite an uncomfortable state. For this reason spiritual teachers should be aware of the possibility of pushing people too hard or too far, of opening them up too much during retreats and similar activities – especially if the next day they go back to the everyday world, back to their jobs and families. People need time to make some headway on the Path of Transformation corresponding to whatever level of the Path of Vision they have experienced.

When we perform the Sevenfold Puja, immediately after the verses of entreaty and supplication we usually have a reading from the scriptures, as is appropriate after opening ourselves to the teaching. In fact, the verses of the puja suggest the attitude with which we should always hear or read the Buddha's words. Immediately after the reading we recite the

Heart Sūtra, which contains the essence of the teaching, at least from a Mahāyāna point of view.[126] There may also be readings at other stages of the puja, according to the nature of the occasion.

If you happen to be asked to do a reading – and it is to be hoped that the leader of the puja will give you plenty of notice of this – you should read through it a few times beforehand to be sure you fully understand the structure of the sentences and where the emphases should come. Readings from the scriptures will be in translation, which often means that the sentence structures are quite awkward and complex, so you need to get the hang of them. If possible it might even be best to read the passage aloud beforehand, preferably with someone listening to offer comments and suggestions. Not many people are able to read well without making this sort of effort.

Tone of voice and enunciation are very important too. A reading should not be delivered in a harsh or discordant tone. It does, however, need to be clear. Oral communication, in readings and in a great many other contexts, is a vital practical element of the spiritual life. For those who are not very skilled at it, it is well worth making the effort to improve, enlisting the help of friends and even undertaking formal training if necessary.

If you are listening to the reading, it is obviously important to remain attentive and receptive throughout. During the reading you are less active than during the verses of the puja itself since you are not reciting or chanting anything, so there may be a temptation to use it as an opportunity to stretch your legs and mentally withdraw somewhat from the puja. But it would be a great pity if, having just declared your openness to the Buddha's teaching, you then failed to receive it.

12

TRANSFERENCE OF MERIT AND
SELF-SURRENDER

May the merit gained
In my acting thus
Go to the alleviation of the suffering of all beings.
My personality throughout my existences,
My possessions,
And my merit in all three ways,
I give up without regard to myself
For the benefit of all beings.

Just as the earth and other elements
Are serviceable in many ways
To the infinite number of beings
Inhabiting limitless space;
So may I become
That which maintains all beings
Situated throughout space,
So long as all have not attained
To peace.

(Bennett)

Having done all this, let me also be a cause of abatement, by
means of whatever good I have achieved, for all of the sorrow of

all creatures.... I sacrifice indifferently my bodies, pleasures, and
goodness, where the three ways cross, past, present and future, for
the complete fulfilment of the welfare of all beings.... As the earth
and other elements are, in various ways, for the enjoyment of
innumerable beings dwelling in all of space; so may I be, in various
ways, the means of sustenance for the living beings occupying
space, for as long a time as all are not satisfied.

(Matics)

There is one difference in interpretation in the second verse. Matics
specifies past, present, and future whereas Bennett's 'merit in all three
ways' refers to another traditional formulation: merit by way of body,
speech, and mind. Whichever of these interpretations we follow, the
general meaning is clear. You give up *all* your merit – past, present,
and future, through body, speech, and mind. You don't want any of it
just for yourself. According to some traditional texts there are three
possible aims in life. You can wish for well-being in this present life;
you can hope for a good and happy rebirth in some future existence;
or you can think in terms of gaining Enlightenment for the benefit of
all beings. In reciting these verses, it is the third kind of motivation you
are trying to cultivate.

Thus the overall feeling of this section is one of altruism and service
to other beings, 'just as the earth and other elements are serviceable in
many ways'. There are many references in Buddhist tradition to the idea
that the elements are for everybody. Everybody can stand on the earth
and make use of the earth; everybody breathes the air; everybody drinks
and makes use of water. They are free to all; they belong to all; they
are completely at the service of all living beings. And the bodhisattva
aspires to be like that – to be available to all living beings, of service
to them, enjoyed by them, without any restriction or limitation. And
just as everybody equally breathes air, in the same way the bodhisattva
wants to be equally of service to all.

The phrase 'that which maintains all beings' refers to *ākāśa*, which
is translated sometimes as 'space', sometimes as 'ether'. It is the subtle
element (as opposed to the gross elements of earth, water, fire, and
air) that sustains the gross elements as they sustain living beings, and
underlies the entire physical universe. So the bodhisattva aspires not

only to be like earth, fire, water, and air but to be like *ākāśa*, which contains and supports the elements themselves. Beyond even that is the idea of Dharma, in the sense here of cosmic law – the word 'Dharma' coming from the verb meaning 'to support'. Ultimately you could say that it is the Dharma that supports everything.

In these verses of transference of merit and self-surrender, you give up not only all your possessions but even your merit. You do not want even to keep your own goodness – your own means, as it were, of getting to Nirvāṇa – for yourself. This is certainly one of the most difficult things to do – to give up your own merits, give up, in a way, your own reputation.

Hakuin, the famous Zen master, is a great example in this respect. According to one story, he was once wrongly accused of making a young woman in the village pregnant, and he thereby lost his reputation as a venerable Zen monk and Zen master. When the child was born, the young woman just put it on the temple doorstep, so Hakuin took it in and brought it up. After some years the woman repented and confessed that she had falsely accused him of being the father of the child in order to shield someone else, so he gave the child back. But in all those years he never said anything about the situation except 'Is it so?' When people said, 'This girl is accusing you of being the father of her child,' he simply said, 'Is it so?' When they said it was his child and he had better bring it up, his response was the same. And when the woman admitted that her accusation had been false and reclaimed the child, again he just said, 'Is it so?' At no point was he concerned about his own reputation as a virtuous Zen master.[127]

Hakuin, then, had no attachment to his own merit, unlike many people who are very attached to their reputations. From an ordinary human point of view such concern for one's own good name is understandable, but from the highest spiritual point of view it is our attachment which must be given up. The bodhisattva doesn't mind appearing not to be a bodhisattva or even not to be a good person, if that is necessary. He certainly doesn't want to keep his merit to himself so that he can get to Nirvāṇa ahead of other beings. If a sense of ego is the principal obstacle standing between you and Enlightenment, how could you ever get to Enlightenment with your ego simply accumulating good actions which it regarded as its own? Clearly that kind of outlook cannot take you all the way.

In this final section of the Sevenfold Puja you say, as it were: 'I know I have performed this puja; I have saluted the Buddhas and bodhisattvas, gone for Refuge, confessed my faults, and rejoiced in merits. I have entreated the Buddhas and bodhisattvas to preach and opened myself to their influence. But I do not claim anything of that merit just for myself. May it redound to the spiritual benefit of all living beings, because that is all I am really interested in.' It is called transference of merit and self-surrender because here you have virtually surrendered yourself. You don't have any selfish interest even in your own good actions. You don't wish to claim them or appropriate them just for yourself. From a Mahāyāna point of view, no virtuous action is really complete until the merit from it has been dedicated to all beings. This practice transforms what would otherwise be a means to a purely individual attainment into something much bigger, much more universal. We should therefore have this attitude of dedicating or transferring the merit gained by any positive activity we undertake, and especially by ritual acts like the puja.

The doctrine of *pariṇāmanā* or transference of merit is not meant to assert that anything has literally been transferred from one person to another. It is to be understood in a more poetic sense; it concerns our inner attitude. For instance, in Burmese temples, whenever anyone makes an offering they ring the bell – the idea being that you wish that whoever hears the bell may share in the merits of the offering that has just been made. The doctrine arises because, owing to the very structure and nature of language, we cannot help speaking about the spiritual life to some extent in terms of accumulation – gaining this, developing that, attaining the other. If we are not careful, this can lead us into a kind of refined selfishness. To counteract that tendency, and to prevent us from thinking of our merits as literally our own, as attaching to our egos, we have this doctrine. It says, 'Yes, develop virtues, acquire all the wonderful bodhisattva qualities, but share them.' The same sort of idea exists, in a simple form, even in Hīnayāna Buddhism.

We cannot of course sincerely wish to transfer our merits unless we feel very positively towards other beings. The transference of merit and self-surrender is therefore a form, or an extension, of the *mettā bhāvanā* practice. It is a training in egolessness and paves the way for the arising of the *bodhicitta*. Indeed the whole Sevenfold Puja is oriented towards encouraging the arising of the *bodhicitta*, towards creating the conditions in which it can arise.

What exactly is meant, then, by the *bodhicitta*? '*Bodhicitta*' literally means 'the thought of or will to Enlightenment', but the main point to grasp is that it is not someone's individual will in the narrow sense. You do, of course, have to start off with an individual will making an individual effort, but the *bodhicitta* is something which as it were supervenes upon that individual spiritual effort when it reaches a very high degree of purity, refinement, positivity, and openness. It is as if the stream or tendency making for Enlightenment takes you over. That is where the surrender comes in. You surrender yourself to it, open yourself to it, become a channel for it. You are no longer 'you' in a narrow egoistic sense. There is something higher working through you. You are still recognizably there as an individual living being functioning in the world, but in fact it is not just you functioning – it is the *bodhicitta* functioning, moving in the direction of the Enlightenment of all beings.

This is why I have sometimes said that the *bodhicitta* manifests within the context of the spiritual community. It is not individual, but it is not collective either; it is in a third category, like the spiritual community itself. The spiritual community, especially to the extent that it is a transcendental community, is an embodiment of the *bodhicitta*. Just as on the ordinary level you can have a wave of emotion that sweeps through a crowd, which is sub-individual, in the same way you can have the *bodhicitta* manifesting in the midst of the spiritual community, which is supra-individual. When that happens you feel that you are working for something greater than yourself, although there is really no distinction between you and it. Even though a number of individuals are involved, it is not a mass thing, precisely because they are individuals. In a sense you cannot have just one lone bodhisattva, although it may seem that you can. By thinking of the *bodhicitta* as arising within the spiritual community, you safeguard yourself against thinking of it as an individual phenomenon. You could say that the *bodhicitta* is something that manifests when a number of individuals in a spiritual community have reached the point represented by the last stage of the Sevenfold Puja. If you have performed your Sevenfold Puja with real feeling, as you reach the end of it there should be an experience somewhat like the arising of the *bodhicitta*.

There is some similarity between this and the Hīnayāna concept of Stream Entry, although it is always very difficult to correlate Hīnayāna doctrinal formulations which have become rather rigid with

Mahāyāna doctrinal formulations which have perhaps become equally rigid. Loosening both concepts up and trying to get at what they were originally referring to, I would say that in the full sense the arising of the *bodhicitta* is something that happens after Stream Entry. You can certainly have an aspiration towards Buddhahood and a very sincere dedication to the bodhisattva way of life long before you become a Stream Entrant, but the arising of the *bodhicitta* as a total experience only takes place, I believe, after Stream Entry. This said, within the context of the spiritual community, individuals who are not Stream Entrants can still get some taste of the *bodhicitta*, so to speak, even though it will not be a full arising. They may not be 'flowers' themselves but they can at least enjoy the fragrance of those who are flowers.

Furthermore, they can act in the bodhisattva spirit to whatever extent they are capable of doing so. Just as the bodhisattva aspires to give whatever support he can to the beings of the whole cosmos, so on your own level, if you are at least trying to practise the bodhisattva ideal, that should naturally involve giving whatever support you can to those within your immediate environment, your spiritual community. If you are not functioning in a supportive way, if you just regard the spiritual community as a sort of convenience to your individual development, you are living more in accordance with the *arhant* ideal, indeed the narrowest interpretation of the *arhant* ideal. Taken in this narrow, extreme form, that ideal becomes self-defeating, because you cannot really help yourself without helping others. If you think in terms of helping yourself to the exclusion of helping others, you have a very rigid idea of self and of others, and as long as that fixed view is there you can't even gain Enlightenment for yourself.

Helping ourselves involves helping others; helping others involves helping ourselves. We cannot separate the two. We cannot really use the spiritual community just as a convenience for our own individual spiritual development, even though we may try to do so. The sharing of merit which helps us move towards the bodhisattva ideal is in accordance with the reality of our situation as living beings.

13
CONCLUDING MANTRAS

The eight mantras that we chant at the end of the puja, each one three times in call and response, are:

oṃ maṇi padme hūṃ (Avalokiteśvara)
oṃ a ra pa ca na dhīḥ (Mañjuśrī)
oṃ vajrapāṇi hūṃ (Vajrapāṇi)
oṃ tāre tuttāre ture svāhā (Tārā)
oṃ amideva hrīḥ (Amitābha)
oṃ muni muni mahā muni śākyamuni svāhā (Śākyamuni)
oṃ āḥ hūṃ vajra guru padma siddhi hūṃ (Padmasambhava)
gate gate pāragate pārasaṃgate bodhi svāhā (Prajñāpāramitā)

There are of course a great many other Buddhas and bodhisattvas, all with their own mantras. These eight include several of the best-known and most prominent of them. But before we are introduced to them, we need to ask a fundamental question. What is a mantra?

The word *mantra* is sometimes translated as 'magic words' or even 'spell', but these renderings have quite the wrong connotations. If we turn to the etymological meaning of the word, that is a little more helpful – but not very much. Etymologically, 'mantra' can be defined as 'that which protects the mind'. The recitation of a mantra undoubtedly does protect the mind, but so does every other spiritual practice, so this definition, whilst not actually misleading, is not nearly specific enough.

Essentially the mantra is a sound symbol – just as the figure of a Buddha or bodhisattva is a form and colour symbol – of a particular aspect of the Enlightened mind. In referring to sound here, I do not just mean the external sound produced by the voice. Mantric sound is also internal – indeed, it is more internal than external. Sometimes the efficacy of mantras is misleadingly explained in terms of physical vibrations. It is said that the recitation of a particular mantra produces a certain number of vibrations per second which is in some way spiritually efficacious, but this is much too crude and materialistic an account. Lama Govinda has pointed out that if mantras were a matter of physical vibrations, one could simply buy a recording of them being chanted and play it over and over again to get all the wonderful spiritual benefits.

So a mantra is essentially an *inner* sound, an inner vibration, even an inner feeling. I am not suggesting that the external physical sound has no meaning at all, or that mantras should not be recited aloud; but the gross repetition of a mantra is only a means to, a catalyst for, the inner feeling of the mantra vibrating through one's being. The relationship between the gross, external, verbal repetition and the subtle, internal, mental repetition is not unlike that between a painted picture of a Buddha or bodhisattva and that same figure visualized during meditation. In each case the gross experience leads towards the subtle experience.

But although the various translations are not much help, there are certain things one can say about a mantra, and these taken together might even add up to a definition. First, it is a string of syllables which sometimes, but not always, form or include a word or words. Whether forming words or not, the syllables of a mantra come from the sixty-four letters of the Sanskrit alphabet. It is customary not to translate mantras. It is sometimes said that they are never translated, but this is not quite correct because occasionally they are. For instance, the Padmasambhava mantra we chant as one of the concluding mantras (*oṃ āḥ hūṃ vajra guru padma siddhi hūṃ*) differs from the one that we often chant earlier in the puja (*oṃ āḥ hūṃ jetsun guru padma siddhi hūṃ*) inasmuch as the latter is derived from the Tibetan chanting and substitutes a Tibetan word for a Sanskrit one. The purely Sanskrit version is really the correct form, but the Tibetans do sometimes translate odd words into their own language when chanting and singing. It is not at all unusual to have different versions of mantras, if only because of mispronunciations. With the Tārā mantra, for instance, Tibetans pronounce *tāre tuttāre* as if it were *tāre tittāre*. Likewise, in the Avalokiteśvara mantra they say *oṃ maṇi peme hūṃ*.

On the other hand some Tibetans chant an alternative version of the Śākyamuni mantra: *oṃ muni muni mahāmuni śākyamuniye svāhā*. And this is quite correct inasmuch as *ye* represents a dative inflexion – i.e. *muniye* means 'to the sage'. But this dative inflexion isn't really necessary in the context of mantras so it can safely be dropped. The one inflexion we do retain is *-me* in *oṃ maṇi padme hūṃ*.

The second thing to say about mantras is that they are not susceptible to logical analysis. In a sense, they are meaningless. Confounding any attribution of conventional meaning is what they are all about. There are certain mantras which contain words that have assignable meanings. There is, for instance, the famous mantra associated with Avalokiteśvara, *oṃ maṇi padme hūṃ*. *Maṇi* means 'jewel' and *padme* means 'in the lotus', so the middle part of the mantra could be given a literal meaning ('the jewel in the lotus'), although the initial '*oṃ*' and the concluding '*hūṃ*' could not be interpreted in any such way. But even though the phrase 'jewel in the lotus' suggests a perfectly good philosophical meaning with all sorts of ramifications in Buddhist thought and practice, it would be a mistake to say that this is what the mantra means.[128] Such a phrase cannot give the real, much less still the total, meaning of the mantra. At best it gives just a facet – and not even the most important facet – of the meaning.

It is even more difficult to give an exact meaning to a word such as *svāhā*, which often comes at the end of mantras. Its conventional meaning is something like 'so be it', or 'that's it'. However, again it would be wrong to say that this is its meaning in the mantra. Perhaps the most we can say is that it carries connotations of affirmation, well-being, and success. And even then it does not carry these connotations for everyone. '*Svāhā*' occurs a great deal in Brahminical rituals and for this reason it would spark off the wrong sort of feelings amongst most Indian Buddhists, especially those once treated by Hinduism as 'Untouchables'. It would be rather like Western Buddhists saying 'amen' in a puja. There is nothing wrong with saying 'amen' if you take it literally – it just means 'yes' – but the connotations and associations are all wrong.

Many mantras contain no words with defined meanings at all. The Tārā mantra, for instance, consists of a series of modulations of the vocative form of the name Tārā, i.e. *tāre*. There is no analysable meaning; reciting the mantra is apparently just juggling with the sound of the name. But mantras are not simply names either – certainly not in the sense of mere labels. Some mantras do include the personal name of the Buddha or bodhisattva to which they 'belong', or variations on that name, but others do not.

Thirdly, and most importantly, a mantra is a sound symbol of a particular divinity, such as a Buddha or bodhisattva. If that divinity could become a sound, which according to Tantric Buddhism it can and does, then that sound is the mantra. Just as the visualized image is the equivalent of the divinity in terms of form and colour, so the mantra is the equivalent in terms of sound. The mantra can therefore be thought of as the true, inherent name of the divinity – regardless of whether it includes the divinity's conventional name. When we call a person by name, he comes; similarly, when we invoke a particular divinity with a mantra, that divinity manifests, becomes present.

Fourthly, using the term 'mantra' in the strict Tantric meaning, a mantra is given by the guru to the disciple at the time of bestowing a Tantric initiation. Usually the disciple repeats the mantra three times after the guru and, through this ritual, spiritual energy is 'transmitted'. If a mantra is not given in this way, it is not truly a mantra. People may read mantras in books, learn them, and start to recite them, and they may even get some benefit from doing so, but what they are reciting is not a mantra. Part of the meaning of mantra is that the practitioner is empowered to use it by the guru, that is, by a more spiritually advanced person than the practitioner with whom he or she is in communication. If it is picked up in any other way, it may be good religious practice, but it is not Tantric recitation of a mantra. Incidentally, the guru may not necessarily be a human living guru. It is possible to receive mantras in dreams or in the course of meditation from a guru-figure.

Fifthly and lastly, a mantra is something that is repeated. It should be repeated regularly and earnestly over a long period, until eventually inner repetition becomes spontaneous, no longer requiring conscious effort. But if it is neglected, the energy originally transmitted by the guru will gradually be lost.

The recitation of mantras occupies an extremely important place in Tantric Buddhism. The Tantra was in fact originally known as the Mantrayāna, 'the way of the mantras'. This distinguished it from the

Mahāyāna which was then known as the Pāramitāyāna, 'the way of the practice of the perfections'. The term Vajrayāna came into use much later, to refer to the more advanced and radical development of the Tantric tradition. It is said that progress is more rapid in the Mantrayāna than in the Pāramitāyāna. The practice of the perfections – giving, morality, patience, vigour, meditation, and wisdom – represents a complete scheme of ethical and spiritual development, but it appeals more to the conscious mind, at least in the early stages. It is an arduous but intelligible path of practice. The Mantrayāna, on the other hand, is directed much more to the unconscious mind. It aims to directly contact the spiritual forces that are latent in the depths of the mind – forces which are ultimately different aspects of the Enlightened mind. These aspects of the Enlightened mind are personified, or, more accurately, crystallized, in the forms of Buddhas, bodhisattvas, and other deities, and according to the Tantra they can be contacted through the practice of visualization of form and colour together with invocation and mantric sound.

The chanting of mantras comes at the end of the Sevenfold Puja. At this point we have already experienced ourselves in relation to the Enlightened mind in a number of ways, represented by the progressive sequence of the seven stages of the puja, and we have felt the strong spiritual emotions and ardent aspirations aroused by seeing ourselves in relation to Enlightenment. Even so, the Enlightened mind may still seem to us to be something quite remote, something of a different order. The chanting of mantras represents the actual presence of Enlightenment, of the Buddhas and bodhisattvas, in the world and in our own being. It indicates the real possibility for our energies to be radically transformed so that we can make manifest the qualities of Enlightenment that are buried deep within us, and become a channel for the arising of the *bodhicitta*. This Tantric touch can lift the whole puja to an altogether higher level.

Although the sevenfold form of puja comes from the Mahāyāna tradition, the version used within the FWBO deliberately includes elements of the Hīnayāna and the Vajrayāna as well. This is not just for the sake of having all three traditional *yānas* represented but because of the spiritual efficacy of doing so.

So now let us meet the eight Buddhas and bodhisattvas whose mantras are chanted at the end of the Sevenfold Puja. The first three are what the Tibetans call the three 'family protectors', the bodhisattvas representing compassion (Avalokiteśvara), wisdom (Mañjuśrī), and spiritual energy (Vajrapāṇi).

The Avalokiteśvara mantra is the most widely known and chanted of all mantras. Avalokiteśvara is the quintessence of compassion, the chief bodhisattva in the Lotus family of which the Buddha Amitābha is the head. He is the active expression of the boundless love which Amitābha represents. He is sometimes envisaged as red, like Amitābha, especially in the form known as Padmapāṇi ('lotus in hand'), but he is more often depicted as pure shining white, most commonly in his four-armed and thousand-armed forms. The many arms of this extraordinary figure reach out in all directions to help suffering beings. His name means 'the lord who looks down', who sees the suffering of beings so that he may respond.

Just as Avalokiteśvara is the embodiment of absolute compassion, so Mañjuśrī, also known as Mañjughoṣa, is the embodiment of transcendental wisdom. Mañjuśrī appears in the form of a beautiful sixteen-year-old youth, a deep, rich yellow in colour and clad in the usual silks and jewels of a bodhisattva. His right arm is uplifted and he flourishes above his head the flaming sword of wisdom with which he cuts the bonds of karma and ignorance. In his left hand, which he presses to his heart, he holds a book of the Perfection of Wisdom. In keeping with his manifestation of supreme wisdom he is known also as 'the lord of speech' and seen as the patron of the arts and sciences.

In order to convey something of the boundless energy that Vajrapāṇi embodies, he is most often depicted in wrathful form, although he also has peaceful forms. In the more popular wrathful form he is dark blue like the midnight sky, stout and strong with thick, short limbs and a protuberant belly. His powerful body is generally naked except for ornaments of human bone, and he wears a crown of human skulls. He has three eyes – the third being in the middle of his forehead – which glare ferociously. Surrounded by a halo of flames, he is trampling triumphantly on two figures which represent ignorance and craving, the evils that he has destroyed. His right arm is raised and in his right hand he grasps, as though ready to hurl it, the vajra or diamond-thunderbolt. Indeed his name means 'thunderbolt in hand'.

Following on from the three family protectors, there is Tārā, the principal feminine bodhisattva or Buddha form. The mantra we chant is particularly that of Tārā in her form of Green Tārā. The other most popular form, that of White Tārā, has a somewhat extended version of the same mantra. Like Avalokiteśvara, Tārā manifests especially the quality of compassion, and her hands make gestures symbolizing giving and the dispelling of fear. Her name means 'the one who ferries across', that is to say the one who ferries beings across the river of birth and death, the river of *samsāra*, to reach the further shore, which is Nirvāṇa. The name Tārā is sometimes translated as 'saviouress', but this is perhaps misleading. Tārā represents more the attitude of helping people to help themselves.

Amitābha, whose mantra comes next, is the red Buddha of the western quarter. His name literally means 'infinite light' and he embodies not just light but warmth, the maturing power of great love, as symbolized by his deep, brilliant red colour. Amitābha's emblem, the lotus flower, symbolizes spiritual unfoldment and growth, a process which is nourished and fostered by love. His hands are in the *mudrā* of meditation. Just as the sun sets in the west in a glorious blaze of red, so the mind withdraws from the cares of the everyday world, quiet but more alive than ever, as it enters a state of meditation.

The next mantra is that of Śākyamuni, the historical Buddha, the extraordinary human being who discovered and opened up for others the way to Enlightenment in our world-age. The central figure in the vast body of Buddhist teaching, devotional practice, and art, Śākyamuni embodies all the innumerable and excellent Buddha-qualities. At the same time his presence reminds us that, as we say in the Short Puja:

The Buddha was born, as we are born.
What the Buddha overcame, we too can overcome;
What the Buddha attained, we too can attain.

Following on from Śākyamuni, we come to Padmasambhava, the archetypal guru. A part-historical, part-mythical figure, Padmasambhava was the single most important influence in the establishment of Buddhism in Tibet, where he is said to have subdued the local gods and demons and converted them to be protectors of the Dharma. He therefore represents, among other things, the ability to deal with and integrate powerful psychic forces. He is a heroic and vigorous figure. In his principal manifestation – he has many others – he is clad in very rich, colourful, and princely garments, and wears on his head the famous lotus cap which terminates in a vajra and a vulture's feather. He holds a skull cup and a golden vajra. In the crook of his left arm there is a long staff with streamers, surmounted by three severed human heads and a trident. His expression is benign and compassionate, although his smile is not without a touch of ferocity.

Finally, there is the mantra of the Perfection of Wisdom, Prajñāpāramitā, which is in a way impersonal and may appeal to those who do not get on very well with 'personal' embodiments of the ideal. Although there *is* a figure of Prajñāpāramitā, she has a different mantra. The normal association of this mantra, which comes from the *Heart Sūtra*, is Prajñāpāramitā, or the Perfection of Wisdom, in the abstract rather than Prajñāpāramitā as a deity that can be visualized. However, there is no hard and fast distinction.

The puja ends, then, with the Perfection of Wisdom, the sublime wisdom that goes beyond, 'holding to nothing whatever' as the *Heart Sūtra* says – the wisdom which is the essence of the Enlightenment of all the Buddhas. Dwelling in the radiance of this last mantra, in the accumulated radiance of all the mantras, we chant just four more words, each in more gentle and attenuated tones than the one before: 'oṃ śānti śānti śānti....' (oṃ, peace, peace, peace...). We experience perhaps a glimmering of that peace which is at once perfectly tranquil and utterly dynamic, brimming with energy and potential. We remain in silence for a short while, or, if we can, for a good long while, to absorb and rejoice in the excellent and propitious emotions aroused by the Sevenfold Puja.

DIALOGUE BETWEEN BUDDHISM
AND CHRISTIANITY

Dialogue Between Buddhism and Christianity *was written for the
'Bouddhisme et Christianisme' issue of the* Revue Internationale
de Theologie Concilium. *When it was reprinted in the Ola Leaves
series the Editor's Foreword noted: 'The actual headings of this essay
represent themes for discussion laid down by the editor of* Concilium.
*Left to his own devices, the author would probably not have chosen to
discuss the subject under these headings at all.' The essay was written
in the first half of 1978. (S) It was originally published in the* Middle
Way, *vol. 61, no. 3, in November 1986.*

Buddhism and Christianity are both universal religions. They are
not, like the old ethnic religions, limited to a particular part of the
earth's surface or to a particular breeding group within the human
population, nor, strictly speaking, is it possible to be born into them.
Although for purposes of communication they adopted – in fact had to
adopt – the outward forms of the culture (Vedic-Śramaṇic and Judaeo-
Hellenic respectively) in the midst of which they originally appeared,
and although they subsequently gave birth to distinctive cultures of
their own, neither of them can be identified with even the most highly
developed culture; nor can they, with justice, be discussed in exclusively
'cultural' terms. In principle, the message of both Buddhism and
Christianity is addressed not to man as a member of a group (family,
tribe, etc.) but to man as an individual who is capable of responding

as an individual and either attaining Nirvāṇa, realizing Buddhahood, etc. or saving his own soul, winning the Kingdom of Heaven, etc. An individual becomes a Buddhist, or becomes a Christian, in the one case through the act of Going for Refuge to the Three Jewels (Buddha, Dharma, and Sangha), in the other by undergoing the rite of baptism. Those who have gone for Refuge, or who have been baptized, form a spiritual community (sangha, church) that is in reality quite distinct from any mundane group to which the Buddhist or the Christian may also belong even when all the other members of that group happen to be Buddhists or Christians.

Although Buddhism and Christianity are both universal religions, and although as universal religions they resemble each other more closely than they resemble any of the ethnic religions, they are, at the same time, about as different from each other as it is possible for them to be. One might in fact say, paradoxically, that it is possible for them to be so different just because they are both universal religions. The differences between them are both intrinsic and extrinsic. Buddhism is not only non-theistic, but the most important representative of the non-theistic group of religions, to which also belong ethnic religions like Taoism and Confucianism, as well as Jainism, which even though it has remained largely confined to the Indian subcontinent is in principle a universal religion. Christianity is of course theistic, and the principal representative of the theistic group of religions, in which are included Judaism, which is an ethnic religion, and Islam, which is a universal religion with strong ethnic features. In fact, on account of its subtle and complex Trinitarian doctrine, Christianity may be considered the theistic religion *par excellence*. On the practical side, Buddhism emphasizes the importance of the part played by meditation and contemplation (*samatha* and *vipaśyanā*) in spiritual development, whereas Christianity insists on the indispensability of the sacraments for the living of the Christian life. In profane historical-phenomenological terms, Christianity is the principal Semitic faith, Buddhism the leading Indo-Aryan teaching. Christianity has dominated the history of Europe, while Buddhism has profoundly influenced the history of Asia. Christianity is the religion of the West; Buddhism is the religion of the East.

Despite the fact that these two great spiritual phenomena grew up in the same world – indeed occupied opposite ends of the same great Eurasian land mass, until very recent times there was no real contact between them. Nestorian Christians and Mahāyāna Buddhists did, of course, have a certain amount of contact in Central Asia, perhaps in China too; a life of the Buddha found its way into medieval Europe as the biography of a Christian saint; Desideri made his way to Lhasa, and wrote a book in Tibetan in which he refuted Buddhism, and St Francis Xavier argued with a Zen monk – and that was about all. [129] Only in very recent times has there been anything like sustained or significant contact between the two religions, and as time goes on such contact is likely to increase rather than diminish. Indeed, it can be expected to play an ever more important part in the spiritual life of mankind.

THE NATURE OF DIALOGUE

According to the dictionary, a dialogue is a conversation between two people. It might therefore be expected that a dialogue between Buddhism and Christianity would be simply a conversation, in the sense of an exchange of views, between the two religions, but in fact this is not so. In the modern ecumenical context – whether as between sects within one and the same religion or as between different religions – the term 'dialogue' has come to possess not only a more specialized but also a richer meaning. This meaning is not unconnected with the fact that many of the sects and religions that nowadays are parties to dialogue, but especially the religions, have hitherto developed in complete isolation. This is particularly so, as we have seen, in the case of Buddhism and Christianity, which for by far the greater part of their careers have remained in almost total ignorance of each other's existence. Because they developed in mutual isolation, and because they moreover met with no decisive spiritual challenge from any other universal religion, both Buddhism and Christianity tended to see themselves as religious absolutes, within whose all-embracing synthesis a place, and an explanation, could be found for all the spiritual facts of existence – including, in theory at least – the teachings of all other religions.

In this respect the position which the two religions adopted on the spiritual plane (and on the earthly plane too, in the case of the medieval papacy) was analogous to the position adopted on the sociological plane by the civilizations of Ancient India and Ancient China. Jambudvīpa was synonymous with the inhabited earth, the Middle Kingdom equivalent to the whole civilized world. When China, in the middle of the nineteenth century, first came in contact with the Western powers, it was forced to recognize that these were not, in fact, outlying dependencies of the Celestial Empire that could be overawed by a few well chosen words from the Dragon Throne, but independent sovereign states whom she was obliged to treat on equal terms. In much the same way, Buddhism and Christianity have been brought face to face, and forced to recognize each other's existence as separate spiritual universes. Christianity can no longer put Buddhism in its place, as it were, by speaking of it as a mere ethical system, or as a form of natural mysticism. Buddhism can no longer relegate Christianity to the *devayāna* with a good-natured comment on the spiritual inadequacies of theism. From now onwards Buddhism and Christianity must take each other more seriously than that. From now onwards they must try to communicate.

But for communication to be possible there must be a medium of communication: there must be a common language. Since the two religions developed in complete independence of each other, however, no such common language exists. Both of them developed, of course, a powerful and flexible 'theological' or 'Buddhological' language which is as adequate to the expression of their own ultimate content (Divine Revelation, Enlightenment) as a language of this sort can by its very nature be, but in each case the language is completely understandable – or fully 'transparent' – only to the members of the spiritual community within which it arose and who habitually use it as their means of communication with one another. What is said in one 'language' cannot be translated into the other without very serious distortion. Even to speak in terms of 'Buddhology', as though there was something in Buddhism corresponding to the Christian notion of theology – even, in fact, to speak of Buddhism as a religion – is already to introduce an element of distortion into the discussion. There is also no question of Buddhism and Christianity alike being translated into some neutral(?) 'universalist' Esperanto[130] and left to communicate with each other through this medium. Were this to be done, the possibility of distortion, and therefore of mutual incomprehension, would be increased to such an extent that even if communication were achieved it could hardly be regarded as a communication between Buddhism and Christianity. Having been brought face to face, and forced to recognize each other's existence, Buddhism and Christianity are in the position of having to communicate without a medium of communication, without a common language. In the ecumenical context, it is in this communication without a medium of communication that the essence of dialogue consists. Less paradoxically, dialogue is that form of communication in which the means of communication has to be created in the course of the process of communication itself.

THE PRINCIPAL OBSTACLE TO DIALOGUE

Obstacles to a fruitful dialogue between Buddhism and Christianity are of many kinds. Even in these days of improved communications, Buddhists and Christians may not always find it easy to meet. There may be difficulties arising out of the special nature of one's vocation, whether as parish priest, meditation master, or social worker. Moreover, the members of one's flock, or one's religious superiors, may not approve of contact between the followers of the two religions. Even when one is face to face with one's partner in dialogue there are still psychological obstacles to be surmounted. Suspicion and prejudice enter only too easily into any human heart, and one may at times be deficient in honesty, in patience, in charity (*maitrī*), and even in common courtesy. More formidable still, there is the inherent difficulty of grasping the real meaning of concepts with which one is totally unfamiliar, as well as of appreciating the significance of symbols that one finds strange and even bizarre. But the principal obstacle to fruitful dialogue consists in confusing dialogue with certain other activities which, though they superficially resemble it, are really quite different. Dialogue can be confused with discussion, with debate, and with diplomacy. Above all, it can be confused with monologue. As long as this confusion persists, no dialogue is possible. Indeed, by creating the illusion of dialogue when, in fact, no dialogue is taking place, it actually postpones the achievement of dialogue indefinitely.

The nature of discussion, debate, and diplomacy, is not difficult to understand. For our present purpose, discussion may be defined as the exchanging of ideas, debate as arguing for victory, and diplomacy as the strategy by which a pseudo-religious power structure seeks to ensure its own survival and aggrandizement, and the destruction of its competitors, by secular means other than that of open violence. A discussion between Buddhism and Christianity, or between Buddhists and Christians, differs from a dialogue in its being conducted, more often than not, on an abstract, not to say an academic, basis, and in its not going deep enough to come up against the fact that they are speaking two different languages and are not, in fact, really intelligible to each other. Similarly, a debate differs from a dialogue inasmuch as because both religions see themselves as absolutes neither victory nor defeat is possible for either. Debate is thus based on a false assumption. As for diplomacy, this is, in reality, not a form of religious activity at all, but arises only to the extent that on its 'institutional' side a religion has, under 'ethnic' influence, sunk from being a spiritual community (sangha, church) to being a secular group among secular groups, that is to say, a political and/or socio-economic power structure among power structures.

Since the broad sense in which discussion, debate, and diplomacy are not dialogue is obvious enough, nothing more need be said about them. But in what sense of the term, exactly, is monologue not dialogue? Apart from the purely formal opposition between the two terms, this is not so obvious, and because it is the confusion of dialogue with monologue, in particular, that is the principal obstacle to dialogue, in this case a few words of explanation are required. As we have already seen, both Buddhism and Christianity tend to see themselves as religious absolutes. Each is a universe in itself. Each speaks its own theological or 'Buddhological' language, as it were, and what is said in one language cannot really be translated into the other. In communicating with each other, therefore, both religions are likely to misunderstand and both are likely to be misunderstood. This may not always be realized. In fact, both parties may be under the impression that they are communicating, and that dialogue is taking place, when this is not so at all. What has happened is that A has taken a word, or a concept, used by B, has attached to it the meaning that it bears for A, and then replied to B as though B had used it in the sense that it would have had for A had A used it. A is therefore not replying to something that B has said but to something that A has said. A is therefore not communicating with B at all. A is communicating with A. What is taking place is not a dialogue but a monologue. Buddhism, for example, may attach to the word 'God', as used by Christianity, the same meaning that it is accustomed to associate with its own Mahābrahma,[131] and may try to continue the communication on those terms. Similarly, Christianity may attach to such words as voidness (śūnyatā), trance (dhyāna), and wisdom (prajñā), meanings quite different from those which they traditionally hold for

Buddhism. Misunderstandings of this sort are much less likely to arise – or if they do arise are much more likely to be corrected – when the two religions meet in the persons of an individual Buddhist and an individual Christian, communicating in the flesh. When they meet only on paper, with the Buddhist or the Christian author trying to communicate with a Christianity or a Buddhism that exists nowhere but in his own brain, the result will be not dialogue but monologue.

THE PROBABLE BEST METHOD OF STARTING DIALOGUE

If dialogue is not to be confused with discussion, debate, or diplomacy, and if Buddhism and Christianity meet in the persons of an individual Buddhist and an individual Christian, the question of the best method of starting dialogue can probably be left to look after itself. Provided that the two parties to the dialogue are open to each other, and provided each really listens to what the other has to say, there is no reason why dialogue should not take place – no reason why they should not be able to communicate even without a medium of communication, that is to say, without a common language, without a mutually acceptable system of concepts, symbols, and values. When dialogue takes place, however, both parties should realize that it is bound to be of a very piecemeal nature, and that they should not expect too much from it. Indeed, they should not expect anything at all from it except the possibility of continued dialogue. If they expect an accession of interesting new ideas, it will become discussion. If they expect victory, or even just the enrichment of, or a positive contribution to, their own (Buddhist or Christian) religious experience, it will become debate. If they expect an accommodation with regard to the practical interests of the secular power structure with which, on their 'institutional' side, they may happen to be identified, it becomes diplomacy.

More important than the question of the best method of starting dialogue is that of the best person to start it. The 'what?' is at bottom a 'who?'. In deciding who is the best person, however, we must be careful not to overlook the obvious fact that a dialogue between Buddhism and Christianity is a dialogue between Buddhism and Christianity. It is dialogue, that is to say, between these two religions in their central, 'classical' forms – not a dialogue between them in any diluted, demythologized, rationalized, and secularized, modern version.

Buddhism and Christianity can, in fact, engage in dialogue only in the persons of the fully committed Buddhist and the firmly believing Christian, and it is these, therefore, who are the best persons to start – and carry on – dialogue between the two religions. On no account can Buddhist–Christian dialogue be regarded as a fashionable exercise for the uncommitted academic, or for those Buddhists or Christians who, uncertain of their own faith, are looking for an intellectually stimulating and professionally rewarding career in the field of 'comparative' religious studies. This does not mean that those who engage in dialogue may not be equipped with a scientific knowledge of Buddhism or of Christianity as, for example, a sociological phenomenon. It means that a scientific knowledge of a religion is not, in itself, a qualification for engaging in dialogue on its behalf.

RELIGIOUS EXPERIENCE AS CHARACTERISTIC OF BUDDHISM AS A STARTING POINT IN DIALOGUE WITH BUDDHISM?

It would seem that, from the Christian point of view, religious experience as characteristic of Buddhism is quite acceptable as a starting point in dialogue with Buddhism. But even if not taken as an actual starting point, once dialogue had really begun the subject of religious experience could hardly fail to be brought up sooner or later. Presumably it would also be possible to take 'religious experience as characteristic of Christianity' as a starting point in dialogue with Buddhism. From a Buddhist point of view, however, the expression 'religious experience' is ambiguous and, therefore, misleading. It could, for instance, be taken to refer either to the experience of concentration and meditation (*śamatha*), or to the experience of insight (*vipaśyanā*); to the act of Going for Refuge to the Three Jewels, to the arising of the *bodhicitta*, or to the 'turning about' (*parāvṛtti*) in the deepest seat (*āśraya*) of consciousness (*vijñāna*). Even if it is taken in the restricted sense of the experience of suffering, and we focus attention on that, serious objections can still be raised against the taking of religious experience as characteristic of Buddhism as a starting point in dialogue at all. Indeed, the identification of 'religious experience' with the experience of suffering and liberation from suffering may serve to reinforce these objections.

Whatever form of communication we engage in, progress is from the simple to the complex, from the shallow to the profound, the peripheral to the central. This is all the more so in the case of the form of communication we call dialogue, wherein religious absolutes confront each other without the benefit of a common language. It would therefore seem that for Christianity to take religious experience as characteristic of Buddhism, especially the experience of liberation from suffering, as a starting point in dialogue with Buddhism, is not really feasible. Indeed, by coming to premature conclusions about the nature of this experience it might even make dialogue between the two religions impossible. Religious experience is an extremely difficult thing to communicate, even when a medium of communication exists, and the experience of liberation from suffering is not an 'experience' in the ordinary sense, not even a 'religious experience'. For Buddhism it is not just liberation from ordinary human wretchedness, but from everything conditioned (*saṃskṛta*) and mundane (*laukika*). As such, it is identical with the attainment of Nirvāṇa or Enlightenment (*bodhi*) or, in other words, with the ultimate goal of Buddhism – a goal that must be realized by one's personal spiritual exertions and which is, we are expressly told, beyond the sphere of reasoning (*atakkāvacara*).

This brings us to a second ambiguity, not one of language but identity. When religious experience as characteristic of Buddhism is put forward as a possible starting point in dialogue with Buddhism, it is not clear whose religious experience is meant. Is it the experience of the Buddhist who is party to the dialogue? (I assume, perhaps wrongly, that his Christian counterpart will have no Buddhist religious experience.) Or is it the experience of some other Buddhist, living or dead, who does not himself actually participate in dialogue? Is it, even, not any particular person's experience at all that is meant, but some general concept of religious experience – a concept which, so far as any actual parties to the Buddhist–Christian dialogue are concerned, may be no more than a matter of words? These questions are raised not in any hair-splitting spirit of pedantry, much less still in order to make dialogue more difficult, but simply as a means of emphasizing the fact that the starting point of dialogue with Buddhism should be something about which at least one of the two parties can speak from personal knowledge. There is a world of difference between taking religious experience as characteristic of Buddhism as a starting point in dialogue and taking as a starting point the words and concepts that traditionally reflect that experience.

In view of these facts it would therefore appear that some more peripheral topic than 'religious experience', or the experience of liberation from suffering, is needed as a starting point for dialogue with Buddhism, i.e. some point of doctrine, or religious practice, or liturgical observance, that is intelligible to, and within the imaginative grasp of, both parties. Religion need not be identified exclusively with 'religious experience'. Indeed, the exaggerated value that is sometimes attached to 'religious experience' in the narrower, more subjective sense, is not a feature of Buddhism. Even if, for some reason, religious experience as characteristic of Buddhism has to be taken as a starting point in dialogue with Buddhism, there can be no question of anyone embarking on a confident exposition of that about which even the Enlightened hesitate to speak. Rather should some more modest, everyday type of religious experience be taken as a starting point. If this is done, and if on both sides there is sufficient openness and sufficient awareness of their own limitations, then there may be some hope that there will begin between Buddhism and Christianity a truly fruitful dialogue, that is to say, a dialogue that will not degenerate into monologue but which will continue.

ASPECTS OF BUDDHIST MORALITY

Aspects of Buddhist Morality *was written at the beginning of 1978 as a contribution to a special volume, on morality in world religions, of the Roman Catholic journal* Studia Missionalia. *It was written at the invitation of the editor, the Rev. Father Dhavamony. (S)*

In 1949, shortly after my ordination as a *sāmaṇera* or 'novice monk' at Kusinārā, the site of the Buddha's 'Great Decease',[132] I fared 'with bowl and robe' from the plains of northern India through the forests of the Terai and so up into the foothills of Nepal. The purpose of the journey was to visit the Newar Buddhists of Butaol and Palpa-Tansen, who were lay disciples of my own preceptor.[133] On the way I not only had to stop and beg my food but also ask for directions. At one village at which I stopped the villagers not only fed me and put me on the right road but, thinking that I was a Hindu like themselves, warned me that the Newar Buddhists were very strange people. 'They don't like to hear about God,' they explained. 'They don't like to hear about the glorious exploits of his *avatāras*, or about *bhakti*.[134] All they want to hear about is dull, dry morality.' It is with this same 'dull, dry morality' that the present article is concerned. I hope to show that, while morality occupies as important a place in Buddhism as my story suggests, for Buddhists at least it is not so dull and dry a topic as my Hindu hosts supposed.

The Indian Buddhist term that is translated, generally, by the Western-Christian 'morality' or 'ethics' is, of course, *śīla* (Sanskrit) or *sīla* (Pāli). The extent to which *sīla* is an integral part – though only a part – of the Buddha's Dharma is sufficiently attested by the fact that it is included in some of the most ancient and important formulations of the Buddhist spiritual path, as well as among some of the most important sets of spiritual practices. Thus *sīla* is the first of the three *śikṣās* (Pāli *sikkhās*) or 'trainings' to be undergone by the disciple, the second and third of them being *samādhi* or 'concentration' and *prajñā* (Pāli *paññā*) or 'wisdom'. It is these three 'trainings' that were, according to the *Mahāparinibbāna Sutta*, the substance of the Buddha's farewell address to his disciples – an address that he repeated in eleven out of the fourteen places he visited on his final tour:

> Such and such is morality (*sīla*), such and such is meditation
> (*samādhi*), such and such is wisdom (*paññā*). Great becomes the
> fruit, great the advantage of meditation, when it is set round
> with morality. Great becomes the fruit, great the advantage of
> wisdom, when it is set round with meditation. The mind set round
> with wisdom is set quite free from the biases (*āsavas*), that is to
> say, from the bias towards sensuous experience (*kāma*), towards
> conditioned existence (*bhava*), towards speculative opinions
> (*diṭṭhi*), and towards ignorance (*avijjā*).[135]

Sīla is also one of the three 'items of meritorious action' (Sanskrit *puṇya-kriyā-vastūni*, Pāli *puñña-kiriya-vatthuni*), coming after *dāna* or generosity and before *bhāvanā* or 'development (of higher states of consciousness)', i.e. 'meditation'. In addition to featuring in these two important triads, *sīla* or morality is reckoned as one of the three, four, five, or seven *ariyadhanas* or 'spiritual treasures' of man. Moreover, 'purification of morality' is the first of the seven successive 'purifications' (*visuddhi*) described in the *Rathavinīta Sutta*[136] and 'recollections of morality' the fourth of the ten 'recollections' (*anussati*) commented on by Bhadantācariya Buddhaghosa in the *Visuddhimagga*.[137] Although *sīla* does not occur as one of the 'members' of the Aryan Eight-membered Way, the fact that the eight members of the Way are traditionally included in the three 'trainings', with right speech, right action, and right livelihood being grouped together under the heading of *sīla*, means that *sīla* is, in fact, part of this well-known formulation too.[138] All the formulations of the Path and sets of spiritual practices so far mentioned belong, if not to the earliest, at least to the very early days of Buddhism, and are the common property of Hīnayāna and Mahāyāna alike. The six or ten 'perfections' or 'transcending virtues' (*pāramitās*) are as a group – though only as a group – of somewhat later origin.[139] As the special practices of the bodhisattva, the spiritual hero of the Mahāyāna, who aims not just at his own liberation from suffering but at Supreme Enlightenment for the benefit of all sentient beings, they constitute the principal formulation of the Path for all the Mahāyāna schools and are, therefore, the common foundation of their entire spiritual life and spiritual practice. *Śīla* or morality is the second of these 'perfections', although strictly speaking it becomes such only when united with 'wisdom' (*prajñā*), which is really the only *pāramitā*. From these examples, which are no more than 'a handful of *siṃsapā* leaves',[140] it is obvious that *śīla* or morality is, in fact, an integral part of the Buddha's Dharma, and that throughout Buddhist history it has occupied a prominent place in the teaching of all schools. Indeed, illuminated and illustrated as it has been by a glorious succession of sages and saints – as well as upheld by an ocean-wide variety of ordinary folk, living under all kinds of conditions – it is one of the richest, most fruitful, and most fascinating fields of study in the entire range of Buddhism. In a short article like this it is quite impossible to do it anything like justice. I shall therefore confine myself to some of the more prominent aspects of the subject, and offer a few remarks on (1) the nature of morality, (2) morality and the spiritual ideal, (3) morality mundane and transcendental, (4) patterns of morality, (5) the fruits of morality, and (6) determinants of morality. While they are not arranged in any logical order, all these aspects are related, and some of them overlap.

1. THE NATURE OF MORALITY

One way of approaching this aspect of the subject is by looking at the word *śīla*. In its primary sense *śīla* denotes 'nature, character, habit, behaviour' in general, as when a person of stingy or illiberal character is spoken of as *adānaśīla*, or when one who is in the habit of speaking is said to be *bhaṇanaśīla*. Its secondary sense, which is the one with which we are really concerned here, is 'moral practice, good character, Buddhist ethics, code of morality'. This is the *śīla* of one who is *suśīla* or of 'good' nature, character, habit, behaviour, as opposed to *duḥśīla* or of that which is 'bad'. But what do we mean by 'good'? What do we mean by 'bad'? What is it, the presence or absence of which makes it possible for us to speak of morality or non-morality at all? The short Buddhist answer to these questions is to be found in the term *kuśala* (Pāli *kusala*), and in its opposite *akuśala* (Pāli *akusala*). When an action is accompanied by volitions and mental factors which are *kuśala* it is said to be good and when it is accompanied by volitions and mental factors which are *akuśala* it is said to be bad. The literal meaning of *kuśala* and *akuśala* is 'skilful' and 'unskilful', but as terms in moral discourse and ethics *kuśala* signifies associated with disinterestedness (*alobha*), friendliness (*adveṣa*, Pāli *adosa*), and wisdom (*amoha*) and *akuśala* signifies associated with greed (*lobha*), hatred (*dveṣa*, Pāli *dosa*), and delusion (*moha*). What is meant by *śīla* in the sense of good action or good behaviour is now clear. It is that action or behaviour which is accompanied by, or is the expression of, volitions and mental factors which are *kuśala*, that is to say, which are characterized by disinterestedness, friendliness, and wisdom. Buddhist morality is thus a morality of intention. This is not to say, of course, that it is a matter simply of 'good intentions', or that it consists in a semi-serious, semi-sentimental *wish* to do what is good or right. On the contrary, *śīla* or Buddhist morality is essentially a matter of volition and action, of action which, since the volition in question is *skilful*, cannot be in any way uncertain or inept. It must also be emphasized that *śīla* is a matter not just of the occasional good deed but of good behaviour: it is *habitual* good action. This habitual good action is not bodily only but, in accordance with the well-known Buddhist threefold division of man into body, speech, and mind, also vocal and mental. *Buddhist morality can therefore be said to consist in the habitual performance of bodily, vocal, and mental actions expressive of volitions associated with disinterestedness, friendliness, and wisdom.* More specifically, it consists in the observance of the ten *śīlas*, or of the ten 'ways of skilful action' (*kuśala-karma-pathas*). In respect of bodily action, one abstains from the taking of life, from theft, and from sexual misconduct; in respect of vocal action, one abstains from untruthfulness, from harsh speech, from idle gossip, and from tale-bearing and backbiting; in respect of mental action, one abstains from indulgence in greed, hatred, and wrong views. One also practises the corresponding positive virtues. One cherishes life, is generous, and remains content with one's own married or celibate state; one speaks what is true, speaks with affection, speaks what is useful and timely, and speaks in such a way as to promote harmony and concord; and one cultivates thoughts which are disinterested, friendly, and based on right views.

The nature of morality is also made clear in various 'scholastic' discussions of the subject. According to the *Paṭisambhidāmagga*, 'There is morality (*sīla*) as volition, morality as consciousness-factor, morality as restraint, morality as non-transgression.'[141] As Buddhaghosa explains, morality as volition and morality as consciousness-factor consist in the ten 'ways of skilful action' considered in the one instance as acts of abstention (from unskilful ways) and in the other as states of abstaining. Morality as restraint (*saṃvara-sīla*) should be understood as fivefold: restraint by the 'monastic rules' (*pāṭimokkha*), restraint by mindfulness, restraint by knowledge, restraint by patience, and restraint by energy. Morality as non-transgression is the non-transgression of the precepts of morality that have been undertaken (i.e. by way of 'ordination', whether as a 'lay' disciple or as a 'monk').[142] Of these four kinds of morality – or senses of the term morality – the first and second have been dealt with in the previous paragraph, while the fourth will be touched upon in the section on 'Patterns of Morality'. According to the *Bodhisattvabhūmi*, as quoted (in Tibetan translation) by Gampopa:

> One must know that the essence of ethics and manners [i.e. *śīla*] comprises the following four qualities: (1) to accept properly from others; (2) to be inspired by pure motivation; (3) to mend one's own ways once one has fallen from one's code [of morality]; and (4) to avoid falling by being mindful and devoted.

As Gampopa explains, the first of these qualities consists in acceptance, i.e. the acceptance of the precepts of morality from a teacher in the traditional manner, and the remainder in preservation, i.e. the preservation of what has been thus accepted.[143]

2. MORALITY AND THE SPIRITUAL IDEAL

Morality does not exist in isolation. As the fact of its being included as a separate stage in various formulations of the Buddhist spiritual path – as well as included among different sets of spiritual practices – is sufficient to indicate, it exists as part of a larger and more complex whole. The whole is the path or way itself, considered as the sum total of all stages and all practices whatsoever, whether elementary or advanced, mundane or transcendental. From the standpoint of common sense at least, a path is something that proceeds in a certain direction, or towards a certain fixed point: a path that does not lead anywhere is a contradiction in terms. As complement or counterpart of the path or way, therefore, there also exists the goal. The goal is generally known as Nirvāṇa (Pāli *nibbāna*), or the complete cessation of thirst or craving (Sanskrit *tṛṣṇā*, Pāli *taṇhā*) and, therefore, of suffering (Sanskrit *duḥkha*, Pāli *dukkha*) – though as I have pointed out elsewhere, cessation is far from being the last word of Buddhism.[144] As realized by an individual human being, particularly as realized by the historical 'founder' of Buddhism, this goal is known as Enlightenment (*bodhi*) or as Perfect Enlightenment (*sambodhi*), and the 'founder' himself as the Buddha or the Perfectly Enlightened One. Since for Buddhism it is axiomatic that what one human being has realized can be realized by other human beings too, if they only exert themselves in the right way, the Buddha, by virtue of his Enlightenment, i.e. by virtue of his having realized the goal, becomes the great exemplar for all those who wish to realize the goal for themselves as he realized it for himself. In other words, the Buddha becomes the spiritual ideal. Because he is the spiritual ideal – the supreme object of spiritual endeavour – the Buddha is also the ultimate Refuge, that is to say, he is the supreme object of that Going for Refuge which is the central and definitive act of the Buddhist life. In the words of Gampopa,

> He is the ultimate refuge because He possesses the *dharmakāya*
> and the devotees of the three paths [i.e. the three *yānas*:
> *śrāvakayāna, pratyekabuddhayāna*, and *bodhisattvayāna*] also find
> their fulfilment in Him by obtaining the final pure *dharmakāya*.[145]

Though there are commonly said to be three Refuges, i.e. the Buddha, the Dharma, and the Sangha, inasmuch as the Dharma is revealed by the Buddha, and the Sangha made up of those who have realized the path by following the Dharma, in the ultimate sense there is only one Refuge, i.e. the Buddha.

The connection between morality and the spiritual ideal is now clear. Morality is one of the three great stages of the path, the others being meditation and wisdom, and consists in the habitual performance of bodily, vocal, and mental actions expressive of skilful volitions. Since the Buddha, by virtue of his having realized the goal, is the spiritual ideal, and therefore the sole Refuge, and since morality is one of the three great stages of the path, it follows that, inasmuch as the path has for its object the goal, the indirect object of the skilful volitions in the expression of which morality consists is the Buddha. Thus morality does not exist in isolation not only because it is connected, as one of the stages of the path, with the goal, but because as skilful volition it is connected with the spiritual ideal, with the Buddha, i.e. has the Buddha as its ultimate object. It is, in fact, only those actions of body, speech, and mind that are expressive of skilful volitions that have the Buddha, as spiritual ideal, as their object, which can properly be said to constitute Buddhist morality. Actions that have as their ultimate object a good rebirth, whether here on Earth or in some higher heavenly world, or which are performed solely for reasons of social propriety or legal obligation, do not constitute Buddhist morality, even though *as actions*, externally considered, they may appear to be no different from the actions which make up Buddhist morality, i.e. which are expressive of skilful volitions having the Buddha as object.

The fact that *śīla* or morality has the Buddha as its ultimate object is illustrated by what takes place at the most important of all Buddhist ceremonies, that of Going for Refuge, when the threefold refuge formula is repeated thrice after whoever is presiding on the occasion. Immediately after the Going for Refuge (*śaraṇa-gamana*) there follows the 'taking of moral precepts' (*śīla-grahaṇa*), five or more in number. In other words, in the act of Going for Refuge one has made the Buddha the object of one's (skilful) volitions, that is to say one has committed oneself to the realization of the spiritual ideal. Such a commitment involves the following of the Path, and this consists – broadly speaking – in the practice of the three successive stages of morality, meditation, and wisdom and the perfecting of them one by one in that order. Only a total commitment, faithfully sustained over a period of many years, will enable one to do this. One is, however, expected to do at least something at once: one is expected to practise *śīla* or morality. The positive volitions of which one has made the Buddha the object should be sufficiently powerful to find expression at least in terms of bodily and vocal action, even if not in terms of mental action. If they are not powerful enough to do this then it is doubtful if one has really made the Buddha the object of one's volitions – has really gone for Refuge. The ceremonial Going for Refuge is therefore followed by the taking of moral precepts as an integral part of the proceedings. Morality, far from existing in isolation, is the initial expression of one's commitment to the spiritual ideal.

3. MORALITY MUNDANE AND TRANSCENDENTAL

In the days when it was taken for granted that Buddhism could be described in terms of Western thought, there was a good deal of discussion as to whether it was a monism or a pantheism, a form of absolutism or a form of relativism, and so on. The discussion came to an end – in intellectually responsible circles at least – when it was recognized that Buddhism could not really be described in any such way because, in the well-known words of Dr Suzuki, its point of view was one from which terms like monism and the rest had no meaning.[146] Yet although Buddhism cannot be described in terms of Western thought, it would not be wrong to say that for practical purposes at least it is a form of dualism, or at any rate is dualistic in character, that is to say, it postulates two 'ultimate' principles and sees the spiritual life as consisting in a process of transition from the one to the other. That this is so is evident from what the Buddha says in the *Ariyapariyesanā Sutta* about the two quests (*pariyesanā*), the noble (*ariya*) and the ignoble (*anariya*). The ignoble quest is when one who is himself subject to birth, ageing, decay, dying, sorrow, and stain, goes in search of what is likewise subject to birth, ageing, decay, dying, sorrow, and stain. The noble quest is the opposite of this, i.e. it is when one who is himself subject to birth, ageing, decay, dying, sorrow, and stain, goes in search of that which is not so subject.[147] Here it is the conditioned (Sanskrit *saṃskṛta*, Pāli *saṅkhata*) and the Unconditioned (Sanskrit *asaṃskṛta*, Pāli *asaṅkhata*) that are the two 'ultimate' principles, and it is they that make possible the two different processes of transition. In the case of the ignoble quest the process of transition is from the conditioned to the conditioned, and in the case of the noble quest it is from the conditioned to the Unconditioned – from *saṃsāra* to *nirvāṇa*. The worldly life is based on the first process, the spiritual life on the second.

Although the conditioned and the Unconditioned, *saṃsāra* and *nirvāṇa*, are both absolutes, in the sense that neither can be derived from, or reduced to, the other, they are nevertheless connected. What connects them is the path. The path consists of a number of different stages, variously reckoned as three, five, seven, ten, thirteen, or fifty-two in all, and these, whatever the total number happens to be, always fall into two groups, or two sections, respectively known as the mundane path and the transcendental path.[148] These two paths, when placed as it were end to end, make up the path in its entirety. The mundane path is so called because the skilful volitions and mental factors that make up the various stages of which it consists are still subject to the deeply-rooted – indeed primordial – tendencies known as the *āsravas* (Pāli *āsavas*), the 'cankers' or 'biases', i.e. the cankers of, or biases toward, sensuous experience (*kāma*), conditioned existence (*bhava*), speculative opinions (*dṛṣṭi*), and ignorance (*avidyā*). Because of the continued presence of the 'biases', regression from the mundane path to the unskilful volitions and mental factors is always possible. For this reason the mundane path is part of *saṃsāra*. Nevertheless it is only in dependence on the mundane path that the transcendental path – from which no regression is possible – can arise. More specifically, it is only in dependence on 'meditation' that 'wisdom' can arise. The mundane path is, therefore, also part of the path. The transcendental path is so called because the 'skilful' volitions and mental factors which make up its various stages are either partly or, in the case of the last stage, wholly free from the 'biases'. Just as the mundane path forms part of *saṃsāra*, therefore, so part of the transcendental path forms *nirvāṇa*. Thus the path in its entirety embraces both *saṃsāra* and *nirvāṇa*, or, in other words, includes both its own starting point and its own goal.

The bearing of this on morality is obvious. As we have seen, morality consists in the habitual performance of bodily, vocal, and mental actions expressive of skilful volitions. Since these volitions may belong either to the mundane path or to the transcendental path, i.e. may be either subject or not subject to the 'biases', it follows that there are two kinds of morality, mundane morality and transcendental morality. In the words of Buddhaghosa,

> All morality subject to *āsavas* is mundane (*lokiya*); that not subject
> to *āsavas* is transcendental (*lokuttara*). Herein, the mundane
> brings about improvement in the future becoming and is a
> prerequisite for the escape from becoming.... The transcendental

brings about escape from becoming and is the plane of 'reviewing knowledge' (*paccavekkhana-ñāna*).[149]

From this it is evident that, much as mundane morality and transcendental morality may resemble each other externally, they are very different in their effects. As we shall see in detail in a later section, mundane morality brings about an improvement in one's future conditioned existence, i.e. one's existence within *saṃsāra*, besides helping to provide a basis for the development of the successive stages of the transcendental path and, therefore, a means of escape from *saṃsāra*. Transcendental morality, on the other hand, brings about escape from *saṃsāra* and is itself an aspect of the goal. There are other differences. Inasmuch as it is expressive of skilful volitions and mental factors that may, at any moment, be overwhelmed by a sudden upsurge of the *āsravas*, mundane morality requires for its maintenance a constant deliberate effort. Transcendental morality requires for its maintenance no effort at all. As the natural expression of volitions which, in the absence of the *āsavas*, cannot be anything but 'skilful', it maintains itself. Mundane morality is a matter of discipline, of conscious adherence to a prescribed pattern of behaviour, or code of conduct. Transcendental morality is completely spontaneous. Mundane morality is the flawed and imperfect morality of the average man or 'worldling' (Sanskrit *pṛthagjana*, Pāli *puthujjana*) which, to the extent that it is not a matter of *habitual* good action – and in the case of mundane morality good action requires constant effort – strictly speaking is not morality at all. Transcendental morality is the pure and perfect morality of the 'saint' (Sanskrit *ārya*, Pāli *ariya*), especially that of the *arhant*, in whom the *āsravas* have been completely destroyed through wisdom and in whom, therefore, there exists no 'bias' toward any form of unskilful behaviour. On the level of formulations of the path, mundane morality is the morality that *precedes* meditation and wisdom. Transcendental morality is the morality that *succeeds* them. From this it follows that, since they come immediately after Perfect Vision and Perfect Emotion – the first and second 'members' of the Āryan Eight-membered Way, which are equivalent to wisdom – Perfect Speech, Perfect Action, Perfect Livelihood – the third, fourth, and fifth 'members' of the Way – are equivalent not to mundane morality but to transcendental morality, a point which is often overlooked.[150]

4. PATTERNS OF MORALITY

Morality is a 'many-splendoured thing', as rich and varied in its manifestations as life itself. Yet basically it is a very simple thing. It consists in no more than the habitual performance of bodily, vocal, and mental actions expressive of volitions which, whether subject to the 'biases' or not, are associated with disinterestedness, friendliness, and wisdom. These actions can, however, be performed in many different ways, by many different kinds of people, under all sorts of conditions, and for all sorts of reasons. Seen not in the abstract but concretely, that is to say, seen not in terms of immutable moral principles but in terms of the actual moral behaviour of millions of individual Buddhists through the ages, morality therefore presents itself as an ever-shifting panorama of actual skilful actions of every conceivable variety, from the most ordinary to the most extraordinary – the humblest to the most heroic and exalted. It is, indeed, a sort of living tapestry, a tapestry glowing with colour and made up of innumerable tiny threads, each thread being a particular skilful action. Looking at it in different ways – from different angles – one perceives in this tapestry various configurations of colours and threads – various configurations of skilful actions. These configurations are the different 'patterns of morality'. They are patterns both in the sense of archetypes or exemplars, and in the sense of complex wholes, characterized by a definite arrangement of parts. Although all the patterns are made up of skilful actions of one kind or another, the particular sort of pattern that skilful actions make is determined by various factors. Broadly speaking, the patterns of morality differ according to the degree of spiritual development, and the socio-ecclesiastical status, that they involve, as well as according to the precise nature of the spiritual ideal toward which the volitions of which their constituent 'skilful' actions are the expression are directed. Only a few of the more important and representative patterns need be mentioned here.

One of the best examples of the way in which the pattern of morality differs according to *the degree of spiritual development* is provided by the so-called 'Tract on Śīla'.[151] This is an ancient document which occurs, in whole or in part, with or without variations, in many places in the Pāli canon. In it the Buddha describes three grades of morality. The lesser morality (*cūla-śīla*) consists in the abstention from the taking of life, from theft, from unchastity, and from false, malicious, disagreeable, and useless speech. In other words, it consists in the observance of the first seven out of the ten 'ways of skilful action', the only difference being that here abstention from sexual misconduct (*kāmesu micchācāra*) is replaced by abstention from unchastity (*abrahmacariya*). This is the pattern of morality of one whose skilful volitions are sufficiently strong to find expression in bodily and vocal action, but not in mental action. The middle morality (*majjhima-sīla*) is more advanced. According to J. Evola's useful summary, its precepts

> deal with a kind of spartanization of life: reduction of needs, cutting away the bond formed by a life of comfort, with particular reference to eating, sleeping, and drowsing. There are also precepts which come under the heading of a 'departure', of a physical or literal leaving of the world: for example, avoidance of business or undertakings, non-acceptance of gifts, abandonment of possessions and refusal to assume fresh ones, and so on. Included in this part of 'right conduct' is abstention from dialectical discussions and speculation....[152]

This is the pattern of morality of one whose skilful volitions are so powerful that they not only find expression in mental action but bring about a complete transformation in his whole way of life. Most advanced of all is the greater morality (*mahā-sīla*). To quote Evola again, it concerns

> not only abstention from practising divination, astrology or mere magic, but also from abandoning oneself to the cult of some divinity or other. One can therefore speak in some measure of surmounting the bond of religion in the sense of a bond that makes one lead the saintly life [i.e. the spiritual life] with the notion 'By means of these rites, vows, mortifications, or renunciations I wish to become a god or a divine being.'[153]

This is the pattern of morality of one whose skilful volitions are the most powerful of all. They are sufficiently powerful, indeed, to cut through the whole dense and luxuriant undergrowth of ethnic religious beliefs and practices. Some of these beliefs and practices are as prevalent nowadays as they were in the Buddha's time. As Evola points out,

The precepts dealing with astrology, divination, and the like, could easily refer to the modern debased practices of like nature in the form of 'occultism', spiritualism, and so on. Measured with the ideal of Awakening [i.e. *bodhi*] all this has thus the character of a dangerous straying.[154]

The pattern of morality also differs according to socio-religious status. By socio-religious status is meant one's technical standing in the Buddhist community as determined by one's sex, whether male or female, and mode of life, whether that of a householder or one who has 'gone forth' from home into the homeless state. One who goes for Refuge, or is 'ordained' (the expressions are synonymous) within the context of a household life is known as a 'lay' disciple or *upasāka* (fem. *upāsikā*), while one who goes for Refuge, or is 'ordained' within the context of homelessness is known as a 'monk' (Sanskrit *bhikṣu*, Pāli *bhikkhu*) or 'nun' (Sanskrit *bhikṣuṇī*, Pāli *bhikkhunī*). The pattern of morality of the lay disciple, male or female – the particular configuration of skilful bodily and vocal actions created by the conditions of household life – is represented by the so-called five precepts (Sanskrit *pañca-śīla*, Pāli *pañca-sīla*). These are the first four out of the ten 'ways of skilful action', considered as 'factors in (moral) training' (Sanskrit *śikṣāpada*, Pāli *sikkhāpada*), plus abstention from intoxicants. On full moon and new moon days a particularly intense moral effort, incompatible with the normal demands of household life, modifies this pattern, and the five precepts become the eight precepts. The eight precepts are the five precepts, with abstention from sexual misconduct changing into abstention from unchastity, plus (6) abstention from untimely meals; (7) abstention from dancing, singing, music, and unseemly shows, from the use of garlands, perfumes, and unguents, and from things that tend to beautify and adorn the person; and (8) abstention from using high and luxurious seats and beds. The pattern of morality of the lay disciple is also represented by the provisions of the *Sigālovāda Sutta*, popularly known as 'the householder's code of discipline' (*gihi-vinaya*).[155] Here the whole duty of man, so far as the lay disciple is concerned, is shown to consist in the proper observance of six relationships, i.e. those with parents, teachers, wife and children, friends and companions, servants and work people, and spiritual teachers and Brahmins. The pattern of morality of the monk – the particular configuration of skilful actions created by the conditions of monastic life – is represented in its earlier, more eremitical, form, by the *prātimokṣa* (Pāli *pātimokkha*) or 150-clause 'rule', and in its later, more coenobitical form by the *skandhaka* (Pāli *khandhaka*) or 'chapters', which together constitute the complete Vinaya or Code of (Monastic) Discipline. The pattern of morality of the nun is similar to that of the monk. Besides abstaining from the taking of life, from theft, from unchastity, and from falsely laying claim to higher spiritual attainments, both the monk and the nun live on alms, possess virtually no personal property other than their three robes and their begging-bowl (though they are entitled to share in the corporate property of the monastic community), and devote themselves exclusively to the study, practice, and teaching of the Dharma. In its specifically Chan or Zen form, the pattern of morality of one who has 'gone forth' is represented by the 'pure standards' of the great Tang Dynasty master Baizhang,[156] who was the first to make manual work for the benefit of the community an integral part of monastic life, declaring, 'A day of no working is a day of no eating.'

Finally, the pattern of morality differs according to the precise nature of the spiritual ideal. This does not mean that there is more than one spiritual ideal – there could not be more than one, for there is only one historical Buddha – but only that for practical purposes the spiritual ideal can be thought of in different ways, or in different terms. In particular it can be thought of in terms of supreme wisdom or in terms of infinite compassion, that is to say, in terms of spiritual individualism or in terms of spiritual altruism. When thought of in terms of spiritual individualism it is known as the *arhant* ideal. When thought of in terms of spiritual altruism it is known as the bodhisattva ideal. The *arhant* ideal represents the spiritual ideal of the Hīnayāna, according to which one should aim at liberation from all suffering for oneself alone. The bodhisattva ideal, on the other hand, represents the spiritual ideal of the Mahāyāna, according to which one should aim at Supreme Enlightenment for the sake of the mundane and spiritual advancement of all living beings. The Mahāyāna attitude finds expression in the bodhisattva vow, one of the shortest and best known versions of which is:

However innumerable beings are, I vow to save them;
However inexhaustible the passions are, I vow to extinguish them;
However immeasurable the Dharmas are, I vow to master them;
However incomparable the Buddha-truth is, I vow to attain it.[157]

Yet striking as the contrast between the two ideals undoubtedly is, spiritual individualism and spiritual altruism are by no means mutually exclusive. Liberation from suffering, even for oneself alone, cannot be achieved without the eradication of craving, and craving cannot be eradicated without recourse to generosity – which is a form of altruism. Similarly, it is hardly possible to gain Supreme Enlightenment, even for the sake of others, without paying attention to one's own spiritual development – which is a form of spiritual individualism. In the long run the two ideals coincide: wisdom and compassion are one, or rather, are not two. Even so, in the early stages of the path the difference between the two spiritual ideals is sufficient to modify the patterns of morality of their respective followers to a considerable degree. The pattern of morality of those who make the *arhant* ideal the supreme object of their spiritual endeavour – the special configuration of skilful actions created by the following of the Hīnayāna – is represented by the literalistic, not to say legalistic, observance of the Code of (Monastic) Discipline, as when a monk refused to pull his own mother up out of a pit into which she had fallen, because this would have involved coming into physical contact with a woman.[158] The pattern of morality of those who make the bodhisattva ideal the supreme object of spiritual endeavour – the special configuration of skilful actions created by the following of the Mahāyāna – is represented by the observance of the five or the eight precepts, or the ten 'ways of skilful action', or the Code of (Monastic) Discipline, and so on, of the Hīnayāna, not just in a 'liberal' manner, but *in the spirit of the Mahāyāna*. In practice this eventually meant the virtual rewriting of the Monastic Code. This resulted in the emergence of a special Mahāyāna code of discipline, a code that represented a pattern of morality in which the nature of the bodhisattva ideal found direct expression, in its own terms, rather than indirect expression, in terms of the Hīnayāna, i.e. in terms of a pattern already created by a particular socio-ecclesiastical status. There are several versions of this code. According to one version, it consists in abstaining from eighteen major and forty-six minor offences. The first two major offences are: (1) to glorify oneself and disparage others for the sake of gains and honours, and (2) to withhold the wealth of the Dharma from others. The first two minor offences are: (1) not to worship the Three Jewels three times a day, and (2) to follow after desires.[159] Besides being thought of in terms of wisdom and compassion, the one spiritual ideal can also be thought of in terms of silence, magical potency, and so on. In addition to the *arhant* ideal and the bodhisattva ideal, therefore, there are various other spiritual ideals. Among these are the archaic *muni* ideal, the later *siddha* or *vidyādhara* ideal of the Vajrayāna, and the Zen Roshi ideal, each of which modifies the pattern of morality of its followers in its own way.

5. THE BENEFITS OF MORALITY

The benefits accruing from the practice of morality are both worldly and spiritual, mundane and transcendental. Moreover, they can be experienced both in the present life and in some other state of existence after death. The most immediate of these benefits is non-remorse (Pāli *avippaṭisāra*), which consists in the consciousness that one's bodily, vocal, and mental actions are all skilful and that one has nothing with which to reproach oneself regarding morals. Buddhism attaches great importance to this state. Not only does non-remorse lead to a higher degree of integration and, therefore, to greater harmony and balance of character, but also, properly reflected upon, it leads to the experience of delight and rapture which, in turn, leads to concentration (*samādhi*) – to insight – to wisdom – to freedom – to Nirvāṇa. For the moral householder there are five benefits in the perfecting of morality: (1) increase of wealth due to non-heedlessness, (2) a good reputation, (3) social confidence, (4) a peaceful death, and (5) rebirth in a happy, heavenly world.[160] So great and glorious are the benefits of morality that Buddhaghosa, having dealt with them in scholastic fashion, and feeling no doubt that something more was needed, bursts into song as it were and eulogizes them in some enthusiastic verses of his own devising:

> The true religion gives to noble sons
> No other stay than virtue [*sīla*]. Who can tell
> The limit of her power? Not Ganga stream
> Nor Yamunā nor babbling Sarabhū,
> Nor Aciravatī nor Mahī's flood,
> Can purify on earth the taints of men.
> But virtue's water can remove the stain
> Of all things living. Necklaces of pearl,
> Rain-bearing breezes, yellow sandalwood,

Gems, nor soft rays of moonlight can destroy
Heart-burnings of a creature. She alone –
Virtue – well-guarded, noble, cool, avails.
What scent else blows with and against the wind?
What stairway leads like her to heaven's gate?
What door into Nibbāna's city opens?
The sage whose virtue is his ornament
Outshines the pomp and pearls of jewelled kings.
In virtuous men virtue destroys self-blame,
Begetting joy and praise. Thus should be known
The sum of all the discourse on the power
Of virtue, root of merit, slayer of faults.[161]

Gampopa, more soberly, says that the results of (the perfection of) morality are:

(1) fulfilment and (2) effectiveness in our situation in life. The first is unsurpassable Enlightenment.... Effectiveness in our temporal life means that we experience the most perfect happiness of *saṃsāra*, even if we do not want it.[162]

Besides conferring benefits within the human or the divine order, or both, mundane morality – the habitual performance of skilful actions subject to the 'biases' – also contributes to the actual maintenance of those orders in existence. This is made clear by the classification of the ten ways of skilful action and the ten ways of unskilful action according to whether they are performed to a great, to a moderate, or to a slight extent. Performed to a great extent, the ten ways of unskilful action lead to rebirth as a tormented being, i.e. to rebirth in hell; performed to a moderate extent to rebirth as a *preta*, or hungry ghost; and performed to a slight extent to rebirth as an animal. Similarly, performed to a slight extent the ten ways of skilful action lead to rebirth as a human being; performed to a moderate extent to rebirth as a desire-world god; and performed to a great extent to rebirth as a form- or formless-world god. If the ten ways of skilful action – if mundane morality – is not practised even to a slight extent, men will not be reborn again as human beings and the human order of conditioned existence will come to an end. Morality is therefore necessary to the maintenance of the human state.

It is necessary to the maintenance of a human society, i.e. a society with human values. Describing the terrible state of affairs that prevails when the moral basis of society has disintegrated, and predicting to the monks that a time will come when human beings will be short-lived and when only an inferior kind of food will be available, the Buddha says:

> Among such humans the ten moral courses of conduct [i.e. the ten ways of skilful action] will altogether disappear, the ten immoral courses of action will flourish excessively; there will be no word for moral among such humans – far less any moral agent. Among such humans, brethren, they who lack filial and religious piety, and show no respect for the head of the clan – 'tis they to whom homage and praise will be given, just as today homage and praise are given to the filial-minded, to the pious, and to they who respect the heads of their clans.

> Among such humans, brethren, there will be no [such thoughts of reverence as are a bar to intermarriage with] mother, or mother's sister, or mother's sister-in-law, or teacher's wife, or father's sister-in-law. The world will fall into promiscuity, like goats and sheep, fowls and swine, dogs and jackals.

> Among such humans, brethren, keen mutual enmity will become the rule, keen ill-will, keen animosity, passionate thoughts, even of killing, in a mother towards her child, in a child towards its mother, in a father towards his child, and a child towards its father, in brother to brother, in brother to sister, in sister to brother. Just as a sportsman feels towards the game that he sees, so will they feel.

> Among such humans, brethren, there will arise a sword-period of seven days, during which they will look on each other as wild beasts; sharp swords will appear ready to their hands, and they, thinking 'this is a wild beast, this is a wild beast,' will with their swords deprive each other of life.[163]

Here it is interesting to see that one of the things that accompanies the disintegration of the moral basis of society and, therefore, the collapse of society itself in the truly human sense, is sexual promiscuity including incest. If such indeed is the case, we could expect to find that the reverse process, the creation by man of a truly human – a morally based – society, would be accompanied by the institution of the incest taboo. According to Cyril Darlington, this is exactly what we find:

> Some races of animals prefer to mate with their likes; others with unlikes. In these circumstances, human stocks which varied towards the rejection of incest would have, not at once but after a few hundred generations, an advantage over those who favoured or allowed incest. For they alone would be variable and adaptable [i.e. because they practised out-breeding and not in-breeding]. They alone would do new things and think in new ways. The future would be with them.[164]

In other words, human society cannot develop unless man is variable and adaptable, and he cannot be variable and adaptable without the incest taboo. Morality, at least to the extent of the incest taboo, is necessary to the very existence of human society. Even genetically speaking, morality is part of the very definition of humanity.

Morality is even more necessary to the existence of divine society, that is to say, to the existence of the world or worlds of the gods, and even more part of the definition of divinity. If a slight practice of the ten ways of skilful action is necessary for rebirth as a human being, and thus for the maintenance of the human order of existence, for rebirth as a god and the replenishment of the divine order of existence – from which beings decease as soon as the stock of merit that caused them to be reborn there is exhausted – the practice of the ten ways of skilful action at least to a moderate extent is required. The gods, we are told, rejoice when a Buddha appears in the (human) world. They rejoice because, as a result of his teaching, there will be a more intensive practice of morality on earth and, therefore, a greater number of men being reborn after death as gods. As a result of this increase in their numbers, the gods will become more powerful. Being more powerful they will be able to overcome the *asuras* or 'titans' in battle. Morality is therefore not just necessary to the maintenance of human society. It is necessary to ensure the preponderance of the forces of good over the forces of evil throughout the universe. Morality is of cosmic significance.

6. DETERMINANTS OF MORALITY

Morality is an integral part of Buddhism. It consists in the habitual performance of skilful actions expressive of skilful volitions, i.e. disinterestedness, friendliness, and wisdom. It is the initial expression of one's commitment to the spiritual ideal, may be subject or not subject to the 'biases', i.e. may be mundane or transcendental, and contains a number of different patterns of observance. Moreover, morality confers benefits both mundane and spiritual, and besides being essential to the maintenance of the human order contributes to the triumph of the forces of good in the universe.

So much we have learned. So much may anyone learn who studies Buddhism. But a theoretical knowledge of morality, even if it covers all aspects of the subject instead of only a few, is a very different thing from the actual habitual performance of skilful actions. How, then, do we make the transition? What is it that induces us to start cultivating skilful rather than unskilful volitions and to lead a moral rather than a non-moral life? In a word, what are the determinants of morality? According to Buddhaghosa, morality is of three kinds, according to whether it arises out of, or gives precedence to, one or another of three factors.

> That practised out of self-regard by one who regards self and desires to abandon what is unbecoming to self is virtue [*sīla*] *giving precedence to self*. That practised out of regard for the world and out of desire to ward off the censure of the world is virtue *giving precedence to the world*. That practised out of regard for the Dhamma (Law) and out of desire to honour the majesty of the Dhamma is virtue *giving precedence to the Dhamma*.[165]

I shall conclude these remarks on Buddhist morality with a few words of explanation on each of these. The fact that the Buddha reached the Goal and gained Enlightenment shows that Enlightenment can be gained by all men, if only they make the effort. The Buddha is therefore the spiritual ideal. All men are potentially Enlightened – because they are men. This potentiality is not a mere abstract possibility but the living seed of Enlightenment actually present in the depths of the human heart, not as a sort of foreign body but as the essenceless essence of human nature itself. It is the presence of this seed that enables the individual human being to develop, i.e. to progress from stage to stage of being and consciousness. Indeed, it is in the unfolding of the seed into shoot, bud, and finally perfect flower, that such progress consists. What is termed morality *giving precedence to self* is thus morality practised out of consciousness of oneself as an evolving being for whom, as an evolving being, some things are appropriate and others not. Here it is the individual's own potentiality for Enlightenment that is the determinant of morality. In addition to being practised out of self-regard, however, morality can be practised out of other-regard. The seed of Enlightenment is present in all men. This means that others are evolving beings as well as oneself. What is termed morality *giving precedence to the world* is thus morality practised out of other-regard or out of consciousness of others as evolving beings. Here it is others' potential for Enlightenment – or even their actual Enlightenment – that is the determinant of morality. In this context 'the world' (*loka*) means not the ordinary human world but the moral and spiritual community, the members of which are not only one's moral exemplars but also sources of inspiration and spiritual guidance. Above the self-regarding and the other-regarding practice of morality there is the Dharma-regarding. Enlightenment is not only immanent in self and world but transcends them. Outside time, and beyond the duality of subject and object, there is the Dharma in the sense of the Goal and the stages of the transcendental path. The Dharma is of such overwhelming greatness that, when one encounters it, one's sole desire is that it should be honoured in a fitting manner. What is termed morality *giving precedence to the Dhamma* is thus morality practised out of the fullness of this desire. Here it is Enlightenment itself – the Unconditioned itself – that is the determinant of morality.

Buddhaghosa's morality *giving precedence to self, to the world,* and *to the Dhamma,* could perhaps be correlated with the pseudo-Aśvaghoṣa's conception of the spiritual life as due to 'Permeation through Manifestation of the Essence of Suchness', to 'Permeation through Influences', and to 'The Influences of Suchness'.[166] But consideration of this topic, interesting as it is, will have to be deferred. If we were to go into it now it would make this article far too long. Even without going into it, however, it should by this time be apparent that Buddhist morality is not so dull or so dry a subject as people sometimes think.

BUDDHISM AND BLASPHEMY

Buddhism and Blasphemy was written in 1978, the 'Year of the Blasphemy Trial', and was my contribution to the debate surrounding the trial and conviction of Denis Lemon and Gay News Ltd for the crime of blasphemous libel. On its publication as a booklet this essay attracted more attention in non-Buddhist circles than any of its companions in this volume.[167] Twice reprinted, it became part of a submission to the Law Commission, which took the views expressed in Buddhism and Blasphemy *into consideration when making its proposals for the reform of the criminal law. It was also quoted from in a debate in the House of Commons, and drew favourable comment from well-known figures in the fields of literature, science, and the performing arts. (S)* Buddhism and Blasphemy *was originally published by Windhorse Publications in 1978.*

In common with most other people, Buddhists in Britain have always believed that they enjoyed complete freedom of expression in religious matters and that punishment for such 'crimes' as heresy and blasphemy was a thing of the past. This belief has now been rudely shattered. In July 1977 the editor and publishers of the newspaper *Gay News* were tried at the Central Criminal Court on a charge of blasphemous libel. Both were found guilty. The editor, Denis Lemon, was sentenced to nine months' suspended imprisonment and fined £500; the publishers, Gay News Ltd, were fined £1,000. In March 1978 their appeals against these convictions were dismissed, although Lemon's nine month suspended sentence was quashed. Shortly before this, Lord Willis had made an unsuccessful attempt to have a bill abolishing the offence of blasphemy passed by the House of Lords.

English law comprises statute law and common law. Statute law is law made by the 'sovereign power', i.e. the Crown in Parliament. Common law is customary law based upon precedent. The statutory offence of blasphemy having been abolished in the law reforms of 1967 and 1969, Lemon and Gay News Ltd were prosecuted under the common law of blasphemy and blasphemous libel (written blasphemy), developed by judges between the years 1676 and 1922, which like the rest of the common law the reforms of the 1960s had left untouched. The last successful prosecution for blasphemy had taken place as long ago as 1922, when W. J. Gott was sentenced to nine months hard labour for distributing *God and Gott, Rib Ticklers,* and pamphlets with similar titles, as well as for 'annoying bystanders'.[168] (He died a few weeks after his release from prison.) It had therefore been widely assumed that the common law of blasphemy was a dead letter whose repeal was unnecessary because it was obsolete. This assumption has now been shown to have been mistaken. No unrepealed law is ever obsolete.

The trial and conviction of Denis Lemon and Gay News Ltd, and the failure of their appeal, surprised and shocked the British public. Meetings protesting against the convictions, and demanding the abolition of the blasphemy laws, were held in London and elsewhere. In August 1977 the Committee Against Blasphemy Law was formed, while in the following year the United Order of Blasphemers, founded in 1844 and since fallen into hebetude, was re-formed with the aim of publishing and distributing works that had resulted in blasphemy prosecutions. At least half a dozen political papers and several student journals republished 'The Love That Dares to Speak Its Name', the 'blasphemous' poem by James Kirkup which was the cause of all the trouble. It was also republished by the Free Speech Movement, thanks to whom thousands of copies of the poem are now in circulation, some of them bearing the signatures of more than a hundred well-known persons. On 4 July 1978, the anniversary of the by now notorious trial, copies of a petition were sent to the Home Office by individuals who had collected signatures. The petition, which had been initiated by the Committee Against Blasphemy Law, deplored the Appeal Court's decision to uphold the convictions of Denis Lemon and Gay News Ltd for blasphemous libel. It also expressed concern at the possibility of the blasphemy law being extended to cover religions other than Christianity.

One of the main reasons for the widespread nature of the concern aroused by the *Gay News* blasphemy trial is the unsatisfactory and uncertain state in which the conviction of the two defendants has left the law of blasphemy, and the fear that it will once again be used to hinder the free expression of opinion about religion. Parliament has never defined blasphemy. In the course of the last three hundred years the offence has been interpreted by various judges and juries in widely different ways. Originally, the mere denial of the truth of the Christian religion, or of any part of it (e.g. miracles, the divine authority of the Bible, the doctrine of the Trinity, the Divinity of Christ), constituted blasphemy and could be punished with fine, imprisonment, and 'infamous corporal punishment'.[169] Later (in 1883), blasphemy was held to consist not in the denial of the truth of Christianity but in 'indecent and offensive attacks on Christianity or the Scriptures or sacred objects or persons, calculated to outrage the feelings of the general body of the community'.[170] Finally, at the hearing of Gott's appeal, it was ruled that the law of blasphemy covers material which 'is offensive to anyone in sympathy with the Christian religion, whether he be a strong Christian, a lukewarm Christian, or merely a person sympathizing with their ideals' who 'might be provoked to a breach of the peace'. Thus between 1883 and 1922 a change in the interpretation of the law of blasphemy took place. In 1883 it was necessary to outrage the feelings of 'the general body of the community'. In 1922 all that one had to do was to offend even a single person sympathetic to Christianity.

At the *Gay News* trial there was a further change in the way the law was interpreted. Ruling against the defence argument about intention, the judge stated that in order to establish that the offence of blasphemy had been committed there was no need to prove intention to attack Christianity, or to cause a breach of the peace. Blasphemy was committed even if there was only a *tendency* to cause a breach of the peace. Despite this ruling, the prosecution produced no evidence that the publication of James Kirkup's poem had in fact had any such tendency. All they did was produce a single witness whose evidence showed that the poem had been published and that one 'sympathizer with Christianity' had been shocked and disgusted by it. *This was sufficient to secure convictions.*

The current interpretation of the law of blasphemy therefore seems to be that blasphemy consists in the publishing of anything that can be proved to have shocked and outraged a single Christian or sympathizer with Christianity. There is no objective criterion of blasphemy. Anything that shocks and disgusts a Christian or sympathizer with Christianity is blasphemous. Therefore, as the Committee Against Blasphemy Law points out, 'It is impossible to know in advance what material concerning religion could be found blasphemous. The main effect of the law is to inhibit free expression about religion in a way which is elsewhere thought to be completely unacceptable.'

This is a state of affairs that gravely concerns every Buddhist in the land. It is well known that the notion of a personal God, the creator and ruler of the universe, has no place in the Buddha's teaching, and that throughout its history Buddhism has in fact rejected the notion as detrimental to the moral and spiritual development of mankind. But such a rejection is undoubtedly painful to the feelings of a great many Christians and sympathizers with Christianity: it shocks and disgusts them. Under the present interpretation of the law any Buddhist bearing public witness to the truth of this fundamental tenet of Buddhism, whether in speech or writing, therefore runs the risk of committing the crime of blasphemy and being punished accordingly. Not only that. Any Buddhist publishing those sections of the Buddhist scriptures in which the notion of an omniscient and omnipotent Supreme Being, the creator and disposer of all, is actually ridiculed by the Buddha in terms which some would regard as being 'indecent and offensive' in the extreme also runs the risk of committing the crime of blasphemy – even though the offending words were spoken five hundred years before Christianity was born.[171]

It will probably be argued that, whatever the law might say, or be interpreted as saying, it is in the highest degree unlikely that in late twentieth-century Britain a Buddhist would be penalized for propagating his religion. Indeed, it will probably be argued that the very idea of such a thing ever happening is absurd. But is it? The Buddhist, as one whose freedom of expression is at stake, may be forgiven for doubting whether the idea is so absurd as some people think – or would like him to think. After all, as a statement issued in December 1976 by the National Secular Society pointed out, 'For the past fifty years whenever the National Secular Society has campaigned for a repeal of the blasphemy laws, we have been assured that this is unnecessary as these laws could never be used again.' Yet they were used again. Within the year Denis Lemon and Gay News Ltd had been tried and convicted, and the worthlessness of all the assurances that had been given the National Secular Society thereby exposed. Indeed, as the Society's statement went on to say, only a few weeks before the blasphemy proceedings against Lemon and Gay News Ltd were initiated, the possibility of invoking the blasphemy laws had been raised, on separate occasions, by the Home Secretary and the Archbishop of Canterbury. Even if no direct link existed between the pronouncements of these two personages and the initiation of the blasphemy proceedings, they certainly helped to create the climate of opinion which made the trial and conviction of Denis Lemon and Gay News Ltd possible and turned 1977 into the Year of the Blasphemy Trial.

The truth of the matter is that so long as the blasphemy laws remain unrepealed they can be used, and so long as they can be used the Buddhist does not enjoy full freedom of expression: he is not free to propagate his beliefs. Even agreeing that it is unlikely, even highly unlikely, that a Buddhist who publicly rejected the notion of the existence of God in terms which Buddhists, through the ages, have been accustomed to reject it, or who criticized the moral character of Christ as defective from the Buddhist point of view, would actually be prosecuted for the offence of blasphemy, the possibility of his being so prosecuted nevertheless does, undeniably, exist, and this possibility introduces into the situation an element of uncertainty that no 'assurance' can dispel. A Damocles will derive little comfort from the argument that the sword suspended above his head by a single hair is *unlikely* to fall. In any case, we probably concede far too much in agreeing that it is unlikely that a Buddhist would be prosecuted for blasphemy in this country. Lord Willis's bill for the abolition of the blasphemy law, put forward in the House of Lords in February 1978, was withdrawn without a vote after strong opposition from their lordships 'like the baying of distant wolves'. Clearly, there are some Christians who wish to retain the blasphemy laws, and presumably those who wish to retain them would not be averse to using them. This is hardly surprising. Christians have never been remarkable for their tolerance, and after the events of 1977 and 1978 no Buddhist – no non-Christian, in fact – can feel really safe so long as the blasphemy laws remain unrepealed. The baying of wolves, however distant, is not a very reassuring sound to more pacific beasts.

That the blasphemy laws will be repealed within the next few years is at least a possibility.[172] The Law Commission is presently reviewing various aspects of the criminal law with the aim of codification, and since this codification necessarily involves the eventual abolition of all offences at common law it will have to consider blasphemy law. If as a result of the Commission's work the offence of blasphemy is abolished, so that the susceptibilities of Christians are no longer given the special protection of the law, Buddhists will have no cause for complaint. If it is not abolished, Buddhists, in common with other non-Christians, will have to consider their position and decide what action, if any, to take. Meanwhile, we cannot do better than try to make clear what the attitude of Buddhism is towards some of the more important issues raised by the *Gay News* trial, and this is what I propose to do in the remainder of this article. In so doing I shall not be concerned with the fact that *Gay News* happens to be a newspaper for homosexuals, or that James Kirkup's poem had 'homosexual' features. The editor and publishers of *Gay News* were tried, convicted, and sentenced for blasphemous libel, and it is solely with the question of blasphemy that I shall be concerned.

The first thing that strikes us in this connection is that for Buddhism there is no such thing as blasphemy. In fact Buddhism does not even have a proper term for blasphemy.[173] This need not astonish us. According to Christian teaching, blasphemy is indignity offered to God in words, writing, or signs. Since in Buddhism there is no place for the notion of God, it follows not only that for Buddhism blasphemy does not exist but that for Buddhists the very concept of blasphemy, and therewith of an offence of blasphemy, is meaningless. St Augustine remarks that 'in blaspheming false things are spoken of God himself'.[174] According to Buddhism it is not speaking a false thing of God to assert that he does not exist, so that from the Buddhist point of view a Buddhist's denial of the existence of God not only is not but cannot be blasphemy. (What would St Augustine have thought of the 'Death of God' theology?)[175] Buddhists are therefore unable to accept that it is possible for them to say, or write, or do, anything blasphemous, and to subject them to the operation of a Christian law of blasphemy means forcing them to recognize the offence of blasphemy and, consequently, the existence of God. It means, in effect, preventing them from being Buddhists and forcing them to be Christians.

But even though the notion of God has no place in Buddhism, might there not be some highest object of veneration occupying a position analogous to that of God, and might there not be, for Buddhists, the possibility of blasphemy in respect of that object? The highest objects of veneration in Buddhism are the Three Jewels, i.e. the Buddha or spiritually enlightened human teacher, the Dharma or teaching of the way to Enlightenment, and the Sangha or spiritual community of disciples practising the teaching and following the way. It is to the Three Jewels that Buddhists 'go for Refuge'. The Three Jewels are the embodiments of the highest values of Buddhism and are, as such, jointly the object of the highest Buddhist aspirations. Indeed, it is commitment to the Three Jewels – to the Three Refuges – that makes anyone a Buddhist at all. Even the material symbols of the Three Jewels, in the form of sacred images, volumes of the scriptures, and 'monks', are objects of veneration. In the case of Buddhism, then, might not blasphemy consist in indignity offered to the Three Jewels? Might not Buddhists be expected to be just as shocked and outraged – just as angry and upset – when the Three Jewels are blasphemed as Christians are when God is blasphemed? For Christianity, of course, the primary blasphemy is denying the existence of God. In the case of Buddhism it would hardly be possible to regard the denial of the historical existence of the Buddha, the Dharma, and the Sangha as constituting blasphemy. In order to blaspheme the Three Jewels it would be necessary to deny the existence, in them, of the attributes which make them what they are, i.e. it would be necessary to deny that the Buddha was the Perfectly Enlightened One, that the Dharma was the way to Enlightenment, and that the Sangha was practising the Dharma and following the Way. Such 'speaking in dispraise' of the Three Jewels, as it is called, is not unknown to Buddhism. Do Buddhists, then, react to it in the same way that Christians react to blasphemy?

The answer to this question can be found at the beginning of the *Brahmajāla Sutta*, the opening *sutta* of the *Dīgha Nikāya* or 'Collection of Long Discourses [of the Buddha]', and it is perhaps not without significance that this *sutta* – in which the Buddha catches as it were in a great net (*brahmajāla*) the sixty-two (wrong) views prevalent in his time – should stand at the very forefront of the entire Pāli canon. The scene of the *sutta* is the high road between Rājagaha (Sanskrit Rājagṛha) and Nālandā, in the then kingdom of Magadha. The Buddha is going along the high road with a great company of about five hundred *bhikkhus*. Behind him come Suppiya the mendicant and young Brahmadatta, his pupil. Suppiya the mendicant is speaking in many ways in dispraise of the Buddha, the Dharma, and the Sangha, while Brahmadatta, even though he is Suppiya's disciple, speaks in praise of them. The same discussion is carried on at the rest-house at which the Buddha and his *bhikkhus*, and Suppiya and Brahmadatta, put up for the night. In the morning the *bhikkhus* tell the Buddha about the unusual exchange that has been going on between master and disciple. The Buddha says:

'Bhikkhus, if outsiders should speak against me, or against the Dharma, or against the Sangha, you should not on that account either bear malice, or suffer heart-burning, or feel ill-will. If you, on that account, should be angry and hurt, that would stand in the way of your own self-conquest. If, when others speak against us, you feel angry at that, and displeased, would you then be able to judge how far that speech of theirs is well said or ill?' 'That would not be so, Sir.'

'But when outsiders speak in dispraise of me, or of the Dharma, or of the Sangha, you should unravel what is false and point it out as wrong, saying: "For this or that reason this is not the fact, that is not so, such a thing is not found among us, is not in us." But also, Bhikkhus, if outsiders should speak in praise of me, in praise of the Dharma, in praise of the Sangha, you should not, on that account, be filled with pleasure or gladness, or be lifted up in heart. Were you to be so that also would stand in the way of your self-conquest. When outsiders speak in praise of me, or of the Dharma, or of the Sangha, you should acknowledge what is right to be the fact, saying: "For this or that reason this is the fact, that is so, such a thing is found among us, is in us."'[176]

How great a difference there is between ancient Magadha and modern Britain! After the suffocating atmosphere of blasphemy laws and blasphemy trials, of convictions for blasphemy and punishments for blasphemy, the words of the Buddha come like a breath of clean, sweet air. This is not to say that in the course of 2,500 years of Buddhist history Buddhists were always and everywhere characterized by the spirit of sweet reasonableness that permeates this passage, but that spirit was always plainly and unmistakably present, and its influence was sufficiently powerful to ensure that the history of Buddhism was never darkened by the enormities that repeatedly disgraced the blood-stained record of Christianity.

Now why should this be so? Why should Buddhism be permeated by sweet reasonableness and Christianity by ferocious unreasonableness? The Three Jewels are as much the highest object of veneration for the one religion as God is for the other. Why, then, should Buddhism react to dispraise of the Three Jewels in such a totally different manner from that in which Christianity reacts to blasphemy against God? Why should there be calm consideration of the truth or untruth of the matter on the part of the one, but shock and outrage on the part of the other? In order to answer this question we shall need to look a little more deeply into the nature of the difference between the two religions.

A clue to the difference, or at least a starting-point for its investigation, is to be found in certain of the Buddha's words to the *bhikkhus* quoted above. If they should feel angry and hurt on hearing outsiders speak against the Three Jewels, he warns them, or elated on hearing them speak in their praise, that would *stand in the way of their own self-conquest*: it would render them incapable of judging the truth or untruth of what had been said. From this it is clear that Buddhism is concerned primarily with the emotional and intellectual – with the 'spiritual' – development of the individual human being, and that the Buddhist's reaction to 'speaking in dispraise' of the Three Jewels must, like his reaction to everything else, be such as to help rather than hinder this process. In other words the centre of reference for Buddhism is man, that is to say, man as a being who, if he makes the effort, is capable of raising himself from the state of unenlightened to that of Enlightened – spiritually Enlightened – humanity or Buddhahood.

The centre of reference of Christianity, on the other hand, is God. Or rather, it is the dignity of God. The traditional concept of blasphemy is that it is indignity offered to God in words, writing, or signs, and as the reactions of Christians to the offence make clear, Christianity is concerned primarily with maintaining the dignity of God and preserving him from indignity. But why should this be so? Why should Christianity be so concerned with maintaining the dignity of God? It would be a manifest absurdity to regard speaking in dispraise of the Three Jewels as offering indignity to the Buddha, the Dharma, and the Sangha. Why is it possible to speak of God in this way? The answer to the question is not far to seek. It is possible because God, the supreme object of veneration for Christianity, is seen as the monarch of the universe (in recent times as a constitutional rather than an absolute one, however). Besides being the Creator of the world, including man, he is its Ruler and its Judge. He possesses in and of his own self absolute power, dominion, and authority. God is king writ large – a sort of cosmic Louis XIV or Ivan the Terrible, sometimes kind, sometimes cruel, but in both his kindness and his cruelty equally despotic.

Theologians trained in the subtleties of the schools will argue that such a conception of God is a travesty of Christian belief. But is it really so? Even a cursory study of Christianity as a historical phenomenon reveals that, despite the conceptual refinements of philosophers and theologians, the religious life of Christianity has always been effectively dominated not by any such abstraction as the Ground of Being[177] but by the grandiose image of a stupendous Power vaguely conceived as somehow personal and as accessible to the blandishments of worshippers. Even now it is this image that looms, with varying degrees of definiteness, in the murky background of a great deal of Western – European and American – life and thought. Sometimes, as in the *Gay News* blasphemy trial, we get a glimpse of it rising behind the barriers of more recent concepts much as Flaubert's Carthaginians saw towering above the roofs of their beleaguered city the monstrous brazen statue of Moloch.[178]

It is because God is seen as a sort of cosmic Louis XIV or Ivan the Terrible that offering indignity to him is such a serious matter – such a grave and terrible offence. Offering indignity to an earthly monarch is bad enough, for it is tantamount to an assault on his authority and as such undermines the whole government of the state. Loyal subjects are therefore shocked and outraged by it and dissociate themselves from it as quickly as possible, while the incensed monarch himself is swift to punish the guilty party with a horrible death. Offering indignity to the monarch of the universe is infinitely worse. It is an attack on the divine majesty itself, and as such undermines not just the government of a single earthly state, but the whole divine government of the universe, the entire established order of things. It is a bomb planted at the foundations of existence. Good Christians are therefore not only shocked and outraged by blasphemy but also frightened. They experience a sudden sense of insecurity, as though the ground had given way beneath their feet. Consequently, they not only dissociate themselves as quickly from blasphemy as loyal subjects from high treason (once punishable in England by hanging, drawing, and quartering), but turn with hysterical fury upon the blasphemer. Blasphemy is theological high treason. The reactions of Christians to blasphemy resemble nothing so much as the reactions of the frightened subjects of a cruel and suspicious tyrant who, in order to demonstrate their own loyalty and avert any imputation of disloyalty, are ready to fall with savage violence upon the slightest manifestation of discontent with his rule.

The penalties for blasphemy have therefore always been severe. Under the Mosaic law the punishment for blasphemy was death by stoning.[179] This precedent was followed by Justinian and the Merovingian and Carolingian kings, who also assigned death as the punishment for the offence, as well as throughout the greater part of Christendom. In France, blasphemy was from very early times punished with particular severity. The punishment was death in various forms, burning alive, mutilation, torture, and corporal punishment. Apart from an occasional pillorying, since the end of the seventeenth century the punishment for blasphemy in England has been a fine and imprisonment. As the *Gay News* trial served to remind us, this punishment is still in force.

The offence of blasphemy being held in such horror, and the penalties attached to it being so severe, one would have thought that, once the nations of the West had been brought into subjection to Christianity, blasphemy would be virtually unknown. Yet, paradoxically, this was not the case. Open and deliberate blasphemy was of course extremely rare, but a tendency to blaspheme seems to have been quite widespread even in those periods when Christianity was most dominant, lurking beneath the threshold of many a Christian consciousness and threatening to break through in moments of emotional stress. Indeed, it was when Christianity was at its most dominant that blasphemy – or the desire to commit blasphemy – seems to have been most widespread. Early Christian ascetics, medieval monks, Counter-Reformation mystics, and Puritan divines, all alike confess to being tempted to commit the terrible offence, some of them in its most extreme and most terrible – because unforgivable – form: blasphemy against the Holy Ghost. As the seventeenth-century author of *The Anatomy of Melancholy* puts it, after painting a lurid picture of the blasphemer's state of mind:

> They cannot, some of them, but thinke evil; they are compelled, *volentes nolentes*, to blaspheme, especially when they come to church to pray, reade, &c such fowl and prodigious suggestions come into their hearts.

> These are abominable, unspeakable offences, and most opposite to God, *tentationes faedae et impiae*; yet in this cause, he or they that shall be tempted and so affected, must know, that no man living is free from such thoughts in part, or at some times; the most divine spirits have been so tempted in some sort.[180]

No man living is free from such thoughts. These few words tell us more about Christianity, and more about its real effect on the human mind, than its sternest critics have been able to do in volumes. According to Burton 'no man living', i.e. no Christian, is wholly free from the compulsion to blaspheme.[181] But why should this be so? Why should any man in his right senses do the very thing from which he shrinks in horror, and for doing which he knows he will be damned – especially when the offence appears to serve no useful purpose whatever? By committing a murder he might ensure his own safety. By stealing he might enrich himself. But there is no possible advantage that he might gain by offering indignity to the all-knowing and all-powerful monarch of the universe, i.e. by committing blasphemy. Why, then, does he do it?

In order to answer this question we shall have to make a distinction between rational blasphemy and irrational blasphemy. Rational blasphemy is blasphemy committed as a logical consequence of one's own beliefs, whether philosophical, religious, or scientific. Thus a Buddhist, believing that no absolute first beginning of the world can be perceived, may deny that the world was ever created and, therefore, that there exists any such being as the Creator of the world, i.e. God. Similarly a Unitarian, believing in the unipersonality of the Godhead, i.e. that the Godhead exists in the person of the Father alone, may deny the Divinity of Christ and the Divinity of the Holy Ghost. Neither the Buddhist nor the Unitarian think of themselves as committing what Christians regard as blasphemy, and their state of mind bears no resemblance to that of which Burton paints so lurid a picture. Indeed for the Buddhist at least, as we have already seen, the offence of blasphemy simply does not exist, its place being taken by the very different concept of speaking in dispraise of the Three Jewels. *Irrational blasphemy is blasphemy committed as the psychological result of the Christian's own largely unconscious resistance to, and reaction against, the very religion in which he believes.* Whereas rational blasphemy is voluntary, irrational blasphemy is involuntary or compulsive. Rational blasphemy is the product of a contradiction between the beliefs of the non-Christian and the Christian, or of the heretical Christian and the orthodox Christian. Irrational blasphemy is the product of a conflict within the soul of the Christian believer himself. Rational blasphemy is extrinsic, irrational blasphemy intrinsic.

The main reason for the Christian's largely unconscious resistance to, and reaction against, Christianity, is to be found in the restrictive and coercive nature of Christianity itself. Christianity is theological monarchism, i.e. God is king writ large. Because God is king writ large the prescriptions of Christianity are not, like those of Buddhism, of the nature of friendly advice freely offered – offered by the Enlightened to the unenlightened – to be just as freely accepted or rejected, but behests which, since they embody the will of the Almighty, are matter not for discussion but only for obedience. In the words of St Augustine, 'God's thundering commands are to be obeyed, not questioned.'[182] These thundering commands pertain to all aspects of human life, from the most important to the most trivial. As mediated by the God-instituted and God-directed church, they oblige the Christian not only to refrain from killing, stealing, and lying, which the state would have obliged him to do anyway, but also – at different times – to hear mass once a week, confess his sins to a priest, gives up one tenth of his income to the Church, fast in Lent, abstain from meat on Fridays, not work on the Sabbath, not play on the Sabbath, and not marry his deceased wife's sister. At the present day the obligations which weigh particularly heavily on the (Roman Catholic) Christian are those pertaining to sex and marriage. Roman Catholics may not limit the size of their families by artificial means, may not engage in any form of sexual activity outside (monogamous) marriage, even within marriage may engage in coitus only in the prescribed manner and for the sake of offspring, and cannot be divorced.

But the obligation which weighs most heavily on the Christian, and which has weighed at all times – the command which thunders loudest in his ears – is the obligation not to think, i.e. not to think for himself in matters of faith and morals. As Cardinal Manning is reported to have said, 'I don't think. The Pope does my thinking for me.'[183] Instead of thinking, the Christian is obliged to believe. He is obliged to believe what the Church – or the Bible – tells him. He is even obliged to be a Christian. In 1864 Pope Pius IX censured as 'one of the principal errors of our time' the opinion that 'every man is free to embrace and profess that religion which, guided by the light of reason, he shall consider true,'[184] while in 1832 Pope Gregory XVI denounced as 'insanity (*deliramentum*)' the opinion 'that liberty of conscience and of worship is the peculiar (or inalienable) right of every man'.[185] Should the Christian refuse to believe what the Church tells him to believe, or even to be a Christian at all, the Church may use force to bring him to a right way of thinking, i.e. to make him believe, the opinion that the Church 'has not the power of using force' being another of the 'principal errors of our time' censured by Pope Pius IX.[186] That the Church rarely hesitates to use force when it is in a position to do so is, of course, a matter of history.

Since God's thundering commands as mediated by the Church deprive him of his freedom of thought and conduct, and force him to believe whatever he is told to believe, the Christian experiences Christianity as an immensely powerful oppressive and coercive force that threatens to crush his nascent individuality or, at the very least, compels it to assume unnatural and distorted forms. A compulsion to commit blasphemy is his response to this situation. Blasphemy, i.e. irrational blasphemy, is the reaction of outraged human nature against a Power external to itself whose demands are incompatible with its own capacity – its own need, in fact – for free and unrestricted development, that is to say, for full actualization of its moral and spiritual potential. Not that some of the demands made by this Power might not be, in respect of their actual content, helpful to the development of the individual; but coming as they do in the shape of commands, rather than as friendly advice, their form tends to negate their content, the medium to contradict the message. Only too often does God seem to be saying to the Christian, 'Love me as I love you – or else!'

Strong as it may sometimes be, however, the Christian's compulsion to commit irrational blasphemy – his resistance to, and reaction against, Christianity – remains largely unconscious. (If it became fully conscious he might have to face up to the fact that he was no longer a Christian!) After all, with his conscious mind at least the Christian believes in God, believes in Christianity. Perhaps, like the unfortunate Cardinal Newman, he believes in God but does not trust him, but that is another matter.[187] Moreover, in some periods of history more than in others, blasphemy cannot be committed with impunity, and the Christian will be uneasily aware that, should he venture to offer indignity to the Almighty in words, writing, or signs – or even in thought – the whole monstrous machinery of repression would at once spring into action against him. This awareness is sufficient to ensure that any tendency to blaspheme is kept largely unconscious. When the ascendency of Christianity is undisputed and the Church able to call on the secular arm to enforce its decrees, or when the mundane interests of the twin 'establishments' of Church and State coincide (from the beginning of the thirteenth century the Church assimilated the crime of high treason against God to that of high treason against temporal rulers), the compulsion to blaspheme disappears from consciousness altogether: it becomes *completely* unconscious. Thus the conflict within the soul of the Christian deepens: the more oppressive and coercive is Christianity, the greater is his compulsion to blaspheme; but the greater is his compulsion to blaspheme, the more necessary is it for him to repress the compulsion. The only way in which he can resolve the dilemma – the only way in which he can give expression to his urge to blaspheme without bringing upon himself the fearful retribution – is by projecting it on other people. As Wolff says, 'Everything unconscious is projected, i.e. it appears as property or behaviour of the object.'[188] Or as Jolan Jacobi puts it, 'Everything of which one is unconscious in one's own psyche appears in such cases projected upon the object, and as long as one does not recognize the projected content as one's own self the object is made into a scapegoat.'[189]

In France and other European countries at the beginning of the four- teenth century many Christians projected their blasphemous fantasies on the Templars, who were accused of renouncing Christ and trampling and spitting on the cross, as well as of other enormities, and who were suppressed in circumstances of extreme cruelty, hundreds of them being burned alive. Similarly, in Europe and North America in the seventeenth century the same fantasies were projected on thousands of harmless old women who were accused of trafficking with the Devil and burned as witches. Even at the present time the soul of the Christian is not free from conflict. The compulsion to blaspheme is, therefore, still projected, and scapegoats are still made. One cannot help wondering whether the *Gay News* trial itself is not a case in point and whether some of the more fanatical supporters of the prosecution of Denis Lemon and Gay News Ltd for publishing James Kirkup's 'blasphemous' poem may not in fact have been struggling to repress their own unconscious resistance to an oppressive and coercive Christianity.

Though the conflict is deepest in the soul of the Christian, it should not be thought that only Christians experience unconscious resistance to Christianity and that, therefore, only Christians experience a compulsion to blaspheme, i.e. to commit irrational blasphemy. Between the Christian and the non-Christian there nowadays stands the ex-Christian. The ex-Christian may be an atheist or an agnostic, a humanist or a rationalist, a secularist or a Marxist – or a spiritualist or a Satanist. He may even be a Buddhist, i.e. a Western Buddhist. Whatever it is he may be, it can be safely asserted that despite the completely genuine nature of his conversion to the new philosophy and the new way of life, in the vast majority of cases he has *not* succeeded in abandoning the religion in which he was born and brought up as completely as he would like to do and that, to some extent, he is at heart still a Christian. The fact need not astonish us. Christianity is not just a matter of abstract ideas but also of emotional attitudes, and easy as it may be to relinquish the one it is often extremely difficult to emancipate oneself from the other. The attitudes in question have, perhaps, been sedulously instilled into one during the most impressionable and formative years of one's life, and little as one may now believe in the monarch of the universe it is sometimes difficult not to feel uneasy when one is actually disobeying his commands – however wicked and pernicious one knows those commands to be. Not without reason has an atheist been defined as a man who does not believe in God but who is afraid of him!

In order to abandon Christianity completely – in order to liberate himself from its oppressive and stultifying influence – it may be necessary for the ex-Christian not only to repudiate Christianity intellectually in the privacy of his own mental consciousness but also to give public expression in words, writing, or signs to his *emotional* rejection of Christianity and the God of Christianity, i.e. it may be necessary for him to commit blasphemy. Such blasphemy is therapeutic blasphemy. Just as the ex-Christian stands between the Christian and the non-Christian, so therapeutic blasphemy stands between the purely rational blasphemy of the non-Christian and the irrational, compulsive blasphemy of the Christian. Therapeutic blasphemy is irrational blasphemy in process of becoming rational blasphemy, just as the so-called ex-Christian is in fact a Christian trying to become a non-Christian, i.e. an imperfect atheist, or agnostic, or (Western) Buddhist, as the case may be, trying to become a perfect one. An imperfect atheist, or agnostic, or (Western) Buddhist, and so on, becomes a perfect one to the extent that he succeeds in transforming his unconscious resistance to, and reaction against, Christianity into an integral part of his conscious attitude. Therapeutic blasphemy helps him to do this.

Christianity – including the Church, especially the Roman Catholic Church – has done a great deal of harm in the world. In Europe particularly, it has done more social and psychological damage than any other system of belief known to history. Crusades, Inquisitions, wars of religion, burning of heretics and witches, and pogroms are only particularly black spots on a record almost uniformly dark. It was because Christianity did so much harm – because its attitude was so cruelly repressive and coercive – that the largely unconscious resistance of many Christians to the religion in which they believed, and their reaction against it, was so strong – and the compulsion to blaspheme so widespread. For the last two hundred years, ever since the rise of the secular state, the power of Christianity to do public mischief has been limited, but even in the twentieth century its capacity to play havoc with the private life of the individual – its capacity to inflict severe emotional damage on those who fall into its hands, continues unabated. James Kirkup, the author of 'The Love That Dares to Speak Its Name', was one of those who suffered in this way. In the course of a statement about his reasons for writing the poem which he gave *Gay News* after the trouble started, but which could not be used at the trial (such evidence being ruled inadmissible by the judge), he gave a moving account of his experience – an experience which could, no doubt, be paralleled by many other people.

When I was a boy, I suffered the misfortune of having to attend a Primitive Methodist Chapel and Sunday School. This dreadful place, like all Christian churches ever since, filled me with gloom, boredom, despondency and sheer terror. I heard the grisly, gory details of the Crucifixion for the first time at Sunday School at the age of five. I was so overcome by revulsion and fright that I fainted with the shock of those gruesome, violent images. When I heard of the fires of Hell and the torments of the damned, my horror expressed itself in outbursts of uncontrollable giggles, my knees shook, and I wet the floor. I, who loathed meat and could not even bear the sight of a cut finger, was informed that I could be 'saved' only if I were to be washed in the Blood of the Lamb – which my poor dear parents considered a Sunday lunchtime luxury. I could never take part in Holy Communion, for the very thought of eating bits of Christ's dead flesh and drinking cups of his blood made me sick. Now I am convinced that young people with impressionable minds should never be exposed to such brutal, sadistic and violent obscenities, whether in church, in books, in the cinema or on television. I wonder how many children were utterly disgusted by Christianity as I was through the constant repetition of these inartistic, tasteless, and crude images.[190]

Having had Christianity inflicted on him as a child in the way he has described, it is hardly surprising that, when he grew up, James Kirkup should have written a 'blasphemous' poem. In so doing he did no more than Blake and Shelley – not to mention Swinburne, Hardy, and James Thomson ('B.V.')[191] – had done before him, and for much the same reasons. Modern literature in fact is replete with 'blasphemy', i.e. therapeutic blasphemy, as through the medium of poem, or novel, or short story, or drama, or autobiography, writer after writer strove to rid himself of the incubus of Christianity and to awaken into the light of a clearer and cleaner day. Not that – except in a few cases – the writer set out with the deliberate intention of committing blasphemy. If, as sometimes happened, he or his publisher was prosecuted for the offence, more often than not he was extremely surprised. The blasphemy was simply incidental to his own free development as a writer and as a man.

But not everybody is a writer. Not everybody is able to purge himself of the fear and guilt that were instilled into him by his Christian upbringing in ways that are not only therapeutic but creative, even if it had not been a criminal offence for him to do so. What then is the ordinary man, the man who is not a writer or an artist – the man who is not a scholar or an academic – to do? In 1883 it was ruled that 'the mere denial of the truth of Christianity is not enough to constitute the offence of blasphemy'[192] (a ruling that has since been superseded, blasphemy being now held to be whatever shocks or disgusts a single Christian or sympathizer with Christianity), and that 'if the decencies of controversy are observed, even the fundamentals of religion may be attacked.' Thus in deciding whether the offence of blasphemy has been committed the point at issue is not the matter but the manner. But can such a distinction in fairness be made? The ordinary man, being neither a biblical scholar nor a theologian, is in most cases unable to deny the truth of Christianity not only without engaging in 'indecent and offensive attacks' but also without engaging in 'licentious and contumelious abuse applied to sacred subjects' and without speaking or writing or publishing 'profane words vilifying or ridiculing God, Jesus Christ, the Holy Ghost, the Old or New Testament or Christianity in general'.[193] If he has to observe 'the decencies of controversy' and is prevented from expressing his rejection of Christianity in the terms which come naturally to him – in terms which are, sometimes, the only ones available to him – he is prevented from expressing his rejection of Christianity at all. He is effectively silenced.

The reason why the law should permit attacks on Christianity which observe 'the decencies of controversy', but not those which do not observe them, i.e. which are expressed in terms of abuse and ridicule, is therefore clear. It prevents the ordinary man, who after all is in the majority, from saying what he thinks. A learned article in an obscure theological journal expressing mild scholarly doubts as to the validity of Aquinas's third proof of the existence of God would not do much harm to the established order of things. But were the ordinary man ever to rise up and proclaim in his own vivid vernacular his abhorrence of God and his utter detestation of Christianity and all its ways the result might be not only a religious but also a social and political revolution. When G. W. Foote founded the *Freethinker* in 1881 he therefore made it clear that the paper was an anti-Christian organ, and therefore chiefly aggressive, and promised that he would use 'weapons of ridicule and sarcasm' as well as 'the arms of science, scholarship, and philosophy'.[194] Ridicule and sarcasm are comprehensible to a far greater number of people than are scientific enquiry, scholarly evidence, and abstract philosophical argument, and attacks on Christianity made with the help of such weapons are likely to be far more effective than those made without them.

It is just because they are so effective that attacks on Christianity which do not observe 'the decencies of controversy', i.e. which make use of the weapons of ridicule, sarcasm, and so on, are prohibited. The point at issue is not the manner rather than the matter of the blasphemy at all. The manner *is* the matter. Ridicule, sarcasm, and the rest are not so much a different way of attacking Christianity as a different kind of attack on it altogether. In deciding whether the offence of blasphemy has been committed, therefore, the real point at issue is not, in fact, whether it has been committed in a certain manner, i.e. decently rather than indecently, but whether it has been committed effectively rather than ineffectively. Ridicule and sarcasm are comprehensible to a greater number of people, and are a different and more effective kind of attack on Christianity, because they are as much emotional as intellectual in character. If one really wants to rid oneself of the fear and guilt instilled by a Christian upbringing – if one really wants to commit therapeutic rather than irrational blasphemy and from being an ex-Christian to become a non-Christian – then a vigorous expression of one's emotional as well as of one's intellectual rejection of Christianity is necessary. It is not enough to deny in private, as an intellectual proposition, that God exists. One must publicly insult him.

This is perhaps a hard saying, and many ex-Christians who are not yet non-Christians, whether atheists, agnostics, humanists, rationalists, or even Western Buddhists, will undoubtedly shrink from the idea of offering indignity to the Power that they were brought up to revere – and fear. Some ex-Christian Western Buddhists, in fact, anxious to show their broadmindedness, not only object to anyone criticizing Christianity but even go out of their way to speak well of it. Any attempt on the part of informed Eastern Buddhists, or less psychologically-conditioned Western Buddhists, to point out the shortcomings of Christianity, or defects in the moral character of Christ, or the absurdity of many Christian doctrines, or even the most obvious differences between Buddhism and Christianity, is met not with calm consideration of the truth of the matter but with accusations of 'narrowmindedness' and 'intolerance' and the assertion that the Christianity about which the critics are talking is not the 'real' Christianity. Such 'Buddhists' are still very much Christians at heart. Though attracted towards certain aspects of Buddhism, they are still afraid of the God in whom they do not believe, and not only shrink from the idea of offering him indignity but try to ingratiate themselves with him by speaking well of Christianity. Criticism of Christianity by Buddhists upsets them because they are afraid of being identified with it and thus incurring the wrath of the Almighty and, perhaps, the displeasure of the secular powers that be. In seeking to suppress or neutralize such criticism they are, in reality, repressing tendencies within themselves which, as yet, they dare not admit into consciousness.

The individual has a right to blaspheme. He has a right to commit rational blasphemy because he has the right to freedom of speech, i.e. to the full and frank expression of his opinions, and he has a right to commit therapeutic blasphemy because he has the right to grow, i.e. to develop his human potential to the uttermost. One who was brought up under the influence of Christianity – under the oppressive and coercive influence of theological monarchism – and who as a result of that influence is tormented by irrational feelings of fear and guilt, has the right to rid himself of those feelings by openly expressing his resentment against the Power that bears the ultimate responsibility for their being instilled into him, i.e. by committing blasphemy. Christianity is not the only form of theological monarchism, of course. Judaism and Islam are also forms of theological monarchism and those who are brought up under their influence often suffer in the same way as those brought up under the influence of Christianity and have, therefore, the same right to blaspheme. At the beginning of this article we saw that the Committee Against Blasphemy Law, in deploring the Appeal Court's decision to uphold the convictions of Denis Lemon and Gay News Ltd for blasphemous libel, also expressed concern at the possibility of the blasphemy law being extended to cover religions other than Christianity. The religions which, in the persons of their official representatives, have so far shown most interest in such an extension, are Judaism and Islam. This is perhaps as one might have expected. In the light of what has just been said, however, it is clear that it would be as wrong for the law of blasphemy to be extended to cover Judaism and Islam as it would be for it to continue to cover Christianity. There is also a practical difficulty in extending the law of blasphemy. Blasphemy is not the same thing in all religions, i.e. in all religions which recognize the possibility of such an offence. For Christianity it is blasphemy to deny the Divinity of Christ. For Islam it is blasphemy to assert it. Hindus are outraged by the slaughter of cows. Muslims are no less outraged if on the festival of Bakri-Id they are not allowed to slaughter cows. Obviously it would be impossible to extend the blasphemy law in such a way as to satisfy the contradictory requirements of all those religions that recognize the possibility of blasphemy or whose followers are capable of being shocked and outraged. In the pluralistic society that now exists in Great Britain the only equitable solution is not to have a law of blasphemy at all.

What the attitude of Buddhism is towards some of the more important issues raised by the *Gay News* blasphemy trial should now be clear. It should be clear that, so far as Buddhism is concerned, there is no such thing as blasphemy, and that so long as blasphemy remains a criminal offence Buddhists, like other non-Christians, do not enjoy complete freedom of expression in religious matters and are, in effect, penalized for their beliefs. For Buddhists in Britain, whether Eastern or Western in origin, it therefore follows that: (1) The law of blasphemy should be abolished altogether. It should not be extended to cover other religions. Buddhism itself does not, in any case, require the protection of any such law. (2) There should be a complete separation of Church and State. The Church of England should be disestablished. There should be no religious instruction (as distinct from teaching about the different religions) in state-run or state-supported schools and no act of religious worship at morning assembly. The sovereign should not be required to be a member of the Anglican communion – or indeed to belong to any Christian denomination, or even to any religion, at all. Reference to the Deity should be expunged from the National Anthem. (3) Blasphemy should be recognized as healthy, and as necessary to the moral and spiritual development of the individual, especially when he has been directly subject to the oppressive and coercive influence of Christianity or any other form of theological monarchism. Far from being prosecuted, it should be encouraged. If these suggestions are acted upon, some of the harm done by Christianity will be undone, Buddhists and non-Buddhists alike will be benefited, and society at large will be happier and healthier than it was in the Year of the Blasphemy Trial.

NEW CURRENTS IN WESTERN BUDDHISM[195]

Pioneer Women's Hall, Auckland, New Zealand, May 1979.

THE INDIVIDUAL AND THE WORLD TODAY

These three talks are about the Friends of the Western Buddhist Order (FWBO), a new spiritual movement affiliated to the great tradition which we know as Buddhism. In referring to the FWBO as a spiritual movement, I am using the word 'movement' advisedly, deliberately avoiding such terms as 'organization', 'society', or 'association', and particularly the word 'group'. I am avoiding these terms because I will not be talking about just another organization, society, or group, but about something I can only describe as a 'current' of positive, emotional, and spiritual energy. In this context the word 'current' seems particularly appropriate. The word is often associated with electricity; if you touch an electric current, you get a shock. If you touch Buddhism you will also get a shock, and if you touch the FWBO, you will certainly get a shock. So the FWBO is a current of spiritual energy which moves from higher to ever higher levels of being and consciousness. It is a current which, with our cooperation, can take hold of us and give us that shock, even radically transform our lives – not only individually, but collectively.

The FWBO is a new spiritual movement first of all in the sense of being comparatively recent; it was founded only in 1967. It is also new in the sense that it is different from existing Buddhist groups in the West; in what way it is different we shall see later on. But the inner meaning of this new movement is revealed in its name, the Friends of the Western Buddhist Order, and in these three talks I am going to explore the meaning of that name. I will try to explain in what sense the FWBO is a movement of *Friends*, in what sense it is a *Western* movement, in what sense it is *Buddhist*, and in what sense it is an *Order*. For the sake of convenience, however, I will not be dealing with them in that order. I will be dealing first of all with the word 'Western', then with the word 'Buddhist', and finally with the words 'Friends' and 'Order' together.

In what sense is our new Buddhist movement *Western?* The FWBO was founded in the UK, just a few hundred yards from Trafalgar Square, in the very heart of London. It started in a tiny basement not more than twelve feet by fourteen, underneath a shop in Monmouth Street. Seven or eight of us used to meet there just once a week, on a Thursday evening. We would meditate for an hour, and then go home. That was how the FWBO began. That was the little seed from which everything sprang. At the moment we have about twenty public centres, some twenty residential communities, about thirty right livelihood business organizations, and we have spread to a number of countries. But we started – almost like mushrooms – in that rather small dark basement in central London.

The FWBO was started in the West, in the midst of a particular kind of society, even of a particular kind of civilization. This was certainly not the sort of civilization I had been living in in India for eighteen years. It was in fact a civilization which differs from all previous civilizations in history. Above all, it differs in being both secularized, and industrialized. Of course, although this 'Western' civilization originated in the West, it is certainly not confined to it. In the course of the past 150 years or so it has spread to most parts of the globe. Although there are signs that this process is being resisted, sporadically, in one or two of the Islamic states, the world of today is a Western world, a world that is either Westernized or in process of Westernization, which is to say of secularization and industrialization. So when I say that the FWBO is Western, I do not mean that it just happens to be geographically located in the West, or that it was started, geographically speaking, in the West; I mean that it has arisen under the conditions of secularized and industrialized Western civilization. And it is with those conditions that the FWBO tries to cope. It tries to make the Buddhist way of life, the spiritual life, even – to drop all such terminology – the truly human life, possible under these conditions.

The FWBO is therefore Western in the sense that it is concerned with the world of today, not with the world of yesterday, however bright that world may have been in some respects. Nor is it primarily concerned with the world of traditional religious culture. That world is a very beautiful world; I recently saw something of it in India and among my Chinese Buddhist friends in Malaysia.[196] But that world has gone, it seems, for ever. The FWBO does not hark back to this beautiful, romantic, traditional, religious culture of the past; it looks forward. In this sense too it is young and new.

The world today has certain special problems, problems that did not exist in the past quite in the way that they exist now. These problems are not entirely new, but they happen to be more acute now, and confront us in a more urgent form – which means that their solution has become more urgent. You may immediately think of economic problems, or ecological problems, according to your particular interest, but the biggest problem of all, at least in human or spiritual terms, is the problem of the *individual*: the survival of the individual.

It is very difficult for the individual to survive nowadays. It is very difficult for the individual to grow and develop. And that which threatens the survival of the individual is clearly, in one word, the *group*. We could therefore say that the FWBO is Western in the sense that it is a spiritual movement of Buddhist origin which is concerned with the protection of the individual from the group.

That the individual – as such – needs to be protected might be a new idea to some people. We are familiar with the idea that children should be protected, we are even familiar with the idea that animals should be protected, but what about the individual? We sometimes forget that, nowadays, the individual too needs to be protected. The individual is threatened by the group, is threatened, even, with extinction.

By now you will have realized that I am using the terms 'group' and 'individual' in a rather special way. To explain what I mean I will have to go back a little in history, even into pre-history, and attempt a few definitions.

The group, of course, came before the individual, before the 'true individual'. Anthropologists tell us that Man has always lived in groups; the group was necessary to survival. This was true not only of Man but of all his pre-hominid ancestors as well: they all lived in groups of various sizes, containing anything from a dozen to two or three dozen members of various ages, and of course of both sexes. In this way they formed a sort of extended family group. This pattern was followed by Man, but with the difference that in the case of Man, the group gradually became bigger. Extended families merged to form tribes, tribes merged to form nations, nations founded states, and states even merged to form empires. This process extended over a period of many hundreds of thousands of years, gradually accelerating towards the end when we reach the period of recordable, datable history, which begins around 8000 BCE.

Whether the group was large or small, in principle it remained unchanged. We can therefore define the group as a collectivity organized for its own survival, in which the interests of the individual are subordinated to those of the collectivity. The group, or collectivity, is also a power structure in which the ultimate sanction is force. The group did not just make survival possible for its members; in the case of humans, it made it possible for them to enjoy higher and higher levels of material prosperity and culture. It made possible the emergence of folk art and ethnic religion; it made possible the emergence of civilization. But there was a price to be paid by the proto-individual, and that price was conformity with the group. The individual was regarded as being essentially a *member of the group*. The individual had no existence separate from the group, or apart from the group.

Let me give you an illustration of this from my own experience. Living in India for eighteen years, I made many Hindu friends. Some of them, being very orthodox and rather old fashioned, used to be rather puzzled by the fact that I did not have a caste. Sometimes they would ask me, 'What is your caste?' because, in their view, I *had* to belong to a caste. When I told them that I did not have a caste, first of all, because I was born in England, where we don't have caste, and secondly, because I was a Buddhist, and in Buddhism we do not recognize the system of hereditary caste, they would say, 'But you *must* have a caste! Every human being must have a caste.' They could not conceive of someone who did not belong to one of the 2,000 or so castes of Hinduism. They could not conceive of someone who did not belong to a group of some kind. There is something a little parallel to this in the West in that we cannot conceive of someone who is not of a particular nationality. But caste is even harder, even stricter, than that.

For the person who is essentially a member of the group, an individual – who does *not* belong to the group, whose being is not totally submerged in the group – is rather difficult to conceive. Because such a person is essentially a member of the group, he does not think for himself, he thinks and even feels just as the group does, and acts as other members of the group act. It does not even *occur* to him that he can do anything else. It does not *occur* to an orthodox Hindu that you need not have a caste. Whether we are talking about prehistoric times or nowadays, a group member, as such, is perfectly content with this state of affairs, because the group member is not an individual – not in the sense of being a *true* individual. He or she may have a separate body, but there is no really independent mind, no independent consciousness. The group member shares in the group consciousness, so to speak. We can call this sort of individual a 'statistical individual'. He can be counted, he can be enumerated, but he doesn't really exist as an individual in the true sense. He is simply a group member.

However, at some stage in Man's history, something remarkable happened. A new type of consciousness started to develop, a type of consciousness that we usually call reflexive consciousness, or self-consciousness, or self-awareness. Reflexive consciousness can be contrasted with 'simple consciousness'. With simple consciousness, you are aware of sights, you are aware of sounds, you are aware of trees, houses, people, books, flowers, and so on, but you are not aware of *being aware*. But in the case of reflexive consciousness, consciousness as it were doubles back upon itself, and one is *aware of being aware*.

When one is aware of being aware, one is conscious of oneself as an individual, conscious of oneself as separate from the group. One is conscious of one's ability to think and feel and act differently from the group, even against the group. An individual of this type is a true individual. Such a person is not only self-aware but is emotionally positive, full of good will towards all living beings. He is also spontaneous and creative because he is not determined in his thinking, feeling, or acting, by previously existing mental, emotional, and psychological patterns – whether his own or those of other people. The true individual is also responsible, aware of his own needs, aware of others' needs, and prepared and willing to act accordingly.

True individuals started appearing on the stage of history in relatively large numbers in the course of what we call – to use Karl Jaspers's term – the Axial Age.[197] This Axial Age, a sort of crucial turning point in human history, was a 300-year period extending very roughly from around 800 BCE to around 500 BCE. The true individuals who started to emerge during this period appeared in Palestine, Greece, Persia, India, and China, in fact in most of the great centres of civilization. Some of them were great thinkers, others were prophets and mystics; others again were poets, sculptors, and founders of religions. In Palestine we have such figures as the prophets Isaiah, Jeremiah, and Amos, as well as the unknown author of the *Book of Job*. In Greece, we have Pythagoras and the great philosopher Plato; we have the Attic dramatists, the great poet Pindar, the sculptor Phidias, and so on. In Persia we have the prophet Zoroaster. In India we have the Upanishadic sages like Yagnavalkya; we have Mahāvīra, the founder of Jainism, and we have the Buddha. In China we have Confucius and Laozi, the two most important individuals to arise in the whole history of Chinese culture. Of course, some of these individuals went far beyond the stage of mere self-consciousness. At least some of them developed what I have called 'transcendental consciousness', and even 'absolute consciousness'.

In this way, the Axial Age was a period of efflorescence of the true individual. Indeed, from this time onwards we can see two factors at work in human cultural, religious, and spiritual history. On the one hand there is the individual, and on the other hand there is the group.

Between the true individual and the group there was always a certain creative tension, the group pulling one way – in the direction of conformity – and the individual pulling the other – in the direction of nonconformity, of freedom, of originality, of spontaneity. In this dialectical relationship, the group provided the individual with his raw material. We find this, for example, in Greek drama. Here, certain myths and legends, themselves a product of the collective unconscious, provided the dramatists with stories which they adapted in such a way as to give expression to their own highly individual vision of existence. In this way the individual influenced the group, reacted upon the group, raising the statistical individuals who still belonged to the group, at least momentarily, to a higher level, bringing them closer to true individuality.

This relationship was in force for about 2,000 years. On the whole it was a lively and a healthy one. Sometimes it broke down, as when the medieval Catholic Church started persecuting those 'heretics' who dared to think differently from the Church. (By this time, of course, the Church was no longer a spiritual community, as it had once been to some extent, but simply a religious group, a sort of ecclesiastical power structure.) But on the whole the relationship between the true individual and the group continued to be fairly healthy for about 2,000 years. Generally speaking, the group at least tolerated the individual – provided he did not impinge too uncomfortably upon the group. During the last 200 years, however, a change has taken place to such an extent that a serious imbalance now prevails between the individual and the group. There are various reasons for this, but I will only summarize some of the more important ones.

To begin with, the population of practically every country in the world has greatly increased in recent years. During the eighteen years I spent in India, for instance, the population of that country doubled! Because we have so many more people in the world, almost everywhere, it has become much more difficult to get away from one's fellows, much more difficult to get away from the group. This is especially the case in small, densely populated countries like Holland and the United Kingdom, and in some parts of the bigger countries.

Secondly, there is the increase in the power of the corporate state. Today's corporate state, we may say, is the group *par excellence*, and it controls so many aspects of our lives. In most countries, this control is increasing rather than decreasing. These corporate states now divide the whole world between them. There is no portion of the Earth's land surface that is not controlled by one or another corporate state, and they have even started staking out claims to the sea. There used to be some nice empty spaces of *terra incognita* between them, where you could go if you wanted to get away from the state, but those spaces no longer exist; there are no spaces anywhere in the world where no state exercises any authority. Every individual has to belong to a state, whether they like it or not. From time to time we hear about a few miserable people who have been declared stateless. Their condition is considered a terrible calamity because, these days, you just have to belong to a state. You have to have a passport, for without one you cannot travel from one state to another. This is a fairly recent development; passports came into general use only after the First World War. Before that it was not so necessary to have one. Now they are really indispensable.

Thirdly, there is the growth of modern technology. This is in many ways a helpful development, but it has its disadvantages. It means that, among other things, the corporate state can now keep track of its citizens far more efficiently. A computer system can be set up to tell its operators a person's date of birth, when he or she last paid taxes, how many parking offences they have ever committed, where they spent their holiday last year, whether they have ever had measles, and so on. With this information at its fingertips, the state finds it much easier to exercise control over the individual.

Fourthly, there is our higher standard of living. This too is a blessing up to a point, but it does make us dependent on the group. We are dependent on the group for such good things of life as cars and televisions, not to speak of petroleum and electricity, since it is very doubtful whether we could produce these things by ourselves. Generally, we are so helpless, so dependent, that we cannot even grow our own food or make our own clothes. The general principle would therefore seem to run thus: the higher our standard of living, the bigger and more complex the state to which we have to belong – and, therefore, the more control it exercises over our lives and the less freedom we have. There is something a little paradoxical about this. If we have a car, for instance, we have greater freedom in the form of more personal mobility. But that freedom is taken away from us in certain other respects by the fact that, in order to possess and to drive a car, we have to be part of a society that is geared to the production of cars – which may not necessarily be the best kind of society.

For these reasons we can now see that there is an imbalance between the individual and the group.

Now I have said that the corporate state is the group *par excellence*. But within the corporate state there are many other smaller groups. The corporate state is in fact a sort of interlocking system of groups, some of which are very powerful indeed when set against the individual. There is the political party, the trade union, the chamber of commerce, the church, the bank, the school. Some of these impinge on us in certain respects more strongly and more directly than does the corporate state itself. The result is that we are left with a virtually powerless individual in a virtually all-powerful state. The group has practically overwhelmed the individual, who feels, very often, that he is quite unable to influence the group, even in those matters that most closely concern his own life.

This is the state of affairs in the world today, especially in the Western democracies, in the old Communist states, and in various military dictatorships. It is a state of affairs that is becoming more and more widespread, and the result is that the true individual is dissatisfied. The 'statistical individual', very often, is not dissatisfied;

very often he is happy with what the group provides, whether it is bread and circuses, as in the case of ancient Rome, or motor cars and television sets as is the case today. His only complaint is that he would like to have more of them more frequently! But the true individual is frustrated. In extreme cases, his frustration may sometimes find expression in violence. We know that violence is on the increase in our cities – and I am certainly not saying that frustration of the kind I've mentioned is the sole cause of this violence – but it is certainly one factor. What, then, are we to do?

To begin with, and above all, we have to restore the balance between the individual and the group. This means that we need a philosophy, a way of looking at things, that can provide the perspective within which we will be able to see the possibility of restoring the balance. We need a philosophy that recognizes the value of the individual, a philosophy that shows the individual how to grow, how to be a true individual. This is where what nowadays we call Buddhism (but which calls itself, in its own habitat, the *Dharma*) comes in.

Buddhism places the individual in the very forefront of its teaching. The Buddha's teaching is concerned solely with the individual, both alone and in free association with other individuals. It shows the individual how to grow, shows him or her, by means of actual methods, how to develop awareness, how to develop emotional positivity, how to live spontaneously and creatively, how to accept responsibility for oneself and for others, how, in other words, to be more and more of a true individual.

Gautama the Buddha, the original teacher, was and is an example of a true individual. He was an individual of the highest kind: an *Enlightened* individual. He was an individual who had developed not only reflexive consciousness, but also 'transcendental' consciousness and 'absolute' consciousness.

If we take even a cursory glance at the Buddha's life we can see how the Buddha's individuality demonstrated itself right from the start. Quite early in his life he cut himself off from the group; that was the first step he took of any significance. He left his parents, left his wife and child, left his city, left his tribe, and gave up his social position to wander alone from place to place. Occasionally he joined various religious groups and cults, but in the end he cut himself off from them too. They too were hindrances, they too were groups. He was left entirely alone – in a way that perhaps no one had ever been alone before. Being alone, he was able to be himself; being himself, he was able to be an individual; being an individual – looking at things as an individual, seeing things as an individual – he was able to see the Truth for himself, able to experience it for himself. Being able to see the Truth, he was able to become what we call a Buddha, an Enlightened individual. And having become an Enlightened individual, he was able to help others to become such. From that moment, we may say, the power of the group, the power of Māra – the power of the gravitational pull of conditioned existence – was diminished.

In the Buddha's day the power of the group was perhaps not so great as it is today, but the Buddha's teaching and example were needed all the same. It is needed, we may say, whenever and wherever the survival of the individual is threatened, wherever there is an imbalance between the individual and the group, especially when that imbalance is as extreme as it is in the world today. There is no political or economic solution to such a problem. There is only a *spiritual* solution, a solution which takes the individual into account. If put into operation, that solution will of course have political and economic implications and consequences, but it has to be a solution that respects and emphasizes the value of the individual.

This is a radical view of things. After all, how many people respect the individual? You can meet so many people who do not respect you as an individual, who don't even *see* you as an individual. You can go into a shop or into a government office and try to deal with the people there. They do not see you as an individual; they see you as a sort of public zombie who has just drifted in. But the solution we need is a solution that *sees* the individual, that respects the individual, that allows the individual, even, to make his own mistakes, that does not hold the individual's hand all the time. This attitude is very well illustrated by an incident in the Buddha's life.

A Brahmin once came to see the Buddha and asked whether he taught all his disciples the way to Nirvāṇa *equally*. When the Buddha affirmed that he did, the Brahmin asked, 'But do they all, equally, *attain* Enlightenment?'

When the Buddha replied that some did, while others did not, the Brahmin was again rather puzzled and asked, 'Well, why is this? If they all get the same teaching, why don't they all realize Nirvāṇa?'

The Buddha therefore gave him the following example: 'Over there', he said, 'is the city of Rājagaha. Now you know the city of Rājagaha; you know the way to the city of Rājagaha. Suppose two men come to you and both ask, "Please tell me the way to Rājagaha." And suppose you give quite detailed instructions: "Go along this road, turn that corner, go through that grove of mango trees, and then you'll get to the city." Suppose you give both of them these directions, and suppose one follows your directions and arrives, but the other does not follow your directions and does not arrive because he makes a mistake, would it be your fault? Would you be to blame for that?'

'No,' said the Brahmin. 'If, after I had given the proper directions, one of them found the way but the other did not, it wouldn't be any fault of mine. I wouldn't be to blame. I am only the shower of the way. I only give directions.'

'It is the same in my case', said the Buddha, 'I am only a shower of the way.'[198]

The Buddha is only the one who shows the way, but it is up to the individual to follow that way, to decide for himself whether he is going to follow that way or not. We may say that this attitude shows tremendous respect for the individual. It shows great confidence in the potential of the individual. It shows an appreciation of the fact that the individual cannot be forced. He must *want* to change; he must *want* to develop. All that one can do is show him *how*, show him an example, encourage him, and, if one can, inspire him. But one can do no more than that. You can't force him, you can't bribe or threaten him; you can only show him the way. That is to say, if you are an individual, and trying to deal with him as an individual, then you can only show him the way and leave it to him to follow or not to follow.

This attitude is the basis for Buddhism's well-known spirit of tolerance. Buddhism is deeply conscious of human differences, deeply conscious of the fact that we are not all the same. We each have our own temperaments, characters, and our different ways of looking at things. We therefore have to be allowed to develop, each one of us, in our own manner. This is why, in the whole of its 2,500-year history, Buddhism has never persecuted anybody for their beliefs. There is no such thing as heresy in Buddhism. There are such things as 'wrong views', views that hold us back and prevent us from developing, but these wrong views are to be corrected – if they are to be corrected at all – by discussion and not by force. Force has absolutely no place in Buddhism, no place in the spiritual life.

At this point, somebody might raise an objection. While agreeing that there is a serious imbalance between the individual and the group that needs to be corrected by spiritual means, they may nevertheless ask why we have to bring in Buddhism. Why should we not do it with the help of Christianity, which is after all traditionally the religion of the West?

I personally think there are three main reasons why Christianity cannot help us correct the imbalance between the individual and the group. The first of these is that Christianity is on the side of the group. That Christianity has no respect for the individual is amply demonstrated by its history. Whenever and wherever Christianity has gained political power it has persecuted those who think differently, those who try to be individuals. We have only to think of the enormities perpetrated by the Inquisition, of the horrors of the Albigensian crusade, of the wars of religion in Europe in the sixteenth and seventeenth centuries, of the burning of witches – that is to say old women – at the stake. (Why were they burnt? Because the Bible says, 'Thou shalt not suffer a witch to live.')[199] Even today, in democratic countries, Christian pressure groups are trying to get laws passed which would compel non-Christians to conform to Christian ideas of right and wrong.

Secondly, Christianity believes in God. It believes in a supreme being, an all-powerful, all-knowing creator of the heavens and the Earth. Buddhism does not believe in God. It teaches that belief in the existence of God is a view that prevents us from developing as true individuals. What is God, after all? If we forget the theological or the more abstract philosophical definitions, and just try to look at God more realistically, more psychologically and existentially, then we must conclude that God is simply the most powerful member of the biggest conceivable group. And we find, in fact, that God enforces group values – or is represented as enforcing group values – such as obedience, conformity, and respect for the powers that be.

Thirdly, people are encouraged to fear God. They are encouraged to feel guilty if they disobey his commands. In this way they are crippled – psychologically and spiritually – sometimes for life. Only too often they become unable to think for themselves, unable to develop. People generally do not realize what a disastrous effect their Christian upbringing, especially their belief in God, has had on them, until –

sometimes – it is too late. They may realize it only when they try to break free from it, only when they try to become individuals. So for these reasons I do not think that Christianity can help us to correct the imbalance between the individual and the group. I do not think it can help us solve the problem of the individual. Christianity, I would say, has exacerbated the problem.

It might of course be said that the Christianity I have been talking about is not true Christianity. I must reply that this is the Christianity of history, the only Christianity that we really know. It is this Christianity which has oppressed us as individuals in the past, and which still oppresses us when it gets the opportunity today. It might be possible to imagine a better Christianity, but this Christianity would have to fulfil four conditions. Firstly, it would have to entirely dissociate itself from what Aldous Huxley called, 'that savage, bronze-age literature' of the Old Testament.[200] Secondly, it would have to give up the belief in God. (Some Christians have in fact already done this, as adroitly as they can, with their 'death of God' theology.) Thirdly, it would have to regard Christ as a teacher rather than as a Saviour. And fourthly, there would have to be an improvement in his teaching.

Until we have a Christianity of this kind we will just have to bring in Buddhism. We will just have to bring in something like the Friends of the Western Buddhist Order, a new spiritual movement which seeks to protect the individual from the group, which tries to correct the imbalance between the individual and the group, and which tries to solve the problem of the individual and the world today.

This spiritual movement will have to be a 'Buddhist' movement because Buddhism recognizes, as I think perhaps no other teaching does, the value of the individual. Buddhism shows the individual how to grow, how to become more and more of an individual; it allows him to develop in his own way. It also gives him the inspiring example of the Buddha and the support of the sangha, or spiritual community, of other *individuals* with whom he is in direct personal contact.

All the same, it is not easy to be a Buddhist. It is certainly not easy to be a Western Buddhist. Historically speaking, at least, Buddhism is an Eastern religion. What the relationship is between Western Buddhists and Eastern Buddhism will be the subject of our next talk.

WESTERN BUDDHISTS AND
EASTERN BUDDHISM

We will now be trying to understand the sense in which the FWBO is a specifically *Buddhist* movement. First of all, however, I must clear up two misunderstandings that could have arisen out of the previous talk.

The first arises in connection with the word 'individual'. You will recall that I spoke of our developing as an individual, even as a 'true individual'. But when I spoke in those terms I was not suggesting that we should become 'individual*ists*'. What, then, is the difference between an individual and an individualist? This distinction is quite crucial.

An individual is someone who has developed a higher level of what we call 'reflexive consciousness'. The individualist still 'shares' the consciousness of the group, the level of consciousness which manifests in all members of the group. The individualist has, we could say, a larger 'share' of this group consciousness than other members of the group, and therefore asserts his or her own interests at the expense of others in the group. The *individual* is therefore alienated from the group in what we may call a vertical direction, while the *individualist* is alienated from the group horizontally. The individualist is a sort of broken-off fragment of the group, reacting, even rebelling, against the group; he is the group writ small, a sort of one-man group – which is really a contradiction in terms, like a one-man band. The individual, on the other hand, has passed, or begun to pass, beyond the group, beyond group consciousness; he is no longer limited by group consciousness.

The second possible misunderstanding relates to the traditional Buddhist teaching of *anātman* (Pāli *anattā*). *Anātman* literally means 'no self', or even 'non-self', depending upon the translation you prefer. But if you have read any sort of textbook on Buddhism you will know that Buddhism recognizes – as I've been insisting – the value of the individual, that it places the individual at the forefront of its teaching. It might therefore be objected that this recognition of the individual contradicts the teaching of 'no self'. Surely, the *anātman* teaching denies the very existence of a self, denies the existence of the individual, treats it as an illusion? What, then, are we to make of all this? Where does the development of the individual fit in?

Fortunately, the difficulty is actually more apparent than real, because the *anātman* teaching does not really reject the existence of the self at all. Indeed, the Buddha specifically denied saying that the self does not exist.[201]

What the *anātman* teaching does deny is the existence of an *unchanging* self, and it does so for two reasons. It denies that there is an unchanging self – with the emphasis on the word 'unchanging' – because an unchanging self would contradict the Buddha's fundamental teaching of the impermanence – the changeful nature – of all conditioned things. Secondly, if the self were unchanging, the *development* of the self, the development of the individual, would be impossible. This would make the spiritual life, and thus Buddhism itself, impossible. However, we must be careful not to think that, because development is possible, there must be an unchanging individual who develops. What we have to realize is that the subject of the verb 'develop' is, in reality, a linguistic fiction.

We can now proceed to the meaning of the word 'Buddhist' in the name of our new spiritual movement, the Friends of the Western Buddhist Order. In what sense is the FWBO a Buddhist movement? Clearly, this very much depends on what we mean by 'Buddhist' – and that depends on what we mean by 'Buddhism'.

There are many different versions of Buddhism, and many interpretations. After all, the word 'Buddhism' itself represents an interpretation. Buddhism was not originally called Buddhism at all. It was certainly never called Buddhism in India, and it was certainly never called Buddhism by the Buddha. It was called *Dharma* in Sanskrit, or *Dhamma* in Pāli. The word *Dharma*, or *Dhamma*, means Reality, or Truth; it means law, doctrine, or teaching. Or, one may say, it represents reality or truth as communicated in the form of a teaching from the Enlightened to the unenlightened mind. The originator of this Dharma, this vision of reality as a teaching, is, of course, Gautama the Buddha. He communicates to his followers a reality, a truth, which he has personally experienced – the experience of which constitutes Enlightenment. Therefore, the Buddha is the best spokesman, the best interpreter, of Buddhism. So what does the Buddha himself say that the Dharma is? In this connection we can refer to an episode in the Pāli scriptures, for the Buddha himself was once asked this very question, namely: 'What is your Dharma? What is your teaching?'

The person who asked this was Mahāpajāpatī Gotami, the Buddha's aunt and foster-mother. She had brought him up since childhood, since the death of his mother when he was just a few days old. In later years Mahāpajāpatī Gotami had not only become a follower of his teaching, but had 'gone forth', as we say, after hearing those teachings from his own lips. She had been so impressed by them that she had wanted to give up all her other interests, connections, and ties, so as to be able to devote her entire life to practising the Dharma. She had therefore gone forth, leaving her home, leaving her family, leaving her husband, leaving the city of Kapilavastu, and wandering from place to place, meditating and seeking to practise the Dharma.

At the time of our episode, Mahāpajāpatī Gotami had passed a period of time without any direct contact with the Buddha, so there was a certain amount of confusion in her mind. She wanted to practise the Dharma, but she was not quite sure what the Dharma was. This is not such an uncommon thing. Sometimes, at least, many of us may find ourselves in the position of wanting to practise the truth, without being quite sure, or even at all sure, what the truth actually is.

Although Mahāpajāpatī Gotami was in contact with some of the Buddha's disciples and was able to ask them what it was that the Buddha taught, the interpretations they gave her were often very different; they each had their own point of view. In the end she decided to go and ask the Buddha himself what it was that he did fundamentally teach. She therefore made the journey to the place where the Buddha was staying and asked, point blank, as it were, 'What is your Dharma? How can we know what you actually do teach? What is the criterion?' Here is a translation of what, according to the tradition, the Buddha said to Mahāpajāpatī Gotami on that occasion:

Gotami, those things of which you know, 'These things lead to passion, not to dispassion; to attachment, not to detachment; to amassing, not to dispersal; to ambition, not to modesty; to discontent, not to content; to association [association with the group, that is], not to seclusion [from the group)]; to idleness, not to energy; to luxury, not to frugality,' of them, you can quite certainly decide. 'This is not the Dharma, this is not the Vinaya, this is not the Master's teaching.'

But those things of which you know, 'These things lead to dispassion, not to passion; to detachment, not to attachment; to dispersal, not to amassing; to modesty, not to ambition; to content, not to discontent; to seclusion (from the group), not to association (with the group); to energy, not to idleness; to frugality, not to luxury,' of them you can quite certainly decide, 'This is the Dharma, this is the Vinaya, this is the master's teaching.' [202]

So here in the Buddha's own words is the criterion; this is the principle. The Dharma is whatever contributes to the spiritual development of the individual. It is whatever the individual finds, in his own experience, does actually contribute to his own spiritual development.

Now in this passage, as in others, individuals are clearly seen to be living, growing, and developing. And in this connection we may also remember the Buddha's 'vision' of humanity immediately after his Enlightenment. At that time, the Buddha was undecided as to whether or not he should actually teach the truth he had discovered. It was, he knew, something very deep, very difficult and abstruse. But he eventually decided that he would go out and teach, he would communicate the truth he had discovered to other beings. And at that moment, we are told, he opened his eyes and looked out over the world to see those living beings as a bed of lotus flowers. [203] It was as if he could see just a vast bed of lotuses spreading in all directions, as far as the eye could reach. This was humanity. This was the human race. Some of these 'flowers' – some of these people – were clearly sunk in the mud. Others had risen just a little way out of it and were struggling free. Others still had broken out of the mud altogether and their heads were rising above the surface of the water so that their petals could open out to receive the light of the sun.

This is how the Buddha saw humanity at that moment. He saw all beings as individuals, and he could see that they were all at different stages of development, all growing but needing the sunlight of the Dharma in order to grow and develop further.

In another passage, in the great Mahāyāna *sutra* called the *Saddharma Puṇḍarīka* or *Lotus Sūtra*, there is another very beautiful comparison. Here, individuals are compared not just to lotuses emerging from the mud and slime, but to many different kinds of plants. They are compared to grass, trees, flowers, and shrubs, while the Buddha's teaching is compared to a great rain cloud.[204] During the winter and summer in India it is very hot and dry for many months. Everything becomes very withered and parched. But then, suddenly, at the beginning of the rainy season, a great black cloud arises in the midst of the sky. There is thunder, lightning, and then the rain falls, very heavily and very steadily, day in and day out, sometimes for weeks on end. And as it rains, everything grows. Everything that was so parched and dry becomes green again and starts springing up. All the leaves, all the grass, trees, flowers, and shrubs, start to grow again. And everything grows in its own way. The tree grows as a tree, the shrub grows as a shrub, the grass grows as grass, the flower grows as a flower; each grows in its own way. This is important to the Buddha's analogy, for the Dharma is just like that rain cloud: it gives us just the nourishment we each need. It leads us from where it finds us, its starting point – so far as we are concerned – being where we are now, because everyone needs the Dharma in his or her own way.

This is also what we find the great Tibetan poet and mystic, Milarepa, saying in one of his songs: everybody needs the Dharma, but they need it in their own way. Here are just a few of the verses which he sang on a certain occasion:

Superior men have need of Dharma;
Without it, they are like eagles –
Even though perched on high,
They have but little meaning.

Average men have need of Dharma;
Without it, they are like tigers –
Though possessing greatest strength,
They are of little value.

Inferior men have need of Dharma;
Without it, they are like pedlar's asses –
Though they carry a big load,
It does them but little good.

Superior women need the Dharma;
Without it, they are like pictures on a wall –
Though they look very pretty,
They have no use or meaning.

Average women need the Dharma;
Without it, they are like little rats –
Though they are clever at getting food,
Their lives have but little meaning.

Inferior women need the Dharma;
Without it, they are just like little vixens –
Though they be deft and cunning,
Their deeds have little value.

Old men need the Dharma; without
It, they are like decaying trees.
Growing youths the Dharma need;
Without it, they are like yoked bulls.
Young maidens need the Dharma; without
It, they are but decorated cows.
All young people need the Dharma; without it
They are like blossoms shut within a shell.
All children need the Dharma; without it
They are like robbers possessed by demons.

Without the Dharma, all one
Does lacks meaning and purpose.
Those who want to live with meaning
Should practice the Buddha's teaching.[205]

Milarepa's song makes it clear that the meaning and purpose of life for the individual is to grow, to rise to a higher level of consciousness, and that this is what the Dharma helps us to do. The Dharma is whatever helps us to rise from wherever we are now, and from whatever we are now. The Dharma is therefore defined as whatever contributes to the development of the individual. That is the criterion.

This may sound rather broad and general, but it is not really so. The Dharma – the Buddha's teaching – is embodied in a number of actual spiritual practices. This is made clear in another episode from the Pāli scriptures. In this particular episode we are reminded that there were a number of spiritual teachers in India during the Buddha's time. One of the best known of these was Nigaṇṭha Nātaputta, as he is called in the Pāli texts, who is usually identified with Mahāvīra, the founder of Jainism. Nigaṇṭha Nātaputta died shortly before the Buddha, and after his death his monk followers split into two factions. These factions disagreed so vehemently about what their master had taught that they almost came to blows. Ānanda, who seems to have been something of a gossip, told the Buddha about this, adding that he hoped there would be no such disputes after the Buddha himself had gone.

The Buddha replied that such a thing would be impossible. He was confident that there were not even two monks among his followers who would describe his teachings discordantly. He then reminded Ānanda what those teachings were. There were the four foundations of mindfulness: mindfulness of the body, of the feelings, thoughts, and of reality. There were the four right efforts: the effort to prevent the arising of unskilful mental states that have not arisen; the effort to abandon unskilful mental states that have arisen; the effort to develop skilful mental states that have not arisen; and the effort to maintain in existence those skilful mental states that have already arisen. He reminded Ānanda about the four bases of success, the five spiritual faculties, the five powers, the seven factors of Enlightenment, the Noble Eightfold Path,... All these things constituted the Dharma that he had taught and about which he was confident there would be no dispute after his death even between two of his disciples.[206]

The immediately noticeable thing about this list of teachings is that they are all practical. They are all actual *practices*. There is nothing theoretical here; the Buddha says nothing about Nirvāṇa, nothing about *śūnyatā*, nothing about the mind. He does not even mention 'dependent origination'. It is as if he is saying that the teachings he has given his disciples are all practical teachings and cannot therefore really be described differently by different people. After all, practical teachings involve actual practice so the experience would be the same for all who practised. It is much the same in ordinary life; we may disagree about theory, but we do not very often disagree about practice. We may disagree, for example, about the nature of electricity, but we are unlikely to disagree about how to replace a fuse. Similarly, the Buddha's disciples might disagree about theoretical teachings, but they could hardly disagree about practical teachings, provided of course that they had actually practised them. So the Dharma is embodied primarily in spiritual practices, in things that you actually do.

There is another interesting point which arises in connection with this episode. Despite the Buddha's answer, Ānanda was not satisfied. He now said, 'Well, even though they may all agree about the teaching, there might still be disputes about livelihood, or there might be disputes about the code of rules'.[207] The Buddha's reply to this was very important. A dispute over livelihood, or a dispute over the code of rules, he said, would be a 'trifling matter'. It is only disputes over the path, or disputes over the way of practice, that would be disastrous.

Now that we have briefly seen what is meant by Buddhism, we can begin to see in what sense the FWBO is a Buddhist movement. It is a Buddhist movement first of all in the sense that it is concerned with the individual. Buddhism values the individual in a way that no other teaching does. And Buddhism is simply whatever helps that individual to grow, whatever helps him or her to develop from lower to higher levels of being and consciousness. At the same time, the Dharma does not represent just a vague general principle of growth; it is embodied in specific spiritual practices.

This last point, however, may leave some people troubled by the following question: If Buddhism is whatever contributes to the development of the individual, does it have to be confined only to what is labelled as 'Buddhism'? Could one not say that whatever contributes to the development of the individual is in fact Buddhism, or at least part of Buddhism?

There are two things that I should perhaps mention in this connection. Some people in the FWBO get a great deal of inspiration from certain Western poets and philosophers, an inspiration which helps them in their spiritual life as Buddhists. I can think of Goethe, of Blake, of Schopenhauer, Nietzsche, Plato, D. H. Lawrence, and Shelley. (Quite a miscellaneous collection, you might think!) Yet other Friends derive inspiration from Western classical music, especially from that of Bach, Beethoven, and Mozart. This is quite in order, and one could certainly count such inspiration as part of Buddhism in the wider sense.

When I say this, however, I am not suggesting that people like Goethe, Blake, and so on – great as they were – were as Enlightened as the Buddha. I am not saying that their poetry or their philosophy or their music can take us as far as can the Dharma – that is to say, the Dharma in the narrower sense. But at present we have to recognize that most people in the FWBO are still at a quite elementary stage in their spiritual life, and they need the help which is appropriate to that stage. Perhaps I should quote the words of Gampopa, the great Tibetan mystic, when he says, 'The greatest benefactor is a spiritual friend in the form of an ordinary human being.'[208] An 'ordinary' human being is ordinary, in this instance, when compared to the Buddhas and the bodhisattvas. By that standard, even Goethe and Blake were ordinary.

Secondly, regardless of the inspiration one may get from these other sources, the principal source of inspiration for the FWBO is nonetheless the Buddha and his teachings. It is from there that we get our idea of what constitutes development; it is from there that we get our ideal of human Enlightenment. So whatever help we get from other sources must be in accordance with that, in harmony with that, and must lead us in the direction of human Enlightenment. This, then, is why we call ourselves the Friends of the Western *Buddhist* Order, rather than something else.

The FWBO is, as we have already seen, a Western spiritual movement, a Western spiritual phenomenon. It seeks to practise Buddhism under the conditions of modern Western civilization, which is a secularized and industrialized civilization. But, historically speaking at least, Buddhism is an Eastern religion. It originated in India, and for 2,500 years it has been virtually confined to the East. It is only quite recently, in the course of the last hundred years in fact, that it has become known in the West at all. So what is the relation between Western Buddhists and Eastern Buddhism?

In attempting to answer this question, the first thing that has to be said is that there is no such thing as Eastern Buddhism. What we actually have is a number of Eastern Buddhisms, in the plural. Broadly speaking there are four of these now extant in the Eastern Buddhist world. There is South-east Asian Buddhism, Chinese Buddhism, Japanese Buddhism, and Tibetan Buddhism.

South-east Asian Buddhism is found in Sri Lanka, Burma, Thailand, and in Cambodia – as well as, here and there, in Singapore and Malaysia. This form of Buddhism belongs to the Theravāda school, whose scriptures are contained in the Pāli Tipiṭaka – in some forty-five volumes in the Royal Thai edition.

Chinese Buddhism is found mainly in China, Taiwan, Korea, Vietnam, and, again, in parts of Singapore and Malaysia. (I am of course ignoring recent political developments which have certainly altered the situation.) Chinese Buddhism belongs to what we may call 'general', or non-sectarian, Mahāyāna, and its scriptures are contained in the Sānzàng, or 'Three Treasuries', corresponding to the Tipiṭaka, in fifty-five volumes. These volumes are very much bigger than the volumes of the Pāli Tipiṭaka. In this particular collection there are no less than 1,662 independent works, a few of which are almost as long as the Bible.

Japanese Buddhism is found, of course, in Japan, but also in Hawaii, and among Japanese immigrants in mainland USA. It comprises various schools of what may be described as 'sectarian' Mahāyāna. The best known of these are Zen and Shin. There are also various modern schools developed even in the present century. The scriptures of Japanese Buddhism are the Chinese Sānzàng plus various Japanese works according to sect – which may in practice sometimes displace the Sānzàng.

Tibetan Buddhism is found in Tibet, Mongolia, Sikkim, Bhutan, Ladakh, parts of China, and even in parts of the USSR. It consists of four main traditions, all of which follow all three of the *yānas* – that is, Hīnayāna, Mahāyāna, and Vajrayāna. The differences between these four traditions occur mainly in respect of Vajrayāna – that is to say Tantric – lineages. Their scriptures are all contained in the Kangyur, which means the 'Buddha-word', in 100 or 108 (according to the edition) xylographed volumes, plus special collections like the *Rinchen-Terma* for the Nyingmapas, or the *Mila Grubum* in the case of the Kagyupas.

These are the four extant Eastern schools of Buddhism. There are many intermediate forms, and sub-forms, and sub-sub-forms, but for the sake of simplicity I have ignored them. For practical purposes Western Buddhists find themselves confronted by four Eastern Buddhisms rather than by just one monolithic Eastern Buddhism with complementary unitary features.

Perhaps I could just add here that they do not find themselves confronted by an Eastern mind, or by an Eastern psychology either. Some writers speak of the Western mind and the Eastern mind as though they were two completely different minds, and it is suggested that it is very difficult for the Eastern mind to understand the Western mind, and vice versa. Buddhism of course is supposed to be a product of the Eastern mind, which is why, we are sometimes told, it is difficult for Westerners to understand Buddhism. Speaking from experience, however, I have found no evidence for any such belief. Wherever I went during my twenty years in the East, whether I was associating with Indians, Tibetans, Mongolians, Thais, or Sinhalese – or even Europeans, I found that I could understand them, and they could understand me. Buddhism is admittedly difficult to understand, but not because it is a product of the 'Eastern mind'. It is difficult to understand because it is a product of the *Enlightened* mind, a mind which transcends the conditionings of both the East and the West.

Another popular myth which I might as well mention in this connection is that there is a 'spiritual' East, and a 'materialistic' West. This really is another myth. The West is no more materialistic than the East. One might say that the West is simply more 'successful' in its pursuit of materialism.

However, to return to the theme of Western Buddhists and the four Eastern Buddhisms, these four Eastern Buddhisms are differentiated from each other in two main ways. They are differentiated, first of all, according to the doctrinal school of Buddhism to which they belong. Secondly, they are differentiated according to the regional or national culture with which they are associated.

From a practical point of view, at least, the second of these is probably the more important since, as a consequence, the Buddhism that most people come across in the West, whether in content or in practice, is not really Buddhism. We could even say that many Western Buddhists never really encounter Buddhism at all. What they encounter is a particular school or sub-school of Buddhism associated with a particular national or regional culture. They may encounter the Theravāda, for instance, which is associated with South-east Asian – specifically Sinhalese – culture. Or they may encounter Zen, which is associated with Japanese culture, and so on.

But the situation is even more complicated than that. Buddhism arose in India, a country with a very rich and ancient culture. From its very beginning, from the moment it emerged from the Buddha's mouth, so to speak, Buddhism was associated with Indian culture, indeed with Indian cultures, because in the course of the 1,500 years during which Buddhism was alive in India, Indian culture went through several different phases of development, each with very strongly marked characteristics.

When Buddhism went on from India to China, what actually 'went' was Buddhism plus Indian culture. Then, in China, Buddhism assumed certain Chinese cultural characteristics before going on to Japan. In Japan, of course, Buddhism assumed certain Japanese characteristics. So today, Japanese Buddhism consists of Buddhism plus Indian culture plus Chinese culture plus Japanese culture. *That* is the Buddhism which is coming to the United States of America, to Britain, to Australia, and so on. Sometimes, of course, the Buddhism succeeds in penetrating all those layers of culture which are superimposed upon it, but sometimes it does not.

Confronted by these different Eastern Buddhisms, the first thing that the Western Buddhist has to do is learn to distinguish what is really Buddhism from what is actually South-east Asian, or Chinese, or Japanese, or Tibetan, or even Indian culture. It is not that there is anything wrong with any of those cultures; they are often very beautiful indeed. But they are not the same thing as Buddhism, not the same thing as the Dharma. When we say that the FWBO is a Buddhist spiritual movement we do not mean that we have adopted some particular form of Eastern culture – though, at the same time, this does not necessarily mean that we reject Eastern Buddhist culture. Some of that culture does express the spirit of Buddhism. One might think, for example, of the Japanese art of flower arrangement – this surely expresses something of the spirit of Buddhism. In the FWBO we are very happy to adopt this kind of Eastern culture, but we adopt it because it can be approached as an expression of *Buddhism*, because it helps us in our spiritual development, and not just because it is Eastern.

However, some Western Buddhists are unable to make this distinction between Buddhism and Eastern culture. They think that they are attracted by Buddhism when in reality they are attracted to an exotic oriental culture. Sometimes they think they are trying to be Buddhists when in reality they are just trying to copy Indians, Japanese, or Tibetans

– or at least to look like them. This is quite harmless of course. There is no harm in dressing up as an Indian, or pretending to be Japanese, or imagining that you are a Tibetan. It is quite harmless – except to the extent that it represents an alienation from your own culture – but it has nothing to do with actually being a Buddhist.

In some parts of the West we now have a very strange situation indeed. All four of the main Eastern Buddhisms have now been introduced. They have their Western followers, all of whom are supposedly Buddhists; but because they follow different Eastern cultures they are unable to live together or to practise Buddhism together.

I remember an example of this sort of thing from the very early days of the FWBO. Not far from London lived a group of English Zen Buddhists. They decided that they would like to join one of our FWBO communities, and, after some discussion, we agreed – even though I had my own misgivings. Almost as soon as they had moved in, a difficulty arose: they refused to join in the puja – that is, the evening devotions. The reason for this was that our puja was recited in Pāli and English, and their guru (who was, incidentally, an English woman who had spent some time in Japan) had told them that they should do their puja only in Japanese.[209] So while some members of the community performed their puja in English and Pāli these English Zen Buddhists waited outside the shrine-room; they would not even sit in the room and listen.

Another example comes to mind in connection with this same guru. Japanese culture is what sociologists call a 'shame culture'. In Japanese culture shame is used as a technique of social control. (Our Western Christian culture is probably a 'guilt culture'.) In traditional Japanese society, when a young person misbehaves, an older person will proceed to imitate him – but greatly exaggerating the misdemeanour. If the young person has been noisy, the older person will be four or five times as noisy. If he has slammed a door the older person must go and slam it three or four times very, very loudly. The young person then feels ashamed; he realizes that he has been corrected and desists from that particular misbehaviour out of shame. At some stage this technique of control through shame was transferred to the Japanese Zen temple. If the disciple misbehaved the master would imitate him. If the disciple slouched during meditation the master would immediately slouch right over; the disciple would notice, feel ashamed, pull himself up straight, and in that way he would learn. The technique was known as 'mirroring'.

Now this English/Japanese Zen guru happened to pass through London some years ago. It seems that she did not very much like what some of the English Buddhists, who had not been to Japan, were doing. So she started mirroring them. Her head monk, an American who was accompanying her, started mirroring them as well. For example, thinking that English Buddhists ate far too much while on retreat, he started mirroring them, and took a second helping of everything, just to show them how greedy they were. However, the English Buddhists, not being Japanese, did not understand what was going on. They thought the poor fellow must be hungry, and gave him a third helping of everything. The guru, I heard, was quite annoyed. She said that English Buddhists were stupid because they could not appreciate her mirroring technique. But really it was she who could not understand that mirroring was part of Japanese culture; it had nothing to do with Buddhism, and it was not appropriate in the West.

The FWBO is definitely a Buddhist spiritual movement. But it does not confuse Buddhism with any of its Eastern cultural forms. In the same way, the FWBO does not identify itself exclusively with any particular sect or school of Buddhism, not with the Hīnayāna, nor with the Mahāyāna, nor with the Vajrayāna, nor with the Theravāda, nor with Zen, Shin, or the Nyingmapas. It is just *Buddhist*. At the same time it does not reject any of the sects or schools that have arisen in the course of the long history of Buddhism. It appreciates them all and seeks to learn from them all, taking from them whatever it can find that contributes to the spiritual development of the individual in the West. As regards meditation practice, for instance, we teach the mindfulness of breathing and the *mettā bhāvanā*, the 'development of universal loving-kindness', which are taken from the Theravāda tradition. We recite the Sevenfold Puja – which comes from the Indian Mahāyāna tradition. We chant mantras which come from the Tibetan tradition. And then of course there is our emphasis on the importance of work in the spiritual life, which is a characteristically Zen emphasis. Naturally, we also have certain emphases that are not to be found in any extant form of Buddhism: for example, our emphasis on right livelihood, on Going for Refuge, and on 'more and more of less and less'.

Although we take what we need from all these sources, our attitude is not one of eclecticism. Eclecticism is a purely intellectual attitude. We may take different things from different forms of Buddhism, but we take them according to our actual spiritual needs, rather than in accordance with any preconceived intellectual ideas. We take whatever will help us *grow* under the conditions of Western life.

We adopt much the same sort of attitude towards the Buddhist scriptures. There are an enormous number of these, as you have already gathered, and it would be impossible to study them all. Actually, we are not in fact meant to; they represent the same basic teachings in varying degrees of expansion and contraction. Instead, we read and study intensively whatever we find most helpful to us in the spiritual life. Our study texts are therefore drawn from all sources: from Pāli, Sanskrit, Chinese, and Tibetan. Among others we study the *Udāna*, which is found in the Pāli Tipiṭaka, the *Bodhicaryāvatāra*, which is a Sanskrit Mahāyāna work compiled in India, *Dhyāna for Beginners*, which is based on the lectures of a Chinese master, *The Jewel Ornament of Liberation*, the work of a Tibetan master, and *The Songs of Milarepa*, the teachings of one of the greatest Tantric yogis of the Buddhist tradition.[210]

We should now be able to see the nature of the relation between Western Buddhists – or at least Western Buddhists in the FWBO – and the various Eastern Buddhisms. But another question might arise at this point. If, as we have seen, the FWBO does not follow Eastern Buddhism as such, is it then trying to create a *distinctively* Western Buddhism? Is it trying to express Buddhism in terms of Western culture?

The answer is both yes and no, and depends very much on what one actually understands by Western culture. As we have already seen, the FWBO is not 'against' Western culture as such: there are certain affinities between the works of the great Western poets, philosophers, and musicians, and certain aspects of Buddhism. But this is not true of Western culture as a whole – in which must be included our social and economic systems. Western culture, as it stands as a whole, is quite incompatible with Buddhism and there can be no question of our seeking to express Buddhism in terms of that culture. It is a question, rather, of Western Buddhism finding expression in a *new* Western culture, a culture which would in its own way, on its own level, help people to develop, if not spiritually then at least psychologically. In creating that culture we would of course keep the best elements of the traditional Western culture, but a lot would have to go.

So far as the FWBO is concerned there is no question of our simply finding a little place for ourselves in the contemporary Western world without trying to change that world. It is not just a question of studying Buddhism and then doing what everybody else does in all practical matters, and living as everybody else lives. This is one of the points that makes the FWBO a new Buddhist movement: it is not content just to inhabit a little niche.

The FWBO was founded in 1967. In those days there were two different kinds of Buddhist group in England. Firstly, there were groups run by Eastern Buddhists – Sinhalese Buddhists, Tibetans, Thais, and so on – who had come here for that purpose. They all propagated Buddhism in a particular Eastern cultural form or setting – sometimes, unfortunately, propagating Eastern culture rather than Buddhism. Secondly, there were groups run by English Buddhists. These tended simply to study Buddhism: to read books, listen to lectures, and maybe in some cases practise a little meditation. I remember, for instance, being told on my return to London in 1964 that English Buddhists were not able to practise more than five minutes meditation at a time, and that I was on no account to try to give them more! That was the standard in those days. People tended simply to study Buddhism, read lots and lots of books about Buddhism, hear lots and lots of lectures about Buddhism, and in some cases practise a very little meditation. But in their everyday life they lived like everybody else, with the same social, economic, and political ideas and ideals as the non-Buddhists (of their own class, that is). Being a Buddhist made no difference in any of these areas; they rarely even practised right livelihood, and didn't even think of practising it. Furthermore, although they studied Buddhism, they rarely studied it from the Buddhist point of view. In many cases they did not even think of themselves as Buddhists. They studied Buddhism, strange as it may sound, from the Christian point of view, or at least with unconscious Christian conditioning.

Very recently a group of students from the Open University, along with their tutor, paid a visit to the London Buddhist Centre. During the course of their visit it emerged that both the students and their tutor – who was a Methodist minister – had some very strange ideas about Buddhism. According to the textbook for their course on Buddhism – which had been written by a Belgian Jesuit priest – the Theravāda was annihilationist, the Mahāyāna was corrupt and degenerate, and the Vajrayāna was just magical nonsense. No wonder they were confused!

This is the sort of thing that is still going on in academic circles, but when I returned to England in 1964, and again in 1967, things were almost as bad in ostensibly Buddhist circles. English Buddhists, for instance, who studied the Pāli scriptures, not only said that the Pāli scriptures were the word of the Buddha, but that *only those scriptures* were the word of the Buddha, and that other Buddhist scriptures were not the word of the Buddha at all. Naturally, one was therefore not allowed to question anything that was recorded in the Pāli scriptures. After all, the Buddha was Enlightened and the Buddha had uttered every word that was found in them. These English Buddhists were in fact Pāli fundamentalists! They adopted towards the Pāli scriptures the same sort of attitude that Christian, especially Protestant, fundamentalists adopt towards the Bible. It was as if they had transferred their Christian attitudes from Christianity to Buddhism without making any real change at all.

The FWBO, I hope, adopts a different attitude. It tries to see Buddhism from the Buddhist point of view. And it seeks to create a new Western civilization and culture, one which will express Buddhist spiritual values, one which will help the individual to develop instead of hindering him or her, and one which will provide the basis for a spiritual community and a new society.

We have now seen that the FWBO is a Buddhist movement in the sense that it is concerned with the individual. We have seen that Buddhism, according to the Buddha, is whatever helps the individual to grow. We have further seen that Buddhism is not exclusively limited to whatever is labelled as 'Buddhism'. At the same time we have seen that Buddhism is not just a vague and general principle of growth, but is embodied in specific spiritual principles and practices. We have also seen that the FWBO distinguishes sharply between Buddhism and Eastern Buddhist culture, and that it is not limited to any sectarian form of Buddhism but appreciates and seeks to learn from – and gain inspiration from – all forms of Buddhism without exception. We have seen too that it seeks to create a new Western culture based on genuine Buddhist values, and that it seeks to see Buddhism in terms of Buddhism – that is to say in terms of the individual evolving in the direction of what we can only call Enlightenment.

COMMITMENT AND SPIRITUAL COMMUNITY

In order to explain the sense in which the Friends of the Western Buddhist Order is based on an *Order*, and the sense in which it is a movement of Friends, I need to offer a little in the way of autobiography. This will help me to explain what it was that led me to start an Order and a movement of friends, rather than just another Buddhist organization of the usual type.

Before returning to England in 1964 I spent altogether twenty years in the East. I spent most of those years in India, initially as a sort of Hindu-Buddhist ascetic, wandering in southern India, meditating, studying, meeting famous teachers, and so on (a part of that story is related in my volume of memoirs, *The Thousand-Petalled Lotus*).[211] I then spent a year in Benares, studying Pāli, Abhidhamma, and logic. Finally, I spent fourteen years in the foothills of the Himalayas in a place called Kalimpong, about 4,000 feet above sea level, sandwiched between Nepal to the west, Bhutan to the east, Sikkim to the north, and, beyond Sikkim of course, Tibet.

Although I kept in touch with various Indian Buddhist organizations during all this time, I did not join any of them. I kept in touch, but I never joined. It was as if some instinct was holding me back. One organization with which I maintained particular contact was quite an old one. It was also fairly well known, for in its day it had done a lot of good work for Buddhism in India.[212] Now I had not been in touch with this organization for very long before I began to feel quite dissatisfied with it. My dealings, both by letter and also from time to time in person, were mainly with the governing body, which, including office bearers, consisted of about forty people. Most of them, I soon discovered, were not Buddhists. This rather surprised me. In those days I was a little inexperienced, not to say naive, and so was rather shocked to find that the majority of the members of the governing body of a prominent Buddhist organization were not even Buddhists.

At first I felt that this must be all right, that these people must be genuinely sympathetic to Buddhism even though they were not actually Buddhists. But in time I found that this was not the case either. Very much to my dismay I discovered that some members of the governing body had no sympathy with Buddhism at all. In some cases they were actually hostile to it, even though they were running the organization's affairs.

Naturally enough, I began to wonder how this had happened, and came to realize that these people were running the affairs of the organization quite simply because they had been *elected* to its governing body. And how had they been elected? They had been elected at an annual general meeting. And how had they come to be present at that annual general meeting? They were there because they were paid-up members of the organization. How had they become members of that organization? Simply by paying a subscription. This, then, seemed to me to be at the root of the trouble: these people had got where they were simply by paying a small sum of money, plus, of course, a bit of string pulling. It seemed a very strange way to run a Buddhist organization; no wonder it was not functioning very well.

You might wonder why it was that people who were not really sympathetic to Buddhism should take the time and trouble to run the affairs of a Buddhist organization. After many years of experience I now know that there are some people who like to belong to organizations, who like to get on to governing bodies and managing committees, whether religious, political, civic, or social. It gives them a feeling of power. They just like to run things and they don't mind very much what it is that they are running.

In the case of this particular Buddhist organization there was yet another factor at work. The organization was quite well known, and used to organize big public meetings, to celebrate the Buddha's birthday for instance. In India public meetings are really very big; you can get

50,000 people, even 100,000 people, coming along. That was the kind of public meeting that this particular organization used to organize, and of course famous politicians and prominent businessmen would be invited to preside over them, so that if you were a member of the governing body you would be sitting up on the platform with all these people, basking in their reflected glory. Naturally you would get to know them, and getting to know these celebrities would be very useful to you in your own political or business life. You might even get some favour in that way, because in India after all, everything is done by personal influence. So, as you can perhaps imagine, what I saw in India made me rather disillusioned with Buddhist organizations.

When I returned to England after twenty years in the East I thought that things would be different. However, as I spent my first two years working with existing Buddhist organizations, mainly in London, I must admit that I found things pretty much the same – only on a very much smaller scale. Again there were plenty of non-Buddhists having quite a big say in the running of Buddhist organizations, and consequently those organizations too were not functioning very well, at least from a Buddhist point of view.

I therefore decided that something had to be done. A new Buddhist organization would have to be started, an organization which would not be an organization. I had already decided to remain in England because I saw that in England – in fact in the West generally – there was scope for a genuinely Buddhist movement, but I now felt the need to start a new one, indeed, a new kind of Buddhist movement altogether. This was of course what was eventually started as the FWBO and the WBO.

It is not as easy to start up something new, not as easy to start a new spiritual movement, as one might think. It is said that a young clergyman once paid a visit to Voltaire, the great French writer and thinker. This clergyman's faith in the Church and Christianity was crumbling and he thought it would be a good idea to start a new religion. So when he was in the presence of the great sage of his time he asked, 'What should I do in order to start a new religion?' Voltaire replied, 'It is really very easy; you just have to do two things. First of all you must get yourself crucified, and then you must rise from the dead.'[213]

It is not as easy to start a new religion as you might think. It is not very easy even to start a new spiritual movement. But although it may not be at all clear at first what *has* to be done, I think I can say that it is usually quite clear how things are *not* to be done. And one thing that was clear to me was that Buddhist organizations could not be run by non-Buddhists. They could not be run simply by people who were good at running things, however efficiently they might do it. And they certainly couldn't be run by people who were merely after power and influence, or name and fame. A Buddhist spiritual movement could be run only by real Buddhists, by those who were actually *committed* to Buddhism and who actually practised the Buddha's teachings, not by those who had merely an intellectual interest in it. Strangely enough, this was not generally realized at the time. People seemed to think that a spiritual movement could be run by people who were not themselves spiritually motivated.

But my view of things presented some important questions. How was one to know who was spiritually motivated? How could one know who was a Buddhist? What in fact *was* a Buddhist? What was the criterion? Eventually, the answer became clear. In a way I had known it all along, but now I saw it in a new light. A Buddhist is one who 'goes for Refuge' to the Buddha, the Dharma, and the Sangha, is one who *commits* himself to the Buddha, the Dharma, and the Sangha, and who commits himself to them totally, with body, speech, and mind.

There are many stories to illustrate what this means in the ancient Buddhist scriptures. When we read those scriptures, especially the Pāli scriptures, we encounter the Buddha as he wanders from place to place, begging his food as he goes. In the course of his wanderings, he might meet somebody under a tree, or in a village, and the two of them get into a conversation. Maybe it's a Brahmin priest, or a farmer, or a well-to-do merchant, or a young man about town. Maybe it's a wandering ascetic, maybe it's a housewife, maybe it's a prince... but in one way or another they get talking.

Sooner or later, this person asks the Buddha a question, perhaps about the meaning of life, or about his teaching, or about what happens after death. The Buddha might reply at considerable length, giving a detailed discourse, or he might reply in just a few words. If he is very inspired he might reply in verse, 'breathing out' what is called an *udāna*. He might even give one of his famous 'lion roars', a full and frank, almost defiant, declaration of his great spiritual experience and the path that he teaches; or he might reply with complete silence – a wordless communication that says so much more than words.[214] But whatever the Buddha says or does not say, if the listener is receptive, the result is the same. He or she feels deeply affected, deeply moved, deeply stirred. They are so stirred, so thrilled, in fact, that their hair might stand on end, or they might shed tears, or be seized by a violent fit of trembling. They feel as if they are seeing a great light; they have a tremendous sense of emancipation; they feel as if a great burden has been lifted from their back, or as though they have been suddenly let out of prison. At such a moment, the listener feels spiritually reborn. And at that extraordinary turning point they respond to the Buddha and to the Dharma with a cry that breaks spontaneously from their lips. According to those ancient Pāli texts, they say; 'Buddhaṃ saraṇaṃ gacchāmi, Dhammaṃ saraṇaṃ gacchāmi, Saṅghaṃ saraṇaṃ gacchāmi,' which means, 'To the Buddha for Refuge I go, to the Dharma for Refuge I go, to the Sangha for Refuge I go.' This is their response: they go for Refuge, commit themselves, because the Buddha has shown them a vision of inner truth, of existence, of life itself in all its depth and complexity. This vision is so great that all one can do is give oneself to it completely, live for it, and if necessary die for it.

But what does one actually mean when one says, 'To the Buddha for Refuge I go; to the Dharma for Refuge I go; to the Sangha for Refuge I go'? The English word 'refuge' is not very satisfactory. It is a literal translation of the Pāli and Sanskrit word saraṇa, but does not give its real meaning. There is certainly no question of running away from anything when one goes for Refuge, no question of taking shelter with anyone. Going for Refuge really means commitment: committing oneself to the Buddha, committing oneself to the Dharma, committing oneself to the Sangha. So what does this mean?

Committing oneself to the Buddha does not mean handing oneself over to the Buddha or blindly obeying the Buddha. It means taking the Buddha as one's ideal, taking Buddhahood as an ideal. The historical Buddha, Gautama, was a human being. By his own human efforts he developed higher and ever higher states of being, states that eventually culminated in what we call 'Enlightenment', the highest conceivable state of moral and spiritual perfection, a state of supreme wisdom, of infinite compassion, and absolute purity. We too are human beings; we too, therefore, according to Buddhism, are capable of developing higher and higher states of being and consciousness. We too are capable of gaining Enlightenment. This is what committing oneself to the Buddha means. It means recognizing the Buddha as the living embodiment of the highest conceivable state of human perfection. It means recognizing Buddhahood as a practical ideal for all human beings, and actually devoting all one's energies towards the realization of that ideal.

What is meant by 'committing oneself to the Dharma'? The Dharma is the teaching of the Buddha, and it is concerned mainly with two things: with the goal of Enlightenment, or Buddhahood, and with the path leading to that state. Committing oneself to the Dharma therefore means actually following the path in order to realize the goal. The path consists of several steps and stages which are variously enumerated according to the particular point of view adopted. One popular enumeration of the stages of the path is that of the three stages of morality, meditation, and wisdom. Another enumeration is that of the Noble Eightfold Path. This is not really a path of eight stages, as is generally thought, but a path of two stages: a stage of vision and a stage of transformation. The stage of vision represents an actual vision of the goal – not just a theoretical idea but an actual spiritual experience – and the stage of transformation represents the gradual transformation of all aspects of one's being, from the highest to the lowest, in accordance with that vision. There is also the path of the six perfections – of generosity, morality, patience, vigour, meditation, and wisdom. So committing oneself to the Dharma means following the path in any of these various ways. It means committing oneself to the process of one's development as an individual by whatsoever means.

The Sangha is the spiritual community – that is, the community of the spiritually committed. The Dharma, as we have seen, is a path that consists of various steps and stages. Naturally, different individuals are on different steps and at different stages. Some are more advanced than we are, some are less advanced, and some are equally advanced. What, then, is our attitude towards these people? We reverence those who are more advanced, we are receptive to their spiritual influence, and assist them in their spiritual work. We help those who are less advanced than we are, giving advice and moral support as and when we can. And we enjoy spiritual friendship with those who are as advanced as ourselves. Indeed, we can enjoy spiritual fellowship with all members of the Sangha in different ways and in differing degrees. This is what we mean by committing ourselves to the Sangha.

Certainly each individual must develop for himself or herself, by his or her own efforts, but we will develop more easily and more enjoyably if we do so in spiritual fellowship with others. We could even say that spiritual fellowship is necessary to individual development. In the spiritual community all help each, and each helps all. In the end, all narrow, pseudo-religious individualism is transcended, there is only a spiritual community of individuals who are, as it were, transparent to each other, individuals through whom the light of Enlightenment shines.

So this is how one can know who is a Buddhist. A Buddhist is one who goes for Refuge in response to the Buddha and his teaching. A Buddhist is one who gives himself or herself to the Buddha and the Dharma and the Sangha. This was the criterion in the Buddha's day 2,500 years ago, and it remains the criterion today.

I had now come to see that a Buddhist organization could be run only by Buddhists, which meant that it could be run only by those who had committed themselves wholeheartedly to the Buddha, the Dharma, and the Sangha. But another thing that then became clear was that a Buddhist organization run by committed Buddhists would no longer be an organization in the ordinary sense of the word. It would be a spiritual movement. In fact it would be what we call a 'spiritual community', an association of committed individuals, freely working together for a common spiritual end.

We can now begin to see in what sense the FWBO is based around an 'order', can begin to see, perhaps, what led me to start an order rather than yet another Buddhist organization of the usual type. An order consists of those who have been ordained. In Buddhist terms 'ordination' means giving full formal expression, in 'concrete' form, to one's commitment to the Buddha, the Dharma, and the Sangha, and having that commitment recognized by others already committed. One can join an organization by paying the required subscription, but one can be received into an order only by way of ordination, only by committing oneself. This was the basis on which our new Buddhist movement was founded, the basis of commitment and spiritual community, or, in more traditional Buddhist language, of 'Going for Refuge' and 'Sangha'. But if this was the only basis on which it could be founded, you might therefore wonder why it had taken me such a long time to see it. You might also wonder why nobody else had thought in terms of commitment and spiritual community, why nobody else, in recent times at least, had started an order instead of yet another Buddhist organization. So far as I can see there are three reasons for this, and I will give a brief account of them so as to offer a clearer idea of the difference between a spiritual community and a religious organization.

The first of these reasons is what I can only describe as inertia and force of habit. Buddhism started to become known in the West, including Westernized India, not much more than a hundred years ago. This was a time when the frontiers of knowledge, and especially of scientific knowledge, were expanding rapidly. Societies were set up at that time for the study of all sorts of things, and it was inevitable that sooner or later there should be societies devoted to the study of Buddhism and the publication of Buddhist texts. This was quite all right, so long as the approach remained purely scientific, purely academic. At this stage I am not questioning the validity of the scientific approach to spiritual traditions, but such an approach is no longer suitable when we are concerned with Buddhism in a more practical, spiritual, even existential way. Unfortunately people did not realize that a new kind of approach was required and assumed that an organization devoted to the practice and spread of Buddhism could have the same structure as an organization devoted to its scientific study. Not only that: the prominent people within those old Buddhist organizations were quite satisfied with things as they were since the existing set-up gave them a certain amount of power and authority which they did not want to relinquish.

The two other reasons are more traditional. The first of these was what we could call the 'devaluation' of the Going for Refuge. Buddhism has a long history. In the course of a thousand years Buddhism spread over practically the whole of Asia, and millions of people became Buddhists, millions of people committed themselves to the Buddha, the Dharma, and the Sangha. So far so good. But as time went by people started reciting the words '*Buddhaṃ saraṇaṃ gacchāmi*' and so on out of habit, or simply because their parents or their grandparents had recited them. They were not real Buddhists; they were not really committed to the ideals of Buddhism. Such people sometimes regard themselves as 'born Buddhists', as though such a thing were not a contradiction in terms. This is the situation today in the Buddhist countries of Asia to a great extent. The Going for Refuge is no longer regarded as an expression of genuine, individual spiritual commitment, but has become a recitation which simply shows that one belongs to a particular social or cultural group.

I had plenty of personal experience of this sort of thing while I was in India. I found Sinhalese, Thai, Burmese, and Indian Buddhists reciting the refuges and the precepts on all sorts of occasions – at big public meetings, at weddings, at funerals.... People would recite the words, and yet nobody bothered about their significance. They recited the refuges and precepts just to show they were good Buddhists or they were respectable citizens. This is why I speak of a devaluation of the Going for Refuge. The Going for Refuge is really the central act of the Buddhist life. It is what makes you a Buddhist. But in popular, modern Buddhism it has largely become something peripheral, something formal, and something of purely cultural significance.

I think this is why it took me such a long time to see that it was on the basis of individual commitment that a new Buddhist movement must be founded. So far as I can remember, no one ever stressed to me the importance of Going for Refuge during the course of my entire stay in India. Some people were very particular indeed about the correct pronunciation of the Pāli refuge formula, but they paid no attention to what the words actually meant. I therefore had to discover the significance of the Going for Refuge for myself. When I had done this I saw that it was in fact the key to everything, saw that it was the basis of our new Buddhist movement. So in the FWBO tremendous emphasis is placed on the Going for Refuge. This is actually the simplest thing in Buddhism, but it is the most important.

The last reason that nobody had thought of starting an order instead of yet another Buddhist organization had to do with an overvaluation of monasticism, especially of formal monasticism. If, nowadays, you were to ask a serious-minded Eastern Buddhist, especially from South-east Asia, what really makes one a Buddhist, more often than not he will say that the real Buddhist is the *monk*. He will say that if you really want to practise Buddhism you must become a monk; a layman cannot practise Buddhism – or he can do so only to a very limited extent. The best thing the layman can do is support the monks, supplying them with food, clothing, shelter, and medicine. In this way the layman can earn some merit and hopefully, on the strength of that merit, be reborn in heaven after his death, or at least be reborn on earth in a rich family.

It would appear that, because the Going for Refuge has been *devalued*, monasticism has been *overvalued*, and overemphasized. Being a Buddhist is no longer a matter of Going for Refuge, no longer a question of committing oneself to the Buddha, the Dharma, and the Sangha. Being a Buddhist means, in effect, becoming a monk. I most certainly do not want to undervalue monasticism or the monastic life – that would be going to the other extreme. I have been a monk myself for more than half my life, and I think that in many ways the life of a monk is the best possible kind of life. But to be a Buddhist it is not necessary to be a monk. What *is* necessary is that one should go for Refuge; what is necessary is the commitment to the Buddha, the Dharma, and the Sangha. That commitment is primary – lifestyle is secondary. For many people, of course, this commitment may find expression in the leading of a monastic life. This was particularly the case in the Buddha's own day, but even then it was not invariably the case. According to the Pāli texts, some of the Buddha's followers attained a high level of spiritual development while continuing to live at home as laymen and laywomen. And of course, when I say that spiritual commitment can be expressed in the leading of the monastic life, I should perhaps add that by this I mean the leading of a *genuinely* monastic life. This unfortunately is not always the case. In many parts of Asia, commitment has been replaced by monasticism. And more often than not this is not genuine monasticism. More often than not genuine monasticism has been replaced by merely formal monasticism. The laity in many parts of the Buddhist world go through the motions of Going for Refuge, while in much the same way the monks go through the motions of being monks – which is to say they recite the monastic rules at intervals, without really asking themselves what those rules mean.

Perhaps we can now see why nobody had thought of starting an order instead of yet another Buddhist organization. Seeing things from their own particular point of view they thought they already had an order when they did not in fact have an order at all. They had, in most places, just a number of people following the same lifestyle in an external, mechanical sort of way. However, as soon as you put the emphasis on Going for Refuge, monasticism is no longer overvalued. It takes its proper place as one possible lifestyle for the committed individual Buddhist.

We now have a clearer idea of the sense in which the WBO is an order. It is a free association of committed individuals, of people who take Enlightenment as their ideal, who try to develop as individuals, who experience for themselves, in themselves, the successive stages of the spiritual path, who enjoy spiritual fellowship with one another, and who help, encourage, and inspire one another.

Some of these committed people in the Western Buddhist Order are old, some are young. Some are men, some are women. Some live in residential semi-monastic communities, others live at home with their families, and a few live on their own. Some live in the cities, some live in the country. Some are quite highly educated, some have no formal education at all. Some have a leaning towards the arts, some towards sciences. Some live in England, some live in Finland, some live in India, some in Europe, some in the USA, some in Australia, and some in New Zealand. But all are committed to the Buddha, all are committed to the Dharma, all are committed to the Sangha; all are united in Going for Refuge. All therefore belong to the same spiritual community, all are 'members' of the Western Buddhist Order.

It is these spiritually committed individuals, and these alone, who are responsible for running the different FWBO centres. It is not that members of the WBO *have* to run the centres – this is a matter of their own free choice. Some Order members have nothing whatever to do with the running of FWBO centres but get on with their own spiritual practice while keeping in regular touch with other Order members. But if, as an Order member, you want to start a centre of the FWBO, you just get together with half a dozen other Order members and agree among yourselves to set it up.

An important point to be made here is that, while there are many different FWBOs in different countries, they are all legally and financially independent. There is no single headquarters for the entire FWBO movement. Orders do not come from above. Actually, they do not come from anywhere. Local activities are run by local Order members. The unity of the movement is therefore spiritual rather than organizational. All Order members everywhere belong to the same Order, and the different centres are therefore run in the same spirit.

At this stage the question might arise as to how one becomes an Order member. In saying just a few words about this, I should also be able to explain the sense in which the FWBO is a movement of friends.

Let us suppose that an FWBO centre has been opened in your part of the world, and starts running meditation classes, yoga classes, lectures, study groups, retreats, and so on – all the usual FWBO activities. And suppose it so happens that you get to know about it and go along in order to sample some of its activities. As soon as you come along you are reckoned as a 'Friend' – with a capital 'F' – of the Movement. You can come along as frequently or as infrequently as you please. You are not asked to join anything, you are not given any responsibility, you can just make whatever use you please of the centre's facilities: you are a Friend. The great majority of people in the FWBO are Friends. There might be quite a few tens of thousands of them who come along every now and then – in some cases for years – attending the odd class or lecture, or the occasional retreat, but without wanting to go any further than that.

Some, however, do want to go further. They start attending classes regularly, start meditating at home every day; they start bringing their working life into line with the principle of right livelihood. Maybe they will also help out at the centre from time to time, and make the effort to get into closer contact with Order members, until, in short, they start feeling that they 'belong' to the FWBO, and want to be more deeply involved. Such people can therefore become what we call 'Mitras'. (The Sanskrit word *mitra* means simply 'friend', but the Sanskrit form is used in order to distinguish Mitras from 'Friends'.) One becomes a Mitra in a simple ceremony in which the Mitra-to-be offers a flower, a lighted candle, and a stick of incense to the Buddha image on the shrine. The ceremony usually takes place in the context of a puja (a sort of devotional ceremony) – usually on the occasion of a Buddhist festival – at the Buddhist centre, or perhaps away on retreat, in the presence of Order members, other Mitras, and Friends.

Some people become Mitras after just a few months as Friends; others wait for two or three or four years. Special study groups and special retreats are arranged for Mitras, allowing them to have more contact with Order members and to intensify their practice. Again, some people find that being a Mitra gives them all that they need, and may not wish to go any further than this. Others, however, will want to go further and will start thinking in terms of actual commitment. They may start thinking they would like to commit their whole life to the Buddha, the Dharma, and the Sangha; that they would like to go for Refuge. There are those who reach this point after just a few months as a Mitra, others reach it after a few years, but sooner or later some of them at least reach the point of asking for ordination within the Western Buddhist Order.

By now you should have a good general picture of the FWBO. As a total movement the FWBO consists of two 'parts'. Firstly, there is the Order, the community of spiritually committed individuals. Secondly, there are the Friends and the Mitras. These Friends and Mitras make up what we could call the 'positive group'. You will of course recall that I had some hard things to say about the group in my first talk. Those were, I believe, fully justified. Nevertheless, we must not forget that there is such a thing as a *positive* group, which consists of people who are happy, healthy, and human. Above all, the positive group is open to the spiritual community. The FWBO is a movement of Friends in the sense that it includes a positive group of this sort, one that is open to the spiritual community.

* * *

In these three talks I have tried to communicate some idea of our new Buddhist movement. I have tried to explain in what sense it is Western, in what sense it is Buddhist, in what sense it is an Order, and in what sense it is a movement of Friends. It may seem as though I have told you quite a lot, but this is not really so. I have really given little more than a glimpse of the FWBO. If you want to know more then you will have to experience it personally, from within. I hope you will do just that, and I hope that, having made contact with the FWBO, you will make a closer and closer contact with that current of spiritual energy which is our new Buddhist movement. And I hope that, sooner or later, you will allow that current to sweep you away.

THE BUDDHA'S VICTORY

THE BUDDHA'S VICTORY

Buddha Day, London, May 1987.

For a Buddhist, the highest values of existence are incarnated in three great ideals. Firstly, there is the ideal of Enlightenment, the ideal of the perfectly developed human being. Secondly, there is the ideal of the path to Enlightenment, the sum total of all the principles, practices, and teachings that help the individual human being in the course of his or her quest for spiritual perfection. Thirdly, there is the ideal of fellowship in pursuing the way to Enlightenment. By this is meant the deriving of encouragement, help, inspiration, and stimulus from other individuals who are also trying to perfect themselves. In traditional terms, these three great ideals are embodied in the Buddha, the Dharma, and the Sangha.

The Buddha embodies the ideal of Enlightenment. The word *Buddha* means 'Enlightened One', humanity perfected. The Dharma, the truth, doctrine, or teaching of the Buddha, embodies the path. The Sangha, the spiritual community of those who follow the path and study and practise the teaching, embodies the fellowship of those treading the path.

These three are known in traditional Buddhist terms as the Three Jewels. They are also known as the Three Refuges or the Triple Gem, or even, in the Chinese tradition, as the Three Treasures. Between them they represent the highest values and ideals of Buddhism. However widely Buddhism has spread over the centuries, however richly it has developed in various ways, everything relates to one or another of these three, or to all of them jointly. Anything that is not connected with the Buddha, the Dharma, or the Sangha, has no real connection with Buddhism at all.

Like all spiritual traditions Buddhism has two aspects: a 'popular' aspect, the aspect of ordinary, everyday practice and observance, and a 'philosophical' aspect, which is concerned with the deeper understanding of the teaching. The popular aspect includes such things as festivals and celebrations. If we look at the Buddhist calendar we see that Buddhism has quite a large number of festivals and celebrations of various kinds. These vary a little from one part of the Buddhist world to another, but the most important are common to all parts of the Buddhist world. Of all these festivals the three most important are all associated with the Three Jewels.

Jewels are generally considered to be the most precious of all material things, while the Buddha, Dharma, and Sangha are considered to be the most precious of all non-material things. Because they are so precious, we rejoice to have them; they give meaning and purpose to our lives, and give orientation to everything we do.

But it is not easy to rejoice all the time, or even to be aware of our good fortune all the time. Tradition has therefore set aside these three days in the year – all full-moon days – on which we make a special effort to remember and rejoice in the Three Jewels. Thus on the full-moon day of May we rejoice in the Buddha jewel, on the full-moon day of July we rejoice in the Dharma jewel, and on the full-moon day of November we rejoice in the Sangha jewel. The fact that these festivals fall on full-moon days, incidentally, is not accidental. It indicates our need to maintain a harmony between ourselves and nature. It reminds us that however far we progress along the path of the 'higher evolution', we must not lose contact with the recurrent rhythms of the 'lower evolution'.

Today is the day on which we rejoice in the Buddha jewel. In particular this means it is the day on which we rejoice in the Buddha's attainment of Enlightenment, rejoice in what it was that actually made the Buddha a Buddha.

We usually call this day Buddha Day, but it is sometimes known as Wesak. *Wesak*, a Sinhalese word, is actually a corruption of the Indian word Vaiśākha, which is in turn short for Vaiśākha Pūrṇimā, which means 'the full moon day of April/May'. In India, especially, Buddha Day is often referred to as Buddha Jayanti, *jayanti* coming from the word *jaya*, meaning 'victory'. Buddha Jayanti therefore means the celebration of the 'Buddha's victory'. But what is this victory?

Victory usually implies victory *over* someone or something. Who or what, then, could this have been in the Buddha's case? The answer is simple: the Buddha conquered Māra, the 'Evil One', and after conquering Māra, attained Enlightenment. In a sense, his conquest of Māra, his *māra-vijaya* as it is called, *was* his attainment of Enlightenment.

It is possible that you have already encountered descriptions of the episode of the conquest of Māra. Perhaps you have seen it depicted in Buddhist art. If so, you will have seen the Buddha-to-be sitting on a heap of *kuśa* grass beneath the spreading branches of the *ficus religiosus*, or sacred fig tree – subsequently known, in honour of the Buddha, as the bodhi tree, or 'tree of Enlightenment'. He is surrounded on all sides by thousands of fearsome figures, all horribly misshapen and deformed. Some of them are whirling enormous clubs; some are spitting fire; some are in the act of hurling great rocks, even whole mountains that they have torn up by the roots; some again are discharging arrows. These are the forces of Māra. Māra himself stands to one side directing his terrible army in its onslaught on the Buddha. But the Buddha himself takes no notice. He is completely surrounded by an aura of golden light. As soon as the various missiles touch this aura they turn into flowers and fall to the ground at the Buddha's feet as though in unintentional worship. The Buddha is undisturbed and carries on meditating. He does not take any notice even when Māra summons his three daughters and orders them to dance in the most seductive manner. So Māra retires defeated, his forces disappear, and his three daughters withdraw in confusion. The Buddha is left alone beneath the bodhi tree on his heap of *kuśa* grass, and carries on meditating. Sitting there in that way he attains Enlightenment.

Such is the well-known episode. But like other well-known episodes in the Buddha's life it is open to misunderstanding. We might of course realize that the episode is symbolic, but we may not understand that the episode of the *māra-vijaya* was not the only episode of its kind to occur in the Buddha's life; may not understand that this was not the Buddha's *only* victory.

Far from being his only victory the *māra-vijaya* represented the culmination of an entire series of victories. This is only to be expected, because spiritual life is like that. One does not develop the fullness of wisdom all at once or the fullness of compassion all at once. One does not develop the fullness of energy and heroism necessary to defeat Māra and his forces all at once. One does not develop any spiritual quality all at once; one develops it gradually. As the Buddha himself said in the *Dhammapada*: 'As a pot becomes full by the constant falling of drops of water, so, little by little, does a man fill himself with good.'[215]

'*Little by little.*' Before the Buddha's great victory there will have been many lesser victories, victories without which the great victory could hardly have taken place. We shall now consider some of those lesser victories – victories that are such only in relation to the *great* victory over Māra. In themselves, these lesser victories are such as we might find hard even to imagine.

The Buddha's first victory, so far as we know at least, is generally described as the 'Going Forth' from home into homelessness. We may not be accustomed to considering this as a victory, but that is what it was. Just suppose that you were the son or daughter of wealthy parents, with high social position and great prestige. Suppose you were young, healthy, and good looking. Suppose too that you were happily married, perhaps with a child.... Would *you* have found it easy to give it all up? Would you have been able to 'go forth' for the sake of you knew not what – for the sake of the 'truth', for the sake of something 'higher', something beyond anything you had yet experienced or imagined? This is exactly what Siddhārtha, the Buddha-to-be, actually did.

There are several accounts of what happened on that occasion, some of them very colourful and romantic. They describe, for instance, how Siddhārtha drew aside a curtain in the inner apartments of his palace and took his last long, lingering look at his peacefully sleeping wife and infant son. They describe how the gods of the various heavens silently opened the gates so that he could depart unseen and unheard. And they describe how those same gods supported the hooves of his horse on the palms of their hands so that there would be no noise.... But the oldest account is actually very simple. Reminiscing in his old age, the Buddha simply said to his disciples:

> Then I, monks, after a time, being young, my hair coal-black, possessed of radiant youth, in the prime of my life – although my unwilling parents wept and wailed – having cut off my hair and beard, having put on yellow robes, went forth from home into homelessness.[216]

Whether the description is elaborate or simple, what actually happened is sufficiently clear. The Buddha-to-be left home. He left his family, left the *group*.

But in what sense was this a victory? What was it a victory *over*? It was a victory over the family, or rather, over the *group* as represented especially by his parents. The Buddha himself once said that he went forth 'against the wishes' of his weeping parents.

But this was also a victory in a deeper sense. It was a victory over his *attachment* to the group. It could not have been easy for Siddhārtha to leave his family; his actual departure must have been preceded by a long internal struggle. But in the end he broke free from the group. This did not just mean leaving the group physically: it meant overcoming group attitudes and group conditioning; it meant taking the initiative, doing something that he wanted to do; it meant thinking for himself, experiencing things for himself; it meant living his own life; it meant being an *individual*. Thus the 'Going Forth' from home into homelessness was a victory over the 'internalized' group.

Having gone forth from home into homelessness, Siddhārtha approached two famous spiritual teachers. These teachers, who seem to have been good and noble men, taught the Buddha everything they knew, taught him what they believed to be the highest truth. Siddhārtha was a very good pupil, and learned what they had to teach. Whatever they taught him, he experienced for himself, very quickly becoming their equal. Realizing this, they offered to share with him the leadership of the communities they had founded. But he refused and, leaving them, returned to his solitary wanderings.

This too was a victory, a victory over spiritual complacency and spiritual ambition. Siddhārtha had experienced for himself everything that his teachers had to teach, but he knew that there was still something 'beyond', something higher which he had not yet realized – and which he wanted to realize. He knew that he was not yet fully Enlightened, despite what his teachers were telling him. In other words, he did not settle down with a limited spiritual experience – even though by ordinary standards it was quite a high experience. It was not the highest, and the Buddha *knew* that it was not the highest. In this way he overcame spiritual complacency. Moreover, his teachers had offered to share with him the leadership of their communities. What an opportunity was this for a young man! But Siddhārtha refused. He was not concerned with leadership. He was concerned with *truth*, he was concerned with *Enlightenment*. In this way he overcame spiritual ambition.

It is interesting to note that Siddhārtha overcame spiritual complacency and spiritual ambition at the same time. The two are actually closely connected. If you are spiritually ambitious, in the sense of seeking a position of spiritual leadership, you are likely to become spiritually complacent. Similarly, if you are spiritually complacent, you will tend to seek a position of spiritual leadership by way of compensation for your lack of real spiritual effort.

Continuing his quest alone, Siddhārtha decided to live in the depths of the forest, far from any human habitation. He lived somewhere where it was very difficult to live, even for those committed to the spiritual life. Furthermore, he stayed in what we would call 'haunted' places, places inhabited, at least according to popular belief, by ghosts and spirits – places in which feelings of fear and terror were likely to arise. And those feelings of panic, fear, and terror *did* arise in his mind. So what did Siddhārtha do on these occasions? If the fear and terror arose while he was walking to and fro, he continued walking to and fro until he had overcome them. He did not run away, did not try to escape from those feelings. Similarly, if they arose while he was sitting still, or while he was lying down, then that is where he faced and overcame them. In this way he was victorious over fear.

Even today, of course, many people have this experience of fear and terror, panic and dread – or of anxiety at least – especially when they are alone. But howsoever and wheresoever we have this sort of experience, it is important to face it. It is important not to run away, whether literally or metaphorically. If we face it we will eventually overcome it, as Siddhārtha did.

Even though Siddhārtha had overcome fear, he had still not attained Enlightenment. He now embarked upon a course of extreme 'self-mortification'. The Buddhist scriptures give us full details of the various torments that he inflicted upon himself. Suffice it to say that he subsequently asserted that no one had gone to such extremes of self-mortification as had he. Indeed, he very nearly died. But there were compensations. He became famous. In those days it was popularly believed that you could attain Enlightenment by means of self-mortification – the more extreme the better. He therefore attracted, in particular, five close disciples, who intended to remain with him until, as a result of his self-mortification, he attained Enlightenment.

But Siddhārtha did not attain Enlightenment in this way. Apparently, he remained as far from Enlightenment as ever. He therefore gave up self-mortification, even though he had been practising it for years, and – to the shock of his disciples – started taking solid food again. The five disciples left him immediately, deeply disappointed that he was not the man they had thought him to be. He had weakened, they thought, and had returned to a life of luxury. Once again Siddhārtha was left alone.

On the face of it this might look like a defeat, but it was actually a great victory. On this instance Siddhārtha had overcome the very human tendency to refuse to admit that one has made a mistake, that one has been on the wrong path, and that one must now retrace one's steps and start all over again. After all, when one has invested a great deal of energy, not to speak of time, money, and all sorts of other things, in making that mistake, one does not like to admit, even to oneself, that all the effort has in a sense been wasted. But Siddhārtha did not mind doing this. He did not mind losing his disciples, he did not mind being on his own again. It would have been easy, in comparison, to continue with his self-mortification, easy to become more and more famous, easy to attract great numbers of disciples. But instead he admitted that he had made a mistake, and continued his quest.

Eventually, his quest took him to the foot of the bodhi tree. There he sat down, as we have seen, and was attacked by Māra and his forces.

But who, or what, is Māra? I have already described this episode as it is depicted in Buddhist art, but I must now pay some attention to its *significance* – even though the symbolic terms in which the episode is described do actually communicate their own message. If we do not understand what Māra represents, we will not be able to understand the true significance of the Buddha's *māra-vijaya*, his victory over Māra.

The word *māra* means 'killing', 'destroying', it means bringing death and pestilence. Māra is therefore the principle of destruction. Sometimes this principle is personified, and thus it happens that the Buddhist texts mention no less than *four* Māras. These are (in Pāli) *maccu-māra*, *khandha-māra*, *kilesa-māra*, and *devaputta-māra*. We will look at each of them in turn.

First of all, comes *maccu-māra*. Here, Māra simply means 'death' or 'destruction'. Death, of course, is usually very unwelcome. Sometimes people are really surprised when it comes, even though they should have known it was coming all the time. Because death is so unwelcome, people tend to regard it as an evil. But in itself death is neither good nor evil: it is just a fact of existence and has to be recognized. That is what *maccu-māra* actually represents.

Secondly, rather more metaphysically, there is *khandha-māra*. This Māra represents a sort of extension of *maccu-māra*. Here we remember that death is not just an abstraction, not just a word. Death is a concrete reality. Death means that there are *things* and *beings* which die, which are destroyed. And these things and beings which die between them constitute a world. In other words, there is a world which is under the sway of death. This is the world of what are called in Sanskrit the *skandhas* (Pāli *khandhas*). These *skandhas*, or 'aggregates', as the word is often translated, are five in number. First of all there is *rūpa*, or material form, then *vedanā*, or feeling, then *saṃjñā*, or perception, then *saṃskāra*, or volition, and finally *vijñāna*, or consciousness. These five *skandhas* are well known; if you know anything at all about Buddhism you will be familiar with them. Between them these five *skandhas* represent the whole of conditioned existence, the whole of mundane existence, the whole of 'relative reality', or, in more traditional terms, the whole of the *saṃsāra*. That is what *khandha-māra* represents.

Thirdly, there is *kilesa-māra*. The Pāli word *kilesa* (Sanskrit *kleśa*) comes from a root meaning 'to adhere' or 'to stick to', and is cognate with the word for 'slime'. *Kleśa* means 'stain', 'soil', or 'impurity'. In an ethical sense it means 'depravity', 'lust', or 'passion'. Broadly speaking, *kleśa* corresponds to what is otherwise called *akuśalacitta* or *akuśalacittāni*, or 'unskilful mental states'. The five principal *kleśas*, or 'defilements', as they are generally called in English, are usually enumerated as craving, aversion, ignorance, conceit, and distraction. The first three of these – craving, aversion, and ignorance – correspond to the three *akuśala-mūlas* or 'roots of unskilfulness', which are represented by the cock, the snake, and the pig that we see at the centre of the Tibetan wheel of life. It is these three that keep the wheel turning. In other words, it is because our minds are dominated by the *kleśas* that we are reborn within the *saṃsāra*, reborn in the world of conditioned existence, the world that is under the sway of death. This is what *kilesa-māra* represents.

And then there is *devaputta-māra*. *Deva* means 'god', with a small 'g', and *putta* means 'son'. So *devaputta* means 'son of a god', which is to say, a god – just as 'son of man' means a man. *Devaputta-māra* is Māra as an actually existent being or person. He is the being who appears in the episode of the Buddha's *māra-vijaya*. Sometimes *devaputta-māra* is regarded as being simply a personification of the *kleśas* or defilements, but *devaputta-māra* cannot really be reduced in this way. Naturally he is dominated by the defilements, just as are most beings within the *saṃsāra*; but at the same time he has his own being and position in the universe. He has his own place in Buddhist mythology.

Buddhism sees the universe as consisting of various planes and worlds. These are the objective counterparts – or correlatives – of mental states, both positive and negative. Just as there is a 'world' of human beings, according to Buddhist cosmology, so also is there a 'world' of animals, a 'world' of gods, a 'world' of demons, and so on. Māra belongs to one of these worlds, in fact to one of the lower heaven worlds. Low though it is, however, Māra rules over this world; indeed, he rules over all the worlds belonging to what is called the *kāmaloka*, or 'realm of sensuous desire', which includes our own human world. In a wider sense, of course, Māra rules over the entire universe, the whole of conditioned existence – because it is subject to *death*, which Māra primarily represents. But he rules particularly over the *kāmaloka*, or realm of sensuous desire.

In order to understand why this should be we must first realize that above the realm of sensuous desire there is the *rūpaloka* or 'realm of archetypal form'. This realm corresponds to the various mental states of higher meditative consciousness. From these states, from the *rūpaloka*, it is possible to gain Enlightenment – which it is not possible to do from the *kāmaloka*. Māra is therefore particularly anxious to stop people reaching the *rūpaloka*, that is, stop them escaping from the *kāmaloka*. This is why Māra, with the help of his forces and his daughters, tried to interrupt the Buddha's meditation beneath the bodhi tree. Perhaps he sometimes tries to interrupt *your* meditation. Perhaps that little distraction which arises in your mind, perhaps even that little tickling sensation that distracts you, is none other than Māra.

Perhaps I have said enough about Māra to place us in a better position to understand what it was that the Buddha actually conquered. We can now return to the *māra-vijaya* itself. As we have seen, there are four *māras*: *maccu-māra*, *khandha-māra*, *kilesa-māra*, and *devaputta-māra*. The Buddha overcame all four of them; his victory was therefore a fourfold victory. Let us look at each of them in turn.

How did the Buddha overcome *maccu-māra*? How did he overcome death? He overcame death by overcoming *birth*, for where there is birth there will inevitably be death. He overcame birth by overcoming the unskilful mental states that lead to birth – that is to say to *rebirth*. In other words, the Buddha overcame death by attaining what in Sanskrit is called the *amṛtapada*, the 'deathless state', the state that is free from death, free from birth – that is, Nirvāna. He overcame death by attaining Enlightenment, a state which is above and beyond conditioned existence. It is not that after attaining Enlightenment the Buddha could not be reborn in the human world if he wanted to be. But he would not be reborn there *out of compulsion*, as a result of previous karma that he had committed. He would be reborn – if he was reborn at all – out of compassion, in order to continue to help ordinary, unenlightened human beings.

How did the Buddha overcome *khandha-māra*? How did he overcome conditioned existence? He overcame conditioned existence by overcoming the *kleśas*, the defilements, which lead one into conditioned existence. He overcame the *kleśas* at the time that he attained Enlightenment. In a sense, the two things were synonymous. According to tradition, however, the Buddha did not finally overcome the *skandhas* until his *parinirvāna* forty-five years later. At the time of his *parinirvāna* he severed all connection with the physical body, severed all connection with the *khandhas*. For this reason the *parinirvāna* is also known as *skandha-nirvāna*, or *anupādisesa-nibbāna*, that is to say, 'Nirvāna without remainder in the form of a physical body'.

But how *did* the Buddha overcome the *kleśas*? So much depends upon this. As we have seen, there are five principal *kleśas*: craving, aversion, ignorance, conceit, and distraction. The Buddha overcame craving by means of tranquillity, aversion by means of friendliness and compassion, ignorance by means of wisdom, conceit by means of selflessness, and distraction by means of awareness, or mindfulness. Naturally it was not easy even for the Buddha to do this. Tranquillity, friendliness, compassion, and so on do not just appear – not even when one is seated beneath the bodhi tree! They have to be developed. But they *can* be developed. Indeed, the fact that they can be developed is one of the central teachings of Buddhism. It is one of the central teachings of Buddhism that our mental states are in our own power and can be changed. Furthermore, Buddhism not only exhorts us to change them, but also tells us just *how* to do this; it gives us specific meditation 'methods'.

Tranquillity is developed by means of the three 'contemplations': the contemplation of the repulsiveness of the physical body, the contemplation of death, and the contemplation of impermanence.

The first of these, the contemplation of the repulsiveness of the physical body, is the most extreme, and generally takes the form of actually contemplating the ten stages in the progressive decomposition of a corpse. Perhaps I should add that it is usually taught only to those who are psychologically and spiritually mature. The other two are less extreme and are therefore taught more widely. But whichever method we practise, whether the contemplation of death or the contemplation of impermanence, or even the contemplation of the repulsiveness of the physical body, we can succeed in developing tranquillity. And by developing tranquillity we overcome craving.

We develop friendliness and compassion by means of *mettā bhāvanā*, or the 'cultivation of universal loving-kindness'. This practice consists in the systematic development of goodwill towards oneself, towards a near and dear friend, towards a 'neutral' person, towards an 'enemy', and, finally, towards all living beings. The *mettā bhāvanā* is one of the best known and most popular of all Buddhist meditation methods. By practising it we can succeed in developing friendliness and compassion, and by developing friendliness and compassion we overcome aversion.

We can develop wisdom by means of the contemplation of the twelve *nidānas*, or 'links'. For a detailed discussion of these, I must refer readers to my other writings (in particular *A Survey of Buddhism* and *The Three Jewels*).[217] Broadly speaking, we develop wisdom by reflecting on the conditionality of mundane existence, on the fact that whatever mundane phenomenon arises or comes into existence does so in dependence on certain definite causes and conditions. Reflection on the conditionality of mundane existence is also roughly tantamount to reflecting on *śūnyatā* or 'voidness'. In these different ways we develop wisdom, and by developing wisdom we overcome ignorance.

We develop selflessness by reflection on the six 'elements'. The six elements are earth, water, fire, air, space, and consciousness. In this practice we reflect that there exists in our own physical body the element *earth* in the form of flesh, bone, and so on. We then further reflect that the earth element in our physical body does not really belong to us. We may point to our bodies and say 'this is me', 'this is mine'. But it does *not* belong to us; the earth element within our physical bodies has been borrowed, literally borrowed, from the earth element in the universe. One day we shall have to give it back. If we see a corpse – even the corpse of a little bird – in the process of decomposition, we can actually see this happening, especially if the corpse is lying on the earth. We can see the flesh and bone that once belonged to the body returning to the soil, returning to the earth, returning to the earth element in the universe from which it came. Similarly, one day, we too shall have to give our body back to the earth element. We should therefore not be attached to it. We should not identify with it by saying 'this body belongs to me'. We then continue to reflect in this way with regard to all of the six elements. As we do so, we develop selflessness, and by developing selflessness we overcome conceit.

Finally, we develop mindfulness, or awareness, by means of *ānāpānasati*, or the mindfulness of breathing. Here we simply 'watch' our breath, without interfering with it in any way, allowing our minds to be increasingly focused, increasingly concentrated on the breath. By practising *ānāpānasati* we develop mindfulness, and by developing mindfulness we overcome distraction, overcome the wandering mind.

Thus the five principal *kleśas* are overcome by these methods of meditation. This is how the Buddha overcame them. He overcame craving by means of tranquillity, aversion by means of friendliness and compassion, ignorance by means of wisdom, conceit by means of selflessness, and distraction by means of mindfulness, or awareness. In this way the Buddha overcame *kilesa-māra*.

There is one Māra left. How did the Buddha overcome *devaputta-māra*, or 'Māra the son of a god'? To understand this we must return to the episode of the *māra-vijaya*, or victory over Māra, as depicted in Buddhist art.

In the traditional representations of this incident we see the Buddha seated beneath the bodhi tree, his eyes closed, or half closed, and we see Māra with his forces and his daughters. The Buddha is not paying Māra any attention at all. We could therefore say that the Buddha overcame *devaputta-māra* simply by ignoring him.

In ordinary life, of course, to ignore someone usually means that we have a rather negative attitude towards them. But the Buddha could not possibly have had a negative attitude towards anyone – not even towards Māra. So we must try to put things a little more positively. It is not so much that the Buddha ignored Māra: rather, he overcame Māra simply *by being himself*. He overcame him by being the Bodhisatta, by being the Buddha. According to the medieval Indian commentator Mallinātha, the word *jayati*, or 'to conquer', means to surpass everything else by means of one's own excellence.[218] It means to be the 'highest'. Thus the Buddha's victory over Māra was not the result of a fight *on Māra's terms*; he defeated Māra simply by being himself, by virtue of the sheer excellence of his moral and spiritual qualities.

Thus the Buddha's victory over Māra was complete. Because it was complete he attained Enlightenment. One would have thought, therefore, that there was nothing left for him to do, nothing left for him to overcome. In a sense this is true, but after the *māra-vijaya* there is in fact another episode, an episode that represents yet another victory, perhaps the ultimate victory. This is the episode of Brahmā's request. Let us now witness it in our mind's eye:

The Buddha has attained Enlightenment; he is enjoying the freedom and bliss of Enlightenment. He is also reflecting that the truth he has discovered is very deep indeed, and therefore very difficult to understand. As he reflects in this way he is inclined not to try to communicate this truth – the Dharma – to other human beings: it will be just too difficult. After all, he reflects, beings are deeply immersed in worldly pleasures, they will not be able to understand the Dharma he has discovered. Just then, Brahmā Sahāmpati, another figure from Buddhist mythology, the 'Lord of a Thousand Worlds', appears. He pleads with the Buddha, pointing out that there are at least a few beings who *will* understand. He implores that for their sake the Buddha should communicate the truth he has discovered. In the end the Buddha agrees, saying: 'Opened for those who hear are the doors of the Deathless, Brahmā, let them give forth their faith.'[219]

Here, the Buddha has overcome the temptation to keep his Enlightenment to himself, or even to think that he *could* keep it to himself. He has overcome spiritual individualism. The Buddha has overcome the Buddha – and has therefore become truly the Buddha. This is the last and greatest of all his victories. He has overcome the group, including the internalized group. He has overcome spiritual complacency and spiritual ambition. He has overcome fear. He has overcome the tendency to refuse to admit that he has made a mistake. He has overcome all four Māras. Now, finally, he has overcome spiritual individualism. He has been victorious all along the line. He is not only the Buddha, not only the Enlightened One, but he is also the *Jina*, the 'Victorious One'.

In the West we are accustomed to using the title 'Buddha'. But we should not forget that the Buddha is also commonly known as the *Jina*. Similarly, followers of the Buddha are usually called 'Buddhists', but perhaps they could just as easily be called 'Jinists': followers of the *Jina*, the Victorious One. The Buddha did in fact once tell his disciples that they were *kṣatriyas*, or 'warriors', fighting for *śīla*, fighting for *samādhi*, fighting for *prajñā*. They were fighting to live an ethical life, fighting for higher states of consciousness, and fighting for transcendental wisdom.[220] According to the Buddha, the spiritual life is an active life, a strenuous life. We might even say that it is a *militant* life. We have to take the offensive against Māra. We should not wait for him to come and tap us on the shoulder. Attack is the best method of defence, prevention is better than cure.

For this reason, Western Buddhists should beware of taking too soft a view of the spiritual life. Perhaps we do not meditate hard enough, study hard enough, work hard enough, even play hard enough. Perhaps we have not committed ourselves to the Three Jewels with sufficient depth and intensity. Perhaps we do not really want to spread the Dharma. Perhaps we are just playing at being Buddhists. If that is the case then we will not get very far: we will not be truly successful or genuinely happy. We will not be real Buddhists, and we certainly won't be real *Jinists*, real spiritual warriors.

Nowadays there is so much to be overcome, both in ourselves and in the world. There is so much to be transformed by the 'golden light'. As the life of the Buddha reminds us, we have to overcome the group; we have to overcome spiritual complacency and spiritual ambition; we have to overcome fear; we have to overcome that very human tendency to refuse to admit that we have made a mistake; we have to overcome Māra; and we have to overcome spiritual individualism. In short, we have to overcome everything that the Buddha overcame so that we can attain Enlightenment just as he did, and benefit the world just as he benefited it.

This is certainly not easy, and no real Buddhist has ever said that it was. But a human being should be ashamed not to attempt that which is difficult rather than easy. A human being should be ashamed not to attempt that which is the most difficult of all. A human being should be ashamed not to be fighting against the odds. Sometimes we may feel that we are being overwhelmed. We may feel that we are having to hack our way through a dense jungle: the jungle of *saṃsāra*, the jungle of conditioned existence. The Buddha must also have felt like that at times. After his Enlightenment he gave some of his disciples the following parable:

Just as if, brethren, a man travelling in a forest, along a mountain height, should come upon an ancient road, an ancient track, traversed by men of former days, and should proceed along it: and as he went should come upon an old-time city, a royal city of olden days, dwelt in by men of bygone ages, laid out with parks and groves and water tanks, and stoutly walled about – a delightful spot.

Then suppose, brethren, that this man should tell of his find to the king or royal minister, thus: 'Pardon me, sire, but I would have you know that while travelling in a forest, along a mountain height, I came upon an ancient road, an ancient track, traversed by men of former days, and proceeded along it. And as I went I came upon an old-time city, a royal city of olden days, dwelt in by men of bygone ages, laid out with parks and groves and water tanks, and stoutly walled about, a delightful spot. Sire, restore that city.'

Then suppose, brethren, that king or royal minister were to restore that city, so that thereafter it became prosperous, fortunate, and populous, crowded with inhabitants, and were to reach growth and increase.

Even so, brethren, have I seen an ancient Path, an ancient track traversed by the Perfectly Enlightened ones of former times. And what is that Path? It is this Ariyan Eightfold Path.[221]

This parable tells us a number of things. It tells us that the Buddha was a pioneer. It tells us that the state of Enlightenment is like a wonderful city inhabited by innumerable people. It tells us that there is a way to that city, a way to that state. Above all, however, the parable reminds us that the Buddha's teaching is something that can be lost. The Three Jewels can be lost. Values can be lost. Fortunately, we are living at a time and in a place where the Dharma is still known, and can still be practised. We can still tread the ancient road to the city, but the jungle has started to encroach. Fewer people now live in the city; parts of the city are in a derelict condition, and entire sections of the road are overgrown.

Even though we are not being called upon to be pioneers in the way that the Buddha was, there is still a lot for us to do. We have to hack away at the jungle; we have to be spiritual warriors; we have to be not just Buddhists, but *Jinists*: we have at least to make an effort to overcome what the Buddha overcame. If we are not prepared to make that effort, then we are not worthy to celebrate Buddha Day, not worthy to celebrate Buddha Jayanti, not worthy to celebrate the Buddha's victory.

THE NEW MAN SPEAKS

Dharmacakra Day, London, 1971.

Two months ago, on the full-moon night of the Indian month of Vaiśākha, we celebrated the Buddha's attainment of Enlightenment. Tonight, we are celebrating Dharmacakra Day, or, to give it its full title, Dharmacakrapravartana Day, the day commemorating the 'setting in motion of the Wheel of the Dharma' – this being the traditional Buddhist idiom for the Buddha's initial promulgation of the truth that he had realized at the time of his Enlightenment. On this occasion, having gained Enlightenment, the Buddha brought out into the open, in the form of words and thoughts, the content of his transcendental realization on the night of Vaiśākha Pūrṇimā.

Two months ago we left the Buddha sitting cross-legged on a heap of grass at the foot of the bodhi tree, enjoying the bliss of emancipation. Sitting there he had fulfilled, after many years of effort and struggle, the entire course of the higher evolution of the individual. He had defeated the forces of Māra and was now a conqueror. He had dissolved all mental defilements, resolved all psychological conditionings. He had seen the Truth, seen Reality. He had not just had a glimpse of the truth but now saw it steadily, all the time, having fully absorbed and assimilated it. He was now an embodiment of the Truth, an embodiment of Reality. He was Reality in human form. He was a new kind of being: a New Man.

A question now arises: what happened next? The Buddha has gained Enlightenment – humanity now has a Buddha on its hands. What does humanity *do* with the Buddha? And what does he do with himself?

At this point, something very mysterious happens. In a way that we cannot hope to understand, *Enlightenment begins to communicate itself.* In other words, the Buddha starts to communicate with other living beings: the New Man speaks. First of all, he simply speaks to himself; then he speaks to the gods; finally, he speaks to human beings.

As for what he says to himself, there are a number of different accounts of this first utterance, but they are substantially the same. According to the oldest Pāli account, the Buddha speaks two verses – of which I must provide two different translations. Buddhadatta's prose translation offers the more or less exact meaning, while Sir Edwin Arnold's verse rendering gives a better impression of the spirit:

Many a birth have I traversed in this round of lives and deaths, vainly seeking the builder of this house. Sorrowful is repeated birth. Oh house builder, you are seen. Never again shall you build the house. All your rafters are broken. Your ridge pole is shattered. My mind has gone to dissolution. I have attained the end of craving.[222]

In Sir Edwin Arnold's much more vigorous version we find:

Many a house of life
Hath held me – seeking ever him who wrought
These prisons of the senses, sorrow-fraught;
　　Sore was my ceaseless strife!

But now,
Thou Builder of this Tabernacle – Thou!
I know Thee! Never shalt Thou build again
　　These walls of pain,
Nor raise the roof-tree of deceits, nor lay
　　Fresh rafters on the clay;
Broken Thy house is, and the ridge-pole split!
　　Delusion fashioned it!
Safe pass I thence – deliverance to obtain.[223]

These two verses constitute what is technically known as an *udāna*. The word *udāna* means 'exhalation', 'a breathing out'. It also means that which *is* breathed out – something spoken under intense emotional pressure. Such utterances are always in metrical form. The Buddha is saying, 'I'm free, I've made it!' His six-year quest is complete. He has broken through. Looking back into the past over hundreds and thousands of lives and seeing where he had been going wrong, where the mistakes and delusions lay, it is not surprising that there should have been a tremendous upsurge of energy and emotion.

Next, the Buddha speaks to the gods – or, rather, speaks to Brahmā Sahāmpati, the 'Lord of a Thousand Worlds':

Opened for those who hear are the doors of the Deathless, Brahmā,
Let them give forth their faith;
Thinking of useless fatigue, Brahmā, I have not preached *dhamma*
Sublime and excellent for men.[224]

In order to understand this verse we have to refer back to the episode in which it occurs. According to the scriptures, after his Enlightenment the Buddha felt inclined to say nothing about it to anyone. He realized that the truth he had discovered went far beyond the capacities of the vast majority of people. He saw that people were immersed in craving and ignorance; they would not be able to understand the Truth even if he uttered it.

To Brahmā Sahāmpati, this was terrible. If the Buddha did not teach, he reflected, then the whole world would perish. It might progress materially, people might become prosperous and happy after a fashion, but there would be no *value* in it if the Buddha would not teach, if there were to be no spiritual element in their existence. So he appeared in front of the Buddha, like a great golden light, and begged him to make known to humanity the truth he had discovered. 'There are just a few', he said, 'whose eyes are covered with only a little dust. For their sake, teach the truth you have realized.'

At that, the Buddha looked out over the world with his eye of intuitive insight. He then saw all the beings who made up the mass of humanity to be like lotus flowers growing in a lake. The vast majority were sunk in the mud beneath the water, but some had grown up a little so as to touch the surface. Just a very few were even standing completely free of the water. Seeing this, he was overwhelmed with compassion and decided that he would teach. It was at that point that he finally addressed Brahmā in the words already quoted: 'Open to them are the doors of the immortal': open to humanity, open to those with just a little dust on their eyes. 'Let them that have ears release their faith.'

One or two points here deserve comment. Firstly, the Buddha uses the term 'immortal'. In early Buddhist texts we do not find the expression *nibbāna* (Sanskrit *nirvāṇa*); more often we find the Pāli term *amata* (Sanskrit *amṛta*). This word means 'nectar of immortality', the deathless, something above and beyond the changes of the world, above and beyond time. It is a sort of synonym for Nirvāṇa, or Enlightenment. The Buddha has now attained Enlightenment; he has broken through into the transcendental dimension of consciousness. Now others can follow his example and his teaching, they too can become Enlightened. The doors to the immortal are now open. Anybody who is prepared to make the effort may enter, anyone who is prepared to release their faith.

In the original Pāli, the phrase 'release their faith' is rather ambiguous. It can mean *giving up* – releasing *wrong faith*, and it can also mean releasing – in the sense of developing – *right* faith.

Faith (Sanskrit *śraddhā*, Pāli *saddhā*) is of great importance in the Buddhist spiritual tradition. This kind of faith is not *blind belief*; in the Buddhist context, faith is the authentic, living, response of the whole being – especially the emotional part of our being – to something which we intuitively perceive to be greater, nobler, more sublime and more worthwhile than ourselves as we are now, something to which we feel we ought to dedicate ourselves, surrender ourselves, something for the sake of which we ought to *live*. Without faith in this sense there is no spiritual life, no development. Unfortunately, this kind of faith is rather lacking nowadays. There is plenty of faith in inferior values, but faith – in the sense of confidence in something higher than ourselves – is comparatively rare.

Finally, the Buddha speaks to human beings. He decides to teach. But *who* is he to teach? Who will be first? Who will learn the doctrine most quickly?

At first the Buddha thought of his first teacher, Āḷāra the Kālāma, a very good and noble man – but one who had not been able to lead him to the highest truth because he had not himself realized it. We are told, however, that a god appeared to tell the Buddha that Āḷāra the Kālāma had died, just a week beforehand. So the Buddha then thought of his second teacher, Uddaka Rāmaputta, under whom he had also learned many useful things. He then became aware that Uddaka Rāmaputta too had died, only the previous evening. Finally, he thought of the five ascetics, his five disciple-companions from the days when he had practised self-mortification. They had stayed with him and looked after him when he was practising those terrible austerities in the hope that they would be able to benefit from his eventual realization. When the Buddha had realized that self-mortification was not the way, and had started taking solid food, they had left him in disgust. But now he thought of them: 'Let me teach the Dharma first of all to these five.'

At that time they were living just a few miles out of Benares, in the deer park at Isipatana. So the Buddha left Bodh Gaya (which was then known as Uruvela), and set off to walk the hundred miles to Benares.

He had not been on the road for very long when he met an ascetic belonging to a sect known as the Ājīvakas. His name was Upaka. When from a distance Upaka saw the Buddha coming, he was very impressed by his appearance. The Buddha had gained Enlightenment only seven weeks beforehand. He was bright, shining, cheerful and happy. As they drew near, they stopped and greeted each other. As is the custom in India, even to this day, Upaka asked two questions: 'Who is your teacher?' and 'Which doctrine do you profess?'

Upaka got rather more than he bargained for, for the Buddha replied in four resounding verses – his first utterance to humanity:

Victorious over all, omniscient am I
Among all things undefiled,
Leaving all, through death of craving freed,
By knowing myself, whom should I point to?

For me there is no teacher,
One like me does not exist,
In the world with its *devas*
No one equals me.

For I am perfected in the world,
A teacher supreme am I,
I alone am all-awakened,
Become cool am I, nibbāna-attained.

To turn the *dhamma*-wheel
I go to Kasi's city,
Beating the drum of deathlessness
In a world that's blind become.[225]

What we cannot fail to notice here, once we've recovered from the shock, is the Buddha's complete self-confidence – a self-confidence that was to last for the rest of his life. There is no false humility, and no false pride either. He makes a simple statement of fact because he knows exactly what has happened, who he is, and what he is going to do. He knows that he has gained Enlightenment; he knows that he is free; he knows that he is a New Man – in that there is as yet no one else like him anywhere in the world; and he knows that he is going to teach.

As if to check that he has heard correctly, Upaka points out that he seems to be claiming to be a *Jina*, a conqueror, a Buddha. The Buddha confirms this in another resounding verse:

Like me, they are victors indeed
Who have won destruction of the cankers [*asavas*];
Vanquished by me are evil things,
Therefore am I, Upaka, a victor.[226]

Upaka thinks for a moment, and simply says, 'Maybe.' Shaking his head, he goes off, we are told, by a by-path.

This incident is very significant. We ourselves are rather like Upaka. We too are confronted, as it were, by the figure of the Buddha, and by his teaching. We too take a look at the Buddha, and listen to the Dharma for a while. Then, just like Upaka, we say, 'Maybe there is something in it.' But then we shake our heads and go off on some little by-path of our own. In this way we miss a great opportunity, perhaps forever.

The Buddha then proceeded to Benares, to the deer park at Isipatana, arriving on a full-moon day. This was a beautiful coincidence. He had been walking for a week, and now, on the full-moon day exactly two lunar months after his Enlightenment, he arrived at the deer park at Isipatana. The five ascetics were there; apparently they had been living there for some time. When they saw the Buddha coming they started to speak among themselves: 'Look, there is that fellow Gautama, the one who gave up, the one who started living luxuriously and taking solid food. He has had the nerve to come back! All right, let him come! If he wants, he even can sit with us for a while, but let's not show him any respect at all.'

As the Buddha came nearer, the five ascetics tried to take no notice. But when he drew close they simply could not help themselves. They rose like humble pupils and moved forward. One politely took his bowl while another took the spare robe he was carrying; another prepared a seat while another brought some water for the Buddha to wash his feet. However, even though they could not help showing respect, they still addressed him by his personal name, Gautama (Pāli Gotama), and addressed him also as *āvuso*, which is a familiar mode of address among monks, meaning 'friend'. In response, the Buddha simply said, 'Do not address me in this way, this is not proper, not appropriate. I am no longer just your friend. I have gained Enlightenment. I teach the Dharma. If you practise according to my teaching you too will gain Enlightenment.'

The five ascetics did not believe him. They could not take him seriously. 'Look here,' they said, 'For all those years you practised self-mortification. You went beyond what anybody else has done in this life. But you did not gain Enlightenment. Now you've gone back to a comfortable, easy, way of living. How do you think you can gain Enlightenment by that means?'

Again the Buddha insisted: 'No. I *am* the Enlightened One. If you follow my teaching you too will become Enlightened.'

They still could not accept what the Buddha was saying. Three times the Buddha therefore made his declaration, and three times they refused to accept his claim. Then he said, 'Look, in all the time that you knew me before, did I ever speak in this way? Have I ever been so certain, so emphatic? Have I ever claimed before that I have gained Enlightenment?' They conceded that he had not. 'All right. Now let me teach you.' In this way he began to convince them, and they became at least open-minded about what he was saying.

The *sutta* describes what happened next very beautifully. Apparently, the Buddha started teaching the ascetics in turns. While two of them remained listening to the Buddha in the deer park, the other three would go out for alms, collecting food from house to house. What the three of them collected, all six would eat. Then the Buddha would teach those three, while the two others went out for alms. So far as we can tell, the six of them lived in this way throughout the rainy season, for twelve or more weeks, taking it in turns to collect food and to receive instruction from the Buddha. At the end of that period, we are told, all five gained Enlightenment. They too became 'New Men'. There were now six New Men in the world.

There is a very important point to be noted here. So far I have been following the oldest account – from the *Majjhima Nikāya*. While this account tells us the way in which the Buddha taught the five ascetics, and tells us that the five ascetics became Enlightened, the *sutta* does not actually tell us *what* the Buddha taught them. We simply do not know what teaching he gave. That remains a mystery.

Later accounts, even in the Pāli canon, try to fill in the blank, especially with a text known as the *Dhammacakkappavattana Sutta* – the *sutta*, or discourse, on the 'setting in motion of the wheel of the doctrine'.[227] This is a useful – if rather stereotyped – summary of the Buddha's teaching which deals with the doctrines of the Middle Way, the Four Noble Truths, and the Noble Eightfold Path. It is quite possible that it represents the substance of a talk actually given by the Buddha on some occasion. But it is important to remember that the *earliest* account of the 'conversion' of those five ascetics makes no mention of any particular teaching at all.

Although some will find this lack of detailed information very unsatisfactory, I personally find it very suggestive. It changes the nature of the whole episode. The Buddha taught the five ascetics; but he teaches *anyone*. He taught *then*, but he teaches *now*. This means that the teaching cannot ever be reduced to a specific formula or set of doctrines. You can never say that you have all of the Buddha's teaching under your thumb, all written down: 'If I learn this and study that, I will *have* Buddhism, *have* the Buddha's teaching.' The teaching is not any specific doctrine. The teaching, as the Buddha himself was to say on another occasion, is whatever conduces to Enlightenment, whatever helps you to grow, whatever helps you to develop.[228]

This is brought out very clearly in a later, Mahāyāna *sūtra*, the *Diamond Sūtra*. Here, the monk Subhūti, speaking under the Buddha's inspiration, says:

The Tathāgata [Buddha] has no formulated teaching to enunciate. Wherefore? Because the Tathāgata has said that Truth is uncontainable and inexpressible. It neither is nor is it not. –

Thus it is that this unformulated principle is the foundation of the different systems of all the sages.[229]

This is only a step away from saying that the Buddha does not actually speak at all, that the New Man remains silent. Another great Mahāyāna *sūtra*, the *Laṅkāvatāra Sūtra*, actually takes this step. The Buddha says here,

> From the night of the Enlightenment to the night of the
> Tathāgata's *parinirvāṇa* [passing away], he has not uttered, nor
> ever will he utter, one word.[230]

In other words, the Buddha has not said anything that can be *identified* as the teaching.

For this reason we can never pin the Buddha's teaching down to any simple formula, to the 'three of this' or the 'four of that', or to any such set of principles. Really, the teaching is nothing verbal, nothing conceptual, at all. The teaching is a realization and an *influence*. It is a communication between the Enlightened and the unenlightened. Certainly, it sometimes makes *use* of words, doctrines, and so on, but it can never be reduced to them.

All this rather alters our picture of what happened in the deer park at Isipatana. We may tend to imagine the Buddha arriving at the deer park, taking out his notes, and giving a lecture to the five ascetics – at the end of which they become Enlightened – then going off to give his lecture somewhere else. Traditional Buddhist art reinforces this view. In traditional works the Buddha is usually depicted sitting cross-legged on a magnificent, ornately decorated, throne, the five ascetics kneeling submissively at his feet while he preaches. But, as we have seen, the Buddha had great difficulty in getting the five ascetics even to listen to him. He certainly did not deliver a formal address, much less still a lecture. He thrashed things out with them, in personal discussion, over a period of weeks and months.

So on the occasion of Dharma Day we do not celebrate the Dharma in the sense of any particular rigid formulation of the Truth, any particular text or scripture – however useful, however ancient, or however inspiring. What we celebrate is the first impact of the Enlightened man on the unenlightened, the first impact of the New Man on the old men.

This impact finds expression in terms of speech, but it is not confined to speech. Today we are celebrating the impact of the New Man on the 'old men' and 'old women' of the *present generation*: upon *ourselves*.

Life today is a complicated and sometimes difficult business. It is full of distractions, as though there are lots of clutching fingers trying to get at us, trying to take hold of us, all the time. Under such conditions it is only too easy to forget what is really the main purpose of human existence. It is only too easy to ignore, or forget, the possibility of developing oneself, of growing in the direction of Enlightenment. Occasions such as this festival help us to remember.

There are many ways in which we can grow and develop. We can grow with the help of meditation, with the help of philosophizing – as an activity of the mind; we can grow with the help of the practice of the arts, and so on. As this process unfolds we will sooner or later find ourselves in contact with others who are also growing, also developing. As we weave a network of relationships with these people, coming subtly more and more in contact with one another, we shall one day wake up to the fact that we collectively form a spiritual community, united by common ideals and a common way of life. If, as a result of the impact of the New Man on our lives, we ourselves start becoming 'new men' and 'new women', evolving together and forming a new spiritual community, then the New Man will not have spoken in vain.

A WREATH OF BLUE LOTUS

Order weekend, Padmaloka, Norfolk, 4 December 1982.

Because there is really only one Going for Refuge, there can really only be one kind of ordination. But ordination may take place in a number of ways. Historically speaking, as we can see from the Pāli scriptures, it could take place when the Buddha, upon meeting and communicating with someone, saw that the person was ready to go for Refuge, ready to commit himself. On such an occasion, the Buddha would simply say, 'Come, O monk! *(ehi bhikkhave!)* Lead the spiritual life *(brahmacariya)* for the destruction of suffering.' And the person was ordained. It could be as simple as that. Similarly, we find that ordination could take place when someone, deeply impressed by the Buddha's teaching, repeated the formula: 'To the Buddha for Refuge I go. To the Dharma for Refuge I go. To the Sangha for Refuge I go,' – and the Buddha accepted that. Otherwise, the ordination could take place when the individual concerned was 'accepted' by an assembly of five or ten monks. However, the episode with which we shall be concerned here centres upon a rather unusual – in fact a quite unique – form of ordination.

At one time the Buddha was staying among the Śākyas of Kapilavastu in a park known as the Banyan Park. The Śākyans were the people among whom the Buddha was born, and among whom he grew up. Kapilavastu was their capital. After the Buddha's Enlightenment many Śākyans became his followers; in particular, many young Śākyan men left home and became 'monks' under his guidance. Among these was of course Ānanda, the Buddha's constant companion in his later years.

While the Buddha was staying at Kapilavastu many people came to see him – including friends and relations he had known before. Among these came Mahāprajāpatī, the Buddha's maternal aunt and foster-mother. (The Buddha's own mother, Māyādevī, had died when he was only a few days old, and it was Mahāprajāpatī who brought him up.)

On this occasion Mahāprajāpatī came with an unusual – even unprecedented – request. This was nothing less than that women should be permitted to go forth from home into the homeless life under the *Dharma-Vinaya* set forth by the Buddha. She wanted to be ordained.

The Buddha's response was a categorical refusal. There was no beating about the bush: he just said no. Three times Mahāprajāpatī made her request and three times the Buddha refused. In fact he asked her not even to wish for such a thing, and, in the end, she just had to go away unsatisfied. The translation of the Pāli text tells us, moreover, that she went away 'sad, sorrowful, tearful, and wailing'.[231]

The second half of the episode takes place some time later. We are not told exactly when it takes place, but it is clear that the Buddha has left Kapilavastu. He has been wandering from place to place and has now come to Vaiśālī and is staying in the Mahāvana, the 'great grove', or 'great forest', at the 'Hall of the Peaked Gable'. Meanwhile, Mahāprajāpatī has not been idle. She has not accepted the Buddha's refusal to allow women to be ordained and proceeds to get her hair cut off, dons saffron robes, and sets off for Vaiśālī with a number of Śākyan women. She is clearly a very determined lady; she won't take no for an answer, even from the Buddha.

Eventually she arrives at the Hall of the Peaked Gable and takes her stand outside the porch. Her feet are of course swollen and dust begrimed after the long journey, and we are told that she is sad, sorrowful, weeping and wailing.

Sooner or later Ānanda finds her. He knows her, of course, because he is also a kinsman of the Buddha and therefore her kinsman too. He asks her what she wants and why she is so upset, and she replies that she is upset because the Buddha will not permit women to go forth from home into the homeless life.

Ānanda is a very sympathetic soul. He feels sorry for Mahāprajāpatī and does his best to help. He goes immediately to see the Buddha, saying that Mahāprajāpatī has come all the way from Kapilavastu and is now standing outside the porch weeping and wailing. He also suggests, out of the kindness of his heart, that the Buddha should grant her request.

But the Buddha refuses Ānanda's request just as categorically as he had refused Mahāprajāpatī's, and asks him not to wish for any such thing. Three times Ānanda makes his request, and three times the Buddha refuses. However, Ānanda does not give up. After all, he knows the Buddha very well, so he argues with him, saying, 'Suppose women *were* to go forth from home into the homeless life under the *Dharma-Vinaya* set forth by the Tathāgata, would they be capable of attaining the fruits of stream entry, or the fruit of once returning, or the fruit of never returning, or the fruit of arhantship?'

When the Buddha admits that women are so capable, Ānanda seizes his opportunity. He reminds the Buddha that Mahāprajāpatī was of great service to the Buddha when he was an infant; on the death of his mother she actually suckled him. It would therefore be a good thing, he says, if women were permitted to go forth from home into the homeless life. The Buddha is unable to resist this argument, and grants Mahāprajāpatī's request.

He grants it, however, on certain conditions. He tells Ānanda that if Mahāprajāpatī will undertake to keep eight important rules, then that will be reckoned as full ordination. The rules are as follows:

> A sister, even if she be a hundred years in the robes, shall salute, shall rise up before, shall bow down before, shall perform all duties of respect unto a brother – even if that brother have only just taken the robes. Let this rule never be broken, but be honoured, esteemed, reverenced, and observed as long as life doth last.

> Secondly, a sister shall not spend the rainy season in a district where there is no brother residing. Let this rule never be broken....

> Thirdly, at the half month let a sister await two things from the Order of Brethren, namely, the appointing of the Sabbath [this is the translator's rather strange word for the *uposatha*] and the coming of a brother to preach the sermon. Let this rule never be broken....

Fourthly, at the end of keeping the rainy season let a sister, in presence of both Orders, of Brethren and of Sisters, invite enquiry in respect of three things, namely, of things seen, heard, and suspected. Let this rule never be broken....

Fifthly, a sister guilty of serious wrong-doing shall do penance for the half-month to both Orders. Let this rule never be broken....

Sixthly, when a sister has passed two seasons in the practice of the Six Rules she may ask for full orders from both Orders. Let this rule never be broken....

Seventhly, a sister shall not in any case abuse or censure a brother. Let this rule never be broken....

Eighthly, henceforth is forbidden the right of a sister to have speech among brethren, but not forbidden is the speaking of brethren unto sisters. Let this rule never be broken, but be honoured, esteemed, reverenced, and observed as long as life doth last.[232]

On hearing this reply, Ānanda goes to Mahāprajāpatī and tells her what the Buddha has said. This is her response:

Just as, lord Ānanda, a woman or a man, youthful, of tender age, fond of self-adornment, having washed the head and having gotten a wreath of blue lotus or of jasmine or of scented-creeper flowers, should take it with both hands and place it atop of the head – even so do I, lord Ānanda, take upon me these Eight Important Rules, never to be broken so long as life doth last.[233]

Ānanda now returns to the Buddha and tells him that Mahāprajāpatī has accepted the eight rules and is therefore now fully ordained.

This, then, is the episode with which we are concerned. This is our wreath of blue lotus. Clearly, it provides us with a good deal of material for reflection. I am going to concentrate on just one important part: the eight important rules. Why did they take the particular form that they did? And what are we to make of Mahāprajāpatī's response to them?

Before looking at the rules, however, we must briefly examine Mahāprajāpatī's behaviour after the Buddha's initial refusal. As we have seen, she gets her hair cut off, dons the saffron robes, and sets off for Vaiśālī with a number of Śākyan women. Finally, she stands outside the porch of the Hall of the Peaked Gable. In doing all this, she seems to be trying to force the Buddha's hand. We might even say that she is trying to present the Buddha with a *fait accompli*. After all, she has left home, shaved her head, and donned the saffron robes. She is in effect now a nun, so the Buddha might as well accept the situation, might as well permit her to do what she has in fact already done.

Now the *fait accompli* is a very interesting phenomenon. Essentially, a *fait accompli* consists in creating a situation in which the other person is, in effect, deprived of their power of choice or decision. I say *in effect* because they are not literally deprived of it; nevertheless, a situation is created in which they can exercise that power only at the cost of a great deal of trouble and even a great deal of unpleasantness. The *fait accompli* involves an element of what we may describe as emotional blackmail, and is thus a form of coercion. This of course means that it is a form of violence, and is hence completely out of place in the spiritual life. If you present someone with a *fait accompli* you are not treating them as an individual. But this is what Mahāprajāpatī did: she tried to force the Buddha's hand. Her desire to go forth was no doubt sincere but, in this connection, she did not treat the Buddha with very much respect.

We are also told that she stood outside the porch 'sad, sorrowful, weeping and wailing'. One can perhaps understand her being sad and sorrowful, but what about the weeping and wailing? It would seem that she was trying to get her way in a rather childish fashion. We can contrast this with Ānanda's attitude. Ānanda argued with the Buddha. He prepared his ground and gave reasons as to why women should be permitted to go forth – with the result that the Buddha was unable to resist his request; he was unable to resist reason, unable to resist argument.

This part of the episode is surely of some significance. The *fait accompli* in fact failed – as it always does in the long run. Emotional blackmail fails, attempted coercion fails. On the other hand, reason suffused with sympathy succeeds. Mahāprajāpatī herself failed to gain her point, but Ānanda gained it for her.

It is now time that we moved on to the eight important rules themselves. Why did they take the particular form they did?

Perhaps the first thing that strikes us about them is that they are quite severe, even quite harsh. We cannot quite help feeling that the Buddha is perhaps being rather unfair towards Mahāprajāpatī – though he no doubt knew her better than we do. Indeed, the Buddha seems to be being quite unjust to women in general. The eight important rules would certainly make the blood of a modern feminist boil with rage, and they might even make some men a little uneasy. Let's go into the matter a little.

If we look at these rules, it is rather obvious that their main function is to subordinate the order of nuns to the order of monks, to make the *bhikkhunīs* completely dependent on the *bhikkhus*. The *bhikkhunīs*, the nuns, are to be kept in a state of perpetual pupilage. What could have been the reason for this?

One scholar has suggested that Mahāprajāpatī's request created an 'organizational problem' for the Buddha. (It seems that even the Buddha had organizational problems!) By this time the order of monks had been in existence for about twenty years. Organizationally speaking, the Buddha was faced with three alternatives. He could admit women to the existing order of monks, thus creating a single unified order, he could create an entirely separate and independent order for women, or he could subordinate the order of nuns to the order of monks.

The first of these options was clearly out of the question. Both monks and nuns were expected to lead lives of celibacy and this would presumably have been rather difficult if they were living together as members of a single unified order. The second alternative was out of the question too. The Buddha could hardly be the head of two quite separate, independent, orders. In any case, he was – externally at least – a man, and a man could hardly be the head of an order of nuns. If it was really to be separate and independent, that order of nuns would have to be headed by a woman. That left only the third alternative, that of subordinating the order of nuns to the order of monks. This, according to the scholar, is the alternative that the Buddha adopted.

This explanation is certainly of interest, there may even be some truth in it, but it does not really suffice to explain the specific form in which the eight important rules were presented. Something more than organizational convenience seems to have been involved. Perhaps it would help if we tried to understand what it was that the rules were intended to prevent. To do this, however, we have to look at rules in general.

If we look at the Vinaya Piṭaka, or *The Book of the Discipline*, we find that it contains many rules, of many different kinds. There are rules for monks, and rules for nuns. According to the Theravāda tradition, there are, altogether, 227 rules for monks, and 311 rules for nuns. How did these rules come to be laid down?

It is certain that the Buddha did not draw them all up in advance. He did not sit down under his bodhi tree and think, 'What sort of Sangha would I like to have? And what sort of rules should it observe? How should it be constituted?' The Buddha laid down rules in response to unskilful behaviour on the part of a member, or members, of the sangha. So long as there was no unskilful behaviour there were no rules; the Buddha was not interested in laying down rules for their own sake. He was interested simply in the moral and spiritual development of the individual, and laid down rules only when 'forced' to do so.

These eight important rules, however, *were* laid down in advance of any offence actually committed by Mahāprajāpatī. But the same principle does perhaps apply.

The effect of these rules is to subordinate the order of nuns to the order of monks. It is to make the *bhikkhunīs* completely dependent, organizationally speaking, on the *bhikkhus*. So what kind of unskilful behaviour are the eight rules meant to prevent? To what kind of possible offences do they refer?

Clearly they are meant to prevent the nuns claiming equality with, or superiority over, monks. That is to say, they are meant to prevent women claiming equality with, or superiority over, men. In other words, we could say that they are meant to prevent an irruption of *feminism* into the order.

To say this does not mean that the Buddha did not believe in equal rights for women in the ordinary social sense. It does not mean that he did not believe that a woman could be spiritually superior to a man. After all, he had told Ānanda quite categorically that women were capable of attaining the fruits of Stream Entry and so on, and, presumably, a woman who was a Stream Entrant was spiritually superior to a man who was still a worldling. So what the Buddha wanted to do, it seems, was to prevent women from going forth *for the wrong reasons*, that is, for social rather than for purely spiritual reasons.

There are indications that this sort of thing did sometimes happen afterwards, despite the Buddha's precautions. A woman might seek ordination because she wanted to be free from her husband, or because she was a widow and wanted to be more highly respected – which as a nun she would be – or because her parents were unable or unwilling to find her a husband. The same sort of thing can happen even in modern times.

I received my *śrāmaṇera* ordination from U Chandramani Mahathera at Kusinārā. U Chandramani – fortunately for me – was very generous with his ordinations. Among others, he ordained a large number of women. He did not ordain them as *śrāmaṇerīs*, since that was no longer possible, but as *anagarikās*. Eventually he ordained so many women that he was begged to stop by his male disciples. The women whom he had ordained were mostly Nepalese and, as I knew from my personal contact with them, they wanted ordination mainly for social reasons. They wanted to enjoy the same rights as men, and saw ordination as a means of achieving this end. In most cases they were not really interested in the spiritual life at all.

This seems to have been the sort of situation that the Buddha wanted to prevent, and this is why he set forth the eight important rules. He was trying to make quite sure that Mahāprajāpatī wanted to go forth for purely spiritual reasons, that she really wanted to go for Refuge, really wanted to gain Enlightenment.

We can take things even further than this. We have seen that Mahāprajāpatī tried to present the Buddha with a *fait accompli*. And we have seen that she tried to get her own way in a rather childish fashion. In Mahāprajāpatī, there was a strong element of what William Blake called the 'Female Will'. In fact, from a certain point of view, she was almost an embodiment of that Female Will. The Buddha saw that before Mahāprajāpatī could truly go forth the Female Will had to annihilated – and the eight important rules were intended to do just that. At this point I should perhaps say a few words about what Blake meant by the Female Will.

According to Blake, in the 'unfallen Individual', reason and emotion, 'masculine' and 'feminine', are united. The feminine 'portion' of the fundamentally bisexual Individual is called the 'Emanation'. With the Fall of Man – to summarize rather rapidly – Reason and Emotion are divided: the Emanation is divided from the Individual and takes the Female form, and Man is left as what Blake calls a 'Dark Spectre'. Worse still, the Emanation acquires a will of her own and this 'Female Will' acts in opposition to her consort. As S. Foster Damon puts it,

The Emanation's self-centred pride seeks dominion over the male. She is jealous of all his activities, and seeks to stop them by denying her husband his freedom.... She is even jealous of her husband's labours, which take his attention from her; so she prevents his working.[234]

It is this kind of spirit, it seems, that the Buddha wanted to prevent from entering the sangha, he wanted to curb the Female Will, and this is why he set forth the eight important rules.

How then does Mahāprajāpatī receive the rules? She says:

> Just as, lord Ānanda, a woman or a man, youthful, of tender age, fond of self-adornment, having washed the head and having gotten a wreath of blue lotus or of jasmine or of scented-creeper flowers, should take it with both hands and place it atop of the head – even so do I, lord Ānanda, take upon me these Eight Important Rules, never to be broken so long as life doth last.

From these words it is clear that Mahāprajāpatī accepts the eight important rules in a completely positive spirit. She passes the test – if it is a test – and the Female Will is annihilated in her. She really did want to go forth, really did want to gain Enlightenment. And gain Enlightenment she eventually did.

In the *Therīgāthā*, or the 'Verses of the Elder Nuns', there are some very interesting verses attributed to Mahāprajāpatī after her attainment of Enlightenment:

> Buddha, Hero, homage to you, O best of all creatures, who
>   released me and many other people from pain.
> All pain is known; craving as the cause is dried up; the Noble Eight-
>   fold Way has been developed; cessation has been attained by me.
> Formerly I was mother, son, father, brother, and grandmother;
>   not having proper knowledge I journeyed on without expiation.
> That blessed one has indeed been seen by me; this is the last
>   body; journeying on from rebirth to rebirth has been completely
>   eliminated; there is now no renewed existence.
> I see the disciples all together putting forth energy, resolute,
>   always with strong effort; this is homage to the Buddhas.

Truly for the sake of many Maya bore Gotama. She thrust away
  the mass of pain of those struck by sickness and death.[235]

The last verse but one is particularly beautiful. Mahāprajāpatī says, 'I
see the disciples all together putting forth energy, resolute, always with
strong effort; this is homage to the Buddhas.' We might say that this
verse could serve as a motto for the entire sangha – past, present, and
future. We could also say that Mahāprajāpatī's acceptance of the eight
important rules and her attainment of Enlightenment are by no means
unconnected. The eight important rules made sure that her going forth
was sincere; they made sure that she really wanted to be ordained, really
wanted to go for Refuge. They made sure that her motivation was not
social but spiritual. The eight important rules are like a great blazing fire,
a fire in which all the impurities in Mahāprajāpatī's wish for ordination
were burned up, were consumed, and from that fire Mahāprajāpatī
emerged triumphant. To her, the eight important rules were not a crown
of thorns but a 'wreath of blue lotus'. They were not something to be
endured, but something to be enjoyed. I am reminded in this connection
of a passage in the *Diamond Sūtra*:

> Moreover, Subhuti, the spot of earth where this Sutra will
> be revealed, that spot of earth will be worthy of worship
> by the whole world with its Gods, men and Asuras, worthy
> of being saluted respectfully, worthy of being honoured by
> circumambulation – like a shrine will be that spot of earth. And
> yet Subhuti, those sons and daughters of good family, who will
> take up these very Sutras, and will bear them in mind, recite and
> study them, they will be humbled – well humbled will they be!
> And why? The impure deeds which these beings have done in their
> former lives, and which are liable to lead them into states of woe
> – in this very life they will, by means of that humiliation, annul
> those impure deeds of their former lives, and they will reach the
> enlightenment of a Buddha.[236]

Before concluding, I would like to generalize a little from the episode
with which we have been concerned. I have spoken of the Buddha
wanting to be quite sure that Mahāprajāpatī wanted to go forth for
purely spiritual reasons. But this should not be seen as applying only to

Mahāprajāpatī, or even only to women. It applies to *all* who want to go forth, to all who want to go for Refuge, to all who want to be ordained.

It is important that one should want to do the right thing for the right reason. Indeed, in the sphere of spiritual life, the right thing is not the right thing *unless* one does it for the right reason. In principle, the eight important rules represent all those factors that prevent us from going forth until we are really ready to do so. To begin with, of course, we may experience those factors not as a wreath of blue lotus, but indeed as a crown of thorns. We may feel very ill-used, very hard done by; we may go around wearing a martyred look. We may even feel angry and resentful that we are not being ordained. But a time comes when we no longer experience the crown of thorns as a crown of thorns but as a wreath of blue lotus. We accept that we are not ready for ordination. Then, paradoxically, we find – or it is found – that we *are* ready.

At this point a question may arise. Must our desire for ordination be perfectly pure before we can be ordained? In the case of Mahāprajāpatī this seems to have been what the Buddha insisted upon – perfect purity of motive at least with regard to what Blake called the Female Will. In modern times, when life is so much more complicated than it was in the Buddha's day, one might say that we cannot expect the desire for ordination always to be perfectly pure. But, at the same time, we can *expect* it to be so, in the sense that we must be prepared to put as much of our energy as we possibly can into the task of spiritual self-development, into the Going for Refuge. Not only that, we must be prepared to take active steps to *put* all our energies into it. If we can do that then we are ready to go forth, ready to go for Refuge.

There is one thing, however, that we must remember. So far as most people are concerned, the Going for Refuge is – to begin with – an 'effective' rather than a 'real' Going for Refuge.[237] Inasmuch as it is only an effective Going for Refuge, we can fall away from it. It is therefore not only necessary to make sure that our desire for ordination is pure, but to make sure that we *keep* it pure. It is also necessary to make sure that our motive for being in the Order remains pure after ordination. We do this by remaining aware and mindful, by remaining emotionally positive, by living and working under conditions that are conducive to our spiritual development, by keeping in close touch with our spiritual friends, and by coming together repeatedly and in large numbers. Otherwise, we may fall by the wayside.

There is just one more point to be made. The eight important rules ensured that Mahāprajāpatī's going forth was sincere. But Going for Refuge is an on-going process. It is not something that we do once and for all. Consequently we all need something like the eight important rules all the time, something that will make sure that our Going for Refuge really is a process that is constantly deepening.

This something is not so difficult to find. We can find it in the positive critical feedback of our spiritual friends – in what has been called 'fierce friendship'.[238] If we are to continue to develop spiritually, if we are to continue to deepen our Going for Refuge, then we will need genuine criticism. I am not of course suggesting that we need nothing *but* criticism – that can be counter-productive: we also need encouragement, appreciation, and inspiration. But we shall upon occasion certainly need criticism too. We shall need criticism that comes from the heart, criticism that is based upon positive emotion, on *mettā*, criticism that is concerned only with our welfare, only with our development.

When we are given that criticism, how shall we receive it? Hopefully we will receive it in the same spirit that Mahāprajāpatī received the eight important rules from the Buddha: not as a crown of thorns, sharp and uncomfortable, but as a wreath of blue lotus resting beautifully on the top of our heads.

A CASE OF DYSENTERY

Men's National Order Weekend, Padmaloka, Norfolk, 3 July 1982.[239]

I am aware that the title of this talk is not like any of my previous titles. It is something of a change from the 'spiritual this', and the 'transcendental that', or the 'creative something else'. Perhaps it will raise a few eyebrows. Perhaps people will think that there has been a dreadful printing mistake or a deplorable lapse of good taste. Others might think that the title is meant to be symbolic or mythic. But there is nothing symbolic about it at all. My theme really is a case of dysentery – in the literal sense.

This is no ordinary case of dysentery, however. This particular case of dysentery is quite an important one, though not from a medical point of view. The case in question took place some 2,500 years ago, and we know about it because it is mentioned in the Vinaya Piṭaka of the Theravāda Pāli canon:

> Now at that time a certain brother was suffering from dysentery
> and lay where he had fallen down in his own excrements. And
> the Exalted One was going His rounds of the lodgings, with the
> venerable Ānanda in attendance, and came to the lodging of that
> brother. Now the Exalted One saw that brother lying where he
> had fallen in his own excrements, and seeing him He went towards
> him, came to him, and said: 'Brother, what ails you?'
>
> 'I have dysentery, Lord.'

'But is there anyone taking care of you, brother?'

'No, Lord.'

'Why is it, brother, that the brethren do not take care of you?'

'I am useless to the brethren, Lord: therefore the brethren do not care for me.'

Then the Exalted One said to the venerable Ānanda: 'Go you, Ānanda, and fetch water. We will wash this brother.'

'Yes, Lord,' replied the venerable Ānanda to the Exalted One. When he had fetched the water, the Exalted One poured it out, while the venerable Ānanda washed that brother all over. Then the Exalted One taking him by the head and the venerable Ānanda taking him by the feet, together they laid him on the bed.

Then the Exalted One, in this connexion and on this occasion, gathered the Order of Brethren together, and questioned the brethren, saying:

'Brethren, is there in such and such a lodging a brother who is sick?'

'There is, Lord.'

'And what ails that brother?'

'Lord, that brother has dysentery.'

'But, brethren, is there anyone taking care of him?'

'No, Lord.'

'Why not? Why do not the brethren take care of him?'

'That brother is useless to the brethren, Lord. That is why the brethren do not take care of him.'

'Brethren, ye have no mother and no father to take care of you. If ye will not take care of each other, who else, I ask, will do so? Brethren, he who would wait on me, let him wait on the sick. If he have a teacher, let his teacher take care of him, so long as he is alive, and wait for his recovery. If he have a tutor or a lodger, a disciple or a fellow-lodger or a fellow-disciple, such should take care of him and await his recovery. If no one takes care of him, it shall be reckoned an offence.'[240]

This passage deals with a significant episode in the collective life of the early Buddhist spiritual community. And, as I am sure you have realized, it deals with the kind of situation which might arise in the collective life of our own order, 2,500 years later, despite the lapse of time and despite the vast cultural differences. In this episode we are able to see how the Buddha responded to a situation of this sort, what advice he gave, what action he took, and so on. The episode is concerned with much more than the treatment of a sick monk; it is concerned with a number of principles of fundamental importance – some of them only *apparently* peripheral to the main issue.

The passage begins rather dramatically:

Now at that time a certain brother was suffering from dysentery and lay where he had fallen down in his own excrements.

This is a dreadful picture! Here is a brother, a *bhikkhu* – we are not told whether he is old or young, we are not even given his name – who is suffering from dysentery. It must be a really serious attack because he has fallen to the ground and is lying in his own excrement. Apparently he is too weak to get up. And he is on his own. There is nobody near, nobody within call, no one to help, no one to give him a drink of water. His condition is very pitiable.

The Exalted One was going His rounds of the lodgings, with the venerable Ānanda in attendance, and came to the lodging of that brother.

There are two points to notice here. The Buddha was going his rounds of the lodgings, and Ānanda was in attendance. Ānanda was the Buddha's cousin. He had known the Buddha – and the Buddha had known him – all his life. They had played together as boys, they had fought together, they had tumbled about together in the dust, they had practised archery together, and, years later, after the Buddha had gained Enlightenment, Ānanda too went forth from home into the homeless life. He became a disciple of the Buddha and advanced steadily on the spiritual path. We know further that Ānanda was the Buddha's constant companion for the last twenty years of his life. Ānanda is usually described as the Buddha's 'attendant'. But why should the Buddha have needed a personal attendant?

The traditional explanations do not seem very adequate. It is simply suggested that the Buddha needed someone to wash his robe, arrange his interviews, and carry messages for him. Ānanda did indeed do all these things, as well as many others. It is also said by the tradition that it was simply the 'custom' for a Buddha to have a personal attendant. Buddhas had always had personal attendants, and that was that – just as they had always had a particular tree under which they gained Enlightenment, or a particular horse, or a particular charioteer, or two particular chief disciples, and so on. Thus Ānanda was the personal attendant of Gautama the Buddha. This is the traditional explanation; but it is not good enough, it does not go deep enough.

Ānanda was not the first of these so-called personal attendants. There was, for example, Meghiya, whom we encounter in the *Udāna*.[241] Meghiya was the Buddha's personal attendant for a while. He was not a very satisfactory one because he went off on his own one day when he should have stayed with the Buddha – with rather disastrous consequences for himself.

Although the Buddha had had some difficulty in finding a satisfactory personal attendant, Ānanda was by no means in a hurry to take on the task. It is as though he realized that it would be no easy matter to be the constant companion of an Enlightened one. Ānanda had made steady progress in the spiritual life. He was certainly a Stream Entrant: he was irreversible from full Enlightenment. But he was not a Buddha. And even for someone like Ānanda, even for a Stream Entrant, even for someone who had grown up with the Buddha, it was a rather awe-inspiring prospect to be the Buddha's constant companion, to be with him, by day and by night, in rain and in sun, year in and year out. Ānanda therefore thought the matter over very carefully. He had seen some previous attendants come somewhat to grief, and was reluctant to give the Buddha any further trouble.

In the end, however, Ānanda decided to accept the challenge, but laid down certain conditions, of which a couple are relevant here. One of these was that he should not be given any share in the various offerings and invitations that were given to the Buddha. He argued that, if people saw him benefiting from the offerings that were made to the Buddha – all the new robes and so on, then they might think he was acting as the Buddha's companion just for the sake of what he could get out of it. He also realized that there would be times when he might have to be away from the Buddha, running errands, taking messages, and so on. While he was away, someone might come to see the Buddha and ask for a teaching. In consequence, the Buddha might give a discourse, might even give an important teaching, in his absence. So another condition he laid down was that the Buddha should repeat whatever teaching he had given during his absence.

The Buddha accepted these conditions,[242] and Ānanda became his constant companion for twenty years. How successful this arrangement was can be seen from an incident that occurred shortly before the Buddha's *parinirvāṇa*, his final passing away. Ānanda was very deeply upset by the prospect of losing the Buddha. Apparently he stood leaning against the door, weeping. As he wept, he said, 'Alas, I am still a pupil with much to be done, and my Master will be passing utterly away, *he who was so kind to me*.'[243] This was Ānanda's impression of the Buddha after twenty years of constant, day to day, companionship. He did not say that the Buddha was *wise*, or *energetic*, but that the Buddha was *kind*.

Fortunately, we also know about the Buddha's impression of Ānanda, for when he was told that Ānanda was weeping outside, he sent for him and spoke the following words of encouragement:

For many a long day, Ānanda, the Tathāgata has been waited on by you with kindly body-service, that is profitable, ease-giving, undivided, and unstinted; waited on with kindly service of speech, that is profitable, ease-giving, undivided, and unstinted; with kindly service of thought, that is profitable, ease-giving, undivided, and unstinted.[244]

Thus the Buddha's predominant impression of Ānanda was that he too was kind, that Ānanda had served him with kindness of body, speech, and mind, that he had kept nothing back, that he had given himself totally. The relation between the Buddha and Ānanda was essentially one of mutual kindness, even though the Buddha was spiritually by far the more developed of the two.

This may seem like a very small thing, but if we reflect we shall realize that it is actually a very big thing that they were kind to each other. Their kindness had never failed, had never been found wanting even for a moment on either side. When two people are constant companions, and when the relation between them is of unfailing mutual kindness, you can only say of them that they are *friends*. Indeed, you can only say that they are *spiritual friends*, because such unfailing mutual kindness over such a long period of time is possible only on a deeply spiritual basis.

To some, it may seem a little strange that the Buddha and Ānanda were friends. It may seem strange, perhaps, that the Buddha should have had a friend. One may wonder whether a Buddha *needs* a friend. But this depends on one's conception of Enlightenment. In response, I can give only a hint.

The Enlightenment experience is not self-contained in a one-sided way. The Enlightenment experience contains an element of 'communication', and contains, therefore, an element of spiritual friendship, even 'transcendental friendship', or friendship of the highest conceivable level. This, perhaps, is the significance of the Buddha's having a constant companion. There is surely no question of the Buddha keeping up the 'dignity' of a Buddha. Ānanda is not a sort of spiritual valet-cum-private-secretary. The fact that he is 'in attendance', as the translator has it, represents the fact that there exists within the Enlightenment experience, within the heart of Reality, an element of communication, an element of spiritual friendship, something that found expression in the later history of Buddhist thought as that rather mysterious concept of *sambhogakāya*.[245]

The Exalted One was going his rounds of the lodgings, with the Venerable Ānanda in attendance, and came to the lodging of that brother.

There is a second point to notice here: the Exalted One was going his rounds of the *lodgings*. In the original, the word for 'lodging' is *vihāra*, and that is all that *vihāra* really means. We must not imagine the Buddha going his rounds of a large, palatial, well-furnished monastery. The lodgings in question were probably just clusters of thatched huts scattered over an area of parkland just a few miles outside the city gates.

The Buddha was making his *rounds* of these lodgings. In other words, he was taking a personal interest in the monks. How were they getting on? What were they doing? How were they passing their time? There was of course no question of them sitting outside their thatched huts reading newspapers, or listening to the radio, or watching television. But they might possibly have been up to other things that they should not have been up to. They might have needed some encouragement, some teaching, or even a little ticking-off. The Buddha was seeing things for himself. In this way, he and Ānanda came to the lodging of that brother.

> Now the Exalted One saw that brother lying where he had fallen
> in his own excrements, and seeing him He went towards him,
> came to him, and said: 'Brother, what ails you?'
>
> 'I have dysentery, Lord.'
>
> 'But is there anyone taking care of you, brother?'
>
> 'No, Lord.'
>
> 'Why is it, brother, that the brethren do not take care of you?'
>
> 'I am useless to the brethren, Lord: therefore the brethren do not
> care for me.'

There are a number of points to be noted here. The Buddha goes towards the sick monk, asks him what is wrong with him, and gets very quickly to the heart of the matter. All of these points could be enlarged upon, but perhaps that is not necessary, their significance being sufficiently clear. The main point of this section is contained in the sick monk's last reply to the Buddha: 'I am useless to the brethren, Lord: therefore the brethren do not care for me.'

This is a very significant statement indeed. It is a shocking, terrible statement. Of course, we have only the bare words of the printed page to go by. We do not know how those words were spoken – and this can of course make a difference. Did the Buddha say, 'Why is it, brother, that the brethren do not take care of you?' indignantly, or with concern, or sadly? And did the sick monk reply with dignity, with resignation, with weariness, or with bitterness and anger? We do not know. All we have is the bleak, shocking, statement itself, 'I am useless to the brethren, Lord: therefore the brethren do not care for me.'

However the words were spoken, they must imply, sadly, that people are interested in you only so long as you are useful to them, only so long as they can get something out of you. It implies that they see you not as a person but as a thing.

To treat a person as a thing is to treat them unethically. And this, apparently, is how the other monks were treating the sick monk. He was not useful to them, so they were not interested in him. He was left lying in his own excrement. No one took care of him. There was no kindness between the sick monk and the other monks as there was between the Buddha and Ānanda. There was no ordinary human friendship – not to speak of spiritual friendship; neither was there any sympathy or sensitivity or awareness. There could not be, because these are qualities that you can experience only in relation to a person whom you actually see as a person. The other monks did not see the sick monk as a person. To them he was like an old worn-out broom or a broken pot. He was useless to them so they did not care for him.

Only too often we ourselves can behave like this. We often consider people primarily in terms of their usefulness. We do this even within the spiritual community. Sometimes we are more interested in someone's talents and capacities – as a bricklayer, accountant, or lecturer – than in what they are in themselves. If you are treated in this way, then, when you are no longer able or willing to employ your talents, you may have the disappointing and disillusioning experience of finding that nobody wants to know you, nobody wants to be friends with you any more. We must therefore learn to see persons as persons. There must be kindness between us, there must be spiritual friendship, as there was between the Buddha and Ānanda. There must be sympathy, sensitivity, and awareness.

There are two principal aspects to persons treating each other as persons. These are communication and taking delight. These two are of the essence of friendship.

Even in the case of ordinary friendship there is the great benefit and blessing of being able to share our thoughts and feelings with another human being. It has been said that self-disclosure, the making of oneself known to another human being – being known by them and knowing that you are known by them – is essential to human health and happiness. If you are shut up in yourself, without any possibility of communication with another person, you don't stay healthy or happy for long.

In the case of spiritual friendship, we share our experience of the Dharma itself. We share our enthusiasm, our inspiration, and our understanding. We even share our mistakes. Here, communication takes the form of confession.

The aspect of 'taking delight' means that we not only see a person as a person, but also *like* what we see, enjoy and take delight in what we see, just as we do with a beautiful painting or poem – except that here the painting or poem is alive: the painting can speak to you, and the beautiful poem can answer back! This makes it very exciting and stimulating indeed. Here we see, we like, we love and appreciate a person entirely for their own sake, and not for the sake of anything useful that we can get out of them. This also happens in ordinary friendship to some extent, but it happens to a far greater extent in spiritual friendship – *kalyāṇa mitratā*. The primary meaning of *kalyāṇa* is 'beautiful'. In spiritual friendship we take delight in the *spiritual* beauty of our friend: we rejoice in his or her merits.

> Then the Exalted One said to the venerable Ānanda: 'Go you, Ānanda, and fetch water. We will wash this brother.'

> 'Yes, Lord,' replied the venerable Ānanda to the Exalted One. When he had fetched the water, the Exalted One poured it out, while the venerable Ānanda washed that brother all over. Then the Exalted One taking him by the head and the venerable Ānanda taking him by the feet, together they laid him on the bed.

There are a number of significant points here. The Buddha acts *instantly*. As a human being he seems to have been of a prompt, decisive, character, not unlike a military commander. At this stage he does not ask anyone how it all happened, but simply sends Ānanda off for water. Then, the Buddha and Ānanda act *together*. Ānanda does not argue with the Buddha; they don't have a long discussion as to who should pour the water and who should wash the sick man, or who should take him by the head and who should take him by the feet. They act together harmoniously, efficiently, and effectively.

Perhaps more importantly, the Buddha and Ānanda *accept responsibility* for the situation, even though it is not of their making. They do not try to hand the responsibility over to anybody else, but take care of the sick monk themselves, doing whatever needs to be done. They make the sick monk comfortable, and only then does the Buddha call the other monks together:

> Then the Exalted One, in this connexion and on this occasion, gathered the Order of Brethren together, and questioned the brethren, saying: 'Brethren, is there in such and such a lodging a brother who is sick?'
>
> 'There is, Lord.'
>
> 'And what ails that brother?'
>
> 'Lord, that brother has dysentery.'
>
> 'But, brethren, is there anyone taking care of him?'
>
> 'No, Lord.'
>
> 'Why not? Why do not the brethren take care of him?'
>
> 'That brother is useless to the brethren, Lord. That is why the brethren do not take care of him.'

There are two points here. First, the Buddha looks into the matter. He does not jump to conclusions. He does not immediately assume that the other monks are guilty of deliberate neglect. He first ascertains the facts of the case, giving the other monks an opportunity to explain, even to defend themselves. He gives them an opportunity to *confess* – and that is what they do.

This is an important lesson. So often we jump to conclusions; we assume that someone is guilty before we have ascertained all the facts. When we don't get a reply to a letter we assume that the person to whom we have written has not replied and conclude that he is not being a good friend. We then write a second, angry, letter. But surely we should first ascertain that our friend did actually *receive* the letter. And we should make sure that he has not in fact replied. Only then should we adopt whatever course seems appropriate.

This is just what the Buddha did, with the result that the monks confessed their mistake. I say that they confessed, but one does rather get the impression from this passage that they did not realize that there was anything wrong with their behaviour. If this was the case, then they must have had a very inadequate conception of the spiritual life, of the spiritual community, and of spiritual friendship. Be that as it may, once they had confessed, the Buddha could exhort them thus:

'Brethren, ye have no mother and no father to take care of you.
If ye will not take care of each other, who else, I ask, will do so?
Brethren, he who would wait on me, let him wait on the sick.'

Here, the Buddha is laying down an important set of principles. He is asserting an absolute discontinuity between the biological family and the spiritual family, between the group and the spiritual community. Once you enter the spiritual community you no longer belong to the group, and you no longer rely upon it. The Buddha does not mean that your mother and father are dead in the literal sense. He means that *spiritually speaking* they no longer exist. In other words, they no longer exist as your mother and father. You can therefore no longer depend upon them to take care of you, no longer take *refuge* in them.

This is what is meant by the 'Going Forth'. It is a going forth 'from home into homelessness'. You go forth from the group to the spiritual community. Spiritually speaking, the group no longer exists. And since it no longer exists, you no longer rely on it or take refuge in it.

Once you enter the spiritual community, only the spiritual community exists. You take refuge solely in the Three Jewels: the Buddha, the Dharma, and the Sangha. You rely only on other members of the spiritual community, and that means that other members of the spiritual community rely on you. You rely on one another, take care of one another, encourage one another, and inspire one another.

All of this certainly applies to our own spiritual community, the Western Buddhist Order. We have in fact no mother and no father to take care of us. What was formerly done by our family must now be done by our spiritual friends – indeed *more* must be done by our spiritual friends.

But suppose it is not done? Suppose someone is ill, or depressed, or experiencing psychological difficulties, or not finding the spiritual life very enjoyable. If that person is left, as the sick monk was left, he may drift back to the group, back to the family, back to mother, wife, or girlfriend. He may go in search of comfort and consolation elsewhere.

It is important that as members of the spiritual community we realize that we have no true refuge except one another, no friends except one another – that is, no *real* friends except spiritual friends. From the group we can expect absolutely nothing – nor should we. We belong *absolutely* to the spiritual community, belong absolutely to one another. We should be prepared, therefore, to live and die for one another – otherwise we have not really gone for Refuge. Our future is with one another; we are one another's future; we have no future apart from one another.

The Buddha says, 'If ye will not take care of each other, who else, I ask, will do so?' If Order members do not love one another, who else will love them? If Order members do not inspire one another, who else will inspire them? If Order members cannot be happy with one another, who else can they be happy with? If they cannot come together with one another, who else can they come together with? Perhaps we should enjoy one another's company more, appreciate one another more, value one another more.

The Buddha certainly valued the brethren highly. He says, 'Brethren, he who would wait on me, let him wait on the sick.' The Buddha is not being mystical or metaphysical here: he is dealing with the realities of life in the spiritual community. By 'the sick', he means sick *brethren* – fellow members of the spiritual community. If one wants to wait upon the Buddha, one should wait upon them. Thus the Buddha in a sense equates members of the spiritual community with himself. It would hardly be possible to value them more highly than that.

'If he have a teacher, let his teacher take care of him, so long as he is alive, and wait for his recovery. If he have a tutor or a lodger, a disciple or a fellow-lodger or a fellow-disciple, such should take care of him and await his recovery.'

Thus all conceivable relationships within the spiritual community are covered. Teacher should take care of pupil, and pupil of teacher; fellow disciple should take care of fellow disciple; occupants of the same *vihāra* (residential spiritual community) should take care of one another. In sickness and in health there should be unfailing kindness and spiritual friendship between them.

'If no one take care of him, it shall be reckoned an offence'. Here, 'offence' means an unskilful action that needs to be confessed. The responsibility for the care of each member rests on the entire spiritual community. Ultimately, all are responsible for each, and each is responsible for all to the extent of his strength. Otherwise there can be no spiritual community.

By now it should be clear that this story is not just about a sick monk being neglected by the brethren. It is not just a simple case of diarrhoea. It is a case of unfailing mutual kindness, a case of personal interest, a case of harmonious and effective action, a case of treating persons as persons, a case of communication and taking delight, a case of recognizing the absolute discontinuity between the group and the spiritual community. Above all it is a case of mutual responsibility and mutual spiritual friendship. It is not a case of something that happened in the past, 2,500 years ago; it is a case of something that is happening *now*, in the present, and something that will happen in the future. It is not a case of something that concerned the ancient brethren; it is something that concerns their modern successors, ourselves.

BETWEEN THE TWIN SĀL TREES

London, 5 February 1983.

There are many Buddhist scriptures: in Pāli, in Sanskrit, in Tibetan, in Chinese, and so on. There are also many Buddhist traditions: Theravāda, Sarvāstivāda, Mahāyāna, and Vajrayāna. And there are very many Buddhist teachings: about the cosmos, about meditation, about the mind, about mental states, about the nature of reality, about different kinds of living beings, about ethics – both personal and social, teachings even about the arts. In fact, there are so many scriptures, traditions, and teachings that one can sometimes get a little bewildered. Sometimes one might think how wonderful it would be if only all those books could be reduced to just one slim pocket volume that one could carry about all the time. How wonderful it would be if one could reduce those multitudinous chapters to just one chapter, all those verses to just one verse, or even reduce all those millions of words to just one magic word upon which alone one could ponder and continually reflect, knowing that if one did so one would be certain of gaining Enlightenment!

I have sometimes thought that this *could* be done, that perhaps all the teachings could be reduced to one teaching, in fact to just one magic, meaningful, word. That word would be 'impermanence'.

In a way, the whole of the Buddha's teaching is contained in that word. If you can understand impermanence it is almost as if you will understand everything that the Buddha ever said. It is not surprising, therefore, that we are told that the trees and birds in Sukhāvatī have nothing else to say, nothing else to sing, than *anitya* (impermanence), *anātman* (selflessness), and *duḥkha* (unsatisfactoriness).[246] One might say that *anitya*, impermanence, would be sufficient since the other two principles are really contained in it. If we understand this one word, impermanence, in sufficient depth, we will see that the whole of the Buddha's teaching, both practical and theoretical, is implied therein.

We very often find, especially in the earlier portions of the Pāli scriptures, that this insight into impermanence is expressed in terms of the realization that whatever has a beginning has an end, that whatever is born must die. If something has a beginning – and of course everything conditioned has a beginning – it must inevitably have an end. Sometimes this is expressed even more precisely and philosophically in the sentence: 'Whatever has by nature an origin, that also by nature has an end.' The end is not accidental, not grafted on: the end is inherent in something inasmuch as it has a beginning. Its beginning *is* its end; the fact that it is a 'beginning-thing' means that it is also an 'ending-thing'. If you are a 'born-thing', you are a 'dying-thing'.

In traditional Buddhist language, this realization is known as 'the opening of the Eye of Truth', or *dharmacakṣus* in Sanskrit (*dhammacakkhu* in Pāli). The opening of the Dharma-Eye, the realization of the truth that whatever has by nature an origin has also by nature an end, is equivalent to Stream Entry. From this fact alone, we can appreciate the great importance of the opening of the Dharma-Eye.

In the course of the Vinaya Piṭaka of the Pāli canon we meet Koṇḍañña, one of the Buddha's first five disciples. It is in connection with him that we hear of the Eye of Truth for the first time. Koṇḍañña had been one of the Buddha's companions earlier on in his career, when the Buddha was practising severe asceticism and self-mortification. When the Buddha gave up that extreme path, Koṇḍañña, like the Buddha's other four companions at that time, left him in disgust and wandered off. The Buddha too went off by himself, and eventually gained Enlightenment.

After gaining Enlightenment, the Buddha thought first of sharing his discovery with his old teachers, but realized that they were now dead. He then thought of his old companions, and realized that they were staying at the deer park at Isipatana, in Sarnarth. So he went to them and, as the story goes, although they had determined not to show him any respect, they were quite unable to stop themselves from doing so when he actually arrived. The Buddha then sat down and talked with them.

They talked for an entire rainy season, the Buddha trying to get his old companions to see the truth that he had seen. This was no easy task. He argued and expostulated; they discussed things vigorously. In the end the Buddha broke through and was able to communicate what he had been trying for so long to communicate. The first to realize that truth was this same Koṇḍañña. He was the first among those five to get a glimpse of Enlightenment. The text says that when the Buddha had finished speaking, the pure and stainless Eye of Truth, the *dhammacakkhu*, arose in Koṇḍañña, and he realized that everything that has by nature an origin has also by nature a cessation. In one overwhelming flash of insight, he realized the truth of impermanence.[247]

At this point the text has a very interesting comment: 'Thus was the Wheel of the Dharma set going by the Blessed One'. In other words, it had not really been set going until there was at least one Stream Entrant in the world. Before that the Buddha had been doing his utmost to communicate the Dharma in words, and maybe in other ways too; but he had not actually set the Wheel of the Dharma in motion. The Buddha had not really *taught* until there was one Stream Entrant in the world.

When this happened, when Koṇḍañña had this great insight and the Buddha *saw* that he had had this great insight – that they shared one and the same insight between them – he was overjoyed. No longer would he have to keep his discovery to himself; it was now, to some extent at least, common property. At that moment, we are told, he let forth an *udāna*, an inspired utterance, a song of ecstasy: 'Koṇḍañña has understood! Koṇḍañña has understood!' The Wheel of the Dharma had been set rolling, and even he could not see where it would stop. Henceforth Koṇḍañña was called *Añña* Koṇḍañña, 'Koṇḍañña who has understood'.

It is interesting to note that the text says nothing about any further attainment beyond the opening of the Dharma-Eye. It simply says of Koṇḍañña that having attained the Dharma, having understood the Dharma, having immersed himself in the Dharma, having left uncertainty behind, having escaped from doubt, having attained confidence and not dependent on others in the doctrine of the teacher, he asked for ordination. And this the Buddha granted. We are told the same thing about all four of the remaining ascetics. In their cases the Buddha had a little more difficulty in breaking through, but he managed in the end. In their cases too the Dharma-Eye arose; they too saw that everything that has by nature an origin has also by nature a cessation. They too asked for ordination, and they too were ordained. In all these cases it was the opening of the Dharma-Eye that seems to have been the real turning point.

Let us therefore return to impermanence. Impermanence is all around us. Everything is impermanent; there is nothing that is not. We see the leaves fall and the flowers fade; everything is impermanent. But the most vivid and the most powerful form in which we encounter impermanence is in death, the dissolution of the physical body – especially in the death of someone near and dear to us.

Buddhism offers a number of practices that are intended to remind us of death, to remind us that, inasmuch as the physical body was 'put together', one day it is going to fall apart.

There is, for instance, the six element practice (or at least the first four stages of that six element practice). Here, we reflect that whatever there is in us of the earth element is borrowed from the earth element that exists all around us in the universe. One day we will have to give it back. Similarly with the water element, the fire element, and with the air element: one day we are going to have to give them all back. That process of giving back, willingly or unwillingly, is the process of dissolution of the physical body, or death.

Then there are the ten so-called 'corpse meditations'. Here, you go along to a cremation, or charnel, ground, and see corpses in various stages of decomposition. You then reflect that as they are, so too will you be one day, because you too are subject to death.

Then again, there is the relatively straightforward practice of the simple recollection of death. Here you just remind yourself that one day you will have to die, just as every other human being will have to die.

These practices all serve to remind us that human beings are subject to death: all must one day die. Even the greatest, even the best, even great heroes, must die – their power does not save them. Great artists and poets must die – their art and poetry does not save them. Sometimes these people die premature, even unpleasant, deaths. One thinks of Keats dying of consumption at 25, of Shelley, drowned at 30, one thinks – in Wordsworth's phrase – of 'mighty poets in their misery dead'.[248] One thinks of Spinoza, a great philosopher, again dying of consumption at the age of about 40. They all die sooner or later, prematurely or in the ripeness of their years. Their political greatness, moral greatness, artistic greatness, philosophical greatness cannot save them.

Even the Buddha had to die. The Buddha was Enlightened, but he was an Enlightened *human being*, and every human being must die because every human being was born. Everything that has a beginning must have an end. It may seem strange that a Buddha should have to die, but inasmuch as he is human, or to the extent that he is human, he must die.

The *Mahāparinibbāna Sutta* is the sixteenth *sutta* of the *Dīgha Nikāya* and gives an account of the last few months, and especially the last day – or rather night – of the Buddha's earthly existence. It is a composite work consisting of a number of different episodes and teachings. I would like to investigate four episodes from this *sutta*. These are the episode of the mirror of the Dharma, the episode of the teaching of 'subjective' and 'objective' refuge, the episode of the untimely flowers, and the episode of the last disciple. The first two episodes took place on the road to Kusinārā, and the second two took place at Kusinārā, or rather just outside Kusinārā, in the *sāl* grove of the Mallas – between the twin *sāl* trees.

The episode of the mirror of the Dharma involves Ānanda; in fact, all four episodes involve Ānanda in one way or another, because Ānanda accompanied the Buddha on his last journey and was present at the *parinibbāna* itself.[249] Ānanda emerges from the Pāli scriptures as a vivid and lovable personality. He also seems to have had a very inquisitive mind – as we shall see.

The episode took place at a little place called Nādikā, where the Buddha was staying at the Brick Hall. The Buddha had a large number of disciples in that area, so no sooner had the Buddha and Ānanda settled down than Ānanda went off to visit them. On his return he told the Buddha that a *bhikkhu* and a *bhikkhunī*, as well as quite a number of lay disciples, had all died since their last visit. Having an inquisitive mind, however, Ānanda was not content just to give the Buddha this information; he wanted to know about the *destiny* of those deceased people. Where had they been reborn? Had they even been reborn at all? The Buddha – and one can imagine him heaving a sort of sigh here – tells Ānanda what he wants to know.

It seems that quite a lot of people have died, so the Buddha's account takes rather a long time. When he has finished, he tells Ānanda that it is becoming wearisome to have to go into this sort of thing every time someone dies. He therefore says that he will teach him how to work these things out for himself. He will teach him the mirror of the Dharma.

Although there is much that could be said about the mirror of the Dharma itself, I am actually concerned here with another point – one that arises in connection with this teaching. I am concerned with the number of *lay* disciples in that place who had, according to the Buddha, become 'non-returners', 'once-returners', and 'Stream Entrants'. The Buddha tells Ānanda that the *bhikkhu*, having become an *arhant*, would not be reborn at all; the *bhikkhunī* had become a non-returner; one lay disciple had become a once-returner; one lay disciple had become a Stream Entrant. Then, he says, there were fifty-seven more lay disciples who had become non-returners, more than ninety who had become once-returners, and more than five hundred who had become Stream Entrants – all in one place, and all apparently since the Buddha's last visit.

All this clearly suggests that Stream Entry, at least, is not such a very rare occurrence as is generally supposed. On the strength of this passage alone, we must conclude that Stream Entry is well within the reach of the serious-minded practising Buddhist, whether living as a 'monk' or 'nun', or as a lay person.

Now comes the episode, or teaching, of 'subjective' and 'objective' refuge. The Buddha and his monk-disciples customarily spent eight or nine months of each year wandering from place to place. Then, for the duration of the rainy season, they would settle in one place. On this particular occasion, they stayed for the three months of the rainy season at the village of Beluva.

While they were staying there, perhaps because it was the rainy season, the Buddha became very ill. However, thinking that it would not be right for him to pass away without taking leave of the order, he made a strong effort of will and suppressed his sickness. He had been staying during this time in a vihara, a lodging – probably a little cottage with no more than one room. On his recovery he came outside and sat in the shade, perhaps just enjoying the fresh air and sunshine.

As he sat there, Ānanda came up to him. Ānanda was quite disturbed by the thought of the Buddha's passing away, so the Buddha took advantage of this opportunity to make certain points, and to give him certain exhortations. In the actual words of the scripture, the Buddha said: 'Therefore, in this regard, Ānanda, abide self-reliant (*attadīpā*), taking refuge in yourself, not taking refuge in others, reliant on the Dharma, taking refuge in the Dharma, not taking refuge in another.'[250] This was the Buddha's exhortation.

There seems to be a sort of contradiction here. On the one hand one is being asked to take refuge in oneself – and on the other hand one is being asked to take refuge in the Dharma. On the one hand there is what I call 'subjective refuge', and on the other there is what I call 'objective refuge'.

Unfortunately, the passage which immediately follows does not help us very much. Here the Buddha simply says that one takes refuge in the self *and* in the Dharma by the practice of the four foundations of mindfulness, the four *satipaṭṭhānas*: mindfulness of the physical body, mindfulness of sensations, mindfulness of thoughts, and mindfulness of *dhammas* (*dhammas* here meaning mental objects, doctrinal categories, or realities). In this way, apparently, the subjective and objective refuges are to be reconciled.

But, to go a little further than this, we could say that 'subjective refuge' represents thinking of the spiritual life in terms of personal – or individual – development, while 'objective refuge' represents thinking of the spiritual life in terms of devotion to a supremely worthwhile *object*. Actually, we have to have both, and we have to hold them in balance.

In our own movement that balance is possibly tilted in favour of the subjective refuge – though I think that this has started to change. We tend to think in terms of something being good for one's own personal spiritual development, in a rather 'precious' sort of way. We tend, perhaps, to ignore the needs of the objective situation. One hears, for instance, of people not attending some business meetings because they don't feel in an 'organizational mood' that morning. Going to the meeting, they seem to think, would be detrimental to their spiritual development. However, as I have said, this has started changing, and people's approach is beginning to be rather more balanced. More weight is being given to the needs of the objective situation, more weight is being given to the Buddhas and bodhisattvas, more weight is being given to other people.

Thirdly, we have the episode of the 'untimely flowers'. This episode took place in the *sāl* grove near Kusinārā, and it took place, as did the succeeding episode, between the twin *sāl* trees. Let us try to visualize the scene.

The Mallas, the tribal people in whose territory Kusinārā was situated, had planted two parallel rows of *sāl* trees, running from east to west. At the eastern end of the two rows, between the last two trees, was a kind of platform which was apparently used for meetings. The Buddha lay down upon this with his head to the north and his feet to the south. Lying down, as he usually did, on his right side, his head to the north and his feet to the south, he would have been facing west, looking right down the great avenue of *sāl* trees. Had you been walking up this avenue, you would have seen the Buddha lying between the last two *sāl* trees right at the very end – a very impressive sight.

We should perhaps note that the Buddha passed away in the open air. According to tradition the Buddha was also born in the open air, gained Enlightenment in open air, and often taught in the open air. In other words, he lived very close to nature throughout his life.

While the Buddha was lying between the twin *sāl* trees, something strange happened. The Buddha himself drew Ānanda's attention to it. The text says:

Then said the Exalted One to the venerable Ānanda:

'See, Ānanda! All abloom are the twin *sāl* trees: with untimely blossoms do they shower down on the body of the Tathāgata, they sprinkle it, cover it up, in worship of the Tathāgata. Moreover, heavenly frankincense comes falling from the sky, showers down upon the body of the Tathāgata, sprinkles it and covers it up, in worship of the Tathāgata. And heavenly music sounds in the sky, in worship of the Tathāgata, and heavenly songs are wafted from the sky in worship of the Tathāgata.

'Yet not thus is the Tathāgata truly honoured, revered, respected, worshipped, and deferred to. Whosoever, Ānanda, be he brother or sister, or lay-brother or lay-sister – whosoever dwells in the fulfilment of the Dhamma, both in its greater and in its lesser duties – whosoever walks uprightly in accordance with the Dhamma – he it is that truly honours, reveres, respects, worships, and defers to the Tathāgata in the perfection of worship.'[251]

Although the heart of the matter seems to be that true worship of the Buddha consists in the practice of his teaching, there is danger of a misunderstanding. The passage seems to fit in very neatly with our Western, rationalistic way of thinking, our rationalistic presuppositions. The passage might seem to be saying that the offering of flowers, lights, and candles is unnecessary. But this is not what the passage is saying at all.

It is true that the offering of flowers and so on is by no means any substitute for the actual practice of the Buddha's teaching: the practice of morality (*śīla*), the practice of meditation (*samādhi*), and the practice of wisdom (*prajñā*). But this does not mean that we should not offer those flowers. Offering flowers is an expression of devotion and thus *strengthens* devotion. If we do not feel any devotion then we will probably not practise the teaching.

We must also remember whom the Buddha was addressing. Ānanda seems to have been an emotional rather than intellectual type of person. Perhaps he was sometimes carried away by his feelings and needed to be reminded that feelings, even devotional feelings, were not everything.

Our position in the modern West is quite different. Many of us find it quite easy to *understand* the Dharma; we even find it easy to practise it up to a point. But we find it very difficult to experience strong devotional feelings. Some of us hardly know what devotional feelings are – they are just things we hear or read about! As a consequence, sooner or later, our spiritual life comes to a halt, or at least stagnates very badly. Unlike Ānanda, and unlike those *sāl* trees, we actually need to offer all the flowers we can, even great armfuls of them. We should certainly not take this passage as condoning a purely rationalistic attitude to spiritual life.

Finally, we have the episode of 'the last disciple'. The name of this last person to be 'converted' by the Buddha himself was Subhadda. Subhadda was a wanderer, a *parivrājaka*, and just happened to be in the vicinity of Kusinārā when he heard that the Buddha was about to pass away. Thinking that he should not miss such an opportunity, he came to where the Buddha was staying.

Ānanda, not wishing the Buddha to be disturbed at such a time, would not allow him to get close enough to the Buddha to speak with him. Overhearing their conversation, however, the Buddha asked Ānanda to let Subhadda approach, and the Buddha and Subhadda entered into conversation. The Buddha taught, and Subhadda was, as we might say, 'converted'. Being converted, he went for Refuge, asked for ordination.[252]

Here we are concerned with just one point, a point not actually mentioned in the text itself, but in Buddhaghosa's commentary to the *sutta*. The text speaks of the Buddha granting Subhadda's request for ordination by telling Ānanda: 'Ordain him'. The commentary then tells us exactly how this was done: what Ānanda did, and what the Buddha did on that occasion. This is very important, because it is clearly based on a very ancient tradition. Here is the passage:

> The Thera (Ānanda), they say, took him (Subhadda) on one side, poured water over his head from a water vessel, made him repeat the formula of meditation on the impermanency of the body, shaved off his hair and beard, clad him in the yellow robes, made him repeat the Three Refuges, and led him back to the Exalted One. The Exalted One himself admitted him then into the higher rank of the brotherhood, and pointed out to him a subject for meditation.[253]

This is particularly interesting because there is a distinct parallel with our own ordination procedure in the Western Buddhist Order. According to Buddhaghosa, Subhadda is first made to go for Refuge, then he is given a meditation subject, his hair and beard are shaved, water is poured over his head, he is clad in yellow robes, and, finally, he is accepted into the ranks of the sangha. All of these elements, except one, are found in our own private and public ordination ceremonies.

First of all, there is the Going for Refuge. This is found in both the private ceremony and the public ceremony. Then there is the giving of a subject for meditation; this is found in the private ordination ceremony when one is given a visualization and mantra recitation practice. Thirdly, comes the shaving of hair and beard. This is not found in the case of the Western Buddhist Order (though some men do sometimes have a very close crop just before ordination). Then comes the pouring of the water; that is found in our public ordination ceremony. Fifthly, being clad in yellow robes corresponds to the investiture with the *kesa* found in the public ordination ceremony. Sixthly and lastly, of course, one's reception into the ranks of the sangha occurs in the course of the public ordination ceremony.

There is thus only one item that is not found in our own ordination procedure, and just one item in our own ordination procedure which is not present in Subhadda's case: the giving of a new name.

All this is quite significant in view of the fact that, in the FWBO and in the WBO, we try to go back to the origins of things, try to base ourselves on what is fundamental in the Buddhist tradition. It is of further interest that T. W. Rhys Davids, the translator of the *Dīgha Nikāya*, has a judicious note on this commentarial passage:

> According to this, no set ceremony for ordination
> (*Saṅghakammaṃ*), as laid down in the Vinaya [which of course
> developed some time later], took place; and it is otherwise
> probable that no such ceremony was usual in the earliest days of
> Buddhism.[254]

The implications of this statement demand to be very well pondered indeed.

The day on which we commemorate the 'great passing away', or *parinirvāṇa*, of the Buddha, is one of the major Buddhist festivals of the year. In recent years, however, I do not believe that we in the FWBO have paid as much attention to this occasion as perhaps we could have done. I would therefore like to conclude this talk by making a few suggestions as to how the day might be marked.

Firstly, if at all possible, we should observe Parinirvāṇa Day throughout the day. We should read the *Mahāparinibbāna Sutta* aloud in the shrine-room, and chant the Vajrasattva mantra. It is perhaps not necessary to read through the *Mahāparinibbāna Sutta* in its entirety on this occasion; one could read only those sections that have a direct bearing on the events leading up to the *parinirvāṇa* itself.

The chanting of the Vajrasattva mantra could be performed at intervals throughout the day. But why the hundred syllable mantra of Vajrasattva? Why not the mantra of Tārā, or Mañjuśrī, or Vajrapāṇi, or Padmasambhava? The answer is quite simple. Vajrasattva is connected with death. The manner in which I first discovered this takes me back to 1958 or 1959, when I was living in Kalimpong.

On one occasion I went up to Gangtok, the capital of Sikkim, to see Jamyang Khyentse Rimpoche, who was one of my Tibetan teachers. He was staying at the Palace Temple, on the outskirts of Gangtok. Upon arriving I was ushered into an antechamber and asked to wait for about half an hour. When I was ushered into his presence he received me, as always, in a very kindly and fatherly sort of way, and apologised for having kept me waiting – adding, by way of explanation, that he had been performing the Vajrasattva puja and recitation of the Vajrasattva mantra on behalf of a lama friend who had just died. As he talked a little more about this, I came to understand that Vajrasattva was connected with death.

A few years later, in the winter of 1966–7, I had a rather strange experience in this connection. I was back in Kalimpong, having spent two years in the West. By now I had decided to settle in England, and was in Kalimpong on a farewell visit, staying at my Triyana Vardhana Vihara.

One night I woke up at about two o'clock in the morning. I really did wake up – this was not a dream or a vision. Everything was bright as if I was in daylight. I sat up on my bed and, looking down towards the side of my bed, I saw a great pit in the floor that certainly had not been there the previous evening. I looked down into the pit. Standing there was an old friend – one who had been dead for several years.

The pit must have been just over six feet deep because he was about six feet tall and was completely contained in the pit. For some minutes I just looked. I knew that he was dead, of course. I also knew that something was wrong and that something had to be done. But what? That was when I thought of Jamyang Khyentse Rimpoche and what he had told me about the Vajrasattva mantra.

Sitting up on my bed, I started repeating the Vajrasattva mantra. As I did so, the words of the mantra – in Tibetan characters – came out of my mouth. They came out of my mouth and formed a sort of garland, or chain, which went right down into the pit and then looped back up again – just within reach of the person in the pit. My friend caught hold of this garland, and so pulled himself out of the pit. He then disappeared.[255]

At that moment I suddenly heard horns being blown just outside. Only then did I remember that it was the night of the new moon and that the Jogis were abroad. The Jogis are a particular caste or sect of the Nepalese, a very strange people. A hereditary duty has been imposed upon them to go around at certain times of the year, on the night of the new moon, to collect the souls of the dead. The Nepalese people keep away from them. Dogs keep away from them too – even the fiercest dog will not touch them. In the morning they come to the houses that they have been clearing of spirits, and you are supposed to give them a little raw rice and some money. Most Nepalese people are so afraid they just throw the money and rice to them from a distance and retreat as quickly as they can.

Since that experience I have had a certain amount of faith in the Vajrasattva mantra in this connection. Vajrasattva is associated not only with death, but with 'hell' – not hell in the Christian sense, of course, but in the sense of lower states of temporary suffering. And Vajrasattva is perhaps associated with hell because he is associated with death, at least so far as 'ordinary' people are concerned, people – that is to say – who have not attained Stream Entry.

To return to the observance of Parinirvāṇa Day, the day should be an occasion for remembering not just the Buddha's *parinirvāṇa*, but also other deceased persons, especially Order members, Mitras, and Friends who have died in the course of the previous year or so. We can perhaps place their photographs on the shrine, below images of Buddhas, bodhisattvas, and gurus. Their full names and the dates of their death should be read out either during or before a Sevenfold Puja.[256] We can also commemorate the friends and relations of Order members, Mitras, and Friends. If anybody wants to bring along the photograph, or hand in the name, of anybody near and dear to them who has died, especially during the course of the past year, they should be free to do that.

There are a number of positive reasons for this suggestion. First of all, the significance of the Parinirvāṇa Day itself will be enhanced. Secondly, we will be reminded that everyone dies, whether Enlightened or unenlightened. Thirdly, in the case of deceased Order members especially, we will be reminded that physical death does not interrupt the spiritual connection. The spiritual community, in the broadest sense, consists of both the 'living' and the 'dead'. In this way we shall be helped to transcend the limitations of the physical body, enabled to realize that the spiritual community is not limited by space and time, and that, in a sense, the dead are not really dead. Fourthly, a commemoration of this sort will help bereaved Order members, Mitras, Friends, and others to come to terms with the fact of death, and come to terms with the fact that they have lost, as it seems, someone near and dear to them. Fifthly, commemorating other people who have recently died will help to remind us that, inasmuch as we may be separated from those near and dear to us at any moment, we should compose our quarrels.

One sometimes hears people saying, 'I am so sad, not just that the person has died, but that we could not resolve a certain misunderstanding before they died.' It might have been one's father or mother, one's brother or sister, or a friend, or a fellow Order member or Mitra, but you feel sorry that that breach, that wound, has not been healed and that the person has died without the two of you having been reconciled. Death may come at any time; it does not always give advance warning. So if there is any misunderstanding unresolved, we should settle it immediately.

In ten days' time we shall be observing that anniversary of the Buddha's *parinirvāṇa*. I hope that what I have said here will, among other things, help to make it an even more significant occasion than usual. I hope that it will give us an even deeper insight into the truth of impermanence. I hope it will give an even deeper realization of the inevitability of death. I hope it will enable us to be 'present' with the Buddha on that occasion, between the twin *sāl* trees.

BUDDHISM AND THE WEST

The Integration of Buddhism into Western Society

Fourth International Congress of the European Buddhist Union,
Berlin, 24–27 September 1992.

'The Integration of Buddhism into Western Society' is a very big subject. To begin with, Buddhism is a very big subject in itself, and it would hardly be possible to speak of the integration of Buddhism into Western society, or into anything else, without first explaining what one understood by the term Buddhism. Is Buddhism a religion, or a philosophy, or a system of ethics, or is it something quite different from any of these? Is it, perhaps, something for which there is no word in our modern Western languages? Does Buddhism exist independently of the various Eastern Buddhist cultures in which it is historically embodied, or is it distinguishable and separable from them? In order to be a Buddhist does one have to transform oneself into a Tibetan, or a Japanese, or a Thai, in accordance with the particular sectarian form of Buddhism one wishes to adopt? Then there is the subject of Western society. That too is a very big subject. Society is 'a system of human organizations generating distinctive cultural patterns and institutions and usually providing protection, security, continuity, and a national identity for its members.'[257] As such, society has a cultural, an economic, a legal, and a political dimension, and if one were to speak of the integration of Buddhism into Western society one would have to deal with its integration in respect of each of these dimensions. Finally, there is the subject of integration which, though not as big a subject as either Buddhism or society, is yet big enough. By the integration of Buddhism into Western society does one mean its bodily incorporation into that society, unchanged, and without its bringing about any change in that society, or does one mean its diffusion throughout Western society?

Thus the subject of the integration of Buddhism into Western society is a very big one, but the organizers of this Congress, besides asking me to speak on it, have allotted me some forty-five or fifty minutes in which to do so. Either they underestimated the dimensions of the subject or overestimated my ability to deal with it in the time allotted. It would be pleasant to think that the latter alternative was the case, but if this is so then I am going to have to disappoint our good organizers, and must ask them and you to forgive me. I am quite unable to deal with the subject of 'The Integration of Buddhism into Western Society' systematically in the space of some forty-five or fifty minutes. Therefore I shall deal with it unsystematically, not to say subjectively. I shall deal with it by telling you the story of my own interaction with Western society, after I had spent twenty years in the East, in the hope that this will shed at least some light on the very big subject of 'The Integration of Buddhism into Western Society'.

I left England in 1944, a few days before my nineteenth birthday. By that time I was already a Buddhist, having discovered Buddhism when I was 16 or 17 and having at once realized that I was, in fact, a Buddhist and always had been. In 1943, the fourth year of the War, I was conscripted into the army, despite my having spent much of my childhood as an invalid, and the following year I was posted to India, the land of the Buddha. There followed postings to Ceylon (Sri Lanka) and to Singapore. In 1947, the war having ended, I left the army and spent two years in South India as a freelance wandering ascetic. At the end of that period I received the lower ordination as a Buddhist monk and the following year, 1950, the higher ordination. During the seventeen years from 1947 to 1964 I studied with Indian, Tibetan, and Chinese Buddhist teachers, meditated, and wrote and lectured on the Dharma, all the time remaining in India and leading the simple life of a Buddhist monk and becoming increasingly Indianized.

1964 saw a dramatic change. In that year I returned to England for what was originally intended to be a short visit, and in 1967, having paid a farewell visit to my teachers and disciples in India, I returned to England for good and started a new Buddhist movement, the Friends of the Western Buddhist Order. Thus after twenty years in the East, seventeen of them as a monk, I was interacting with Western society.

That society seemed very strange to me, as it in many ways still does. It was strange to me for two reasons. In the first place, not only had I been leading the simple life of a Buddhist monk; I had also been leading that life within the context of a society with a traditional culture, and Western society was far from having a traditional culture. In the second place, during the twenty years I had been away, Western society had changed, at least English society had changed. Wartime austerity had been replaced by postwar prosperity. There were more cars on the roads, more telephones, refrigerators, and washing machines in people's homes. There were launderettes and supermarkets – neither of which had I seen before. There was television, with enormous aerials sprouting from the thatched roofs of tiny country cottages. Moreover, manners and morals had changed. People spoke differently, dressed differently, and behaved differently – sometimes in ways that before the war would have been considered quite shocking.

This was the society with which I was now interacting. This was the society into which, after my twenty years in the East, I was trying to integrate Buddhism when I started the Friends of the Western Buddhist Order.

The initial point of interaction was meditation. Mind, one could say, started to interact with individual mind. Within weeks of my final return to England I started conducting weekly meditation classes in a tiny basement room in central London, only a few hundred yards from Trafalgar Square. Subsequently I likened this basement room, in which the FWBO began its existence, to the catacombs in which the early Christians took refuge from their persecutors and where they developed their doctrine. In these meditation classes I taught two methods of meditation, the *ānāpānasati* or 'awareness of in-and-out breathing' and the *mettā bhāvanā* or 'development of loving-kindness' (methods now taught throughout the FWBO), and it was not long before people attending the classes began to experience some of the benefits of these practices. Their minds became calmer and clearer and they felt happier. This was only to be expected. Meditation can be defined, at least provisionally, as the raising of the level of consciousness by working directly on the mind itself, or, alternatively, as the gradual replacement of a succession of unwholesome mental states by a succession of wholesome mental states. Howsoever defined, meditation means change, change for the better, in respect of one's mind, or heart, or consciousness.

Thus the integration of Buddhism into Western society involves, to begin with, raising the level of consciousness of at least some of the people who make up that society. The two methods of meditation I have mentioned are able to raise the level of consciousness only temporarily, but there are other methods, also taught in the FWBO, which are able to raise it permanently, or which are able, alternatively, to replace a succession of unwholesome mental states by a succession of wholesome mental states which, since they are imbued with 'clear vision', will never be replaced by a succession of unwholesome mental states.

When I had been conducting my meditation classes for a few months the FWBO held the first of its retreats. Some fifteen or twenty of us spent a week together in a large house in the countryside, fifty miles from London. We spent part of our time meditating, part of it in devotional practices and discussion. Some people had come because they wanted to deepen their experience of meditation, which with varying degrees of success they were able to do. But this was not all. Without exception, those taking part in the retreat found that simply being away from the city, away from their jobs and families, in the company of other Buddhists, and with nothing to think about except the Dharma, was sufficient to raise their level of consciousness quite dramatically.

Here, then, was another point of interaction. The level of consciousness of the people who make up Western society could be raised not only by meditation, or working directly on the mind itself. It could also be raised by changing the conditions under which they lived. It could be raised by changing the environment. It could be raised, at least to some extent, by changing society. The integration of Buddhism into Western society therefore involves changing Western society. Inasmuch as our level of consciousness is affected by external conditions, it is not enough for us to work directly on the mind itself, through meditation, as though it were possible for us to isolate ourselves from society or to ignore the conditions under which we and others live. We must change Western society, and change it in such a way as to make it easier, or at least less difficult, for us to lead lives dedicated to the Dharma within that society. To the extent that Western society has not been changed by Buddhism, it could be said, to that extent Buddhism has not been integrated into Western society. In order to change Western society it will be necessary for us to create Western Buddhist institutions, Western

Buddhist lifestyles. I shall have something to say about some of these institutions in a minute.

At the time I was conducting meditation classes and leading retreats, during the first few years of the FWBO's existence, I was delivering public lectures, both under the auspices of the FWBO and at the invitation of universities and other outside bodies. In these lectures I sought to communicate the fundamental ideas or concepts of Buddhism in a way that was both intelligible to a Western audience *and* faithful to the spirit, and even to the letter, of Buddhist tradition. Here was yet another point of interaction with Western society, this time one that was of a more intellectual character. The integration of Buddhism into Western society involves the introduction of Buddhist ideas into Western intellectual discourse. By Buddhist ideas I do not mean the doctrinal refinements of the Abhidharma or the philosophical subtleties of the Madhyamaka and Yogācāra schools, though these have begun to attract the attention of professional philosophers and theologians in the West. I am speaking of ideas so fundamental that Buddhists themselves often take them for granted and fail to recognize their full significance. Such, for example, is the idea that religion does not necessarily involve belief in God, the creator and ruler of the universe, and that it is quite possible for one to lead an ethical and spiritual life, and to raise the level of one's consciousness, without invoking the aid of any outside, supernatural power.

If Buddhism is to be integrated into Western society, then Buddhist ideas of this fundamental kind, which have been known to strike those previously unacquainted with them with the force of a revelation, will have to become familiar to all educated Europeans and Americans. Moreover, we shall have to establish, wherever possible, connections between Buddhist ideas and concepts of Western origin, as I have done in the case of the Buddhist idea of conditionality, mundane and transcendental, and the Western concept of evolution. We shall have to be able to recognize the Buddhistic nature of some of the insights of Western philosophers, poets, novelists, and dramatists. Goethe, for example, has some interesting comments on self-education and self-transformation – a subject of central importance in Buddhism. The bridge between East and West must be built from both sides.

But to return to Western Buddhist institutions, which we are under the necessity of creating if Western society is to be changed and

Buddhism integrated into that society: when the FWBO had held a few retreats, some of the people who had taken part in them regularly started to feel that they wanted to prolong the experience, at least to an extent. Even if they were not in a position to move to the countryside, or give up their jobs (though some did give them up), they wanted to live with other Buddhists and have more time for thinking about the Dharma and, of course, more time for practising it. In this way there came into existence what came to be called residential spiritual communities. The members of these communities did not just live under the same roof. They meditated together every morning, ate together, studied the Dharma together, encouraged one another in their Buddhist life, and contributed to the maintenance of the physical basis of the community. That was twenty or more years ago. Now the FWBO has scores of residential spiritual communities, in a number of countries.

These communities are of several different kinds. Some are quite small, consisting of only four or five persons, while others are relatively large, consisting of anything up to thirty persons. Most are situated in the city, though a few, including some of the largest, are to be found in rural areas. Some community members have outside jobs, while others work within the FWBO. The most successful, and perhaps most typical kind of FWBO spiritual community, is the single-sex community consisting of either men only or women only. Mixed sex communities, including those containing families, have not worked very well or lasted very long. Some women's communities, however, contain mothers and children, and this arrangement seems to work. Husbands and wives, as well as lovers, sometimes live in separate, single-sex communities.

Thus we change Western society, thereby integrating Buddhism into that society, by creating Western Buddhist institutions, in this case the institution of the residential spiritual community, which to some extent replaces the institution of the nuclear family. The residential spiritual community, as I have described it, is not an Eastern Buddhist institution. In most Buddhist countries society is divided into two mutually exclusive groups, the monastic and the lay, the latter being very much the larger of the two. The FWBO is neither a monastic movement nor a lay movement, and its communities are neither monastic nor lay communities, though some members of some communities are celibate. I shall have more to say about this aspect of the integration of Buddhism into Western society towards the end of this talk.

Another Western Buddhist institution is the team-based right livelihood business, in which the point of interaction with Western society is economic. Some of the people who were living together in FWBO residential spiritual communities, but who had outside jobs, started to feel that they wanted to work together. In some cases this was because their present job was not of a very ethical nature, and Buddhism attaches great importance to what it terms 'right means of livelihood', the fifth step of the Buddha's Noble Eightfold Path. In others, it was because they did not want to spend their working life in the company of people who were hostile or indifferent to Buddhism or whose behaviour they found offensive. Thus there came into existence the first of what came to be called the FWBO's team-based right livelihood businesses. They were 'team-based' because they consisted of a number of Buddhists working together along broadly cooperative lines, and they were 'right livelihood' because they operated in accordance with Buddhist ethical principles. But there was another factor in their genesis. In 1975 the FWBO embarked on the creation of Sukhavati and the London Buddhist Centre in east London, at present the second largest of its urban centres.[258] Huge sums of money were needed. Instead of appealing for help to wealthy Buddhists in the East, as other groups might have done, the FWBO raised the money itself, partly by setting up team-based right livelihood businesses which donated their profits to the project. Such businesses thus came to do four things. They provided those working in them with material support, they enabled Buddhists to work with one another, they conducted themselves in accordance with Buddhist ethical principles, and they gave financial support to Buddhist activities.

Over the years the FWBO has set up a number of team-based right livelihood businesses, not all of which have survived. Existing economic institutions are immensely powerful, and the integration of Buddhism into the economic life of Western society is therefore a task of enormous difficulty. In the early days of the FWBO I once did a radio interview on Buddhism while walking through the streets of the City, the financial centre of London. Pointing to the Bank of England and the Stock Exchange, I remarked, 'This is what we are up against.' Nonetheless, some of our team-based right livelihood businesses have done extremely well. One of them currently 'employs' more than sixty people and has an annual turnover of £2,000,000.[259]

We can now begin to see what the integration of Buddhism into Western society actually involves. There is what we may term psychological integration, consisting of the raising of the level of consciousness of at least some of the people who make up that society. The level of consciousness is raised by meditation, or working directly on the mind itself, as well as by various indirect methods such as hatha yoga and t'ai chi ch'uan which I have not had time to mention. Since the level of consciousness is affected by the conditions under which we live, we have to change those conditions, change Western society, and in order to change Western society we shall have to create Western Buddhist institutions. We shall have to create, for example, residential spiritual communities, representing the integration of Buddhism into Western society in the narrower sense of the term, and team-based right livelihood businesses, representing the integration of Buddhism into the economic life of Western society. We shall have to integrate Buddhism into Western society intellectually by introducing its fundamental ideas into Western intellectual discourse and making them, in fact, familiar to all educated Europeans and Americans. Unless we do these things, and many other things of the same kind, there can be no question of any integration of Buddhism into Western society and all talk of such integration will be just so much hot air. But though I have spoken of the psychological, the social, the economic, and the intellectual integration of Buddhism, there is one kind of integration of which I have not spoken, even though it is the most important of all, in the sense that all the other kinds of integration of Buddhism into Western society depend upon it and cannot, in fact, exist without it. Before going on to speak of this kind of integration, however, and therewith begin thinking of bringing this talk to an end, I want to say a few words about a broader kind of integration of Buddhism into Western society.

This broader kind of integration is the integration of Buddhism into Western *culture*, in the sense of its integration into the whole body of the fine arts, music, and literature. At the beginning of this talk I referred to my returning to England for good in 1967 and founding the FWBO. Earlier this year the FWBO celebrated its twenty-fifth anniversary. The celebrations included the performance of *Carpe Diem*, a Buddhist oratorio by a member of the Western Buddhist Order, and a performance of *A Face Revealed*, a play based on the first four chapters of the *White Lotus Sūtra*, written by another Order member.[260] While it would be premature to pronounce upon the intrinsic merits of these works, they undoubtedly constitute points of interaction between Buddhism on the one hand and Western music and drama on the other. They represent the integration of Buddhism into Western culture. There are other points of interaction. Over the years, members of the Western Buddhist Order and their friends have produced Buddha images and icons which, while faithful to the spirit of Buddhist tradition, show a sensitivity to Western aesthetic values. A similar integration of Buddhism into Western culture seems to be taking place, perhaps more sporadically, within certain North American Buddhist circles.

But now for the kind of integration on which all the other kinds of integration of Buddhism into Western society depend, and about which I have not yet spoken. This most important integration of all is the integration of the individual, that is, of the individual Buddhist. It is the individual Buddhist who meditates, who goes on retreat, who lives in a spiritual community or works in a team-based right livelihood businesses, and who communicates the fundamental ideas of Buddhism. It is the individual Buddhist who paints pictures, composes music, writes plays and poems, and sculpts Buddha images. Without the individual Buddhist there can be no integration of Buddhism into Western society. The idea of such a thing would, indeed, be absurd. But what is a Buddhist?

First of all let me say what a Buddhist is not. A Buddhist is not someone who has simply been born into a Buddhist family, though being born into a Buddhist family obviously does not prevent one from being a Buddhist. A Buddhist is not someone who has made an academic study of Buddhism and has an exhaustive factual knowledge of the history, doctrines, and institutions of Buddhism. Such a person is no more a Buddhist than the director of an art gallery is an artist or, perhaps I should say, than the caretaker of an art gallery is an artist. Similarly, a Buddhist is not someone who merely dabbles in Buddhism, who has a smattering of knowledge about it, who airs purely subjective views on the subject, and who mixes Buddhism up with Christianity, or Vedānta, or New Ageism, or what not. What, then, is a Buddhist? A Buddhist is someone who goes for Refuge to the Buddha, the Dharma, and the Sangha, and who, as an expression and as a reinforcement of that Going for Refuge, seeks to observe the ethical precepts of Buddhism.

Going for Refuge to the Buddha means accepting the Buddha, and no other, as one's ultimate spiritual guide and exemplar. Going for Refuge to the Dharma means doing one's utmost to understand, practise, and realize the fundamental import of the Buddha's teaching. Going for Refuge to the Sangha means looking for inspiration and guidance to those followers of the Buddha, both past and present, who are spiritually more advanced than oneself. The ethical precepts that one observes as an expression and as a reinforcement of that threefold Going for Refuge are the precept of reverence for life, the precept of generosity, the precept of contentment, and the precepts of truthful, gracious, helpful and harmonious speech, and so on. The word 'refuge', which is the literal translation of the original Indic term, is liable to be misunderstood. It does not have connotations of running away, or of seeking to escape, from the harsh realities of life through losing oneself in pseudo-spiritual fantasies. Rather does it represent (1) the whole-hearted recognition of the fact that permanence, identity, unalloyed bliss, and pure beauty are not to be found anywhere in mundane existence, but only in the transcendental nirvāṇic realm, and (2) the wholehearted resolve to make the great transition from the one to the other.

Such is the Buddhist. Such is the individual without whom there can be no integration of Buddhism into Western society. But the individual, the individual Buddhist, does not go for Refuge to the Buddha, the Dharma, and the Sangha alone or in isolation. He or she goes for Refuge in the company of other individuals who also go for Refuge. He or she is a member of the sangha or spiritual community in the wider sense, and it is this sangha, and not so much the individual Buddhist alone or in isolation, that raises the level of consciousness of people living in Western society, changes that society by creating Western Buddhist institutions, introduces the fundamental ideas of Buddhism into Western intellectual discourse, and interacts with Western fine arts, music, and literature. It is this wider spiritual community that effects the psychological, social, economic, and cultural integration of Buddhism into Western society.

This brings me back to the aspect of the integration of Buddhism into Western society to which I referred earlier on, when I spoke of the FWBO as being neither a monastic movement nor a lay movement. It also brings me very nearly to the end of this talk. At the time that I started the FWBO a Buddhist movement had been in existence in Britain for about fifty years. It was a very small movement, and one of the reasons for its smallness was that it was to a great extent controlled by people who, though sympathetic to Buddhism, were not actually Buddhists, and who could not bring to the work of making known the Dharma the energy and conviction of Buddhists. A year after starting the FWBO I therefore founded not another Buddhist society but a spiritual community, a sangha, an order. I founded the Western Buddhist Order or WBO, all the members of which are Buddhists, in that they all go for Refuge to the Buddha, the Dharma, and the Sangha, and undertake to observe the ten fundamental precepts of ethical behaviour. It is this Order that directs FWBO activities and institutions in more than a dozen countries, including Germany, and which I believe offers a paradigm for the integration of Buddhism into Western society. Without such an Order, their common membership of which enables individual Buddhists to cooperate on the closest terms, there can be no integration of Buddhism into Western society such as I have described. It is therefore good to know that membership of the European Buddhist Union, which together with the German Buddhist Union has organized this Congress, is open only to *bona fide* Buddhist organizations whose membership is predominantly Buddhist and whose council or board is under the control of professed Buddhists. This is a move in the right direction and one that augurs well for the future of Buddhism in Europe.

But while there can be no integration of Buddhism into Western society without an order, equally that order itself must be an integrated order in the sense of being without serious internal divisions, that is, divisions between Buddhists of different kinds. It must be a unified order. The Western Buddhist Order is a unified order in three important respects. Firstly, it is an order of Buddhists, that is, of individuals who go for Refuge to the Buddha, the Dharma, and the Sangha, and who undertake to observe the ten ethical precepts. It is neither a monastic order nor a lay order, which is why the FWBO is neither a monastic movement nor a lay movement. In the WBO and FWBO, commitment, in the sense of Going for Refuge, is primary, and lifestyle, in the sense of living more as a monk or nun or more as a layman or laywoman, is secondary. This does not mean that lifestyle is unimportant but only that it is less important than commitment or Going for Refuge, the latter being the central or definitive act of the Buddhist life and as such the fundamental basis of unity and union among Buddhists. Secondly, the Western Buddhist Order is an order of both men and women, who are admitted on equal terms. Men and women receive the same ordination, engage in the same spiritual practices, and undertake the same organizational responsibilities. Thirdly and lastly, the Western Buddhist Order is not a sectarian order, in that it does not identify itself with any one form of Buddhism. Instead, it rejoices in the riches of the whole Buddhist tradition and seeks to draw from those riches whatever is of value for its own practice of the Dharma here in the West. Thus the Western Buddhist Order is a unified order, an integrated order, and it is because it is an integrated order that it has been able to make its contribution to the integration of Buddhism into Western society and, indeed, to offer a paradigm for that integration.

As I observed at the beginning of this talk, 'The Integration of Buddhism into Western Society' is a very big subject, and I hope that by telling you the story of my own – and the FWBO's – interaction with Western society I have been able to shed at least some light on it. This Congress is being held in Berlin, and I am addressing you not far from the area which, three years ago, saw the dismantling of a notorious symbol of disunion and disintegration. Happily East and West Berlin, and East and West Germany, are now unified or, as we may say, integrated. We, the Buddhists of Europe and America, are concerned with a different kind of integration – the integration of Buddhism into Western society. Let us therefore do away with our divisions. Let us do away with the divisions between monastic and lay Buddhists, between men and women Buddhists, and between the followers of different sects and schools of Buddhism. Let us have an integrated Buddhism and an integrated Buddhist community. Let us base ourselves firmly and unmistakably upon our common Going for Refuge to the Buddha, the Dharma, and the Sangha.

One last word. I have spoken on the integration of Buddhism into Western society because that is what I was asked to speak on. But as my talk proceeded it will have become obvious to you that what we really have to do is integrate Western society into Buddhism. There is much in Western society that needs changing. Buddhism can help us change it. May this Congress be a step in that direction.

PART II
ARTICLES, INTERVIEWS, AND TALKS
1965–2005

Sangharakshita at his desk at Padmaloka. 1970s

THE BUDDHIST

The Buddhist *was the journal of the English Sangha Association.*
Sangharakshita took over the editing of the magazine, then called
Sangha, *in September 1964. The name was changed to* The
Buddhist *for the January 1965 issue (vol. 9, no. 1). Sangharakshita*
explained that there was a 'need for a title that will be immediately
comprehensible to those knowing little, if anything, about Buddhism.'
(p. 3). Editorship passed to Maurice Walshe in 1966 prior to
Sangharakshita's return to India for his farewell tour in 1967.

Buddhist Society Summer School at High Leigh in Essex, England, 1964. (L–R) John Blofeld, Dr Malalasekara (Sri Lanka High Commissioner), Stella Coe, Sangharakshita, Bhikkhu Piyadassi, Trungpa Rimpoche, and a Sinhalese bhikkhu, 1964

SANGHA AND LAITY

The Buddhist, *February 1965, p. 29.*

The Buddhist community consists of four groups or sections: *bhikṣus* or 'monks', *bhikṣunīs* or 'nuns', *upāsakas* or male lay disciples, and *upāsikās* or female lay disciples. In the early days of the Buddhist movement in this country only the third and fourth groups were represented, visits by members of the sangha being, as those of angels are said to be, 'short and far between'.[261] Gradually, however, the situation has changed, and now, fifty-seven years after the return of the first fully ordained British *bhikṣu* to the land of his birth, the beginnings of a permanently resident native-born sangha are beginning to be discerned.[262] Despite the fact that the second constituent of the Buddhist community, the *bhikṣunīs* or nuns, is as yet unrepresented, it would seem time to remind ourselves what the respective duties of the sangha and the laity are and what the relations between them should be.

Let it first of all be observed that, to the extent that they too have gone for Refuge to the Buddha, the Dharma, and the Sangha, the laity are as much Buddhists as are the members of the monastic order and that the two sets of groups together form one great spiritual family. At the same time there is a difference in the degree of commitment and, therefore, a difference of duties. William James has remarked that everybody has religious experiences but that the religious man is one who makes them the centre of his existence.[263] Similarly all Buddhists aim at Enlightenment; but whereas the monk devotes *all* his energies to its attainment, the lay disciple devotes only as much of them as he can spare from secular activities.

The duties of the monk are traditionally three in number, consisting of the study, practice, and dissemination of the Buddha's teaching, while those of the lay disciple are two, consisting of the giving of material support to the sangha and fulfilling at least the basic ethical requirements of the Buddhist way of life. Sangha and laity are therefore mutually dependent. The monk, out of compassion, shares his deeper knowledge and experience of the Dharma with the layman; the layman, out of gratitude, shares with the monk his material resources. Mutual respect and love are therefore consolidated.

At this stage of the development of the Buddhist movement in England it is unlikely that the traditional pattern of sangha–laity relations will be perpetuated in the extreme form that it has taken in some parts of the Buddhist world, which is perhaps undesirable even if it were possible. The few *bhikṣus* present in this country have, inevitably, to be more deeply involved in organizational problems than they might care to be, while the laity – as witness the newly formed speakers' class – are obliged to take a more active part in the propagation of the Dharma than they might really feel qualified for. Nevertheless, if without confusing their distinctive functions this development helps to bring sangha and laity closer together, and strengthens their common devotion to the Three Jewels, it will be fully justified.

THE FIVE SPIRITUAL FACULTIES[264]

The Buddhist, *March 1965, pp. 57–9.*

One of the most important aspects of the Middle Way, in the following of which the practice of Buddhism consists, is the attainment of a state of perfect mental and spiritual equilibrium, harmony, and balance. This state is traditionally described in terms of the 'evenness' (*samatha*) of the five spiritual faculties (*indriyas*) of faith (*śraddhā*), wisdom (*prajñā*), vigour (*vīrya*), concentration (*samādhi*), and mindfulness (*smṛti*).

The first pair of faculties, faith and wisdom, represent respectively the emotional and devotional and the cognitive and gnostic aspects of the spiritual life, which must be equally well developed. If faith is developed one-sidedly, to the detriment of wisdom, it becomes 'blind faith', narrow, dogmatic, bigoted, and intolerant, such as one only too often encounters among the followers of the theistic religions. On the other hand, if wisdom is cultivated at the expense of faith, it hardens into the cold and lifeless intellectualism common in Western academic circles. Wisdom must therefore illumine faith, and faith vivify wisdom.

The second pair of faculties, vigour and concentration, may be regarded as representing the extravert and the introvert tendencies of the human psyche. Unless balanced by concentration, in the more technical Buddhist sense of an experience of higher levels of awareness, vigour degenerates into restlessness and one's energies are dissipated in a multiplicity of directions. Divorced from vigour, concentration lapses into a passive, dreamlike state of self-preoccupation.

Mindfulness, the fifth of the spiritual faculties, requires no counter-poise, being by its very nature incapable of extreme development. In the words of the Buddha, 'Mindfulness is always useful.'[265] As not always is the case with other good things, one cannot have too much of it. It is, in fact, the regulative principle, by the presence of which balance and harmony are maintained between the devotional and the cognitive, the introvert and the extravert, aspects of the Buddhist life.

So much is a commonplace of the Buddha's teaching in all schools. What is less generally realized is that there should be an 'equilibrium of the faculties' not only in the spiritual life of the individual Buddhist but in the activities of Buddhist groups as well. Some at least of the difficulties that beset the Buddhist movement in this country, for instance, are in part attributable to the fact that, in certain cases, one or another of the spiritual faculties has been stressed to the virtual exclusion of its complementary principle.

A balanced and harmonious Buddhist movement, whether in this country or in any other part of the world, should make provision for activities conducive to the development of *all* the faculties. *Faith* is developed by the ceremonial taking of the Three Refuges and Five Precepts, by congregational worship of the Buddha, by celebrating Buddhist festivals such as the Vaiśākha Pūrṇimā or full-moon day of May, by treating with reverence the Buddha image, the sacred scriptures, and the members of the Order, as well as by rendering personal service to one's spiritual teacher. *Wisdom* is developed through lectures and classes, study groups and discussion. The faculty of *vigour* is stimulated by various forms of 'social service', undertaken not only from humanitarian motives but as a means to Enlightenment. These include doing odd jobs at the vihara (cooking, cleaning, gardening, repair and maintenance work), visiting the old, the sick, and the infirm, raising funds for refugees and other deserving causes, and helping out with the routine administrative chores which, in most organizations, are left in the hands of the devoted and overworked few. The cultivation of *concentration* is provided for by meditation classes, as well as by longer or shorter periods of retreat at a meditation centre.

No separate activities are prescribed for the development of the remaining faculty. 'Always useful' as it is, *mindfulness* is developed by truly mindful participation in *all* Buddhist activities, whether those connected with faith, wisdom, vigour, or concentration.

An individual in whom the five spiritual faculties are harmoniously developed is sure of progressing along the Middle Way. A Buddhist movement in which the corresponding types of activity are properly balanced will continue to consolidate itself and expand.

THE SPIRIT AND THE LETTER

The Buddhist, *April 1965, pp. 85–7.*

The distinction between the spirit and the letter of a religious teaching is well known, and well known, too, is the fact that the letter may sometimes be cultivated at the expense of the spirit or even mistaken for it altogether. Such a confusion can occur with regard to any aspect of the teaching concerned, or, in the case of one consisting of successive stages, at any stage.

The teaching of the Buddha is a path leading to Supreme Enlightenment, a state of direct experience of Reality. As this path consists of the stages of *śīla* or moral observance, *samādhi* or concentration and meditation, and *prajñā* or transcendental wisdom, within which are included all the doctrines and practices of Buddhism without exception, the confusion to which we have alluded can occur, so far as this teaching is concerned, with regard to any one of these three great divisions of the spiritual life.

While the spirit of *śīla* is to be found in kindly, generous, contented, honest, and mindful conduct, its letter consists in observing the five negative rules of ethical behaviour: abstention from violence, from taking what is not given, from sexual misconduct, from false speech, and from indulgence in intoxicants. Confusion between the two arises when the rules are observed scrupulously but without the cultivation of their positive counterparts or in such a way as to circumvent the purpose for which they are prescribed. Thus one may make a statement which, though factually correct, one knows to be misleading, or one may remain technically guiltless of the offence of taking life while in reality participating in it through one's wilful addiction to flesh diet.

At the level of *samādhi* the spirit of the teaching consists in an experience of psychical wholeness wherein, abstracted from sensuous impressions and discursive thought, consciousness abides in a state of absolute purity, blissful and serene. By the letter is meant the practice of concentration exercises such as mindfulness of breathing, repetition of the mantra or sacred formula, and the cultivation of love towards all sentient beings. Here the mistake consists in reducing concentration and meditation to the practice of concentration exercises, as well as in thinking that success can be achieved without any moral or spiritual preparation, merely by the forcible application of a technique, and even in the absence of any genuinely religious aspiration. Closely connected with this misunderstanding is the idea that the teaching of meditation means the imparting of a technique and that no spiritual qualifications on the part of the teacher, and no spiritual link between him and his pupil, are required.

The spirit of *prajñā* consists in non-conceptual insight into the Unconditioned, its letter in the doctrinal formulations in which that insight finds conceptual expression. Among these formulations are the three characteristics of existence: *duḥkha* or unsatisfactoriness, *anitya* or impermanence, and *anātman* or insubstantiality, the four kinds of *śūnyatā* or emptiness, and so on. At this stage of the path confusion arises between the spirit and the letter of the teaching when one thinks that, because one has intellectually understood the doctrinal formulations, one has developed wisdom. In other words book knowledge is mistaken for transcendental insight.

While it is true that spirit must be distinguished from letter at every stage, to conclude therefrom that the letter is dispensable would be to commit a mistake no less gross than confusing the two. The path to Enlightenment is a middle path, and such at every stage and in every respect. Though the letter of the teaching is ultimately meaningless without the spirit, the spirit can be realized only with the support of the letter. Rigid adherence to the letter is one extreme; premature rejection of it the other. Remembering that the Buddha taught the Dharma under the figure of a raft,[266] the wise and skilful Buddhist, realizing the spirit with the help of the letter at every stage, follows the middle path and nears Enlightenment.

THE BUDDHA'S ENLIGHTENMENT

The Buddhist, *May 1965, pp. 109–11.*

The historical fact of the Buddha's Enlightenment beneath the bodhi tree at Bodh Gaya is the alpha and omega, the beginning and the end, of the entire system of Buddhism.

It is the beginning inasmuch as the Dharma taught by the Buddha is not the product of mere unillumined mental activity, a philosophical system in the mundane sense of the term, to be accepted or rejected at will, but a transcription into conceptual symbols of his own truly ineffable inner experience of Reality. Nor was this transcription made with the slightest intention of gratifying idle, albeit philosophically camouflaged, curiosity, but with the sole object of affording adequate practical guidance to whoso, possessed of faith, were desirous of treading in the footsteps of the Buddha and obtaining Enlightenment for themselves even as he had obtained it for himself.

It is in this sense that Enlightenment is to be regarded as the end, the final term, of the Buddha-Dharma. We take refuge in the Buddha, believing that he himself was fully Enlightened; in the Dharma, with the conviction that, as the expression of his Enlightenment in conceptual terms, it is capable of guiding us thereto; and in the sangha, confident that as the living embodiment of the tradition they are capable of expounding it theoretically by their teachings and exemplifying it practically in their lives.

It therefore follows that any attempt to elucidate Buddhist doctrines that is not based upon the full acceptance of the root reality of the

Buddha's Enlightenment, with all the momentous consequences that stem therefrom, is wholly unacceptable to a believing and practising Buddhist and, moreover, foredoomed from the beginning to miserable failure, leaving out, as it does, the one supreme and all-explaining fact whence the whole system issues and into which it finally returns.

From this fatal omission arises the whole sticky web of 'contradictions' and 'difficulties' which the profane, academic mind delights to elaborate, spider-like, from the abysm of its own learned ignorance, and wherein the unwary student becomes speedily entrapped. The Buddha was not an agnostic, a social reformer, a humanitarian, nor anything else to be adequately described by attaching to it any such fashionable label, but simply a man who had, by his own efforts, become the Buddha, the Enlightened One.

Those who are for any reason unable to accept him as such had better leave him and his religion strictly alone, since however 'learned' they may be they will never be able to understand more than the superficialities of either. A Sinhalese peasant or a Tibetan muleteer has a better chance of comprehension than they, for the feet of the devotee are on the path, however short the distance they have traversed, and their eyes have caught a glimpse of the Goal, from however far away they may have beheld the beam of its splendour.

The academic approach to Buddhism is not simply neutral with regard to the possibility of Enlightenment, despite all its protestations of objectivity and impartiality, but, in fact, definitely hostile to it, since what it really endeavours to do is to judge the wisdom of the Buddha in accordance with the perverted standards of its own unillumined and deluded mentality, thereby seeking to subordinate knowledge to ignorance and striving to drag egolessness down to the level of egoism.

We are not to shape Buddhism in accordance with our understanding of it, but to mould our understanding in accordance with Buddhism. Otherwise, instead of taking refuge in the Buddha, the Dharma, and the Sangha, we should be expecting them to take refuge in us! Such is the difference between the attitude of the devout, however unscholarly, and that of the undevout, however scholarly.

Such an inversion of the legitimate hierarchy of things, wherein Enlightenment occupies the topmost position, and wherein all other varieties of knowledge and experience are ranged in higher or lower degrees in accordance with the extent to which they conduce or do not conduce to its attainment, is characteristic of the present age, when things sacred are subordinated to things profane, and when the worldling, with all his ignorance and desires, dares to sit in judgement on the wisdom of Buddhas and bodhisattvas.

BUDDHISM IN ENGLAND[267]

The Buddhist, *June 1965, pp. 141–3.*

Though Buddhism has been known in this country for a hundred years or more, its introduction may be said to date from 1908, when the English elder Ananda Metteyya (Allan Bennett) arrived at the head of the first Buddhist mission to England.[268] The event was unique in several respects. For one thing, whereas in the case of all the Asian Buddhist lands it was foreign monk-missioners who were responsible for the full-scale introduction of the Dharma (Mahinda in Ceylon, Kāśyapa Mātaṅga in China, Padmasambhava and Śāntarakṣita in Tibet, etc.), in the case of England it was introduced by an Englishman who had gone to the East with the sole idea of undergoing the training necessary for the purpose, and who possessed, moreover, a clear understanding of the historical and spiritual significance of what he was doing. Thus the English can almost be said to have converted themselves to Buddhism. This circumstance may partly account for the fact that English Buddhism, while willing – indeed eager – to learn from all available Eastern Buddhist spiritual and cultural traditions, has increasingly tended to be a sturdily independent growth with an attitude and outlook of its own.

This is particularly true with regard to the vexed question of the different, sometimes rival, claims of various schools of Buddhism. In the course of the fifty-seven years that have passed since the landing of Ananda Metteyya's mission we have not only witnessed the introduction of the Theravāda as a living tradition and the laying of the foundations of an indigenous Chan/Zen movement, but also had our first direct contact with Tibetan Buddhism, besides hearing something of Shin. From all these forms of Buddhism the English Buddhist feels he has much to learn. True, he may, and indeed often does, specialize in one or another of them, the one to which he feels most strongly drawn, but his loyalties are not exclusive, and occasional lapses from grace apart he refuses to carry with him over into Buddhism the narrow sectarianism which disgusted him in Christianity and which was, perhaps, one of the main reasons for his abandoning that religion.

Such liberal-mindedness may disappoint, even irritate, those Eastern Buddhists who, failing to understand both the spirit of Buddhism and the realities of the current situation, would like to see their own school of Buddhism and their own version of the Dharma established in the West to the exclusion of all others; but for the English Buddhist, with his wider (sometimes deeper) knowledge of the Buddha's teaching, and his greater objectivity, no other attitude than one of liberal-mindedness is possible.

A similar outlook of independence is discernible in connection with the various national cultures with which, in the East, Buddhism is associated and with which it sometimes tends to be identified. The English Buddhist has, most often, been attracted to Buddhism on account of the spiritual principles of which it is the embodiment – principles which he tries, with varying degrees of success, to put into practice in his own life. He is much less interested in the various national cultures wherein, throughout the various traditionally Buddhist countries of the East, these principles are embedded. Generally he tends to believe that, as the Dharma becomes acclimatized in this country, it will tend more and more to express itself, through the mouths of its qualified native exponents, in terms of the best indigenous thought and culture. English Buddhism, he hopes, far from remaining a frail transplant carefully sheltered from the chill northern blast in some secluded pseudo-oriental hothouse, will in time develop into a sturdy and vigorous growth true both to its own high spiritual ancestry and the conditions under which it has now to live and propagate its kind. Almost the last thing English Buddhists want Buddhism in this country to be is a feeble replica of any of its Eastern prototypes, however admirable these might have been in their own time and place and however inspiring and instructive now as examples.

Time will no doubt show (and the next few decades will probably be decisive in this respect) that the Buddhists of this country, drawing upon the streams of all available Buddhist traditions, and resolving their differences at the highest attainable level of spiritual experience, are capable of creating a form of Buddhism which, finding comprehensive expression in terms of the best of Western thought and culture, will be able to meet the deepest needs of Western man.

THE SIGNIFICANCE OF VAIŚĀKHA

The Buddhist, *May 1966, pp. 157–9.*

The festival of the full-moon day of the Indian month Vaiśākha, commemorating the Enlightenment of the Indian prince who became the Buddha, is the principal event of the entire Buddhist year. Being like the Christian Easter a lunar festival, its date varies from year to year, and this year it falls on Wednesday 4 May. In India the great festival is nowadays popularly known as 'Buddha Jayanti', the word *jayanti* being used in the sense of a joyous 'victory' celebration, and as the Vaiśākha Pūrṇimā or full-moon day of Vaiśākha. Elsewhere in the Buddhist world other terms are in use. In Tibet, for example, it is referred to as 'Saga Dawa', i.e. Śākya Pūrṇimā or the full-moon day of the Buddha Śākyamuni, and in Ceylon as Wesak, a Sinhalese corruption of Vesākha, the Pāli equivalent of Vaiśākha. Though these differences of nomenclature have created a certain amount of confusion, not to say uncertainty, it can be affirmed quite categorically that what we all celebrated on 4 May was the anniversary of the Buddha's Enlightenment, whether known as Vaiśākha or by any other name. Some Buddhists believe that, by an extraordinary coincidence, the Buddha was born, gained Enlightenment, *and* passed away on the full-moon day of the month Vaiśākha – in different years of course. This is, however, a comparatively recent Sinhalese innovation and is not borne out by the evidence of the Pāli canon. According to the ancient Indian tradition, the festival of Vaiśākha commemorates the Buddha's Enlightenment, and his Enlightenment only.

It is on the Enlightenment, therefore, that we must reflect and meditate in order to understand the significance of Vaiśākha. By Enlightenment, or Perfect Enlightenment, or Great Enlightenment (*bodhi, sambodhi, mahābodhi*), as it is variously termed, of the Buddha, is meant his complete emancipation from all subjective conditioning, whether intellectual or emotional, together with the eternal light of infinite wisdom and boundless compassion and resultant liberation from the bondage of recurrent phenomenal existence. What the Buddha attained 2,500 years ago, in that faraway corner of north-eastern India, we too can attain, here and now, if we only follow the path of ethical conduct, concentration and meditation, and transcendental wisdom prescribed and exemplified by him. The festival of Vaiśākha therefore not only celebrates the Buddha's actual past Enlightenment, but our own potential future Enlightenment. It reminds us not only of what he has done, but of what we must try to do if we are to consider ourselves true followers of the Enlightened One. Vaiśākha should therefore be a time of moral and spiritual stocktaking, of ruthless self-examination, for all of us. How far along the path have we been able, so far, to progress? How far have we still to go? What faults and weaknesses remain to be corrected, what virtues to be developed? Are we really *trying*? What progress, if any, have we made since Vaiśākha last year?

The festival of Vaiśākha is not only a time of individual but of collective stocktaking. In some parts of the Buddhist world the new year commences at this time. Buddhist groups take the opportunity of surveying the progress made during the previous twelve months. While complacency would be out of place, the English Buddhist movement as centred on the Hampstead Buddhist Vihara can look back over the past year with a feeling of sober satisfaction. Systematic teaching of the Dharma, together with the regular practice of guided group meditation, attendance at the speakers' class, and participation in the devotional meetings, have between them not only built up membership of the Association but helped to create the nucleus of a spiritual community of people who, taking Enlightenment as exemplified by the Buddha as their ideal, his Dharma as their way of life, and the members of the Sangha as their guides, are gradually coming to constitute a living presence of Buddhism in Great Britain. Various Buddhist traditions have contributed to this development. Theravāda, Mahāyāna, Tibetan Buddhism, and Zen are all honoured at the Vihara. If anything has become clear during the last year it is the fact that while English Buddhism, or British Buddhism as some prefer to call it, will draw gratefully on all Buddhist traditions, it will not confine itself exclusively to any one of them. Indeed, it is clear that a distinctive Western Buddhism, a Buddhism adapted to the spiritual needs of the West, is already in process of emergence.

THE BUDDHA

The Buddhist, *May 1966, pp. 166–8.*

From the traditional point of view Buddhism begins with Going for Refuge to the Three Jewels (*triratna*), the first of which is the Buddha. Although there is no longer any doubt about his historical existence, the exact dates of his birth and *parinirvāṇa* are still the subject of controversy. In all probability those given by the *Dīpavaṃsa* and the *Mahāvaṃsa* (excluding its continuation the *Cūlavaṃsa*, the dates of which are sixty years out), equivalent to 563–483 BCE, are not far wrong.[269] The events of his life are too well known to be recounted in detail. Born in Lumbini, in the territory of the Śākya republic, of wealthy patrician stock, he went forth 'from home into the homeless life' at the age of 29, attained Supreme Enlightenment at Bodh Gaya at the age of 35, and passed away at Kuśinagara at the age of 80. During his lifetime his teaching spread throughout the kingdoms of Magadha and Kośala (corresponding to the modern Bihar and Uttar Pradesh), as well as in the circumjacent principalities and republics. From kings, merchant princes, and orthodox Brahmins, to outcastes, courtesans, robbers, and naked ascetics, his disciples were recruited from all classes of society, and included both men and women. Besides instructing an extensive circle of lay adherents, he trained up a smaller, more select band of monks (and nuns) who constituted the sangha proper and upon whom, after the *parinirvāṇa*, the responsibility for carrying on his mission mainly devolved. His personality, as it emerges from the ancient records, was a unique combination of dignity and affability, wisdom and kindliness.

Together with a majesty that awed and daunted kings, he possessed a tenderness that could stoop to comfort the bereaved and console the afflicted. His serenity was unshakeable, his self-confidence unfailing. Ever mindful and self-possessed, he faced opposition and hostility, even personal danger, with a calm and compassionate smile that has lingered down the ages. In debate he was urbane and courteous, though not without a vein of irony, and almost invariably succeeded in winning over his opponent. Such was his success in this direction that he was accused of enticing people by means of spells.

In addition to the 'historical facts' of the Buddha's career, notice must be taken of the myths and legends from which, in the traditional biographies, these facts are inseparable. When Buddhism first came within the purview of Western learning it was generally assumed that myth and legend were synonymous with fiction and that, except as illustrations of primitive mentality, they were valueless. Since then we have begun to know better. Some incidents in the Buddha's biography, which appeared as 'legendary' within the materialistic framework of nineteenth-century science – such as those describing his exercise of supernormal powers – are now, with the expansion of that framework, seen to have been based, in all probability, on actual occurrences. Others apparently relate to a different order of reality and a different type of truth altogether, being poetic rather than scientific statements of psychological processes and spiritual experiences. Yet others are of the nature of illuminations struck out by the tremendous impact of the Buddha's personality on the minds of his disciples and express the greatness of that personality subjectively in terms of the feelings of rapturous adoration which it evoked.

This introduces the great question of the alleged 'deification' of the Buddha.[270] According to some modern scholars the Buddha was a human teacher whom the devotion of his followers turned into a god, or God. Based as it is on assumptions quite different from those of Buddhism such an interpretation of an important doctrinal development must be rejected outright. Within the context of a non-theistic religion the concept of deification has no meaning. The Buddha claimed to be a fully Enlightened human being, superior even to the gods, and as such he has invariably been regarded. Since he was already the highest being in the universe there remained no higher position to which he could subsequently be exalted. What really happened was that the Buddha, having realized the truth, thereby becoming its embodiment and symbol, reality came to be interpreted concretely in terms of Buddhahood and its attributes, as well as abstractly in terms of *sūnyatā*, *tathatā*, etc. At the same time, the devotion with which the Buddha was worshipped was analogous to that which, in the theistic religions, is the prerogative of the Creator.

No deification of an originally 'merely human' teacher ever having taken place, we must also dismiss as impertinent the several theories according to which the Buddha was in reality an ethical teacher like Socrates or Confucius, a rationalist, a humanist, a social reformer, and so on.

MESSAGE FROM THE HEAD OF THE ENGLISH SANGHA[271]

The Buddhist, *October 1966, pp. 300–2.*

Dear Members and Friends. In August 1964, at the invitation of the English Sangha Trust, I returned to this country after an absence of twenty years in order to take charge of the Hampstead Buddhist Vihara and its associated activities. At that time it was my intention that the visit should be a comparatively short one, and before leaving India I told my friends and fellow workers there that they could expect me back within six months. However, I had not been here for many weeks before I realized how much in the way of reorganization was needed and that my visit would have to be considerably longer than I had anticipated. Moreover, as the months went by, attendance at meetings and classes steadily increased and I found it difficult to abandon those who, they said, were still dependent on me for guidance. In this way six months became a year, and a year more than two years. After thinking the matter over, I have recently come to the conclusion that the progress made during this period is sufficient to justify my shifting my working headquarters from India to England. By the time this issue of *The Buddhist* is published, therefore, I shall be in India on a short visit making arrangements for the transfer of some of my responsibilities in that country to other hands.

During my absence lectures and classes will all continue as usual. Ven. Chien Chau, who has been with us since April, and who is already well known here, with the assistance of Sāmaṇera Viriya, will be looking after the Vihara until my return.[272] He will also take the guided group meditation classes, his deputies being Ruth Walshe for the classes held at the Buddhist Society; and Ruth Walshe, Jack Ireland, and Owen Jenkins for those held at the Vihara. Our chairman, Maurice Walshe, will be in charge of the fortnightly discussion group (formerly the 'speakers class'), which will continue to meet alternately at the Vihara and the Buddhist Society. For the highly popular Sunday afternoon lectures, most of which I have given myself during the last two years, we have secured the cooperation of a number of well-known speakers. Besides Ven. Chien Chau, they include Dr Carmen Blacker, Gerald Yorke, Tom Harris, John Hipkin, and John Elliott, as well as Ruth and Maurice Walshe. This magazine will be the joint responsibility of Mike Hookham and Jack Ireland, assisted by Francoise Strachan, and time permitting I hope to send the editorial articles as well as news of my travels in India. There is no reason, therefore, why the Vihara should not only consolidate its position during the coming months but even make fresh gains. I appeal to all of you to extend your full cooperation to Ven. Chien Chau and Sāmaṇera Viriya, and help to make this period one of the most successful chapters in the history of our movement.

After my return to this country, which will be on or about 1 February, I propose to divide my time between London and Biddulph, spending the winter and spring at the Vihara for lectures and classes, and the summer and autumn at Old Hall for meditation courses, literary work, and contacts with the Midland and Northern Buddhist groups. Full details of the Biddulph programme for 1967 will be announced early in the new year.[273]

May the blessings of the Buddha, Dharma, and Sangha be upon you all.

SELF-AFFIRMATION AND SELF-DENIAL:
A Buddhist View[274]

The Buddhist, *November 1966, pp. 329–33.*

When I started thinking about the subject of this talk, the first thing that struck me was that it is extremely difficult for one religion or one system of thought to operate with the concepts of another. A Christian would, no doubt, be hard put to it to give an adequate account of what he calls salvation in terms of the Buddhist concept of Nirvāṇa. It is no less difficult for the Buddhist to speak in terms of the Christian, or at any rate Western, concepts of self-affirmation and self-denial – concepts that Buddhism not only does not use, but which it even, in a sense, repudiates. In his first discourse, delivered two months after his Great Enlightenment or awakening to the truth, the Buddha laid down the principle of the middle way, one of the cornerstones of his teaching. An intelligent person, he told his first five disciples, should *avoid extremes.* So far as the religious life is concerned, the extremes are those of self-indulgence on the one hand, and self-mortification on the other – or, we may say, *self-affirmation* and *self-denial.* Each of these extremes had its followers in ancient India, and the Buddha himself, before his Enlightenment, had personal experience of them both. Born of wealthy and aristocratic parents, he led, up to his twenty-ninth year, a life of luxury and pleasure. Then, renouncing the world, he lived for six years in the forest as an ascetic, systematically reducing food and sleep and practising other austerities. Only after abandoning *both* these extremes and following the middle way did he attain Enlightenment, thus becoming the Buddha or Enlightened One.

Now the reason the Buddha gave up both self-affirmation *and* self-denial was that he saw that the two are, at bottom, the same. 'Extremes meet'[275] says the proverb, and although one extreme affirms, even asserts, the self, while the other seeks to deny or negate it, they are identical inasmuch as both regard the self as real, as a sort of ultimate fact of existence, if not as *the* fact. According to the Buddha, however, our thinking, feeling, willing self – what we usually refer to as 'I' and 'me' – is not real but unreal, not an ultimate fact of existence but only, as it were, a provisional one. If this seems difficult to understand and even harder to accept, as it does to most people, we can perhaps rephrase the Buddha's teaching and say that what we ordinarily regard as the self is unreal means not that we are less than we thought we were but that we are more. In the words of the poet, 'We are greater than we know.'[276] From a different point of view, and within a narrower context, this is the conclusion reached by modern psychology, especially psychoanalysis. What it terms the unconscious is as much 'us' as the conscious mind with which we usually identify ourselves – sometimes, perhaps, even a bit more. Buddhism goes further than this. Besides the unconscious, existing as it were below the surface of the conscious mind, there extends a whole vast new range of possibilities 'above' it. So much do these possibilities surpass our present everyday self, that the Buddha never speaks of them as constituting a higher self, though there is no doubt that in a sense they are, or can be, us. The concepts of self-affirmation and self-denial are thus superseded by that of self-transcendence, by which is meant a process of continuous openness to, and achievement of, ever higher modes of being and consciousness. The culmination of this process is what is called Enlightenment. The Buddha also points out that, like all contraries, the two extremes of self-affirmation and self-denial tend to change into each other. As the study of history reveals, periods of moral licence alternate with periods of repression. The Puritan interregnum is succeeded by Good King Charles's golden days, after the gaiety of the Regency comes the gloom of the Victorian period, and so on. Both extremes are moreover capable of assuming a variety of disguises. The desire for personal immortality, or perpetual post-mortem existence in heaven, for example, far from being a genuinely religious aspiration is, according to Buddhism, a subtle form of self-affirmation and as such to be discarded.

The Buddha's path to self-transcendence or middle way is often spoken of as being made up of eight parts. For this reason it is termed the Noble Eightfold Path – 'noble' here meaning spiritual or transcendental. The eight parts, which are to be practised both successively and simultaneously, are: Perfect View, consisting in a true understanding of the meaning and purpose of life; Perfect Resolve, or the development of non-attachment, love, and compassion; Perfect Speech, which is truthful, kindly, helpful, and conducive to peace and harmony; Perfect Action, consisting of abstention from injury to living things, from taking what is not given, from sexual misconduct, from false speech, and from intoxicating drinks and drugs; Perfect Livelihood, by which one earns one's living in a way that does no harm, either directly or indirectly, to any living being; Perfect Exertion, consisting in the unremitting effort to eliminate lower and cultivate higher states of consciousness; Perfect Recollection, or continuous awareness of one's bodily movements, emotional states, and thoughts; and finally, Perfect *Samādhi*, an untranslatable term covering the whole field of what is generally referred to as mind-development.[277] These eight parts of the Noble Eightfold Path – or middle way – are distributed under three headings corresponding to the three main stages in the process of self-transcendence. Perfect Speech, Action, and Livelihood make up the stage of morality; Perfect Effort, Recollection, and *Samādhi* the stage of concentration and meditation; while Perfect View and Resolve make up the final stage of wisdom. Of these, morality is the preliminary stage of intelligent self-control, in which one tries to lead a life of purity, simplicity, and unobtrusive helpfulness. Wisdom, usually defined as seeing things as they are, is the final stage. When fully developed it is equivalent to Enlightenment or Nirvāna. In between comes the stage of concentration and meditation, which constitutes the centre, indeed the very heart, of the Buddhist spiritual life. So much, indeed, on the practical side, is Buddhism organized around this stage, that it might well be called the Religion of Meditation. Some of you might have heard of Zen Buddhism. Zen means simply meditation. It is that form of Buddhism that specializes, as it were, in the practice of meditation, leaving the study of Buddhist philosophy to other schools. You might also have seen images or pictures of the Buddha. Most of them show him sitting, with half-closed eyes, cross-legged in what is called the lotus posture – the meditation posture. A word or two about meditation, the central stage of the Buddhist path of self-transcendence, will perhaps not be out of place before I close.

Meditation is not dreamy reverie, nor a matter of auto-suggestion or auto-hypnosis. It has nothing to do with the development of occult powers or with sitting and making the mind a complete blank. Though Buddhism originated in India, it is not a peculiarly Eastern practice. Many English people practise meditation regularly. At Biddulph, in Staffordshire, we in fact have a Buddhist meditation centre where special courses are held every year. Essentially, meditation is the progressive self-transformation, in awareness, of one's total being and consciousness. In the course of this process, scattered psychophysical energies are neither allowed to rampage unchecked nor merely be repressed. Instead they are unified and refined, and one increasingly experiences peace, bliss, and inner illumination. All mental conflicts are resolved. Self-transformation paves the way for self-transcendence. Both self-affirmation and self-denial have been left far behind.

THE FWBO NEWSLETTER

The FWBO Newsletter *was a quarterly publication that ran from May 1968 until winter 1985/6 when it was superseded by* Golden Drum. *It was set up by Ananda and Sudata with Ashvajit as its editor. Nagabodhi took over as editor in the summer of 1975 and brought out subsequent editions until the arrival of* Golden Drum, *again under his editorship.*

Friends of the Western Buddhist Order

The NEWSLETTER

Number 62

Price 80p

Sangharakshita:
Twenty years in the West

FWBO Newsletter no. 62

A LETTER FROM THE PRESIDENT

FWBO Newsletter *no. 1, Spring 1968, p. 2.*

Dear Friends. If you are reading this *Newsletter* it means you are either attending classes or other activities of the Friends, or you are giving your support in some other way; possibly you have just expressed interest in what we are doing. Whatever the reason we are pleased that you want to know more about what is going on. Recent events have shown that it is possible for a community to come into being which is in harmony with both the nature and the spirit of Buddhism, and which meets at least some of the needs of those who wish to draw nearer to the teaching of the Buddha. A new and, indeed, crucial phase of Buddhism in the West was reached with the recent ordinations; much remains to be done. Meanwhile, among the Friends, we have discovered that the traditional relationship between a spiritual teacher and those who are being taught, and relationships between those who are receiving the teaching, can have much power and vitality.

As President of the Friends of the Western Buddhist Order I meet many people different in ages, backgrounds, aspirations, and degrees of spiritual advancement. But all have one thing in common: a desire to know more about the incomparable Buddha Dharma.

Buddhists are not 'special' people; they are, as the Friends show, varied and differing people, yet many will come to have a special view of life. Whatever understanding, insight, and discovery is made in classes, in meditation, in retreats and other activities among the Friends, these are not, in essence, things provided by the teacher. They are the result of personal striving. Guidance, advice, and information are there for the asking – and, of course, for the effort on the part of those who seek these things.

I welcome the opportunity that the *Newsletter* gives us of reaching more of those who share our work, as I welcome the more limited personal contact which I have with many of you. We are doing something new and exciting together, yet as old and profound as man's search for Enlightenment which received its impetus from the Buddha nearly 2,500 years ago. Yours in the Dharma, Sangharakshita.

MAN AND REALITY

FWBO Newsletter *no. 4, March 1969, pp. 1–2, extracted from a lecture entitled 'The Bodhisattva Hierarchy' given at Centre House, London, on 7 March 1969, the seventh in a series on 'Aspects of the Bodhisattva Ideal'.*

Reality is beyond thought and speech. The Buddha and the great spiritual masters of the Buddhist tradition describe it, from different points of view, as Nirvāṇa, the Void, the One Mind, and so on, but essentially it remains beyond conception and expression, to be intuited within ourselves, in the depths of our own self-transcending spiritual experience.

Man is related to this inexpressible reality in two ways: directly and indirectly. He is related to it directly by being connected with it at the very roots of his being. What is ultimate in him flows as it were into what is ultimate in the universe, continuous with it and ultimately one with it. This direct relation between man and reality is realized in its fullness only by the Enlightened Ones, the Buddhas.

Indirectly, man is related to reality in two ways. In the first place, he is related to it through all those things that stand lower than himself in the hierarchy of being, or which represent a lower degree of manifestation of reality than he does. Among these things are the elements, the sun and the moon, the stars, minerals, plants, birds, and beasts – indeed, all the products of the evolutionary process up to and including ordinary unenlightened human beings.

In the second place, man is also related to reality indirectly through all these forms of life that stand higher than himself in the hierarchy of existence, through all those beings who represent a higher degree of manifestation of reality than he does.

The first kind of indirect relation to reality is like seeing a brilliant light through a thick veil, a veil which in places is so dense as to be impenetrable. The second kind of indirect relation to reality is like seeing the same light through a very thin veil, one that is so fine as to be diaphanous, or in which there are here and there rents through which it is possible to catch a glimpse of the naked light itself shining beyond.

The 'thin veil' represents the spiritual hierarchy, especially the hierarchy of bodhisattvas, inasmuch as they have become, in their life and work, as it were transparent to the light of reality. Reality shines through them more brightly than it does through other people. Through them we see reality itself more clearly.

If we aspire to Enlightenment, to knowing reality in its fullness, and knowing it directly, it is therefore important that we should be in contact with those who are spiritually more advanced than ourselves, who make up part of the 'thin veil' and through whom the light of reality shines with more than ordinary brilliance. Such persons are known as our 'spiritual friends'.

Reliance on spiritual friends is stressed by all branches of the Buddhist tradition, and nowhere more than in the Mahāyāna. We all need help in leading the spiritual life, in following the path, even if only to the extent of receiving moral support. So long as we remain entirely on our own very little real spiritual progress, if any, is likely to be made. How difficult it would be for *you*, for example, if from one year's end to another you never saw the face of a fellow Buddhist, if there were no meditation classes, lectures, and retreats for you to attend, and even no Buddhist literature for you to study!

The help that we need in leading the spiritual life we get by associating with those whose ideals are the same as our own, who follow a similar way of life. Above all, we get it by associating with those who are spiritually more advanced than we are, or who are simply more authentically human. In other words, we receive sustenance and support in our long journey to Enlightenment from contact with spiritual friends.

In our own movement, as represented by the WBO and FWBO, great emphasis is placed on the principle of spiritual hierarchy, as well as on its corollary, the principle of spiritual brotherhood. This means, in practical terms, adopting an attitude of receptivity towards those who are 'above' us in the spiritual hierarchy, of kindness and generosity towards those who are 'below', and of mutuality and reciprocity towards those who stand on the same level. These three attitudes correspond to the three great spiritual emotions of faith and devotion, compassion, and love. Faith and devotion is directed upwards, towards the senior members of the hierarchy, the Buddhas and bodhisattvas and great spiritual masters, whose 'gift-waves' we seek in perfect openness of spirit to receive. Compassion is directed downwards, towards pupils and newcomers, as well as towards the mentally distressed and perplexed, whom we wish to help. Love is radiated all around, towards Friends and fellow members of the Order – ultimately, in ever-widening circles, to all sentient beings.

Though we speak, for the sake of convenience of expression, in terms of those who are 'above' or 'below' us in the hierarchy of being, it must be emphasized that there is no question of any 'official grading'. Indeed, even to think, 'I'm higher up in the hierarchy than you are' or 'You're lower down than I am – let me give you a little compassion,' would be destructive of the principle of spiritual hierarchy, and with it of the principle of spiritual brotherhood. Whether in relation to those who are 'above', or 'below', or 'around' us, the appropriate spiritual emotion flows forth naturally, spontaneously, and unselfconsciously.

People in different stages of spiritual development adorn the spiritual hierarchy like half-open and fully-blown flowers all blooming on a single rose bush. Or they all constitute a family, a family of which the Buddha is the ultimate head and the great bodhisattvas the elder brothers. Everyone gives what he can; everyone receives what he needs. The whole multidimensional network of relationships is pervaded by a spirit of joy, by freedom, light, and warmth. Living and growing within a context such as this man passes, eventually, from an indirect to a direct relation with reality.

THE STUDY OF BUDDHISM

Towards the end of 1971 Sangharakshita was invited by Dr Howard Marratt to become a member of the British Council of Churches Working Party on interfaith dialogue. In response to questions posed by this group, he produced the following two short papers. Both were published in the FWBO Newsletter *no. 15, April 1972, pp. 5–8.*

The systematic discipline of the study of Buddhism is a demanding one. It requires not only intellectual penetration and emotional sensitivity but also, above all else, wholehearted dedication to the task of ethical and spiritual self-development. The study and teaching of Buddhism as a 'subject' separate from one's own life and experience is, strictly speaking, an impossibility. This should always be borne in mind in any discussion of such study and teaching.

The study and teaching of Buddhism in the West is beset by special difficulties of its own. These are both objective and subjective in character.

1. Objective Difficulties

Throughout its history, Buddhism has attached great importance to freedom of individual judgement. Consequently, though the views of eminent teachers, both past and present, may command wide acceptance, there is no central ecclesiastical authority to determine what Buddhism is and what it is not, much less still to enforce doctrinal conformity. Neither is there a single body of scriptures recognized as authentic by all Buddhists in the way that all Christians recognize the Bible and all Muslims the Koran. The nature of Buddhism has to be determined empirically, i.e. by examining the actual beliefs and practices of the various Buddhist communities down the ages. This means that an encyclopedic, not to say ecumenical, approach is unavoidable – with all the additional work that this entails.

2. Subjective Difficulties

In the West the student and future teacher of Buddhism is almost bound to be conditioned, either positively or negatively, by his Christian background. This may well make any understanding of certain aspects of Buddhism virtually impossible. For instance, in all its diverse forms Buddhism remains a non-theistic ethical and spiritual teaching. This sharply differentiates it from Judaism, Christianity, Islam, and some forms of Hinduism, and allies it with Marxism and Humanism. Theists and ex-theists find it extremely difficult to imagine how Buddhism can be both non-theistic and a religion. Others, recognizing that it is a religion, will maintain that it must be theistic. In either case, serious distortion occurs.

Buddhism is also grossly distorted by being discussed in Christian religious terms such as 'faith', 'belief', 'salvation', 'sin', 'guilt', 'soul', 'worship', and 'prayer'. Some Buddhists are even of opinion that Buddhism is distorted by being discussed in terms of religion at all – a viewpoint that would remove it from the sphere of the present inquiry altogether.

There is also the danger that, within the western educational context, Buddhism will be presented as a sort of exotic anthropological curiosity, that is to say, not as a teaching demanding respectful intellectual consideration, but as a collection of quaint customs and curious beliefs.

More specifically, the systematic discipline of the study of Buddhism involves (a) intellectual study, (b) personal practice, and (c) contact with the Buddhist community.

a. Intellectual study

This would cover (i) selections from the three major collections of Buddhist canonical literature (Pāli Tipiṭaka, Chinese Sānzàng, and Tibetan Kangyur), as well as important individual texts (the *Dhammapada, Sutta-Nipāta, Vajracchedikā Prajñāpāramitā Sūtra, Saddharma Puṇḍarīka Sūtra, Laṅkāvatāra Sūtra*, etc.); (ii) basic teachings accepted by all forms of Buddhism (dependent origination, the four noble truths, the Noble Eightfold Path, the three characteristics of existence, Nirvāṇa, karma and rebirth, etc; (iii) a survey of the history of Buddhism in India, South-east Asia, China, Japan, Tibet, etc. including some reference to Buddhist achievements in the fine arts, literature, and social life; (iv) distinctive tenets of important individual schools of Buddhism (Theravāda, Sarvāstivāda, Madhyamaka, Yogācāra, Tendai, Zen, Shin, etc.); and (v) rudiments of at least one Buddhist canonical or quasi-canonical language (Pāli, Sanskrit, Chinese, Japanese, Tibetan).

b. Personal practice

Besides the leading of the ethical life, this would consist in the regular practice – under an experienced teacher – of such elementary Buddhist concentration exercises as the mindfulness of breathing and the development of universal loving-kindness. The student would also be encouraged to face, and if possible resolve, whatever personal psychological and spiritual problems might emerge as a result of this practice.

c. Contact with the Buddhist community

This would involve spiritual contact and exchange with other Buddhists or students of Buddhism, both individually and in groups. The student would live for a time as a member of a Buddhist community, whether monastic or lay, and participate in its daily routine, including group meditation, chanting, observance of silence, performance of the Sevenfold Puja, cooking and cleaning, etc.

BUDDHISM AND ITS ORIGINAL
CULTURAL ENVIRONMENT

The relationship between Buddhism and its original cultural environment cannot be understood without a clear understanding of the nature of Buddhism itself. Indeed, once the nature of Buddhism has been understood, the nature of its relationship not only with its original cultural environment but with *any* cultural environment will immediately become clear.

According to the modern science of comparative religion, Buddhism is the name of a religion founded in the sixth century BCE by an Indian teacher known as the Buddha. The word 'Buddha' derives from a verbal root meaning 'to know' or 'to understand', and is not a personal name but a title. A Buddha is one who knows, or who understands the truth, who has personally experienced absolute reality in its fullness and become, as it were, one with that reality.

Having understood the truth, having experienced absolute reality, the Buddha does not keep the experience to himself, but makes it known to other living beings in such a way that, by their own efforts, they can come to achieve it for themselves. *Sambodhi* or Perfect Enlightenment is thus an experience that seeks as it were to communicate itself. In traditional terms, it is not only wisdom (*prajñā*) but compassion (*karuṇā*), not only knowledge but love.

The Buddha's communication of his Enlightenment experience to other living beings is embodied in the Dharma or teaching, and it is this and the Enlightenment experience itself which between them make up what is known today as Buddhism.

We are now in a position to understand, in principle, the relationship between Buddhism and its original cultural environment.

The Buddha is trying to communicate. After the unique experience that has transformed him from an unenlightened to an Enlightened human being, he is trying to convey to ordinary people something of the nature of that experience, trying to share with them at least a moiety of the riches he has discovered. In order to do this, he has no alternative but to express himself in the words that ordinary people habitually use, to have recourse to their language, in the fullest sense of the term, i.e. as comprising not only words but concepts, images, attitudes, and institutions. The Buddha's medium for the communication of his Enlightenment experience is thus the whole of contemporary Indian culture. From this it follows that the relationship between Buddhism and its original cultural environment is, from the Buddhist point of view, a relationship between message and medium – and in this instance the medium is *not* the message.

Some media are of course better adapted to the transmission of a particular message than others. In the case of the original cultural environment of Buddhism, which was partly Brahminical and partly non-Brahminical, or 'popular', some elements were more pervious to the Enlightenment experience than others. Concepts such as those of a personal creator God (*īśvara*), or an unchanging immortal soul (*ātman*), could function as a medium for the transmission of the Buddha's message only by being negated. Other elements, such as the ideal of the Brahmin, or the teaching concerning karma and rebirth, had to be modified in various ways. Others again, such as the hierarchy of higher states of consciousness known as the *dhyānas* needed little or no modification at all.

Indian Buddhism may be defined as the Buddha's experience of Enlightenment as communicated through the medium of Indian culture, the medium itself, of course, being increasingly modified by the message it was transmitting. Much that is thought of as characteristically Buddhist is, in fact, merely Indian, and has no necessary connection with the Enlightenment experience. Examples that may be cited are (a) the highly 'intellectual' analytical form in which a great deal of Buddhist teaching has come down to us, and (b) the somewhat rigid separation of 'monks' and 'laity' – a separation that corresponds to the distinction between '*parivrājakas*' and '*gṛhasthas*' in ancient Indian society rather than to any fundamental difference among the members of the Buddhist spiritual community.

To what extent 'Buddhism' is in fact Indian culture may be seen by considering the principle non-Indian forms of Buddhism, especially Chinese Buddhism. Chinese Buddhism may be defined as the Enlightenment experience as communicated in terms of Chinese culture. Probably the most important form of Chinese Buddhism is Chan or Zen. This, it is well known, is non-intellectual, not to say anti-intellectual, and tends to minimize the difference between monks and laity. In other words, it differs strikingly from Indian Buddhism. Yet, at the same time, it is no less truly Buddhist; indeed, it may even be argued that it is more Buddhist, which would mean, in effect, that Chinese culture was a better medium for the communication of the Buddha's message than Indian culture.

From the above discussion it should be clear, incidentally, that Buddhism is not *a priori* opposed to any form of culture, including the religious beliefs and practices of that culture. Buddhism seeks to communicate the Enlightenment experience – in a sense *is* that communication – and as such is prepared to adopt whatever means of communication may be available. Towards the original cultural environment, as well as towards all the different cultural environments it has enjoyed in the course of its long history, its attitude has been one of appreciation and acceptance rather than condemnation and rejection. For this and other reasons, therefore, religious intolerance and persecution have ever been unknown to it. Recognizing that even its own teachings are only a means to an end – only the medium, not the content, of the communication – it respects other teachings even when it is unable to agree with them.

It should also be clear that in 'teaching Buddhism' there can be no question of 'abstracting the teachings and thought of Buddhism and presenting it divorced from the context in which it arose'. Rather it is a question of oneself experiencing something at least of the spirit of Buddhism – of the Enlightenment experience – and communicating it to others through the medium of either Eastern or Western culture – or indeed, in any way that one can.

A PERSONAL MESSAGE TO ALL FRIENDS

FWBO Newsletter *no. 18, Spring 1973, pp. 5–7.*

For the last six years (ever since the foundation of the FWBO in fact), out of the thousand or so classes and meetings that have been held, there have been scarcely half a dozen in which I have not participated – in which, indeed, I have not taken a prominent part. Now, however, a change has taken place. As reported in the supplement to the last *Newsletter*, I have decided to take a 'sabbatical' and release myself from all the programmed activities for the coming year. What is the basis for this decision? Those who are in any way involved with our movement, whether as regular participants or simply as sympathetic observers, may well welcome a few words of personal explanation.

First of all, let me correct two wrong impressions that have been heard among the Friends during the last two or three months, and which have gained, perhaps, limited currency and credence. (1) 'Bhante is tired and needs a rest.' This is certainly not the case. Throughout the whole of 1972, but especially from about the middle of the year, I felt more full of energy than I have ever done in my life. The sabbatical is not to be interpreted, therefore, as being in the nature of a rest-cure for a tired and worn-out *bhikṣu* who, fatigued by his labours in the big city, feels a need to 'get away from it all' for a while; (2) 'Bhante is disappointed by the slow progress of the Movement, and the lack of enthusiasm shown by many of the Friends.' That the Movement is as yet functioning at only a fraction of its optimum capacity, and that the majority of members are lukewarm in their commitment to the Three

Jewels and lax in their practice of the Path, is of course known to no one better than myself. At the same time, I am far from disappointed at the progress that has so far been made. The handful of people who, six years ago, met and meditated together for the first time in a tiny basement in Monmouth Street started something – or were started by something – the vast potential of which is only just now beginning to be realized. I am convinced that, whatever its present limitations may be, the FWBO is not only the most important factor in all our lives, but *one of the main growing points of the Higher Evolution in the western hemisphere,*[278] and that, as such, it demands our wholehearted allegiance. The sabbatical does not, therefore, represent a withdrawal in a dudgeon, much less still any disposition to seek out less stony soil on which to sow the seed of the Dharma.

What, then, *is* the sabbatical? Why have I decided to withdraw, for at least a year, from all programmed activities? The key to the mystery is to be found in the word 'programmed'. As the Movement grew, and as activities steadily increased, I found myself involved for longer and longer periods of time in an unintermitting round of classes, lectures, retreats, personal interviews, and so on. Sometimes for months on end I did not have a free evening, i.e. an evening when I could do whatever I felt like doing. Indeed, it eventually became obvious that, if I was not careful, the whole of my life was going to be planned for me at least one year in advance, and that for eighteen hours a day, 365 days of the year, all my activities would be scheduled activities. From the point of view of the Movement, of course, this was not a bad thing. Indeed, it was a good thing, and a necessary thing. Like a tender growing plant, a movement as young as ours needed constant attention, and this, as the only full-time gardener then available, I felt perfectly happy to give. But energy cannot be programmed indefinitely; indeed, some kinds of energy cannot be programmed at all, and must either function unprogrammed or remain quiescent. *It is principally in order to release this unprogrammed and unprogrammable energy, long accumulating within me, that I have decided to take a sabbatical.* What this energy will do, once released, no one can say, least of all myself: it is a spirit, and being a spirit it is like the wind, that bloweth where it listeth; but whatever it does will undoubtedly be for the greater good of the Movement in general, of myself individually, and all those who come in personal contact with me.

That it is now possible for me to take a year off from tending the healthy six-year-old peepul sapling that is the FWBO is due, above all else, to the fact that, within the last two or three years, several assistant gardeners have appeared. To them the care of the sapling has, from now onwards, been entrusted. Theirs will be the responsibility for seeing that it gets both rain and sunshine in the right quantities, that the soil in which it grows is kept well aerated, that caterpillars are picked off the leaves, and that, periodically, its branches are sprayed with insecticide. Even had it not been necessary for me to take a year off, a development of this kind would have been a highly desirable thing. If assistant gardeners are ever to blossom into gardeners, and gardeners into master gardeners, it is imperative that, having undergone a certain amount of preliminary training, they should eventually be freed from all petty routine supervision and encouraged to function independently, on their own initiative. Before such a development can take place, however, there is a condition to be fulfilled: for a time at least, the head gardener must withdraw from the scene. Only when they are no longer working under supervision, and *feel* free and independent, will it be possible for the gardeners of the future to accept real responsibility and, giving of the best that is in them, to be a source of blessing to everything that lives and grows within the compass of the garden. Far from being simply an opportunity for me to cultivate a few choice blossoms of my own, important as that may be, the sabbatical therefore constitutes, coincidentally, a definite stage in the training of the Order members and other Friends. Indeed, it is even more than that; dropping all metaphor and speaking plainly, it may be said to constitute a phase of reappraisal, consolidation, and further evolution for the whole spiritual movement that is the FWBO.

The sabbatical also has a more *personal* significance, in the sense of a significance that is relevant not just to me individually but to me *as* an individual. The proverb tells us that familiarity breeds contempt. This may or may not be true, but it is certainly true that when we have enjoyed for a long time the uninterrupted possession of certain facilities and advantages, perhaps even of certain privileges, we almost invariably tend to develop towards them an attitude of indifference and 'taking for granted'. My own continued presence within the Movement is a case in point. So constant was I in my attendance, so much of a permanent fixture, that in the eyes of some people I became a piece of spiritual furniture, useful indeed, even necessary, but not to be taken any particular notice of or shown any particular regard. As I remarked once at an Order meeting, jokingly but with an underlying seriousness, I often felt as though I was being treated not as an individual but as a piece of well-oiled religious clockwork – as a machine in fact, for giving lectures and taking classes, for answering people's questions about Buddhism and solving their personal problems. If you thought the machine was not working properly, that it was not giving you the right answers, then if you were in a bad mood that day you gave it a good hard kick to make it function better. Now that the piece of furniture has got up and walked away, it will be possible, I hope, for people to realize that it was not a piece of furniture after all but a human being. They will undoubtedly get more out of me by treating me as an individual than by treating me as a machine, even a spiritual machine. And I shall undoubtedly get more out of them. Indeed, I hope that it will now be possible for some at least of my 'unprogrammed energy' to flow into an ever-expanding network of spiritual friendships.

Perhaps that network is even now in process of formation. As I write these lines, a vision rises before me, a vision of a figure multiple-faced and multitudinously-armed. It is Avalokiteśvara, 'the Lord who Looks Down', the embodiment of compassion, the bodhisattva who par excellence among the bodhisattvas of the *dharmakāya* is the incarnation of the cosmic will to Enlightenment – not indeed, in his more familiar two-armed or four-armed form, but in the most universal and (to us in the West at least) most bizarre of all his manifestations, the manifestation in which eleven radiant countenances look with smiles of compassion in the eleven directions of space, and a thousand arms, radiating like so many light rays from their single sun-like source, extend their benign operations into the remotest corners of the universe. Much as the full moon in all its glory may be reflected in a puddle, it is a tiny reflection of this figure that the FWBO aspires to be. May the present sabbatical help all of us to cooperate towards this end!

Sangharakshita, Cornwall, 7 March 1973.

YESTERDAY, TODAY, AND TOMORROW

FWBO Newsletter no. 34, Spring 1977, pp. 12–17. Ten years after the dedication of the Movement's first shrine-room in London's Monmouth Street, Nagabodhi, Buddhadasa, and Devamitra interviewed Sangharakshita about the developments of the preceding decade, and what he would like to see happening during the next.

You spent eighteen years in India, Bhante. During this period did you ever think of returning to the West to teach?
No, quite definitely not. I took it for granted that I would spend the rest of my days out in the East, in India. It was only in 1963 that the idea of returning was put into my head at all. At that time there were difficulties in London within the English Buddhist movement – mainly conflict between the Hampstead Buddhist Vihara and the Buddhist Society – and some people began thinking that, if I came over, inasmuch as I was the seniormost *bhikkhu* of English origin, or of British origin, I might be able to reconcile the two factions and bring people together. This was why they thought of inviting me. When the suggestion was first made I rejected it out of hand, but I was gradually persuaded, and thought, 'Perhaps I do have some responsibility. Perhaps I could help.' Before that I had no plan of doing anything in the West, or of contributing to the development of Buddhism in the West in any way, other than through my writings. There was another factor. I was under the impression, in India, that Buddhism in Britain was going very well. It did not occur to me that it might need my attention. For instance, I used to get the *Middle Way*, and this gave me a totally wrong impression, because it contained so many good articles. I did not realize that this was all purely a façade. There was no Buddhist movement corresponding to the *Middle Way*, as it were. The *Middle Way* featured articles from Buddhists from all over the place, and it gave the impression, being the journal of the Buddhist Society, that there was a

thriving Buddhist movement in Britain. Consequently I tended to think, 'Well, they're getting on all right.' It was only when I got back, and had been here for some time, that I saw that though the field was very fertile hardly anything had been done to cultivate it.

This was when you returned in 1966?
No, when I first returned, in 1964. The reason I did not think of returning to the West was not that I did not care about the West, or did not care about Buddhism in Britain, but that I thought it was being adequately looked after by the Buddhist Society and the other smaller groups that sprang up later.

Did you think it was a more fertile situation than the situation you left in the East?
In a sense, yes. I felt that the emphasis in India was almost entirely on material improvement, material development – that that was now the dominant trend. But here, I felt, there were sufficient people who had become disillusioned with all that, and who were thinking much more in terms of other values.

Did you consult anybody in India about this? Did you talk to any of your own teachers?
Only when I returned to India for a farewell visit in 1967, having by that time made up my mind to settle permanently in the West. I consulted them then, especially in view of the efforts that were being made to prevent me coming back to England at the end of my visit as planned. They were all quite emphatic that I should come back and work in Britain. As for the difficulties that I was having with the Sangha Trust, and with some of the people at the Buddhist Society, I remember Dhardo Rimpoche, for instance, simply dismissing them and saying, 'That's nothing at all. Ignore it. Just carry on with your own work.' He seemed to attach no importance whatever to the opposition I was encountering.

But when you first came back in 1964, did you have any idea that you might be starting your own movement?
No. I originally agreed to come over on a four-month visit. This gradually lengthened to two years, and towards the end of that period I saw that,

quite clearly, a new Buddhist movement was needed. But I did not see how this was to be done, in the sense that I did not see how I could start up something independent, because even people who were quite friendly and well disposed to me said, 'Why have another movement?' I saw that the Buddhist Society could not be changed, that the Hampstead Buddhist Vihara could not be changed. At the time I saw that if the Buddhist movement in this country was really to develop, something new was definitely needed. But I also knew that the majority of English Buddhists, even those in contact with me, would say, 'Why start up something new? Why not work with the existing organizations?' I saw that it was not possible to work with the existing organizations, but they did not – probably because they had no real idea of what was needed. When some of those who considered themselves the leaders of British Buddhism decided they did not want me back (the vast majority of ordinary Buddhists did want me back), and did their best to prevent my returning, they gave me the perfect excuse to start up something new. I was delighted. Despite the fact that, owing to their machinations, the situation was for a time rather unpleasant, it did make it possible for me to start up something completely new, which is what I wanted to do anyway. After I had come back some of my friends were still trying to get me back into the Hampstead Buddhist Vihara. My one prayer was that they would not succeed, and of course they didn't.

So you did establish the 'Friends' after that point?
Immediately after I came back. I was quite sure that we could, and should, and must, start a new Buddhist movement in this country – indeed, in the West generally. I had no doubt about it at all.

1977 is the tenth anniversary year of the FWBO. *Are you satisfied with the way things have developed in the last ten years?*
That's a very big question. I would say I am contented, but not satisfied. Things have certainly gone in the right direction – I'm quite satisfied on that score – but we still have quite a long way to go, and we have to broaden out quite a lot.

In retrospect are there many things that you would have done differently?
There has been only one really unforeseen development of any importance, and this has been a very positive one. When the 'Friends'

was started I took it for granted that it would be a mixed movement. The Order of course is mixed: it contains both *upāsakas* and *upāsikās*. I tended to assume that, inasmuch as this was the West, that was the correct and proper way to do things. Experience has definitely shown otherwise, however. It has shown that, if those concerned are to progress beyond a certain point in their spiritual development, we need – even in the West – to separate the sexes in the traditional way. I don't think we can say that separation of the sexes, in connection with spiritual activities, is merely a part of Eastern culture. Actually, it is one of the necessities of the spiritual life. I think I tended to assume, in the early days of the Movement, that it was just a part of Indian culture, a part of Eastern culture, and that it wasn't necessary for us in the West. Here men and women could develop spiritually, together, as it were side by side, all along the way. But experience has shown that this is not possible. This is the one thing, I think, that I had not foreseen.

It seems, actually, that none of the other Buddhist movements in the West have seen this either.
Well, they haven't come to the point that we have come to. They haven't got far enough spiritually. It's as simple as that. Some are even deluding themselves, especially the pseudo-Tantric ones. But the fact is that there has been no real spiritual development in the case of these groups. In the 'Friends' we've got where we have because both men and women have been working on themselves, and because they've come to the point when, in order to progress further, they've just got to see less of each other, especially on occasions like retreats when one is trying to make a more intensive effort spiritually and needs to be as free from distractions as possible.

The next question ties in with the last one. What do you consider to be the main areas of difficulty in bringing the Dharma to the West?
I think the biggest area of difficulty is what one can only describe as false and muddled thinking. This is basically what one is up against – unclear thinking, confused thinking. In particular there is the ideology of what I call pseudo-liberalism, which one is supposed to take for granted and regard as the truth, even though its pronouncements are not always very consistent with one another. For instance, there is the

view that men and women must always do everything together, and that this represents the enjoyment of some kind of 'equality'.

Are there any others that you can think of?
There is, of course, the fact of modern industrialization. Having to live in the big city certainly doesn't help one spiritually. Whether this is a specifically Western difficulty now, I don't know. You encounter it in Japan, and even in India to some extent. Putting it bluntly, I'd say that the real obstacle in bringing the Dharma to the West was *micchā-diṭṭhis* – false views.

What would you like to see happening in the next ten years?
First, I'd like to see the Order grow. I would really like there to be, say by the end of the next ten years, upwards of a thousand Order members. Then we would be really getting somewhere. Obviously one isn't just thinking in terms of numbers, but of the more intense spiritual interaction that a larger number of Order members makes possible, as well as of the greater impact on society that it would have. Some people have warned that the bigger the Order, the greater the danger of a diminution of quality, but this has not happened so far. Numbers have increased over the last ten years, and the quality of Order members has increased steadily too. There's no doubt about this. I think it's going to be quite a long time, if ever, before we reach a point where increase of numbers will automatically mean decrease of quality. We have organized ourselves in such a way that you can't get into the 'Friends' simply by paying a subscription and becoming a 'member'. Moreover, the Order itself has a certain kind of strength which, more and more, draws the right sort of people. Also, as the Order grows, and as the interaction within it becomes more and more intense, the Order becomes more and more demanding, and thus draws people of ever higher calibre. So I don't think we should allow ourselves to be scared by the bogey of 'Be careful you don't get too big. Don't get the wrong kind of people.' I see no danger at all, at the moment, of this sort of thing happening. Consequently I'd like to see upwards of a thousand Order members by the end of another ten years. After all, the FWBO is directly dependent on the WBO – they are, indeed, the organs through which different teams of Order members carry on their work in the world – and the bigger and more spiritually alive the Order is the more widely and the

more effectively it will be able to communicate the Dharma to people in the West.

When you say that you would like to see upwards of a thousand Order members, does this mean upāsakas *and* upāsikās *or are you thinking in terms of a new level of ordination?*
I think that there will be, within the Order, people who, for want of a better word, will be called monks. But I'm not happy about these monks being like the *bhikkhus*. There's quite a lot of monastic formalism in the East. People accept rules, or make vows, which they know that they are not going to be observing, and this has a very undermining effect on the spiritual life. Some of these rules are not very relevant to us in the West anyway. Nevertheless I think we shall see the emergence in the Order – this is already happening to some extent – of people who are really committed to the spiritual life and devoted full-time to Dharma work. Such people will be free from family responsibilities, free from emotional ties. They will lead purely spiritual lives, being involved, at any given time, either with their own meditation and study, or with the work of an FWBO centre – or with a combination of both. These people will in fact be 'monks'. We can't prevent monks from arising within the Order, whether we have a separate ordination for them or not. The main thing, I think, is that we safeguard the unique importance of the Going for Refuge as the basic act of the Buddhist life. In many parts of the East, as we know, more importance is given to becoming a monk, with the result that the Going for Refuge is undervalued. This is because the ordinary lay follower, who more often than not is a merely nominal Buddhist, also chants the Refuges, thus obscuring their real significance. Even if we do have a monastic ordination, that will have to be seen as an extension of the Going for Refuge. This will have to be made completely clear. How we shall do that I don't as yet know: I think the problem will resolve itself. Monks are emerging – monks in the real sense – and will continue to emerge. There will be this contingent of 'monks', as it were, within the Order. The unity of the Order will be maintained by stressing the common Going for Refuge. This means that those who are Going for Refuge in the context of the household life will have to be quite certain that they are really Going for Refuge, really keeping up with their commitment, and that they are not just becoming more or less nominal Buddhists. If they do, then obviously the gap between the

'monk' Buddhists and the others will widen. You therefore need to do two things. On the one hand, stress the fact that being a 'monk' is a fuller implementation of the original Going for Refuge, and on the other, that those who go for Refuge and remain householders must be absolutely certain that they are really Going for Refuge, and really implementing that, to the utmost, within their particular lives as householders.

As well as the Order, I'd like to see the FWBO itself expanding. So far as this country is concerned, we are virtually confined to the south-east and the east, and I'm not at all happy about that. I'd like to see us expanding into the Midlands and the industrial north, as well as extending our activities in Scotland and planting ourselves quite firmly in Wales and the West Country. I'd also like to see us very definitely established on the Continent, especially in Sweden, where we have one Order member now. Also in Holland and Denmark – especially in Copenhagen. Then I'd like to see us stretching out across the Atlantic to the United States, perhaps starting up in Boston, which would seem to be a good place to begin. And also to Australia. We have been talking about a party of Order members and Friends going out to Sydney. I think Sydney would be a very good place to have a centre.

There are other things. I'd like to see some meditation centres. Though meditation plays an extremely important part in all our centres and communities, we don't as yet have even one meditation centre as such – a place in a really secluded part of the country devoted exclusively to meditation.

I would also like to see more of our own businesses. At Sukhavati we've been developing this scheme of Order members and others setting up businesses which will give them, firstly, an opportunity of working together, secondly, a means of right livelihood, and thirdly, a medium for making contact with people in the world so that our ideals can be put across. I'd like to see the Friends becoming a whole world within a world, and self-sufficient in every way.

Would this suggest schools and farms?
Yes, and even light industries – all in accordance with the principles of right livelihood. You would have people in the spiritual community working together and ploughing back all profits into the Movement and, perhaps, supporting the full-time workers and meditators – the 'monks'. A start has been made, but it's mainly Sukhavati-based. I'd like to see it

spread throughout the Movement. Another thing I would like to see in the next ten years is more publications, especially the edited transcripts of the study seminars, as well as other things I shall be writing. We have a lot of work to do in this field.

Then I would like to see the FWBO projecting itself a little bit more. It is becoming increasingly clear that the FWBO *is* the British Buddhist movement – that there isn't really anything else worth mentioning. We have deliberately kept a low profile during our first ten years, but I don't think we need to do that so much during the coming ten. We have a lot to offer and we should not hesitate to make that clear. Neither should we hesitate to correct people who claim to speak in the name of Western Buddhists, or British Buddhists, when in fact they have very little contact with them.

You mean we should blow our own trumpet a bit more loudly?
You could put it that way. We haven't blown our trumpet at all yet. I'm not suggesting we should go to the other extreme and blow it just loudly, but certainly we should blow it sweetly and distinctly. We undoubtedly have the largest active membership of any Buddhist movement in the country. We have an Order of 82 committed people, about 150 Mitras, and several hundred Friends who are quite active and involved.

The Movement is still very dependent on you for guidance. Do you think that this will change very much in the next ten years?
I personally have more hope of, say, ten or twelve senior Order members being able to take over from me as it were collectively, rather than of any one person being able to take my place. One may emerge – there's plenty of time – but I'm quite confident that in ten or fifteen years' time the ten or twelve most senior and experienced Order members could collectively – though that's not such a good word – take over my responsibilities quite easily and quite smoothly.

How significant do you think it was to leave us to our own devices when you went away to Cornwall in 1973?
Well clearly the consequences were very positive indeed, and the experiment – if one sees it in that way – a complete success. A very great deal happened immediately afterwards, culminating in Sukhavati. When I went away we virtually had only one centre, the Archway Centre.

All our other centres and branches started up afterwards – with the possible exception of Auckland, where Akshobhya was already holding meetings in his own home. So much has happened, all in the last four years! Let's see what happens while I'm away this time, in Scotland. Probably all sorts of developments will take place.

When there are more centres, in all parts of the world, do you think you will have to do a lot of travelling?
I don't know. At the moment I don't feel like doing a lot of travelling. I wouldn't feel obliged to travel just because we had a lot of centres.

Do you feel that people ought to be able to develop without your presence? In Helsinki a question constantly heard is 'When is Sangharakshita coming?'
As the Movement expands, obviously it will be more and more difficult for me to get around. I'm not even sure that that is the most useful thing I can do for the Movement. I feel more and more, nowadays, that the best thing I can do is to write – to give people material to read and to study. Most of the things I've written on Buddhism reflect, not so much an earlier point of view, but they are not intended specifically to meet the needs of the existing movement. I'm thinking mainly in terms of writing books and articles that would meet the intellectual and spiritual needs of people within the 'Friends' – especially Order members.

Does this include the next volume of your memoirs?
I hope to be able, within the next ten years, to do more than one volume – though I think the memoirs are of only secondary importance. What I would really like to produce is a systematic work on our own way of looking at Buddhism, but expressed not exclusively in traditional terms. It would be more like an exposition of our 'philosophy of life', as it were. I would also like to write some specifically 'Buddhist' things, like a book on the *Sūtra of Golden Light*. These are some of the projects that I have in mind.

So you won't be appearing so much in the various centres of the Movement?
Not during the coming year, at least. After that I don't know. I may feel quite different then. But at the moment I feel I can most usefully spend

my time in relative seclusion, corresponding with people certainly, but devoting most of my time to literary work related to the needs of the Movement. There is a lot that hasn't been expressed clearly and fully yet that people need to know about and to understand.

Do you ever miss India?
Frankly, I can't say that I do. Not even the sunshine! I don't even know that I'd like to go back. Probably I shall one day, just to see old friends, and see what's happened. Possibly when Order members get something started out there I shall pay visits every now and then. I'd like us to do something in India, and have centres in some of the Buddhist holy places, you know, to serve Order members and Friends who were in India on pilgrimage. I'd also like us to do something for the Indian Buddhists, especially the ex-Untouchables. I'm sure we could do a lot of work among them and that our approach to the Dharma would be a very good and positive one for them. In fact, I think they would welcome it.

And this would be a continuation of the work that you were doing in India?
Well, yes. I'm quite sorry I had to stop that, but I felt that my time and energy could be more creatively put into the Buddhist movement in the West. But I certainly haven't forgotten India, and I would very much like some Order members to go there, eventually, and continue my work.

Is India conducive to the spiritual life these days, or do we have a better chance over here?
You definitely have a better chance here. I don't think that, as regards teaching, there is available over there what is available here, now. Quite a lot of the tradition has to be reassessed and recreated: I'm not suggesting changes in the Dharma itself, but the Dharma that has come down to us is not so much the principial Dharma as the Dharma as presented in a certain way, at a certain time, for the benefit of a certain kind of people. England does have some advantages. It's much easier to work for Buddhism here. People are more reliable. Working in India can be very frustrating, because there people can be very lackadaisical. I've certainly succeeded in doing much more here in ten years than I did in twenty over there – leaving aside the fact that I am more experienced

now. Eventually, though, I think the 'Friends' could have quite an effect on Buddhists in the East. Probably not many people, even in the Order, realize exactly what they are involved with, and what is really happening. Maybe they do in a way, but not very vividly or concretely. I think this will dawn on them only after some years. You can't see it when you are so close to it, so much a part of it. Our main objective should be to make the whole Movement a world within a world, a culture within a culture, a community within a community, where everything is as it should be, or at any rate as near to it as we can get. And this world, this culture, should grow and extend until it is virtually coterminous with society itself. That is the ideal. We are certainly achieving it in a very small way already, and I hope that during the next ten years we will achieve it on an even larger scale. I am sure we can do it.

DR CONZE: A PERSONAL APPRECIATION

FWBO Newsletter *no. 45, Spring 1980, pp. 23–5.*

I met Dr Conze for the first time in 1964, only a few months after my return to England after an absence of twenty years. We met in Oxford, where he was then living and teaching and where I had been invited by the University Buddhist Society to give a lecture. Dr Conze attended this lecture, which was on 'The Spiritual Ideal in Buddhism', sitting at the back of the room and following everything I said with great intentness. Afterwards we exchanged a few words of cordial greeting. Those who knew Dr Conze personally, and especially those who have been the objects of what he himself terms his 'disinterested *krodha*',[279] may be surprised to learn that my first impression of this formidable old scholar – an impression that registered instantly, as soon as our eyes met – was that he was an essentially kindly person. Since experience has taught me to trust my first impressions of people, I am convinced that, in the case of Edward Conze, this impression of essential kindliness was correct, and I would still be convinced of its correctness even if I had not experienced nothing but kindness at his hands.

Although the meeting after the lecture was the first time we had come face to face, we had been in fairly regular correspondence for a number of years. How the correspondence started I no longer recollect, but it probably had something to do with the magazine *Stepping-Stones*,[280] which I edited from 1950 to 1952 from the Himalayan township of Kalimpong, where I had settled in 1950 and where I was to remain for fourteen years. At any rate, the last issue of *Stepping-Stones* carried the first instalment of Dr Conze's *Selected Sayings from the Perfection of Wisdom*, afterwards published in book form by the Buddhist Society.[281] It was one of my greatest regrets, when *Stepping-Stones* came to an end, that we were unable to continue the serialization of this important work. However, Dr Conze bore me no ill will for having let him down in this way, and our correspondence continued. After taking over the editorship of the *Maha Bodhi*, I invited him to contribute to that journal, which he did on several occasions, the most interesting of his articles probably being the one on 'Love, Hate and Perfect Wisdom' (reprinted in his *Thirty Years of Buddhist Studies*).[282] In 1960 he agreed to my bringing out *A Short History of Buddhism*, originally contributed in Italian to a publication on the civilization of the East, as the third volume in the Buddhist Library series, which I was then editing for Chetana Ltd of Bombay.[283] Meanwhile, in 1957 or 1958, he had reviewed *A Survey of Buddhism* in terms so eulogistic that I was both surprised and delighted.[284] However, our correspondence was by no means confined to the publication of articles and books. He commented freely on events and personalities in the tiny world of British Buddhism, and by the time we actually met in Oxford it was clear that we were, as he was afterwards to write, 'kindred spirits'.

That first meeting in Oxford was not to be our last. We met whenever I lectured for the University Buddhist Society, which I did several times during the two years (1964–1966) that I was based at the Hampstead Buddhist Vihara. In the course of one visit I attended Dr Conze's lectures on the Madhyamaka school at Manchester College, which is not really a college but a hall of residence and as such not part of the University. I was surprised to see how few people turned up: there could not have been more than twenty. Dr Conze did not seem to be as much appreciated in the venerable 'home of lost causes' as he should have been. Indeed, Buddhism itself did not seem to be very much appreciated. When I naively remarked to Dr Conze that Buddhist philosophy must surely be appreciated in a place like Oxford he sourly replied, 'All they're interested in here is linguistic analysis.' Life was made difficult for him in other ways. With what seemed extraordinary petty-mindedness, his lectures were officially listed as being by 'Mr Conze'. This, I was told, was because although he had, of course, a doctorate in philosophy, it was his misfortune to have obtained it neither from Oxford nor from Cambridge. Moreover, since he had not been able to get a divorce from his first wife, a Roman Catholic, he was at that time not legally married to his second wife, Muriel. So far as the University was concerned, therefore, Muriel did not exist, and she was not included in official invitations. The first time I had lunch with them at their flat he introduced her with what I thought was a slight air of constraint, as though not quite sure how I would react to the situation. He need not have worried. So far as I was concerned, if you lived with someone you were married to them, and I was only sorry that, as it seemed, he felt unable to raise the subject with me openly so that I could tell him exactly where I stood. Indeed it pained me that a man of Dr Conze's eminence should have been made to feel embarrassed for reasons that had nothing whatever to do with genuine morality. Despite the shabby way in which the University establishment treated him, however, life in Oxford was not without its compensations. He and Muriel had a number of friends, among them Guy and Freda Wint, at whose house it was I first realized what a deep and abiding interest Dr Conze had in astrology. From remarks that passed between him and our hostess I gathered that he had cast the horoscope of practically every person present, and that he had been greatly struck by the fact that a high percentage of English Buddhists were Virgoans.

After my farewell visit to India and my final return to England at the beginning of 1967 Edward Conze and I did not see each other again. He was away much of the time in the United States, while I was busy launching the FWBO and WBO in London. However, we exchanged letters occasionally and did each other little friendly services whenever we could. When in the winter of 1969–70 I went to Yale as Visiting Lecturer in Philosophy, it was due partly to his support that I was given my teaching title. By the time he settled permanently in Sherborne, which was in 1973 or 1974, I had left London and was living, initially, in Cornwall. It would then have been possible for us to meet, especially as I sometimes made the journey between Cornwall and London, or between Cornwall and Norfolk, but for some reason or other we never did. Correspondence, however, became more regular, and more animated, and we always sent each other copies of the offprints of our latest articles. (In the academic world, I am told, great importance is attached to the ritual exchange of offprints, the omission of the courtesy sometimes leading to deadly feuds.) All this time I was, of course, keeping him informed about the progress of the FWBO. In view of his well-known antipathy for what he termed 'Western Sectarian Buddhism' it was not surprising that his attitude towards us should at first have been one of reserve, or that he should have made it clear that he had no time to do anything for us, but he soon came round. Before long he was subscribing to the *Newsletter*, which he clearly read with avidity, and not only sending us cheques for small amounts but lamenting that he was not rich enough to give more generously. In later years, especially when he had been writing about the misdeeds of certain Buddhist organizations, he would often conclude his letters with a heartfelt 'Thank heavens for the FWBO!'

After remaining at a respectable plateau for several years, in the early part of 1977 correspondence between us suddenly reached a bit of a peak. I was at that time 'on retreat' on the Isle of Arran, devoting myself mainly to literary work. Dr Conze, in response to Professor de Jong's questions about his life up to 1948, was writing – or rather dictating – his autobiography. Being in some doubt as to whether he should continue with the work, he wrote to ask whether, in my opinion, such an account would harm or benefit the cause of Buddhism, and what alterations might be desirable. After considering the pros and cons of the matter (the pros far outnumbered the cons) I came down in favour of publication, and urged him to continue the story. Indeed, I went further and suggested that he work the account up into a full-scale autobiography along the lines of Karl Popper's *The Unended Quest*,[285] at the same time expressing the hope that Popper was not one of his *bêtes noires*. (He was!) I also suggested that he should give a more detailed account of his early intellectual development, his involvement with politics, and his transition from Marxism to Buddhism. Correspondence relating to *The Memoirs of a Modern Gnostic*,[286] as the autobiography came to be called, eventually reached such proportions, especially after Dr Conze had decided to publish it himself and asked our help with the distribution, that I handed it over to Kulananda and Nagabodhi. Thus a contact that had lasted for more than a quarter of a century came to an end.

On my return from New Zealand in the middle of June I found Part I of the *Memoirs* already on sale at the London Buddhist Centre bookstall, and Part II followed soon afterwards. Though I had seen the greater part of the work in its original duplicated form it was good to see it in its final samizdat dress, with the smart black covers (symbolic of the forces of evil?) on which the figure of Mañjuśrī, the Bodhisattva of Wisdom, picked out in white, brandished his flaming sword – as he did at the top of Dr Conze's personal notepaper. It was good to know that my old friend had been able to finish writing the story of his life and that his autobiography was now complete, or at least as complete as the laws of libel would allow. All the same, I was not wholly satisfied with the result of his labours. The *Memoirs* were less well written than I had hoped (probably Dr Conze did not think it worth his while to spend too much time and energy on mere artistry), and the course of his intellectual and spiritual development was charted in less detail than might have been expected. Still, there were abundant compensations, both in Part I: 'Life and Letters', and Part II: 'Politics, People and Places'. We learn, for instance, about the London-born author's Protestant/capitalist German background, about his special gift for learning languages (fourteen by the age of 24), about his first-remembered contact with Buddhism (not unlike my own, in that it involved the *Diamond Sūtra*), about his aversion to Nazism, about his arrival in England in 1933 with only the suit on his back and £4 in his pocket, about what it was like being a German abroad, about his first contact with Marxism, and later doubts about it, about his rediscovery of Buddhism and discovery of astrology, and about the inception, writing, and publication of all his books. We are also given thumbnail sketches of friends and colleagues and accounts of visits to Italy, the Soviet Union, and the USA, besides being treated to typically Conzean observations on such topics as feminism, social democracy, and people in general. Through the self-denigration and the intellectual pyrotechnics we discern, in luminous outline, the figure of a highly sensitive, intensely energetic, exceptionally talented man of uncompromising honesty and absolute intellectual integrity who never hesitated to sacrifice personal advantage rather than his principles, who invariably spoke as he thought, and who never suffered fools gladly. We are also able to see what it is that makes a Modern Gnostic, or rather, in what sense he describes himself in these terms – a point that had puzzled me for some time. Comparing himself to E. F. Schumacher, economic adviser to the National Coal Board and later on author of *Small is Beautiful*,[287] he says,

> My memoirs clearly show that I am [an] elitist, anarchist person
> who rejects the world and all that is in it, including most of its
> human inhabitants, and feels a kinship with small groups of the
> perfect, in the style of the Pythagoreans, Cathari, Dokhobors, etc.

He, following the Church rather than the Gnostics, is a friend of the ordinary man and acts within society.... Where I work for a spiritual life, so he for a society which makes one possible. My eremitic ways have been forced on me by temperament, social accidents and the general godlessness all around me. I probably would have achieved more [if] I had not been so isolated and on my defensive all the time.[288]

Altogether the *Memoirs* were a fascinating performance and gave me a more rounded, or perhaps I should say a more many-cornered, portrait of their distinguished subject than had emerged either from our meetings in Oxford or from our long correspondence. Despite minor disappointments I was therefore glad to be holding the two slim volumes in my hands at last. Leafing through them, however, I recalled with something like dismay that Dr Conze was expecting me to give his autobiography a 'leg up' (his own phrase) by writing one of what, in a reminder addressed to Kulananda, he ironically referred to as my 'celebrated reviews'. Alas, I had been away on my travels, and the required leg up had not yet been given. Since time was now running out, and Dr Conze was sure to be growing impatient, I started toying with the idea of reviewing the *Memoirs* jointly with Christmas Humphreys' *Both Sides of the Circle*,[289] for which I was expected to perform a similar service, at the same time wondering what Dr Conze (or indeed Christmas Humphreys) would think of the idea. I was still wondering when I heard that Dr Conze had died a few days earlier, on 24 September, and that the funeral would be at Yeovil on 2 October, two days before I started giving my lectures on the *Vimalakīrti-nirdeśa*.[290] Since I was unable to be present personally, I asked Subhuti and Buddhadasa to go and represent me and the Order, which they did, taking with them a large wreath of orange-coloured chrysanthemums. On their return they reported that although Dr Conze had been cremated in accordance with Buddhist rites, there had been no mention of his achievements as a Buddhist scholar or of his services to the cause of Buddhism.

The omission surprised me. Dr Conze's contribution to our fuller understanding and deeper appreciation of the Dharma was of the highest significance, and so far as the English-speaking world at least is concerned it is unparalleled in recent years. This applies especially to *Buddhist Thought in India* (1962),[291] which at the time of writing his *Memoirs* he still viewed as his 'greatest achievement',[292] and his translations and elucidations of the historically important and spiritually indispensable Perfection of Wisdom texts. As he writes in the *Memoirs*,

> The publication in 1974 of *The Short Prajñāpāramitā Texts*
> by Luzac brought me nearer the goal which I had set myself in
> 1938, i.e. to translate all the 42 PP texts into English. In 1938 the
> *Prajñāpāramitā* could be read in five languages, i.e. in Tibetan,
> Mongol, Chinese, Manchu, and Japanese. Now in 1978 about
> 90% of it is also accessible in English, the new World Language.[293]

For these and other services, the consequences of which we cannot even begin to foresee, Western Buddhists, and I think members of the WBO and FWBO in particular, will always be profoundly grateful to Edward Conze. Though wrathful in form, he was truly a bodhisattva. From the realms where he now rests for a while from his labours – realms in which, so one hopes, there is no occasion for *saeva indignatio*[294] – may he look down with approval on all those who are still working for the wider dissemination of the Dharma.

BRAHMACHARYA

FWBO Newsletter *no. 55, pp. 9–10 (Autumn 1982). An extract from a seminar on the 'Chapter of the Snake' from the Sutta-Nipāta held at Pundarika, North London, in 1975.*

SANGHARAKSHITA: What does *brahmacarya* mean? This is very important. *Brahma* literally means sublime, noble, superior, and pertains to higher, sublime, and noble states of consciousness. In other words, to states of meditative consciousness. And the Brahmas as mythological entities are those beings, or gods if you like, who dwell on the higher cosmological planes corresponding to those states. (You can speak subjectively of a state, objectively of a plane, and, in terms of individuals, of a god dwelling on that plane or born or reborn on that plane.) *Carya* means walking, faring, living, practising. A *brahmacārin* is one who is walking like Brahmā, one who is dwelling in sublime states of consciousness, one whose life is rooted in higher, noble, meditative states of consciousness, and who is living out of, and in accordance with, those states. *Brahmacarya* therefore means something like the spiritual life. That is why it is sometimes translated as 'the holy life'. But in the original Pāli and Sanskrit the term doesn't convey the same connotations as the expression 'holy life' in English. It is also sometimes translated as 'the godly life', which doesn't help us very much either. In the Pāli texts, especially in the earlier ones, *brahmacarya* is the word for the whole spiritual life. Following the spiritual path *is* the *brahmacarya*. Later on the word *brahmacarya* underwent a change, and came to mean the practice of celibacy or complete sexual abstinence – a meaning which it had had in an applied or secondary sense even from the beginning. As the third of the eight precepts observed by lay Buddhists on the four fast days of the month and of the ten precepts observed by the novice monk (as well as of the different set of ten precepts observed by the *anagārika*), *abrahmacarya* consists in abstention from non-celibacy, in other words, in the practice of celibacy. What is the connection between *brahmacarya* in the first sense and *brahmacarya* in the second, more applied sense?

SAGARAMATI: Well, you have to be celibate in a meditative state of consciousness.

SANGHARAKSHITA: The celibacy is the natural expression of the meditative state of consciousness, because at that particular time you feel happy and contented within yourself. For instance, if you are actually meditating, and thoroughly enjoying the meditation, then you won't have any sexual feelings, because the meditation experience is more enjoyable. Therefore there won't be any sexual activity. But if you come out of that meditative state of consciousness, then sexual feelings may arise. This is the connection between the two senses of the term. *Brahmacarya* in the sense of celibacy is an application, ideally a natural application, of *brahmacarya* in the first sense. Here there is no conception of *brahmacarya* as a penance, or as a price that has to be paid. The restrictions that you observe in this connection are simply avoidances of stimuli. It is just taking sensible, as it were hygienic, precautions. If you know that you are susceptible to flu, then you stay away from those places where lots of germs are circulating. So if you find that you are sexually susceptible, you will stay away from those situations in which your sexual susceptibilities are intensified. It is just a common-sense precaution until such time as you so firmly dwell in the *dhyāna* states that sex doesn't bother you any more....

The important point in connection with *brahmacarya* is that it is a state of mind, a higher mode or level of consciousness, the effects of which must be manifested more and more in actual action. It is not a discipline imposed as it were from without.

SIDDHIRATNA: Actual actions in one sense would be the beginning of wanting to be celibate, or of celibacy.

SANGHARAKSHITA: You could want to be celibate in the sense of wanting to experience higher states of consciousness, as a result of which you would tend to be naturally celibate, or you could want to be celibate for the sake of celibacy, out of feelings of guilt, inadequacy, etc.

I sometimes say that there are two kinds of sexuality: neurotic and non-neurotic. The non-neurotic is non-neurotic. The non-neurotic is when there is sexual activity, not through any need for security, for example, through the 'relationship', but just because you are young and healthy. Neurotic sexuality is where there is not only the actual sexual urge, but also an infantile craving for security, contact, warmth, and so on, through sexual relationship or activity. It may be, in the case of some people, that they do experience higher states of consciousness, *dhyāna* states, yet at the same time a certain amount of sexual activity may go on, but this will certainly be non-neurotic. However, one must be very careful that one doesn't, as it were, leave a loophole and deceive oneself here. The great test is how you feel if the relationship breaks up. If your partner, or lover, or whatever, says, 'Bye-bye! I've found somebody else.' If you can say, 'That's great! See you tomorrow,' and just accept it happily, then you had no neurotic craving along with your sexual relationship and activity. But if you are cut up, upset, and disturbed and can't meditate for months, well, obviously there has been a strong neurotic element. So that is the criterion.

SUVRATA: There are also another person's feelings involved. They might be getting neurotically involved, and you might do them harm, even if your own involvement was non-neurotic.

SANGHARAKSHITA: Sure, you must consider that too. One doesn't want to lay down hard and fast rules. A lot depends upon temperament, physical state, and so on. It may well be that some people, once they get absorbed into higher states of consciousness, and once those states become normal, may not feel like engaging in any sexual activity at all, ever. Others may have the same experience of the meditative states, but their physical type may be different. They may be more healthy, more vital, and a certain amount of physical sexual activity may continue. But, certainly, in neither case will there be any neurotic craving – this is the really important thing. There is not much point in giving up sex as a sort of discipline when the neurotic craving and dependence is still there and maybe finding outlets in other ways. You may still be just as neurotically attached to your dog or cat. But one must again emphasize that one must be very honest with oneself, and not indulge in any sort of self-deception, which is so easy: 'Oh, I am free. I am not attached. I don't really care if it ends tomorrow.' But if it *does* end tomorrow, well, that's quite another story....

PADMAPANI: Presumably if one had a neurotic relationship, and the relationship broke up, the sexual urge or drive could go into other things, like pleasures of a material nature. Would you say that was so?

SANGHARAKSHITA: You can invest your energy and your sense of security in completely material things – even objects. Like the houseproud woman who may be quite frigid sexually, but completely neurotically dependent, as it were, on her three-piece suite and all the rest of it.

PADMAPANI: One's new car....

SANGHARAKSHITA: One's new car, one's stamp collection – so many things. But for most people the neurotic craving to a very great extent goes along with sex. So it is usually there that one has to watch it most. The great criterion is whether one can remain happy whatever happens, whatever storms may come. If the storm does pour down and sweeps things away, and if you are still happy, then you can be sure there was no neurotic element in your attachment.

PADMAPANI: Couldn't you have a neurotic relationship, and the actual fact of its ending precipitate a breakthrough?

SANGHARAKSHITA: Well, it always does happen that it ends, because you lose everything in the end. To what extent you can respond healthily, and get good out of it, depends on the sort of person you basically are. Some people, at least as far as this life is concerned, are destroyed by the break-up, be it of a relationship, job, or a particular ambition; simply destroyed. But others respond in a healthier way, and even develop a sort of insight. They see what happened and grow because of it. But growth is not automatic. When all your castles in the air come tumbling down, you may be buried beneath them and never get up again – not as regards this lifetime. You can sometimes meet people like that. Their marriage has broken up, or their business has failed, or they have lost their money:

they can't do anything. But others are more resilient. It depends on one's basic health or unhealthiness, in the ordinary human sense. Certainly you can have a breakthrough at such times, but that doesn't justify the previous attachment. One has to be very careful of that. Some people try to argue that attachments are good, because when they break up you get a real insight. Be very careful of this line of thought. I think that for the average Westerner, trying to follow a spiritual path, this whole question of sex and so on is one of the most touchy of all. You have to be very careful that people don't fall victim to the current *micchā-diṭṭhis*. At the same time, you don't want to encourage feelings of guilt. One has to follow a middle path, which is very, very difficult.

TOBY AS I KNEW HIM

Personal Reminiscences of Christmas Humphreys

FWBO Newsletter *no. 58, Summer 1983, p. 22.*

Christmas Humphreys was born in 1901 and died in 1983. He was president of the Buddhist Society for over fifty years, and author of the Penguin *Buddhism* – one of the most popular studies of the subject ever written. Six months after his death it is much too early to try to assess the nature and significance of his contribution to Western Buddhism. A few personal reminiscences may, however, be in order.[295]

I met Christmas Humphreys for the first time in 1942, at the Society's premises in Great Russell Street, not far from the British Museum. He was turned 40, and I was still very much in my teens. It was, of course, wartime. Meetings were held once a week and I remember that at one meeting, while we were 'meditating', a doodlebug exploded nearby, causing the windows to rattle; but nobody stirred.[296] After meetings we often adjourned to a nearby restaurant for a meal. On one such occasion Toby (as he already was) treated the whole class to dinner. There were only seven or eight of us – virtually the whole effective Buddhist movement in Britain. Forty years later I would not like to have to take the whole present effective FWBO membership out to dinner. At least, I would not like to have to foot the bill. After the meal was over Toby recited his own French translation of a sonnet he had written, and a discussion ensued between him and one of the ladies present as to the best way of rendering one particular line, which so far as I remember was about his heart being 'caught in one of her tresses' (presumably a reference to Mrs Humphreys, who was not present). We all thought Toby very clever.

After my departure for India with the army in August 1944 Toby and I corresponded fairly regularly, though my real confidante continued to be Clare Cameron,[297] the rather enigmatic editor of the *Middle Way*. The correspondence continued even when Toby himself went to Japan as junior prosecuting counsel in the War Crimes Trials. Like Clare Cameron and several other English Buddhists I thought that for him to function in this way was inconsistent with his position as president of the Buddhist Society, and wrote and told him so. Toby sharply disagreed. The Japanese saw no inconsistency, he wrote, and he saw no reason why I should. Even as early as that, it would seem, he had formulated his famous theory of the law – and the lawyer – as the appointed instrument of karmic retribution.

Correspondence continued after my settlement in Kalimpong in 1950, and in 1956 we met in New Delhi. The occasion was, of course, the government-sponsored celebration of the 2500th anniversary of Buddhism. Toby was particularly keen to meet the Dalai and Panchen Lamas, both of whom were coming to India specially for the occasion. We in fact met the Dalai Lama together (thereby hangs a tale, but I will keep it for another time.)[298] Subsequently I saw Toby in his room at the Ashoka Hotel. Perhaps because I had now lived in India for more than a decade, what struck me most about him was his extreme coldness of manner. He seemed the archetypal icy Englishman. Some time later he visited me at my vihara in Kalimpong, and I took him to see Dhardo Rimpoche. On this occasion he thawed a little, though the only time he really softened was when he spoke of Puck (i.e. Mrs H.), for whom he bought a pair of tigerstone earrings. 'She's an old lady with white hair,' he murmured sentimentally, half to himself.

In 1964 I returned to England, partly at Toby's suggestion, though hardly at his invitation. From 1964 to 1966, when I returned to India for four months, I naturally saw quite a lot of him. One of my earliest reminiscences from this period relates to an incident that took place at the Buddhist Society's summer school, which I attended some ten days after my arrival. Turning up at the lecture hall one morning to give my first talk I found Toby waiting for me with every sign of impatience. 'You're two minutes late!' he snapped, looking up at the clock above the door. 'I'm sorry, but I don't have a watch,' I explained. I had not owned a watch for years. (Wrist-watches are regarded by the modern Theravāda as a form of jewellery, and may not be worn by monks.)

'You don't have a watch?' exclaimed Toby, thoroughly scandalized. The upshot was that the Society bought me a watch for my birthday, which fell a few days later. Nineteen years on I am still wearing that watch, a symbol of my bondage to clock time.

Every few weeks Toby visited me at the Hampstead Buddhist Vihara, just to make sure I was doing things in the right way. Usually he came with a long list of matters that required some kind of joint decision, as between the Society and the Vihara (between whom there existed a good deal of bad feeling that both he and I were anxious to dispel). 'I'm sure you will agree that...' he would say, rattling through the items on his list, and ticking them off one by one without giving me a chance to say anything. I shall never forget his look of genuine surprise when, after two or three such visits, I said, 'Wait a minute Toby, I'm not sure that I quite agree with that.' He was clearly unaccustomed to such treatment at the Buddhist Society. After that we always discussed things. Similarly I shall never forget the occasion on which he told me, in all seriousness, that I should think of myself as the Buddhist equivalent of the vicar of Hampstead. (Was he aware that to some irreverent English Buddhists *he* was known as the Pope of Eccleston Square?)

After my return to England in 1967 and the establishment of the FWBO, there followed several years during which we did not see each other at all, but gradually contact was re-established. During the last seven or eight years of his life we met at least once or twice a year. I could not help noticing that after the death of Puck – indeed, after her disappearance into a nursing home – he mellowed considerably. Each time we met he seemed more glad to see me than ever, and exuded greater warmth and friendliness. This was partly because there were few English Buddhists he had known for so long, or with whom he shared so many recollections. Sometimes he forgot exactly how long we really had known each other. 'Do you remember that time in 1933,' he would say, 'when the Society...' 'But Toby, I didn't start coming along until 1942,' I would gently protest. 'Of course, of course,' he would mutter, not very pleased that he had been caught out. 'Stupid of me. I should have remembered.'

During the last three or four years of his life Toby was fascinated, indeed almost obsessed, by the subject of the FWBO, and would cross-examine me at length about it. With some difficulty he was able to grasp the difference between membership of the Order and membership of a

Buddhist society, but at the time of his death he was still puzzling over what the FWBO actually taught. 'But what do you *teach*?' he would ask me whenever we met, as though it was an impenetrable mystery. 'Buddhism,' I would reply, just to tease him, but this of course did not satisfy him at all. Perhaps Subhuti's book,[299] about which he displayed intense curiosity, and which he wanted to see in manuscript (Subhuti did, in fact, send him a chapter or two) would have answered his question. It is 'symbolic' that he should have died only a few days after it was published.

I last saw Toby in the summer of 1982, shortly before my departure for Italy. As we said goodbye on the doorstep of 56 Marlborough Place, where we had said goodbye so many times before, I felt the warmth and friendliness of his parting 'look after yourself' more strongly than ever, and the thought crossed my mind that we might not meet again – and we didn't.

JUST LIVING MY LIFE

An interview with Sangharakshita

FWBO Newsletter *no. 62, Summer 1984, pp. 9–15. The questions were put by the editor, Nagabodhi.*

In a lecture you once gave, 'The Nucleus of a New Society',[300] you said that until you received an invitation from the English Sangha Trust you had no plans at all for returning to the West. Is that really true?
Not only had I never thought of returning, I had quite consciously, definitely, and deliberately made up my mind that I would be staying in India. I liked India. I liked the Indians. India was, after all, the original homeland of Buddhism. I was quite happy with my whole way of life there and what I was doing. So, that being the case, I had no plans to return.

But you did come back, originally for just a visit.
Officially it was just to be a four-month visit. When I received the invitation my initial response was to say no. But it was Bhikkhu Khantipālo[301] who put it to me that perhaps I did have a sort of responsibility towards the Buddhist movement in England. At that time the Buddhist movement in England – though perhaps I should say London – was divided into two camps, so to speak, and there was a lot of tension between them. Khantipālo suggested that a visit from me could perhaps help to heal the rift, and he put it to me that I had a sort of duty to do what I could.

Had you kept in touch with developments in the Western Buddhist world during your time in India?

I had *been* kept in touch. For instance, I received the *Middle Way*, and had been reading that year after year. I was in correspondence to a limited extent with Christmas Humphreys, and a few other people like Jack Austin, Dr Conze, and Adrienne Bennett. Also, Christmas Humphreys had been out to India twice, where I had met him. He had been out to Kalimpong.[302]

What were your impressions of the English Buddhist movement on your return?

I had got the impression that the British Buddhist movement was very much bigger and more vigorous than it actually was. The *Middle Way* was quite a good Buddhist magazine but, as I discovered after my return, it was not really the product of the British Buddhist movement at all. It drew on a much wider range of talent than was actually contained within the active Buddhist movement in Britain.

Did you find that the rifts and the difficulties were as serious as you had been led to believe?

I don't find it very easy to recall. I think I found that the difficulties were much more complicated. There were, on the whole, two main camps: one based on the Buddhist Society, and the other based on the Hampstead Buddhist Vihara. But there were several people who had a foot in each camp, as it were, without necessarily always agreeing among themselves. There were also complicating factors like the Chiswick Vihara (the Maha Bodhi Society's centre), and the Thai *bhikkhus*; and of course, personalities played quite a part. So there were in fact quite a number of rifts over a number of issues, some of which overlapped. It was sometimes quite difficult to get to the bottom of things and find out what had gone wrong.

Broadly speaking, the Buddhist Society stood for a more ecumenical approach to Buddhism, and the Hampstead Vihara stood for an exclusively Theravāda approach. But to complicate matters, there were some people connected with the Buddhist Society who were quite strongly sympathetic to the Theravāda, and there were one or two Theravādins who had Zen sympathies in a rather inconsistent sort of way. In addition, of course, there were people who were involved with psychological approaches of various kinds.

A big issue when I arrived was the question of the so-called *vipassanā* meditation. Some people in the Buddhist Society were seriously worried about this – I think quite rightly – because the way in which it was being taught by some of the people connected with the Hampstead Vihara was certainly very extreme, and they had had a number of quite severe psychological casualties. This had, perhaps, crystallized the issue between the two groups.

Did you see yourself as having the specific job of trying to heal the rift, and then returning to India?
I didn't see it in such specific terms, but it had been put to me that I could be of help. I was, as it were, an outsider; I was a fairly well-known Buddhist of English origin, of some standing and of some seniority in the order. Actually, it didn't work out quite as simply as that.

In both camps there were moderate, reasonable people, and there were extremists. Some people connected with the Hampstead Vihara didn't like the fact that I used to go along to the Buddhist Society on friendly terms, and even give classes and lectures there. On the other hand, there were people at the Buddhist Society who were very displeased that someone from the 'enemy camp', as they saw it – because I was living at the Hampstead Buddhist Vihara – was actually having the audacity to come to the Society.

So although I may have succeeded in bringing together the moderate people, I think that in the course of two years I offended the extremists in both camps!

In 1967 you returned to India for a 'farewell visit' before turning to work in the West. But during that visit you received a letter from the English Sangha Trust discontinuing the invitation to work in England. You have said that when you read that letter you immediately saw that it signified a new Buddhist movement. Had you not already seen the need for such a movement?
I had definitely seen the need, but I had not really seen my way through to getting a new movement going. I had talked about the matter with some friends, and had even made some provisional plans to start what might turn into the beginning of a new Buddhist movement.

I definitely felt the need for some kind of new departure, but I knew quite well that the situation in London was such that even my strongest supporters would not welcome the idea of a new Buddhist group or movement. The general feeling was that it was unfortunate that the Buddhist movement was split already, and that there were already quite a number of groups not getting on. People didn't want another one, even if it was a good one.

So, in a way, the letter cleared the ground?
I felt that I now had, so to speak, the perfect excuse. I had tried to heal the rifts, but now no one could blame me for starting up something new.

I wonder, having read some of the things you wrote in the East, whether you had already formulated a blueprint for a new Buddhist movement?
I had thought about it quite a lot. For instance, there were two articles I wrote in the early sixties entitled 'Wanted: A New Type of *Upāsaka*', and 'Wanted: A New Type of *Bhikkhu*'.[303] Those two articles alone show the way my mind was moving. Even earlier, there were all the strictures, especially on the Theravāda, in *A Survey of Buddhism*.[304] But perhaps I should say that even those two articles were 'reformist' rather than, to use the term, 'revolutionary'. They didn't represent thinking in terms of a new Buddhist movement so much as in terms of updating the old one. I was thinking of a reformed sangha, rather than a sangha put on a completely different, that is to say its *original*, basis, as we have now in the Western Buddhist Order.

So when you actually began to set up the new movement, in 1967, to what extent did you feel that you were following circumstances, devising it as you went along, and to what extent did you feel that you had thought it through already?
I can't say that I followed circumstance, but on the other hand I can't really say that I had thought it through. Looking back on my life, it doesn't seem that I have operated in these two ways, actually. I have always had a very strong sense of the general direction in which I am moving, but I have never been bothered about the details. So when I look back over my life I can see that I am very definitely moving in a certain direction, but I rarely think in what direction I am moving in any sort of specific way. It is as though, if I do what just lies to hand, the fact that I have some overall ideals and principles leads to the creation of a pattern. So I wasn't simply reacting to circumstances, nor did I

have a sort of clear-cut plan thought up in advance. You may say that there were these archetypes operative within me, in accordance with which I responded to circumstances, and which therefore resulted in the creation of certain kind of pattern and the creation of a certain type of movement.

But were you aware at the time of what a unique project you were engaged in?

I was certainly aware of it being different. Though perhaps even that statement has to be made with reservations, because I certainly saw the FWBO as a traditional Buddhist movement. I am by nature, you might say, a traditionalist. I don't think of myself as an innovator or revolutionary, or anything of that sort. If I am a revolutionary, it is a reluctant revolutionary: a revolutionary by force of circumstances. But I was very conscious of certain things that I didn't want to happen in the FWBO. I didn't want it to be the sort of Buddhist group or movement that I had so far experienced in England. On the other hand, I was very clear about the basic Buddhist principles that I wanted to see followed.

It seems that at the time you were working very much alone.

One must remember that I was quite accustomed to functioning on my own in India. It wasn't as though I had had the support of a very strong sangha there; far from it. I had very worthwhile contact with certain individuals like Bhikkhu Kashyap, and later on with Dhardo Rimpoche and other Tibetan teachers, but I certainly never functioned as part of a team. I was quite accustomed to working on my own.

In India, where I've heard you teaching among the new Buddhists, the medium of communication for the Dharma seems to be predominantly social: the Dharma as a social force. Here in the West, the language seems to have been predominantly personal, individual, psychological: the language of individual growth. Do you feel that this is closer to your own, personal approach?

Oh no. Not at all. I think by nature I'm not especially sympathetic to the psychological approach, nor am I particularly sympathetic to the social approach. My own interest is more definitely spiritual, doctrinal, metaphysical. I get onto these sorts of topics as quickly as I can, using the psychological and the social simply as means of approach. I certainly don't think that Buddhism is all about psychology in the modern sense, nor do I think it is all about social life, again in the modern sense.

Having said that, I should add that after coming to England I did develop some limited interest in psychology, and did study a little of it. Similarly, as a result of my contact with the ex-Untouchables, I did become more aware of the social dimension of Buddhism.

So did you feel frustrated by a lack of appropriate conceptual models or cultural keys in the West that could serve as a medium for the communication of the Dharma?
No. I can't say that because I did, after all, use the evolutionary model. If I've ever felt frustrated by anything, it has been simply lack of time – including the lack of time to acquaint myself with the various models of Western thought.

In the very early days you did seem to cast your net quite widely. You would quote from the Gospels, Jung, Fromm, Maslow...
Those names were very much in the air at that time. A lot of people who came along to classes and lectures had read those particular authors. I just wanted to create a sort of atmosphere of being at home with those authors, recognizing a certain amount of common ground, even using them as bridges. I must say my personal interest in all these writers rather quickly waned.

So you were in no way looking for a synthesis between the Dharma and those current models?
I never had any idea of creating a synthesis between the Dharma and those things. I never saw them as being on anything like the same level as the Dharma. If you think of the Dharma as the expression of the Enlightened consciousness, and these other things, however interesting, as the product of groupings of unenlightened minds, the idea of any synthesis between the two would have seemed really quite absurd.

At that time, those books and ideas were to some extent tied up with the hippy culture. You seemed to be making yourself quite accessible to that culture.
Clearly one was addressing people who were looking for something, people who weren't able to find what they wanted, or what they needed,

within the existing social system or religious framework. So, in a sense, one was addressing people who had to some extent 'dropped out'.[305] I think that the majority of people who were coming along were not hippies in the literal sense, but people who were looking for an alternative and had in some cases already looked at the various alternatives.

Nevertheless, some people did think you were getting a bit too close for their comfort to the hippy generation, and even now the FWBO is sometimes regarded as being a bit of a hangover from that era.

I remember someone who became very upset about what he referred to as hippies who were 'taking over' the FWBO, so one day I sat down with him and we went through all the people who were coming to classes (there weren't many of them in those days), looking at the individuals concerned, and he had to admit that, after all, only one of them could perhaps have been described as a hippy. So I think it was almost entirely projection. In the case of this particular person, clearly he saw the hippy as wild, undisciplined, dirty, erotic – all those things which he had suppressed, I think, in his own life.

But really, one is not going to recruit one's members from convinced Christians or regular churchgoers! You have to recruit them from people who have, as it were, dropped out. They may still have their jobs and their families, but spiritually speaking, one might say, they have dropped out. The mere fact that you have a Buddhist movement at all means that you recruit from these people. Any Eastern tradition that takes root in the West necessarily, by definition, is alternative, and draws on that pool of alternative people. So to say that the FWBO is an alternative movement is a truism. So is everything that is not Christianity in this country. The Buddhist Society itself is alternative.

Are you generally content with the way in which the Movement has developed?

Well, yes and no. So far so good. Of course I feel that things have not gone nearly far enough yet. There are a lot of things that I would like to see happening. Order members emerge at a much slower rate than I would like to see. We haven't really effectively covered the United Kingdom, not to speak of Europe, not to speak of the world. We are mainly established in the south-east corner of England, and we have a very long way to go yet.

Have you felt frustrated by this slowness?
I have sometimes wondered why progress isn't quicker. Sometimes it has seemed that progress is unnecessarily slow, especially when I see people who have been exposed to the influence of the FWBO for quite a while but who don't seem to have such a great appreciation of the urgency of the situation as one would expect.

It is sometimes suggested that when you took a year away from direct involvement with centre activities, in 1973, there was something of an ultimatum involved. Some people thought that if we didn't pull together and get things moving you might even return to India.
I don't think that possibility crossed my mind. There were other factors which perhaps people did not appreciate. One was that I had been fully involved in active Buddhist work for quite a number of years. Before my six years with the FWBO there had been two very busy and active years with the Hampstead Buddhist Vihara, and before that my work in India. And, of course, I had my memoirs to be finished. One of the very important reasons I went to Cornwall was that I wanted to finish them. Which I did.

I believe you quite recently said that you have often been surprised to realize how hard some people find it to change.
I do know that there are quite a number of sincere people who have been involved with the FWBO, perhaps for five, six, seven, and even ten years or more, who try quite hard, who struggle quite hard, but who nonetheless seem unable to change very much at all. This does sometimes surprise me.

Of course, there are on the other hand quite a few people who do change quite dramatically as a result of their exposure to the FWBO, and their involvement with meditation, spiritual friendship, and so on.

You seem to be one of those! From what I know about you it would seem that you have always been 100% clear, 100% committed – to the extent that I sometimes find myself wondering, 'What's different about him? When did you struggle? When did you have trouble with your commitment?' Can you remember such times?
I can certainly look back and remember some things with regard to which I can connect with others in this way. I had to make a definite

effort, even to struggle, with things like mindfulness. I've worked on mindfulness for years together. Not that I was especially unmindful, but I was very, very conscious that I needed to be much more mindful than I was. So I can certainly remember having to struggle with certain things. But I've certainly never had any sort of doubt as regards my overall direction, or about my – for want of a better term – involvement with the spiritual life. I think I can also say that whenever I came to exercise my mind, I was able to understand the Dharma. One of the things that surprises me most about people is their inability to think clearly. I think I can say, without claiming too much, that this has been natural to me.

Again, it seems remarkable about you, so far as one gathers, that you don't seem to have suffered from the absence of emotional clarity that perhaps gives rise to unclear thinking in others.
I think I've always had confidence in my own basic direction, so that I did not have to be overscrupulous, for instance, about my interest in things like poetry. Some people whom I knew clearly regarded that as a sort of deviation from the spiritual path. I didn't really think that, although I was influenced by that way of thinking for a while. But eventually I had sufficient faith in myself to feel that my interest in poetry was not inconsistent with my commitment to spiritual life. I think I was to a great extent free from emotional conflict because I had this confidence in myself and in the fact that the direction in which I was moving was the right one.

The more I have been left to my own devices and the less I have had to do with other people, the easier have I found things. So, in a sense, the latter part of my life has been the least easy because I've become increasingly involved with people, and therefore increasingly involved with their problems and difficulties – which are not my own, and have never been my own. I'm often quite surprised by people's lack of conscientiousness, their unreliability, and so on.

How, then, have you managed to avoid becoming cynical?
I can understand people being cynical. But what is cynicism? Cynicism arises when there is a lack of emotional positivity to safeguard one from cynicism. But I can also see that, despite their lapses and backslidings, and stumbling and straying, people do very often make, at least intermittently, a very sincere effort. So one appreciates that too. It's not

as though the backslide is the whole of the story. I'm also very conscious of the fact that a lot of people have had a very unfavourable start in life, so one can't help feeling for them, and understanding, certainly in some cases, why they find it so difficult to make progress, and why there are so many things to be sorted out.

After the founding of the FWBO it seems that you devoted the first few years to explaining and introducing Buddhism; then a period followed when you put a lot of thought and direction into the more material superstructure: the centres, cooperatives, and communities. More lately, perhaps, your main input has been in the tracking down of woolly thinking, wrong views, and so on. Has this just been a matter of historical circumstance, or would you see that order as representing a hierarchy of priorities in your mind?

It didn't represent a conscious hierarchy of priorities. In fact I don't think that I had had any idea that I would have to direct my mind to things like co-ops. I directed my mind to those things because they were needed. Certainly I would have preferred to study another poet, or something of that sort.

I sometimes get the impression that you are taking a view of the Movement's development that extends, literally, hundreds of years into the future. Is this the case?

I would agree, yes. There are quite a lot of things that I say, or things that we say in the FWBO, the more far-reaching implications of which hardly anybody realizes – apart from myself. But I suppose that is only natural. This is a more conscious thing; it is tied up with my historical sense. I've always been interested in history, so I think I can say that my sense of history is very well developed. I'm very conscious, therefore, of the position of the FWBO and the WBO in the broader context of history and of Buddhism itself. Within that context, twenty years seems to be a very short time indeed.

Do you think it has been long enough for us to come up against the major obstacles that we will have to face?

That's very difficult to say. We have to bear in mind that we have limited ourselves to a great extent. You know, we have started the Movement in England, which is perhaps the easiest country to start something like the

FWBO in. If we had tried to start in a Communist country, or an Islamic country, it would have been a very different matter. We have had a very easy time so far, in the sense that we haven't come up against any real opposition at all. But clearly we will have to move into more difficult areas.

For much of its history the FWBO has been small, financially poor, 'low-profile' in terms of public image, and very dependent on the input of people with a high level of commitment. But now we seem to be growing bigger, a little richer, and there are more levels of involvement available. We seem to be broadening out. I think this is something you've said in the past that you would welcome. But how do you think we will best maintain the radical spiritual integrity of the Movement as we do broaden out?

One could think of course in terms of our just broadening out in the sense of dilution; that is to say, with the average level of commitment becoming lower. I don't want to see that sort of broadening. The other kind of broadening is a broadening in the sense of the small committed group operating along a broader front. I see that as something quite different. So when I say I'm happy to see the Movement broadening out, what I mean is that I'm happy to see the committed nucleus operating along that broader front.

But our centres will doubtless attract into their orbit people whose level of commitment is less than that of, say, Order members. Is not some kind of dilution inevitable?

I don't think that need represent a dilution. The whole structure of the FWBO is such as to keep 'power', for want of a better term, effectively in the hands of Order members – the spiritually committed – so that they have a deciding voice in everything. As long as we maintain that principle and that structure there is no danger of dilution, however many people there are involved with the Movement. That is, of course, provided that the Order itself maintains its present vitality. There can be no built-in guarantee for that because that rests on the sense of responsibility, or the spiritual awareness, of each individual.

But could there develop a 'split' between the strongly and the not-so-strongly committed, perhaps akin to the 'monk–laity' split encountered in the East?

I think there is that possibility. It is there all the time when one does have radically different lifestyles. But such a split will not develop if people maintain the same level of commitment, regardless of lifestyle. I think the danger very definitely lies with those who are committed to, for want of a better term, the family and the domestic lifestyle. There is a definite danger that, owing to that sort of lifestyle, that sort of situation, there will come about some weakening of their commitment. If that happens – if there are too many people involved in that sort of lifestyle and with a weakened commitment – a split will develop, so to speak, between them and those people who are not following that sort of lifestyle, and whose commitment is more vigorous and more alive.

So I think the first point is that the split will not come about at all if Order members equally, regardless of lifestyle, keep up a full commitment to the Three Jewels and, secondly, if those who are involved with a family and domestic type of life especially are careful to see that they do maintain their full commitment.

It is the responsibility of Order members to keep each other up to scratch. This will be one of the main responsibilities of the Order chapters. Where the Order chapters are not conterminous with a single-sex community it will be good to have a mix of people in them: a balance of people – those who are living in small, single-sex communities, and those who are living at home with their spouses and families.

Over the next twenty years, would you envisage consistent steady growth along the lines that we are witnessing at the moment, or would you envisage any kind of quantum leap in the Movement's development?

I would like to see a few more quantum leaps. I think they can be expected from time to time in the life of the Movement, just as in the life of the individual. It would be surprising if there weren't any quantum leaps in the Movement. Such a leap did take place with the creation of the Sukhavati and London Buddhist Centre complex. Again, a quantum leap took place with the establishment of the Tuscany preordination course. You could say that the whole Aid For India project was a quantum leap. It seems to me that such leaps are likely to be associated with particularly capable or gifted individuals.

With regard to the future, I'm thinking here of someone perhaps becoming involved, becoming an Order member, who is, for example, a very gifted poet or novelist, who is widely recognized as such, who through his poetry or his fiction could achieve a breakthrough into the whole world of literature for the FWBO. It could of course be into the world of film, or business, economics, and so on.

So could we be doing more to create the conditions for those quantum leaps?
Well, the more alive the Movement generally, the more alive the people it will attract. Certainly the standard has improved over the years. We are now attracting more healthy, capable, and balanced people than we formerly did. So it is to be hoped that we will likewise attract in the future more and more people who are positively talented and highly skilled – which will represent a very great increment to the Movement.

Do you think it is at all possible yet to isolate any trends in the FWBO that may give a clue to the more final nature of Western Buddhism?
I think it's probably too early. Before then I would like to see the single-sex communities multiplying much more than they have done, and I would like to see the women's retreat centre emerging. I would like to see much more activity on that front.

When Subhuti's *Buddhism for Today* was published I saw this as a landmark not only for the Movement but for me also.[306] I felt that something had been passed on that would continue. In some ways I was as happy with the publication of Subhuti's book as Subhuti was himself!

You have often said that you would like to see Order members conducting ordinations. Do you have any idea how long it will be before that is happening?
I can't say. I would like it to be this year but I know it's not going to be this year. It is, in a sense, a responsibility I want to hand on, to leave myself free for other things. I've enjoyed giving ordinations, I love going to Tuscany, I enjoy ordination retreats, but now I see other things as being even more important.

If I look back to the very early retreats, in those days I couldn't even entrust the evening puja to anybody – not even to an Order member. There were evenings when I had to rush up to London from a retreat to take a class there and then rush back – hoping that nothing had gone wrong during my absence – in time to take the evening puja, because nobody else could do it.

So consider the tremendous difference between then and now! I don't have anything at all to do with retreats, except to go along and give ordinations. And it's not as if the retreats now are only as good as they were when I was taking them; they are far better, because they now have the weight of the Movement behind them. So, yes, I can envisage the responsibility for ordinations being taken over by the more experienced Order members sooner or later.

What are the things to which you want to give priority now?
As I see things at present I want to give priority to my writing for two or three years. I also want to keep in touch with India; I see myself making regular visits there for as long as I can, if only to give ordinations and give a few lectures. I also want to operate, personally, along a broader front, if I possibly can, and make more contacts in the outside world. Last year, for instance, I had contacts with groups of clergymen, and I gave a lecture to the Wrekin Trust's 'Mystics and Scientists' conference.[307] So I shall perhaps be trying to do more of that sort of thing if the opportunity arises. But my main priority is, of course, my literary work.

One last question. Do you ever stand back from your work and recognize how much you've achieved, how much you've given?
By the very nature of the part I've played it's very difficult for me to do this. I'm just living my life, doing what is natural for me to do. I must say that in recent years I have received so many letters from people in the Movement expressing their appreciation of the FWBO, and their appreciation of me for having started the FWBO, that I can no longer really ignore the fact that I really have started something.

You never allow yourself a glow of contentment?
I can't say that I experience anything of that sort. To me it seems that I'm just living my life; I'm doing what I want to do and what I think it is right to do, and that's that. – Just as, on another level one might say, the ordinary person doesn't think, 'Well here am I; I have held this job for all these years, and I've brought up these two children and...' He

doesn't look back on that with a tremendous glow of pride, because it's just his life.

Yes, but that is a life lived more reactively – in reaction to certain instincts and conditionings; whereas you have lived your life creatively. Surely there's more individual initiative involved?
Yes, but in the same way that the reactivity is natural for him, creativity is natural for me. So it doesn't seem such a big deal. Do you see what I mean?

LAST CORRESPONDENCE BETWEEN LAMA GOVINDA AND SANGHARAKSHITA

FWBO Newsletter *no. 65, Spring 1985, pp. 13–14. On 14 January 1985, in California, USA, Lama Govinda died at the age of 86. He lived for many years in India where he developed a strong friendship with Sangharakshita. The last in this exchange of letters between Lama Govinda and Sangharakshita is dated four days before the lama's death.*

122 Lomita Drive, Mill Valley, California 94941
6 September 1984

My dear Sangharakshita-ji, What a pleasant surprise to receive your recent publications, your *Ten Pillars of Buddhism* and your essay about *World Peace and Nuclear War*.[308] For such a long time we have not heard from you or about your activities that we are happy to know that you are well and still busy with your writings which we have always enjoyed. After my book on *The Inner Structure of the I Ching* some years ago,[309] I have not been able to write much, except two books in German: one a collection of unpublished essays and another on the dynamic attitude of Buddhism and the bodhisattva ideal, with special reference to Western philosophy and life.[310] I do not intend to write further books. My eyes are two weak for sustained work or even painting, and I can only move about in a wheelchair, since my legs are partially paralyzed due to a stroke. But otherwise I am all right. Last May the Arya Maitreya

Mandala[311] organized a month-long exhibition of some of my paintings and books, together with lectures by well-known Indologists and prominent representatives of our Order (AMM). The Mayor of Stuttgart and one of the German ministers opened the exhibition in the town hall of Stuttgart. The exhibition, as well as the lectures, attracted much interest and a lot of publicity for the AMM and Buddhism in general. As I am now 86 years old, I have appointed Dr Gottmann (Advayavajra) to be my successor and leader of the AMM. We emphasize, like you, the fundamentals of Buddhism, without rejecting its different forms and interpretations, thus making it possible for Westerners to adopt it as a modern way of life. Theravāda, Mahāyāna, and Vajrayāna are equally represented and studied, because we feel that each branch of Buddhism has some valuable contributions to the Dharma. The AMM, which is steadily growing, is now more than fifty years old and has become one of the most influential organizations in central Europe. Now it is up to the next generation to take Buddhism out of the merely academic atmosphere and make it a matter of living experience.

With all good wishes and kindest regards, also from Li Gotami, affectionately yours, Lama Govinda.

Padmaloka, Lesingham House, Surlingham, Norwich, NR14 7AL
10 December 1984

Dear Lama Govinda, On my return from Italy a few days ago I was delighted to find your letter dated 6 September 1984, which brought quite a flood of very precious memories of you and Li and of the times that the three of us spent together in Ghoom, at Sanchi, at Deolali, and finally at Almora.[312] I was very glad indeed to have direct news of you, and to know that you are as well as can be expected at 86, and hope that you are not too incommoded by the stroke which, you say, has left you partially paralyzed. You are two years younger than my mother, who I see regularly and who at 88 is still healthy and active. My father died about twelve years ago. I have not yet seen your book on *The Inner Structure of the I Ching* (has it appeared in English?) though I well remember you talking about your researches into this great classic and saying that your last major literary work would be devoted to it. Several of our friends here in England study, and teach, t'ai chi, and some of them are rather puzzled as to the relation, on the philosophical and spiritual level, between Taoism on the one hand and Buddhism on the other. It occurs to me that your book could be of some use to them.

For the last four years I have spent the three autumn months in Italy, on retreat in a former Augustinian convent, and as a result have developed a great love for Italy, especially for Tuscany. I believe you knew that part of the world well in your younger days.[313] Before and after each retreat I devote a few days to sightseeing, and in this way have seen, and to some extent explored, Florence, Venice, Siena, Ravenna, Pisa, and Rome. This year I was particularly impressed by the fourteenth-century frescos in the Campo Santo, Pisa, which I expect are well known to you. My favourite city is, I think, Siena, which I have visited at least four times, and which is still relatively unspoiled. As a Buddhist, I feel no inclination whatever to neglect Europe's vast treasure-store of culture. On the contrary, in fact.

During the last ten years I have paid four visits to India, the most recent being a three-week visit last December. You will be interested to know that the FWBO is now the most active Buddhist organization in India. We have centres in Bombay, Poona, Ahmedabad, and Aurangabad, as well as a meditation and retreat centre at Bhaja, near Lonavala, about a mile from the celebrated Buddhist caves. During the last five or six years we have brought out a number of books and pamphlets, mostly in Marathi, and also publish a Marathi Buddhist magazine called *Buddhayan* which prints 4–5,000 copies each quarter.[314] The MBS is virtually defunct. Jinaratana died a year ago, as I expect you know, and Dhammaratana – a good friend of ours – is now General Secretary.[315] Bombay continues to deteriorate year by year, and were it not for our tens of thousands of Buddhist friends there I would not care to visit it again. The polluted air always gives me an attack of bronchitis.

Most of my time is spent here in Norfolk, where I have lived for the last ten years. It is a quiet, mainly agricultural county, and Norwich, the capital, which is only six miles away, is an ancient and very civilized city with a (modern) university and a lot of cultural activities – including an FWBO centre. Padmaloka itself is a sort of country house, with five acres of grounds, which we have turned into a community and retreat centre. About twenty men live here, mostly Order members, though on special occasions (as last weekend) we can accommodate up to 110. Norfolk is very flat, like Holland, which it resembles in many ways, but though I miss the mountains I am quite happy here. Having established the FWBO on what I hope is a sound basis, I am now trying to devote the greater part of my time to literary work. In the coming year I hope to continue work on a second volume of memoirs, which will cover the period 1950–1957. As you perhaps know, there is now a branch of the FWBO in Essen, and it seems to be doing quite well. The two Order members there are in touch with the AMM,[316] and of course over the years Advayavajra has kept in regular friendly contact with us. Several of our members have, in fact, visited him, and from time to time he has sent me news of you. Nevertheless, I am very glad indeed to be in personal contact with you again, even if only through letters. You are well aware, I am sure, that when in India I did not feel spiritually and intellectually (and culturally!) closer to anyone than I did to you, and in many ways that feeling continues. I am very happy that in this life our paths should have crossed, though I very much regret that they could not have crossed more often. Whether we shall ever meet again in our present bodies it is impossible to say, but I should like to say how greatly I value the limited contact we have had and what a source of inspiration your life and work have been to me. I often think of you, and of Li, and think of you both with very great affection.

With very warmest regards, Yours ever, Sangharakshita

122 Lomita Drive, Mill Valley, California 94941
10 January 1985

My dear Sangharakshita-ji, What a joy to have your dear long letter and to know that you are well and active as ever. Many, many thanks! Though my eyes are too weak to write long letters, I am happy that we have re-established our contact. I have asked my publishers to send you immediately a review copy of my *I Ching*. As far as I know, it was published also in England, but I cannot remember the name of the publisher. There were also requests from Swedish and Italian publishers. Last year one of my books was published in Germany and is being now translated in Italian, while another one is being edited by Ven. Advayavajra, who has taken over the leadership of the Arya Maitreya Mandala as Mandalācarya. I cannot be bothered any more with proof-reading and negotiations with publishers, and must leave all this to him. But he is a very conscientious and reliable person, with a thorough knowledge of Buddhist literature. How wonderful that you have been so many times to Italy. It is my favourite country in Europe. I had my home in Capri near Naples, but I have frequently been to Venice, Florence, Siena, Pisa, and Rome. I am a great admirer of Italian art and, like you, I always uphold the importance of European culture. Without knowing the root of our own culture, how can we absorb the essence of Buddhist culture?

    With all good wishes, also from Li,
    Affectionately yours, Lama Govinda

GOLDEN DRUM

'By this resounding of the sound of the drum may all troubles in the world be suppressed.'

from the *Sūtra of Golden Light*.[317]

Golden Drum *began publication in the winter of 1985/6 under the editorship of Nagabodhi. It was the successor to the quarterly* FWBO Newsletter *with higher production values and a wider circulation.*

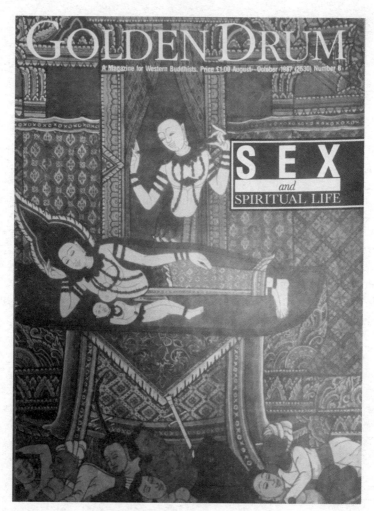

Golden Drum no. 6, October 1987

SEX AND THE SPIRITUAL LIFE

Golden Drum *no. 6, August 1987, pp. 4–14. The questions were put by the editor, Nagabodhi.*

The five precepts are the common 'minimal' ethical observance of Buddhists throughout the world. The third precept, kāmesu micchācārā veramaṇī-sikkhāpadaṃ samādiyāmi, *is translated: 'I undertake the training principle of refraining from sexual misconduct'. What is the essential meaning of this precept?*

There is a personal aspect and a social aspect. One must avoid sexual behaviour which is socially disruptive, and one must at the very least avoid engaging in sexual behaviour of any kind to such an extent that one's ethical and spiritual progress is seriously impeded.

In the Buddhist East this precept is often taken to mean simply the avoidance of rape, abduction, and adultery.

This is really quite a narrow view. The thought that immediately springs to mind is that of prostitution in Bangkok. Bangkok is almost the world capital of prostitution, so much of it goes on there. Yet Thailand is a Buddhist country, and the prostitutes in Thailand are all, presumably, good Buddhists. So those who engage in prostitution – assuming they are not married women doing it for a bit of extra housekeeping money – are not committing rape, they're not committing adultery, and are therefore, according to the current, popular Buddhist understanding, not committing any breach of the third precept. But one certainly couldn't feel that by having recourse to prostitution they were really leading ethical lives from a Buddhist point of view!

Why has the precept come to be interpreted in such a narrow way?
I think people in the Buddhist East, including parts of India, don't really examine their sexual behaviour in any detail. At least until recently, you simply conformed to tradition and custom, rather than trying to work out what was ethical or non-ethical for yourself. More often than not, tradition and custom kept you on the right track – one has to acknowledge that – but perhaps not in a very intelligent way. People wouldn't usually examine their sexual conduct any more than they usually examined any other aspect of their behaviour. They'd be concerned only with *social* approval or disapproval. And, naturally, the group interprets the precept in a rather social sort of way.

Generally speaking, in the Buddhist East, they don't worry too much about what goes on between consenting adults in private, provided it does not amount to rape, adultery, or anything of that sort. Certainly, in Buddhism, there isn't that preoccupation with the minutiae of sexual behaviour that we have had in the West, as a subject for gossip and enquiry, nor even, perhaps, for ethical scrutiny.

Perhaps it should also be said that, in those countries, there is no very serious expectation that the lay person will lead a spiritual life. The monks or nuns, on the other hand, *are* expected to lead a spiritual life, and for them there is the Vinaya, in which the precept is explored in far greater detail, probably to make it clear that absolutely all forms of sexual behaviour are excluded.

To what extent can the rules of the Vinaya be taken as the Buddha's own words, or as representing a detailed working out of his views on the subject of sex?
Whether or not they are *Buddhavacana* in all their details can be debated; I am not at all sure that the Vinaya offers a fair representation of the Buddha's thoughts on the subject. It is very legalistic in tone, and I don't think the Buddha could have viewed anything in a purely legalistic way. But I think the Vinaya does give legalistic expression to an attitude, or a principle, which was the attitude of the Buddha himself.

There can be no serious doubt that the Buddha expected his monk disciples – those who had gone forth from their spouses and families – to be celibate. That seems to have been understood, not only by the Buddha himself, but by others of his day. One who had gone forth from home into the homeless life did so probably because he or she wanted to be free from all entanglements. So even if one disregarded the personal aspect of sexual ethics – if one disregarded the effect of sex upon the mind – one would still have to avoid sexual activity if one wanted to be free from worldly (in the sense of household) entanglements. If one did engage in sex, a sexual relationship might develop, children might be produced, and you would be back where you had started.

From this point of view, such abstention from sexual activity would be the concomitant of a certain *lifestyle*, rather than of the spiritual life as such. The Buddha certainly wouldn't say that one who hadn't completely given up sexual activity couldn't make any spiritual progress, and it wasn't that you couldn't make spiritual progress without being a monk. The Buddha had householder disciples who were Stream Entrants, who appear not to have given up sexual activity. But, if you did follow the lifestyle of a monk, it would have been contradictory to engage in sexual activities in a society where there were no contraceptives.

When you were in the East, living as a monk, what part did chastity play in your own personal practice?
I'm not so sure that it played a very active part. I knew I was expected to be celibate, and so I was. I accepted it as part of the deal, part of the spiritual life; but looking back, I don't think I regarded chastity as a *practice*, something I should *work* on.

I was chaste for many, many years, in body, and I think in speech. Unchastity of speech always displeased me from a quite early age. But I don't think I made a particular effort to eliminate sexual thoughts. I was more concerned with eradicating unmindfulness, and was much more distressed by angry or violent thoughts than I was by sexual thoughts – which I tended to think of as being more 'natural'.

Even when I was in the army, these feelings, though strong, were very much at the background of my mind. I was finding the East so interesting. I was reading whatever Buddhist books I could get hold of; I was writing – it was a very exciting time for me. So even sexual *thoughts* played a very minor part in my life. It was only when my thirst for such things as the Dharma, literature, poetry, and philosophy had been slaked to some extent that I started thinking about sex, towards the end of my stay in India.

In your experience of the modern Theravāda, did the monks seem to be spotless in their practice of chastity?
Some of them did talk to me about these things, and from what they said I gained the impression that most Theravāda monks had committed minor breaches of celibacy, at least from time to time. I even met and heard of a few Theravāda monks who had wives and children – though they kept them as secret as they could – but who nonetheless continued to wear the yellow robe and expected to be treated as monks.

Minor breaches of celibacy were generally overlooked, as if it was almost too much to expect of ordinary human beings that they should be completely celibate in body, even though they were monks. Among themselves, the attitude was fairly forgiving. After all, many of them had become monks purely for social reasons: because their parents wanted them to become monks, or because, by becoming monks, they could be sure of receiving a good education, or of achieving economic security. So there would be no question of any conflict between their breach of the precept and their spiritual aspiration. They were usually only concerned with what might happen if they were found out by the lay people.

Even so, in many traditional Buddhist countries, sex is the 'great divider', perhaps the major point of difference between the life of the monk and the life of the lay person. The monk is chaste; the lay person is not. Is this a fair observation?
It is certainly fair with regard to the Theravāda countries and those Mahāyāna countries where they do have celibate monks. But it wouldn't be a fair observation with regard to Japan, where celibate monks ceased to exist centuries ago, or to some of the sects of Tibetan Buddhism who do not emphasize the monastic life, and therefore do not emphasize celibacy.

In the Theravāda world, the monks and the laity seem to have very little in common. They certainly don't seem be following one and the same spiritual path. The Mahāyāna's main emphasis, though, is on the bodhisattva ideal, and therefore on the development of the *bodhicitta* or 'will to Enlightenment'.

In the early days of the Mahāyāna there was a very strong conviction that the Buddha had taught what was, essentially, one path for all: not only in the sense of his having taught one *yāna* instead of three, but also in the sense of his having taught a spiritual path that could be followed regardless of lifestyle. The *bodhicitta* can be developed both by the monk and by the layman; the emphasis was very much on following the path of the *pāramitās* or perfections, and on becoming a bodhisattva. Celibacy and non-celibacy thus became less important issues. One did not have to be a monk – or a layman – to develop spiritually. In our FWBO terminology, we would say that commitment was primary and lifestyle was secondary.

A further development was of course that of the Vajrayāna. There were great teachers, even in India, who were not monks. Candragomin, who composed the 'Hymn to Tārā', was a layman.[318] We have the famous example of Vimalakīrti, who was a bodhisattva *appearing* as a layman. Marpa too is a famous example – though his most celebrated disciple, Milarepa, led an extremely ascetic life and was certainly celibate. In this way, the ground was prepared for the 'married lamas' of the Vajrayāna.

Do you think the Theravāda has placed too much emphasis on the importance of chastity in the monk's life?
I think it would be difficult to attach too much importance to chastity. It is, however, possible to attach too much importance to being a monk, in whose life chastity occupies an important place. You could say that the Theravāda places too much emphasis on monasticism, too much emphasis on chastity as an aspect of monasticism, and, therefore, too much emphasis on chastity of *body*: on chastity in a purely *technical* sense.

You see, it's not as if you've got the chaste as the sheep, as it were, and the rest as the goats. We shouldn't think of chastity and non-chastity as if they were white and black, and as though you were either one or the other. There are degrees. To begin with, there's chastity of body, chastity of speech, and chastity of mind. We can't divide Buddhists into those who are chaste and those who are not chaste. We can't even divide them into those who are bodily chaste and those who are not. One certainly can't associate chastity exclusively with the monk and non-chastity exclusively with the layman. I would prefer to say that there are infinite gradations, and that everybody is chaste to some extent and everybody is non-chaste to some extent.

I believe the Buddha once said, 'If there was another human passion as powerful as the sexual urge, there would be no hope of Enlightenment for human beings'.[319] *What do you think he meant by that?*

One *could* argue that the Buddha was simply trying to point out how powerful that passion is, so that his disciples would guard against it. But I take it quite literally. The sex drive is very powerful. From a common-sense point of view, the sex drive is what enables the human race to perpetuate itself; it would seem to be nature's great con-trick. If there was no sex drive, and we were asked, on rational grounds, to do what the sex-drive impels us to do instinctively, most likely we wouldn't do it! If you didn't have any sex urge, or sex drive, would you *really* want to be responsible for bringing into the world, and supporting, and educating, children? You'd have to be quite altruistic to want to do that on purely rational grounds!

Then again, the sex drive can have a very destructive effect. It can be a source of very strong feelings of attachment and possessiveness, of jealousy, hatred, and despair. It can completely overwhelm people, making it impossible for them to follow the spiritual life, or even think in terms of any higher human development.

I suppose the Buddha's view was that sexual desire is a form of craving. Craving is, of course, an unskilful mental state, and unskilful states hold us back from gaining Enlightenment. For Buddhism – certainly for early Buddhism, and certainly for the Theravāda – sexual desire is thus axiomatically unskilful. I doubt very much whether it is anywhere considered that you can engage in sexual activity without, at least to some extent, that activity being an expression of an unskilful mental state.

Under no circumstances or conditions?

It would seem so, yes. The emphasis of Buddhism in this respect – its realization that sex is, or can be, an obstacle to spiritual life – is virtually unique. The theistic religions tend to believe that God created everything in the world: he created human beings, and he created their bodies – including the reproductive organs. So, in a way, God is *behind* sex, and approves of sex. In some religions, God even blesses sex (though the Christian position is ambiguous because the Fall has rather spoiled things).

In the case of Buddhism, however, there is no creator god, no god responsible for sex. So who *is* responsible for sex? *You* are. Your past desires – 'past' in the sense of desires experienced in a previous existence – have brought you, in this life, into the gross material human body, equipped with sexual organs, by means of which you can give expression to the desires you have carried from your previous existence.

People are not aware of how powerful this force is. You experience the strength of a force when you oppose it. Usually people tend to go along with their sexual drives, and so don't experience their strength – except, perhaps, when they come up against external obstacles, in the form of parental disapproval, or something of that sort.

So since Buddhism regards sexual desires (along with others) as binding you to the wheel of life and causing you to be reborn again and again, it therefore teaches that, if you are serious about not being reborn, if you are serious about following a spiritual path and attaining Nirvāṇa, then you will need to avoid sex, not simply in the sense of abstaining from sexual activity, but in the sense of overcoming, eventually, those particular desires or cravings that find expression through sexual activity.

You have been using the words 'desire' and 'craving'. Craving is usually understood to imply a neurotic element, as distinct from 'desire' – which is sometimes understood to suggest more of a healthy appetite. Is sexual desire always to be regarded as a form of craving?
I think traditional Buddhism, especially Theravāda Buddhism, would maintain that even a healthy appetite for sex is the expression of an unskilful mental state. It follows from Buddhist principles that one could be Enlightened and at the same time enjoy one's food without any associated craving. But I doubt if that principle could be extended to cover sexual experience. Buddhists might well acknowledge that even an Enlightened person has to eat; but an Enlightened person does not have to engage in sexual activity, he does not have to procreate.

Then, of course, the sexual appetite usually involves other people. When one comes into close physical, or emotional, contact with another person within the context of a sexual relationship, usually all sorts of psychological projections take place, and sometimes a very complicated, even negative situation develops – which doesn't happen with regard to food, say, or to sleep. Even the so-called 'healthy appetite' for sex, if satisfied, very quickly leads to the development of attachment. That attachment can lead to the arising of very strong emotions of possessiveness, jealousy, hatred, and so on.

It could of course be argued that it is possible for someone to enjoy sex without any of these things arising. But then there would very likely be present in the mind of that person, the unskilful states, not so much of sexual craving, as of indifference, lack of positive emotion, and exploitiveness.

To return to the five precepts for a moment, you once composed a 'Tantric version', in which the third precept was rendered: 'Do not misuse energy.'[320] Could you expand on that?
The third precept represents an important form of ethical discipline. I discovered that a lot of young people in the West didn't take very kindly to the idea of discipline, so it wasn't very easy to talk about the importance of the precept in disciplinary terms.

What I had in mind was that sexual energy was a sort of paradigm of energy in general. I don't think there is, specifically, a special, separate, 'sexual energy'. The psychophysical organism is itself an expression of energy, and sexual activity is simply one form in which that energy manifests itself. It's obviously important that energy should not be wasted, so if you can point out that sexual energy is a form of energy, then it becomes immediately obvious that that energy should not be wasted.

Some people argue that sexual activity – and particularly the orgasm – bestows energy, and that its denial depletes. Could you comment on this?
I rather doubt whether sex does actually give people energy, as they maintain. At the time of orgasm there is an expenditure of energy; you experience yourself as spending energy, and therefore you experience yourself as being 'energy full' – as you might when you throw a cricket ball.

When people talk of sex and orgasm actually giving them energy, they are talking about something quite different. I think, especially in the case of men, that when they experience orgasm, there's a sort of sense of achievement, as if they've had their way: they've done something that they consider worthwhile. Their ego becomes a bit bloated and swollen, and this they interpret as a sort of access of energy. It isn't at all a healthy or positive state.

When one has experienced orgasm, one is often left in a state of what could be called 'enervation'. Having made the effort that the approach to orgasm involves, your natural tendency is simply to rest. If you want to meditate, to overcome the hindrances, to concentrate the mind, and enter the *dhyānas*, you have to make a very great effort, and after an orgasm, you won't feel like making an effort. Some people may not feel like making an effort – especially that mental effort – for many hours afterwards; for others it might be quite a few days. They are just not able to get their mental energies together. It's not that they feel physically weak, or even mentally exhausted: they have lost a certain cutting edge, not only in relation to meditation, but to all sorts of other areas. They need to give their energies, and especially their mental energies, time to build up again and to want to express themselves.

You sometimes hear it said that, at the moment of orgasm, one experiences a dissolution of ego and a sense of union with one's partner. There seems to be a confusion here between sinking below the ego and transcending it. Ego is lost in deep sleep; you are not self-conscious in all sorts of situations, not because you've transcended the ego, but because you've temporarily reverted to a state lower than that of the ego, or self-consciousness.

As for 'union', the very idea is nonsensical. Often, those very people who feel this sense of union at the time of orgasm are fighting and quarrelling five minutes later! So where is the union? What has been achieved? If one really achieved unity in a spiritual sense, not just by way of mutual unconsciousness, then one's attitude to the other person would be completely transformed: one would be positive, affectionate, and caring – which ordinary human sexual relationships rarely are.

Even so, sex is usually regarded as a vital route – even the vital route to emotional fulfilment and satisfaction.
I wonder whether people really do get emotional satisfaction and fulfilment out of sex. Certainly there is a *measure* of satisfaction and fulfilment, but it's usually very short-lived.

Emotional satisfaction and fulfilment is quite a big thing. From a philosophical point of view, Buddhism sees man's predicament as stemming from the fact that he is looking for absolute happiness in something which is quite unable to give absolute happiness. He's looking for permanence in something which is quite unable to give him permanence, looking for the real in the midst of the unreal. No finite thing is capable of giving infinite and unlimited satisfaction and fulfilment – emotional or otherwise. But this is very often what people are looking for in sex. So sex may give them a measure of satisfaction, a measure of fulfilment; but it can't give satisfaction and fulfilment to the degree that people expect or hope.

But people look to sex at least for the enjoyment of emotional intimacy. Well there is certainly physical intimacy in sex. Whether there is emotional intimacy is quite another matter. It is well known that all sorts of misunderstandings and confusions occur between people who are involved in sexual relationships. When a sexual relationship comes to an end, it often does so in a very unfortunate and emotionally negative way: the two people separate, perhaps with fairly negative feelings towards each other; their so-called intimacy might never have been.

So when people speak of their sexual partners as being their best friends, do you think they are absolutely deluded?
Friendship and sexual infatuation are two very different things. Sexual infatuation can arise and reach its physical consummation very, very rapidly. Friendship is a plant of much slower growth; it takes much longer to develop. You become friends with someone as you really get to know them, as you develop confidence in them, as you come to feel that they really do know and understand you. This is very different from the process of sexual infatuation.

It may be that, when sexual infatuation subsides, if the two people are reasonably healthy, and if they have certain things in common, including the raising of a family, or if they have religious and spiritual ideals in common, they *may* be able to develop a friendship in the long run, especially as they get older. But, even so, a sexual relationship is a very different thing from a friendship. If anybody ever tells me that their wife is their best friend, or their girlfriend is their best friend, or their husband is their best friend, or their boyfriend is their best friend, I can't help feeling that they are using the word 'friendship' in a totally different sense from the sense in which I use it.

I believe you once said that the worst thing you can do to someone is to fall in love with them. Could you explain what you meant?
Falling in love implies psychological projection, or seeing in the other

person qualities and aspects which are in fact qualities and aspects of yourself, but of which you are unconscious. This means that you do not see the other person as they really are; in a way, you're not treating them as a human being; you are treating them as an object, a thing. Perhaps you're both treating each other in that way, and it may be that by that means you satisfy certain appetites. But there won't be any question of your development as a human being, much less still of any spiritual development.

Presumably you have had to spend a fair amount of time over the years discussing this aspect of your pupils' lives?
In the early days of the FWBO, especially, when people tended to bring their more everyday problems to me rather than to Order members, roughly a third of my discussion time would be devoted to the subject of sex, and particularly to sexual relationships that had gone wrong or broken down.

Did you find that men and women have different problems and preoccupations in this area?
It's not easy to generalize, but it does seem that achieving a sexual *relationship* was more important for women than for men. In the case of men, it was perhaps more a matter of gaining sexual satisfaction – not necessarily with one and the same woman.

In the case of women, sexual desire is very much bound up with the desire for children. At the back of the woman's mind all the time is the desire for a child, and there is therefore the desire to have someone to help her, and look after her, when she is having the child. That question doesn't arise in the case of the man – who has to be wary of adopting a purely self-indulgent and exploitative attitude with regard to sex. Men may want children, but rarely in the passionate sort of way that women very often do.

Over the years, I came very much to the conclusion that the reason sexual relationships were so difficult, and sometimes ended so disastrously, was that people were investing far too much in them. Very often they seemed to have built their lives around their sexual relationships, and had no other serious relationships: not with their parents, for example, and certainly not with their friends.

Is this a particularly Western syndrome? Or did you have to deal with similar problems in India?

I don't remember having to, partly because people – if they did have problems concerning sex – might well have considered it inappropriate to bring them to me, a celibate monk. But I also think that people did not have that sort of problem – certainly the non-westernized people – because most Indians lived as members of a joint family; there was a good spread of relationships, even of important relationships, in their lives.

Could there be a lesson in that for us?

In the FWBO we sometimes talk in terms of the mandala. The mandala is your whole life, and what is within your mandala represents the contents of your life. A mandala has a centre, so there will be, in the mandala of your life, something that occupies a central position: the interest, activity, idea, or ideal around which your life is centred. Then we include the other interests and activities of our lives, putting them nearer to the centre as they are more important, and nearer to the periphery as they are less important.

So with regard to sex, I think we could say that, for most people, sex has a legitimate place somewhere near the periphery of the personal mandala. It certainly shouldn't be at the centre of the mandala; *there* we place the Buddha, representing the ideal of Enlightenment.

It is possible for a human being to develop spiritually while still engaging in a certain amount of sexual activity, but that is provided that not too much importance is attached to that activity, that our emotions are not invested in that sexual activity to a very great extent, and provided especially that there is a strong spiritual ideal seated right at the centre of the mandala.

Obviously, we have here to be very careful that we don't engage in rationalization – which is why I am sometimes very reluctant to admit that sex has a place in the mandala at all! I've heard so many men and women say that they are not very deeply involved in their sexual relationships, but who nonetheless absolutely broke down and were completely demoralized when their sexual partner left them.

But how is one to know when one is over-investing?

You should ask your spiritual friends to tell you. It is very difficult to tell yourself. Of course, if you want to spend as much time as you possibly can with your sexual partner, then you've probably put them in the centre of your mandala.

You may also notice – or your friends will notice – that if you have a sexual partner and are very attached to them, you tend to relate in a certain way, engage in almost meaningless communication simply to reassure yourself that the other is still there. You find that people who are involved in a sexual relationship often do this. This suggests quite deep attachment and emotional dependence, which is not at all desirable.

Then, if you want to make sure that your sexual relationship really is towards the periphery of your mandala, you should be very careful not to spend too much time with the person you're having the sexual relationship with, and preferably not live with them. And you should ensure that you have strong friendships with members of your own sex.

In the FWBO, as you know, people who are having sexual relationships often live in separate communities, the man living in a men's community, the woman living in a women's community. I would say that this not only helps to ensure that the sexual relationship occupies only a peripheral place in those two people's mandalas, but also assures a happier, more truly human relationship between them, because they allow themselves space.

Would fidelity be an important factor in a 'successful' relationship?
Fidelity is faithfulness over a long period of time, especially in the absence of the friend or sexual partner. It implies not only time: it implies space. It implies the ability, or the capacity, to behave in the absence of a friend, or a sexual partner, as though they were present. And you can only behave as though they were present if you have a strong sense of their existence when they're not actually there with you.

For this to be possible you must dwell much more on the 'mental' level – using that term in the Buddhist sense – than on the physical. You must be less susceptible to every passing physical stimulation, be less carried away by the senses, and live less in the present in a forgetful sort of way. Fidelity is a very human, very individual quality, like friendship or 'impersonal' love in the sense of *mettā*. You are able to look ahead, able to imagine – or to feel – the presence of another person who is not physically with you. This suggests that you don't just see the other person as a body: you have some consciousness of them as a mind, as a 'spirit' if you like, and you relate to them in that way and on that level.

Fidelity is of course different from attachment. Perhaps it isn't always easy to distinguish between the two. Fidelity is a positive quality, whereas attachment is not. When you practise fidelity towards someone, you are, as it were, valuing them for their own sake. But when you're attached to them, you are wanting something from them for *your* sake.

So I've observed that men and women can have very happy relationships, including sexual relationships, provided they live quite independent lives, and see each other just from time to time. When the man and the woman have each placed Enlightenment firmly at the centre of their mandala, they've got something to get on with; their lives don't centre around their sexual partners. Then, paradoxically, the relationship becomes more satisfactory, and they can relate more as human beings. You have to strike a sort of happy balance, where you see someone sufficiently often to keep up a continuity of contact, but not so often that you become attached, or become bored with each other's company.

Then, if you are committed to a spiritual way of life, or if you are committed to your personal development, and if you do see your sexual partner infrequently, and if you do both live in single-sex spiritual communities, and if you have strong friendships with members of your own sex, and if you are making a very determined effort to develop spiritually, with the help of meditation, with the help of Dharma study, altruistic activity, retreats, and so on, then the danger of over-investment in a sexual relationship will be far less.

Obviously, many couples live together in order to bring up a family. They might argue that having and nurturing children is itself a spiritually challenging activity. Would you agree?
Well, every human activity can be regarded as having a spiritually demanding aspect. There is always the possibility of a skilful, positive response or of an unskilful, negative response. Suppose it rains. You can have a positive response to the fact that it is raining, but does that mean that rain is, as such, a spiritual experience? In the same way, if you have children, you can be patient, forbearing, kindly – and that can be a spiritual experience. But that does not mean that having children is, itself, a spiritual experience any more than the weather is.

Raising children and helping them to get on in the world can be a challenging and creative pursuit, but I would say that there are already far too many beings in the world who have never had that help, and who need that help; it would probably be much better for us to direct our attention towards *them*.

Even so, as you mentioned a moment ago, bearing children is a major issue – and a major source of conflict – for some women. Is there any general advice that you would offer?

Some years ago I wouldn't have ventured to give a piece of general advice. Now I very definitely do. Quite a few women in the FWBO have experienced tremendous conflict between the very genuine desire to lead a spiritual life, and the desire for a child. I have come to the conclusion, after discussing the matter with quite a number of women, and observing women in the Movement who have children, that, if a woman has a genuine desire for the spiritual life, then having a child will not in the long run get in the way.

Of course, for two or three years, she will be very tied down by the child. She won't be able to go on retreats; she may not even be able to attend classes at the Centre, or able to attend Order meetings. She will have to be patient. But that period of almost total dependence of the child on its mother does come to an end; the mother does become more free with the passing of every year, and if the mother's original interest in, or commitment to, the spiritual life has been genuine or sincere, it will re-emerge and be free to express itself again.

Of course, if her involvement isn't very strong, the likelihood is that, even if she doesn't have a child, she will drift away from the spiritual life. Men often drift away from the spiritual life without even thinking about having children!

I believe you have said that heterosexual sexual activity and attitudes can have a polarizing effect on the individual, leading him or her to a one-sided kind of development. Could you say a bit more about this?

If you're involved in a heterosexual relationship, you think of yourself as a man, the other person as a woman, or of yourself as a woman, the other person as a man. In other words, you don't relate to your partner so much as an individual, but as just a man or just a woman. So within that relationship only half your total 'nature' has an opportunity to express itself – because a human being is not 'just a man', or 'just a woman': there are other potentialities too.

Then, if one relates predominantly as a member of *this* sex or *that* sex, the qualities and characteristics associated with the opposite sex are not developed; one becomes one-sided in one's psychological, and possibly even in one's spiritual, development. Thus you get the very 'macho' man and the extravagantly feminine woman, in whom the complementary qualities of the opposite sex have no opportunity to develop.

A human being should try to develop the whole range of human qualities: the so-called 'masculine' and the so-called 'feminine', and in this way become – to talk in these 'sexual' terms – androgynous. This doesn't necessarily mean that a man will become bisexual or a woman will become bisexual; they may continue to confine their sexual activities to partners of the opposite sex. But, nonetheless, they will have developed – if they're truly, psychologically androgynous – the psychological and spiritual qualities of, so to speak, both sexes.

Is there less risk of polarization, attachment, or psychological projection in homosexual relationships than in heterosexual ones?
It's very difficult to generalize. I get the impression that among men who might be described as 'professionally gay' sexual relationships can become quite turbulent. But where the men concerned are not actually gay, or not gay in an extremely one-sided way, it is possible for them to have a relationship in which sex may play a part, but not a very important part.

The case of women is rather different. So far as I've observed – and of course I am generalizing – sexual relationships between women can result in very powerful emotional attachments of a very 'heavy' kind. Sex, and the emotions associated with sex, play a much more important, and in a way constant, part in the life of a woman than in the life of a man. So when two women come together, you tend to get a much more emotionally charged relationship.

But do you think that people who are looking for a clearer sexual mode might at least benefit from experimenting with homosexuality?
I don't think one can experiment with homosexuality – or even with heterosexuality come to that – on purely rational grounds. It simply doesn't work. The essence of the matter is that there is a natural, spontaneous attraction, whether sexual or non-sexual.

But is anybody 100% heterosexual or homosexual?

There are people who appear to be 100% heterosexual and to have not even the slightest homosexual inclination; but it is very hard to be sure. The least one can say is that the majority of people, under certain conditions, would be able to find at least some sexual satisfaction with members of their own sex.

But, you see, we've made it all into such a big deal; we've classified and labelled people as 'heterosexual' and 'homosexual'. You can speak of certain actions as homosexual actions, or others as heterosexual, but can you speak of individuals as either 'homosexual' or 'heterosexual'?

I don't like people being spoken of as 'gay', or speaking of themselves as 'gay', as though their sexual identity is the most important thing about them. I don't blame them too much, because that attitude is a reaction against years – even centuries – of oppression of people engaged in homosexual activities by people who did not engage in homosexual activities, but it is nevertheless unfortunate.

This raises an issue which is, I think, quite a serious problem for Western men, and especially perhaps for those involved in Buddhism. Spiritual friendship is important, and it can only arise on a basis of ordinary friendship. Friendship implies closeness, mutual confidence, intimacy, and even physical contact.

For most people in the West it would seem that physical contact occurs in association with sex. We consequently seem to confuse the two, or to regard the two as being inseparable. Purely physical contact is therefore quite difficult for people to obtain, especially, I think, for men to obtain from other men. Normally, in the case of other men, there's no 'danger' of sexual involvement. Even so, men find it quite difficult to experience physical contact with other men because of their fear of homosexuality.

I've observed cases where men are even afraid to give each other a brotherly hug! It may take them years to get through that. And when they succeed in doing it, they are quite overwhelmed and overjoyed, as if they've had a real breakthrough! This illustrates the terrible mess we've got ourselves into; such a simple thing has become an enormous problem.

During the time when I was living at the Hampstead Buddhist Vihara, I was quite celibate. Even so, I remember how bothered some people were by my close friendship with Terry Delamare. Actually, as they really ought to have taken for granted, that was a completely Platonic relationship – in fact it wasn't a relationship in the ordinary sense at all, and certainly not a sexual relationship. The crux of the matter seemed to be people's inability to believe that there could be a close friendship between two men without their being a sexual element.

Women, generally, seem much less inhibited in this respect. They don't hesitate to put their arms round each other's waists or hug each other; they even kiss each other quite freely. Men normally would not dream of doing such things, and limit their contact. Because of that, they very often limit the possibilities of friendship with other men. And so, because they don't develop friendship with other men, they don't develop *spiritual* friendship with other men. And because they don't develop spiritual friendship with other men, they're not able to develop what the Buddha declared to be the most important element in the spiritual life.

So what can Western men do about this?
They must break down their fear of homosexuality, by facing it, and by not being afraid of sexual contact with other men. This is not necessarily to say that they should have sexual contact with men, but at least that they should not be afraid of the idea. They have to realize that physical, and even sexual, contact between men is *just* physical or sexual contact between men. It is a quite ordinary thing, and one's fear of that should not be allowed to get in the way of one's friendships.

Some while ago, I believe you did engage in some sexual 'experimentation' yourself. Could you say something about that?
In 1967, when I returned from India to start the FWBO, there was a lot of talk about the place of sex in communication. I therefore thought I should perhaps experiment a little in this field. In those days, everything seemed to be in the melting pot. I was, in a sense, free to do what I wanted, free to do whatever I felt was best. It was a very important period, a creative period: I was giving all those classes, all those lectures. This was also the period of my experimentation with psychedelic drugs, the period when I let my hair grow.... You could say I was feeling my way, feeling my way around.

I think I've always been guided by instinct or intuition. I very much tend to *do*, and then worry about the implications afterwards. I'm sure that appetite did play some part in the 'experimentation', but it was all definitely more to do with intuition than appetite.

The ancient Greeks encouraged 'educative', erotically charged, friendships, especially between older and younger men. Did you have something like this in mind?
No, I don't think it was from this point of view at all. I have had hundreds of pupils and disciples without there being any sexual element entering into the relationship. When I engaged in my period of 'experimentation', it wasn't so much within a pedagogic context, as just in a context of ordinary friendship. Of course one can learn from friends, but the experimentation wasn't part of the education of some other person. I was just exploring certain things for my own benefit, for the satisfaction of my own curiosity.

But even now, I don't think I could really explain what it was that I was intuitively reaching for – without setting myself to write about it seriously, when I can really 'dig around' and ask myself what I really felt about things. I do in fact intend to describe this period in a volume of memoirs, which I hope to write in the next few years.

Did you come away from that period of experimentation with any conclusions?
One of my conclusions was that sex didn't really play much of a part in human communication. Bodily contact sometimes functioned as a *means* of breakthrough in communication, but it didn't result in a permanent breakthrough: it only gave one a certain opportunity, which one then had to develop. Sometimes the breakthrough came to an end and things were as they were before. In fact, that was almost always the same. So I came to the conclusion that sexual contact wasn't really much help in developing human communication, and again I ended up celibate.

At the same time, I *can* definitely say that, in the case of certain people, I found that having physical contact with them (and I'm speaking now of physical, not sexual contact) certainly did release them from their fear of homosexuality, and enabled them to develop friendships – by which I mean non-sexual friendships – with other men more easily.

In the early days of the FWBO you seemed to be very patient with our tendencies to sexual distraction and sexual indulgence. Were you as tolerant and patient as you seemed?

I had no choice but to be patient! I was starting out – in the 'permissive' sixties – with people who were, on the whole, completely fresh to Buddhism. I was more concerned that people should develop some sympathy for Buddhist ideals, and gradually bring their conduct into line with those ideals. I didn't take the view that, 'Well, you've got to give up all your present unskilful actions and mental attitudes, and *then* we can start thinking about Buddhism.' That would simply not have worked. So I mainly followed what I afterwards called the 'path of irregular steps'.

Were you ever afraid that the FWBO might disappear in a cloud of sexual permissiveness?

Well sexual permissiveness is not the only danger. We mustn't dwell too much upon that, even though we are at present dealing with the subject of sex. The FWBO could dissolve for all sorts of reasons, and there will always be the danger of it dissolving so long as, within the FWBO, and within the Order especially, we don't have a sufficient number of Stream Entrants. If you're not a Stream Entrant you can resile from the spiritual life, you can resile from your commitment to the Three Jewels; you can become anything, do anything.

But do you think that we in the West need to work harder at our understanding of the third precept than those from a more traditional, Eastern culture?

I think we have to fight against a cultural message that overvalues sex and regards sex as an unqualified good. A lot of people still think that so long as you don't actually harm people you can have – should have – as much sex as you please. Because of this attitude, there's no understanding of the fact that if you want to develop spiritually, then sex has to take a peripheral place.

We're living in a transitional period. Formerly the great disincentive, particularly for the woman, was the fear of pregnancy. That fear has been largely removed, and people find themselves (or, at least until the advent of AIDS, found themselves) free to engage in sexual activity without the fear of consequences. This has certainly altered attitudes towards sex. But there have been side-effects: the contraceptive pill does have certain physical dangers for some women; then, it may be doubted whether promiscuous sex is necessarily very psychologically satisfying, or even healthy. Perhaps the freedom with which people can now have sex has resulted in an altogether disproportionate amount of attention being given to it.

More recently, you have been encouraging us to think more seriously about, and to aim ourselves more decidedly towards, celibacy.
Well, in the early days, most of our early members were in their twenties or even in their late teens. One could not really expect or demand celibacy of people of that age. But those who were 25 or even younger when they joined us are now in their forties. People of that age can certainly start thinking seriously about celibacy – and I have asked people to do no more than that: just to think about it seriously.

Though you do seem content that a few people are taking the anagārika *precepts – which include a 'vow' of celibacy.*
I'm not only content: I'm very pleased that they are. They are really nailing their colours, their saffron colours if you like, to the mast. But I never urge anyone to take a vow of celibacy. When people tell me they want to take such a vow, I almost invariably ask them to think about it for a while longer.

One can be a member of the Western Buddhist Order without being celibate. One is only asked to keep one's sex life at the periphery, or towards the periphery, of one's personal mandala – or at the very least not too near the centre. But if one can be celibate in a non-neurotic way, in a positive and healthy way, I'm sure that will enable one – other factors being equal – to develop spiritually more rapidly, and enable one to be more free to be of use to the Dharma and of use to other human beings.

What would be the distinction between a 'neurotic' and a healthy, 'non-neurotic' celibacy?
You could be celibate because you were so absorbed by the beauty and attractiveness of the spiritual ideal that sex just didn't interest you. That would be a very healthy sexual mode. But then you could be celibate out of guilt, or for the sake of some material advantage. You could be

celibate for all sorts of quite negative reasons, which would be neurotic.

It certainly isn't just a question of being celibate. Being physically celibate by itself probably has very little value. What is more valuable is being *relatively* celibate because the main object of one's emotional energies is something of a higher order. You can't be healthily and happily celibate unless you are celibate for the sake of a higher cultural, artistic, humanitarian, or spiritual interest. You could even say that sexual frustration takes place when you don't have at the centre of your mandala an interest or an ideal that absorbs your emotional energies.

In the Udāna, *Nanda complains that his mind is always dwelling on the beautiful girl he left behind when he became a monk.*[321] *The Buddha takes him to a heavenly realm, and shows him goddesses of even greater beauty. What is the teaching there for us?*
Nanda's experience represents an experience of beauty more refined than ordinary human beauty. So he becomes less attracted, less attached, to lower, human beauty. I don't think that while still remaining on the level of ordinary human beauty you can simply put it all behind you. You only have a reason for doing that if you have a glimpse of a higher, heavenly beauty.

So what are we to do? Pay more visits to the art gallery?
A visit to the local art gallery is not to be despised. Then there is refined music, or engaging in a creative activity. This can certainly absorb one's energies. Then of course there is meditation. So long as you haven't developed insight you will be swaying between engaging in sex and experiencing sexual craving, and being free from that craving. So in order to make spiritual progress while continuing to have sex, you have to ensure that the sex is peripheral, and that you are mentally free from the hindrance of sexual desire for sufficient periods, from time to time, to be able to achieve higher states of consciousness, and on that basis develop insight. Once insight starts being developed, then of course you are attacking the craving at the source. The more you do of that, then the weaker any craving will become.

So there is a sort of gradual path to celibacy: taking some of these things on, developing insight, adding these refined elements to our lives?
Yes indeed! – Like a caterpillar passing from leaf to leaf. While with its

rear legs it is still adhering to one leaf, with its front legs it is grasping hold of another. And it doesn't pull its rear legs forward onto the new leaf until it has planted its front legs very securely on the front leaf.

It is quite impossible to give up everything all at once, though some spiritual disciplines seem to demand that: 'Give up everything to God: give up everything to the guru....' I don't think that is humanly possible; you may have a nervous breakdown if you try. But at least seize hold of the spiritual, just like the caterpillar seizing hold of that leaf with its front legs. In a sense, it doesn't matter if you've got two front legs on that new leaf and twenty legs back on the old leaf: at least you've grasped hold of that new leaf. Then you can proceed to haul yourself slowly forward.

Psychologically and spiritually speaking, it's not so much a question of just giving up the old, but of seizing hold of the new while you are still, to some extent, involved with the old, even trapped in the old. Just make sure you do seize hold of the new, and try to seize hold of it more and more. Don't think there's no point in seizing hold of the new because you haven't yet completely relaxed your hold on the old. There are degrees of celibacy. Everybody is celibate to some extent, and everybody is non-celibate to some extent. No one is engaging in sexual activity all the time (I'm speaking here about physical celibacy), and nobody – except for Buddhas and bodhisattvas – is celibate in body, speech, and mind all the time.

One should therefore understand the *principle* of celibacy, which in Buddhism is called *brahmacarya*. This can be translated as the 'divine life', or even the 'angelic life'. It represents a transition from a lower to a higher sphere, from the *kāmaloka* to the *rūpaloka*, from the *rūpaloka* to the *brahmaloka*. *Brahmacarya* means, literally, walking with, or 'faring' with Brahmā – Brahmā meaning a very lofty, spiritual state. When you are celibate in body, speech, and mind, well, you dwell in that state. But you're *trying* to dwell in that state all the time. Some people make a nearer approach to it, others don't succeed in approaching so near, but everybody, one might say, is to some extent on their way – even if only by accident.

Of course, if you're leading a specifically spiritual life, if you've taken up the *brahmacarya*, you can try to be more and more celibate. If, for instance, you normally engage in sexual intercourse once a week, then try to make it once a fortnight, or once a month, or even once a year, as some of our friends do. In that way you gradually detach yourself from attachment to the material world, from the senses, from unskilful pleasures, and you experience skilful pleasures more and more intensely, and pursue them.

I see the FWBO – and the Order especially – as never standing still. I would like to see everybody involved with the Movement, everybody involved with the Order, becoming more and more celibate, every day if you like.

I'm not asking anyone to give up sex all at once; I'm not expecting them to do that. But inasmuch as I expect people to progress a little every day, then I expect them, in a way, to give up a little bit of sex every day, so that over the years there is an appreciable difference – so that overt sexual activity plays a smaller and smaller part in their lives.

You've said from time to time that, so far as you can see, the monk's life is the happiest life you can imagine. To what extent is their celibacy a factor in that?
Well, I must first define what I mean by 'the monk's life'. I don't mean a formally monastic life; I don't mean simply wearing yellow robes and shaving one's head; and I certainly don't mean being celibate in a neurotic way. By the monk's life I mean a life totally devoted to the Dharma, in one way or another, a life which is, so to speak, wedded to the Dharma. I certainly see *that* as the happiest life, and I've certainly seen many, many very happy monks – in the formal sense – in the East. Very often they did seem to be much happier than the lay people who were presumably indulging in the enjoyment of all the worldly pleasures. I won't say that the monks were always strictly celibate; sometimes they weren't, but they were certainly much more celibate than the lay people! And, at the very least, they were to that extent happier.

MORE TO COME

Golden Drum *no. 10, August 1988, p. 7. The questions were put by the editor, Nagabodhi.*

In an issue of the FWBO Newsletter, *you envisaged a network of viharas spreading to wherever there are ex-Untouchable Buddhists:*

> The Western Buddhist Order is well suited to the task.
> Dr Ambedkar himself saw the need for a new kind of *bhikkhu*:
> educated, in touch with the modern world, and free to act, free to
> go out and do Dharma work. There is no reason why the general
> lines on which the FWBO operates in the West should not be valid
> out there. Bhante also hopes to see us doing something on the
> material plane, such as supporting a medical team to work among
> the poor people. Before long there will no doubt be Indian Order
> members.

That extract provides a glimpse of your vision for the Movement's development in India ten years ago. Are you surprised that things have gone so well?
I can't say I'm surprised. I knew the need of the ex-Untouchables for the Dharma, and I was quite confident that the kind of approach developed by the FWBO in the West would be suitable for India.

But did you expect the TBMSG *to have more trouble establishing its name, or its credentials, given that it was founded by Westerners?*
Not really. I knew that the ex-Untouchable Buddhists on the whole

had no prejudice against Westerners – least of all against Western Buddhists. I also knew that from the very beginning they had been desperately looking to Buddhists outside India, hoping for some gesture of friendship and solidarity. But they have on the whole been very bitterly disappointed by the Buddhist countries of South-east Asia. Virtually no help, not even any encouragement, has come from those quarters, except for the occasional *bhikkhu*, perhaps, trying to do something – but no more than that. There has certainly not come the sustained and solid support that Ambedkar expected. It's probably not an exaggeration to say that all the Buddhist countries of South-east Asia combined have not contributed even a tenth as much, even financially, to the ex-Untouchable Buddhists as have Western Buddhists, especially those in England.

Can you say which of the past ten years' developments have pleased you most?
One has certainly been that we now have so many Order members of Indian origin. I've been very pleased to see how very effectively many of those have been able to work despite – in most cases – having families, full-time jobs, and so on.

We now have centres in Maharashtra and Gujarat, and we're beginning to spread towards the states of Andhra Pradesh and Karnataka; we have medical teams and some educational work, and the Order has grown quite quickly. Are there any major areas of activity that you are still waiting to see being tackled?
I'd like to see much more literature being published in all the major Indian languages. We are still lagging behind quite seriously in this respect. We've brought out quite a few pamphlets, and a few books even, in Marathi, but not much in any other language.

That suggests that you would like to see the conversion movement gathering momentum, and spreading further afield.
This is something we should think about very seriously. At present the conversion movement remains more or less confined to the Mahars [Dr Ambedkar's own caste], but if it is to achieve Ambedkar's original objectives it will have to spread to other communities as well: beyond the ex-Untouchables and beyond the Scheduled Caste communities,

even. We do already have just a handful of caste-Hindu sympathizers, and a few of those do consider themselves to be Buddhists. That is a very good thing because, if 'Buddhist' becomes just a synonym for 'Mahar', then the Mahars themselves will not really have broken out of the caste system.

As our work in India becomes better known in the Buddhist world, it is possible that other organizations may wake up to the potential of the situation. Do you feel it would be a good thing if some of them started to work there?
It would depend entirely on the nature of those movements. If they wanted to work entirely along traditional Theravāda lines, they'd best not bother. Frankly, they'd do more harm than good. In the South-east Asian Buddhist countries, *bhikkhus* have largely become more or less like the Indian Brahmins, and the ex-Untouchable Buddhists, having shaken off the yoke of one set of Brahmins, don't want another! They want the Dharma, which the majority of *bhikkhus* in South-east Asia are just not really able to practise or to preach.

So is there any way in which you would like to see our own movement progressing?
Well I'd obviously like to see it progressing on all fronts! I'd like to see more viharas, more medical centres, and more hostels. I'd like to see a small hospital; I'd like to see more meditation centres; I'd like to see more publications; I'd like to see more classes and courses and retreats and lectures, and public meetings! I'd just like to see more of everything!

Is there any particular message you would like to pass on to our Indian friends on this anniversary occasion?
Clearly, I'd like all the Order members, Mitras, and other Friends in India just to go on working as hard as they possibly can. I would like them to know that they have the full sympathy and support, at least the moral support, of all members of the Order and of the Movement in the West, and especially my own sympathy and support. I would also like them to know that we look to them not only to do what is good for India, and for people in India who wish to come into contact with the Dharma, but also to be a source of inspiration to us here in the West. We know very well that they are working under much more difficult

conditions than we have to face here, so we admire them all the more for what they are able to achieve.

One last question: Are you hoping to return to India yourself?
I do hope to go back. When and how I can't say at the moment. But I would be very disappointed if I couldn't pay at least one more visit to India, and probably more.

WORKING WITH THE INEVITABLE

Golden Drum no. 26, August 1992, pp. 8–9. The questions were put by the editor, Nagabodhi.

Bhante, were there ever any times when you didn't think the FWBO would last twenty-five years, when you despaired?
I certainly never despaired. But I can't say I thought we were definitely going to last twenty-five years or not last twenty-five years. I simply thought in terms of carrying on from day to day, week to week, class to class, retreat to retreat, confident that we would survive.

Because you were determined that we would?
Not in any 'wilful' sense. It was more that I saw it as being 'inevitable' – almost in the nature of things – that there should be a movement like the FWBO. This was the intuitive feeling on the basis of which I carried on working.

Have you been surprised or disappointed by the Movement's development so far?
If I look back to those very small beginnings, then I am definitely somewhat surprised that we could have expanded to such an extent and in such a variety of ways in just twenty-five years. But if I consider all the needs that the FWBO is not in a position to meet – when I think of the vast number of people who could benefit from the FWBO but to whom we haven't as yet been able to make ourselves available – then I feel rather disappointed.

Would you single out any particular groups of people, or are you thinking of the general mass of humanity?
I'm thinking of the general mass of humanity, but when there's an accident you give your attention first of all to the most seriously wounded. So in India we are more concerned with the ex-Untouchables, the more seriously wounded in a social sense. In the West we often have to give more immediate attention to those who are wounded psychologically. They are often the ones who come to us, because they feel in need of some kind of spiritual healing.

Should we be doing more to contact those who do not particularly experience life as something painful but who would benefit from the Dharma?
I'm sure there's a lot more we could be doing in this way. Perhaps we should target specific groups more accurately than we do at present. One recent development that has pleased me has been that one or two Order members have been going out specifically to black women and to gay people, people who might have been shy of approaching us. But there is the question of human resources: our centres are kept busy by the people who are already making their own way to them.

Of all the developments that have taken place in the last twenty-five years, which have especially pleased you?
I am particularly pleased that the FWBO has taken root in India. This is partly for personal reasons. I myself spent so much time in India. Those eighteen years constituted a central part of my life. But that development also pleases me because it has taken place mainly among the ex-Untouchable followers of Dr Ambedkar. If anybody on the face of this Earth needed something like Buddhism to lift them out of their condition of social deprivation and give them some faith in themselves and an ethical and spiritual path to follow, it was them. I am also aware that this involvement is a two-way process. The interaction between the Eastern and Western wings of the FWBO has been, and will continue to be, very fruitful indeed.

Another surprise was the development of our team-based right livelihood businesses. Even in the very early days I used to speak of right livelihood, but I was thinking of it in the traditional terms of an *individual's* right livelihood in the midst of a non-Buddhist secular society. When, some years later, our right livelihood businesses began to emerge and to reveal the extent of their spiritual implications, it all happened on the initiative of certain Order members; I couldn't have been responsible for more than one per cent of it. This was quite unanticipated – and all the more of a pleasant surprise because of its being unanticipated. It showed that the Movement had its own independent life and growth.

Very recently I have been pleased – and a little surprised – by a sudden 'interest' in celibacy and in becoming an *anagārika*. In the past months fifteen men in India and England have become *anagārikas*, and I believe that some more might be on their way. The life of the *anagārika* represents a freedom to follow the spiritual life and respond to the needs of others which one doesn't have to the same extent if one is either married or in a regular sexual relationship.

Though I've always strongly recommended celibacy I have never pushed it: it must be an entirely voluntary decision that one takes in the interest of one's own spiritual development and something which is not annexed to any sort of post or position. I have therefore been all the more pleased because this development has been so spontaneous. It is the result of the reflection, the momentum, the spiritual experience and life of those particular people, and not a result of any instigation of mine.

In 1967 the FWBO was virtually unique in offering Westerners an opportunity to encounter Buddhism on the basis of practice and commitment. In the last twenty-five years a number of active Buddhist movements have emerged with some highly committed people in their ranks. As Western Buddhism evolves, what distinctive contribution do you think the FWBO has been making?

Twenty-five years is a very short time. We won't really be able to say much about our contribution for quite a few more years. I suspect, though, that our main contribution will be seen to be our emphasis on the central importance of Going for Refuge.

I just don't know to what extent we have yet had an effect on the Western Buddhist movement generally. I have become aware over the past couple of years that a number of groups in the United States have begun to take some of our more typical ideas, institutions, and practices seriously, but it remains to be seen to what extent they, or Buddhist groups elsewhere in the West, will be influenced by them.

Which of its features do you think particularly justify the FWBO's continued existence and appeal?
It's the FWBO as a whole. One can't single out the single-sex 'principle', or its right livelihood businesses, or its emphasis on spiritual friendship.... All these things hang together as part of a unified system. So we justify our existence, and our appeal – if they need justification at all – by what we are totally, and not by any specific features.

With so many serious Buddhist organizations around these days, do you feel less alone as a Dharma teacher?
I can't say that I do. If there was no FWBO I think I would be as alone as ever. I'm not alone any more simply because I've been able to convince at least some people that the way in which I perceive Buddhism is – so far as one can see at present anyway – the best and truest way in which to see it. I don't really think people make contact with the same thing through other Buddhist groups as they make contact with through us. Sometimes the Dharma is presented elsewhere in such a way as to *obscure* it.

Could you be more specific?
It is often a question of confusing lifestyle with spiritual commitment. Very often the Dharma is presented in more or less exclusively monastic terms, so that one is left with the feeling that if one does not become a monk it's not really worth one's while to practise Buddhism at all.

Again, sometimes the Dharma is disguised by Eastern culture. This happens most of all in the case of Tibetan Buddhism. Those involved with Tibetan Buddhist groups are sometimes quite confused by the Tibetan culture, and find it very difficult to discern the Dharma – the spirit of Buddhism as it were – in the midst of this very rich and elaborate – and to us alien – culture.

I meet quite a lot of people who are new to the FWBO. Many of them seem to have 'shopped around' other Buddhist groups before making contact with the FWBO. They've certainly nothing against the other Buddhist groups, but when I ask them why they have opted for the FWBO, they usually say first of all that the FWBO presents the Dharma in a more *accessible* manner. They also say that some of the teachers – especially some of the monk-teachers – in some of the other groups, communicate from behind a barrier which cannot be crossed, and which makes communication difficult. They do not find this to be the case with our Order members.

It has sometimes been suggested that the FWBO is a new school. I once even heard somebody claim that we are a new yāna! *How would you respond?*

Traditionally, especially in Tibetan Buddhism, the *yānas* are regarded as being successive. The Mahāyāna is believed to go somewhat beyond the Hīnayāna, and the Vajrayāna is believed to go beyond the Mahāyāna. So if we were a new *yāna* we would have to be claiming to go beyond the Vajrayāna. I certainly don't think we are a new *yāna* in that sense. Nowadays, anyway, I tend to question the Tibetan *triyāna* conception itself. According to that conception, the Going for Refuge is said to be representative of the Hīnayāna, the arising of the *bodhicitta* of the Mahāyāna, and so on – which suggests that you can go beyond the Going for Refuge. That is something I do not recognize.

I would therefore prefer to think of the FWBO as going back to what is central from what is peripheral, inasmuch as we stress the centrality of the Going for Refuge in the Buddhist life, and inasmuch as we see the arising of the *bodhicitta* not as a going *beyond* the Going for Refuge, but as the positive, altruistic dimension of the Going for Refuge itself. So if we *are* eventually to be seen by ourselves and others as a new development, or as a new school, it will be in the sense that we represent a distinctive assemblage of *emphases* from within the Buddhist tradition.

Twenty-five years is about one percent of Buddhist history. Have we yet made any contribution to the total Buddhist tradition? Are we even on our way to making such a contribution?

I hope we are. Whether we will make a contribution, as distinct from being an 'independent development', I don't know. The mere fact that we have existed represents a contribution to Buddhist history. But to what extent it is significant, useful, or valuable remains to be seen. I would hope that others in the Buddhist world – whether individuals or groups – will avail themselves of such insights and experience as we have managed to achieve or acquire, just as I hope we will avail ourselves of whatever insights and experiences are available within the wider Buddhist world.

Do you think we should be communicating our own insights and experience more energetically?

We have a duty to communicate, full stop. We have a duty to communicate the Dharma to those who wish to hear the Dharma or who would benefit from hearing it and putting it into practice. At present our constituency is with the 'unchurched' – with ex-Christians, ex-Hindus, ex-Jews, and even a few ex-Muslims. But I would like that constituency to expand. I would like people who already consider themselves Buddhists to harken to what we have to say, and to consider whether it might not be applicable to their own situation. Some of our Buddhist friends, especially in the East, are very set in their ways. But if they do not address some of the problems we have addressed their form of Buddhism may well not survive.

What sort of problems are you thinking of?

There is the problem of the monk–laity divide, and there is the problem essentially of 'restating' the fundamental truths of Buddhism in such a way as to be intelligible and appealing to people in our modern, secular world. Young people particularly, even in the Buddhist East, often do not heed the message of Buddhism when it is couched in traditional terms.

Do you see yourself as a reformer of the Buddhist tradition?

I have put forward certain ideas and insights. The FWBO acts upon those ideas and insights. If others in the Buddhist world were to act upon them I'd be very pleased, but it's not my job to reform them. You can't reform people by force. It's for them to take advantage of what you offer – or not. I would expect that some groups around the world will be somewhat influenced by our example, and may make little changes – though they may not always recognize where those particular ideas came from.

Although you are not an old man, for at least ten years you have been attending to the issue of 'succession'. Did any development – within the FWBO or elsewhere – spark that process off?

I certainly heard about disagreements arising within particular Buddhist groups after the deaths of their founders, but nothing like that really sparked me off. I was just aware that I was growing older, and I was aware of the issue of succession as a part of the whole question of the continued survival and development of the FWBO.

In some ways it is more difficult to be the successor to something already established than it is to start something completely new. I therefore want to make things as easy for my successors as possible. Ideally, I would like to live long enough to see my own successor, or successors, handing things over, after a period of ten or fifteen years, to *their* successor or successors. I don't see myself as simply handing things over to a successor or successors and then disappearing from the scene, but as 'supervising' at least two stages of succession. I would then feel that the FWBO, and the Order, had been really firmly established. That is why I've started thinking about the question of succession earlier than people might have expected. It's not the sort of thing one should be thinking about on one's deathbed!

But have there been times in recent years when you have felt you were the only person who could see something that needed urgent attention?
That is certainly the case, and it's still the case to some extent. But it is less and less the case as the years go by. That is why I'm always very pleased when I hear of Order members tackling issues in a way that I might have tackled them myself, or tackling them in a way that gives me complete satisfaction. It gives me great joy when I listen to talks by Order members, when I can tell that their grasp of the Dharma is really very sound, and that they can be relied upon to sort out even philosophical problems without any help from me.

But do you ever fear that without your guidance we might still lose our bearings?
As far as I can see, there's no question of the Movement losing its bearings in any very general or radical sort of way. I don't see that as a possibility, really, in view of the quite experienced and insightful people that we now have within the Movement – and also when I see the confidence that some of them enjoy on the part of the Movement as a whole.

I once heard it suggested that the FWBO is heavily dependent upon you for its philosophical, scholarly input, that our knowledge of the Dharma is perhaps over-reliant on you....

Well you don't need to be a scholar to comb the scriptures. I am not a scholar in the academic sense; I am merely well read. So, yes, I would certainly encourage at least some Order members to be well read and to comb the scriptures for teachings and insights that may have particular value and relevance for us.

I would also be quite pleased if there were – as in fact there now are – a few real scholars within the Movement to act as a sort of liaison between ourselves and traditional Buddhism. They will not only help us to draw upon the various treasuries of Buddhist teachings in Pāli, Sanskrit, Chinese, Tibetan, and so on, but will help us explain ourselves in traditional terms to those who *are* Buddhists – whether in the East or the West – and who are perhaps unable to see the value of our features on their own merits. For our part we need to know when we are deviating from tradition, so that we deviate from it knowingly, and know *why* we deviate from it.

What do you think will be the ultimate guarantees of the Movement's integrity, survival, and success?

Obviously it's important that Order members keep up the practice of the Dharma. That is obvious, I know, but I had better say it anyway because Buddhist history shows that it has sometimes been overlooked. So, yes, Order members must keep alive and deepen their Going for Refuge. They must be scrupulous in their observance of the precepts, keep up their practice of meditation, and so on.

The Movement's survival will depend too on a willingness to share the Dharma, to communicate it because you realize that other people could benefit from it, and you want them to benefit; you don't just want to keep what you've discovered to yourself. Then, of course, the Movement must be permeated on all levels by spiritual friendship. That is an absolute essential.

There is something else which may come as a surprise. There is what I would tentatively call 'respect for elders'. This is not very much in accordance with contemporary ideology, I know, but it is important for the integrity and survival of the Movement that Order members, Mitras, and others feel a genuine respect for those who are older in the sense of being more experienced, more insightful, and so on. It would be difficult for the Movement to survive or maintain its integrity without that. This respect is of course something that you yourself must feel – and must be willing and open to feel – for other people. If people are not ready and willing to recognize a greater degree of experience and insight than their own when they encounter it, then one cannot entertain very great hopes for the continued integrity, survival, and success of the Movement.

Having started what people sometimes refer to as a 'withdrawal', do you ever feel a conflict between the pull of your writing, say, and a desire, or need, to stay in touch with the day-to-day life of the Movement?
Objectively, of course, there is a conflict, if only in terms of my time. But I don't feel ambivalent. I am quite happy to do my best in both respects so long as that is necessary. But I have been able to devote more time to my writing and study and reflection over the last few years than was possible before. That does seem to be the way things are moving.

Has twenty-five years given us – given you – a chance to appreciate more fully the sort of forces that we are up against?
There is, of course, human weakness. That is always with us! The three poisons are always with us, so we're always up against those. But we are also up against contemporary ideologies such as egalitarianism and the intellectual leftovers of a discredited Marxism. We're up against pseudo-liberalism, and I would say we're up against some of the more extreme developments in Feminism – by which I don't mean that I am not in favour of all avenues being open to women which they are capable of following and willing to follow. We are up against all sorts of ideologies and attitudes that are inimical and contradictory to the Dharma – as well as our own greed, hatred, and delusion. Very often, of course, those ideologies represent a rationalization of those particular poisons.

Which elements of 'discredited Marxism' do you have in mind? Would you not say, for instance, that the maxim 'Take what you need, give what you can' is as relevant as ever?
Yes indeed, though the question would be how to make it *operative*, how to make people *willing* to take only what they needed, and to give what they could. This is a psychological and spiritual question. The

mechanics of it may be a matter of economics, but mechanics alone are not going to solve our problems in this area.

Just to make myself clear, what has been discredited is, perhaps more correctly, socialism in the sense of centralized planning, the idea that you can direct an economy from a single command centre. The more general, 'free-floating' view that has arisen in its wake is that any kind of difficulty or problem is other people's fault. You are the *victim*, so you've got to change the system, you've got to change society: *you* haven't got to change, you don't even think in those terms. All you have to do – if you don't actually instigate the revolution – is take advantage of it and participate in its goodies.

But what about the other end of the spectrum, the kind of heightened economic individualism that has been such a feature of the past decade in many countries?
Well the whole idea of private vices as public benefits is an old one, isn't it.[322] But even if private vices *are* public benefits, we're not in favour of the cultivation of private vices, are we? We would rather cultivate private virtues and try to see in what way *they* can be made to work out in the form of public benefits. That, I think, has not yet been tried.

Perhaps our team-based right livelihood businesses are a step in this direction. But there's infinitely more to do. Although they provide a Buddhistic working environment and spiritual friendships for those who work in them, although they donate money to the Movement, and although they function ethically, by and large they are part of the old structure, the old financial system.

In this connection I would like to see some people taking a thorough look at that financial system, seeing what it is, how it works, how it relates or doesn't relate to the Dharma, asking, for example, what is the function – even the meaning – of money. Money is a bit like electricity, in the sense that we all make use of it without really knowing what it actually is. This is an area we haven't even begun to explore. We need to understand the old structures and try to see whether they might not be replaceable by structures which would be more beneficial to us and to society at large.[323]

Are there any ways in which Western society has become more supportive to what we are doing over the last twenty-five years?
I wouldn't say more supportive, but more open in the sense of being more permeable. There's less resistance. People are more willing and ready to consider, say, doing yoga, or meditating, or being vegetarian.

Or being a Buddhist?
Or even being a Buddhist. Yes, it no longer raises eyebrows. When I returned to Britain in 1964 there were people coming along to the Hampstead Buddhist Vihara who were *proud* of the fact that even their best friends didn't know that they were Buddhists!

REFLECTIONS ON THE USA

Golden Drum *no. 31, November 1993, pp. 20–1. The questions were put by the editor, Nagabodhi.*

Did you have any general impressions of the American Buddhist scene prior to your recent visit?[324]

Over the years I've had a certain amount of correspondence with a few American Buddhists, and I've been receiving American Buddhist magazines, so I have been able to form a few very general impressions. I have noticed, for instance, that Tibetan Buddhism has become an increasingly strong and vigorous influence. When I stayed at Yale in 1970, the dominant influence was that of Japanese Zen; there was hardly any trace of Tibetan Buddhism. Then there is the phenomenon of the Buddhist scholars – scholars in Buddhism who are themselves practising Buddhists. That can only be a positive development. I have also noticed, especially latterly, that the older generations of Asian teachers are in some cases being succeeded by native-born American teachers – and sometimes even by the American disciples of those American teachers. This certainly represents a development – one could perhaps even speak of an 'Americanization' of Buddhism.[325]

There is a positive aspect to this. It means that, in the case of some groups, Buddhism is shedding a few of its Eastern cultural trappings and becoming more approachable and accessible. But there is a negative aspect as well, inasmuch as Buddhism seems to be becoming, to some extent, rather assimilated into the American way of life – which is not of course necessarily very Buddhist at all.

I was particularly struck, for example, by the promotion of 'vipassanā' meditation as a technique quite dissociated from its foundations in Buddhism, and associated instead with a very worldly, almost secular sort of Western outlook. There seems also to be some talk of a 'family-based' Buddhism. Here it would seem that the American idealization of the family has infiltrated some Buddhist circles. In the East, even where the Buddhism is very ethnic, no one ever talks in such terms. One can also see, judging especially from advertisements in the Buddhist press, that there is a good deal of commercialization involved. There are all sorts of fringe products associated with the Buddhist movement: 'lucky Buddhas', expensive, luxurious meditation cushions, all kinds of religious paraphernalia, even insurance and legal services, and real estate. Some people are clearly making a lot of money out of all this. One might even mention Tantric initiations.

That takes us back to an earlier point. Why do you think there is so much enthusiasm for Tibetan Buddhism?
I think it's just that hordes of teachers have come across. To take a slightly realistic view, they are refugees, they've got to make a living, so they do it mainly through teaching the Dharma and handing out Tantric initiations, with more or less of altruistic inspiration.

That's a pretty strong statement!
Well, they never came out of Tibet before. They never even thought of it. So inasmuch as they professedly upheld the bodhisattva ideal, one rather wonders why they didn't bother.

Did you find that you or the FWBO are at all well known in America?
It certainly transpired that I was well known through my writings. Quite a lot of people were familiar with *A Survey of Buddhism* and *The Three Jewels*. People were very welcoming and appreciative indeed. I was somewhat surprised to find myself being hailed wherever I went, quite explicitly and spontaneously, as an 'elder of the Western Buddhist movement'. The FWBO is probably rather less known. But with the establishment of an FWBO centre in San Francisco, and now that I have met personally several of the more important leaders in the States, I think there will be a greater awareness of the FWBO and what it stands for than hitherto.

What aspects of the FWBO *seem to be attracting those who are getting involved?*

Although the majority of those who have joined the FWBO, at whatever level, have had substantial experience of other Buddhist groups, I kept hearing how much they appreciated the clarity of our teaching – of the Dharma in general and of meditation in particular. They also valued our emphasis on the importance of sangha and spiritual friendship, and appreciated the friendly atmosphere of the FWBO – though I must say that wherever I went, among other Buddhist groups, I found the atmosphere generally friendly.

Are people being drawn by our experiments with residential communities and right livelihood?

Most of the local Buddhist centres have retreat centres with associated communities, and even residential communities in cities. But they are all somewhat caught up with the family. You always seem to find married couples with children living at the retreat centres and city centres. There is no conception of the 'single-sex' situation or community. Even the Theravādin movement there is predominantly a lay movement. I would say that they have still to address the question of what we would regard as real spiritual communities, based on the single-sex principle.

There are certainly people engaged in right livelihood, though I don't think the ideal of right livelihood has been addressed in the same 'total' way as we've addressed it here. The main exception I encountered was Dharma Publishing. The people working there were completely committed to Dharma Publishing and its ancillary bodies. I am sure they also meditate and study, but they seemed to regard working for, with, and in Dharma Publishing as constituting a whole way of life, a whole spiritual commitment in itself – in a way that corresponded quite closely to our own attitude to right livelihood. I was very impressed by them.[326]

Were any of your meetings with leading Buddhists particularly stimulating? Did you encounter any particular preoccupations among the people working there?

I found all my meetings quite stimulating and very agreeable. People were sincerely interested and willing to listen – but very ready to express their own ideas as well. Although there was too little time to go into many things in sufficient depth, I think the preoccupation I encountered most often was one with issues of authority, with power and the abuse of power. In certain cases the abuse of power has led to disaster. This has been particularly the case when authority has been associated with institutional centralization – even over-centralization – with all authority, power, and financial resources being concentrated at the top of a pyramid, as it were, and in the hands, sometimes, of just one person. A lot of the Buddhists I met were concerned to find an alternative model. They were therefore interested in the FWBO's principle of decentralization, of having a large number of FWBO institutions that are legally and financially autonomous, instead of having just one big FWBO with branches that are controlled from the centre.

An allied theme to which we returned again and again was the importance of 'horizontal' spiritual friendship in addition to the 'vertical'. The man at the top of the organizational and spiritual structure was, in most cases, the guru. So they were interested that in the FWBO we balance the vertical spiritual friendship with the horizontal.

Were people able to talk about their problems very freely?
The people at San Francisco Zen Center and at Green Gulch Farm were particularly open about their difficulties. They have already been reviewing their structures for some years, and I certainly got the impression that if they found anything that would be useful to them in our FWBO experience they would not hesitate to adopt it. Others spoke in a more general way.

There seems to be a fairly 'ecumenical' mood among West Coast Buddhists, quite a lot of mutual awareness and friendly contact.
Well, you use the word 'ecumenical', a term of Christian origin which means 'tending to promote unity'. Within the Christian context, this means unity among the churches. In a Buddhist context it would mean unity among different Buddhist groups. But what constitutes the basis for unity among Buddhists? So far as I see it, promoting the unity of different Buddhist groups could only come about through promoting an understanding of the centrality of the act of Going for Refuge. I don't think there is an ecumenical movement in American Buddhism in that sense.

Abbot Tenshin Anderson recently wrote a very interesting article for *Tricycle* in which he made the point very strongly that American Zen

Buddhists have concentrated on other aspects to such an extent as to lose sight of the Going for Refuge, but to what extent American Buddhists have made the Going for Refuge central, and if they do try to make it central, to what extent that will result in the modification – even the complete overhaul – of the tradition to which they belong, remains to be seen. One mustn't confuse being ecumenical with just being friendly. The Buddhist groups in the Bay area are certainly friendly. They were friendly towards me and I think they are friendly among themselves. But whether they could be said to be ecumenical is another question.

That friendliness gives rise to quite a lot of mutual contact and 'networking'. Does this seem to have a diluting effect?
As regards some people, the networking could lead to superficiality, but not in all cases. It was quite clear that each centre had a nucleus of quite devoted practitioners who, while having a friendly attitude to members of other groups, were quite clearly getting on with their personal practice in the context of their own tradition. Dilution may be the case with some people, particularly perhaps those who are into the arts and who just draw on a little bit of Zen or Tibetan Buddhism for inspiration. But this by no means affects everybody.

In some of your talks on the 'Rain of the Dharma' you referred to 'cotton candy Buddhism' and the 'acid rain of the Dharma'. Can you say a little about this?[327]
I coined the term 'candyfloss – or cotton candy – Buddhism' after listening to some of the talks at the European Buddhist Union Congress in Berlin last year.[328] Really, I was continuing a line of thought that began to develop there, but I thought a word of warning might be appropriate in the States.

Cotton candy is, first of all, pink – pink being the colour of pseudo-liberalism. It's sticky, it's sweet, and there appears to be a lot of it without there being any real substance. As taught by some people Buddhism seems to be rather like that. As for the 'acid rain': when talking about the 'Rain of the Dharma' I emphasized that it must be pure rain, pure Dharma. The 'acid rain' of the Dharma is a rain of the Dharma in which the purity of the rain is polluted by foreign elements, by isms and ideologies that have nothing to do with the Dharma; they are in fact quite opposed to it, and deprive it of its specific identity. I referred, for instance, to Catholicism; I know that Philip Kapleau has complained about the integrity of the Zen tradition being threatened by teachers sanctioning Catholic priests and nuns as well as rabbis and ministers to teach Zen. Then of course there are those who mix up Buddhism with Feminism (with a capital F)[329] and with all sorts of confused political ideas about egalitarianism. One could say that 'cotton candy Buddhism' represents Buddhism in a very weak and dilute form, whereas the 'acid rain of the Dharma' represents Buddhism as mixed not just with extraneous, but even with hostile, elements.

IDOLS OF THE MARKET PLACE

Golden Drum *no. 33, May 1994, p. 28.*

Sir Francis Bacon (the philosopher, not the artist) spoke of the deep-seated limitations of the human mind as idols.[330] An idol was a false god that was set up and worshipped in place of truth. There were idols of the Tribe, idols of the Den (or Cave), idols of the Market Place, and idols of the Theatre. Numerous enough in Bacon's own day, such idols are even more numerous in ours. This is particularly true of the idols of the Market Place, or those words and phrases that corrupt and muddle our thinking.

In recent years three particularly monstrous idols of the Market Place have been set up on the other side of the Atlantic, and now Western Buddhists are being invited to fall down and worship them. If one does not do so one is in danger of being branded as unprogressive and reactionary and even as un-Buddhist. The three new idols are Democratization, Feminization, and Integration.

Representative democracy is probably the best form of government humanity has succeeded in devising, despite its evident shortcomings in certain respects. The democratization of Buddhism is quite another matter. Buddhism is a spiritual teaching. It is a teaching about a path – a path leading from *saṃsāra* to *nirvāṇa*, from the mundane to the transcendental. That path consists of a number of successive stages, and those who tread that path – the true followers of the Buddha – occupy positions on one or another of those stages, either a higher one or a lower one. Thus there is a hierarchy of stages, or experiences, and a hierarchy of persons. This hierarchy is a spiritual hierarchy, and is not to be confused with the purely ecclesiastical hierarchy of (largely self-styled) Holinesses and Eminences and their appointees, even though in the person of certain exceptional individuals the two may occasionally coincide. A Buddhism that was democratized to the extent of refusing to recognize the existence of a spiritual hierarchy would not be Buddhism at all, for it would have abandoned the principle of the path with its successive stages, and have ceased, therefore, really to practise the Dharma.

Feminization means, in effect, refashioning the Buddha in the image of that darling of the women's pages the so-called New Man, with his much-advertised vulnerability, his touching efforts to domesticate himself, and his pathetic emotional dependence on women – and hence refashioning Buddhism accordingly. It means creating a 'nice' Buddhism, an inoffensive, unchallenging teaching in which there would be no place for initiative, boldness, daring, courage, adventurousness, and enterprise, or for any of the more typically masculine qualities and virtues. It would be a Buddhism for eunuchs, not men, and probably would not appeal to the majority of women either. The feminization of Buddhism follows from its democratization. Since women (it is argued) form fifty percent of the Buddhist community they ought to have an equal share in determining the general character of the religion. It also follows from the demonization of the masculine and the (alleged) necessity of its redemption by the feminine consciousness.

Integration means the integration of Buddhism into the world, or the practice of the path to liberation without withdrawing from worldly life. In practice this amounts, only too often, to trying to develop spiritually without giving up one's affluent North American or West European lifestyle. Such integration is also spoken of in terms of the creation of a lay Buddhism as distinct from the predominantly monastic Buddhism of the East. What is really wanted is a Buddhism that is neither lay nor monastic in the traditional sense but which is firmly based on the centrality for the Buddhist life of the act of Going for Refuge supported by the observance of the fundamental ethical precepts. The integration that is needed is not the integration of Buddhism into the world, but of the world into Buddhism.

Rather than falling down and worshipping the monstrous idols of Democratization, Feminization, and Integration as we have been invited to do, let us take to them the hammer of right view and reduce them and all other idols of the Market Place to a heap of rubble, however fashionable for the moment they may happen to be.

SANGHARAKSHITA AT SEVENTY

Golden Drum *no. 38, August 1995, pp. 2–9. The questions were put by Vidyadevi.*

First of all, what led you to decide to appoint a College of Preceptors and a Council as a way of handing on your responsibilities?[331]
It's really quite simple. I have a lot of responsibilities which have to be handed on. Either I hand them over to one person or to a number of people. I thought it would be better to hand them over to a number of people working together in cooperation, partly because the responsibilities are growing all the time and I don't think it would have been fair to hand them all just to one person.

And perhaps there are also benefits from having a number of people sharing that responsibility?
Yes, provided, of course, that those people are the more senior and more experienced members of the Order, and that they are able to work smoothly and harmoniously together on a basis of mutual friendship.

Are there any precedents for this?
In a sense there are precedents everywhere. Although some Buddhist traditions do emphasize the guru, and although there is often a formal or ceremonial head of a tradition or lineage, it is usually in fact a body of senior and more experienced people who give general guidance to the direction of that particular tradition.

What areas of the FWBO do you feel the College members should pay attention to over the next few years?
That's rather a big question. I'll say just a few general things. I think the first thing that the members of the College have to do is to strengthen their own friendships and learn to work harmoniously together. Some of them, of course, will be living together, the men in one community, the women in another. So that's the first thing. They need to really work upon and deepen their friendships among themselves. In a way everything flows from that. Then they need to look carefully at the Movement as a whole, and the preceptors especially have to make sure that the standards represented by effective and possibly by real Going for Refuge are maintained throughout the Movement, and throughout the Order especially. They have to make sure that the same standards are observed throughout the Movement with regard to meditation, to study, to team-based right livelihood, and so on. In this way they will act as a unifying influence.

The time may come when our conditions will be much more difficult, and that depth of friendship may be the thing that will hold us together.
Yes indeed. There might be a war, for instance, or a severe economic decline, or a very hostile non-Buddhist religious movement trying to wipe us out, if not in one country, in another.

It's your wish that a library be built in your memory. Why?
It's more that I have a wish that the books I've collected over the years should be preserved for the benefit of the Movement. That's the basis of it. Quite a few of the books I've collected are out of print or difficult to get hold of or very expensive. The collection needs to be housed and catalogued properly, and it also needs proper care and expansion. There are big gaps in the Buddhist collection that I would like to see filled.

When you think of your life, do you think of yourself as having been involved with a series of projects, the FWBO having been just one of them, or is that not how you see it?
I don't really see it like that at all. It's all within the scope of the Dharma – practising the Dharma, studying the Dharma, trying to spread and communicate the Dharma. It's as though there's just one big, continuous, ongoing project which is still going on. I certainly don't think that the

'FWBO project' is now more or less complete as far as I am concerned. Even if I do get on with some more writing after my withdrawal from organizational responsibilities, that writing, I hope, will be relevant to the Movement.

Do you feel you've succeeded with the FWBO in terms of what you set out to do?
I didn't set out at the beginning with some sort of blueprint, so there's no question of whether or not I have been able to execute that blueprint. But things have grown, things have developed. I think that I – or we – have been reasonably successful, certainly not unsuccessful, but there is so much still to be done, so many possibilities of further expansion, that I feel no inclination either to sit on my own laurels, such as they are, or to encourage others to sit on their laurels, those that have them. I hope that everybody will carry on doing more and more – not in a superficial activist way, but in a very genuine way, on the basis of their own understanding and experience, and in cooperation and harmony with each other.

Subhuti has recently made a connection between spiritual hierarchy and the taking on of responsibility in an organizational sense. Is there any danger of taking something on in an external way as a substitute for commitment to the development of one's inner life?
Clearly there must be both. Sometimes it's the other way round – you escape into subjectivity in order to evade objective responsibility. So yes, one has to avoid both those dangers.

Can it be right for Order members to be giving the impression of being busy all the time?
Well, if they are busy they can't help giving the impression of being busy, but one should never try to give the impression that one is very busy as a way of increasing one's importance in other people's eyes. On the other hand, if someone is very busy externally, one shouldn't assume that they're 'out of touch with themselves'. And if they don't seem to be doing very much, one shouldn't assume that they are very much *in* touch with themselves.

You are withdrawing from your responsibilities to the FWBO. *How far away, so to speak, are you going?*

I've always said I will be withdrawing from *organizational* responsibilities, though by 'organizational' I don't mean something very mundane and unspiritual – perhaps 'practical' would be a better word. I don't intend to withdraw from contact with people within the Movement. I may well be seeing quite a lot of Order members and Mitras and others, as well as Buddhists outside the Movement. The assumption would seem to be that I'm going away to some little cave somewhere and will be completely incommunicado, but that is not my idea at all. I may go away from time to time, say to somewhere like Guhyaloka, but I don't see that as being my permanent lifestyle.[332]

Would you wish it to be?

I'd quite like to spend time on my own from time to time, but at present I have the greater part of the day on my own and I'm quite happy with that. I get on with my writing.

So you don't mind too much where you are?

If it was a possibility without jeopardizing other things I wanted to do, obviously I'd prefer to be surrounded by beautiful scenery, but that's certainly not a determining factor. Sometimes I'm a bit surprised that Order members who are thinking of going here or there, or setting up a centre here or there, seem to think first of all about whether it's the sort of place they'd like to live in, not whether it's the sort of place that really needs the Dharma. This is not very bodhisattva-like, one might say. It's a bit self-indulgent.

But don't we need to consider how much we're affected by our surroundings?

As a practising Buddhist you shouldn't really be too strongly affected by your surroundings, or too dependent on having very supportive conditions. You don't want to put yourself into unnecessarily difficult situations, obviously, but you should have a certain independence from external conditions. Your moods should not depend upon whether you are surrounded by trees or whether you've got nice neighbours, whether you live in a nice street in a nice area in a nice part of town.

Being a nice Buddhist!
Yes.

That brings to mind another question. It seems that we are looking to spread the Dharma first to places which are more settled, more stable. Would it just be impractical to go to, say, Bosnia, where conditions are very difficult, and attempt to teach meditation?[333]
I think we should go to places not only where we're most needed, but where we could most fruitfully employ our energy, and not just waste it. At present that means going to situations which are stable enough for us to get something started, to plant something that is going to last. If, on the other hand, an individual Order member has a strong urge to go to Bosnia and teach meditation to people there regardless, I'm not going to discourage them.

Subhuti says in his recent biography, Bringing Buddhism to the West, *that you are considering what he calls 'a work that will place all your thinking in a clear philosophical context'.*[334] *That sounds intriguing.*
That does sound rather ambitious. What I'm going to do initially is to try to clarify my own terminology. In the past, in lectures and seminars, I think my English terminology has been rather loose and inconsistent. I tend to do my Buddhist thinking in Pāli and Sanskrit – not of course just in Pāli and Sanskrit, but using Pāli and Sanskrit key terms, which I translate into English as I go along. But there are some English terms that I use which don't exactly correspond to any Pāli or Sanskrit term, but which give expression to a very definitely Buddhist attitude or set of ideas. I think my English terminology needs straightening out. I'm thinking of words like 'individual' and 'person', 'conditioned' and 'unconditioned', 'positive' and 'negative', and even terms like 'Enlightenment' and 'the Transcendental'. 'Transcendental' has a meaning in Western philosophical thought, but when I use the term I always use it as the English equivalent of the term *lokuttara*. So I want initially to clarify my own terminology, and then see whether that leads to any more general considerations of a philosophical nature. If anybody comes across a term that I use regularly but inconsistently, or the meaning of which is not clear, they can write to me and ask me to include it in this list.

In your essay on Buddhism and William Blake you wrote 'Buddhism will not really spread in the West until it speaks the language of Western culture.'[335] *In recent times arts events have become a very important part of* FWBO *activities. How do you see this development?*

Frankly I don't see arts events as having very much to do with Buddhism speaking the language of Western culture. For that, there needs first of all to be a very deep experience of Buddhism, and perhaps within the FWBO collectively we don't yet have that. Perhaps a few individuals approach it, but no more than that. And then there has to be a very deep immersion in Western culture, even the creation of a new Western culture.

I've always encouraged the practice of the arts, and I have always seen the serious practice of any of the arts as constituting a spiritual discipline, but I emphasize the *serious* practising. I think both inside and especially outside the FWBO there's a lot of dabbling in art, whether it's writing, painting, or whatever. If you dabble in Buddhism and dabble in one or other of the arts, that's really got nothing to do with Buddhism learning to speak the language of Western culture. If we're not careful that expression can become a bit of a cliché.

So how can Buddhism learn to speak the language of Western culture?

Well, it comes down to individuals. When one speaks of Buddhism, one means practising Buddhists. So Western Buddhists have to deepen their experience of the Dharma, and communicate that as best they can to people in the West who want to hear about it. They will therefore need to develop media of communication, including communicating through the arts – because the arts in the widest sense, including literature, do have a very powerful appeal, and reach far beyond the boundaries of organized religion. But it's not as though there's an art there ready to be used. You probably have to create the medium that you want to use; it has to grow out of your practice and experience of the Dharma.

There are two approaches to art: the passive or receptive, and the creative. The passive – the enjoyment of great works of art, great literature, great paintings, great music – can certainly help refine our emotional state. But that is not what I'm talking about. I'm talking about the more creative side of artistic activity, communication of Buddhist values through the medium of the arts, not in an artificial or didactic way, but a communication which takes place out of a deep involvement with Buddhism and with one or another of the arts.

I think the arts events taking place in the FWBO fall more into the former category – which is fine. Encouraging people to refine their emotional life through appreciating and enjoying the arts does contribute to their spiritual development. But the communication of the Dharma through works of art which you yourself create is another matter. Also, despite the language I've been using, I don't want to draw too hard and fast a distinction between the Dharma that you communicate and the work of art through which you communicate it. The two should be a sort of seamless garment, as it were.

Are there any developments in the area of the arts that you'd particularly like to see?
I'd just like to see them all develop. I'd like us to be producing works of visual art and music. For instance, I'd like to see a really good musical setting of the Sevenfold Puja, creating an appropriate mood for each of its seven stages. And I'd like to see the Buddha's life being illustrated. Of course there are some beautiful Buddha images that have been made by Order members and Friends. Perhaps that is one of the areas where we have produced something reasonably good. At the very least they are a step in the right direction.

At the end of Bringing Buddhism to the West *Subhuti says that you 'regard these present times as largely ones of degeneracy and increasing barbarism'.*[336] *There is a teaching that whole civilizations, being impermanent, will inevitably decline. In these 'barbaric' times, what do you think about that traditional teaching?*
Some Buddhist schools in the Far East seem to believe that decline is inevitable – there's nothing we can do about it, we live in the age of decay, the dark age, the *kali-yuga*. But that's more a Hindu teaching than a Buddhist one, though I'm afraid this line of thought does rather disfigure some of Dr Conze's writings. I certainly don't believe that decay and decline are inevitable, whether for the collective or for the individual. Circumstances may be very difficult but that doesn't mean you have to resign yourself to them. You can struggle against them, overcome them, even reverse them.

This raises the question 'What conditions are conducive to spiritual development?' Difficult times might be conducive.

And would perhaps call forth more faith, more energy, more determination, more devotion. So yes, there is that question too. What, ultimately speaking, are difficult conditions? Life itself is a difficult condition because it's subject to suffering, to old age, disease, and death. If you're not going to be able to do anything worthwhile under unfavourable conditions, you might as well give up in view of the fact that you have been born, are going to grow old (with or without illness), and die. What could be more difficult than that?

So we should be confident that positive actions will have a positive effect.

And that there can be a positive response even to apparently unfavourable conditions. Say someone we know is dying of AIDS. Well, that's a very difficult situation, certainly difficult for that person. But that difficult situation may call forth so much love and sympathy and support from the friends and family of the person who is ill that in a sense the situation becomes very positive. Obviously one doesn't wish that anybody should get AIDS so that all that love may be called forth, but when something like that does happen, one doesn't have to just fold one's hands and lament. There can be a positive response on the part of all concerned.

There's the idea that the teachings of one Buddha will disappear before the arising of another.

That may well happen, but it doesn't have to happen. You can practise the Dharma in any situation, however apparently difficult. The Dharma is not like a rock that is gradually, inevitably, worn away by the wind and the rain. It exists in the lives and hearts of people – to the extent that we practise it. Inasmuch as we have free will according to Buddhism, there's nothing to stop us practising the Dharma, so no individual is bound to decline.

Do you think that in the FWBO in the West we place too much importance on having good conditions?

I think perhaps we do. I think we've become too accustomed to comfort. Yes, it is good to have conditions that conduce to one's personal spiritual development, but it's very easy to begin to see that in terms of having easy, comfortable conditions. If you don't feel easy or comfortable with a certain set of conditions, you might think that they're not helpful to your spiritual development, and then you start thinking that you need better conditions. In that way, instead of thinking in terms of what *really* conduces to your spiritual development, you think in terms of what you like and what you dislike. There's a subtle shift. I think this is a trap into which people sometimes fall.

In Sangharakshita: A New Voice in the Buddhist Tradition, *Subhuti says 'Unless the new society starts to influence its environment, it will become increasingly isolated and therefore increasingly vulnerable.'*[337] *As we move into the twenty-first century, to what extent is it a priority for us to begin to influence our environment in social, economic, and political ways?*
This is the sort of complex question that I will just leave the members of the College and the Council to sort out. Whether or not I myself will see the twenty-first century is an open question. By the way, don't forget it isn't our Buddhist twenty-first century, just as it isn't going to be our second millennium. That belongs to a quite different chronology. So we mustn't think too much in these terms.

Are there any specific areas in which we might begin to have an effect on our environment?
It depends on the scale upon which one is thinking. Certainly one should try to have a good effect on one's immediate environment. I think it's a question of taking it step by step.

I know that there are places where FWBO *groups are thinking of building their own Buddhist centres rather than converting existing buildings.*
I think this would certainly be good, because then we'd be creating something more adapted to our own requirements. We've done this fairly successfully in India; we could do it in the West too. We've created our own images; why not create our own temples, centres, communities, to house them?

*It would be an opportunity for us to express ourselves in a new way –
there are limits to what you can do to an existing building.*
Yes. If, for instance, we built a community house, it would be built in
accordance with our own lifestyle, so it would express that lifestyle, just
as a monastery does. It would have a shrine-room and a common room,
study-bedrooms – some for one person, some for two or three – and
a guest room and a spacious kitchen, a garden and a workshop. That
would be an expression of the way we live, so that from the outside we
don't look just like a family even down to the lace curtains. Just thinking
off the top of my head, I think we should start by asking ourselves what
our practical requirements are, and build accordingly. The development
of a particular architectural style can come later.

*You've said that Order members should remember that we are citizens.
How does that relate to being an* anagārika, *a cityless one?*
Anagārika literally means 'homeless one'. It is literally possible to get away
from home in the narrow sense, but nowadays you can't get away from
the state. In the Buddha's time in India perhaps you could, because there
were forests where the king's writ didn't run, but nowadays every part of
the Earth's surface belongs to one or another sovereign state which has its
own government and its own laws. If you live within that state, you can't
escape from those laws. You may disagree with them, you may disobey
them if you think that they are wrong or unjust, but you will have to suffer
the consequences. So the *anagārika*, though he or she may leave home,
can't literally leave the state. You may have an international outlook, you
may not identify yourself mentally or emotionally with any particular
state or nation or country or tribe or caste, but the world doesn't let you
get away with that. And since we are perforce citizens, we have rights
and we have duties. It's our responsibility as Buddhists to exercise those
rights and perform those duties in a way which is most in accordance
with the Dharma and most furthers the purposes of the Dharma.

Although I say 'remember that you're a citizen',[338] I'm not suggesting
that you are likely to forget, because you are always going to receive
your tax returns, for instance, or in some countries your call-up papers
and so forth. But we need to remember that we are citizens in the sense
that we try to connect our rights and duties as citizens with our practice
of Buddhism, rather than somehow keeping the two things in separate
compartments of our lives.

You said once that you'd like to be remembered as a clear thinker.
I didn't mean of course that I would like to be remembered only for
that.

*No, no. But why clear thinking in particular? What's so special about
clarity of thought?*
I think I've been inclined to emphasize clarity of thought because in the
course of my life, both in India and in the West, I've come up against so
much muddled thinking. If you don't think clearly, if your thinking is
muddled and confused, you can't develop right view. And if you don't
develop right view, you can't develop Perfect Vision. It's as simple as
that. So clear thinking, leading to right view, leading to Perfect Vision,
seems to be a particular need of the times.

*But in your teaching about Perfect Vision, you say that the arising of
glimpses of vision need not be anything to do with thought.*
That is true. It doesn't have to have anything to do with thought. It
can arise independently of clear thinking, but not in the presence of
muddled thinking.

So it is more to do with untangling muddled thinking.
Yes – and letting your imagination shine forth.

*In his talk on FWBO Day this year Kamalashila said he thought that in
general people in the FWBO lack mindfulness. Do you agree?*
Yes. In fact I have made the point myself more than once. I think
people in the FWBO are not nearly mindful enough, and I include
Order members in that. There's not enough mindfulness, awareness,
in the affairs of everyday life, in carrying out one's ordinary everyday
activities, and in speaking. There's a lot of unmindful talk. Fairly
recently I was concerned to learn that some Order members still
indulged sometimes in bad language. That means that there isn't
sufficient awareness of how one is speaking. I think it's very necessary
to be aware of the person to whom we are speaking, and whether what
we say is appropriate and skilful, conducive to harmony, and so on.
And even, just to come down to quite ordinary, everyday situations,
I've sometimes not been very happy to see how unmindfully people
eat. I'm certainly not happy to see Order members walking along the

street stuffing things into their mouths in the most unmindful way. That's the sort of thing I'm thinking of.

There are possibly two reasons why people in the FWBO don't seem to attach sufficient importance to mindfulness. I think they are rightly concerned not to develop alienated awareness, but that doesn't mean you should not develop awareness at all. And then I think – as a leftover, perhaps, from the sixties – there's an idea that you should be spontaneous and natural, and that being very mindful is somehow unnatural, as though mindfulness is almost *per se* alienated. So the practice of mindfulness tends to be undervalued. But as the Buddha said, mindfulness is always useful.[339]

Which living person do you most admire?
Oh dear. Well, I'm glad you said 'most' because I can't say that there are many living persons that I admire at all. It's easy to admire someone for a particular trait, but you might not admire them as a total person. As I look around the world, even the Buddhist world, I can't say there are many people whom I admire at all, but if I was pressed, I would say Allen Ginsberg. It's not that I admire everything about him. It's not that I particularly like his poetry – in fact I think I rather don't like it. And it's not that I necessarily agree with all his ideas. But I do admire his honesty, and that is a very rare quality these days. It seems to me that Allen Ginsberg has always been completely honest, and I admire him very much for that.[340]

Do you admire the Dalai Lama?
I think 'admire' is too strong a word. I certainly appreciate him, I appreciate the non-violent stand he has taken in connection with Tibet and China.

And within our own movement?
There are a lot of people I admire within the Movement and within the Order because I know their history. I know what difficult backgrounds they've come from, and what sufferings they've undergone before coming into contact with the Movement and changing their lives. So yes, there are lots of relatively unknown people, certainly unknown to the outside world, within our own Movement, our own Order, whom

I do admire very much for the effort they've made over so many years, and are still making.

Have you any particular travel plans over the next few years? And is there anywhere in particular you'd like to visit?
I very definitely have travel plans, principally in fulfilment of a long-standing promise. I have been promising for years to visit New Zealand and Australia, and I think the time has come for me to keep that promise. So, all being well, I shall be leaving some time in the late summer or early autumn of next year, and visiting first of all America and our centres there, then going across to Australia to visit our Sydney and Melbourne centres, and to New Zealand to visit our Auckland and Wellington centres. I have no plans to give talks or lead retreats or anything like that. I just want to see something of those two countries, do a little sightseeing in each, and of course meet up with people.[341]

As for wishing to see places, I think it's rather late in life for that. These days I only do sightseeing as it were in the course of duty, just as side interest. I would have liked to have seen, among other places, Istanbul and New Mexico, but it looks rather doubtful as to whether I'll see either.

Why New Mexico particularly?
I'm interested in New Mexico through my interest in D. H. Lawrence, because he has described it so beautifully in some of his writings, especially the country above Santa Fe. If there is any possibility of FWBO activities starting up there I may go. But I'm doubtful as to whether there will be FWBO activities in Istanbul just yet, though of course one doesn't know.

Do you see travelling round FWBO centres as part of your future, or is this a 'farewell tour'?
Well, it's obviously something I can always do. There are so many centres even in Britain, and a few more in Europe, and I know I'm welcome at each and every one of them. My priority definitely will be to get on with writing, so if I do any visiting of that sort – and I always enjoy my visits to FWBO centres – it'll be in the intervals between chapters or between books.

What are your impressions – on the strength of your most recent visit – of Buddhism in America? And what particular contributions do you think the FWBO could make to the practice of the Dharma there?

I do hope the FWBO can have a very strong and positive presence in the States. And I hope that we can have friendly contact with all the other Buddhist traditions and groups there, and have a positive influence on them, especially in the way of helping them to clarify the centrality of Going for Refuge in the Buddhist way of life. There are some that emphasize being a monk more, some that emphasize meditation more, some that emphasize receiving Tantric initiation more – and if any of these things is placed at the centre and made the dominating factor in Buddhism, that is obviously one-sided. I would like us to assist those Buddhist groups and traditions to see the centrality of Going for Refuge to a greater extent than most of them do at present.

A lot of thought is being put into what is to happen after your death. How does it feel to have your own death discussed so much?

To me it doesn't feel anything in particular. After all, I know that I'm going to die, and it's of some significance to the Movement, so why shouldn't people talk about it? I've been accustomed to that for years. At Padmaloka years ago people used to discuss it around the meal-table very freely, and I just listened as though in a sense they were talking about another person – not in an alienated way, I hope. I'm quite happy that people should talk about it. It seems quite sensible – it's not as though my death won't make any difference to anybody.

Sometimes people think about who they'd like to have present at their death, what funeral arrangements they'd like, and so on.

I don't have any particular wishes. I'm quite happy to leave it to whoever will be responsible. If I think of anything I'll let people know, but at the moment I've no particular wish for this piece of music to be played or that text to be read. Let people do as they please. It will be their funeral, not mine!

And how about your future rebirth?

I never think about it.

So not for you the whole business of incarnations and tulkus?
I assume that I will be reborn somewhere, and no doubt that will be determined by what I've done in the course of this lifetime. My concern is much more to do what is right in this lifetime than to bother about where I'll be reborn or what as. Look after the cause and the effect will look after itself.

Presumably that would be good general advice.
Yes indeed. One need have no unhealthy curiosity about previous lives or future lives. This life is enough for us to be getting on with. And if this life is right, how can any future life not be right?

Sogyal Rimpoche's book The Tibetan Book of Living and Dying, *which deals with the Tibetan approach to death and the various practices recommended by the Tibetan tradition, has sold very well. But how useful is that approach for Western people? I have to admit that when facing the death of somebody I know, I find the* Tibetan Book of the Dead *a bit foreign.*[342] *Do you think we're going to need to find ways to relate to that, or will we need to come up with our own rituals and texts?*
I think we just need to learn to relate to the fact of death, our own death and the death of other people. As regards our own death we have to learn to approach it as mindfully as we possibly can and in the best possible circumstances, so that we give ourselves the opportunity of a positive send-off. So far as other people are concerned, we should try to make them comfortable, try to develop a positive atmosphere around them, and – both before they actually die, while they are dying, and after they're dead for some time – direct our positive thoughts of *mettā* towards them. That, I think, is the essence of the matter: mindfulness and *mettā*.

DAKINI

The first Dakini *magazine appeared in 1976, just a few gestetnered pages stapled together. Informal and unedited, its articles and poems were contributed by the relatively few women then involved with the* FWBO. *Some years later the new* Dakini *was brought into life as a printed magazine by Kalyanaprabha, and she and Vajrapushpa were its general editors. It was relaunched in 1995 as* Lotus Realm: a new voice for Buddhist Women, *and came out two or three times a year until 2002, playing a significant part in the life of women in the* FWBO, *and exploring issues relevant to and from the point of view of women practising the Dharma. Themes included women and motherhood, women and work, women and power, women speaking out, social action, meditation and transformation, women and art, women and the heroic ideal, and so on. The news section provides posterity with a close-up view of the development of the women's wing of the Order and Movement. Book reviews and sometimes poetry were also features, as were the illustrations, carefully selected by Dharmottara. Digitised copies can be found at https://adhisthana.org/digitised-periodicals/.*

The interview that follows comes from Dakini *No. 12, on the theme of spiritual life and beauty. To give a flavour of that issue, it included an article by Vajrapushpa entitled 'Beauty is something that does not exist', with other articles by Sobhana (on ethics), Gunabhadri (on transcending the human predicament), and artist Rupachitta (on seeing things as they really are). The central feature of the issue was the following interview with Sangharakshita, conducted by Sinhadevi.*

DAKINI

WINTER 1993 ISSUE TWELVE £2

SPIRITUAL LIFE AND BEAUTY

SPECIAL FEATURE

Sangharakshita talks about women
...feminism
...public life
...ordination

and more

The Friends of the Western Buddhist Order

Dakini *no. 12, December 1993*

SANGHARAKSHITA TALKS ABOUT WOMEN

Dakini no. 12, December 1993, pp. 12–17. Sinhadevi puts questions from women Order members to Sangharakshita.

Is there a woman who particularly stands out for you in the history of religion and from whom we can learn?

I don't think that there's a woman who stands out in the way that Confucius or the Buddha or Mohammed or Jesus stand out. That leaves us with the saints. I can't think of a woman from the East who particularly stands out as a saint, but there are some in the West. Catherine of Siena, for example, was an outstanding figure in her day, and did exert considerable historical influence. She persuaded – or cajoled, or bullied – the pope of the time to leave Avignon (where the papacy had been established for nearly seventy years) and move back to Rome – a move which had considerable historical and religious significance. I have always been interested in Catherine, and have in fact visited her birthplace. One can visit the house where she grew up and the Dominican monastery where they have her head on show. (Her body was kept in Rome where she died.)

Physically she was very frail – she suffered from what we would nowadays call anorexia, and died in her early thirties – but she had a very forceful character. Although she was a woman, not at all from a distinguished family, and a nun, through sheer force of personality she influenced events in her day to a very great extent. If there is a lesson to be learned from her life, it's how much the individual can do.

She does seem to have been a bit impatient with women. One of the points she constantly made was that women need to be heroic. Not just women, of course – she emphasized the need for heroism to both her male and her female disciples. She was very fond of the word 'heroic'.

So although, obviously, I don't subscribe to all her views, Catherine is a woman who stands out for me in the history of religion as someone from whom we can learn.

Which woman writer do you most admire, and why?
I don't think I could say which one woman writer I admire most. One admires different writers at different times in one's life. I have certainly admired Jane Austen and George Eliot, and I think I have read all their novels. In the seventies I admired Anaïs Nin – not for her diaries, which I found rather self-indulgent, but for her stories. I liked their vivid, impressionistic character. More recently I've admired Rose Macaulay, particularly for two of her later novels, *The World My Wilderness* and *The Towers of Trebizond*, which were both written in the 1950s. She is an intelligent, witty, humorous writer with a very good literary style, a very educated and cultured woman. Judging by her biography she was a woman of great independence. She was never a feminist, but she went her own way and lived her own life in the way that she wanted to – a balanced, human, intelligent way. Not that her life was without difficulty or sadness. She didn't find it easy to go her own way and start on her career as a writer. For one thing, she had a lot of domestic responsibilities, mainly connected with her parents. (She never married, although she had one long-standing relationship.)

A book I've come to admire recently is *The Tale of Genji* by Murasaki Shikibu. She is a Japanese writer who began her writing career at the end of the tenth century. Her writing is very fine indeed – subtle, poetic, and allusive, with great psychological penetration. She is considered the greatest Japanese novelist ever on the strength of this one novel, which is about the length of *War and Peace*.

Does her work have a similar breadth of vision to Tolstoy's?
No, her vision is, in a way, very narrow – but it's very deep. It's narrow in the sense that all the characters – and there are a lot of them – belong to the highest circles of Japanese aristocracy. But within this narrow circle she explores human relationships very deeply, critically, and objectively. She seems to have some insight into masculine as well as feminine psychology – the hero of the novel, Genji, is a man.

If we include poets among the women writers I admire, I would mention Christina Rossetti. Some critics consider her the best – not the greatest but the best – poet of the nineteenth century. She led rather a sad life, or at least rather an unfulfilled one, but she produced some very fine poetry.

Do you think that participation in public life is an important aspect in the development of individuality? If so, why?
Yes, I do. Formerly, of course, women were virtually excluded from public life, tied as they were to the domestic sphere and the practical business of bringing up children and looking after the home. But obviously there are many women these days who are relatively free from those occupations who do have the opportunity of entering public life.

We mustn't forget that both men and women exist as part of a wider community. If one has the vote, if one is a citizen, one has the responsibility of exercising that vote.

Another point is that if one takes part in public life, one is usually associating with other people for the sake of some objective aim or goal, which helps the individual in the development of objectivity. One is lifted out of one's personal concerns into wider interests, even though they may still be mundane in the sense of being social, cultural, or political rather than spiritual. One also gains in self-confidence by engaging in public life. Making a speech in front of a number of people, for example, can be a great help in building up confidence. So I think that participation in public life does have quite an important part to play in the development of individuality. Now that women, at least in the West, have the opportunity to play a part in public life, I think they should take that opportunity.

In the case of the FWBO, a woman can participate in public life through helping to run the local centre. *Dhammacārinīs* can become members of the centre council, or even become chairmen. In this way one participates in the more public aspect of the FWBO. One isn't just staying at home meditating and doing pujas, or even just going along to classes as a participant. One has a responsible part to play in the public life of the FWBO. Playing such a part broadens one's outlook and contributes to one's maturity.

Do you think it's important for women to take a leading role in FWBO *centres even though the women's wing of the Movement has its own particular needs, which could easily take up all our time and attention?*
Well if we had no women in positions of responsibility at our public centres, what message would that communicate to women who were coming along? One needs to consider that. We know very well that women coming along to a centre, especially when they are new, feel that something is amiss if they never see a *dhammacārinī*. The unspoken message is 'This is not for you.' You may be told that *dhammacārinīs* exist, but you don't quite believe it, because you don't see them. If you're told that in the FWBO there is the same ordination for men and women, and men and women both have the opportunity to take responsibility, but you don't actually see a woman at a public centre exercising responsibility, you end up feeling there are two messages coming across.

So although I recognize the need to put energy into the women's wing, especially the women's ordination process, I don't think it would be wise to encourage *dhammacārinīs* and women Mitras to put all their energies into 'women only' activities. I think their presence in and around the centres is also important, for the sake of new women coming along. You need to be able to see some sort of role model around, otherwise it can take years for women to realize that there are women deeply involved in the FWBO. They can end up thinking that it is just for men, and that can be quite discouraging.

For Buddhists, abortion is clearly a serious breach of the first precept. Do you think there's a case for members of the FWBO *campaigning for abortion to be made illegal?*
No, I don't think there is – partly because there are so many other things for us to do, and also because I don't think that making abortion illegal is going to stop it. If one does feel moved to do anything about it, there would be more point in inculcating a greater reverence for life, and we do that anyway by teaching the Dharma. I would not encourage anybody to campaign for abortion to be made illegal.

What about airing our views more publicly through the newspapers and other media?
Certainly individuals could contribute to the debate by writing to the papers. But campaigning takes a lot of time and energy and money,

and I don't think this is one of our priorities. And as I said, I'm pretty certain that making abortion illegal wouldn't stop it. It would still go on. It's been illegal in Ireland all these years, but what happens? When a woman wants an abortion, she comes over to Britain.

It is generally held that women find it relatively easy to develop friendships. In your view, what are the pitfalls that women need to guard against in developing spiritual friendships?
I don't think I can give you a whole list of pitfalls, but I can tell you one thing I've noticed. Sometimes women seem to become emotionally attached to their friends in a way that men, as far as I have observed, do not. I'm not talking here about lesbian relationships. Even non-lesbian relationships between women can become very intense and exclusive in an unhealthy way. I also think that women can slide, almost imperceptibly, from an emotional relationship to one in which there is a certain amount of physical contact – to something that is quasi-lesbian – without realizing what is happening. For most men there is a definite dividing line between a friendship and a gay relationship, but for women the line of distinction can be blurred.

What should we do to guard against that sort of sliding into lesbian relationships?
I'm not saying that you shouldn't have lesbian relationships. But one should not confuse a lesbian relationship, if that is what it is, with a spiritual friendship, although obviously within a sexual relationship there are elements of friendship. It is this blurring of the distinction between a lesbian relationship and a friendship that can be a pitfall.

Even when a friendship doesn't tend towards lesbianism, it can become what I call 'sticky' – emotional, exclusive, possessive, unhealthy – in a way that doesn't happen between men, at least not outside gay relationships. This 'stickiness' is not necessarily sexual – it can exist quite independently. (If there is an element of sexuality in a friendship, it just has to be acknowledged.) But I think stickiness is in fact more dangerous than a sexual element because it is bound up (as sexuality can also be) with exclusiveness, possessiveness, and jealousy. What I am saying is that one mustn't think, in the case of women, that possessiveness and exclusivity are characteristic only of sexual relationships. The fact that two women have an intense emotional relationship which is not sexual does not necessarily mean that it is a spiritual friendship. It can still be bound up with all sorts of feelings of attachment, even when there is no sexual element present. If both the sexual and the emotional elements are there, of course, those feelings are compounded, and sometimes give rise to extensive difficulties between women in a lesbian relationship.

Do you think there is any difference between a man's and a woman's capacity to develop friendship?
Well, that's quite a big question. One difference seems to be that women are less likely to develop friendship through a working relationship. Women don't seem to think of friendship as something to which working together contributes, whereas men find it quite easy to think of developing friendship in that way. I think women may tend to think in more narrowly personal terms, thinking of the development of friendship more along romantic lines, in the way in which a sexual relationship develops – getting closer to someone, or becoming more intimate with them – rather than working together for a common objective in the way men tend naturally to do.

In your lecture, 'A Wreath of Blue Lotus',[343] you say that one of the reasons that the Buddha introduced the eight garudhammas *was to prevent the irruption of feminism into the order. I believe you have made a distinction between Feminism with a capital F and feminism with a small f. Could you say what the distinction is between the two forms of feminism and what aspects of feminism you consider to be a hindrance to one's spiritual development?*
When I said that one of the reasons the Buddha introduced the eight *garudhammas* was to prevent the irruption of feminism into the order, I didn't, of course, mean it to be taken literally, because there was no such thing as feminism in the Buddha's day – not in the modern sense of the term. One should take the spirit and not the letter of that remark.

Yes, I do make a distinction between Feminism and feminism. Feminism with a small 'f' I take to mean the attitude that a woman, no less than a man, should be free to develop whatever capacities and interests she has. There is nothing inconsistent with Buddhism in that. I have no quarrel with feminism with a small 'f'. But I distinguish that from Feminism with a capital F, which covers many other attitudes. One of these attitudes which I am not happy about is the tendency to see woman as victim. There's no doubt that women have suffered in various ways in the course of history, and are still suffering. (It is also true that men have suffered – in different ways – and are still suffering.) But I don't think the fact that women have suffered should lead one to think of woman primarily in terms of her being a victim – whether of rape, or male oppression, or whatever. I don't think it helps in one's individual development, whether one is a man or a woman, to think of oneself primarily as a victim.

The tendency of Feminism with a capital F to see woman essentially – at least in historical terms – as victim, and therefore to see man as victimizer, tends to result in the development of hatred towards men, and it is obviously not in accord with the Dharma that one should hate anybody for any reason. I remember hearing some years ago that there were some women on a newcomers' retreat at Taraloka who resisted the idea of developing *mettā* for men in the *mettā bhāvanā* meditation because, they said, men should be hated, not loved. That is rather extreme, and actually I think some of them were persuaded to develop *mettā* towards men in the end, but that is the sort of attitude which is part of Feminism with a capital F.

To have this attitude is also to refuse to see men as individuals, so that a man's point of view is ignored simply because he is a man. Some Feminists would say that men can't possibly understand women, so nothing men say about women has got any validity. I can't accept this, because it suggests that there is an immovable barrier to communication and understanding between men and women. I don't believe there is such a barrier. After all, even in ordinary biological terms there are clearly more similarities between men and women than there are differences.

All this, I think, makes it pretty obvious that some aspects of Feminism (with a capital F) inhibit spiritual development.

What do you think of positive discrimination in favour of women?
I see parallels with the situation in India, where there is positive discrimination for Scheduled Caste people. It does help to some extent, so one can't rule out its use completely, at least in the short term. On the other hand, it doesn't conduce to someone's self-respect to know that they have been given certain advantages not because they deserve them or have earned them but because they belong to a particular community or, in this case, a particular sex.

Presumably positive discrimination has no place in the FWBO?
It doesn't need a place because everything is open to women anyway. Positive discrimination is meant to counter a tendency – whether conscious or unconscious – to keep women out, but in the FWBO it's just the opposite. Women can't be persuaded to do enough sometimes – or at least to do certain things and accept certain responsibilities. If we did have positive discrimination it would be to encourage women to do certain things they don't want to do but which would be good for them.

We know that language changes and develops with time. In recent years feminists have been making efforts to promote changes in the use of language that they consider to be exclusive. Do you think there is any justification for this?
I must say I don't think there is any real justification for it. What is important is that there is clarity in communication, and not misunderstanding. In my own writings and lectures I say 'men and women' if I think it is not clear from the context whether or not women are included, but I don't go out of my way to say that as a concession to Feminists when it is quite clear anyway that women are included in what is being said. I think some Feminists exclude themselves and then make a great point of being included in some special way. I am quite sure that such Feminists really know that the language does include them but, in accordance with Feminist ideology, make a point of its being exclusive. They then want to develop an artificial language which they claim does not exclude them.

I am not happy about this sort of deliberate attempt to change language. For one thing, it introduces too great a discontinuity with the language and literature of the past.

Some people would say that the use of 'he or she' and 'men and women' is so common nowadays that choosing not to use it makes a point.
I don't think it's used as widely as all that. It depends what sort of literature you read.

What's in my mind is that when some women have read, for example, Subhuti's book, The Buddhist Vision,[344] *in which he uses 'he' and 'man' throughout, they have felt that this kind of language wasn't standard usage, and that Subhuti must have been making some kind of deliberate point in using it.*

It's difficult to know what is standard. Different publishing houses use different conventions. People sometimes seem to think that American publications are a model of 'political correctness' in their use of 'non-exclusive' language, but in fact if you read scholarly or literary American books, more often than not you find no trace of the kind of language we are discussing. For the most part, you only find it in Feminist works, or works written by Feminist sympathizers. I've come across a couple of books in which 'he' and 'she' are used alternately, but that really reads rather oddly.

My own approach is to spell out what I am trying to say if there is genuine ambiguity. Otherwise, I just follow the standard procedure. If the Feminists do succeed in changing language, presumably we will have to spell it out every time, but they haven't succeeded in doing that yet. If there is genuine doubt, of course it should be made clear that women are not excluded, in fact that they are included. But I think we should also be aware that to include someone in too conscious a way is to exclude them. It's like saying, 'Develop *mettā* to all living beings – and black people too, of course.' How would a black person feel about being 'included' in that sort of way?

The Western Buddhist Order has the same ordination for men and women. However, in other religious traditions, including Buddhist traditions, there is something of a controversy over the ordination of women. Would you care to comment?

There's a controversy over *bhikkhunī* ordination because in most countries where it once existed the tradition has died out and it is generally believed that it cannot be revived. *Bhikkhunī* ordination persists only in China (including Taiwan) and in Korea, which is part of the Chinese tradition. I think the *bhikkhunī* ordination issue is a bit of a red herring for women in the West. The real solution to the problem is not to bother about *bhikkhunī* ordination, but to recognize (as we do in the FWBO) that there is really just one ordination which consists in effectively Going for Refuge, and that it is just the same for men and women, for those who lead monastic lives and those who lead non-monastic lives. Looking at it like that you don't need to bother about *bhikkhunī* ordination. (I have gone into this in my recently published book, *Forty-Three Years Ago: Reflections On My Bhikkhu Ordination.*)[345]

I think there is a contradiction in the position of some of the Western women who are agitated about the question of *bhikkhunī* ordination. If you have *bhikkhunī* ordination you have to observe *bhikkhunī* rules, and some of those rules relate to the complete subordination of *bhikkhunīs* to *bhikkhus*. Is this really what women want? And if it isn't, why bother with the *bhikkhunī* ordination at all? Why not fall back on, say, the FWBO position? Let there be one ordination for all – for men and women, monastics and non-monastics alike. I think our solution is neat and simple. The fact that some Western women are indulging in a lot of heart-burning over not being able to get *bhikkhunī* ordination when there are so many rules which they would not want to observe anyway suggests that they are concerned more with status than with the actual observance of those rules or the living of that kind of life. Why not start afresh? One former *bhikkhunī* in the States has done that. Having had contact with the FWBO, she has given up her *bhikkhunī* ordination and become an *anagarikā*, observing the ten precepts as we do in the Western Buddhist Order.

The remarks about the sangha not lasting more than 500 years due to the ordination of women, though attributed to the Buddha, are regarded by many scholars as a later interpolation to the text. Is it in your opinion a later interpolation? What truth, if any, is there in the Buddha's prophecy? What implications might there be for the FWBO? And how and why did such interpolations come about?
I'm not sure it's true to say that 'many scholars' regard it as a later interpolation; scholars are usually a bit cautious about saying such things. (And when I say 'scholars', by the way, I mean scholars, not just people who disagree with the sentiments expressed in the passage and think the Buddha simply could not have uttered them.) It is very difficult to find out whether or not something has been interpolated at a later date. In the case of the Pāli canon we can only distinguish very roughly between earlier and later parts of the text on the basis of slight differences of language and terminology, and as far as I know those criteria have not yet been applied to this particular passage.

The prophecy is that if women had not been ordained within the sangha, the Dharma would have lasted for a thousand years. We know, of course, that in fact the Dharma lasted in India for well *over* a thousand years. Some people might argue that there are different levels at which it lasted, and maybe in the later centuries no Enlightened beings were produced, but I don't think there's anything to show that the presence of women in the sangha in its early days had anything to do with its later decline.

I think the likelihood is that this prophecy is not a later interpolation. Rather than dismissing it as such, we need to look for the reasons the Buddha might have had for making those remarks. He says,

> Just as clans with many women and few men are easily ruined by robbers and bandits, so too in the Law and Discipline in which women obtain the Going Forth the Holy Life does not last long.[346]

That suggests that the sangha is more vulnerable when there are women in it. But why should it be more vulnerable? As far as I can see it would only be more vulnerable if the women in it – as well as the men – had ceased to attain the higher spiritual paths. Perhaps what the Buddha is saying is that at a time of deterioration in the sangha, when it is no longer made up of highly developed people, the possibility of further deterioration would be greater if women formed a considerable part of the sangha – in the same way that a clan with many women and few men is liable to deteriorate.

I sometimes say that when there is something in the Buddha's teaching that is not clear, one has to interpret it in the light of what *is* clear, and what the Buddha makes quite clear in this passage is that women are capable of attaining higher spiritual levels, transcendental states. It was for other, social reasons that he was reluctant to ordain them, not because they lacked spiritual potential. In the same way, if there is any question of the sangha not enduring due to the presence of women, that would be for social reasons rather than spiritual ones. After all, how *could* the sangha decline if the women within it were spiritually developed and had attained to higher spiritual states?

So there's nothing to suggest that women would inherently cause a degeneration?
No. If we look at the passage, we find that it gives three comparisons:

Just as when the blight called grey mildew falls on a field of
ripening grain, that field of ripening grain does not last long –
just as when the blight called red rust falls on a field of ripening
sugarcane, that field of ripening sugarcane does not last long – so
too in the Law and Discipline in which women obtain the Going
Forth, the Holy Life does not last long.

But the Buddha goes on to say,

As a man might construct in advance an embankment so that
the waters of a great reservoir should not cause a flood, so I too
have made known in advance these eight great capital points for
bhikkhunīs, not to be transgressed as long as life lasts.[347]

Now to me there's quite a big difference between these sets of
comparisons. To speak in terms of building an embankment so that
waters don't go beyond their proper level is quite different from
speaking in terms of mildew or blight on crops. In the case of the
third comparison the Buddha is simply safeguarding against possible
unhelpful development. He is not saying that water is bad, only that
a certain restraint is necessary. But there's nothing good about mildew
or blight; they are wholly bad. So if there is an interpolation I suspect
it might be here. The Buddha's teachings were passed on by word of
mouth for hundreds of years before they were ever written down, and
it would have been easy for someone to have added another simile just
to make the point more strongly. As I say, there does seem to be an
inconsistency between the first two comparisons and the third; they seem
to communicate something quite different.

Do you think it's just an innocent elaboration?
It doesn't sound innocent! You could well say that the presence of women
in the sangha is like water, and just as water needs to be contained
within a reservoir, so certain limits have to be placed if women join the
sangha, but you don't place limits on mildew and blight – you try to get
rid of them completely. It could well have been the monks who were
responsible for this kind of attitude creeping in. They were rather wary
of women generally in a way that the Buddha wasn't.

Do you think the monks were right to be wary of women?
They were right to be wary of them individually – for the sake of their own spiritual practice – but not in the sense of trying to exclude women from monastic life. Of course, the monks did have some responsibility for the women in the sangha. That might have been necessary in those days for social reasons, but today, when those social conditions no longer obtain, *bhikkhus* can sometimes tend to take too much responsibility for women in the sangha, in the sense of assuming authority over them.

We mustn't forget, on the other hand – and I don't think this point has ever been made – that it was the *bhikkhus* who preserved the *Therīgāthā*, the verses concerning the lives of the early *bhikkhunīs*. They weren't handed down by the *bhikkhunī* sangha. In fact we don't know whether the *bhikkhunīs* handed down any teachings at all. All the information we have about the early *bhikkhunīs*, the *theris*, including their own *gāthas*, was handed down within the *bhikkhu* sangha. Discourses by women, including the one by Dhammadinnā, the well-known *arhant* disciple of the Buddha, were also preserved by the *bhikkhus*. So the *bhikkhus* can't have been all that negatively disposed towards the *bhikkhunīs*. If it wasn't for them, we wouldn't know anything about the *bhikkhunīs* of those early days, women such as Mahāpajāpatī, Dhammadinnā, and so on.

What developments in the women's wing of the FWBO over the last ten years have impressed you most?
Well, I suppose I have to say the establishment of Taraloka – it's certainly a very impressive achievement.[348] Then more recently there has been the further development of the women's ordination process. And perhaps I could mention *Dakini*. I'm very pleased with the way that has developed over the last couple of years. It's the only magazine of its kind for Buddhist women in the western world.

And what would you like to see being developed in the women's wing over the next ten years?
Just more of everything! More and more women being prepared for ordination, an extension of facilities for women of every kind. I would particularly like to see more development in India. I would like to see a women's vihara and retreat centre established there, somewhere outside the city where women could hold their own retreats and where there

could be a permanent community of women who wanted to live in that way, especially, perhaps, older women who had become *anagarikās*. And, coming back to *Dakini*, I would like to see it become a much bigger magazine, and much more widely distributed.

Thank you very much.

DHARMA LIFE

Dharma Life *was a print magazine sold in bookshops. More upmarket than its predecessors, it was published three times a year and included news and comment, interviews with leading figures from Buddhist traditions, personal stories, book reviews, and features. The magazine was edited initially by Vishvapani and latterly by Vajrasara and it ran for 26 issues.*

dharma life

BUDDHISM FOR TODAY

Zen at War
Vishvapani investigates

Sangharakshita
on Writing

Thomas Cleary
on the Perfection of Wisdom

London's Buddhist
Psychotherapist

finding the truth
THE BUDDHIST PATH TO WISDOM

Dharma Life *no. 14, Winter 2000*

WHERE THERE'S A WILL

Dharma Life no. 3, Winter 1996, pp. 30–1. In a talk at the opening of a new Buddhist centre in Turner Street, Manchester, Sangharakshita stresses the power of conscious intention.

Over the years I have written quite a few books, given many talks, and expressed opinions on all sorts of subjects. But even though a great deal of this has now been committed to writing it should not be assumed that I have stopped thinking, or that my thinking has stopped changing, or much less still that I consider my thought to be complete. In fact I spend quite a bit of my time just thinking. I enjoy reflecting. I find there are many things to reflect upon and I especially think about things that have a bearing on the FWBO and on the Dharma – which is the basis of the FWBO. So on this occasion I would like to share with you some of my current thinking about the Dharma and the vitally important subject of Going for Refuge to the Three Jewels.

I have said much about this subject in the past. Going for Refuge to the Buddha, the Dharma, and the Sangha is the central act of Buddhism but, when we talk about it, it can become rather abstract. Going for Refuge is the act of commitment to the ideals of Buddhism, and it can only be undertaken by the individual. In that sense it is a function of the mind, and the mind has three distinct aspects. There is the intellectual aspect, the emotional aspect, and the volitional aspect or the will. That is to say we think, we feel, and we will.

Of these three aspects I suspect that the will has had a particularly bad press among Buddhists in the West. Often if someone is not getting on very well with meditation or they are having difficulties in personal relationships they are told, 'You are being too wilful. Don't try so hard.'

Sometimes it is necessary to relax, and real wilfulness is, of course, a weakness. But strong and steady willing is quite a different thing. *Cetanā* in the sense of will or conscious intention plays a crucial part in the Buddhist life and I have always rendered *bodhicitta* as 'the will to Enlightenment' rather than as 'the thought of Enlightenment'. Similarly, dhyānic states – states of meditative superconsciousness – are states of willing. They represent mental activity which has highly positive karmic consequences.

When we come to take up spiritual life, it would seem that the three aspects of the mind do not all come into play equally. This is because we are divided beings and this division affects the way in which we go for Refuge. In the case of the Buddha, we first acquire an intellectual knowledge through reading about the historical facts of the Buddha's life. However, you can have this kind of knowledge without any feeling and without being a Buddhist. But if you become sufficiently acquainted with those facts and dwell on certain episodes in the Buddha's life you start having a feeling for the Buddha's compassion, his wisdom, and his energy. And when you reflect like this the emotions start to come into play. It is a traditional practice to then go on to contemplate the attributes of the Buddha quite systematically in order to build up your feeling for him. Performing a puja in which one expresses feelings of devotion has much the same effect. What then happens is that, feeling drawn towards the Buddha, you want to become more like him. In this way will comes into play. It is not an easy thing to become like the Buddha; you have to make an effort and this implies the will. It is only when all three of these faculties – intellect, emotion, and will – come into play that one is able effectively to go for Refuge to the Buddha.

Similarly it is quite possible to engage in intellectual study of the Dharma without having a feeling for it, much less any desire to embody the Dharma in one's own life. It is also possible, while staying on this level, to write books about Buddhism and there are many such books around, but in one's reading it is important to distinguish books that are on a purely academic level from books that have a real feeling for the Dharma. When we have such feeling, real interest in Dharma study starts to develop. And when the will comes into play we will want to make the Dharma operative in our own lives.

We also speak of Going for Refuge to the Sangha but, strictly speaking, there are two sanghas. Firstly, there is the Āryasaṅgha, which includes all those who have gained the path leading directly to Nirvāṇa – the great bodhisattvas, the Stream Entrants, and so on. Again we start by coming to know about the lives of the Āryasaṅgha or the characteristics of the great bodhisattvas. We can read about the lives of Milarepa or Hakuin, for example. As we contemplate the example of their lives a feeling for them develops, and this grows into a will to be like them.

The sangha of non-Āryans is all those who are practising Buddhism but who have not yet reached the transcendental path. For practical purposes this means all those who are practising the Dharma with whom we are in actual personal contact. Again we need to be active. It is not enough to attend classes at a Buddhist centre and not make any friends. You have to enter into some sort of positive relationship with other people and generate positive feelings towards them. A Buddhist centre should be an oasis of friendliness in a world which can often be a rather unfriendly place. That said, so far as centres are concerned the near enemy of spiritual friendship is mere socializing. We should remember that a Buddhist centre is not a social centre and we should not treat it as such. As it says in our dedication ceremony, 'Here may no idle word be spoken.' Just as we leave our shoes outside the shrine-room we should leave other concerns and distractions with them. In this way we can truly go for Refuge to the Sangha in the broader sense of the term.

We should not underestimate the role of will in spiritual life. It is not enough to have feeling for the Buddha. We have to will to be *like* the Buddha. One might even say there is no spiritual life without will. Indeed, spiritual life could be defined as the constant willing of the good in all circumstances.

I will soon be leaving this country to visit FWBO centres in the United States, Canada, Australia, and New Zealand. I will be meeting people informally and doing a little sightseeing but I am not intending to make any formal public appearances. I shall be away for six or seven months. This will be the longest period for which I will have been away from the UK since the FWBO was started, and during that time anything may happen. I am very aware of the fact that I am now nearly 71, which means that, even in the ordinary course of nature, I may not come back. This may be my last public appearance. We must never forget that death may come to any one of us at any time, and the older you get the greater are the odds against your continuing to exist. This applies not just to me but to each and every one of us.

We should make the best possible use of our time and practise the Dharma. Sometimes I think we do not realize how lucky we are. My first real access to the Dharma was during the war when I joined the Buddhist Society and started to attend its classes. At that time it was the only Buddhist organization in Britain and it had about a dozen regular members. Now the Dharma is easily accessible to us in the West.

As the bomb that exploded in Manchester a few weeks ago so painfully reminded us, we are living in difficult times.[349] I am not a prophet and I have no crystal ball, but I suspect the next few decades will not be easy. We shall need the Dharma more than ever. So let us make full use of the Dharma and let us practise it.

WISDOM WITHIN WORDS

Dharma Life *no. 10, Spring 1999, pp. 28–32. The questions were put by the editor, Vishvapani.*

Sometimes wisdom is regarded as beyond concepts and beliefs, but you stress the importance of looking at one's beliefs in the light of Buddhist teachings and cultivating what Buddhism calls right view. This seems a rather unfashionable emphasis; why do you make it?

I emphasize the importance of looking at one's views because in the modern world wrong views of various kinds are so predominant. If you seriously entertain wrong views, and if your actions are based on them, then according to Buddhist teaching one is not able to follow the spiritual path or achieve Enlightenment. Right view is therefore regarded as absolutely crucial in Buddhism, whether understood in terms of comprehension of the four noble truths or of any of the other traditional formulations of the Buddha's teaching. All are different conceptual expressions of the same spiritual realization and go to make up the conceptual content, so to speak, of right view.

I am interested in the relationship between the concepts Buddhism teaches, and which Buddhists try to understand, and the realization that lies behind them. Sometimes I use the term right view and sometimes I speak of Perfect Vision, and the difference between the two points to a very important distinction. Perfect Vision is often explained in Buddhist texts in terms of full comprehension of the four noble truths. This is not a merely theoretical or intellectual understanding, but actual insight into that to which the teaching of the truths refers. It is a liberating spiritual experience. One person, having had that experience of Perfect Vision, seeks to communicate it to another in conceptual terms, and one of the ways in which he does this is by saying, 'I have seen the four noble truths.' In other words, the content of his liberating spiritual experience finds expression in terms of that particular formulation. Another person, hearing him explain the truths, may understand them conceptually, and thus may have right view. But he understands them only theoretically, without having the deep, comprehensive experiential realization that, for example, the Buddha had. He only understands the truths. So when it is a matter of the Buddha's full comprehension – his realization of the four noble truths – I render *sammā-diṭṭhi* as Perfect Vision; when it is a case of the purely or largely understanding on the part of the unenlightened disciple, I render the term as right view. Right view is important because it is on the basis of right view that one practises the Dharma and comes to realize Perfect Vision.

Is there a danger that emphasizing right view can lead to literalism or dogmatism, that emphasis on ideas can get in the way of direct practice and experience?
Some people believe that insistence on the correctness of any particular view is 'dogmatic', but I think this is a misuse of the word. Right view – as distinct from Perfect View – is a matter of theoretical understanding, and with regard to the theoretical understanding of any spiritual teaching there is always the danger of literalism. It is as though the human mind has an inbuilt tendency to slip into literalism, however many warnings are given against it. So yes, there is certainly a possibility that teachings which are conceptual expressions of the Buddha's spiritual experience, such as the four noble truths, may be taken literalistically, but that should not be used as an argument against emphasizing the importance of right view. Emphasizing the importance of right view means drawing attention to the fact that without right view there can be no Perfect Vision and that wrong views, therefore, are positively dangerous. If the importance of right view is emphasized in this way – if it is seen as a means to an end – such an emphasis will not lead to literalism.

Speaking of right and wrong views raises the question of authority. Who defines what is right, and on what basis? How do you see your own authority to make such judgements, especially in relation to your disciples?

For me as a Buddhist, the Buddha has Perfect Vision and he gives expression to that Vision in terms of right view. Thus the ultimate authority is the Buddha. I define right view, in the first place, by referring to the Buddhist scriptures, especially those which, so far as we can make out, are nearest in time to the Buddha himself or are most likely to reflect what he actually taught. Next we have to draw upon our own understanding of those teachings. We also have to draw upon our personal experience, so far as it goes – experience that may be spiritual to some extent, or more mundane.

In my opinion no Buddhist teacher, whether in the East or in the West, is entitled to do more than that. I don't agree with the view, taken by at least some Tibetan Buddhists, that authority resides wholly in the lama, and that you have to accept as the truth whatever the lama says. Such a sacrifice of individual judgement goes against the spirit of the Dharma and against the Buddha's own words as they have come down to us.

In relation to my own disciples, I simply apply these principles. I have studied the Buddhist scriptures to some extent; I have tried to put their teachings into practice; I have some experience of spiritual life and some experience of dealing with people. To that extent I have some 'authority' to make judgements about right and wrong views. I can't enforce my conclusions (nor would I wish to do so), but those people who have confidence in me, especially those who say they are my disciples, will at least give careful consideration to the conclusions at which I have arrived.

Wisdom is spoken of in different ways in Buddhism. Sometimes it is seen as a goal that is far above us and which we must struggle to reach; sometimes becoming wise seems to be a matter of waking up to something within us and which we already know. Borrowing terms from theology, you could call these the transcendent and immanent approaches to wisdom. What is your own approach?

There are, indeed, different ways of speaking of wisdom, and the Buddhist tradition contains examples of both the immanent and transcendent ways. For instance, the Buddha tells us that the Dharma is deep, that it is subtle, and this could be seen as describing it in terms of immanence. My own emphasis derives from a consideration of the nature and structure of the Buddhist path. In the broadest sense, the path is threefold: it consists of ethics, meditation, and wisdom. Meditation goes beyond ethics, and wisdom goes beyond meditation, just as Enlightenment goes beyond wisdom.

You thus have a path of ascent, where the stages are not merely successive, like the stages along a road, but like those of a path going up the side of a mountain. At each stage you go not further, but higher, and of course the last stage is regarded as the highest of all. Here each stage transcends the previous one, though incorporating it. It is a path of perpetual transcendence and, since the pilgrim is the path, of perpetual self-transcendence. The goal can therefore be described as the transcendental – meaning that which transcends everything else, especially all previous stages.

In speaking of the Transcendental is there a danger that we turn it into a thing or a place?
Well there is a danger of reifying any abstract noun. One just has to be aware of that; one can't simply stop using such terms. But it ought to be clear from the context that one is not, in fact, reifying, and therefore that what one is saying is not to be taken literally. If one talks about the Dharma at all one can't help using abstract terms. Moreover, one shouldn't forget that the Buddhist tradition speaks of the *nirvāṇa-dhātu* or 'sphere of Nirvāṇa', Nirvāṇa being not just a state of mind, so to speak, but an objectively existing reality that one intuits through wisdom. Therefore one shouldn't abandon language, such as that of the Transcendental, too readily. One simply has to be aware that language has its limitations and perhaps use such terms 'poetically' rather than in the strict metaphysical or ontological sense.

Why do you think so many other western Buddhist teachers emphasize the immanent?
There may now be two to three hundred western Buddhist teachers, and as far as I am aware no survey has been done to ascertain their views in this respect. But I would say that if they do not emphasize the transcendent nature of the path they can hardly be Buddhist teachers.

Not that in the Buddhist scriptures there is no mention of immanence. Even in the Pāli scriptures there are two references to the fact that the mind is by nature pure.[350] Later in the history of Buddhism, there is the *tathāgatagarbha* doctrine, according to which Buddha-nature is inherent within each individual. Some western Buddhist teachers emphasize immanence in this sense, but that is a dangerous thing to do. If people are told they have Buddha-nature, they will almost inevitably think of that as something added on to their ego-personality as a sort of possession, and that misunderstanding may well prevent them from making any real effort in the direction of Enlightenment. That is not to say that there may not be some justification, philosophically, for using the language of immanence, but from a purely practical point of view it is unwise to do so.

If it is true that the language of immanence is more popular, the reason is evident. People like to be told that they are Buddha: it flatters them. Perhaps it makes them think that they don't have much more work to do. They just have to sit there thinking – because in their case it can only be a matter of thinking – that they are Enlightened already.

Similarly, there is a popular emphasis on the importance of being in the present. Some Zen practitioners try to see the whole of life in this way. They might do that when they are meditating, but how did they come to be there sitting on that cushion? At some point in their day they had to stop 'being in the present' and start thinking about getting into the car and going along to the *zendō*. It's nonsense to talk about just remaining in the present all the time in this sort of way. Actions have consequences, and this principle connects us to both the past and the future, which means that we have to think about them at times, whether we like it or not.

A similar issue arises in the metaphors that are used for spiritual paths. Certain teachers, perhaps influenced by western psychology, suggest we have to explore the depths of the mind. You emphasize ascent to the heights of spiritual life. What lies behind this?
Buddhism itself emphasizes the heights rather than the depths, in the sense that it emphasizes the importance of going from a lower to a higher stage of ethical and spiritual development. If one is a Buddhist at all, one will therefore emphasize the heights in that way. Emphasizing the depths can only mean emphasizing going down in the opposite direction, that is to say, from the skilful to the unskilful. In Buddhism one doesn't speak of a spiritual path that goes 'down'. In the *Sallekha Sutta* the Buddha says:

Just as all unwholesome states lead downwards and all wholesome states lead upwards, so too a person given to cruelty has non-cruelty to lead him upwards. One given to killing living beings has abstention from killing living beings to lead him upwards. One given to taking what is not given has abstention from taking what is not given to lead him upwards.[351]

One can speak of certain mental states being lower, but in Buddhism such states are called hindrances. If one has within a Buddhist context the conception of a path that goes from stage to stage in an upward direction, then clearly going down means going from a relatively higher to a relatively lower stage of ethical and spiritual development – which is the direct opposite of the Buddhist life. So it's not wise to use the language of going down into the unconscious in this connection; one should use the traditional Buddhist language, and speak of overcoming the hindrances. Clearly you are conscious of them, at least to an extent, otherwise you wouldn't be able to overcome them.

When people talk about contacting their depths rather than rising to the heights, they're often referring to the difficult, painful aspects of reality. Doesn't this language have value from that point of view?
We certainly have to look at difficult and painful things. If we have to look at our own weaknesses, and even at disastrous happenings in the world, that may be difficult and painful. But in doing so we don't have to speak of going down into the depths in the psychological sense, as that particular usage of the language of heights and depths is incompatible with the traditional Buddhist usage of it. Moreover, one must not forget that in depth psychology itself 'depth' is just a metaphor. One must therefore be careful not to take it too literally or to oppose the 'going down' of depth psychology to a 'going up' that is of a wholly different order.

What is the particular significance for you of speaking of the heights?
When one says higher one really means of greater value. The conception of the path is inseparable from a sense of values. In following the path you feel you are going from something of lesser value to something of greater value.

How significant are these issues around the metaphors we use to describe and even understand the spiritual life?

Language is only language. Even when one speaks of the Buddhist path it is only a figure of speech, but it is a very useful figure of speech and one that lies at the heart of Buddhism. If you take the figure of the path too literally you will think that when you move on to the succeeding stage you leave behind the preceding stage. But that would be transferring what is true of the path in the literal sense to the path in the metaphorical sense. We cannot but speak metaphorically, but we have to remain aware that we are speaking metaphorically. It is not just that metaphorical language is useful – it is indispensable.

ALL IN ORDER

Dharma Life *no. 13, Summer 2000, pp. 32–9.* Dharma Life *invited Jamie Cresswell – an academic scholar of Buddhism in the West and a Nichiren Buddhist – to interview Sangharakshita about a lifetime of bringing Buddhism to the West.*

On your seventy-fifth birthday on 26 August 2000 you will hand on the headship of the Western Buddhist Order. What is the significance of that change?
The process of handing on my responsibilities has been an ongoing one. For some years Order members, both men and women, have been performing ordinations, but what happens on 26 August will mark a definite watershed. I will then publicly make it clear to whom I am handing on my remaining responsibilities. More than that I won't say now, as I will be making a full statement in August.

What will you be doing after that?
I shall continue to do many of the things I'm doing at present. I meditate, I write, I see people, I engage in correspondence, I visit Buddhist centres, I keep up contact with Buddhist friends. I was recently approached by the Roman Catholic Archbishop of Birmingham's Interfaith Commission to engage in interfaith dialogue with them. I'm looking forward to doing more of that sort of thing. But I shall no longer be 'in charge'. My contact with the FWBO will be more through personal connections than through any kind of organizational responsibility, though no doubt I shall find it difficult not to keep my eye on the Movement as a whole.

The FWBO and the WBO have been your life's work. How do you feel about this process of handing on?

I certainly don't feel excited, nor that I am losing anything. But I'm well aware that I will die one day. If I had continued to carry total responsibility for the FWBO and had the deciding voice in every issue until the day I died, others would have to take up those responsibilities without any preparation. That would not be fair to those people, nor to the Movement as a whole. I saw that the greater part of my remaining responsibilities would devolve upon the more senior and experienced Order members, with some of whom I have been in close contact for thirty years.

Even that did not seem enough, so I asked as many of them as possible to come and live together here in Birmingham, while I moved in next door. It was important that they should learn to function as a team so that they could harmoniously fulfil the responsibilities I was handing on. This is the Preceptors College, and the associated Council.

Are you feeling happy with this process?

I'm reasonably satisfied, which is not to say that mistakes may not be made, because it is difficult to understand other human beings. And it's not to say I haven't made mistakes myself in the past. But you have to accept that because you don't know how people are going to develop. You can only judge to the best of your ability, to the extent of your knowledge of them.

There is a proposal to change the name of the FWBO. What do you think about that?

I'm happy to leave it in the hands of those to whom I am handing on responsibility. There's no point in my handing on responsibility and then saying, you mustn't do this, or you mustn't do that. This is no doubt the temptation of all people who retire.

Going back to the origins of the FWBO, I'd like to ask a very basic question. What did you set out to create in 1968?

The main point is that I set out to create an order, not a society. My experience of Buddhist organizations, both in India and in Britain, was of Buddhist societies. Non-Buddhists could become members just because they were interested in Buddhism, and their influence was not always in the best interests of Buddhism. I concluded that one needed a sangha, a community of people who actually practised Buddhism.

Then the question arose, what is a Buddhist? I thought about this for many years. There are doctrinal differences between Buddhists, so one cannot say that Buddhism is this or that doctrine. It is an act: the act of Going for Refuge to the Three Jewels, the Buddha, Dharma, and Sangha. And the implications of that act are tremendous, because it involves understanding the Buddha, the supreme exemplar for Buddhists, and Buddhahood itself; the Dharma, the Buddha's teachings and the reality they indicate; and the Sangha, the assembly of those who embody the Dharma.

I concluded that a Buddhist is one who goes for Refuge to the Buddha, Dharma, and Sangha. All Buddhists would accept that, but in many traditional Buddhist countries the refuges and precepts are recited as a formality. In a fuller sense, though, a Buddhist is one who makes Going for Refuge to the Three Jewels the centre of their spiritual life. Out of that realization emerged much of what is distinctive about the FWBO's approach to the Dharma.

We don't see ourselves as either lay or monastic. To us, being a layman or a monk is a matter of lifestyle, and both lifestyles are acceptable. What is fundamental is to go for Refuge: we see ourselves simply as a spiritual community of people who go for Refuge to the Buddha, Dharma, and Sangha.

When you had this vision of setting up the Western Buddhist Order back in 1968, you must have had some thoughts of how you wished it to be in the future. Has it lived up to those dreams?
I didn't have a vision of the Movement. I went step by step. I started meditation classes and lectures, and after a while there were retreats. Then some of those people who'd been on retreats wanted to start living together, so communities were formed. Some people decided to work together, so right livelihood businesses were started, and in that way it all snowballed. Our development was organic. So I cannot say I am satisfied, or that my vision was fulfilled, or that I am dissatisfied, though I am well aware that there is a great deal of room for improvement on all fronts.

Have you had disappointments?

Sometimes one is disappointed when individuals of whom one had great hopes don't fulfil those expectations, but such is human nature that one must not be too disappointed. I can't say I've had any great disappointments, because I didn't expect too much. I wasn't thinking at the beginning of building up a big organization, just of communicating my understanding of the Dharma to people whom I regarded as friends.

What improvements could there be?

I would like to see people meditating more deeply, studying the Dharma more intensely, going on more retreats, and writing better English! I would like to see more development of the arts, more communication with other Buddhists. Just more and more of all those kinds of things.

What does the Order reflect of you?

That's difficult for me to say, but one of the things I've said many times is that I don't want the Order to be Sangharakshita writ large. For example, my own sympathies are on the side of the arts and not the sciences, but I don't want personal limitations of that kind to be reflected in the Movement.

What issues have been central in setting up a spiritual community?

Communication and friendship. Those are much more important than organizational structures, important though such structures are.

With hindsight, would you approach the setting up a spiritual community differently?

I'm not sure, because there is the fact of one's own limitations. Some movements are set up on the basis of personal charisma, but I never had any charisma. I had to rely on the straightforward teaching of meditation and giving of lectures. Fortunately I have some facility in writing, but I am not a 'popular' writer.

It seems surprising for there to be a Western Buddhist Order in India where Buddhism first started. Why has the WBO gone back to India?

I am the link. I was in India until 1964 and I was associated with Dr Ambedkar's movement of mass conversion from Hinduism among the people who were considered 'Untouchables'. I knew Dr Ambedkar personally. On more than one occasion he said that there were only two *bhikkhus* his followers could trust, and one of them was Sangharakshita. That carried a lot of weight with his followers. But he died six weeks after the first mass conversion ceremony, and in the ensuing years I spent a lot of time among these followers.

Then I was invited to Britain and eventually decided that my future was here. But I kept up correspondence with some of those who had been associated with me in India, and twelve years after I left, Lokamitra, a senior member of the Western Buddhist Order, went to Poona and his lectures and classes grew into the Indian wing of the FWBO. Now there are 220 Order members in India, and thousands of others are involved.

In that the FWBO has been established to translate Buddhism into a Western context, is it being retranslated as it goes back to India?
No, not at all. In the West the FWBO is not creating a western form of Buddhism so much as finding a way of practising traditional Buddhism in the new conditions of modern western life: urbanized, industrialized, secularized, and so on. In India people increasingly live under such conditions, and many are alienated from traditional Hindu culture. They like our form of Buddhism because it is not reminiscent of Hinduism.

Over the years the FWBO, and indeed you personally, have received a certain amount of criticism and hostility. How have the criticisms affected you?
I've been accustomed to criticism throughout my career. Even when I was in India I was criticized by Theravādin monks for my interest in the Mahāyāna, while some of the Mahāyānists did not like my being a Theravādin monk. Hindus criticized me because I wouldn't agree that all religions are one, and at the same time I was criticized by the Christian missionaries for being a Buddhist at all. So I wasn't altogether surprised when, starting up this new Buddhist movement, I was criticized again. It isn't pleasant, especially when one feels that the criticism is unjustified.

On the other hand, I have been the object of the warm and friendly feelings of a lot of people, even though others have been hostile. I have seen this as an opportunity to develop evenness of mind. One should not be upset when one is criticized; one should not be elated when one is praised.

What do you think has opened the FWBO and yourself to such criticism?
When criticism is rational one can respond. An example of rational criticism is when some Theravādins have said, 'Sangharakshita is against monasticism.' My response to that has always been that I am not against monasticism. I have criticized it on just two scores. In the 1950s I criticized what I called monastic formalism – observing monastic rules in the letter but not the spirit, as when monks did not actually handle gold and silver, which is forbidden, but had no objection to handling currency notes. Secondly, when I came to understand the primacy of Going for Refuge, I was critical of the idea that monasticism was the most valid form of Buddhist life. But within the FWBO I've encouraged a sort of slimmed down monasticism for those who are ready for it. That means being an *anagārika*, who is celibate, leads as simple a life as possible, has no career, and is cutting down on personal possessions.

But some of the hostility directed against the FWBO is irrational, and I don't understand it. It has been disappointing to be the object of the hostility of fellow Buddhists. I can understand people disagreeing with, even criticizing, what one is doing, but it is disappointing when hostility is expressed in extreme language, unjustified accusations, and even dirty tricks.

You seem very capable of putting forward your own views, yet there's been a huge amount of misunderstanding. Why have you been so misunderstood?
I have noticed that my critics seem not to read what I have written – and I have written a lot. Sometimes people criticize the Movement when all they may need to do is ask a few simple questions. I've made my position clear on all sorts of issues, sometimes in response to criticism or misrepresentation.

There was a time when apparently you were neither a monk nor a lay person, but you were still wearing robes. Do you regret that lack of clarity?
I can only say that I was a transitional figure, neither a monk nor a lay person in the traditional sense. For a long time now I have been an *anagārika* in the sense I described, but there was a period when I was not an *anagārika*. If I'd stopped wearing a robe, people would have said, 'He has ceased to be a monk, he is now a layman.' I was between

the devil and the deep blue sea. I hope it is now clear where I stand: that for the last so many years I have been an *anagārika*. But circumstances being what they were then, I had no option but to proceed as I did.

You have had Dharma teachers from a range of lineages and traditions. What is your relationship with those traditions?
I was greatly inspired by my contact with those teachers, and I am grateful to them, but I don't regard myself as representing them, or as passing on those lineages as such. I regard myself as just a Buddhist, and I see them simply as Buddhists, not as representing this or that lineage. For instance, I had close contact with Dhardo Rimpoche over many years. I saw him as a completely mindful and compassionate person, and I was inspired by him. I hope something of that rubbed off on me, and it is that that I am hoping to pass on, not a particular technique or tradition.

How do Order members view you?
You'll have to ask them. Some don't bother about such things at all, and others do.

But how would you like them to see you?
That isn't something I think about. They no doubt see me in the light of their experience of me, whether directly or through my lectures and books.

Do you not consider yourself to be a Buddhist teacher, or a guru?
No, I have repudiated the idea of being a guru, because of the associations that cling to that term. I'm happy to be thought of as a spiritual friend or even just as a friend. I am rather critical of the emphasis on the guru among Tibetan groups. I don't think it's good for the guru, who can get inflated ideas, or the disciples, who can become dependent and dogmatic about their guru's attainments.

When you meet another person you must not assume that you are more developed than they are, or that they are more developed than you. If you enter into communication deeply enough it will become evident whether one of you is more developed, at least in certain respects. But this cannot be posited in advance. I don't think it is possible simply to accept it when someone says, 'Lama so-and-so is a tremendous teacher!'

That knowledge can only come from communication, from getting to know Lama so-and-so. If you yourself regard him as more developed, that's fair enough, but you cannot insist that others see him in that way, especially on the grounds of his occupying a certain ecclesiastical position.

Some people have questioned your authority and hence the authenticity of the Movement. How do you respond?
I don't think of myself as possessing authority. As a result of my studies and practice I have a certain understanding of the Dharma, and a certain ability to communicate that, and that's what I've been doing. If people find what I say reasonable and if, when they put it into practice, they find that it works, they may choose to accept it. That was the Buddha's approach, and on my own level I do the same.

My appeal is to people's reason and experience; ultimately that is the authority. If there are conflicting authorities, you can only decide between them in the light of your own reason and experience, especially spiritual experience.

But isn't there some sort of authority in the WBO?
I know that Order members take what I say seriously. But many Order members don't hesitate to disagree with me, and I don't think that is an unhealthy sign. Of course, if they were to disagree on absolute fundamentals – for instance, if they decided that monasticism was of overriding importance and asked for monastic ordination outside the Order – we would bid them a friendly farewell.

So you don't consider your word sacrosanct?
Even the Buddha did not consider his word sacrosanct. He said, 'Test my words as gold is tested in the fire.'[352] How can one say more than that?

Is the Order a lineage now?
I don't use that term, but some people would see a lineage of Going for Refuge. That will be continued mainly through ordination, and I have already handed on the responsibility for ordaining people to a College of Order members whom I regard as playing a crucial role. In time, others will no doubt be admitted to that College, while some of the

preceptors may withdraw, especially once they have ordained a number of people and feel they should spend more time looking after them.

The Order's Refuge tree includes a number of historical Buddhist teachers and your relation to them. That suggests a lineage.
But what one is continuing is not so much specific teachings as the inspiration that comes from them, which is concentrated in the Going for Refuge that is common to them all. That's what I see myself as passing on. The idea of lineage has become bound up with ideas of feudal origin, especially among the Tibetans. Artificial lineages are constructed, and people are proud to belong to an especially 'powerful' lineage, as if that confers power on them.

If your teachers' inspiration comes to Order members through you, will they look to other teachers for inspiration once you've gone?
An important teaching, the four reliances, tells us to depend on the teaching (*dharma*), not the person (*pudgala*). If people aren't gaining inspiration from the teachings they have received within the FWBO, one might ask why. Sometimes people get bored with their meditation practice and think things would be different with another teacher. That is to be expected, and it may happen after I'm gone – it has occasionally happened while I've been around. But I hope that people will continue to derive more and more inspiration from the teaching they have already received.

The Buddha himself, when asked who would be his successor, replied, 'The Dharma I have taught will be my successor.' (See endnote 359.) If after my death people go haring off after another teacher, it would suggest they are not placing enough importance on the Dharma.

What is the locus of the purity of the Movement?
In a general sense it is the whole Order, but more specifically it is the College of Preceptors and the presidents, who will be mainly responsible for ensuring harmony between different aspects of the Movement and fidelity to my teachings. The members of the College have been particularly close to me over the years, and they know my mind.

Is the canon of the Order now closed?
Not at all. The FWBO is only just over thirty years old, which is no time at all in terms of the Buddhist tradition.

As people mature and find their own ways to practise the Dharma, what will keep everything together?

Doctrinally what will keep things together is the teaching of the centrality of Going for Refuge, and everything that stems from that. That emphasis is indispensable, and it distinguishes us from other forms of Buddhism. In practice what holds us together above all is the observance of the ten ethical precepts. And in organizational terms there are the preceptors and presidents working in collaboration with the different elements of the Movement.

As each FWBO centre is autonomous, might people take certain aspects and set up independent centres?

That may happen. But I deliberately established the legal and financial autonomy of FWBO centres from the very beginning. Centres must run their own affairs. The unifying factor is the Order because centres are run by Order members, but it is a spiritual, not an organizational, unity. There is no organizational headquarters that directs these different 'branches'.

What is your hope for people in the FWBO?

I hope they will progress on the path to Enlightenment, that's the main thing. I hope they will make progress in that direction not just for their own individual sakes, but so they can help other people.

And what does the FWBO offer the world as a whole?

Neither we nor any other Buddhist movement could offer more than the path to Enlightenment. In India there's also a need for practical and material help, but in the West the need is for spiritual education.

How do you see your place in the Buddhist world as a whole? Do you feel part of the Buddhist community in this country?

I can't say I think about my place in the Buddhist world. I just do my job, so to speak, from day to day.

Of the hundreds of teachers in the West, from whom would you say you have gained spiritually?

The person with whom I had most contact in recent years was Ayya Khema. It started in 1992 at the European Buddhist Union Congress in

Berlin. At the end Ayya Khema came across to me, and said, 'I admire your courage. I am a bold woman, but I could not have said what you said.' What she so admired was that I had publicly disagreed with something Thich Nhat Hanh had said. I thought, 'What have we come to? Just because someone is a prominent teacher, can't one disagree with him in a friendly way? That was the start of our friendship. After 1992 we met regularly whenever she came to England, and we corresponded until she died a couple of years ago. We didn't agree about everything, but we agreed about a lot of things.

Do you think westerners will always have a superficial understanding of Buddhism?
Well they've had a superficial understanding of Christianity all these hundreds of years, haven't they? The more widely something is known the more misunderstanding there is bound to be. One can only hope there will be a minority of people with a deeper understanding.

But people brought up in a Buddhist culture will have a deeper understanding of it in some sense.
Such Buddhists may know the manners and customs and how to be respectful to monks, but they may not understand the basic principles of Buddhism. There is a good and a bad side to being brought up in a popular Buddhist culture. Sometimes you miss what the Dharma is really all about.

There is a lot of talk about non-sectarianism in Buddhism. Has the FWBO itself become a sect?
If by 'sect' one means an independent religious organization, then I suppose we are one. But I don't think the term should be used pejoratively. The real question is what one means by sectarianism. One can't say that it simply consists in believing that your particular teaching is true, or even that it is the only truth. It means taking undue advantage of people with other religious affiliations for the benefit of your own sect. In that sense there has been sectarianism in Northern Ireland, but I wouldn't say that Protestantism or Catholicism itself is necessarily sectarian.

Nowadays people think that if you don't believe that all religions teach the same thing you are sectarian and intolerant, but this is just confused thinking. Indeed, that view is itself intolerant. I used to find in India that if you didn't agree that all religions teach the same thing as Hinduism, people would become annoyed and oppose you.

For me, tolerance is the ability to accept differences without difference giving rise to unskilful mental states. We should be able to recognize that someone else has a different view and have no inclination to change it except through rational means. Certainly differences should not be used as a reason to oppress people or feel negatively towards them.

If you felt strongly that someone's religion is damaging them, how do you deal with that?
You have to give them more light. One can only use discussion and debate.

As you approach your seventy-fifth birthday, what are your thoughts and feelings about old age and death?
I'm very aware that I don't have the energy I used to have. Recently I looked at some old diaries and I saw that I was sometimes giving five or six lectures a day. I don't have that energy these days, and one has to accept that as gracefully as possible. Unless I become ill I don't see any likelihood of my present way of life changing. I will hopefully write a bit more, and travel a bit. But I accept that my energies will be running down.

I wouldn't like to die at the end of a long, lingering illness, but of course I don't have the choice, and if that happens I will have to accept it as best I can. And I would prefer not to suddenly drop dead in the midst of everything. I would like a few days of preparation at least. But I may not get that. One has to be prepared for all eventualities. That's old age. That's life. I enjoy my old age and I don't hanker after my youth, even though I sometimes wish I could do more. But that's part of handing on: accepting that it is up to others to carry the torch.

What in your life has given you most joy?
When I was in India working with the new Buddhists I sometimes asked people what difference Buddhism had made. Their faces would light up, and they would say, 'Now I feel free.' That gave me great joy. It's the same in principle in the West, although the conditions are different. What gives me most joy now is getting letters from people telling me what a difference the Dharma has made to their lives, especially when I

know what a dreadful life they had before. I then think my life has been to some extent worthwhile.

And how would you like to be remembered after you die?
I haven't really thought about that.

Well, now's the time...
I would like to be remembered as someone who did something for the ex-Untouchables, because I did feel very strongly for them. And I would like to be remembered as someone who did something to help bring the Dharma to the West.

TRUE COMMUNICATION

Dharma Life *no. 14, Winter 2000, pp. 44–7. Sangharakshita responds to an invitation to write on his 'entrance to the spiritual realm'.*

The request to write on the theme of 'What is your entrance/access to a spiritual dimension/realm' did not evoke an immediate response. As a Buddhist, my principal 'entrance' to the dimension or realm in question has been through Buddhism or, perhaps I should say, through being a Buddhist, in the sense of being one who goes for Refuge to the Three Jewels: the Buddha or perfectly Enlightened teacher, the Dharma or principial means to Enlightenment, and the Sangha or spiritual community of all Buddhists, past, present, and future. Basically, my 'entrance' has been the act of Going for Refuge, as that deepens from provisional to effective Going for Refuge, and from effective to real. I did not want, however, to write on Buddhism, or even on Going for Refuge. Having written over the years a number of books on different aspects of Buddhism, including one entitled *The History of My Going for Refuge*,[353] I preferred not to go over ground already covered more than once.

Nonetheless, the theme on which I had been invited to write must have remained at the back of my mind, for two days ago I had a kind of *eureka* experience, as it may be called. The thought struck me that besides Buddhism and Going for Refuge I had another entrance to a spiritual dimension – an entrance that had in fact been under my nose all the time and on which it might be possible for me to offer a few reflections. This other entrance was the experience of writing – the experience of transferring ideas and emotions to the written and, eventually, the printed page.

After all, writing had long been an important part of my life. Over the years I must have spent thousands of hours at my desk, and the written and printed word had been, with the spoken word, the principal means by which I had communicated the Dharma – the Buddha's teaching – to hundreds of thousands of people in both the East and the West. Let me, therefore, try to explain how it is that, for me, writing is an entrance or access to a spiritual dimension or realm.

Before that, I would like to explain what I understand by spiritual, as well as by dimensions or realms. Though the word 'spiritual' is widely used, its meaning is not very clear. According to the dictionary it means, primarily, 'relating to the spirit or soul and not to physical nature or matter; intangible'. This leaves us none the wiser, as we are not informed what the spirit or soul (apparently the two terms are synonymous) is in itself. In my own usage, standardized over many years, the word 'spiritual' has two meanings, one narrower than the other. In its narrower sense, 'spiritual' corresponds to the Buddhist term *kuśala*, literally, skilful (sometimes translated as 'wholesome') which means characterized by the mental states of freedom from craving, freedom from aversion, and freedom from delusion or, more positively, by contentment, (non-erotic) love, and wisdom.

Thus the spiritual life is a life devoted to the cultivation of such states, a spiritual practice one that conduces to their development, and a spiritual teaching one that is concerned with them either theoretically or practically or both. In its broader sense 'spiritual' corresponds, in my personal usage, not only to the term *kuśala* but also to the still more important term *lokuttara*, literally, '(the) beyond-world' or, as we may say, the transcendental or nirvāṇic. When the word spiritual is taken in this broader sense, the spiritual life is one that is devoted not only to the cultivation of skilful mental states but also to the attainment of the transcendental or nirvāṇic state. For Buddhism it is axiomatic that there is no attainment of the transcendental or nirvāṇic state except on the basis of a mind dominated by the skilful mental states of freedom from craving, freedom from aversion, and freedom from delusion

How literally one is meant to take the distinction between spiritual dimension and spiritual realm I do not know, but to me the former has a more psychological and the latter a more metaphysical connotation.

In what way, then, does writing, for me, constitute an entrance into a spiritual dimension or realm? Nowadays a distinction is often made, at least implicitly, between 'creative writing', as it is called, and writing that is not creative. I doubt very much if the distinction is a hard and fast one. Creative writing does not form a distinct genre, as a piece of writing in any genre may be either creative or non-creative. Nonetheless certain genres undeniably give greater scope to pure creativity than do others. Such, for example, are the poem, the novel and short story, and the drama. Others, like the scientific treatise and the business letter, give it minimal scope. As for genres such as history and biography (including autobiography and memoirs), these come somewhere in the middle, for though all are concerned with facts the author has a good deal of freedom in the arrangement and presentation of those facts.

Now the book on which I was working when I received my invitation to contribute to the present publication happened to be a third volume of memoirs.[354] Thus the writing in which I was engaged was, on the whole, of the semi-creative variety. In trying to describe how writing constitutes, for me, an entry into a spiritual dimension or realm I shall be drawing principally on my experience in writing this volume of memoirs, an experience which lasted, on and off, for three years, and is still fresh in my memory.

In the first place, writing involves concentration. By concentration I do not mean the forcible fixation of one's attention on a single object but, rather, the gradual mobilization of one's energies around a single point, which for me as a writer is the point where pen meets paper and inner experience is transformed into outer expression. My usual practice is to write in the morning, starting immediately after breakfast. Especially when I have been writing daily for several weeks, I find that I become concentrated as soon as I sit down at my desk and take up my pen, or rather my biro, having not yet succumbed to the blandishments of modern technology in the form of the word processor.

Here there is a definite parallel with my experience as a meditator, for especially when I have been meditating regularly I find, more often than not, that I become concentrated as soon as I sit down on my cushion, cross my legs, and close my eyes. The parallelism illustrates the fact that writing, like meditation, is able to form an entrance to a spiritual dimension by virtue of the element of concentration it involves, though it should be emphasized that for writing, as for meditation, the concentration in question is 'skilful' concentration, i.e. concentration that is associated with the mental states of freedom from craving, freedom from aversion, and freedom from delusion. The writing of a pornographic novel, for instance, would not be an entrance to a spiritual dimension inasmuch as the concentration involved would be associated with unskilful mental states.

My life has consisted of a series of incidents and experiences, and writing my memoirs means writing about these incidents and experiences. But first they have to be recalled. This I do not find too difficult, at least in certain respects; for instance I have a good visual memory, and can recall the way certain people and places looked, even though I saw them forty and more years ago. What I cannot recall so easily are conversations. I can recall the substance of what was said, whether by myself or others, but very rarely can I recall the actual words that were spoken, much less still a whole series of verbal exchanges. My memoirs therefore contain no conversations, which from a purely literary point of view is a serious defect. On the few occasions when I do place my own or another person's remarks within quotation marks the reader may be sure that the words quoted were spoken exactly as given, and that I must have remembered them because they made a deep impression on me at the time.

Autobiographies and memoirs often contain conversations. A few of them consist of little else. In some cases the author may have had a good memory for conversation, or have made notes or kept a diary; in others, I suspect, he or she simply invented the conversations and dialogue, thus doing with real life characters what the novelist does with imaginary ones. In writing my own memoirs I was determined to include nothing that was not factual even if that meant leaving some unsightly gaps in my narrative. I was determined not to usurp the function of the novelist. With regard to each incident and experience I asked myself, 'What actually happened?' and only when this was clear did I describe it. In other words I was concerned that my memoirs should be strictly truthful, and truthfulness is an entrance to a spiritual dimension. Certainly there can be no entry to such a dimension without it.

But truth is subjective as well as objective. One can be truthful not only with regard to outer events but also with regard to inner feelings. In writing my memoirs I therefore had to ask myself not only what actually happened, but also what I actually felt on a particular occasion, or in a certain situation. Sometimes this was obvious. Sometimes, however, it was not, and I had to recall the occasion or situation in detail, dwell upon it, and coax forth into present consciousness the feeling I had then experienced. Only when I had done this did I seek to describe the feeling.

Occasionally it so happened that I was able to coax forth feelings of which I had not been fully cognisant at the time or to which I had been unwilling to admit. For example, I saw that there were occasions when my real feeling had not been just one of mild annoyance, as I then thought, but actually one of anger. I was also able to see more deeply into the motives that had led me to adopt a particular course of action or behave in a certain way. I saw how I had missed opportunities and failed to take full advantage of favourable circumstances. All this meant that in writing my memoirs I got to know myself better, at least as I had been in the past; and that self-knowledge is a means of entrance to a spiritual dimension there can be little doubt.

As I described incidents and experiences, seeking to ascertain feelings and exploring motives, and as I got to know my past self better, I began to see my life more as a whole or at least to see more as a whole the part of it covered by my third volume of memoirs. Seeing it as a whole I was able to see it more objectively and, in a way, even to distance myself from it. Distancing myself from it I could see how one thing had led to another and how in dependence on events which were, in themselves, seemingly insignificant, there had arisen others that were of considerable importance.

In a word I saw my life as conditioned, and to the extent that one truly sees the conditioned as conditioned one is free from the conditioned, in the sense of being free from attachment to it, and has access to the Unconditioned. The Unconditioned being synonymous with the spiritual in the broader sense of the term, seeing one's life as a whole and as wholly conditioned is an entrance to a spiritual dimension. Not that one can see one's life as a whole only if one writes an autobiography or memoirs, or that writing these will necessarily enable one to see one's life as a whole and as conditioned, but writing them certainly enables one to focus on one's life in a sustained and systematic way that otherwise is hardly possible outside meditation.

Concentration, truthfulness both objective and subjective, and self-knowledge, are all entrances to a spiritual dimension or realm, and as writing, including the (semi-creative) writing of memoirs, can involve all three, writing itself can be an entrance to that dimension. I for one have certainly found it to be so in the course of the past three years.

IMAGE CONSCIOUS

Dharma Life *no. 21, Autumn 2003, pp. 17–22.*

In the course of 1,500 years Indian Buddhism passed through three great phases. The first phase was named the Hīnayāna, the 'lesser way', by followers of later Buddhist schools, but we can think of it simply as early Buddhism. In this first flowering of the Buddhist tradition, the emphasis was placed on ethical observance and psychological analysis. With the development of what became known – at least to its own adherents – as the Mahāyāna, the 'great way', the focus shifted to devotional practice and what could be called metaphysics, although it was of a rather different kind from the metaphysics of the western tradition. But the third phase, the Vajrayāna, the diamond way, also called the Tantric path – placed special emphasis on the use of symbols, ritual, and meditation.

Each phase emerged in response to, or even reaction against, existing tradition, but did not entirely replace it; the essential features of the preceding traditions were preserved in each new synthesis of the teaching. Even when a change of cultural setting was involved, when the Vajrayāna or Tantra was introduced into Tibet, the Tibetans elaborated upon the Indian Tantric tradition rather than changing it in any substantial way. The only real innovation was the incorporation of indigenous Tibetan deities into mandalas, but those figures never occupied a prominent position. Even the songs of Milarepa, which seem so distinctively Tibetan, have antecedents in Indian literature.

The Tantra went on developing in the Indian Buddhist community until the final disappearance of Buddhism from India. But the Indian tradition was always just one step ahead of developments in Tibet. For several hundred years Tibetan monks and scholars were coming down into India and eagerly enquiring after the latest Tantric teaching, so that they could study it, practise it, and take it back to Tibet. The Tibetans did not rely entirely on Indian forms of practice; they assimilated the spirit of the teachings and practised them in their own way.

But before the introduction of Buddhism the Tibetans had very little culture of their own, so their culture has always been mainly Buddhist, and that included the adoption of Indian cultural forms. The situation was more or less the same in Sri Lanka, and even in Japan. The great exception was China. The Chinese did not always take kindly to the Indian culture that came along with Buddhism because they already had a highly developed culture of their own.

Our own position, as we adopt Buddhism in the West, is most akin to that of the Chinese; we too have a highly developed culture already, and that will have its effect on the way we approach Buddhism. We may be as eager, as were the Tibetans all those centuries ago, to acquire the latest teachings, but we may find that we experience – in a way the Tibetans never did – a clash between Buddhist tradition and the culture in which we have been born and which has exerted its influence on us throughout our lives.

This is perhaps especially true when we try to understand Tantric Buddhism, with all its symbols, rituals, and apparently arcane practices. The increasingly rationalistic and secular outlook of western society has given many people a thirst for myth and symbol. All the same, we will need to make a special kind of effort if we are to grasp the true nature of those myths and symbols, so that they can become part of our lives in a creative and natural way.

This has been my own experience, anyway. When I first encountered the Tantra I was living in Kalimpong, a small town in the foothills of the eastern Himalayas. Thus I was surrounded by the great kingdoms of Tantric Buddhism – Sikkim, Bhutan, Nepal, Tibet – and Kalimpong itself was full of Tantric practitioners, mostly Tibetan refugees who had fled the Chinese invasion. But although I was surrounded by the Tantra, it took me some time to understand what that meant. At that time, in the 1940s and 1950s, I had been a committed Buddhist for a number of years, but nothing had prepared me for the Tantra, and there were no reliable books on it in English. But in Kalimpong I began to meet people who were actually engaged in the practice of the Tantric path. I came in contact, a little later on, with Tantric art and ritual, and I eventually met a number of great Tantric gurus, and came to experience Tantric initiation and practice for myself.

As I tried to penetrate a little into the Tantra I felt that it was a jungle in which one could easily get lost. There were so many different traditions, so many meditation methods and forms of ritual observance, so many kinds of offerings, scroll paintings, so many figures of Buddhas, bodhisattvas, and gurus, and *ḍākas*, *ḍākinīs*, and *dharmapālas*.

This is likely to be the experience of any westerner beginning to investigate the Tantra. The impression of richness and variety, growth, fertility, and abundance is quite bewildering to begin with. But to become intellectually lost in the context of the Tantra is quite a positive thing. One may find oneself moved by the symbols without being able to say exactly how or why. With more experience, one comes to discover that the Tantra is not really the jungle it appears to be. It is more like a garden or, rather, a complex of gardens. Despite the exuberance of the Tantra there is a pattern running through it, or a number of interlocking patterns. These patterns are not intellectual, but spiritual. They are not imposed on the Tantra from the outside, but unfold from within it, expressing its innermost nature and essential purpose.

Tantric Buddhism is concerned not with theories or speculations, not with formal religiosity or external piety, but with the direct experience, in the depths of one's being, of what one truly and essentially is. It seeks to reveal to us our essential nature – not just psychologically but existentially, even transcendentally. So far as the Tantra is concerned, this experience cannot be mediated by concepts. In fact, concepts give no idea of it at all. It is beyond words, thought, and the conscious mind and personality. But this direct experience can be evoked, or at least glimpsed, with the help of symbols. The whole Tantric path to Enlightenment is strewn with symbolic images, mantras, and rituals; indeed it largely consists of them. And they are all intended to give a glimpse of this direct experience.

What is a symbol? The very nature of symbols makes it impossible to define them; it is best to let them speak for themselves. But we can at least make one generalization: a symbol is not a sign. It does not stand for something that could be known in some other way. You can only get at what the symbol represents, or develop any feeling for it, through the symbol itself. You don't know what it stands for, because your only means of access to it is through the symbol.

You can give a meaning to a symbol if you like, but that is not to say that you have got in touch with what the symbol stands for. Symbols are not concepts, so their meaning cannot be exhausted conceptually. There is usually something quite concrete about them – they have form and colour – and they do communicate something, but it is not easy to put what they communicate into words. They are like dreams, which leave a vivid impression, but cannot be expressed in conceptual terms.

To take one of Buddhism's favourite symbols, consider the lotus. Let your mind dwell on it, and then ask yourself what you are experiencing. What is this flower? What does it mean? Clearly it is not just a botanical specimen. It conveys something; it gives you a certain feeling that goes beyond its botanical characteristics. That is what makes it a symbol. But how does that work? Is it that we invest the innocent flower with qualities it does not possess, or does it really have some quality of its own, apart from our projection onto it?

When you see the lotus as a symbol, you are seeing it as being illuminated by some other, higher, dimension of reality. This reality is described in some Buddhist texts by the term *śūnyatā* (emptiness) which is a synonym for the unfathomable, indefinable mystery of the true nature of things. However, we cannot come at that mystery except through what is around us every day. As the Perfection of Wisdom *sūtras* put it, we cannot experience *śūnyatā* except through *rūpa* ('form'), referring to the objects we can perceive through our senses. A symbol is an object seen or felt or experienced as possessing a heightened significance that cannot be reduced to words or concepts. There is something there other than that form, that colour, or that sound, which is both communicated through that form and inseparable from it.

So it isn't quite accurate to say that a symbol stands for something. It is more that the symbol is that thing as it appears under a certain set of conditions, in a certain mode. What determines how something appears is the quality of perception of the person who sees it. For example, the figure of the Buddha is well known to be a symbol of Enlightenment. But how do we know that? We are unlikely to be able to recognize it from our personal knowledge of the Enlightened state. We may have some conception of what Enlightenment is, and we may also, if we are receptive, get some inkling of Enlightenment through the Buddha's symbolism of it. But that inkling will not necessarily coincide with our conception of Enlightenment.

And to get even an inkling, we have to be receptive to the symbol. It isn't that it definitely means this, that, or the other, and will deliver its meaning to us automatically. The symbolism is in the eye of the beholder. That is one of the differences between a symbol and a concept. In certain states of mind – the kind of states of mind developed in meditation – all experience is symbolic, and everything is seen as possessing a heightened significance. To continue to use the language of the Perfection of Wisdom, in as much as all forms are empty (all *rūpas* are *śūnyatā*), whenever we are in contact with *rūpa* we are in contact with *śūnyatā*. Everything we see – a tree, the sky, the clouds – is therefore symbolic: 'huge cloudy symbols of a high romance', as Keats says.[355]

Ultimately, nothing is any more significant than anything else. Things can't be divided into symbols and non-symbols. They simply become symbolic under certain conditions; a symbol is a particular thing seen under particular circumstances or in a particular way. In principle, anything can be a symbol. One might say that everything is symbolic but some things are more symbolic than others. It is partly that we experience some things as being more significant than others for subjective reasons. Most people can see the significance of a beautiful sunset more readily than that of a heap of ashes.

One cannot say that a lotus is more real than a dandelion, or that in itself it possesses more significance, but for subjective or cultural reasons it may make a more appropriate symbol. There may also be some objective reason – the way the lotus grows unsullied out of the muddy water, for example – that makes it an especially appropriate symbol for purity. But one must be careful that the association is not just intellectual. You have to *feel* the purity of the lotus.

A symbol is not an inadequate copy of something that exists quite separately on some higher plane. It is not that the lotus symbolizes something that is quite other than a lotus and could just as well have been symbolized by something else. What we speak of as being symbolized by the lotus is in fact a deeper dimension of the lotus, so that when you see the lotus as a symbol, you are seeing it in a deeper and truer way.

This is what the spiritual life is about: trying to find more significance in our daily lives. When you can do that, there is never a dull moment.

This is the experience of mystics and meditators who speak of seeing literally everything as being lit up from within, glowing with light. Light, significance, meaning, inner depth, symbolism – it all amounts to the same thing. In a certain state of mind, everything you see has significance. Not that the significance is reducible to a conceptual meaning – it just is significant.

We each need to explore what it is that makes something symbolic for us personally. We might all agree that a lotus – or indeed a dandelion – is symbolic in some way, but what is your actual experience of it? Setting aside whatever it is conventionally said to mean, what does it symbolize for you as an individual? Quite often one finds oneself exploring the meaning of one symbol through others. For example, the significance of a particular Buddha figure may become clearer when we consider what he is holding in his hands.

In any case, the effect of symbolism is not entirely subjective. Whereas a sign simply points towards a reality, a symbol to a degree participates in it. And, as I said, some symbols are more symbolic than others. Some, as Carl Jung discovered, are universal, archetypal, to be found in all cultures in various forms. There is what might be called a hierarchy of symbolism, and for Buddhists, the images of Buddhas and bodhisattvas are certainly to be found at the top of that hierarchy. But in what sense are these figures truly symbols for us? We may have their pictures on our walls. We may even visualize them in meditation. But they are not necessarily symbols for us in the sense of being fully, powerfully, and emotionally stimulating. A symbol isn't just something you put up on a wall. It's only a symbol to the extent that you respond to it.

Developing a feeling for a symbol may therefore mean establishing links from whatever we do have a feeling for, however mundane it may be, to more refined things, making them more real to us. The Buddha image is the symbol of spiritual growth par excellence, the most elevated symbol available to us, but we may still find it easiest to approach it through other symbols. For example, a certain Buddha figure may be associated with the symbol of the elephant. While the Buddha may be beyond the reach of your vision, you may for some reason feel an attraction to elephants, and make your connection that way. Its profusion of symbols means the Tantra contains something to appeal to everybody.

At the beginning, we may have to accept that the Buddha image is not a symbol for us, but only a picture. It may represent an inspiring ideal for us, but, to begin with, it is just that – an ideal – something conceived of mentally. If the Buddha image were really a symbol for us, it would rouse and harness all our energies. If we just admire it as a striking picture or conceive of it as an abstract intellectual ideal, it is clearly not a symbol for us yet.

If we dwell upon and are receptive to them Tantric symbols will affect us, work on us, and transform us. They stand for something of which we are not yet conscious, but of which we can become conscious, which we can come to know in a spiritual sense. Symbols are not dead, inert counters. They are full of energy, and give birth to life, spiritual life, within us. They are by their very nature creative. The creative symbols of Tantric Buddhism are not just of historical interest. They are not just creative in the abstract, or in the past, or in Tibet and India. They are creative for us. They can act on us, energize us, spark off developments in our own spiritual life, here and now, right now.

THE LONG VIEW

Dharma Life *no. 26, Summer 2005, pp. 42–6. In Sangharakshita's eightieth year, Vajrasara went to his home in Birmingham to discuss his life, his vision, and his legacy.*

INSOMNIA

Sleep deprivation is a peculiar experience; it does strange things to you. For over a year I suffered chronic insomnia and felt very unwell. I was aware of difficult changes – physical and emotional. I could stand back and observe them, but I couldn't do much to affect them; I had so little energy. I needed to focus on the medication, and getting better.

I kept up with as many activities as I could manage; I saw a few people, and went for walks each day. I did some editing and, slowly and with difficulty, I did finish *Living with Awareness* and *Living with Kindness.*[356] Most importantly I kept up Dharma study almost daily with my companion Nityabandhu. The Dharma seemed more relevant than ever and it was consoling to be reminded of it.

Throughout that period I had brilliant dreams: frequently in beautiful mountains, in green fields or by the sea contemplating its deep blue colour. They were Turneresque scenes.[357] Often I was with monks, sometimes with old friends or my teachers, chanting with them and watching them perform pujas. Perhaps it was a natural compensation for the suffering of sleep deprivation. Fortunately, last year my energy returned and my sleep improved, although since I've been sleeping better, I've seldom had such vivid dreams.

Old age has certainly contributed to my illnesses. Sleep deprivation is often caused by ageing. And my sudden eyesight failure (macular degeneration) two years earlier was also an effect of old age. I adjusted to seeing very little quite easily. I was hardly disturbed at all, which surprised some people, given how much I have always read. Nature is reminding me that I'm pretty old, and I accept that. I now have greater opportunity to reflect.

I don't really feel old within myself, but there's a difference in the way other people regard you. Old people are less important; I've noticed this even within our Buddhist movement. For instance, when I handed on my responsibilities for the Order and Movement in 2000, I specifically used the term 'handing on'. But people kept referring to me 'stepping down'. I believe this is because some people saw me as the teacher formally placed 'up there' – in their eyes I was 'in charge' and held power. I never felt I held power, but I know very well that some disciples did see me in that way; they projected power onto me. When I handed on my responsibilities, they saw me as having handed on that power. Accordingly, I became less important, and that meant they needn't take so much notice of me!

I contemplate these aspects of ageing. It's why, in one letter to the Order newsletter, I referred to *King Lear*. Shakespeare's play is about old age – an extreme example of an old man being ill-treated after stepping down. You see a similar attitude shift in families towards grandparents, when they're no longer the breadwinners. And it's one reason why dictators are often reluctant to give up power; it's unsafe for them to step down. I felt quite safe to hand on – confident that no one would assassinate me! It may be the minority who viewed me that way but in the early days I was seen as the one with the 'power to make you an Order member'. A few people have found it difficult to drop that type of thinking. And that attitude lingers in the way some Mitras relate to the ordination teams, which is unfortunate.

I may be 80 this year but in a sense I am not 'retired' – nor do I wish to be. I've certainly handed on my organizational responsibilities but, as founder, I feel responsible in a spiritual way for the FWBO. I cannot be indifferent to it. I still reply to letters and see disciples individually and in small groups. I am always happy to be consulted on Dharmic principles. Five years ago I said that I wanted to 'be free to be a disruptive influence', by which I meant that I wanted to help to keep us on our toes – to ensure the Order does not settle down, or ossify. Thus far circumstances have not allowed things to stay still. So I haven't yet needed to be disruptive!

ACCOMPLISHMENTS

As for what I've achieved, I could be paradoxical and say I personally haven't 'achieved' anything. However, I feel that something – work for the Dharma – has been achieved through me. I've often had this sense of being an instrument of some force. In the past I've remarked that I wasn't the best person to start a new Buddhist movement in the West, but one was needed and I was the only western Dharma teacher available in Britain. I suppose mine has been a life of communication, of translation – allowing myself to be a channel for something beyond me.

It has certainly been satisfying work. If it had just been 'my achievement', probably it wouldn't have been worth much. But what has been created in the broad sense, collectively, has been valuable. I have felt myself a channel more strongly at certain times than others. I felt it most intensely in the West when giving lecture series in the 1970s, particularly on Mahāyāna *sutras*. By bringing in the poetic and imaginative element, these *sutras* lent themselves to an opening up on my part to something higher. I also felt myself a channel very intensely in India, while working among the followers of Dr Ambedkar.

In setting up something new – non-denominational and separate from established traditions – I was primarily concerned with the people I met. They were evidently suffering, and I was communicating the Dharma to *them*. So meeting their needs determined the outward form of my approach. I've regularly had letters from western Buddhists saying that if they'd met the Dharma in a traditional Asian form it wouldn't have felt accessible. Some have explored traditional groups and couldn't connect with them, but many others evidently find the traditional approaches appeal to them.

In the FWBO I've continually emphasized 'clear Dharma teaching and a sense of sangha'. Again and again in letters of gratitude these are the two factors I singled out. They seem to be our strength. Of course the Movement could have been set up in all sorts of different ways. And it has evolved in surprising ways over its thirty-eight years. But clearly this approach enables many people to benefit from the Dharma.

TRANSFORMATION

Obviously I hope the FWBO survives but that depends on those who comprise it. We all need to go deeper into the fundamental teachings. If Order members remain committed to embodying the Three Jewels in their own lives, then it will survive. The FWBO is part of a worldwide Buddhist movement, so it will be affected by what happens elsewhere, as well as by broader political and economic factors. I imagine more and more people will find Buddhism attractive. But then many Muslims are making converts in the West outside their racial groups. Perhaps some ex-Christians who might have been drawn to Buddhism will take to Islam instead, especially its mystical Sufi side. We just don't know. However, within the broader Buddhist context I hope the FWBO will maintain its distinctive character, especially of *mettā* and spiritual friendship.

Although I'm less visible these days, I still hear a lot about what's going on. I wasn't well informed during my year of illness. But now, as well as visitors, I have the Order newsletter read to me and a great many people write to me – I even hear things I'm not meant to. So I feel I'm in touch with the grass roots of the Movement, and I don't rely on any one source of information.

For instance, I am aware of the current questioning of the developmental model of meditation. Actually this model is an integral part of the Buddha's teaching. To the extent you get away from that model you move away from Buddhism itself. You need to face the fact that transformation takes work. If you look closely into the lives and experience of those who claim to be following a non-developmental or formless approach, you find they are in fact practising a developmental model, but in a somewhat different or subtle way.

Take one of the figures on the FWBO Refuge Tree: the Japanese master Shinran. I wouldn't say that Shinran simply abandoned himself to the 'other power'. In the Pure Land tradition you have to put yourself into a frame of mind in which you are receptive to the other power, and that is not easy; that requires a whole series of steps, a series of efforts, before you can open yourself up in that way. So I don't take this talk of rejecting the developmental model too seriously. It's a fashion that will pass.

Perhaps people could ask themselves whether they have a correct view of the developmental model or a caricature. It's often more subtle and less gung-ho than people realize. Some people see it very one-sidedly; there is a potential weakness in each model. Opening up to 'other power', or immanence, certainly does have its place, but we cannot solely rely on it.

We can't really get away from the need for right effort – it's integral to the Noble Eightfold Path. But there are different ways of practising the four right efforts. According to the Buddha, you can watch an unskilful thought, letting it pass like a cloud in the sky. This is one way of applying right effort, though some might describe this as pure awareness. But of course if it's a powerful unskilful mental state, impelling you to act, simply watching it may not be enough. You will need to apply other methods.

You ask why I've been cautious about the Buddha-nature approach. In the early days people read Zen books and seized the idea that they were already Buddhas. I saw how very unhelpful this was. Taking an example from the *Tathāgatagarbha Sūtra* of the golden statue covered in dirt: some people would imagine the golden image was there not just in potential but already developed.[358] Yes, it might sound naive, and most people would understand they needed to work to purify themselves, but not all. I have learned not to underestimate people's capacity to be literal-minded.

DIRECTION

Taking another current development, I was pleased to learn of the appointment of more public and private preceptors. To me it seems an obvious need. I know the existing preceptors have been overburdened; so it is a logical step. It's also interesting that some thought I might be displeased. Why would they imagine I'd want things to stay as they were? I would be more concerned if things *did* stay the same. Stasis is not the answer. I am glad there's a substantial body of experienced practitioners willing to take on such a significant responsibility.

I also know there's currently concern about coherence. My impression is that there's quite a lot of coherence. Order unity consists in the fact that we are all Going for Refuge to the Three Jewels, we're all meditating, trying to practise the ten ethical precepts, and studying the Dharma; our urban centres are flourishing, many live in Buddhist communities, most Order members attend chapter meetings and Order weekends. There are more and more *kalyāṇa mitra* relationships, and large numbers are getting ordained each year. I don't think we need to worry. Coherence isn't ensured through organizational frameworks. All the spiritual elements are in place, they just need to be maintained, and deepened.

As for the question of leadership, I don't think we need a single head of the Order. I think it's mistaken to think in those terms. I never thought of myself as 'leading' the Order. The Movement is large and widespread; it won't take 'orders' from any one person. I hope we never have a leader: that would suggest we'd become politicized. We can look to the Buddha for a model; he didn't appoint one successor. When asked who would lead the monks after his death, he said the Dharma would be their guide.[359]

Likewise, our direction is determined by our practice. If Order members are faithful to the Dharma, and if we collectively maintain our distinctiveness, I feel confident the FWBO will go in the right direction (to the extent that we are going in any direction). We must beware of importing political terms into a spiritual context. As individuals we have the ideal of Enlightenment – freedom from greed, hatred, and delusion– and our institutions are intended purely to facilitate us moving in that direction.

DRAWING INSPIRATION

My current sources of inspiration lie primarily in the Dharma. Memories of my teachers also sustain me; I recall them all a great deal. As for archetypal figures, well, I have been reflecting more than usual on the historical Buddha. I have recently been studying the Pāli scriptures again. I believe we don't have a strong enough sense of Śākyamuni in our movement, of his historical presence and his 'achievement'. It is vital that Śākyamuni becomes a living figure and exemplar for us. Pilgrimage to the holy places in India can certainly help to bring him alive. And it is important to study deeply the Buddha's teachings in the Pāli scriptures. It will strengthen our understanding that Buddhism's unity stems from the Buddha.

Unfortunately Buddha images are usually so idealized that we have little impression of how he looked. We know he was tall, dark-haired, fair-skinned, and well built. But some images depict him like a modern *bhikkhu* with laundered robes and a shoulder bag! He certainly would have looked far more unkempt and worn, in ragged robes more like the sadhus wandering in India today.

Speaking of my own teachers, during the week before I officially handed on my responsibilities in 2000 I had unusually vivid dreams. Every night I dreamt sometimes multiple dreams of my teachers. I dreamt of them all a number of times. Each morning I told the dreams to a friend who wrote them down. These dreams stopped the day after the handing-on ceremony. They felt very significant – visionary or archetypal. I understood them to mean I had the blessings of my teachers in taking that step. I certainly feel I've kept in touch with my teachers, especially through the *sādhanas* I've done, and still do sometimes. And I'm still in contact with Chattrul Sangye Dorje,[360] the only one who is alive; he sends me messages from Nepal from time to time.

It has occurred to me that I could write more about these teachers. Perhaps a little book, not a scholarly study but personal reminiscences and impressions, on what these teachers from so many different traditions meant to me. Maybe I will; I can see how it might help my disciples to feel part of our lineage and linked to the wider tradition.

Although I'm a Buddhist, I was brought up a Christian and I am working in a post-Christian environment. Recently I have been writing some reflections on Buddhism and Christianity.[361] It's not an academic study, more a short review of my contact with Christians over the decades, some comparison of the two teachings, some art appreciation, critical comment, and so on; I don't know if it will be published. This is the first time I've given Christianity such sustained attention.

BIRTH AND REBIRTH

Looking back over my eighty years, I'd say the happiest time was spreading the Dharma among the Buddhists in central and western India. I felt this especially after the sudden death of Dr Ambedkar in 1956, when I stepped in to support and guide the grieving millions, and to bring hope to those newly converted Buddhists. As I wrote in my memoirs, I felt very much like a channel for a positive force working through me, so I was able to rise to that challenging situation almost effortlessly. It was deeply satisfying.³⁶² The saddest time was in England in 1969 when a close friend, Terry Delamare, committed suicide. That was a very painful period of my life.

Would I like to be reborn near an FWBO centre? Well, I suppose there would be a karmic link! But it's all so unknown. For instance, I don't know how soon I'd be reborn. Above all, I hope to remain in contact with the Dharma – somewhere it is genuinely being practised. It wouldn't really matter where, or which tradition. (And of course, it might be disconcerting if I were to appear at an FWBO centre as a child and chide people for not teaching the Dharma properly!) I'm not sure about monastic life – I have experienced both the benefits and the defects. I would want to be a full-time Buddhist, though. I certainly wouldn't want a worldly life in the ordinary sense.

I have no particular plans for whatever time remains to me. I shall simply carry on doing what I do which is a fair bit for my age. Writing, studying, reflecting, editing seminars, listening to music, talking to people. As long as I'm alive and have energy I'll keep working, though I don't regard it as work. It is simply my life, and I certainly enjoy it.

PART III

LATER TALKS, 2007–2009

Sangharakshita relaxes after the dedication of the Tara Cabin at Taraloka Retreat Centre, Shropshire, England, May 2007

THE MEANING OF FRIENDSHIP
IN BUDDHISM

Buddhistisches Tor, Berlin, Germany, 1992.

I'm very glad to be addressing you on this, the occasion of my first visit to the undivided Berlin, and especially happy to be in the midst of all our friends. It's natural that we should gather together in this way, because humans are social animals, and we are all necessarily related to each other in many different ways. Our earliest human relationships make up the family circle, and of these, our very first connection is with our mother. It is an intimate relationship, and its effects remain with us for the rest of our lives. Then as we become a little older, father appears, and then brothers and sisters, if we have them, and, if we're fortunate, also grandparents. We might have aunts and uncles – I personally had about twenty – and if so, there will usually be cousins. Beyond that, our next-door neighbours come into view and people in the same street. When we start school, teachers and school friends become important and, as we enter adult life, employers and work-mates, government officials, even rulers. And in most cases as we grow up, we become husbands and wives, and have children of our own, so by the time we reach maturity, we might be directly related to scores, perhaps hundreds, of people, and indirectly to very many more.

This network of relationships is the subject matter of a very important Pāli text. It is found in the *Dīgha Nikāya* or 'Collection of Long Discourses', and we can be reasonably certain it goes back to the Buddha himself. It is the *Sigālaka* or *Sigālovāda Sutta*, the Buddha's discourse of advice to Sigāla, a young Brahmin, or member of the priestly caste that was very influential in the Buddha's day. The *sutta* tells us that the Buddha happened to meet Sigāla early one morning, just as the young Brahmin had taken his ritual bath. The Brahmins attached great importance to these rituals, purifying themselves by dipping in the river and reciting mantras, and if you go to Benares you can see this even today. So, having taken his bath, Sigāla is engaged in the ritual worship of the six directions, comprising the four points of the compass, plus the zenith above and the nadir below. We are told that his father, at the time of his death, had instructed Sigāla to do this as a means of protecting himself from harm, and being a very pious son, Sigāla was obeying that instruction. Nonetheless, his father had given no further explanation and when the Buddha asked him why he was doing it, Sigāla couldn't say. He was just doing the ritual blindly. The Buddha therefore offered his advice. He said that what Sigāla was doing was not bad in itself, but because he hadn't understood what the worship of the six directions really amounted to, it was not the right way to protect yourself. Thereupon the Buddha proceeded to explain, and with that the *sutta* proper begins.

Each of the six directions can be taken to represent something, said the Buddha. The east is the direction in which the sun rises, and since one takes one's own origins from one's parents, the east can stand for one's mother and father. In the same way, one's teachers can be represented by the southerly direction; child and wife by the west; friends and companions by the north; servants and workers by the nadir below; and ascetics and holy men by the zenith above. This, said the Buddha, is the true worship of the directions. Recognizing one's duties towards all these six kinds of persons offers true protection, because one is acting ethically, and ethical action is what produces happiness. The Buddha's advice to Sigāla places the human being at the centre of a fairly wide network of human relationships. He does not enumerate all the many possibilities, only these six primary relationships of human life, and even though they may not all be of exactly equal importance, he seems to give them an equal emphasis.

The Buddha's advice to the young Brahmin is highly appropriate for the culture of north-east India of the sixth century BCE. But not all cultures are the same, and those in other parts of the world, and in other ages, are rather different in this respect. In ancient China, for example, great emphasis was placed on filial piety, or the duties of children towards their parents. According to Confucius this was the greatest of all the virtues, and in ancient classical China sons and daughters who were conspicuous examples of filial piety could be officially rewarded with a title, or given a large piece of land, or an archway might be named after them. This is rather different from our own era, we may note. Similarly, in the feudal system of medieval Europe, the great virtue was loyalty to your feudal superior, especially to your immediate superior. If you were a great lord it would be the king. If you were a small landowner it would be the local lord, or if you were an ordinary serf it would be your knight. But whoever it was, loyalty to your feudal superior had the greatest emphasis, so great that you'd be ready and willing to die for them if you had to.

When we come to the modern era, we find a rather different emphasis. In our case, in the West, importance is often placed on one's relationship with one's sexual partner. This is the so-called romantic relationship, and it is central, as we know very well, to many people's lives, even though one's partner may not always remain the same person. Perhaps you may not be prepared to die for your lover, but very often you declare that you cannot live without them. It is this romantic relationship which, for many people, gives meaning and colour to life. It is the subject matter of films, novels, plays, and poems and we're so accustomed to seeing it as central to life that we accept this simply as 'the way things are'. We think it is perfectly natural and that it has always been like that everywhere in the world. However, that's not the case. You might even say that this is a distinctly abnormal state of affairs, and, quite apart from the neglect of other relationships, it has one unfortunate result. It results in our 'overloading' the sexual-romantic relationship so that we expect from our sexual partner far more than he or she is able to give. If we're not careful, they have to be everything for us, sexual partner, friend, companion, mother – at least in the case of men – father, advisor, counsellor, and much else. We expect love from them, security, happiness, fulfilment and, in a word, we expect the sexual-romantic relationship to give meaning to our lives. In this way it becomes overloaded, and just like an electric wire when the current is too great, it very often breaks down under the strain, bringing all kinds of difficulties.

This is why we need a greater spread of relationships, a network of different kinds of connection, all of which are important to us, and to all of which we can give care and attention. The emphasis on one's sexual relationship means that other relationships are very often neglected, especially those involving our parents and friends. Not only do we not take them seriously, we may not even notice that this is happening. Among these primary human relationships, friendship is probably the most neglected of all, but from the Buddhist point of view, friendship is extremely important. It has, according to Buddhist tradition, a direct connection with spiritual life, as we shall see. So let us return to the Buddha's advice to the young Brahmin Sigāla and specifically to what the Buddha says about friendship.

Friends and companions, says the Buddha, are like lords, and they are to be served according to five duties which, if we perform them, will keep our friendships alive and flourishing. The first is generosity, which includes not only giving but also sharing. We should share whatever we have with our friends, whether it is time, resources, interest, energy, or even money. Some of those living in our FWBO communities have decided on a common purse, for example, and this isn't an easy thing to do, especially when some people find it difficult to share even a book, or just a cup and saucer. But easy or not, generosity is the first of the five duties outlined by the Buddha.

Secondly, we should speak kindly and compassionately to our friends, never harshly or bitterly. In Buddhism, we have a number of ethical precepts, and in the list of ten, only one applies to action, while no less than four precepts cover acts of speech. It indicates how easy it is to use our faculty of speech in a harmful way, speaking roughly, harshly even, to those close to us. So the Buddha says the second duty we have is to speak kindly and affectionately to our friends, and never be disparaging or sarcastic. It is not enough even to speak in an indifferent way. We should choose our words with respect and kindness towards those dear to us, and do so all the time. This is kindly speech, the second duty.

Thirdly, we should look after the welfare of our friends. In the most simple way, we should just see that they're all right, looking after their health and their economic well-being. Should they have any sort of difficulty, we help them, but this is especially true of their spiritual welfare, helping them to grow and develop as human beings. This is our third duty, according to the Buddha: looking after our friends' welfare.

The fourth duty is that we should treat our friends in exactly the same way that we treat ourselves. This is highly significant because it means breaking down the barriers between ourselves and other people.

The *Bodhicaryāvatāra* of Śāntideva, an important Mahāyāna Buddhist text, deals with this very topic in considerable depth, and in the course of the last twenty years Nagabodhi, the editor of *Golden Drum*, has given seminars on this particular text practically all over the world, and people have found them very inspiring indeed. So if ever Nagabodhi gives his seminar on the *Bodhicaryāvatāra* in Germany, make sure you attend. It'll really show you how to treat others, especially your friends, just like your own self. And that's the fourth of the five duties outlined by the Buddha.

The fifth duty is simply that we should keep our word to our friends. Very often we are quite careless about our undertakings, and sometimes that's because we make promises without thinking. But once we've given our word and made a promise, we should adhere to that, come what may. If we say we'll do something, we must do it.

These are the five duties towards our friends that the Buddha sets out and they are by no means a one-way matter. According to the Buddha, all human relationships are reciprocal, and that also goes for our duties. So friends and companions minister to each other, serve each other, and reciprocate in all kinds of ways. They watch over us when we're encountering difficulties, and when we're sick they watch over our property. In other words, where our possessions are concerned, they take more care of them than we do ourselves and that's surely a sign of friendship. Our friends are also our refuge in times of fear and can help allay our anxieties. If we have objective cause for fear they help remove it and when we are in trouble, they do not forsake us. As the English proverb says, 'A friend in need is a friend indeed.' If we have children, our friends are concerned for them also, or if we have disciples our friends, our fellow gurus and teachers, are concerned for them. Between them, these ten reciprocal duties between friend and friend represent a very high ideal. So let us spend a little more time with them, particularly with the first set of five, because if we know something about Buddhism, when we look at them we will notice something interesting.

The first four of these duties between friend and friend are identical with another well-known set of categories, one that occupies an important place, especially in Mahāyāna Buddhism. These are the four *saṃgraha-vastus* or 'elements of conversion', and they are significant in that they also appear as part of what is called *upāya pāramitā* or the perfection of skilful means. The perfections, or *pāramitās*, are ten in number and the bodhisattva practises them all so as to pass through ten stages of development. Since *upāya* is the seventh of the ten perfections, the fact that the four *saṃgraha-vastus* are called the 'elements of conversion' is quite noteworthy. It suggests that the most skilful means of converting someone, or winning them over, is simply by being a friend to them.

It's not uncommon to find people trying to convert us to their point of view, especially to their religion. They might knock on our door to ask if we have heard 'the Word' (whatever the Word might be). Quite a few people have tried to convert me in that way and I'm glad to tell you they didn't succeed. In Buddhism, by contrast, bringing pressure to bear on others, sometimes almost forcibly, is not the right path. In Buddhism we convert people – if that is even the right word – simply by being friendly. We just make friends, and there's no need to preach to them. So if you want to win someone over, just be a friend. Be generous, share with them whatever you have, and speak kindly and affectionately, show concern for their welfare, especially their spiritual welfare, keep your word to them, and treat them in the same way that you treat yourself. These five things in themselves communicate the Dharma. In fact you could even go so far as to say that friendship actually *is* the Dharma. Just as William Blake, the great English artist and mystic, says in one place that 'Brotherhood is Religion',[363] so for us, the Dharma is friendship. If you're practising friendliness you're not only practising the Dharma, you're spreading the Dharma without having to preach anything at all.

Let me say just a few more words about our fourth duty to friends and companions. This fourth element of conversion is *samānārthatā* in Sanskrit, meaning treating our friends and companions like our own selves, treating them equally. *Samāna* means equal, so we could say that a friend is, almost by definition, one whom you treat equally. It is noteworthy in this connection that the English word 'friend' is etymologically connected with the word 'free' through its roots in the Old Teutonic language, and perhaps this is also true of German.[364] Friendship is a relationship that can exist only between free people, that is to say people who are equals. The ancient Greeks realized this, and their axiom that there could be no friendship between a free man and a slave can be taken both metaphorically and literally.

This brings us to another very important point – the relation between master and slave is based upon power. It is an expression of what we sometimes call in the FWBO the 'power mode'. But friendship is not like that. It is an expression of what we've come to call the 'love mode'.[365] Here I'm using 'love' as the equivalent of the Pāli *mettā* which is where *mitta*, the Pāli word for friend, comes from. Unfortunately the English word 'love' is highly ambiguous. In both Pāli and Sanskrit, *mettā* or *maitrī* is very sharply distinguished from *pema* (Sanskrit *prema*) which is what we may call 'attachment love', characterized by clinging and possessiveness. It is fundamentally selfish, and that's why sexual love, being very often of this kind, can easily turn into hatred. *Mettā* is very different, being concerned only with the happiness and the well-being of the other person, and is unselfish, and non-attached. Friendship, therefore, is an expression of the '*mettā* mode', as we might call it.

The Pāli word *mettā* will already be familiar to you if you've practised the *mettā bhāvanā* meditation, the development of strong positive feelings of friendliness towards all living beings. First of all, you develop *mettā* towards yourself, then in the next stage towards a near and dear friend, though not to a sexual partner. In the third stage you develop that same feeling of *mettā*, which by this time is quite strong, towards a neutral person – someone you know fairly well but you neither particularly like nor dislike them, and then in the fourth stage you develop that same *mettā* towards someone whom you regard as an enemy or perhaps who regards you as one, or both. It might sound incredible that you could develop *mettā* towards an enemy, but people who have done the *mettā bhāvanā* practice know from their own experience that it is actually possible. In the fifth and final stage you develop *mettā* equally towards all four persons – to yourself, friend, neutral person, enemy – before radiating that same *mettā* out to all the people in the room, all the people in the house, in the neighbourhood, in your country, the whole continent, then all men and all women. And you end up directing your *mettā* not just to human beings, but also towards animals, or even to all 'gods and men' because in the Buddhist tradition even the gods need *mettā*.

With the help of the *mettā bhāvanā* practice we develop what we may call a friendly attitude, shifting to a new footing, and away from the 'power mode', where we are concerned only with getting what we want. Only too often we operate in accordance with the power mode. We might do this by means of deception, cheating, emotional blackmail, lying, even by force if necessary. But usually we do it less directly. We manipulate others and try to get them to do what *we* want them to do, and not for their benefit so much as for our own. We try to coerce them, not openly, but subtly. Some people are so good at this that you hardly know they are manipulating you, and very often they don't even know it themselves, it is so indirect. But in *mettā*, in friendship, there's nothing of this, only unselfish affection, concern for the happiness and well-being of the other person. There's no question of operating in accordance with the power mode or of using force of any kind, and this is mutual, because in friendship there's only equality.

We can now perhaps begin to see that there's more in the idea of friendship than we thought, and that it has a very definite spiritual dimension. So let's go a little further, and turn to another Buddhist text, one that may be even earlier than the *Sigālovāda Sutta*, called the *Udāna*.[366] Chapter 4 of the *Udāna* finds the Buddha staying at a place called *Cālikā* with a single companion, a young monk by the name of Meghiya. One day, Meghiya happens to see a beautiful grove of mango trees, a far from unusual sight on the outskirts of an Indian village even today. Mangoes are very beautiful trees, and apart from their delicious fruit, their dark green leaves provide very welcome shade in the heat of the Indian summer. Meghiya clearly thought it would be an ideal place in which to sit in the cool and meditate, and asked the Buddha for his permission to go and spend time there. The Buddha, however, didn't agree. Even Buddhas, when they get old, need a bit of looking after, so he asked Meghiya to wait until some other monk arrived. Meghiya was apparently quite a young monk, but what he lacked in years he certainly seems to have made up for in confidence. He simply disagreed with the Buddha, I'm sorry to say, and put to him a clever argument. He asked the Buddha whether he was Enlightened, to which the Buddha replied that, yes, he was. In that case, said Meghiya, 'I need to meditate much more than you do, because I'm not Enlightened yet.' Disciples are very good at catching their teachers out in this way, and in the end what could the Buddha say? He had to agree. Meghiya went off to the mango grove and the poor old Buddha was left to fend for himself.[367]

The mango grove was a fine, peaceful place and Meghiya sat down with high hopes for his meditation. But once there, a strange thing happened – or maybe not so strange. As soon as he started to practise, his mind was overwhelmed by greed, jealousy, lust, false views, and all kinds of negative thoughts. Not knowing how to deal with them, Meghiya just couldn't seem to get started so he came back to report to the Buddha, who responded not with blame, but with a teaching. The Buddha taught the spiritually immature Meghiya five things that conduce to spiritual maturity. The first of these is spiritual friendship, because Meghiya had disregarded the spiritual friendship and companionship of the Buddha. The second is the practice of ethical action; the third, serious discussion of the Dharma; fourthly, the application of energy to eliminate negative mental states and develop positive ones; and then, fifthly, there is insight, the deep understanding of universal impermanence. In Meghiya's case, it is noteworthy that the Buddha put spiritual friendship first. Meghiya just hadn't realized the extent to which he was dependent on the spiritual friendship and companionship of the Buddha, but instead thought he was ready to go off and meditate on his own, only to discover quite quickly that he wasn't ready at all.

We ourselves are in much the same position. Like Meghiya, we need spiritual friends and it is very difficult to make any spiritual progress without them, although for us, personal contact with the Buddha himself is no longer a possibility. Nonetheless, even if it were, we would probably end up behaving little differently from Meghiya due to our lack of receptivity, but we do have one another, and that is enough. We can develop spiritual friendship amongst ourselves, giving help and encouragement in our practice of the Dharma. We can confess our faults and weaknesses to our spiritual friends, sharing our understandings and rejoicing in one another's merits. It goes without saying that we need also to practise the Dharma ourselves. No one can practise it for us, but even so, we do not have to practise on our own. We can live our Dharma lives in the company of other like-minded people, and this is the best way to practise. In fact we may say that for us it is the only way. In his teaching to Meghiya, the Buddha made this very clear.

On another occasion, apparently some years later, the Buddha was staying at a place called Sakkara, and while he was there his disciple and cousin, Ānanda, came to see him. Ānanda happened to say that he thought that spiritual friendship must be half the spiritual life. The Buddha immediately told him not to speak in such a way. 'Spiritual friendship is not half the spiritual life,' said the Buddha, 'it is the *whole* of the spiritual life.'[368] This is a statement that we may find rather puzzling. We can understand that friendship is important, being one of the six primary relationships of human life. But the idea that friendship, even spiritual friendship, should be the whole of the spiritual life, we might find difficult to fathom.

To make things clearer, we need to look at the language the Buddha uses. The Pāli term that I've translated as 'spiritual friendship' is *kalyāṇa mittatā* (Sanskrit *kalyāṇa mitratā*), a very expressive term that is more poetic than philosophic. *Kalyāṇa* means beautiful, charming, auspicious, helpful, morally good. The connotation is both aesthetic and moral and covers much the same ground as the Greek expression '*kalos*' meaning 'beautiful', 'good', and 'noble'. Taken together with *mitratā*, or companionship, the phrase *kalyāṇa mitratā* gives us 'beautiful friendship', 'morally good companionship', or as I've translated it, 'spiritual friendship'. It is this 'spiritual friendship' or *kalyāṇa mitratā* that the Buddha has declared to be the whole of what I've translated as 'the spiritual life', which appears in the Pāli as *brahmacariya* (Sanskrit *brahmacarya*). This sometimes means celibacy or chastity, that is to say abstention from sex, but its meaning here is much wider. *Brahmacarya* consists of two parts and the first, *brahma*, means high, noble, best, sublime, or even real. It also means divine, not in the theistic sense, but as the embodiment of all the best and noblest qualities and virtues. The second part, *carya*, means walking, faring, practising, experiencing, and also living. So *brahmacarya* can mean 'practising the best', 'experiencing the ideal', living 'the divine life', or as I translate it here, 'the spiritual life'. To gain a fuller sense of this, we shall have to look a little more into the Pāli terminology. In early Buddhism there's a whole series of terms beginning with this word '*brahma*' including in particular *brahmaloka*, meaning 'sublime realm', 'divine world', or 'spiritual world' in the highest sense. The *brahmacarya* or spiritual life is therefore that way of life that leads to the *brahmaloka* or spiritual world. But by virtue of what quality is it able to do so?

We find the answer to this question in the *Mahāgovinda Sutta,* another early Buddhist text. In this *sutta,* a question is asked regarding how a mortal being might be able to reach the immortal – *brahma* – world, passing from the transient to become eternal.[369] The answer given is short and simple. One reaches the *brahma* world by giving up all possessive thoughts, all thoughts of egotism and selfishness. In other words, one reaches the *brahmaloka* by giving up any sense of 'I'. Now we have our answer to the question of why spiritual friendship is the whole of the spiritual life. As we saw earlier, you share everything with your spiritual friends. You speak to them kindly and affectionately and show concern for their welfare, especially their spiritual welfare. You treat your spiritual friends in the same way that you treat yourself. You treat them equally. Spiritual friendship is, therefore, a training in unselfishness, and it is in egolessness that the true meaning of spiritual friendship consists.

In *kalyāṇa mitratā*, you relate to your spiritual friends in accordance with the *mettā* mode and thus you learn gradually to relate to all living beings in just the same way. This is why we regard it as a training, because relating to all beings in accordance with the *mettā* mode is by no means easy. It goes against the grain of our natural selfishness. The development of spiritual friendship is very difficult. In fact, leading the spiritual life, and being a Buddhist – a real Buddhist – is itself very difficult. That's why we need help, and we get it, as I've said, from one another. Even though we can't perhaps be with our spiritual teacher all the time, we can be with our spiritual friends at least much of the time. We can work with them in what is called in the FWBO a team-based right livelihood business. We can live with them in a spiritual community, especially a single-sex spiritual community. As we spend time with spiritual friends in this way, we will get to know each other much better and learn to be more open, more honest. We will also be brought up against our own weaknesses, especially against our natural inborn tendency to operate in accordance with the power mode. But if we have spiritual friends, they will help us to learn to operate in accordance with the *mettā* mode and become less selfish, more egoless. We will begin to see that spiritual friendship is indeed the whole of the religious life, and to realize from our own experience what true friendship in Buddhism really means.

ENTERING THE SANGHA

Buddhafield festival, Devon, Summer 2007.[370]

To be here this weekend is a happy event. I've been hearing about Buddhafield for the last twelve years but this is the first time I've actually been able to see it with my own eyes, and to sit in the Padmasambhava yurt, tour around the healing area, and have lunch in the restaurant.

When I was told that I'd be giving my talk in the 'Dharma Parlour' tent, I thought it very appropriate, because the word '*pāla*' means protector: protector of the Dharma. But then I learned that the words were not '*Dharma pāla*', but 'Dharma Parlour', 'parlour' being a good old-fashioned English word with quite another meaning. I remember from my childhood a nursery rhyme that began: 'Will you walk into my parlour, said the spider to the fly.' So here I am in your parlour, in the centre of your web. We are in – or on – Buddhafield, in the Dharma Parlour tent, and all talking about sangha. So we've got Buddha, Dharma, and Sangha. That was very neat on the part of the organizers I'm sure.

A few words about Dharma. People often ask what we mean by Buddhism. What is it? What does it stand for? What are its teachings? In more than one passage in the Pāli scriptures the Buddha speaks in terms of what he calls the *Dharma-Vinaya*, *Dharma* meaning the more theoretical, or principial, aspect, whereas '*Vinaya*' means not just the monastic code but the more practical side of his teaching. On one occasion, when the Buddha addressed his disciples to explain what his *Dharma-Vinaya* was like, his explanation wasn't abstract or theoretical, but took the form of an image. My *Dharma-Vinaya*, he said, is like the great ocean. Just as the land slopes down gradually little by little into the great ocean depths, he said, in the same way, my teaching offers no sudden penetration. You go step-by-step, little by little.[371] This is an emphasis that we find throughout the Buddha's teaching. For instance, in the Noble Eightfold Path there are eight stages by which you penetrate gradually into the depths of the *Dharma-Vinaya*. And again, the Buddha said, in the great ocean there are many treasures: gold, silver, jewels – all sorts of wonderful and beautiful things. In the same way, he said, in my *Dharma-Vinaya* there are the treasures of the four noble truths, the Noble Eightfold Path, and the teachings on meditation and ethics, wisdom and compassion.

The teachings of the Buddha have already become quite well known in the West. In fact, there are now so many sources of information that sometimes we don't realize the great value of what we already have but instead go off to read all about the Theravāda, Zen, or Dzogchen looking for something further. But we must not overlook the fact that the Buddha, Dharma, and Sangha are themselves of inestimable spiritual value, and the fact that we refer to them as the Three Jewels is by no means without significance.

Again, the Buddha said, from whichever part of the great ocean you take water it all has the taste of salt. In the same way, whichever aspect of my teaching you encounter, it will lead to freedom, to *vimukti*. If it doesn't have that taste, he said, it isn't my teaching. This is a very important characteristic of the *Dharma-Vinaya* and something that we should be looking for, and using, so to speak, to help us to become free in the deepest and truest sense. Freedom can be understood on many levels and usually we can't approach it in its deepest and truest meaning straight away. The Buddha is talking here of liberation or *vimukti*, the ultimate freedom, but freedom is also essential on lower levels of experience, such as in the social, religious, or economic sphere. One needs the freedom to think, and to believe, and we cannot do without them.

We all need freedom, just as we need air, and my own experience years ago in India reminded me very forcibly of its importance to human beings. This was in the 1950s, when a widespread movement of conversion to Buddhism was taking place on the part of the former 'Untouchables', people living on the lowest level, socially and economically speaking, of the Indian caste system. This was – and to a great extent still is – a very rigid structure. There are those of high caste and those of low caste, and there are even people whose caste is so low that they don't have a proper caste at all. They were regarded as impure, and since any contact with this so-called Untouchable caste pollutes, the caste Hindu would avoid contact with anyone belonging to that community. Traditionally, the 'ex-Untouchables' were excluded from the temples and schools and were forbidden to engage in any kind of work other than the most menial and servile tasks.

This extreme oppression is to some extent still going on even today, but in 1956 an event of tremendous importance took place, not only for India, but even for some of us here in the West. A leader emerged from among the ex-Untouchables themselves by the name of Bhimrao Ambedkar.[372] Although he was born an Untouchable and suffered all the consequences of being one, he was nevertheless a kind of genius and he managed to educate himself and rise to one of the highest positions in Indian political life. He also became the leader of a very large section of the ex-Untouchables in Central and Western India. Dr Ambedkar saw at first hand the oppression and exclusion of his people in caste Hindu society, and he came to the conclusion that there was no future for them within the Hindu fold. If they wanted to improve themselves they would have to change their religion.

So fifty years ago, in Nagpur, Dr Ambedkar announced his own conversion to Buddhism, along with 400,000 of his followers who all took the same step with him. It was a momentous occasion. Many hundreds of thousands of others soon followed their example, and all of them, at a stroke, were no longer Hindus, but Buddhists. In this unprecedented situation, they naturally looked to their leader Dr Ambedkar for guidance, but very soon afterwards, disaster struck. Only a few weeks later, Dr Ambedkar died and, at least from the point of view of the Dharma, this left them with nowhere to turn. I was present in India at that time, and I and some others decided that we had to act quickly. From then onwards, much of my time in the 1950s was spent moving about different parts of India, giving Dharma talks and lectures to different groups of these new Buddhists. I am reminded of that very much today because they were always sitting on the floor just as you are now.

In my travels I sometimes asked people what difference it had made to them, now that they had become Buddhists, and I always got the same answer. Nobody ever said, 'I'm a bit better educated now' or 'now I can go to a Buddhist temple'. No, they all said that 'now I'm a Buddhist I feel free'. It was this sense of freedom that was psychologically and spiritually most important to them. As Buddhists they felt free not only to take charge of their own lives, but to make progress in every respect. Even outside observers have noted that those ex-Untouchables who became Buddhists have progressed much further than those who did not convert, making headway not just in religious terms but also socially and economically.

This is the importance of a sense of freedom, and I expect it is one of the reasons why you come to Buddhafield: to get away from the city and be free to do things that perhaps you wouldn't be able to do at home. People really value that feeling of freedom to breathe, to run around, to get away from the usual routine, and this is especially good for children. When I was a child I was always out playing in the street but I have heard it said that children aren't allowed to do that any longer because it's too dangerous. Here, of course, children are also free to play, roam, and run around. Buddhafield is such a safe place for children that it has a high reputation with parents and that's a really great testimony to the people who have been organizing and running it all these years. It is one of Buddhafield's many virtues.

Freedom, however, has its opposite, and that is restriction, even imprisonment. Sometimes we feel as though we're living in captivity all the time, there are so many things we can't do, places we can't go, so many prohibitions of every kind. It has even been said that human life itself is like a prison, with so many limitations, and people try to deal with this in different ways. Some might not even realize it's a prison, but be quite happy trying to make things more comfortable rather than planning an escape. Others, well aware of their confinement, might try to show their defiance by writing things on the wall, perhaps even really rude things, but since they remain imprisoned it's not defiance in the truest sense. This brings to mind the famous simile in Plato's *Republic* of the cave and the prisoners who live there. According to Plato it's a deep, dark cave and the people sit facing the rear wall, bound and shackled so that they can't turn around. Behind them shines a light, but they can't see it directly, nor the shapes and objects moving in it; all they can see are the shadows cast on the wall in front of them.[373] In this way Plato gives us a vivid sense of our own existential situation.

We are in captivity, bound and fettered, and we see only shadows, not the realities of things.

This idea is also present in the Buddha's teaching. When the Buddha speaks of the opposite of freedom, or *vimukti*, he uses the Pāli word *saṃyojana*, which roughly translates as fetter or bond.[374] It's a significant image, and if we want to make any progress at all on the spiritual path, there are certain fetters that we simply have to break, especially the first few that we encounter. The first fetter is what the Buddha calls *satkāya-dṛṣṭi*, rendered literally as 'fixed personality view'. It's the sort of fixed view that identifies us as being this or that, a particular nationality, say, or a parent, or an artist, and we identify very strongly with it in the belief that it is 'us'. But the fixed view that thinks 'this is me' and clings to it militates against the possibility of change. And so, because the fixed view tends to limit us, we have to adopt a creative attitude in the conviction that we are free to remake ourselves as we wish.

In this regard I recently came across a book entitled *The First Man-Made Man*.[375] It was about the transsexual, the person who, perhaps by means of surgical operations or hormone treatment, effects a change from his or her sex at birth, hence the 'man-made man'. I was especially interested because many years ago someone who had undergone this change, in his case from female to male, came to stay with me at my vihara in Kalimpong.[376] This was the first time I had come across this, and I remember our having a number of conversations as I tried to find out what had made a 'her' want to be a 'him'. In the end, I came to the conclusion that this way of bringing about change was rather forced and external. I felt that it was not so much the body that had to be worked on and changed, but the mind, so as to bring about transformation at a deeper level. And while there are all sorts of ways to work on the mind, one of the principal methods is meditation. Through meditation we can transmute our ordinary everyday consciousness into something higher, even into something sublime.

So that's 'fixed personality view', the idea that 'we are what we are' and, since that's what we are, 'that's the way we are going to stay'. This is the first fetter that has to be broken, and it involves radical transformation, which is not nearly as easy as many people think. We may sometimes say to ourselves that we want to change and develop, but deep down there often remains very strong resistance indeed. In fact, once you decide upon really radical change, you have a battle on your hands. This fundamental change, this radical transformation, not only of consciousness but also of the will, is what the spiritual life, from the Buddhist point of view, is largely concerned with. That's the challenge of the first fetter. There are a number of other fetters, but I'll just mention two more.

The second of the fetters is called in Sanskrit *vicikitsā*, and this is usually translated as doubt. But *vicikitsā* is more than just uncertainty. In your heart of hearts, it's that you don't actually want to find out the truth, whatever it may be, and this is why one of the translations of *vicikitsā* is 'sceptical doubt'. You are resistant to the truth and put forward all sorts of excuses and objections. In meditation, for instance, you might start having doubts about how effective it is and wondering whether some other meditation or even some entirely different activity might be better. And that sceptical doubt produces an uncertainty which prevents you from committing yourself wholeheartedly to what you are doing. Your mind waivers as you go from this idea to that, continually questioning whatever it is you have set your mind to do.[377]

The third and last fetter that I'm going to speak about is *śīlavrata-parāmarśa*, usually translated as 'attachment to rules and observances'. Just as with the first fetter, you have to interpret rather than translate to find the real meaning, and this is perhaps paraphrased best as 'just going through the motions'. You might have taken up the practice of puja, for instance, or meditation, and maybe you do it every day for a while, but as time goes on you might sense that you're not really 'doing' it any more, but just going through the stages of the practice in a superficial manner. You may well believe that to 'go through the motions' in that way must be doing you good, but if that is your view, it has become another fetter holding you back. No spiritual practice will do you any good unless you can do it with your whole heart and soul, and that is what this third fetter is all about. It's the fetter of doing your meditation or puja just half-heartedly, not putting the whole of yourself into it. There's a verse in the Bible – I do sometimes quote the Bible – that goes, 'Whatever your hand finds to do, do it with all your might.'[378] I think that's the secret of success in many fields, and that includes spiritual practice. You don't necessarily have to devote a lot of time to meditation or Dharma study, but whatever time you do devote to it, you must put your whole heart into it. After all, if you really do believe in what you're doing, you will do it with the whole of yourself. It's only that sort of practice that can help us break this fetter of *śīlavrata-parāmarśa*.

All these kinds of wrong attitude – fixed view, sceptical doubt, and going through the motions – are fetters that inhibit our practice of the Dharma. They prevent us in the end from realizing *vimukti* or freedom and we need to break them. So I would like to give my own version of these three fetters that emphasizes their positive counterparts. These are what I call three Cs: let's be creative, be clear, and be committed. Be creative, first of all, in the sense of constantly working to recreate oneself, trying to fashion a better person, a more universal, more spacious person, and working to produce that higher kind of self from day to day. And then, secondly, be clear. Try to clarify your ideas, don't be vague or woolly in your thinking, and don't allow yourself to be overpowered by sceptical doubt, but be absolutely clear. And then lastly, be committed. Whatever you do, commit yourself to it, especially any form of religious practice, such as meditation, and any relationship, especially friendship. Commit yourself to it wholeheartedly and without reservation; be committed.

If, on higher and higher levels, you can be creative, clear, and committed then you can be sure that before long you will be able to enjoy a deep understanding of freedom, the true meaning of the Buddha's teaching. Once you have achieved that freedom, then you will be able not only to benefit from that understanding yourself, but also to benefit others with it, and help them also to achieve *vimukti*, the freedom that is the highest spiritual goal.

THE REFUGE TREE

Taraloka, Shropshire, England. Chairs' Assembly, January 2009.

The idea of the refuge tree became familiar to me when I was in Kalimpong, where at one point I possessed a large and magnificent thangka of the Refuge Tree executed in accordance with the Gelugpa tradition. It showed Tsongkhapa as the central figure, accompanied by all the important gurus and teachers of that particular tradition. It was heavily stylized, with Tsongkhapa in the middle, his successors below him, and his spiritual ancestors above. To the left were the bodhisattvas, to the right the *arhants*. From a distance it looked rather like a cross (which I didn't think was quite appropriate). I no longer have that thangka; one of my Tibetan friends, Rechung Rimpoche, a Gelugpa, begged it from me because he didn't have one and he thought it quite important. As he was a Gelugpa and I was not, I thought he should have it.

After that I saw quite a number of different Refuge Trees, not only of the Gelugpa lineage but also of the Nyingmapa and Kagyupa traditions. Decades later, when I was back in England and had started the Western Buddhist Order, it suddenly occurred to me one day that we ought to have a Refuge Tree of our own, but one that was a bit different from the Tibetan Refuge Trees with which I was familiar. All those Refuge Trees were sectarian, relating to one particular school or lineage of teachers and disciples, and I decided that our Refuge Tree should be rather broader, more ecumenical – though I'm not completely happy to use that word. It's true that I used it to describe one of the six distinctive emphases of the FWBO, but 'ecumenical' derives from the Christian tradition, and I hope that over time we will able to find a more appropriate term.

From its original home in India, the Dharma spread to Tibet, China, South-east Asia, and Japan, and many great spiritual luminaries have arisen in all those countries and given important teachings and lived very inspiring lives. I wanted a Refuge Tree that would represent the whole history of Buddhism in the East, including the principal representative figures, especially those who were founders of schools or important spiritual traditions. There are hundreds, even thousands, of such teachers, and our Refuge Tree couldn't contain them all, so I decided to limit the number to those figures who were the best known and the most important historically and spiritually. In that way I arrived at the selection of figures of the teachers of the past which is now on our Refuge Tree. What I had in mind was not that we should be following all the teachings and practices of every one of those teachers. That would be rather a lot. I was thinking in a much more general way that they were all figures by whom we could be inspired. They were all great teachers, great spiritual figures, but they lived very different lives, and we could be inspired by all of them in different ways.

I think, for instance, of Atīśa and that occasion when he was invited by the king of Western Tibet to visit his country. Atīśa consulted his *yidam* or *iṣṭa devatā*, the bodhisattva Tārā.[379] We don't know how she spoke to him, whether it was in a vision or whether he cast lots which he interpreted, but howsoever it was, Tārā said to him, 'It's a good idea that you should go to Tibet in response to the invitation that you've received. But I must tell you that if you do go, your life will be shortened by twelve years.' Atīśa thought, 'It's for the sake of spreading the Dharma in a country where the Dharma has scarcely taken root, so never mind. Let me sacrifice twelve years of my life, it doesn't matter.' When I think of Atīśa I don't think so much of the teachings he gave or of the books he wrote, some of which are still available. I think of his willingness to sacrifice a whole slice of his life for the sake of spreading the Dharma in Tibet. That is what inspires me when I think of him.

And then there's that other well-known figure connected with Tibet: Padmasambhava. There are several biographies of Padmasambhava, and there are a mass of legends and miracles and strange phenomena connected with him. But when I think of Padmasambhava, when I remember and visualize him, it's not by those wonders that I am so much impressed. For me, Padmasambhava means something a little different. I think of the story of how Śāntarakṣita, the bodhisattva abbot as he was called, was trying to build the great monastery of Samye, but how the walls the workmen built each day were destroyed overnight by the demons of Tibet, who weren't very happy with the introduction of this new religion, Buddhism. So Padmasambhava was called upon. He made his way to Tibet and we're told he succeeded in bringing the demons of Tibet under control. To my mind that's the most significant feature of Padmasambhava's life.[380]

But what do we mean by the demons of Tibet? What are demons? I have an open mind about the objective existence of demons, having seen what I think were one or two. But I think the demons of Tibet really stood for all those deeply-rooted ethnic Tibetan attitudes that stood in the way of the practice of the Dharma. They had to be overcome, both in their collective and their individual forms, before the Dharma could be introduced and really practised. In the West, too, there are all sorts of demons that we have to battle with and try to overcome. I don't wish to cast Christianity in the role of demon. It has acted demonically on occasion in the past, but there are other more deeply-seated demons. We've been hearing about them in the course of the last few weeks in connection with the economic life of the world, where it seems there has been a great big demon of greed abroad. That's one of the biggest demons that needs to be controlled, even exorcized. When I started teaching in the West and talking about the Buddha's Noble Eightfold Path it occurred to me that we had to develop right means of livelihood. It wasn't enough that Buddhists in the West should simply abstain from obviously unethical means of livelihood; we had to have a much more radical economic vision than that. We therefore developed the idea of team-based right livelihood as one of the ways in which we can help bring under control the demon of economic greed. That's what Padmasambhava stands for, so far as I am concerned, and what inspires me when I think of him: his bringing under control the deep-seated demons of unskilfulness, greed, hatred, and delusion.

Going across to China, there's Huineng, the sixth patriarch of the Zen tradition. In the opening chapter of the *Platform Sūtra*, the text by which I was so deeply influenced in my early days, Huineng gives a brief autobiographical sketch. We learn how he came from a very poor family and earned his livelihood selling firewood, and how one day he heard someone reciting the *Diamond Sūtra* and had a sort of awakening. It wasn't a full or total awakening – that came much later – but it set him on the spiritual path. He joined a monastery and, being a simple, uneducated man, he was given the task of chopping firewood and pounding rice. So he spent eight months pounding rice ... pounding rice ... pounding rice. That in a way was his spiritual practice. He'd had this insight and perhaps he was turning it over and over in his mind as he pounded away. Then one day he caused to be written on the wall of the meeting hall a stanza which showed that indeed he had some insight. The abbot recognized this, and it was eventually this humble illiterate man who became the Sixth Patriarch. I find the story of Huineng's life very inspiring as it shows that even without book knowledge it's possible to go a very long way in the spiritual life. I used to stress this in the early days of the Movement because some of the people who came to us weren't as highly educated as the rest and they sometimes felt that there wasn't much hope for them in the spiritual life. This was quite a wrong view, and to counter it I used to emphasize the example of Huineng. I've always been inspired by his story. What it conveys for me is that ultimately what we want is not book learning, or even culture, but a spiritual awakening: clear vision, *vipaśyanā*.

Staying in China, there's also the figure of Zhiyi, a great spiritual teacher, and a very remarkable man intellectually.[381] By his time, in the sixth century CE, an enormous mass of Buddhist scriptures had been translated into Chinese. There were hundreds and hundreds of them, Hīnayāna scriptures and Mahāyāna *śāstras* and *sūtras*. Zhiyi was quite puzzled by the fact that these scriptures didn't give the same teaching, and some of them even seemed to contradict one another, so he set himself to study all of them and eventually he organized them into different periods. First of all, he said, the Buddha taught one particular *sūtra*, the *Avataṃsaka*, but because it was so difficult for people to understand, he decided to teach what in Pāli we have as the four *Nikāyas*, corresponding in Sanskrit to the *Āgamas* of the Sarvāstivādins. This was what Zhiyi called the Buddha's 'Deer Park' period. Then, in the second period of his teaching, the Buddha taught mixed Hīnayāna and Mahāyāna, and in the last period, he taught pure Mahāyāna, especially the *White Lotus Sūtra*. In this way, Zhiyi tried to make sense of the Buddhist scriptures on the basis of his belief that all this mass of *sūtras*, Hīnayāna and Mahāyāna both, had quite literally been personally preached by the Buddha at different stages of his life. We can't any longer accept Zhiyi's classification, but in principle he offers us a great example. In the West we too are confronted by a great mass of Buddhist scriptures, perhaps an even greater number than Zhiyi had access to, and we also have to make some sense of them and try to understand how they relate to one another as well as to the Buddha's original teaching. For me, Zhiyi represents the spirit of inquiry into the Buddhist scriptures. He is a great exemplar and source of inspiration as regards this more ecumenical attitude to the Buddhist scriptures.

In this way, the teachers of the past on the Refuge Tree are sources of spiritual inspiration. I'm not so much inspired by the specific teachings of this or that figure as by the story of their lives. It is not that I intended that the Western Buddhist Order should be a platform for all the different teachings and practices of those teachers of the past. In fact, it is very difficult to follow all the different teachings simultaneously. While not exactly contradictory, some of them disagree with others. We can't imagine Buddhaghosa agreeing with Shinran, for instance. So far as I'm concerned it's more a question of our being inspired by them in different ways and as a result of that inspiration doing what we can, here and now, to practise and spread the Dharma.

The most inspiring figure on the whole refuge tree is of course that of the Buddha himself, and it's very important that we should know as much as we can about his life. There are several traditional biographies of the Buddha, but broadly speaking the closest we can get to him as a historical personality is through the older portions of the Pāli canon. If we can become acquainted with those parts of the canon and get to know as much as we can about his life, the Buddha becomes a living figure for us, not just some distant personage vaguely seen in the remote distance of history.

There's another way in which we can get a deeper sense of the Buddha, even of the presence of the Buddha, and that is by visiting the principal places associated with his life, and in particular the four great holy places: Lumbini, where the Buddha was born; Bodh Gaya, where he gained Enlightenment; Sarnath, where he gave his first teaching; and Kusinārā, where he passed away. I can certainly remember my own association with these places. During my time in India I visited them all, two of them a number of times, although not quite in the correct order for purely accidental reasons. The first that I visited was Sarnath, then came Kusinārā, where I received my *śrāmaṇera* ordination, then Lumbini, and fourthly and lastly came Bodh Gaya.

Bodh Gaya has recently been very much in the consciousness of the Order, because that is where our international Order convention is going to be held later this year. I won't be going myself for various reasons, mainly age and health, but I hope that the Western wing of the Order will be very well represented. I know that to have so many of their Western brothers and sisters with them on that occasion will mean a very great deal to our Indian Order members. Some of them have been able to take part in our UK conventions in past years but, for obvious financial reasons, only in very small numbers. However, on this occasion they will be very well represented indeed and I hope that the Western wing of the Order will be no less so. For those who haven't been to Bodh Gaya before, it will also be an opportunity to make a pilgrimage to that place and perhaps to other places as well.

I have spoken about the Refuge Tree in general, about some of the teachers of the past, and about the Buddha, but something else can be seen on the Refuge Tree that I haven't yet touched upon. On the Refuge Tree we also have a lot of books. All the scriptures are there, all the *sūtras* that have come down to us, whether in the original Pāli or translated from Sanskrit into Chinese, or Tibetan, or Japanese. We're in the fortunate position of having access to far more of the scriptures than perhaps any previous generation of Buddhists. While that can be inspiring, it can also be quite confusing. Are some more important than others, or more relevant to us than others? Which should we study? To help with this, I want to mention an important principle that was enunciated in one of the scriptures, and which I have spoken about in the past: the four reliances.

These are reliance on the Dharma not on the person, reliance on the spirit as opposed to the letter of the Dharma, reliance on the scriptures of obvious meaning rather than the scriptures of recondite meaning, and reliance on *jñāna* or wisdom rather than *vijñāna*.[382] We are concerned here with the third reliance, reliance on *nītārtha* rather than *neyārtha* scriptures. Very broadly, there are two classes of scriptures: those the meaning of which is quite obvious and those whose meaning requires some explanation if they are not to be misunderstood. For example, when the *Dhammapada* says that 'hatred does not cease by hatred, it ceases only by love', that is to be taken quite literally. It doesn't require any explanation, we just have to try to practise it. But also in the *Dhammapada* there's a verse which says that 'after killing mother and father, the monk or the Brahmin goes free'.³⁸³ This certainly requires some explanation, the explanation being that the 'mother' and the 'father' are ignorance and greed. This is a very obvious example, but we need to apply this principle much more broadly. When we look at the whole mass of Buddhist scriptures, we should direct our attention primarily to those texts the meaning of which is clear and obvious and in no need of explanation. Those that apparently require explanation should be interpreted and understood in the light of the teachings of those scriptures the meaning of which is quite clear.

When we apply this criterion to the Pāli scriptures, to the four *Nikāyas* plus the *Udāna*, *Sutta-Nipāta*, *Dhammapada*, and so on, it's very clear that there's not much that needs explanation. Some of it may be difficult to understand or difficult to practise – that's another matter – but there's not much that needs explanation, much less still that needs to be explained away. Perhaps in the case of some of the supernormal phenomena some explanation is required, but the actual teachings, such as that of the Noble Eightfold Path, don't require much explanation. All they require is that we should do our best to practise them. There are some occasions when the Buddha does give a teaching that requires explanation, but then he at once proceeds to give the explanation himself, so again there's no problem. For instance, having told the parable of the smouldering anthill, he proceeds to explain what the smouldering anthill is, why it smoulders, and so on, and when he tells the parable of the blind men and the elephant, he goes on to explain what he means by it.³⁸⁴ On the whole, the Buddha's teachings in the *Nikāyas* of the Pāli canon either require no explanation or are explained within the text itself.

When we come to the Mahāyāna *sūtras* it's a different story. There are some that don't require explanation. The Perfection of Wisdom *sūtras* are difficult, but they don't have to be explained in the sense of a deeper recondite meaning having to be brought forth, a meaning that is different from the surface meaning. But many of the Mahāyāna scriptures do require explanation. I'm thinking for instance of the *Sūtra of Golden Light*, which is especially important on account of its chapter on confession. I gave a series of talks on this *sūtra* under the heading

'Transforming Self and World'[385] and several people have told me that had I not given those talks, they wouldn't have been able to make head or tail of the *sūtra*. The *Sūtra of Golden Light* requires quite a lot of explanation and also interpretation.

Perhaps I should make a distinction here between explanation and interpretation. Parts of the Perfection of Wisdom teachings may require explanation, but they don't require interpretation. The *Sūtra of Golden Light*, like a lot of other *sūtras*, requires interpretation because it contains so much symbolism. So we are to interpret those *sūtras* that require interpretation in the light of those that do not. We can conclude that, very broadly speaking, the Mahāyāna scriptures require interpretation in the light of the – I don't like to say 'Hīnayāna' or 'Theravāda' – but in the light of the *Nikāyas*, and that will give us a criterion. Sometimes we may find that when we try to interpret some Mahāyāna texts they are not in accordance with the teachings in the *Nikāyas*, or even represent a departure from the Buddha's original teaching, and this is quite important. But if we use the *Nikāya* teachings to interpret the Mahāyāna teachings, that will ensure a greater consistency in our teaching and in the way we communicate the Dharma.

Going back to the figures of the past, as I said, when I included them on the Refuge Tree I did not mean to suggest that we would necessarily be practising all their different teachings. Their value is of a different kind. When I think of those teachers, I think of their lives, and it is their lives that I find inspiring. It's the same with the teachers of the present. I had the good fortune, especially when I was in Kalimpong, to come into contact with some very highly developed and important teachers, but when I look back to my contact with them it seems to me that what was important for me then, and perhaps even more so now, was not so much the teachings and *sādhanas* I received from them, but the inspiration I received from them and from contemplating what they were. What they were was more important to me than what they said. It was as though what they were was much bigger than what they taught. Nowadays, if I happen to do a *sādhana* that I was given by one or another of them, as soon as I start the *sādhana* they at once spring to mind and I have a very vivid sense of their presence. It's as though they transcend their own teaching. Life can never find full expression, and in the case of a spiritual teacher, his or her spiritual teaching never fully expresses their realization. If one has personal contact with a teacher, one gets much closer to him or her than one does through their teaching, especially if that teaching comes only through words. I can certainly say that when I contemplate the teachers of the past and the teachers of the present – who with one exception are now also teachers of the past – I gain great inspiration from them.[386] I'm not so much concerned with the details of their teachings. I'm much more concerned with them as sources of inspiration. They inspire me to do what I can for the Dharma, just as they all did in very different circumstances and in the course of their very different lives.

LIVING WITH ETHICS

Sangharakshita launches Living Ethically *at the Birmingham Buddhist Centre, FWBO Day celebration, 11 April 2009.*

When I was preparing this talk on ethics, the Pāli word *kataññutā* floated into my mind.[387] It means gratitude, appreciating all the efforts that people have made on one's behalf. Very often we express our gratitude by thanking people and appreciating what they've given us, and that's what I want to do this evening, first of all towards Vidyadevi. When I first suggested that Vidyadevi should undertake the editing of what was then to be called *The Sangharakshita Reader*, she readily and graciously assented. But that was three or more years ago, and while progress was not exactly slow, there was a lot to do. I used to phone Vidyadevi from time to time to ask how she was getting on and the day finally came when she had assembled all her material, arranged it into an aesthetic form, and sent it off to Wisdom Publications, and even though it was twice the length they had originally been thinking of, Wisdom accepted it as it was. I am very grateful to Vidyadevi for what she has done in creating the collection, which was published under the title *The Essential Sangharakshita*.[388]

Somebody else I want to thank is Samacitta, who worked with me on the final editing of *Living Ethically*.[389] Much work had already been done on the seminar transcript on which the book is based, but there was still more to do. Samacitta used to come along whenever she could, once or twice a day, and read me what had been edited. I dictated additions and clarifications, and also quite ruthlessly cut some of the stories and even some of the digressions which, though quite good in themselves, didn't really belong in that particular work. I reasoned that they'd impede the flow of the exposition, and in any case I've told them elsewhere. It was a great joy to work with Samacitta, because she was not only regular in coming, and not only intelligent, but also a very cheerful presence. Sometimes when people come to see me they can be a little downcast, or even depressed, but not Samacitta. She was always bright, always ready to start work straight away. I am very grateful to her for what she has done in this connection, and I thank her heartily for the many pleasant and enjoyable hours that we spent together working on what eventually became *Living Ethically*.

A word or two now about the book itself. *Living Ethically* is based on a seminar I gave in 1976 on the *Ratnamāla* or *Precious Garland* by Nāgārjuna.[390] This is a work of some five hundred Sanskrit verses, and *Living Ethically* is based upon half of them. The reason for this is that the *Ratnamāla* is rather a medley, a mixture of ethical teachings and teachings about wisdom, and at an earlier stage of the process, Vidyadevi – her finger is in this little pie too – very deftly separated out the teachings about ethics and arranged them as a separate book. In *Living Ethically* we have Nāgārjuna's exposition of the ten precepts, with my own commentary, and my application of some of them to the conditions of modern life. The book is the latest in a series which began with *Living with Awareness*, continued with *Living with Kindness*, and continuing in a way with *The Yogi's Joy*, now carries on with *Living Ethically*.[391]

After Samacitta and I had concluded our work, I started to reflect more about ethics, not so much as presented by Nāgārjuna but in the sense that we often regard the ethical status of an action as dependent upon the state of mind by which it's accompanied. Thus if our actions spring from greed, hatred, or delusion, they're called unskilful, and if they spring from the opposite of those states, we call them wholesome, or, if you like, ethical. However, I felt there should really be something more to it than that, because if we look at the precepts, we find that they're not really so much about our own mental state as about our attitude towards other people and the way in which we treat them. The first precept, for instance, is not just a matter of keeping our own minds free from feelings of anger or hatred, though it is that also, but perhaps even more importantly it's about treating others in a way that not only doesn't harm them, but actually brings them benefit. The same is true of the second precept. Regardless of our intentions, if we take something that doesn't belong to us, we've affected other people and as a result they suffer. Conversely, if we practise generosity, the corresponding positive precept, then we affect others positively by being helpful to them.

We can look at all the precepts in this way. They're not only concerned with the purity of our own mental state but with our attitudes towards others, the way we treat them and feel for them. They're concerned, in other words, with putting ourselves in another person's shoes, although this isn't nearly as easy as it sounds. We can often be so wrapped up in how things affect us that we don't give sufficient thought to how our actions are affecting other people, and this amounts to a certain indifference with regard to them. So how can we make it easier to think, or even experience, what it's really like to be that other person? I believe the faculty we need is imagination. It is the imaginative faculty that enables us to bridge this gap between self and other. There's much that could be said on this subject, but this evening I'd like us to think of imagination as being of two kinds: the horizontal and the vertical.

In what I'm calling horizontal imagination, our imaginative faculty can be highly active but nonetheless limited to an ordinary level of consciousness. This is the sort of imagination about which Samuel Johnson writes in his philosophical novel *Rasselas*, in a chapter entitled 'The Dangerous Prevalence of Imagination'.[392] The mind's wonderful propensity for thinking up schemes and situations can easily be activated by emotions such as greed, as when your mind strays towards what it would be like to win the lottery. Within a matter of seconds you are working out the practicalities of buying the biggest and most expensive car, a holiday in the Bahamas, or a trip round the world. If activated by fearful thoughts, on the other hand, you might start to ponder your prospects for survival if there was an earthquake, or what would happen if you lost all your money and you became a pauper. How would people treat you? How would you manage? Falling prey to fear can easily activate the horizontal imagination, even to the extent of paranoia, and in all sorts of other ways, too, our emotions can set the imagination wandering. Then we become immersed in our fantasies, and forget the reality of where we actually are. This is what I am calling the horizontal imagination, but what of the vertical dimension?

If the horizontal imagination is confined to the flat plane of worldly activity, the vertical imagination goes upwards, taking flight in search of higher things. This is imagination understood in the more creative sense of which the English Romantic poets wrote. Think, for example, of William Blake's famous lines,

> When the Sun rises do you not see a round Disk of fire somewhat
> like a Guinea? O no no. I see an Innumerable company of
> the Heavenly host, crying 'Holy Holy Holy is the Lord God
> Almighty.'[393]

The vertical imaginative faculty lifts us out of ourselves and enables us to identify, to some extent at least, with other people, and to put ourselves in their place. The Pāli scriptures do not appear at first glance to have a word for this kind of vertical imagination as I've called it, but something nonetheless corresponds to it. This is what's sometimes called the *divya-cakṣu*, or 'divine eye'.

Buddhist literature speaks of a whole series of eyes. We find the eye of the flesh, and then the divine eye, and beyond that the Dharma eye and the Buddha eye, but it is with the divine eye that we are concerned at the moment, and this is what I've identified with the vertical imagination. The Buddha possessed the divine eye, as well as the other eyes, and it is with that divine eye that the Buddha, after his Enlightenment, looked out upon humanity. But when he did so, what did he see? Certainly not a world of nasty grovelling little creatures, as Swift might perhaps have seen them.[394] No, with the eye of imagination, with his divine eye, the Buddha saw a world of lotus flowers, all in different stages of development. He recognized the potential that every ordinary human being has within them and it was on that account that he decided to proclaim the Dharma for the benefit of beings. So that's why it's important that we follow the Buddha and try to develop just a little of that kind of imagination, the vertical imagination that puts us in the place of other people, which is able to appreciate them as living, growing, beings who aspire to something spiritual.

I've already spoken of my initial thoughts of gratitude, or *kataññutā*, as it is called in Pāli, and this is clearly relevant here. But something else also came to me: one final aphoristic thought concerning the relationship between ethics and non-duality. You may remember there's a chapter on non-duality in the talks I gave on the *Vimalakīrti-nirdeśa*,[395] and in that chapter I spoke of non-duality with regard to different pairs of opposites. In duality you have A as opposed to B, this as opposed to that. You have a pair of opposites, and we are all in the midst of this sort of experience most, if not all, of the time. But it also has a very direct ethical application, because alongside A as opposed to B, one also has self and other, you and me. So what is the entrance, here, to non-duality if we want to live more ethically? The door to non-duality here is surely imagination, the vertical imagination, about which I've been speaking. If we can develop this kind of imagination, even in some degree, then we shall be able to live more ethically, more wisely, and be able to put into practice the teachings that Nāgārjuna gives us in *Living Ethically*.

THE FWBO AND THE PATH OF
SPIRITUAL DEVELOPMENT

Buddhistische Zentrum Essen (Essen Buddhist Centre), Germany,
6 April 2009.

INTRODUCTION

Returning to Essen after so many years brings back vivid memories of my first visit more than two decades ago. At that time Dharmapriya had already set to work, and although a proper FWBO centre had yet to be set up, there were regular classes and also a community of sorts. I remember in particular the walks I had in Essen at that time. It's always been my habit to go for a morning walk, and in this case I would take the air in a large cemetery not far from where I was staying. It was a very well-kept cemetery, clean and tidy, with well-swept paths and a great many flowers on the graves, and it made quite an impression on me. I thought that, clearly, the people of Essen remember their dead and appreciate them, and they remember their anniversaries also. So it's fitting that today, here in Essen, we celebrate an anniversary of our own.

I. EARLY DAYS

Today is the forty-second anniversary of the founding of the FWBO. Twice forty-two is eighty-four, and since 84 is my age this year, it follows that I've spent the second half of my life entirely devoted to the FWBO. That I remember its beginnings quite clearly will perhaps come as no surprise to you. It all began right in the centre of London, not far from Trafalgar Square, in a basement room so small that it couldn't hold more than twenty people at most, squeezed together down a little winding stair that led from a shop upstairs.[396] I used to joke sometimes that we were holding our activities in the catacombs, just like the early Christians in Rome.

Once a week, I led two meditation practices, the mindfulness of breathing and the *mettā bhāvanā*, and alongside those classes I was also giving public lectures in central London, in places such as Kingsway Hall and Conway Hall. These were also attracting more and more people and gradually, as our activities expanded, we held classes on different evenings of the week. After a year or two, we arranged our first retreats in the countryside, hiring premises because we had no retreat centre of our own. These retreats were held during the Easter and summer holidays, and even though they lasted just one week I began to notice something interesting about the people who were coming along.

When they first arrived, the participants usually looked tired, sometimes even depressed, because in those days everybody had regular jobs and they had come straight from work. But as the days went by, people started to relax and became happier and more communicative, so that by the end of the week they looked really quite different. I found this amazing. We had done some meditation, but not much. I'd given a few talks, we'd done some communication exercises, and people had taken walks together and developed friendships. But these few simple things had been enough to create real change. So yes, I had to admit that the Dharma really does work.

I knew that it had worked in India, and certainly in the Buddha's time, but I wasn't so sure that it would be the same in the West. Nonetheless, the experience of these early retreats dispelled any doubts I may have had. You don't need to know all about esoteric meditation practices, or the philosophy of the Abhidharma, all you need to know are the basic teachings of the Buddha and be willing to practise them. That will be quite enough for you to develop as a human being and to start treading the spiritual path. A little Dharma goes a long way.

From these simple beginnings, in a tiny basement shrine-room, the FWBO grew. And that was forty-two years ago. I sometimes surprise myself with the thought that such an impressive movement could have had so humble a foundation. That's why, when people start a new centre of the FWBO and only a few people come along at first, I always tell them not to worry. That was just how we found things too, at the start.

Perhaps I should also mention that the FWBO began in the 1960s and 1970s, a time of change, even of revolution, quite literally with the 1968 Paris uprising, and the student demonstrations in the United States.[397] We had the beatniks and then the hippies, and all sorts of strange and unconventional things were going on. These were exciting times and people were thinking, yes, it's possible for things to change – it's possible for *us* to change. The Zeitgeist, to use the German word, was on our side, and we were going with the stream. All this contributed to the atmosphere in which the FWBO developed in its early stages, but inevitably, after perhaps a decade or two, the Zeitgeist changed. Perhaps it became more conservative, but in any case it was no longer quite so supportive of a new Buddhist movement such as ours was. We nonetheless carried on, and began gradually to attract more and more young people. One of the myths about the FWBO was that we *started* with young people, but that's not quite correct. Right at the beginning, people were not so youthful, let us say, and later on some of them dropped out. But when we had been going for five or six years a new wave of young, idealistic people appeared, and some of those are still with us. They may not be as young today as they were then, but they are still enthusiastic and no less idealistic. People like Lokamitra in India, Subhuti, Buddhadasa, Dhammadinna, and Malini are still very much with us and even though their hair might have turned as grey as mine is now, they're still young and idealistic at heart, and continuing to make a significant contribution to our movement.[398]

So even though the Zeitgeist was not always in our favour, as in the 1980s, we still carried on, and the FWBO continued to expand. Centres sprang up in different parts of Europe, in the USA, Australia, and New Zealand, and I visited all of them. On my first visit to Germany, I visited Aachen, Charlemagne's capital, the founder of the Holy Roman Empire. Subsequent visits to Germany took me to other important places in European history such as Weimar, which I had wanted to visit ever since my teens. Weimar was the city of Goethe, of Schiller, Beethoven, and Schopenhauer and, despite its modest size, it was a city of great cultural significance. I was nonetheless primarily based in England, where I was writing books and also giving more and more talks, some of which were subsequently published by the 'Spoken Word Project'.[399] I don't know exactly how many books I've written in my life, though it is quite a large number, but tonight I'd like to talk about one particular book, one that caused a certain question to arise in my mind. What that question was will become apparent later on.

2. PUBLICATION: THE ESSENCE OF THE TEACHINGS

A few years ago I was approached by Wisdom Publications, an American publishing house, to bring out a volume of selections from my writings to be called *The Sangharakshita Reader*. I was quite happy to agree. Vidyadevi, an English *dhammacārinī*, took on the responsibility of making the selection and organizing them into a suitable shape. Vidyadevi was working on this project for at least three years and during that time the publisher started thinking that a better title might be *The Pocket Sangharakshita*. Vidyadevi had to point out to them that she had accumulated so much material that it wasn't going to be a pocket volume, so a more appropriate title was needed. It was eventually agreed that it should be *The Essential Sangharakshita*, those parts of Sangharakshita's writings that you really must have, and it was published this year in January. *The Essential Sangharakshita* is now a volume of 800 pages, containing more than 160 extracts from, I'm told, 38 different books. Vidyadevi gave much thought to how to arrange that mass of material and eventually decided to organize it into five main sections, each of them presided over, as it were, by one of the five Jinas. Akṣobhya would preside over my more philosophical writings, Ratnasambhava over my writings on the arts, Amitābha would preside over my writings about friendship and meditation, and so on.

The book is now published, but with 800 pages and over 160 different extracts, *The Essential Sangharakshita* is still quite large. And this is when the question arose in my mind. If this represents the essence of my teachings, I wondered, what is the essence of this essence? What is it that I've been trying to communicate in the course of these last forty-two years? Whatever it was, the truth is that I had been trying to communicate it even before the days of the FWBO, because some of the extracts in *The Essential Sangharakshita* are from books and lectures I gave even before the Movement began. And the essence, I eventually decided, had to be that of human spiritual development, a process that I see proceeding by way of a series of stages. The Buddhist scriptures describe the stages of spiritual development in many places and in many ways, but they all represent different stages on a single path of spiritual development. Today, I would like to focus on three particularly significant stages in that process, the stages of integration, positive emotion, and spiritual death.[400]

THE STAGES OF THE PATH

1. Integration

If we were to single out the very first thing that we have to do in order to make any meaningful spiritual progress, it would be to bring our conflicting thoughts and emotions together into an integrated whole. If we look at our minds, and our lives, we find that we're pulled in so many different directions. Sometimes we want to do this kind of thing, at another time we want to do something entirely different, even quite contrary. Our energies are scattered, lacking integration. So the first thing that we have to try to do is to gather our scattered energies together, to bring them to bear on a single focus, a single leading principle, which for Buddhists is the ideal of Enlightenment. In practical terms, this begins with mindfulness. If we want to integrate ourselves we have to be aware of what is going on. I've sometimes spoken of four dimensions of mindfulness or awareness, and the first of these is what I'm calling awareness of our selves.

a. Self-awareness

Throughout all our activities, we need to be aware of what we're doing, what we're saying, and what we're thinking. It's very important that we pay attention to the totality of our activities, even though for most of the time that is not really the case. For example, at the moment I am standing here at this rostrum. I'm aware of my two hands resting on it, of my feet firmly planted on the floor, and of my whole body standing here. This is bodily awareness, which we need to try to maintain all the time, not only in our posture but also in our movements. If we wave our hand, we should be aware that, yes, we are waving our hand. If we're blowing our nose, yes, be aware of that also. If we practise mindfulness of the body and its movements in this way, it will help us develop a more integrated kind of awareness. It will probably also have the effect of slowing us down a little, because under the conditions of modern life we do things much too quickly, rushing from one activity to another, and that is conducive neither to calmness nor peace of mind.

After cultivating awareness of the body and its movements, we should seek to be aware of our feelings. Ask yourself how you feel. What sort of mood are you in? Are you happy or sad? Depressed, angry, bored? Or are you simply indifferent? If we can only become more aware of our passing emotional states we'll be less likely to act impulsively. Many of our actions are without thought, and sometimes we can't even say why we did a particular action or said a certain thing.

Thirdly, we need to be aware of what we're thinking. If I were to ask you, sitting here, what you are thinking about, what would you say? You might perhaps say you were following what I was saying, but is that actually the case? If you look more closely you might find you have been thinking about something else at the same time, perhaps your lunch, or a friend you were going to see this afternoon. You might even have been thinking, 'I hope Bhante doesn't go on talking for too long.' Whatever the case, we need to keep watch over our thinking and if the process can be slowed down in this way, when we meditate we'll find it easier to get into a concentrated state. So this is the first of our three dimensions of awareness, being mindful of our body, our emotions, and our thoughts. One more aspect of self-awareness will be mentioned later, but for now, let's move from self-awareness to look at two more dimensions that are essential if consciousness is to become integrated.

b. Awareness of others

Along with mindfulness of oneself, one needs to be aware of other people. You might think this goes without saying, and that we are always aware of others, and in a sense that is true. But in another sense we're not really aware of others at all other than perhaps only as objects, a bit like statues or waxworks. We are aware of others in so far as they can be useful to us, but we're very rarely aware of what they are in themselves, or of how they may be affected by what we say and do. So we need to cultivate more of this awareness of other people *as* other people with their own needs and interests and desires, and take these also into consideration.

c. Environmental awareness

The third dimension of awareness, as I've called it, is awareness of our environment. We need to be aware of the material conditions by which we are surrounded, of the city in which we live, of the countryside, and aware of the world. I need not say much about this because people currently, especially younger people, are becoming much more aware of the environment. We can see the harm that the human race has been doing to our world over so many centuries and the problems of climate change and pollution. It's our responsibility to be more aware of the impact that we have upon our surroundings, not just as citizens but also as Buddhists, and make sure that our actions do as little harm as possible in that regard.

These three dimensions, awareness of self, awareness of others, and awareness of our environment, go to make up the first great stage of the spiritual path, the stage of integration. The second stage in the path of spiritual development is that of emotional positivity and we can also view this by way of three dimensions. These are what are known in Sanskrit as *maitrī*, *śraddhā*, and *muditā*.

2. Positive Emotion

Maitrī

From the Buddhist point of view, *maitrī* (Pāli *mettā*) is the basis for all positive emotion. *Maitrī* is sometimes translated as 'love', although this might be a source of misunderstanding in English, and perhaps in German also, as we will see. *Maitrī* is an intense and warm desire for the happiness and welfare of other beings, and it is closely associated with the term *mitra*, meaning friend. So we could also say that *maitrī* denotes the cultivation of an attitude of friendliness, in a very strong and positive way, towards other living beings. *Maitrī* is the cardinal Buddhist virtue, exemplified in the Buddhist slogan, *sabbe sattā sukhī hontu*, which expresses the heartfelt wish of all Buddhists that 'all sentient beings be happy'. *Maitrī* can have different aspects depending on its focus. When *maitrī* is directed towards those who are more or less on the same level as ourselves, we speak of it more as friendliness or friendship, but when it is directed towards those who are in difficulty, we start feeling their suffering as our own and *maitrī* becomes *karuṇā* or compassion; and in the same way, when our *maitrī* is directed towards those who are happy and successful it becomes *pramuditā* or joy.

Muditā

When *maitrī* becomes *muditā*, or sympathetic joy, we are conscious of the good qualities in others and rejoice in their merits. From time to time it's customary in the FWBO to do this in a formal way. We rejoice in someone's merits at the memorial service after they have died, for example, and I know of several occasions when the non-Buddhist relations of the dead person have been impressed by the way their Buddhist friends have spoken in appreciation of a son or daughter, brother or sister, and publicly rejoiced in their merits. But why wait until someone dies before we voice our appreciation? We should be doing it during their lifetime and if we see or hear of someone doing something positive and ethically skilful, let's be happy and congratulate them. Remembering also the Buddha's teaching that the greatest gift is the gift of the Dharma, if we see or hear someone communicating the Dharma, even in a small way, let us be especially willing to rejoice in their merits.

Śraddhā

Maitrī shows itself in a further direction. Friendliness and appreciation expand outwards to others, but *maitrī* can also go upwards, ascending towards something higher than ourselves, something ideal, even transcendental. When the positive emotion of *maitrī* looks upwards in this way, we call it *śraddhā* or faith, but it involves much more than simple belief. *Śraddhā* is our heartfelt response to something more developed, more spiritual. In England, and perhaps this may be true of other countries, there's a growing cynicism toward people engaged in positive activities. Often, when people hear of acts of selflessness and altruism, they try to find some negative motivation for it. This cynical attitude is very unpleasant and highly undesirable. Far from trying to disparage something positive that others are doing, we should join in, and try to follow their example if we can possibly do so.

Towards the beginning of the nineteenth century, a new word entered the English language. This was phrenology, the science, or pseudoscience, of bumps on the head, and it became quite popular. Different emotions or attitudes were identified with different bumps, so if you had a bump here you were more intellectual, if you had a bump there you tended to be jealous and so on. Now one of the bumps is called the bump of veneration and if you had this bump you were inclined to look up to and appreciate whatever was higher than yourself. I must have been born with a big bump of veneration, because even when I was young, I responded very positively to what was higher, and better, and more beautiful, not only in the religious sense but also in poetry and art and music. To some extent this tendency is what led me to appreciate the Dharma and of course the Buddha. So I naturally dislike the cynical modern tendency to pull what is higher down to one's own level. We should be trying to lift ourselves up to join those who are seen as occupying that higher standing. This is faith, *śraddhā*, and along with *maitrī*, friendliness, and with *muditā*, or sympathetic joy, it contributes to the third dimension of positive emotion.

Integrated awareness and positive emotion make up the first two stages on the path of spiritual development, and most people spend most of their Buddhist lives trying to practise just these two. Nonetheless, further, higher, stages are available to us, and of these I'll mention one more. The third great stage on the path is what I call the stage of spiritual death, the death of the 'I', the passing away of the ego. This is the stage of really serious spiritual life and spiritual effort. A number of Buddhist practices, especially in meditation, help us undermine this false sense of ego and some of you will be familiar with them. But I'm not going into any of these today. I'll just say one thing about this particular stage.

3. Spiritual Death

If one wants to put it in simple language, spiritual death really means practising unselfishness. In the decisions we make and the things we do we usually put ourselves first, but when we practise selflessness we do our best to put other people first, to consider *their* convenience, and consider *their* happiness, and sometimes even put it before our own. To engage in abstruse meditation exercises on the nature of self will not be enough. We have to try to be less selfish, less self-centred, than we usually are. The ego is tough, it won't die easily, it'll put up a lot of resistance. But if it is to die it is much more likely to die by what we may call the death of a thousand cuts. Every time you consider others more than yourself, whenever you give up your own convenience for the sake of others, you've made a little cut to the ego. There's a beautiful line from the English Romantic poet William Wordsworth, who speaks of 'little, nameless, unremembered acts of kindness and of love'.[401] When repeated again and again, day after day, month after month, year after year, these are what will undermine the ego, and bring us nearer to Enlightenment.

I have spoken of integration, positive emotion, and spiritual death as the great stages of spiritual development that will bring us nearer to Enlightenment. But one need not think in terms of results. Don't bother *too* much about whether you're going to become a Stream Entrant next week or not, just immerse yourself in the Dharma, and if you practise these stages, forgetting about yourself as it were, you will lead a truly happy life, and have nothing to regret when you die. The practice of the Dharma is itself happiness of a kind and you don't really need anything else. During my own last forty-two years, the second half of my life, I have devoted myself entirely to the FWBO and I must say it's been a very happy time. Of course it's had its difficulties and its disappointments, but nonetheless I look back on these forty-two years as years of achievement, happiness, and fulfilment. They have been forty-two years of working for the Dharma, and I can assure you from my own experience that there's nothing better or more satisfying, nothing more fulfilling than that.

NOTES AND REFERENCES

Notes appended with (S) were written by Sangharakshita.

EDITORIAL NOTE

1 Jinananda and Vidyadevi initiated the Spoken Word Project in 1990, with the aim of publishing Sangharakshita's lectures and seminars in edited form. With the help of several other editors, they produced sixteen books including *Who is the Buddha?*, *What is the Dharma?*, and *What is the Sangha?* (*Complete Works*, vol. 3).

FOREWORD

2 *A Stream of Stars, Complete Works*, vol. 26, p. 55.

3 See *Buddhism in England*, p. 485 below.

4 *The Taste of Freedom*, pp. 42–3 below.

5 *Wisdom Within Words*, p. 653 below.

6 *The Taste of Freedom*, pp. 47 and 50 below.

7 See *Facing Mount Kanchenjunga, Complete Works*, vol. 21, p. 523; and *Ambedkar and Buddhism*, vol. 9, pp. 21–3. Sangharakshita recounts in detail the events subsequent to Dr Ambedkar's death in *In the Sign of the Golden Wheel, Complete Works*, vol. 22, pp. 360–4, also quoting from a letter to his friend, Dinoo Dubash, which was written just over a week after the event.

8 *Entering the Sangha*, p. 708 below.

9 Subhuti, *Bringing Buddhism to The West*, Windhorse Publications, Birmingham 1995, p. 111.

10 *Yesterday, Today, and Tomorrow*, p. 520 below.

11 *Toby as I Knew Him*, p. 543 below.
12 *Mind – Reactive and Creative*, p. 32 below.
13 *Buddhism for Today – and Tomorrow*, p. 181 below.
14 *Sangharakshita at Seventy*, p. 617 below.

BUDDHA MIND
15 *Dhammapada* 1.
16 For more on the range of negative mental states understood from an Abhidharma perspective, see *Know Your Mind, Complete Works,* vol. 17, pp. 643–82.
17 Sangharakshita goes into the Yogācāra system in greater detail in *The Meaning of Conversion in Buddhism, Complete Works,* vol. 2, pp. 279–83.
18 For a detailed exploration of the Perfection of Wisdom, see *Wisdom Beyond Words* in *Complete Works*, vol. 14.

19 The mere scholar cannot believe that the Dharma was rediscovered by the Buddha, because he does not accept the 'legendary' or 'mythical' (words for him synonymous with imaginary) Buddhist accounts of its existence in previous world-periods.

A Survey of Buddhism, Complete Works, vol. 1, p. 56.
20 The Buddha's descent of the celestial ladder can be found in Eugene Watson Burlingame (ed.), *Buddhist Legends*, part 3, Luzac, London 1969, p. 53.

According to the *Lalitavistara Sūtra*, after his birth the Buddha-to-be took seven steps in each of the directions, each time uttering words expressive of a great intention. See G. Bays (trans.), *The Voice of the Buddha*, vol. i, Dharma Publishing, Berkeley 1983, pp. 131–2. The arising of the Earth Goddess to bear witness to the depth of Siddhārtha's practice appears in the *Lalitavistara Sūtra*, ibid. pp. 481–2. For the story of how the serpent king Mucalinda protects the Buddha after his Enlightenment see *Udāna* 2.1 in John D. Ireland (trans.), *The Udāna and the Itivuttaka*, Buddhist Publication Society, Kandy 1997, pp. 23–4.
21 From the *Lalitavistara Sūtra*. See Gwendolyn Bays (trans.), *The Voice of the Buddha*, vol. ii, Dharma Publishing, Berkeley 1983, p. 439. See also Aśvaghoṣa, *Buddhacarita*, E. H. Johnston (trans.), Motilal Banarsidass, Delhi 1984, p. 186, and the *Appaṭivāṇa Sutta, Aṅguttara Nikāya* i.50: see Bhikkhu Bodhi (trans.), *Numerical Discourses of the Buddha*, Wisdom Publications, Boston 2012, p. 142; or F. L. Woodward (trans.), *The Book of the Gradual Sayings*, vol. i, Pali Text Society, Oxford 2000, p. 45.
22 See Francesca Fremantle and Chogyam Trungpa (trans.), *The Tibetan Book of the*

Dead, Shambhala Publications, Boston and London, p. 37.

23 From a verse that stands above the introductory plate to William Blake's *Jerusalem*, headed 'To the Christians'. See William Blake, *Jerusalem: The Emanation of the Giant Albion*, chapter 1, plate 77.

24 Sangharakshita (trans.), *Dhammapada* 1–2, in *Complete Works*, vol. 15, p. 9.

25 This verse is attributed to Bodhidharma. See D. T. Suzuki, *Essays in Zen Buddhism* (First Series), Rider & Company, London 1949, pp. 20, 176. For Sangharakshita's commentary on the verse, see *The Essence of Zen, Complete Works*, vol. 13, pp. 335–64.

26 From 'The Clod and the Pebble' by William Blake.

27 E. W. Burlingame (ed.), *Buddhist Legends*, part 3, Luzac, London 1969, p. 53.

28 The seven factors of Enlightenment, or *bodhyaṅgas*, are enumerated in, for example, the *Mahāsatipaṭṭhāna Sutta*, *Dīgha Nikāya* 22 (ii.303–4); see M. Walshe (trans.), *The Long Discourses of the Buddha*, Wisdom Publications, Boston 1995, p. 343; or T. W. and C. A. F. Rhys Davids (trans.), *Dialogues of the Buddha*, part 2, Pali Text Society, London 1971, pp. 336–7. See also the *Ānāpānasati Sutta, Majjhima Nikāya* 118 (iii.85–7); Bhikkhu Ñāṇamoli and Bhikkhu Bodhi (trans.), *The Middle Length Discourses of the Buddha*, Wisdom Publications, Boston 1995, pp. 946–8; or I. B. Horner (trans.), *The Collection of the Middle Length Sayings*, vol. iii, Pali Text Society, Oxford 1993, pp. 128–9.

29 Sangharakshita (trans.), *Maṅgala Sutta, Sutta-Nipāta* 2.4, in *Complete Works*, vol. 15, p. 62.

30 The *locus classicus* for the teaching on mindfulness and its various aspects is the *Satipaṭṭhāna Sutta, Majjhima Nikāya* 10 (i.55–63). I. B. Horner (trans.), *The Collection of the Middle Length Sayings*, vol. i, Pali Text Society, London 1976, pp. 70–82; or Bhikkhu Ñāṇamoli and Bhikkhu Bodhi (trans.), *The Middle Length Discourses of the Buddha*, Wisdom Publications, Boston 1995, pp. 145–55. See also Sangharakshita's commentary on the *sutta: Living with Awareness*, in *Complete Works*, vol. 15, pp. 27ff).

31 *Alagaddūpama Sutta, Majjhima Nikāya* 22 (i.134). See I. B. Horner (trans.), *The Collection of the Middle Length Sayings*, vol. i, Pali Text Society, London 1976, pp. 173–4; or Bhikkhu Ñāṇamoli and Bhikkhu Bodhi (trans.), *The Middle Length Discourses of the Buddha*, Wisdom Publications, Boston 1995, pp. 228–9.

32 For this episode, see *The Uposatha Sutta, Udāna* 5.5. John D. Ireland (trans.), *The Udāna and the Itivuttaka*, Buddhist Publication Society, Kandy 2007, p. 68.

33 Mātṛceṭa quoted in Edward Conze (ed.), *Buddhist Texts Through the Ages*, Bruno Cassirer, Oxford 1954, p. 194. For more about Mātṛceṭa, an Indian poet-monk of the third century CE, see Robert Buswell and Donald Lopez Jr (eds), *Princeton Dictionary of Buddhism*, Princeton 2014, p. 903. See also Mātṛceṭa's 'Letter to the Great King Kaniṣka' in Michael Hahn (ed.), *Invitation to Enlightenment*, Dharma Publishing, Berkeley 1999.

34 Plato, *Theaetetus* 155c–d.

35 The traditional order is *satkāya-dṛṣṭi, vicikitsā*, and *śīlavrata-parāmarśa*, which correspond to habit, vagueness, and superficiality. In the original lecture and book, these were presented in the order 'habit, superficiality, and vagueness'. Sangharakshita acknowledged that this was unintentional and the arrangement has been revised for this *Complete Works* edition.

36 From the poem 'The Scholar-Gipsy' by Matthew Arnold (1822–1888).

37 Zhiyi (538–597 CE), the fourth Tiantai patriarch, is regarded as the first major figure of Chinese Buddhism to make a significant discontinuity with the Indian tradition.

38 Samuel Taylor Coleridge, *Table Talk*, 15 May 1833, in *Table Talk and Omniana*, Humphrey Milford, Oxford 1917, p. 241.

39 Goethe, *Maxims and Reflections*, Macmillan, New York 1906, p. 200.

40 The full title of Wordsworth's poem is 'Lines Composed a Few Miles above Tintern Abbey, on Revisiting the Banks of the Wye during a Tour. July 13, 1798'.

41 The phrase 'noble wisdom' occurs throughout Suzuki's translation of *Laṅkāvatāra Sūtra*. D. T. Suzuki, *The Laṅkāvatāra Sūtra*, Prajna Press, Boulder 1978.

42 Ibid.

43 Matthew Arnold, *Literature and Dogma*, Watts & Co, London 1903, p. 21.

44 More recently available as Edwin Arnold, *The Light of Asia*, Windhorse Publications, Birmingham 1999.

45 *The Wheel of Fortune* (1871–1885) by English Pre-Raphaelite painter Edward Burne-Jones (1833–1898) hangs in the National Gallery of Victoria, Melbourne, Australia.

46 From William Blake's poem 'London', one of his *Songs of Innocence and Experience*, first published in 1794.

47 The New Burman Satipaṭṭhāna Method refers to *vipassanā* meditation as taught by the

Burmese school of Mahasi Sayadaw during the latter half of the twentieth century. The preface to the first American edition of *A Survey of Buddhism* offers a mental health warning to all would-be practitioners of this method. (Sangharakshita, *A Survey of Buddhism*, Shambhala Publications, Boulder 1980, p. xv.) Lama Govinda also wrote critically of such practices. See Lama Anagarika Govinda, *Creative Meditation and Multi-Dimensional Consciousness*, Unwin Mandala Books, London 1976, p. 125.

48 *Dhammapada* 204.

49 *Saṃyutta Nikāya* i.138. See Bhikkhu Bodhi (trans.), *The Connected Discourses of the Buddha*, Wisdom Publications, Boston 2000, p. 233; or C. A. F. Rhys Davids (trans.), *The Book of the Kindred Sayings*, part 1, Pali Text Society, London 1979, p. 174.

50 A detailed visualization of the Lotus Throne comes as the 'seventh contemplation' in the *Amitābha Visualization Sūtra*. See Ratnaguna and Śraddhāpa, *Great Faith, Great Wisdom*, Windhorse Publications, Cambridge 2016.

51 See *Tibetan Buddhism, Complete Works*, vol. 13, pp.76–80.

52 See Bunnō Katō et al. (trans.), *The Threefold Lotus Sūtra*, Kōsei Publishing Company,

Tokyo 1995, pp. 126–34, where the parable is entitled 'the Parable of the Herbs'. For Sangharakshita's commentary, see *Drama of Cosmic Enlightenment, Complete Works*, vol. 16, pp. 116–30.

53 See *A Survey of Buddhism, Complete Works*, vol. 1, p. 246.

54 Ibid. pp. 218, 360.

55 From *Wilhelm Meister's Journeyman Years* (1829), in J. W. von Goethe, *Maxims and Reflections*, trans. E. Stopp, Penguin, Harmondsworth 1998, p. 66.

HUMAN ENLIGHTENMENT

56 The Ideal Home Exhibition was later rebranded as the Ideal Home Show.

57 *Karaṇīyamettā Sutta, Sutta-Nipāta* 1.8. See H. Saddhatissa (trans.), *The Sutta-Nipāta*, Curson Press, London 1985, pp. 15–16. Sangharakshita's commentary on the *sutta* is published as *Living with Kindness* in *Complete Works*, vol. 15, pp. 245ff.

58 *Mahāparinibbāna Sutta, Dīgha Nikāya* 16; see M. Walshe (trans.), *The Long Discourses of the Buddha*, Wisdom Publications, Boston 1995, pp. 231–77; or T. W. and C. A. F. Rhys Davids (trans.), *Dialogues of the Buddha*, part 2, Pali Text Society, London 1971, pp. 78–191.

59 See, for example, the *Lalitavistara Sūtra*, published

as Gwendolyn Bays (trans.),
The Voice of the Buddha,
Dharma Publishing, Berkeley
1983; and Aśvaghoṣa,
The Buddhacarita, trans.
E. H. Johnston, Motilal
Banarsidass, Delhi 1984.

60 Henry Ford (1863–1947) was
a United States industrialist
who formed the Ford Motor
Company in 1903.

61 St Augustine, *Confessions*,
Dover Press, New York 2002,
p. 1.

62 T. R. V. Murti, *The Central
Philosophy of Buddhism*,
George Allen and Unwin,
London 1955, p. 280.
Sangharakshita has more to say
on this topic in *The Meaning
of Orthodoxy in Buddhism*,
Complete Works, vol. 7,
pp. 535–7.

63 In the *Pāṭika Sutta* the Buddha
explains to Bhaggava how
the idea of a Creator is a
wrong view and will hold
him back along with other
erroneous views about the
origin of the universe. See
Dīgha Nikāya 24 (ii.28–35) in
M. Walshe (trans.), *The Long
Discourses of the Buddha*,
Wisdom Publications, Boston
1995, pp. 381–3; or T. W. and
C. A. F. Rhys Davids (trans.),
Dialogues of the Buddha,
part 3, Pali Text Society,
London 1971, pp. 25–32. The
Buddha speaks more strongly
about the unfortunate effects
of believing in a creator God
at *Aṅguttara Nikāya* i.173–4.
See Bhikkhu Bodhi (trans.), *The

*Numerical Discourses of the
Buddha*, Wisdom Publications,
Somerville 2012, pp. 266–7;
or F. L. Woodward, (trans.),
Gradual Sayings, vol. i, Pali
Text Society, Oxford 2000,
pp. 158.

64 For 'heirs to spiritual things'
see *Itivuttaka* 100, in John
D. Ireland (trans.), *The Udāna
and the Itivuttaka*, Buddhist
Publication Society, Kandy
1997, p. 226. For the Buddha
compared to a chick helping
others to hatch see Vinaya
Piṭaka iii.3–4 (*Pārājika* 1.1) in
I. B. Horner (trans.), *The Book
of the Discipline*, part 1, Pali
Text Society, Oxford 1996,
pp. 6–7.

65 Vinaya Piṭaka ii.258–9
(*Cullavagga* 10.5); see
I. B. Horner (trans.), ibid.,
part 5, Pali Text Society,
Oxford 1975, p. 359. See also
Aṅguttara Nikāya iv.280, in
E. M. Hare (trans.), *The Book
of the Gradual Sayings*, vol. iv,
Pali Text Society, Oxford
1995, pp. 186–7; or Bhikkhu
Bodhi (trans.), The *Numerical
Discourses of the Buddha*,
Wisdom Publications, Boston
2012, p. 1193.

66 *Ariyapariyesanā Sutta*,
Majjhima Nikāya 26 (i.169);
see Bhikkhu Ñāṇamoli and
Bhikkhu Bodhi (trans.), *The
Middle Length Discourses
of the Buddha*, Wisdom
Publications, Boston 1995,
pp. 261–2; or I. B. Horner
(trans.), *The Collection of the
Middle Length Sayings*, vol. i,

Pali Text Society, London
1976, p. 212.

67 See Edward Conze, *Buddhism:
Its Essence and Development*,
Windhorse Publications,
Birmingham 2001, p. 135.

68 See *Saṅgārava Sutta,
Saṃyutta Nikāya* v.90–3 in
F. L. Woodward (trans.), *The
Book of the Kindred Sayings*,
part 5, Pali Text Society,
London 1979, pp. 76–8; or
Bhikkhu Bodhi (trans.), *The
Connected Discourses of the
Buddha*, Wisdom Publications,
Boston 2000, pp. 1611–3.
See also the *Saṅgārava Sutta,
Aṅguttara Nikāya* iii.232 in
E. M. Hare (trans.), *The Book
of the Gradual Sayings*, vol. iii,
Pali Text Society, Oxford
1995, pp. 168–70; or Bhikkhu
Bodhi (trans.), *The Numerical
Discourses of the Buddha*,
Wisdom Publications, Boston
2012, pp. 807–8.

69 The similes for the four
dhyānas are found in various
places including the *Mahā-
assapura Sutta, Majjhima
Nikāya* 39 (i.276–9); see
Bhikkhu Ñāṇamoli and
Bhikkhu Bodhi (trans.), *The
Middle Length Discourses
of the Buddha*, Wisdom
Publications, Boston 1995,
pp. 367–9; or I. B. Horner
(trans.), *The Collection of
the Middle Length Sayings*,
vol. i, Pali Text Society,
London 1976, pp. 330–2.
See also the *Mahāsakuludāyi
Sutta, Majjhima Nikāya* 77
(ii.15–17); Bhikkhu Ñāṇamoli

and Bhikkhu Bodhi, ibid.
pp. 641–2; or I. B. Horner
(trans.), *The Collection of the
Middle Length Sayings*, vol. ii,
Pali Text Society, Oxford 1994,
pp. 216–7.

BUDDHISM FOR TODAY –
AND TOMORROW

70 Alexander Pope (1688–1744),
Essays on Criticism, part 2
(1711).

71 G. Lowes Dickinson, *A Modern
Symposium*, George Allen &
Unwin, London 1905, p. 173.

72 See note 69 above.

73 These are the four *brahma
vihāras*, and the Buddha
is recorded as describing
them in the *Tevijja Sutta,
Dīgha Nikāya* 13 (i.251).
See M. Walshe (trans.), *The
Long Discourses of the
Buddha*, Wisdom Publications,
Boston 1995, p. 194; or
T. W. Rhys Davids (trans.),
Dialogues of the Buddha,
part 1, Pali Text Society,
London 1973, pp. 317– 8. For
Sangharakshita's advice on
the practices, see *Complete
Works*, vol. 5, pp. 191–219;
also *Living with Kindness*
in *Complete Works*, vol. 15,
pp. 245ff.

74 See Sangharakshita, *The
Meaning of Conversion in
Buddhsim*, *Complete Works*,
vol. 2, pp. 275–85.

75 Deliverance through wisdom
(*paññā-vimutti*) is the
knowledge (*ñāṇa*) bound
up with the fruition of
arhantship. See Nyanatiloka,

Buddhist Dictionary, Buddhist Publication Society, Kandy 1980.

76 See, for example, the *Cūlagopālaka Sutta*, *Majjhima Nikāya* 34 (i.227) in Bhikkhu Ñāṇamoli and Bhikkhu Bodhi (trans.), *The Middle Length Discourses of the Buddha*, Wisdom Publications, Boston 1995, p. 321; or I. B. Horner (trans.), *The Collection of the Middle Length Sayings*, vol. i, Pali Text Society, London 1976, p. 279.

77 See S. Radhakrishnan, *A History of Indian Philosophy*, Cambridge 1922, vol. ii.

78 Proverbs 29:18.

79 *Ariyapariyesanā Sutta*, *Majjhima Nikāya* 26 (i.168); I. B. Horner (trans.), *The Collection of the Middle Length Sayings*, vol. i, Pali Text Society, London 1976, p. 212; or Bhikkhu Bodhi (trans.), *The Middle Length Discourses of the Buddha*, Wisdom Publications, Boston 2000, p. 261.

80 The story of the Buddha and the sick monk is told at Vinaya Piṭaka i.301–3 (*Mahāvagga* 8.26); see I. B. Horner (trans.), *The Book of the Discipline*, part 4, Pali Text Society, Oxford 1996, pp. 431–4. The rogue elephant appears at Vinaya Piṭaka ii.193–5 (*Cullavagga* 7.3); see I. B. Horner (ibid.), part 5, Pali Text Society, London 1975, pp. 271–4. The

legendary story of the Buddha holding up a flower at which Mahākāśyapa 'sees' is in D. T. Suzuki, *Essays in Zen Buddhism* (First Series), Rider & Company, London 1949, p. 167.

81 Chapter 2 of the *Shulchan Aruch*, the Code of Jewish Law authored in 1563, consists of 'Laws Relating to Dressing', including a section on the putting on of shoes and the tying of laces. Its focus is the correspondence between general codes of ethics and the practical matters of day-to-day living, especially the significance of seemingly unimportant actions. See also Sangharakshita's seminar on 'Ethics and Manners', chapter 13 of *The Jewel Ornament of Liberation*, 1980.

82 Vinaya Piṭaka i.39–40 (*Mahāvagga* 1.23); see I. B. Horner (trans.), *The Book of the Discipline*, part 4, Pali Text Society, Oxford 1996, pp. 52–4.

83 From 'Song of Myself' by Walt Whitman.

84 The TBMSG, or Trailokya Bauddha Mahasangha Sahayak Gana, was the original name of the Indian wing of the FWBO. In 2010 the Order and Movement were renamed so that they would have the same names worldwide, and the TBMSG became the Triratna Bauddha Mahasangha Sahayak Gana.

RITUAL AND DEVOTION IN
BUDDHISM

85 For the origins of the content
of *Ritual and Devotion in
Buddhism*, see the editorial
note on p. xiv.

86 This popular quotation is
almost certainly apocryphal.
Something approaching its
meaning can be found in
Meno, a Socratic dialogue
by Plato, in which Socrates
suggests that 'virtue is
knowledge' (Meno 87c)
although there, the knowledge
in question is that possessed
by the gods.

87 See Aristotle, *De Anima*,
especially chapter 4.

88 Within a specifically spiritual
context these become 'higher
centres': a higher thinking or
even intuitive or visionary
centre; a positive emotional
centre; and a centre of spiritual
practice and experience. (S)

89 Jean-Jacques Rousseau (1712–
1778) was a French political
theorist of the Enlightenment
whose writings inspired the
artists, poets, and thinkers
of the Romantic movement.
Rousseauism extols the virtues
of a radical return to simpler
ways of life.

90 Early communism, otherwise
known as anarchist
communism, is discussed
by Bertrand Russell in his
Proposed Roads to Freedom,
Manor Press, Rockville 2008
pp. 33ff.

91 P. D. Ouspensky, *In Search of
the Miraculous*, Routledge &
Kegan Paul, London 1950.

92 'Prends l'éloquence et tords-lui
son cou!' from the poem 'L'Art
Poétique' by Paul Verlaine
(1844–1896). Valerie Laurent
(ed.), *Paul Verlaine Textes
Choisis*, Éditions de Seuil, Paris
2004, pp. 110–11.

93 The higher thinking faculty is

> a knowledge that is derived
> not from the senses and
> reason alone, but from
> a fusion of reason with
> emotion in a higher faculty
> of archetypal knowledge
> which we may call 'vision',
> 'insight' or 'imagination'.

Sangharakshita, *Who is the
Buddha?*, *Complete Works*,
vol. 3, p. 11.

94 Rationalist philosophers of
the European Enlightenment
include Descartes, Leibniz, and
Spinoza.

95 Erich Fromm, *Psychoanalysis
and Religion*, Yale University
Press, New Haven 1950,
p. 108.

96 For information about the
life of Dhardo Rimpoche
see Suvajra, *The Wheel and
the Diamond*, Windhorse
Publications, Glasgow 1991.

97 *Torma* are small objects
made of flour and butter used
in rituals or as offerings in
Tibetan Buddhism.

98 See note 95 above, p. 109.

99 Sangharakshita's experiences
at the summer school are
described in *Moving Against*

the Stream, Complete Works, vol. 23, pp. 32–8.

100 For more on bodhicitta, see The Bodhisattva Ideal, Complete Works, vol. 4, pp. 27–54.

101 See Śāntideva, Bodhicaryāvatāra, trans. Kate Crosby and Andrew Skilton, Oxford University Press, Oxford 1996; also Marion L. Matics (trans.), Entering the Path of Enlightenment, Allen & Unwin, London 1970. See also Stephen Batchelor's translation A Guide to the Bodhisattva's Way of Life, Library of Tibetan Works and Archives, Dharamsala 1981.

102 Complete Works, vol. 1, pp. 406ff.

103 Sangharakshita's contact with Adrienne Bennett is described in Moving Against the Stream, Complete Works, vol. 23, pp. 54–5. The Sevenfold and Threefold Pujas are in Sangharakshita (ed.), Puja: the Triratna Book of Buddhist Devotional Texts, Windhorse Publications, Cambridge 2008.

104 Marion L. Matics (trans.), Entering the Path of Enlightenment, George Allen and Unwin Ltd, London 1970.

105 Stephen Batchelor (trans.). See the end of note 101 above.

106 R. E. Emmerick (trans.), Sūtra of Golden Light, Pali Text Society, London 1979. See also Sangharakshita's commentary on this sūtra:

Transforming Self and World, in Complete Works, vol. 16. Sangharakshita's arrangement of verses based on this text is published as the 'Suvarnabhasottama Puja', in Lokabandhu (comp.), Puja Readings and Other Texts, Triratna Inhouse Publications, 2014, p. 582.

107 Sangharakshita composed the Short or Threefold Puja for the Finnish sangha, who sought a more down-to-earth ritual.

> Vajrabodhi, I remembered, had once told me about Finnish Friends who were not happy reciting the Sevenfold Puja because they were not actually offering mandārava flowers, lamps encrusted with jewels, etc.

Travel Letters, Complete Works, vol. 24, p. 49.

108 See for example, T. Cleary (trans.), The Flower Ornament Scripture (Avataṃsaka Sūtra), Shambhala Publications, Boston 1987.

109 This and all subsequent quotations from Matics are taken from Marion L. Matics (trans.), Entering the Path of Enlightenment, George Allen and Unwin Ltd, London 1970. Adrienne Bennett's translation remains unpublished.

110 Sangharakshita's six-month stay at the guest cottage of Prince K. M. Latthakin or 'Burma Raja' as he was known, is recounted in Facing Mount Kanchenjunga,

Complete Works, vol. 21, pp. 124–36.

111 This expression originally referred to the sweet smell said to be exhaled by the bodies of dead saints. More recently, it has taken on the derogatory meaning of a sanctimonious, holier-than-thou attitude.

112 Lama Govinda, *Foundations of Tibetan Mysticism*, Samuel Weiser, New York 1960, p. 90.

113 For more on the relationship between Buddhism and animism, see Sangharakshita's analysis of the elements, or *mahābhūta*, in *Living with Awareness*, *Complete Works*, vol. 15, pp. 132–9.

114 Ani-La, the French nun, appears many times in Sangharakshita's memoirs of his Kalimpong days. See, for example, *In the Sign of the Golden Wheel*, *Complete Works*, vol. 22, pp. 193–5, 219–24, 396–7.

115 For more background on these historical disputes and divisions, see Andrew Skilton, *A Concise History of Buddhism*, Windhorse Publications, Birmingham 1994, especially chapter 11.

116 The *Saddharma Puṇḍarīka Sūtra* is available in several translations. For Sangharakshita's commentary on the *sūtra*, see *The Drama of Cosmic Enlightenment* in *Complete Works*, vol. 16.

117 *Śrāmaṇera* precepts: the ten precepts undertaken by novice monks or *śrāmaṇeras* include the five precepts listed in chapter 8, with the modification that instead of undertaking to abstain from sexual misconduct, *śrāmaṇeras* undertake to refrain from all sexual activity. The remaining five precepts include abstaining from eating after midday, music and dancing, luxurious beds, wearing garlands, scent, or jewellery, and handling money.

118 See, for example, the *Sāleyyaka Sutta*, *Majjhima Nikāya* 41 (i.289); Bhikkhu Ñāṇamoli and Bhikkhu Bodhi (trans.), *The Middle Length Discourses of the Buddha*, Wisdom Publications, Boston 1995, p. 384; or I. B. Horner (trans.), *The Collection of the Middle Length Sayings*, vol. i, Pali Text Society, London 1976, p. 348.

119 For more about the ten precepts observed by members of the Triratna Buddhist Order, see *The Ten Pillars of Buddhism* in *Complete Works*, vol. 2, pp. 307–96.

120 See *Dasadhamma Sutta*, *Aṅguttara Nikāya* v.88 (10.48). See Bhikkhu Bodhi (trans.), *The Numerical Discourses of the Buddha*, Wisdom Publications, Boston 2012, p. 1399; or F. L. Woodward (trans.), *The Book of the Gradual Sayings*, vol. 5, Pali Text Society, Oxford 1996, p. 62.

121 For a fuller treatment of karma, including what it is

not, see *Who is the Buddha?*,
Complete Works, vol. 3,
pp. 92–115.

122 Sangharakshita introduces
the terms 'faith-follower'
(*saddhānusārin*) and 'doctrine-
follower' (*dhammānusārin*)
at the beginning of his talk 'A
Vision of Human Existence',
published in *Buddhism for
Today and Tomorrow*, below,
pp. 157–8. For a canonical
reference see the *Cūḷagopālaka
Sutta, Majjhima Nikāya* 34
(i.227); Bhikkhu Ñāṇamoli
and Bhikkhu Bodhi (trans.),
*The Middle Length Discourses
of the Buddha*, Wisdom
Publications, Boston 1995,
p. 321; or I. B. Horner (trans.),
*The Collection of the Middle
Length Sayings*, vol. i, Pali
Text Society, London 1976,
p. 279.

123 *Brahmasaṃyutta, Saṃyutta
Nikāya* i.138. C. A. F. Rhys
Davids (trans.), *The Book of
the Kindred Sayings*, part 1,
Pali Text Society, London
1979, pp. 173–4. See also
Bhikkhu Bodhi (trans.), *The
Connected Discourses of the
Buddha*, Wisdom Publications,
Boston 2000, p. 233.

124 *Mahāparinibbāna Sutta,
Dīgha Nikāya* 16 (ii.103–4).
T. W. and C. A. F. Rhys
Davids (trans.), *Dialogues of
the Buddha*, part 2, Pali Text
Society, London 1971, pp.110–
11; or M. Walshe (trans.),
*The Long Discourses of the
Buddha*, Wisdom Publications,
Boston 1995, p. 246.

125 Paul Reps, *Zen Flesh
Zen Bones*, Penguin,
Harmondsworth 1972, p. 17.

126 Sangharakshita's commentary
on the *Heart Sūtra* appears
in *Complete Works,* vol. 14,
pp. 357–67.

127 Paul Reps, *Zen Flesh Zen
Bones*, Harmondsworth,
Penguin 1972, p. 19.

128 *Padme* isn't a locative but a
vocative, so a literal translation
is simply 'jewel lotus'. Donald
Lopez devotes an entire chapter
of *Prisoners of Shangri-la*
(University of Chicago Press,
1999) to a discussion of
how this mantra has been
misconstrued in the West.

DIALOGUE BETWEEN
BUDDHISM AND
CHRISTIANITY

129 For an overview of early
contact between Buddhism
and Christianity in Central
Asia see Andrew Skilton,
*A Concise History of
Buddhism*, Windhorse
Publications, Birmingham
1994, ch. 28.

   For the medieval story
whose origin is in the life
of the Buddha, see *From
Genesis to the Diamond Sūtra*,
Complete Works, vol. 13,
pp. 653–4.

   Ippolito Desideri (1684
–1733) was an Italian Jesuit
missionary who travelled
to Tibet and gained an
understanding of its language
and culture. See Donald
S. Lopez, Jr. and Thupten

Jinpa, *Dispelling the Darkness*, Harvard University Press, 2017.

Francis Xavier (1506–1553) was a Spanish Jesuit priest who first arrived at Goa in 1542. His missionary work also took him to Malaysia and Japan.

130 Esperanto is an international language invented in the late 1800s to foster global communication and understanding.

131 In Buddhist cosmology *Mahābrahmā*, or Great Brahmā, is the ruler of the *brahmaloka*. He is considered a *dharmapāla*, or protector of Buddhist teachings, but not in any sense a creator god.

ASPECTS OF BUDDHIST MORALITY

132 Sangharakshita's *śrāmaṇera* ordination, and his receiving the name 'Sangharakshita', is described in *The Rainbow Road from Tooting Broadway to Kalimpong, Complete Works*, vol. 20, pp. 402–13.

133 Sangharakshita's preceptor was the Venerable U Chandramani (1876–1972), a Burmese *bhikkhu*. For more on the journey to Nepal, see ibid. pp. 424–41.

134 *Bhagavad Gītā* 4.8. *Bhakti* refers to the practice of devotional worship.

135 e.g. *Dīgha Nikāya* ii.91; see T. W. and C. A. F. Rhys Davids (trans.), *Dialogues of the Buddha*, part 2, Luzac, London 1971, p. 97; or M. Walshe

(trans.), *The Long Discourses of the Buddha*, Wisdom Publications, Boston 1995, p. 240.

136 *Rathavinīta Sutta, Majjhima Nikāya* 24; see Bhikkhu Ñāṇamoli and Bhikkhu Bodhi (trans.), *The Middle Length Discourses of the Buddha*, Wisdom Publications, Boston 1995, pp. 240–5; or I. B. Horner (trans.), *Middle Length Sayings*, vol. i, Pali Text Society, Oxford 1957, pp. 187–94.

137 *Visuddhimagga* 221–2 (vii.101–6). See Bhikkhu Ñāṇamoli (trans.), *The Path of Purification*, Buddhist Publication Society, Kandy 1991, pp. 218–9.

138 See *A Survey of Buddhism, Complete Works*, vol. 1, p. 424.

139 Ibid. pp. 394 et seq.

140 In the Pāli canon, the Buddha says that, just as the *siṃsapā* leaves which he held in his hand were few compared to the trees of the forest, so was the knowledge he had revealed to them compared with the knowledge of which he had not spoken. *Siṃsapā Sutta, Saṃyutta Nikāya* v.437–8 (56.31); Bhikkhu Bodhi (trans.), *Connected Discourses of the Buddha*, Wisdom Publications, Boston 2000, pp. 1857–8; or F. L. Woodward (trans.), *The Book of the Kindred Sayings*, part 5, Pali Text Society, London 1979, p. 370.

141 *Paṭisambhidāmagga* i.44. The
Paṭisambhidāmagga is the
twelfth book of the *Khuddaka
Nikāya*, translated by Bhikkhu
Ñāṇamoli and published as *The
Path of Discrimination* (Pali
Text Society, London 1982).

142 *Visuddhimagga* 6–8
(i.17–18). See Bhikkhu
Ñāṇamoli (trans.), *The Path
of Purification*, Buddhist
Publication Society, Kandy
1991, pp. 10–11.

143 Gampopa, *The Jewel
Ornament of Liberation*, trans.
Herbert V. Guenther, Rider,
London 1970, pp. 164–5.

144 See, for example, *Crossing
The Stream, Complete Works*,
vol. 7, pp. 385 et seq. and *A
Survey of Buddhism*, vol. 1,
pp. 114 et seq.

145 Gampopa, *The Jewel
Ornament of Liberation*, trans.
Herbert V. Guenther, Rider,
London 1970, p. 101.

146 Being a matter of direct
experience, the truth is
inexpressible. It is therefore
said that from the night of his
Enlightenment till the night of
his *parinirvāṇa* the Tathāgata
did not utter a single word.
See D. T. Suzuki (trans.), *The
Laṅkāvatāra Sūtra*, George
Routledge, London 1932,
pp. 124–5.

147 *Visuddhimagga* 13 (i.32). See
Bhikkhu Ñāṇamoli (trans.),
The Path of Purification,
Buddhist Publication Society,
Kandy 1991, p. 16–17.

148 The three principal aspects
of the path: renunciation,

bodhicitta, and wisdom
realizing emptiness. See
Tsongkhapa, *The Principal
Teachings of Buddhism*, trans.
Geshe Lobsang Tharchin,
Classics of Middle Asia, New
Jersey 1998.

The 'five paths' (*lam-
lnga*) of accumulation,
joining, seeing, cultivation,
and the path beyond
training. See Edward Conze,
Abhisamayālankāra, Is.M.E.O,
Rome 1954.

The seven stages of
purification: of moral virtue,
mind, views, overcoming
doubt, knowledge and vision
of the path and the not-path,
knowledge and vision of the
way, knowledge, and vision. See
*Rathavinīta Sutta, Majjhima
Nikāya* 24; Bhikkhu Ñāṇamoli
and Bhikkhu Bodhi (trans.),
*The Middle Length Discourses
of the Buddha*, Wisdom
Publications, Boston 1995,
pp. 240–5; or I. B. Horner
(trans.), *The Collection of
the Middle Length Sayings*,
vol. i, Pali Text Society,
London 1976, pp. 187–94. For
Sangharakshita's account of
these seven stages, see *What is
the Dharma?, Complete Works*,
vol. 3, pp. 290–4.

The ten bodhisattva
bhūmis are the very joyous
(*pramuditā*), the stainless
(*vimalā*), the light-maker
(*prabhākarī*), the radiant
intellect (*arciṣmatī*), the
difficult to master (*sudurjayā*),
the manifest (*abhimukhī*),

the gone afar (*dūraṃgamā*),
the immovable (*acalā*), the
good intelligence (*sādhumatī*),
and the cloud of doctrine
(*dharmameghā*). See Thomas
Cleary (trans.), *The Flower
Ornament Scripture*,
Shambhala Publications,
Boston and London 1993,
pp. 695–811.

Thirteen *bhūmis* appear
in a Mahāmudrā formulation
made up of the ten stages
outlined above plus universal
light, the lotus of non-
attachment, and the vajra
holder. See Tsele Natsok
Rangdrol, *Heart Lamp of
Mahamudra*, Rangjung Yeshe
Publications, Kathmandu
2011.

The fifty-two stages of
bodhisattva cultivation are
to be found in the *Jewelled
Necklace Sūtra*, a fourth-
century scripture from the
Chinese canon that has yet
to be translated into English.
The *sūtra*'s fifty-two stages
comprise ten stages of faith,
ten stages of security, ten
stages of practice, ten stages
of devotion, ten stages of
development, the stage of near-
perfect Enlightenment, and the
stage of perfect Enlightenment.

149 *Visuddhimagga* 13 (i.32). See
Bhikkhu Ñāṇamoli (trans.),
The Path of Purification,
Buddhist Publication Society,
Kandy 1991, p. 16–17.

150 See also *A Survey of
Buddhism*, *Complete Works*,
vol. 1, p. 136.

151 For example, see *Brahmajāla
Sutta*, *Dīgha Nikaya* 1
(i.4–13). See M. Walshe
(trans.), *The Long Discourses
of the Buddha*, Wisdom
Publications, Boston 1995, pp.
68–73.

152 J. Evola, *The Doctrine of
Awakening*, Luzac, London
1951, p. 151.

153 Ibid.

154 Ibid.

155 *Sigālovāda Sutta*, *Dīgha
Nikāya* 31 (iii.188). See also
M. Walshe (trans.), *The Long
Discourses of the Buddha*,
Wisdom Publications,
Boston 1995, p. 467. For an
alternative translation, see
T. W. Rhys Davids (trans.),
Dialogues of the Buddha, part
3, Pali Text Society, Oxford
1991, p. 180.

156 Baizhang Huaihai (720–814).

157 For more on the bodhisattva
vows see *The Bodhisattva
Ideal*, *Complete Works*, vol. 4,
pp. 27–83.

158 Whereas the case of a
bhikkhu who touches a
woman for reasons other than
desire is not mentioned in
the Vinaya, the commentary
cautions that, should one's
mother fall into a river, under
no circumstances should
one grab hold of her. 'If she
happens to grab hold of her
son the *bhikkhu*', it goes on,
'he should not shake her off,
but should simply let her
hold on as he swims back to
shore.' Thānissaro Bhikkhu
(Geoffrey DeGraff) (trans.),

The *Buddhist Monastic Code*,
vol. i, third edition, *Mettā*
Forest Monastery, Valley
Center, 2013, pp. 161–2. See
also the commentary on the
Vimanavatthu (sixth book
of the *Khuddhaka Nikāya*)
113, Peter Masefield (trans),
Vimana Stories, Pali Text
Society, Bristol 1989.

159 Gampopa, *The Jewel
Ornament of Liberation*, trans.
Herbert V. Guenther, Rider,
London 1970, pp. 165 et seq.

160 *Dīgha Nikāya* ii.86. see T. W.
and C. A. F. Rhys Davids
(trans.), *Dialogues of the
Buddha*, part 2, Luzac, London
1971, p. 91; or M. Walshe
(trans.), *The Long Discourses
of the Buddha*, Wisdom
Publications, Boston 1995,
pp. 236–7.

161 *Visuddhimagga* 10 (1.24)
in Pe Maung Tin (trans.),
The Path of Purity, Pali Text
Society, London 1923, p. 12.

162 Gampopa, *The Jewel
Ornament of Liberation*, trans.
Herbert V. Guenther, Rider,
London 1970, p. 170.

163 *Dīgha Nikāya* iii.73. See
T. W. and C. A. F. Rhys Davids
(trans.), *Dialogues of the
Buddha*, part 3, Luzac, London
1971, p. 71.; or M. Walshe
(trans.), *The Long Discourses
of the Buddha*, Wisdom
Publications, Boston 1995,
p. 402.

164 C. D. Darlington, *The
Evolution of Man and Society*,
George Allen & Unwin,
London 1969, p. 53.

165 *Visuddhimagga* 13–14 (1.34)
in Bhikkhu Ñāṇamoli (trans.),
The Path of Purification,
Buddhist Publication Society,
Kandy 1991, p. 17.

166 Yoshito S. Hakeda (trans.), *The
Awakening of Faith*, Columbia
University Press, New York &
London 1967, pp. 56 et seq.
Aśvaghoṣa was previously
believed to have been the
author of this work, but
modern scholars agree that the
text was composed in China.

BUDDHISM AND
BLASPHEMY

167 The volume referred to
here is a 1993 anthology of
Sangharakshita's writings
entitled *The Priceless Jewel*.

168 For more on W. J. Gott, see
David Nash, *Acts Against
God*, Reaktion Books, London
2020, pp. 140ff.

169 Sir William Blackstone (1723–
1780), English jurist and Tory
politician, quoted in Theodore
Schroeder, *Constitutional Free
Speech Defined and Defended
in an Unfinished Argument
in a Case of Blasphemy*, Free
Speech League, New York
1919, p. 169.

170 Regina v Ramsay and Foote
(1883), 15 Cox CC 231.

171 See, for example, *Kevaddha
Sutta, Dīgha Nikāya* 11
(i.222) in M. Walshe (trans.),
*The Long Discourses of the
Buddha*, Wisdom Publications,
Boston 1995, pp. 178–9; or
T. W. Rhys Davids (trans.),
Dialogues of the Buddha, part

1, Pali Text Society, London 1973, p. 282.

172 Blasphemy laws were abolished in England and Wales in 2008, and in Scotland in 2021, while Northern Ireland still maintains 'blasphemy' provisions. Worldwide, seven countries retain the death sentence for blasphemy, and a further seventy-seven countries impose a prison sentence or a fine. To date (2023), blasphemy laws have been repealed in only nine countries.

173 Buddhadatta's *English–Pāli Dictionary* does indeed give *ariyupavada* as the equivalent of blasphemy, but this is a recent coinage not found in, for example, the Pali Text Society's *Pāli–English Dictionary*.

174 Contra Mendacium 39 in *Seventeen Short Treatises of S. Augustine, Bishop of Hippo*, Walter Smith (late Mozley), London 1884, p. 466.

175 Also known as Radical Theology, the 1960s 'death of God' theology hypothesized that, at best, a transcendent creator God could not be known and at worst does not exist at all. Christian thinkers associated with this movement include Thomas J. J. Altizer, William Hamilton, and Paul van Buren.

176 *Dīgha Nikāya* 1, in *Dialogues of the Buddha*, part 1, trans. T. W. Rhys Davids, Pali Text Society, London 1973, pp. 2–3.

177 The 'ground of being' appears in the work of Paul Johannes Tillich (1886–1965), a German-American Christian existentialist philosopher and theologian. Critical of arguments put forward by traditional theology, Tillich affirms God as the 'ground of being', meaning the underlying precondition for the existence of anything at all.

178 Gustave Flaubert (1821–1880) set his historical novel *Salammbô* (1862) during the siege of Carthage in 240–237 BCE. In chapter 13 of the novel, Carthaginian children are sacrificed to the god-monster Moloch.

179 *Leviticus* 24:16:

> And he that blasphemeth the name of the Lord, he shall surely be put to death, and all the congregation shall certainly stone him: as well the stranger, as he that is born in the land, when he blasphemeth the name of the Lord, shall be put to death.

180 Robert Burton, *The Anatomy of Melancholy*, vol. ii, Longman and others, London 1827, p. 587.

181 Ibid.

182 *De Civitatis Dei*, lib. XVI, cap. xxxi.

183 Archbishop Henry Edward Manning (1808–1892) devotes an entire volume to the justification of papal infallibility. See H. E. Manning, *The Vatican*

Council and Its Definitions, D. & J. Sadlier, New York, 1871.

184 Anne Fremantle, *The Papal Encyclicals in their Historical Context*, Mentor, New York 1960, p. 145.

185 Ibid. p. 137.

186 Ibid. p. 146.

187 Sangharakshita refers here to an analysis of Newman's devout treatise *Apologia pro Vita Sua* by John Middleton Murry, who concludes that Newman 'believed in God, but he did not trust Him: he was afraid of Him'. John Middleton Murry, *Things to Come*, Ayer Publishing, 1928, p. 34.

188 Quoted Jolan Jacobi, *The Psychology of Jung*, Kegan Paul Trench Trubner, London 1942, p. 88.

189 Ibid.

190 Quoted in Nicolas Walter, *Blasphemy in Britain*, Rationalist Press Association, London 1977, pp. 9–10.

191 William Blake (1757–1827) objected to orthodox Christianity's suppression of natural desire in the name of morality to the extent that, in the opening lines of *The Everlasting Gospel*, he states, 'The vision of Christ that thou dost see/Is my vision's greatest enemy.'

The poet Percy Bysshe Shelley (1792–1822), an avowed atheist and political radical, was expelled from Oxford for co-authoring *The Necessity of Atheism*.

The work of Algernon Charles Swinburne (1837–1909) frequently satirizes the Christian establishment, which he viewed as a source of repression.

The Scottish poet and freethinker James Thomson (1834–1882) published under the pseudonym Bysshe Vanolis (B. V.) Thomson and harboured a lifelong animosity toward organized religion.

The novels of Thomas Hardy (1840–1928) include much implicit criticism of the harm caused in the name of Christian virtue. See, for example, the tragic result of Angel Clare's moral inflexibility in Hardy's *Tess of the D'Urbervilles*.

192 *Regina v Ramsay and Foote* (1883); 15 Cox CC 231.

193 Ibid.

194 For more on the luckless Foote and the fate of the *Freethinker*, see David Nash, *Acts Against God*, Reaktion Books, London 2020, pp. 129–35.

NEW CURRENTS IN
WESTERN BUDDHISM

195 For details of Sangharakshita's preparation and delivery of these three talks, see *Travel Letters, Complete Works,* vol. 24, pp. 91ff.

196 For Sangharakshita's experiences in Malaysia, ibid., pp. 34–46, 53–4.

197 The idea of the Axial Period, or Age, comes from the existentialist philosopher

Karl Jaspers (1883–1969). Sangharakshita's account of the theory in relation to Buddhism appears in *What is the Sangha?*, *Complete Works*, vol. 3, pp. 424–517. See also Karl Jaspers, *The Origin and Goal of History*, Routledge and Kegan Paul, London 1953.

198 *Gaṇakamoggallāna Sutta, Majjhima Nikāya* 107 (iii.6) in I. B. Horner (trans.), *The Collection of the Middle Length Sayings*, vol. iii, Pali Text Society, Oxford 1993, p. 56.

199 The Inquisition began in the mid-thirteenth century with the Albigensian Crusade, directed towards a French Christian sect known as the Cathars. In three subsequent centuries of religious persecution, thousands of women convicted of heresy across Catholic Europe were executed under the direction of the Curia of the Roman Catholic Church with the justification that 'thou shalt not suffer a witch to live' (Exodus 22:18). See also Arthur Guirdham's *The Great Heresy*, Neville Spearman, Jersey 1977, reviewed by Sangharakshita in *Alternative Traditions*, *Complete Works*, vol. 8, pp. 421–5.

200 Aldous Huxley, *Ends and Means*, Chatto and Windus, London 1946, p. 93.

201 The Buddha's doctrine of *anattā* holds that none the five *skandhas* is self. (See, for example, the *Pañcavaggi Sutta, Saṃyutta Nikāya* iii.66–7 (22.59).) Nor are the six senses self. (See the *Girimānanda Sutta, Aṅguttara Nikāya* v.109 (10.60).) However, the question of whether the self actually exists or not is one the Buddha instructed his followers to avoid, since it would lead to views such as 'I have a self' or 'I have no self'. The Buddha regards these as 'a thicket of views, a writhing of views, a contortion of views' (*Sabbāsava Sutta, Majjhima Nikāya* i.8) that present an obstacle to awakening. Thanissaro Bhikkhu attributes such polarized thinking to what he calls 'the debate culture of ancient India', where

> Religious teachers often held public debates on the hot questions of the day, both to draw adherents and to angle for royal patronage. The Buddha warned his followers not to enter into these debates [*Pasūra Sutta, Sutta-Nipāta* 4.8] partly because once the sponsor of a debate had set a question, the debaters couldn't follow the Buddha's policy of putting useless questions aside.

Thanissaro Bhikkhu, 'There is No Self', in *Tricycle*, Spring 2014.

202 *Aṅguttara Nikāya* iv.280 (8.53). See E. M. Hare

(trans.), *The Book of the Gradual Sayings*, vol. iv, Pali Text Society, Oxford 1995, pp. 186–7; or Bhikkhu Bodhi (trans.), *The Numerical Discourses of the Buddha*, Wisdom Publications, Boston 2012, p. 1193.

203 See note 49 as well as note 66 above. Also Vinaya Piṭaka i.6; see I. B. Horner (trans.), *The Book of the Discipline*, part 4, Pali Text Society, Oxford 1996, p. 9.

204 See Bunnō Katō et al. (trans.), *The Threefold Lotus Sūtra*, Kōsei Publishing Company, Tokyo 1995, pp. 126–34.

205 From the Jetsun Milarepa's sojourn in the Stone House of Drin, 'The Song of Good Companions' in Garma C. C. Chang, *The Hundred Thousand Songs of Milarepa*, Shambhala Publications, Boston and London 1977, pp. 653–654.

206 *Sāmagāma Sutta, Majjhīma Nikāya* 104 (ii.243–5), Bhikkhu Bodhi (trans.), *The Middle Length Discourses of the Buddha*, Wisdom Publications, Boston 2000, pp. 853–4; or I. B. Horner (trans.), *The Collection of the Middle Length Sayings*, vol. iii, Pali Text Society, Oxford 1993, pp. 29-31. In the text Mahāvīra is referred to as 'the Nigaṇṭha, Nātha's son'.

207 Pāli: *pātimokkha*, the hundred-and-fifty rules observed by the monks, still observed in many cases. (S)

208 Gampopa, *The Jewel Ornament of Liberation*, trans. Herbert V. Guenther, Shambhala Publications, London 1986, p. 33.

209 These were members of the Order of Buddhist Contemplatives, whose English founder, Jiyu-Kennett Rōshi, had been ordained in Japan and moved to the USA. Their British retreat centre, Throssel Hole Priory, was established in 1972.

210 For transcripts of Sangharakshita's seminars see freebuddhistaudio.com; for edited versions relating to some of these texts, see *Complete Works*, volumes 4, 10, 18, and 19.

211 This was the title provided by Heinemann, the original publisher; the *Complete Works* edition bears the title Sangharakshita originally intended: *The Rainbow Road from Tooting Broadway to Kalimpong* (*Complete Works*, vol. 20).

212 This was the Maha Bodhi Society, the governing body of which was dominated by caste Hindus. See *Beating the Drum* in *Complete Works*, vol. 8.

213 This anecdote, widely attributed to Voltaire, is likely to be apocryphal.

214 The Buddha's *udānas* are collected in the *Udāna*, see John D. Ireland (trans.), *The Udāna and the Itivuttaka*, Buddhist Publication Society, Kandy 2007. The lion is a

traditional epithet for the
Buddha. See *Aṅguttara Nikāya*
v.33; Bhikkhu Bodhi (trans.),
*The Numerical Discourses
of the Buddha*, Wisdom
Publications, Boston 2012,
p. 1362; or F. L. Woodward
(trans.), *The Book of the
Gradual Sayings*, vol. v, Pali
Text Society, Oxford 1996,
pp. 23–4.

THE BUDDHA'S VICTORY

215 *Dhammapada* 122.

216 *Ariyapariyesanā Sutta,
Majjhima Nikāya* 1 in
I. B. Horner (trans.), *The
Collection of the Middle
Length Sayings*, vol. i, Pali Text
Society, London 1976, p. 207.

217 For a full exposition by
Sangharakshita of the twelve
cyclical *nidānas* see *Complete
Works*, vol. 1, pp. 105–14 and
vol. 2, pp. 74–6. For canonical
sources, for example, see
sections 17–21 of the
*Mahātaṇhāsaṅkhaya Sutta,
Majjhima Nikāya* 38 (i.261–
4). See Bhikkhu Ñāṇamoli and
Bhikkhu Bodhi (trans.), *The
Middle Length Discourses
of the Buddha*, Wisdom
Publications, Boston 1995,
pp. 353–7; or I. B.Horner
(trans.), *The Collection of
the Middle Length Sayings*,
vol. i, Pali Text Society,
London 1976, pp. 318–9.
Alternatively, sections 1–9 of
the *Mahānidāna Sutta, Dīgha
Nikāya* 15 (ii.55–9). See
M. Walshe (trans.), *The Long
Discourses of the Buddha*,

Wisdom Publications,
Boston 1995, pp. 223–4; or
T. W. Rhys Davids (trans.),
Dialogues of the Buddha, part
2, Pali Text Society, London
1971, pp. 50–5.

218 Mallinātha Sūri was a critic
known for his clarifications
of the five *mahākāvyas* (great
classical epics) of Sanskrit
and on śāstric works. Based
on the evidence of various
inscriptions, it is probable that
he lived c. 1350–1450 CE.

219 *Ariyapariyesanā Sutta,
Majjhima Nikāya* 26 (i.168).
See I. B. Horner (trans.), *The
Collection of the Middle
Length Sayings*, vol. i, Pali
Text Society, London 1976,
p. 212; or Bhikkhu Bodhi
(trans.), *The Connected
Discourses of the Buddha*,
Wisdom Publications, Boston
2000, p. 261.

220 Quoted in Dr B. R. Ambedkar,
The Buddha and his Dhamma,
Siddharth Publications,
Bombay 1991, p. 327, and
Christmas Humphreys, *Zen
Buddhism*, Unwin, London
1984, p. 27. In neither case,
however, is a canonical source
given.

221 *Saṃyutta Nikāya* ii.105–6, in
F. L. Woodward (trans.), *Some
Sayings of the Buddha*, Oxford
University Press, London 1939,
pp. 25–6.

222 *Dhammapada* 153–4 in
Buddhadatta Maha Thero
(trans.), *Dhammapada*,
Colombo, Colombo
Apothecaries' Co. n.d.

223 Sir Edwin Arnold, *The Light of Asia*, Windhorse Publications, Birmingham 1999, pp. 131–2.

224 *Ariyapariyesanā Sutta, Majjhima Nikāya* 26 (i.169) in I. B. Horner (trans.), *The Collection of the Middle Length Sayings*, vol. i, Pali Text Society, London 1976, p. 213.

225 *Majjhima Nikāya* i.171 in ibid. p. 214–5.

226 Ibid. p. 215.

227 *Saccasaṃyutta, Saṃyutta Nikāya* v.420; F. L. Woodward (trans.), *The Book of the Kindred Sayings*, part 5, Pali Text Society, London 1979, p. 360; also Bhikkhu Bodhi (trans.), *The Connected Discourses of the Buddha*, Wisdom Publications, Boston 2000, p. 1847.

228 See note 202.

229 A. F. Price (trans.), *The Diamond Sūtra*, Shambhala Publications, Boston 1990, p. 24.

230 D. Goddard (ed.), *A Buddhist Bible*, Beacon Press, Boston 1970, p. 348.

231 Vinaya Piṭaka ii.254–5 (*Cullavagga* 10.1). See I. B. Horner (trans.), *The Book of the Discipline*, part 5, Pali Text Society, London 1975, pp. 354–5.

232 Vinaya Piṭaka ii.254–5 (*Cullavagga* 10.1) in F. L. Woodward (trans.), *Some Sayings of the Buddha*, Oxford University Press, London 1973, p. 81.

233 Ibid. pp. 81–2.

234 S. Foster Damon, *A Blake Dictionary*, London 1979, p. 121.

235 K. R. Norman (trans.), *The Elders' Verses II (Therīgāthā)*, Luzac & Co. London 1971, p. 18.

236 E. Conze, *Buddhist Wisdom Books*, George Allen & Unwin, London 1958, p. 56.

237 In his 1978 lecture, 'Levels of Going for Refuge', Sangharakshita describes six levels: cultural, provisional, effective, real, ultimate, and cosmic. See *Complete Works*, vol. 12, pp. 310–15.

238 'Fierce friendship' was much talked about at a certain period of Triratna's history. An article in *FWBO Newsletter* 47 (Autumn 1980) explained the role of criticism in friendship, declaring robustly that 'the offering of criticism by a spiritual friend, unlike dispraise, really is an act of friendship, for it shows a living concern for the person being criticized, a refusal to be indifferent to their shortcomings. What could be more loving than that?' This kind of approach could obviously be used insensitively, as Sangharakshita points out.

239 This was the first men's national Order weekend Sangharakshita attended and the third in the history of the Order, the first occurring while he was in India, the second while he was in London.

240 Vinaya Piṭaka i.301–2
(*Mahāvagga* 8.26) in F. L.
Woodward (trans.), *Some
Sayings of the Buddha*, Oxford
University Press, London 1973,
pp. 84–5.

241 *Meghiya Sutta*, *Udāna* 4.1,
in F. L. Woodward (trans.),
*The Minor Anthologies of
the Pāli Canon*, part 2, Pali
Text Society, Oxford 1996,
p. 41. See also 'The Meaning
of Friendship in Buddhism',
pp. 695ff. below.

242 *Theragāthā* 17:3. See C. A. F.
Rhys Davids (trans.), *Psalms
of the Brethren*, Oxford
University Press, Oxford 1913,
pp. 350–1.

243 *Mahāparinibbāna Sutta*,
Dīgha Nikāya 16 (ii.143); see
M. Walshe (trans.), *The Long
Discourses of the Buddha*,
Wisdom Publications, Boston
1995, p. 265; or T. W. and
C. A. F. Rhys Davids (trans.),
Dialogues of the Buddha,
part 2, Pali Text Society,
London 1971, p. 158.

244 *Dīgha Nikāya* ii.144 in F. L.
Woodward (trans.), *Some
Sayings of the Buddha*, Oxford
University Press, London 1973,
p. 233.

245 *Sambhogakāya* is a term
from the *trikāya* doctrine
of the Mahāyāna, referring
to archetypal Buddhas,
as distinct from historical
Buddhas. For an account of
the Mahāyāna *trikāya* doctrine
see, for example, *A Survey of
Buddhism*, *Complete Works*,
vol. 1, pp. 250–64.

246 Sukhāvatī is the Buddha
Amitābha's Pure Land. For
more on the Pure Land
sūtras, see ibid., pp. 326ff.
For Śraddhāpa's translations
of three of the Pure Land
sūtras, see Ratnaguna and
Śraddhāpa, *Great Faith,
Great Wisdom*, Windhorse
Publications, Cambridge
2016.

247 Vinaya Piṭaka i.11
(*Mahāvagga* 1.6). See
I. B. Horner (trans.), *The Book
of the Discipline*, part 4, Pali
Text Society, Oxford 1996,
p. 17.

248 From 'Resolution and
Independence' (1802) by
William Wordsworth.

249 *Mahāparinibbāna Sutta*, *Dīgha
Nikāya* 16 (ii.94); Maurice
Walshe (trans.), *The Long
Discourses of the Buddha*,
Wisdom Publications, Boston
1995, p. 241; or T. W. and
C. A. F. Rhys Davids (trans.),
Dialogues of the Buddha,
part 2, Pali Text Society,
London 1971, pp. 99–100.

250 *Dīgha Nikāya* ii.100: see
M. Walshe (trans.), *The Long
Discourses of the Buddha*,
Wisdom Publications, Boston
1995, p. 245; or T. W. and
C. A. F. Rhys Davids (trans.),
Dialogues of the Buddha,
part 2, Pali Text Society,
London 1971, p. 108.

251 *Dīgha Nikāya* ii.138;
see M. Walshe (trans.),
ibid., p. 262; or T. W. and
C. A. F. Rhys Davids (trans.),
ibid., p. 150.

252 *Dīgha Nikāya* ii.148–53;
see M. Walshe (trans.), ibid.,
pp. 267–9; or T. W. and
C. A. F. Rhys Davids (trans.),
ibid, pp. 164–9.

253 Buddhaghosa in T. W. Rhys
Davids (trans.), *Dialogues of
the Buddha*, Oxford University
Press 1910, vol. ii, pp. 169–70
fn.

254 Ibid.

255 The friend was Jivaka. For
more detail, see 'The Man in
the Pit', *Moving Against the
Stream, Complete Works*,
vol. 23, pp. 387–91.

256 See Sangharakshita, *Ritual and
Devotion in Buddhism* above
pp. 192ff. above.

BUDDHISM AND THE WEST

257 *Collins English Dictionary*,
Harper Collins, Glasgow 1991.

258 Sukhavati was the name
given to the building that
was to become a residential
community and the London
Buddhist Centre. The building
project to turn this derelict fire
station into a Buddhist centre
began in 1976 and the centre
was opened in 1978.

259 Windhorse Trading (later
Windhorse:Evolution) had
grown from a market stall
into a major source of income
for the Triratna Buddhist
Community. (See Vajragupta,
The Triratna Story, Windhorse
Publications, Cambridge
2010.) The company was
dissolved in 2015, after thirty-
five years of trading. For more
on team-based right livelihood

as a spiritual practice, see
Padmasuri, *Transforming
Work*, Windhorse Publications,
Birmingham 2003.

260 The oratorio *Carpe Diem* was
composed by Bodhivajra, and
A Face Revealed was written
and directed by Kovida.

THE BUDDHIST

261 From the poem, 'The Grave'
(line 588), by the Scottish
writer Robert Blair (1699
–1746).

262 Allan Bennett, ordained in
1901 as Ananda Metteyya,
was in all likelihood the first
English *bhikkhu* to return
to England, but the first
British *bhikkhu* was probably
H. Gordon Douglas, who was
ordained in Siam in 1899 or
1900, but never returned to
Britain. See Stephen Batchelor,
The Awakening of the West,
Parallax Press, Berkeley 1994,
p. 41. Douglas himself may
have been preceded by U
Dhammaloka (c.1856–c.1914),
who was originally from
Dublin. See the special issue
of *Contemporary Buddhism*
entitled 'U Dhammaloka, the
Irish Buddhist', especially
Alicia Turner et al. 'Rewriting
the History of Early Western
Buddhist Monastics',
Contemporary Buddhism,
November 2010, 11 (2):125–
47.

263 William James, *Varieties of
Religious Experience*, The
Modern Library, New York
1902, p. 193.

264 For more on five spiritual faculties see also *The Way to Wisdom* in *Complete Works*, vol. 17.

265 See *Bojjhaṅgasaṃyutta*, *Saṃyutta Nikāya* v.115 (*Mahāvagga* 46.53); Bhikkhu Bodhi (trans.), *Connected Discourses of the Buddha*, Wisdom Publications, Boston 2000, p. 1607; or F. L. Woodward (trans.), *The Book of the Kindred Sayings*, part 5, Pali Text Society, London 1979, p. 98.

266 See the *Alagaddūpama Sutta*, *Majjhima Nikāya* 22 (i.134–5); Bhikkhu Ñāṇamoli and Bhikkhu Bodhi (trans.), *The Middle Length Discourses of the Buddha*, Wisdom Publications, Boston 1995, pp. 228–9; or I. B. Horner (trans.), *The Collection of the Middle Length Sayings*, vol. i, Pali Text Society, London 1976, pp. 173–4.

267 'Buddhism in England' was reprinted as 'Buddhism in Britain' in the *FWBO Newsletter* no. 62, summer 1984.

268 See note 262 above.

269 More recent research, based upon the *Dīpavaṃsa*, suggests that he was most likely born c.485 BCE. See R. Gombrich, 'Dating the Buddha: A Red Herring Revealed', in *The Dating of the Historical Buddha*, part 2, ed. H. Bechert, Gottingen 1992, pp. 237–59.

270 See T. R. V. Murti, *The Central Philosophy of Buddhism*, George Allen and Unwin, London 1955, p. 280, and A. C. Banerjee, in P. V. Bapat, *2500 Years of Buddhism*, Ministry of Information and Broadcasting Publications Division, New Delhi 1956, pp. 118–19. Sangharakshita has more to say on this topic in *The Meaning of Orthodoxy in Buddhism*, *Complete Works*, vol. 7, pp. 535–7.

271 Sangharakshita writes about this trip to India, and what followed, in *Moving Against the Stream*, *Complete Works*, vol. 23, pp. 333–42.

272 See Sangharakshita's memoir, ibid., vol. 23. For details of Ven. Chien Chau see pp. 228–31; for Sāmaṇera Viriya see pp. 236–41.

273 The English Sangha Trust owned Old Hall, in Biddulph, Staffordshire, which they ran as a meditation and retreat centre from 1963 until 1969.

274 A radio talk broadcast via the BBC to sixth form students on 25 October 1966. (S)

275 The saying is found in Pascal's *Pensées*, for example.

276 From the closing lines of William Wordsworth's 'River Duddon' (1820).

277 Readers familiar with Sangharakshita's *The Buddha's Noble Eightfold Path* will note the reference here to the stages of the path as 'Perfect' rather than 'right'. The distinction is clarified in *Wisdom Within Words* on p. 653 below.

278 See Sangharakshita's 1969 lecture series on 'The Higher Evolution of Man' in *What is the Sangha?*, *Complete Works*, vol. 3, which also contains some of the lectures in the 1970 series 'Aspects of the Higher Evolution of the Individual'.

279 *Krodha* is a Sanskrit term meaning 'indignation' or 'rage', one of the twenty negative mental events (*upakleśa*) discussed in *Know Your Mind*, *Complete Works*, vol. 17, pp. 643–5.

280 *Stepping-Stones* was a monthly magazine that came to a premature end due to lack of funds. Sangharakshita subsequently took a number of its contributors with him to the *Maha Bodhi*, of which he was editor for over ten years. See *Complete Works*, vol. 7 for a number of Sangharakshita's articles from *Stepping-Stones*.

281 E. Conze, *Selected Sayings from the Perfection of Wisdom*, Buddhist Society, London 1955.

282 Edward Conze, *Thirty Years of Buddhist Studies*, Bruno Cassirer, Oxford 1967, pp. 185–90.

283 Later published in the UK as Edward Conze, *A Short History of Buddhism*, George Allen & Unwin, London 1980.

284 For Conze's review, see *Complete Works,* vol. 21, p. 545.

285 Karl R. Popper, *The Unended Quest*, rev. ed, Routledge, London 2002.

286 E. Conze, *The Memoirs of a Modern Gnostic*, Samizdat Publ. Co, Sherborne 1979.

287 E. F. Schumacher, *Small is Beautiful*, Blond & Briggs, London 1973.

288 See note 286, part 2, p. 65.

289 Christmas Humphreys, *Both Sides of the Circle*, Allen & Unwin, London 1978.

290 Published as *The Inconceivable Emancipation* in *Complete Works*, vol. 16, pp. 437–582.

291 E. Conze, *Buddhist Thought in India*, Allen and Unwin, London, October 1983.

292 See note 286, part 1, p. 107.

293 Ibid. p. 135.

294 Latin: 'savage indignation', or *krodha* (Sanskrit).

295 More reminiscences are to be found in *Moving Against the Stream*, *Complete Works*, vol. 23.

296 The V-1 flying bomb, or doodlebug, was a jet-propelled missile first launched for the terror bombing of London in 1944.

297 Sangharakshita writes about his friendship with Clare Cameron in *The Rainbow Road from Tooting Broadway to Kalimpong*, *Complete Works*, vol. 20, pp. 87, 100, 103, 150. See also *Facing Mount Kanchenjunga*, *Complete Works*, vol. 21, p. 338.

298 This tale is related in *In the Sign of the Golden Wheel*, *Complete Works*, vol. 22, pp. 354–5.

299 Subhuti, *Buddhism for Today*, originally published

by Element Books, 1983, and then Windhorse Publications, Glasgow 1988.

300 This lecture appears as chapter 3 of *Buddhism for Today and Tomorrow*, on pp. 169ff. above.

301 Bhikkhu Khantipālo (born Laurence Mills in 1932) was an Englishman ordained in the Thai monastic tradition who spent a year in Kalimpong with Sangharakshita in the early 1960s. See Khantipālo, *Noble Friendship*, Windhorse Publications, Birmingham 2002, pp. 140–8, and *In the Sign of the Golden Wheel*, *Complete Works*, vol. 22, pp. 526–43.

302 Jack Austin (1917–1993) was a member of the board of the Buddhist Society in the early 1950s and joined Lama Govinda's Arya Maitreya Mandala in 1952. Sangharakshita mentions Jack Austin in ibid., p. 173.

For more about Edward Conze, see 'Dr Conze, A Personal Appreciation', pp. 529ff. above.

Adrienne Bennett was the Maha Bodhi's representative in Europe and the Americas, and Sangharakshita writes about her in *Moving Against the Stream*, *Complete Works*, vol. 23, pp. 54ff and vol. 8, p. 636. She was also the translator of *Long Discourses of the Buddha* (*Dīgha Nikāya* I–XVI), Chetana, Bombay 1964.

303 These were published in the *Maha Bodhi* and are included in *Complete Works*, vol. 8, pp. 327–35.

304 See Sangharakshita's critique of monastic formalism in *Complete Works*, vol. 1, pp. 11, 147, 187, 227ff.

305 'Turn on, tune in, drop out' was a slogan made popular in 1966 by Timothy Leary, who writes in his memoirs: 'Drop Out meant self-reliance, a discovery of one's singularity, a commitment to mobility, choice, and change.' Timothy Leary, *Flashbacks*, Putnam, New York 1990, p. 253.

306 See note 299 above.

307 Sangharakshita recounts his experiences at the Wrekin Trust's conference in *Travel Letters*, *Complete Works*, vol. 24, pp. 194ff.

308 *The Ten Pillars of Buddhism* and *World Peace and Nuclear War* are included in *Complete Works*, vols. 2 & 12 respectively.

309 Lama Govinda, *The Inner Structure of the I Ching*, Weatherhill, Tokyo 1981.

310 Lama Govinda, *A Living Buddhism for the West*, Shambhala Publications, Boston 1989; Lama Govinda, *Buddhist Reflections*, Motilal Banarsidass, New Delhi 1993.

311 The Arya Maitreya Mandala was founded by Lama Govinda in 1933. The order's activities were concentrated on India until 1952, when branches of

the order were set up in East Asia and Europe.

312 For an account of Sangharakshita's time in India with Lama Govinda and Li Gotami, see *In the Sign of the Golden Wheel* in *Complete Works*, vol. 22.

313 For more on Lama Govinda's travels, see Ken Winkler, *A Thousand Journeys: The Biography of Lama Anagarika Govinda*, Element Books, London 1990.

314 *Buddhayan* is the Marathi quarterly journal of the Triratna Buddhist Order and Community, which is circulated in Maharashtra and beyond. The circulation in 2021 was 8,500 copies.

315 Dr U Dhammaratana was a lecturer at the Nava Nalanda Mahavihara. For his highly accessible introduction to the *Visuddhimagga*, see U Dhammaratana, *Guide Through the Visuddhimagga*, Buddhist Publication Society, Kandy 2011. For more on Jinaratana, see *The Rainbow Road, from Tooting Brodway to Kalimpong*, *Complete Works*, vol. 20, pp. 165, 170.

316 The two Order members were Dharmapriya and Dhammaloka, who moved to Germany and eventually founded Germany's first Triratna Buddhist centre in Essen in 1988. In 1990, Kulanandi, Gunavati, Jayacitta, and Jayaprabha

arrived to initiate women's activities there.

GOLDEN DRUM

317 R. E. Emmerick (trans.), *The Sūtra of Golden Light*, Pali Text Society, Oxford 2001, p. 9.

318 For more on Candragomin, see M. Tatz, 'The Life of Candragomin in Tibetan Historical Tradition' (1982) in *Tibet Journal*, 7 (3), 3–22. Candragomin's writings include the *Śiṣyalekha* or 'Letter to a Disciple' published in Michael Hahn (trans.), *Invitation to Enlightenment*, Dharma Publishing, Berkeley 1999. Sangharakshita's translation of Candragomin's 'Flower-Garland Hymn to the Goddess Tārā' can be found in *Complete Works*, vol. 17, p. 143.

319 *Sūtra of Forty-Two Sections* 23, in Samuel Beal, *A Catena of Buddhist Scriptures*, Trubner & Co. London 1871, p. 198, and John Blofeld (trans), *The Sūtra of Forty-Two Sections*, Buddhist Society, London 1977, p. 18.

320 See *Complete Works*, vol. 26, p. 8.

321 *Udāna* 3.2. See Peter Masefield (trans.) *The Udāna*, Pali Text Society, Oxford 1997, p. 40; or John Ireland (trans.), *The Udāna and the Itivuttaka*, Buddhist Publication Society, Kandy 1997, pp. 35–9.

322 This phrase originates with political economist and satirist

Bernard de Mandeville (1670 –1733). In his poem 'The Grumbling Hive' (1705) a colony of bees demonstrates, at least to Mandeville's satisfaction, that without private vice there can exist no public benefit.

323 Order members' more recent explorations of personal finance and its implications for practice include Kulananda and Dominic Houlder, *Mindfulness and Money*, Penguin Random House, London 2003. For an examination of world economics from a Buddhist moral standpoint, see Vaddhaka Lynn, *The Buddha on Wall Street*, Windhorse Publications, Cambridge 2015.

324 For an account of Sangharakshita's visit to the USA in the following year (1994), see 'Impressions of America', in *Through Buddhist Eyes, Complete Works*, vol. 24, pp. 468–89.

325 In addition to the more recent varieties of 'Western Buddhism' mentioned here, the USA has long-standing communities of Asian-American Buddhists. For an account of Buddhism in the USA seen from an Asian-American perspective, see Chenxing Han, *Be the Refuge*, North Atlantic Books, Berkeley 2021.

326 Dharma Publishing is the publishing wing of the Nyingma Institute of Berkeley,

California, whose teacher is Tarthang Tulku (b.1935). There remains a strong connection between Triratna and the Nyingma Institute due to the fact that Jamyang Khyentse was teacher to both Tarthang Tulku and Sangharakshita. Dharma Publishing's titles were distributed in Europe by Windhorse Publications until 2003.

327 This talk appears in *Complete Works*, vol. 12, pp. 492–517.

328 This was the European Buddhist Union Congress of 1992. Alongside Sangharakshita, the speakers included Sogyal Rimpoche, Thich Nhat Hanh, and Dr Rewata Dhamma. The text of Sangharakshita's address can be found above under the title *Buddhism and the West*, pp. 459ff.

329 For Sangharakshita's distinction between feminism and Feminism see pp. 638–41 below.

330 Francis Bacon (1561–1626) was an English philosopher and statesman. For Bacon's conception of idols, see Francis Bacon, *The New Organon and Related Writings*, Liberal Arts Press, New York 1960.

331 For more on the College of Public Preceptors in 1993, see chapter 9 of Vajragupta, *The Triratna Story*, Windhorse Publications, Cambridge 2010.

332 Guhyaloka is a men's retreat centre in the Alicante mountains in southern Spain.

333 At that time, Bosnia was the scene of widespread ethnic violence following the collapse of the Socialist Federal Republic of Yugoslavia.

334 Subhuti, *Bringing Buddhism to the West*, Windhorse Publications, Birmingham 1995, p. 186.

335 *Alternative Traditions, Complete Works*, vol. 8, p. 553.

336 See note 334 above, p. 188.

337 Subhuti, *Sangharakshita: A New Voice In The Buddhist Tradition*, Windhorse Publications, Birmingham 1994, p. 240.

338 This is an allusion to one of Sangharakshita's 'Fifteen Points for Old – and New – Order Members', in *Complete Works*, vol. 12, p. 488.

339 See note 265. For more on the distinction Sangharakshita draws between integrated and alienated awareness see, for example, ibid., pp. 258ff.

340 American beat poet Allen Ginsberg (1926–1997) first met Sangharakshita in Kalimpong in June 1962; see 'With Allen Ginsberg in Kalimpong', in *Complete Works*, vol. 22, pp. 563–8. See also *Moving Against the Stream, Complete Works*, vol. 23, p. 123, and Sangharakshita's poem, 'In Memory of Allen Ginsberg' in *Complete Works*, vol. 25 p. 413.

341 Sangharakshita's further travels are recorded in *Through Buddhist Eyes, Complete Works*, vol. 24.

342 Sogyal Rimpoche, *The Tibetan Book of Living and Dying*, Rider Books, London 2017; Frances Fremantle and Chögyam Trungpa (trans.), *The Tibetan Book of the Dead*, Shambhala Publications, Berkeley and London 1975.

DAKINI

343 Above, pp. 420ff.

344 Subhuti, *The Buddhist Vision*, Rider, London 1994.

345 *Complete Works*, vol. 2, pp. 575–614.

346 *Aṅguttara Nikāya* iv.274–6; see Bhikkhu Bodhi (trans.), *The Numerical Discourses of the Buddha*, Wisdom Publications, Boston 2012, pp. 1189–90; or E. M. Hare (trans.), *The Book of the Gradual Sayings*, vol. iv, Pali Text Society, Oxford 1995, pp. 181–5.

347 Ibid.

348 Taraloka is a women's retreat centre in Shropshire founded in the 1980s. For more on Taraloka's early years, see Dayanandi, 'Building Tārā's Realm: The Story of Taraloka Women's Retreat Centre' in Kalyanavaca (ed.), *The Moon and Flowers*, Windhorse Publications, Birmingham 1997.

DHARMA LIFE

349 On 15 June 1996, an IRA bomb exploded about 400 metres from the Manchester

Buddhist Centre. It caused significant damage, but no fatalities.

350 *Aṅguttara Nikāya* i.10: Bhikkhu Bodhi (trans.), The *Numerical Discourses of the Buddha*, Wisdom Publications 2012, p. 97; and F. L. Woodward (trans.), *The Book of the Gradual Sayings*, vol. i, Pali Text Society, Oxford 2000, p. 8.

351 *Sallekha Sutta, Majjhima Nikāya* 8 (i.44). See Bhikkhu Ñāṇamoli and Bhikkhu Bodhi (trans.), *The Middle Length Discourses of the Buddha*, Wisdom Publications, Boston 1995, p. 130; or I. B. Horner (trans.), *Middle Length Sayings*, vol. i, Pali Text Society, London 1976, p. 56.

352 See Ganganatha Jha (trans.), *The Tattvasaṅgraha of Shāntarakṣita*, Motilal Banarsidass, Delhi 1986, vol. ii, p. 1558, text 3588.

353 *Complete Works*, vol. 2, pp. 397–503.

354 *Moving Against the Stream*, in *Complete Works*, vol. 23.

355 From John Keats (1795–1821), 'When I Have Fears That I May Cease to Be'.

356 *Living with Awareness* (2003) and *Living with Kindness* (2004) in *Complete Works*, vol. 15.

357 A reference to English landscape painter J. M. W. Turner (1775–1851).

358 See William H. Grosnick, *The Tathāgatagarbha Sūtra* in Donald S. Lopez Jr.

(ed.), *Buddhism in Practice*, Princeton University Press, 1995, p. 92.

359 *Mahāparinibbāna Sutta, Dīgha Nikāya* 16 (ii.154). See M. Walshe (trans.), *The Long Discourses of the Buddha*, Wisdom Publications, Boston 1995, pp. 269–70; or T. W. and C. A. F. Rhys Davids (trans.), *Dialogues of the Buddha*, part 2, Pali Text Society, London 1971, p. 171.

360 Chattrul Sangye Dorje Rimpoche (1913–2015) was a Tibetan Dzogchen master in the Nyingma tradition. See *Precious Teachers, Complete Works*, vol. 22, pp. 390–5.

361 *From Genesis to the Diamond Sūtra*, in *Complete Works*, vol. 13, pp. 519–672.

362 See Sangharakshita's account of the events subsequent to Dr Ambedkar's death in *In the Sign of the Golden Wheel, Complete Works*, vol. 22, pp. 360–4.

THE MEANING OF FRIENDSHIP IN BUDDHISM

363 William Blake, *Jerusalem* xxiii.

364 The *Shorter Oxford English Dictionary* traces the word 'free' to the Old Teutonic *frijo*, also meaning 'free', and to the Old English *fréon*, meaning 'to love', whence 'friend'. Both are etymologically connected to the Old Aryan *priyo*- represented by the Sanskrit *priya*, meaning 'dear'.

365 For an account of the love mode and the power mode,

see Sangharakshita, *The Ten Pillars of Buddhism, Complete Works*, vol. 2, pp. 361–3.

366 See John D. Ireland (trans.), *The Udāna and the Itivuttaka*, Buddhist Publication Society, Kandy 2007.

367 See note 241.

368 *Maggasaṃyutta, Saṃyutta Nikāya* v.2 (5.1). See Bhikkhu Bodhi (trans.), *The Connected Discourses of the Buddha*, Wisdom Publications, Boston 2000, pp. 1524–5; or F. L. Woodward (trans.), *The Book of the Kindred Sayings*, part 5, Pali Text Society, London 1979, p. 2.

369 *Mahāgovinda Sutta, Dīgha Nikāya* 19 (ii.240–1). See M. Walshe (trans.), *The Long Discourses of the Buddha*, Wisdom Publications, Boston 1995, pp. 307–8; or T. W. and C. A. F. Rhys Davids (trans.), *Dialogues of the Buddha*, part 2, Pali Text Society, London 1971, pp. 273–4.

ENTERING THE SANGHA

370 The Buddhafield festival takes place each year at the height of the English summer.

371 *Uposatha Sutta, Udāna* 5.5. See John D. Ireland (trans.), *The Udāna and the Itivuttaka*, Buddhist Publication Society, Kandy 2007, p. 68. See also Sangharakshita's talk 'The Taste of Freedom', pp. 39ff. above.

372 See *Ambedkar and Buddhism* in *Complete Works*, vol. 9.

373 Plato, *The Republic*, book 7.

374 For more on the fetters, see pp. 47ff. above.

375 Pagan Kennedy, *The First Man-Made Man*, Bloomsbury Publishing, London 2008.

376 The friend was Jivaka; for an account of his stay in Kalimpong see *Precious Teachers, Complete Works*, vol. 22, pp. 434–45. *The First Man-Made Man* tells Jivaka's story.

377 The order of the fetters has been revised for this *Complete Works* edition. See note 35.

378 Ecclesiastes 9:10.

THE REFUGE TREE

379 For more on King Lha-btsun-pa's invitation, see Alaka Chattopadhya, *Atisa and Tibet*, Indian Studies, Calcutta 1967, pp. 416–7. For the divination concerning Tārā and the yogini, see ibid. pp. 417–8.

380 For the story of the demons of Tibet, their subjugation by Padmasambhava, and their becoming *dharmapālas*, see canto 60 of *The Life and Liberation of Padmasambhava*, Dharma Publishing, Emeryville 1978, p. 370.

381 Zhiyi (538–597 CE) is also spelled Chih-I according to the Wade-Giles romanization system used in Taiwan.

382 For more on the four reliances, see Sangharakshita, *The Inconceivable Emancipation, Complete Works*, vol. 16, pp. 567–82.

383 *Dhammapada* 294–5. These
verses are explained in the
Dhammapada commentary.
See Daw Mya Tin (trans.),
*The Dhammapada Verses
and Stories*, Yangon,
Myanmar Pitaka Association,
2009, pp. 362–3; and
S. Radhakrishnan,
Dhammapada, Oxford
University Press, London 1950,
pp. 152–3.

384 The parable of the ever-
smouldering anthill is
found in the *Vammika
Sutta, Majjhima Nikāya*
23 (i.143–5): see Bhikkhu
Ñāṇamoli and Bhikkhu
Bodhi (trans.), *The Middle
Length Discourses of the
Buddha*, Wisdom Publications,
Boston 1995, pp. 237–9; or
I. B. Horner (trans.), *Middle
Length Sayings*, vol. i, Pali
Text Society, London 1976,
pp. 183–6. For the parable
of the blind men and the
elephant, see *Udāna* 6.4
(*Paṭhamanānātitthiya Sutta*),
in John D. Ireland (trans.),
The Udāna and the Itivuttaka,
Buddhist Publication Society,
Kandy 2007, pp. 81–4.

385 These lectures formed the
basis of Sangharakshita,
Transforming Self and World
(*Complete Works*, vol. 16).

386 The exception was Chattrul
Sangye Dorje (1913–2015)
who was still alive at the time
of this talk.

387 A few years ago I gave a talk
that went into the meaning of
that word at some length and
what I said on that occasion
has appeared in *What is the
Sangha?* in the form of chapter
19. (S) See *Complete Works*,
vol. 3, pp. 595ff.

388 *The Essential Sangharakshita*
is also published as *Complete
Works*, vol. 6.

389 *Living Ethically* appears in
Complete Works, vol. 17.

390 For the original text, see
Nāgārjuna, *The Precious
Garland and the Song of the
Four Mindfulnesses*, trans.
Jeffrey Hopkins and Lati
Rimpoche with Anne Klein,
Harper & Row, New York
1975.

391 *Living with Awareness* and
Living with Kindness are
included in *Complete Works*,
vol. 15; for *The Yogi's Joy*, see
Complete Works, vol. 19.

392 Samuel Johnson, *Rasselas*,
Oxford University Press,
Oxford 2009, chapter 44.

393 From 'A Vision of the Last
Judgment, page 70, for the
year 1810, "Additions to
Blake's Catalogue of Pictures
etc."' quoted in David
Erdman (ed), *The Poetry
and Prose of William Blake*,
Doubleday, New York, 1970,
p. 555.

394 Jonathan Swift (1667–1745)
was an Irish poet and satirist.
His works paint a grim picture
of humanity, whose innate
reasoning faculty is put to use

merely in pursuit of greed and other base impulses.

395 See *The Inconceivable Emancipation*, *Complete Works*, vol. 16, pp. 535–50.

THE FWBO AND THE
PATH OF SPIRITUAL
DEVELOPMENT

396 The Movement's first 'meditation and shrine room' opened on 6 April 1967 in Monmouth Street, central London. See *Moving Against the Stream*, *Complete Works*, vol. 23, pp. 426–31.

397 In May 1968 student demonstrations in Paris escalated within days into a general strike, bringing the economy to a virtual standstill. In the USA, opposition to the war in Vietnam included large-scale resistance to military conscription, eventually forcing an end to US combat operations.

398 Lokamitra moved to India in 1978, inspired by the work of Dr B. R. Ambedkar among the Dalit communities of Maharashtra, and helped to establish what later became known as the Triratna Bauddha Mahasangha Sahayak Gana (TBMSG).

   Subhuti was involved with Pundarika, the original Triratna Buddhist centre in North London, and the London Buddhist Centre in London's East End. During the 1980s, Subhuti lived at Padmaloka Men's

Retreat Centre where he was Sangharakshita's secretary, helping also to establish ordination training for men.

   Buddhadasa first met Sangharakshita in 1969 in the London basement described above and was active in the founding of the Pundarika centre and the London Buddhist Centre. In 1987 Buddhadasa founded the Melbourne Buddhist Centre and men's community.

   Dhammadinna was secretary of the first North London Buddhist Centre in Archway, later moving to Tiratanaloka retreat centre for women in the Brecon Beacons, where she remained for many years. She became a private and public preceptor in the late 1990s.

   Malini was chair of the Glasgow Buddhist Centre before helping to organize some of the Movement's first retreats exclusively for women in Norfolk, England. Malini later moved to London, and then to New Zealand in 1989, where she spent the next quarter-century training women for ordination.

399 See note 1.

400 For more on this topic, see 'A System of Meditation', *Complete Works*, vol. 5, pp. 29–35.

401 From William Wordsworth, 'Lines Composed a Few Miles above Tintern Abbey'.

INDEX

Abhidharma 463, 728, 738n
abortion 636–7
the Absolute 81, 126; *see also* the
    Unconditioned
absorption 124–6, 131, 150; *see also*
    dhyānas; *samādhi*
Advayavajra, Ven. 561, 563
aesthetic
  aspect of (*kalyāna*) 440, 704
  sense and ritual 211, 224, 232–3, 240
Āgamas 716
Aid For India (later Karuna Trust) 556
Akshobhya, Dharmachari 94, 526
Akṣobhya 730
Alagaddūpama Sutta 37, 481, 739n, 761n
Ālāra the Kālāma 398–9, 413
Alexander the Great 250
alienation or alienated awareness 79, 81,
    121, 626, 766n
alms 40, 166, 187–8, 318, 416
altruism 282, 734
altruistic, and individual aspects of
    spiritual life 255, 271–2, 318–19,
    451
altruistic activity, *see* helping other people;
    social service
Amaradakini xxii
Ambedkar, B. R. 591, 708, 737n, 757n,
    770n
  death of xix, 691, 708, 737n, 767n
  followers of 592, 596, 687, 708
  and mass conversion 663–4, 708
  Sangharakshita and 663–4
Ambedkar and Buddhism 737n, 768n
Amitābha 287, 292, 293, 730, 759n
  Pure Land of, *see* Sukhāvatī
Amitābha Visualization Sūtra 87, 741n
anagārika
  precepts 176, 316, 537, 587

Sangharakshita as 665–6
anagārikas, anagarikās 427, 537, 624,
    642; *see also* celibacy
  in WBO/TBM 587, 597, 646, 665
Ānanda 276, 369–70, 420, 421–4, 426,
    428, 432–3, 434–7, 438, 440–1,
    449–54, 703
Ananda, Dharmachari 501
Ananda Metteyya (Allan Bennett) xvi,
    475, 485, 760n
ānāpānasati, see mindfulness of breathing
Ānāpānasati Sutta 31, 739n
anātman (Pāli *anattā*) 48, 58, 364, 446,
    481, 755n; *see also* selflessness; views,
    wrong, of self
Anderson, Tenshin 609–10
anger 84, 130, 164, 332–4, 430, 442,
    569, 677; *see also* hatred
Aṅguttara Nikāya 16, 109, 123, 364, 366,
    383, 643, 656–7, 738n, 742n, 743n,
    747n, 755–6n, 756–7n, 766n, 767n
Ani-La (French nun) 250, 747n
animals 154, 701
  instincts 197
  realm 28, 166, 195, 321, 402
animism 247–8, 747n
animosity 256; *see also* hatred
archetypal 16
  Buddhas and bodhisattvas, *see* Buddhas
    and bodhisattvas
  dreams 691
  power 228
  realms or worlds, *see under* worlds
  symbols 683; *see also* symbols
archetypes 315, 549; *see also* myths;
    patterns
arhant ideal or path 254–5, 286, 318–20
arhants 42, 57, 107, 167, 254–5, 314,
    450, 645, 713

arhantship 422, 743n
Aristotle 192, 745n
Ariyapariyesanā Sutta 109, 161, 312, 397,
    406, 412, 742n, 744n, 757n, 758n
Arnold, Edwin 76, 411, 740n, 758n
Arnold, Matthew 49–50, 75, 740n
arts 25, 33, 75, 118, 177, 195, 203, 204,
    292, 390, 510, 588, 610
  FWBO and the 148, 186, 390, 466–7,
    620–1, 631, 663
Arya Maitreya Mandala (AMM) 560–1,
    563, 763n
Āryasaṅgha or transcendental community
    134, 234, 254, 650–1; *see also* noble
    ones
ascetics 41, 170, 188, 414, 496, 696
  five 163, 400, 414–18, 446
Ashvajit, Dharmachari 501
astrology 80, 316–17, 531, 533
asuras 28, 165, 323, 429
Aśvaghoṣa 16, 103, 738n, 742n
  pseudo- 325, 752n
Aśvajit 163
Atīśa 714, 768n
ātman 512; *see also anātman*
attachment 283, 366, 398, 538–40,
    572–3, 580, 590, 637–8, 677
  love (*pema* (Sanskrit *prema*) 701
  non- *see* detachment
  to observances, *see* fetters, third
Auckland 93–5, 177, 349, 526, 627
Augustine, Saint 105, 331, 338, 742n, 753n
Austen, Jane 634
Austin, Jack 546, 763n
Australia 374, 390, 651, 729
authority 19, 185, 335, 387, 609, 645,
    654–5, 667
Avalokiteśvara 243, 292, 293, 517
  mantra 242, 287, 289, 292
  Sangharakshita vision of F/WBO as 517
Avataṃsaka Sūtra 225, 716, 746n
aversion 27, 37, 129–30, 401, 403–4,
    674; *see also* hatred
awakening xviii, 105, 716; *see also*
    Enlightenment
The Awakening of Faith 325, 752n
awareness (*smṛti* (Pāli *sati*)) 12, 13, 17,
    26, 31, 65, 101, 115, 164, 258; *see
    also* mindfulness
  alienated 81, 626, 766n
  of environment 733
  four kinds or levels of 36–7
  mutual 26
  perfect or transcendental 21, 31
  pure 689

Axial Age 354–5, 755n
Ayya Khema 669–70

Bach, J. S. 204, 228, 371
Bacon, F. 612, 765n
Baizhang Huaihai 318, 751n
Batchelor, S. 219, 760n
beauty 204, 222, 232–3, 468, 587–8, 631;
    see also kalyāṇa
  ritual and 211, 222, 227, 240
Beethoven, L. van 371, 729
Benares 380, 696
  Isipatana 414–15, 418, 446
Bennett, A. A. G. 218, 219, 546, 746n,
    763n
Bennett, Allan, *see* Ananda Metteyya
Berlin 459, 470, 610, 670, 695
Bhaja retreat centre 562
bhāvanā 153, 306
bhikkhu/bhikkhunī, ordination 68,
    317; *see also* ordination, monastic;
    ordination, of women
bhikkhunīs (Sanskrit *bhikṣuṇīs*) 68, 317,
    449–50, 475, 644–5; *see also* nuns
bhikkhus (Sanskrit *bhikṣus*) 39–40,
    187–8, 548, 591, 593; *see also* monks
  British xvi, 475, 485, 545, 760n, 763n
  and ethics, *see* monastic code
bhūmis
  ten 217, 313, 750n
  thirteen 313, 751n
biases *āsravas* (Pāli *āsavas*) 46, 306,
    313–14, 321, 324
  destruction of 30, 46, 314, 415
Bible xvi, 328, 339, 361, 379, 508, 711
  Leviticus 336, 753n
  Proverbs 161, 744n
bisexuality 427, 582
Blacker, C. 495
Blair, R. 475, 760n
Blake, W. 19, 25, 78, 343, 370–1, 427–8,
    430, 620, 700, 725, 739n, 740n,
    754n, 758n, 767n, 769n
blasphemy 326–33, 335–9, 343–7, 753n
  law of 327–9, 331, 346–7, 752n
    abolition 327, 330–1, 753n
  rational and irrational 337–9, 341–2,
    345–6
  therapeutic 341–3, 346, 347
blessings 516, 691
  as 'gift waves' 507
bliss 45–6, 86, 125, 149
Blofeld, J. 474, 764n
Bodh Gaya 171, 414, 482, 491, 717–18
bodhi, see Enlightenment

Buddhist scriptures 372, 377, 379, 445,
508, 655, 716–20; *see also* Kangyur;
Mahāyāna *sūtras*; Pāli Canon
myths and legends in 15, 738n
Buddhist Society
London, *see* London Buddhist Society
Oxford University 529, 530
Reading University 19
Buddhist teachers 70, 460, 655, 656–7,
668; *see also* spiritual teachers
Buddhist tradition 222, 467, 470, 487,
490, 678–9
FWBO and xix, 51, 209, 258, 455, 463,
549, 599–600, 602; *see also under*
ecumenism; *yānas*
The Buddhist Vision 640–1, 766n
Burma 236, 247–8, 372
Burne-Jones, E. 77, 740n
Burton, R. 336–7, 753n

Calcutta 171, 172
Cameron, C. 542, 762n
Candragomin 571, 764n
Carpe Diem 466, 760n
caste 41, 353–4, 592–3, 624
Hindus 593, 708, 756n; *see also*
Brahmins
Scheduled 592–3, 639
system 593, 707–8
Catherine of Siena 633–4
Catholicism 214, 228, 251, 260, 305,
338–9, 342, 355, 611, 670, 755n
celibacy 176, 308, 425, 464, 536–8,
570–1, 587–90, 597, 704, 747n;
see also anagārikas; *brahmacarya*;
chastity
centres, FWBO 94, 186, 239, 351, 390,
523, 525–6, 554, 623, 627, 636, 651,
728–9; *see also* London Buddhist
Centre; Pundarika; retreat centres
in Australia (Melbourne & Sydney) 524,
627, 770n
autonomy of 609, 669
in Germany (Berlin and Essen) 563, 695,
727, 764n
Glasgow 770n
in India 592
Manchester 649, 652, 766–7n
Norwich 562
in USA 524, 607, 627–8
cessation (*nirodha*) 86, 163, 310, 428,
447–8
Ceylon xvi, 170, 460, 485, 488; *see also*
Sri Lanka
Chan 170, 214, 318, 485, 513
Chandramani, U 305, 427, 749n

chanting 119, 209, 211–12, 221, 227,
229, 288, 291, 510, 685; *see also*
mantras
chastity 315, 316, 317, 318, 569–71, 704;
see also celibacy
Chattrul Sangye Dorje 691, 767n, 769n
Chien Chau 494–5, 761n
Chih-I, *see* Zhiyi
China 20, 170, 270, 297–8, 355, 372,
374, 485, 510, 626, 641, 696–7, 714,
715, 752n
Chinese Buddhism 372, 374, 513, 679,
740n; *see also* Chan; Tiantai
Christianity 75–6, 106–7, 199, 214,
334–43, 361–2, 486; *see also*
Catholicism; Protestantism
and blasphemy 329–47
and Buddhism 214, 295–304, 334–5,
338, 345, 467, 551, 691, 748n
Christians, ex- 341–2, 345
citta, *see* mind
civilization 197, 270–1, 351, 353, 355,
621
climate change 733
Coleridge, S. T. 56–7, 740n
commitment xix, 40, 49–50, 221, 257,
391, 552–3, 555, 617
and lifestyle, *see* lifestyle and
commitment
to the Three Jewels 67–70, 134, 136,
176–9, 189, 311–12, 332, 475, 586,
712; *see also* Going for Refuge,
ordination
communication 33, 139, 186, 440, 549,
639, 663; *see also* language; speech
Buddha and 161–5, 383–4, 417–18,
437, 511–13, 653–4; *see also* Buddha,
teaching
effect on energy 196, 199, 200, 202
exercises 200, 728
sex and 575, 579, 584–5
communism 197, 745n
communities, residential 44–5, 135,
176–8, 189, 351, 390, 444, 464–6,
554, 608, 624, 662, 690, 698, 727
single-sex 189, 464, 556, 557, 579–80,
616, 705, 760n, 770n
compassion (*karuṇā*) 6, 11, 13, 64,
102–3, 104, 155, 257, 403, 507, 734
bodhisattva of, *see* Avalokiteśvara
and wisdom 156, 160, 319, 489, 511, 707
conceit 5, 401, 403, 405
concentration 65, 120–4, 148–50, 477,
478, 481, 675–6; *see also samādhi*
skilful and unskilful 675–6

conditionality 163, 404, 463, 677; see
also dependent origination
cyclic, twelve links of (nidānas) 28–9,
35–6, 166, 404, 757n; see also wheel,
of life
cyclic and spiral xxii–xxiii, 163–4, 167,
179
described as 'becoming' 29, 36, 162–3,
313–14
spiral, twelve links of 30; see also
nidānas, positive; path, spiral
the conditioned (saṃskṛta) 126, 303; see
also saṃsāra
and the unconditioned (asaṃskṛta) 11,
312–13, 619, 677
conditioned existence, see existence,
conditioned
conditioning 58–9, 81, 205, 239, 398, 489
psychological 5, 6–8, 11, 12, 13–14, 410
religious 7, 106–7, 199, 260, 262,
341–3, 345–6, 361–2, 378–9, 509
conditions
difficult 16–17, 622–3
external 183–4, 197, 462, 618, 733
supportive 279, 430, 618
confession 217, 218, 219, 243, 259–64,
268, 440, 442, 444, 703, 719
Confucianism 296
Confucius 355, 493, 697
consciousness, see also vijñāna
absolute 115–16, 134, 355, 358
developing or raising level of 146, 160,
306, 334, 355
direct and indirect methods 94,
116–20, 123, 148, 461–2, 466
feminine 613
group 354, 363
hierarchy of 31–2, 130
individual or relative 21, 29, 35
levels of, see also dhyānas; worlds
four 115, 131
higher 46, 61, 80–1, 119, 122, 148–9,
152, 497–8, 588
reflexive or self- xxii, 32, 115–16, 121,
145–7, 354, 358, 363, 575, 731–2
sense- 115–16, 148, 225
subjective, and objective descriptions of
536, 656
'third order of', see awareness, mutual
transcendental 18, 115, 116, 355, 358, 413
transformation of 710–11
turning about in... (parāvṛtti) 156, 302
contact (sparśa) 29, 35, 36, 86
contentment 28, 32, 37, 63, 129, 140,
256, 257, 674

conversion 21, 341, 417, 454, 700
elements of (saṃgraha-vastus) 699–700
mass
Dr Ambedkar and 663–4, 708
movement 171, 592, 663–4, 707; see
also ex-'Untouchables'
Conze, E. 529–35, 546, 621, 740n, 743n,
750n, 758n, 762n, 763n
cosmology, Buddhist 28, 323, 402, 749n;
see also planes; realms; worlds
covetousness 256, 257
craving 5–6, 28, 46, 129, 292, 401, 403,
412, 428; see also desire, greed
aversion and delusion 27, 32, 37,
129–30, 674
for experience 79–80, 82–4
and grasping, in cyclic nidānas 29, 36
overcoming 310, 319, 404, 411, 414
sex and 538–9, 572–4, 588
creativity 25, 31–2, 50, 77–8, 102, 559,
675, 712; see also mind, creative
Cresswell, J. 660
criticism 201, 431, 758n
of Sangharakshita and the FWBO 664–5
Crusade, Albigensian 361, 755n
Cūḷagopālaka Sutta 157, 268, 744n, 748n
culture
1960s alternative 550–1, 586, 626, 729,
763n
Buddhism, and, see under Buddhism
Western 370–1, 377, 379, 463, 466–7,
513, 562, 564, 620
cynicism 553, 734

dākas 42, 43, 167, 680
Dakini magazine 631–2, 632, 645, 646
dākinīs 42, 43, 52, 87, 151, 167, 680
Dalai Lama 542, 626
dāna 12, 244, 306; see also generosity
Darlington, C. D. 323, 752n
Dasadhamma Sutta 263, 747n
Dayanandi 766n
death 17, 29, 455–8, 628–9
contemplation of 404, 448
Māra as (maccu-māra) 400–1, 402, 403
and rejoicing in merits 734
spiritual 731, 735–6
deathlessness, drum of 415
deathless state 403, 406, 412, 413; see
also Nirvāṇa
debate 299–301, 636, 671, 755n
defilements, see kleśas
deities
indigenous Tibetan 678
wrathful 17–18, 243, 292
Delamare, Terry 583, 692

delight 45, 164, 222, 320, 440; *see also* joy

delusion (*moha*) 27, 32, 129–30, 258, 274, 276, 308, 674, 715, 723; *see also* ignorance

Democratization, Feminization, and Integration 612–13

demon, of impermanence 29, 167

demons 293, 368, 715, 768n
  world of 402; *see also* hell

dependent origination 369, 509; *see also* conditionality

Descartes, R. 745n

Desideri, I. 297, 748n

desire 122, 319, 497, 577; *see also* craving
  sexual 572–3, 588
  world of (*kāmaloka*), *see* worlds, of sensuous desire

detachment or disinterestedness (*alobha*) 109, 308, 315, 324, 366

Devamitra 518

devaputta-māra 400, 402–3, 405

devas 42, 236–7, 402, 414; *see also* gods

development
  clarification of use of term 364
  personal 145–7, 153; *see also* spiritual development

devotion 155, 229, 451, 453, 622, 650, 751n; *see also* faith and devotion, reverence

devotional practice 148, 206, 293, 462, 678; *see also* puja, ritual

devotional worship, Hindu (*bhakti*) 305, 749n

Dhammacakkappavattana Sutta 417

dhammacāris/dhammacārinīs xiv, 255–7, 635–6; *see also* Order Members

Dhammadinnā (*arhant*) 645

Dhammadinna, Dharmacharini 729, 770n

Dhammaloka, Dharmachari 563, 764n

Dhammaloka, U 760n

Dhammapada 3, 20, 21, 85, 397, 411, 509, 718–19, 738n, 739n, 741n, 757n, 769n

Dhammaratana, U 562, 764n

dhammas, mindfulness of 451

Dhardo Rimpoche 210–12, 519, 542, 549, 666, 745n

Dharma 19–20, 245, 246, 253–4, 278, 283, 307, 325, 364–5, 367–8, 482
  basic, *see* Buddhism, basic/original teachings
  can be lost 409, 622
  definition of 109, 365–6, 417–18
  or Dharmacakra Day 395, 410, 418

dispute about 369–70

embodied in practices 369–70

eye (*dharmacakṣus*) 446–7, 725

friendship and 700, 703–4

Going for Refuge to 67, 175, 385, 451, 468, 482, 650, 668

like rain 87, 367, 610–11

like the ocean 39–43, 51, 707

mirror of the 449–50

misunderstanding, *see* Buddhism, misunderstanding of; literalism

'mythical bits' 15, 738n; *see also* myth

protectors of, *see* dharmapālas

psychological approach to, *see* psychological approach

as a raft 37–8, 481

as a social force 549–50; *see also* social service; society, new

spreading and working for 407, 619, 687, 691, 700, 714, 717, 736; *see also* FWBO, expansion

study, *see* study

summary of 163

using four reliances to interpret 718–20

wheel of 218, 410, 417, 447
  first turning 161, 218

Dharma-farers, *see* dhammacāris/ dhammacārinīs; Order members

dharmakāya 226, 310; *see also* trikāya
  bodhisattvas of 517

Dharma Life magazine 647, 648

dharmapālas 42, 293, 680, 706, 749n, 768n

Dharmapriya 563, 727, 764n

dharma-vicaya, *see* mental states, investigation of

Dharma-Vinaya 39–45, 47, 50–2, 421, 422, 706–7

Dhyāna for Beginners 377

dhyānas 63–4, 65, 512, 537–8, 575, 650; *see also* absorption; consciousness, levels of
  four 149–53, 743n
  translated as 'trance' 112, 300

Diamond Sūtra (Vajracchedikā Prajñāpāramitā Sūtra) 170, 417–18, 429, 509, 533, 716, 758n

Dīgha Nikāya 102, 107, 155, 276, 306, 320, 322, 332–3, 436, 449, 452, 453–4, 455, 690, 695, 704, 739n, 741n, 742n, 743n, 748n, 749n, 751n, 752n, 753n, 757n, 759n, 760n, 763n, 767n, 768n

Dīpaṅkara 246

Dīpavaṃsa 491n, 761n

disciple, way of (*śrāvakayāna*) 255, 310
disciples
of the Buddha 41, 407, 435, 438, 449,
450, 453–4, 491, 492, 568–9, 645, 702
first five 163, 400, 414–18, 446–8, 496
and sick monk, *see* monks, sick
care for our friends' 699
and guru, *see* gurus
lay, *see* lay disciples; *upāsakas/upāsikās*
Sangharakshita's 585, 655, 686, 691; *see
also* Order Members
discipline, *see* spiritual discipline
dismal-jimmyism 201
dispassion 46, 109, 366
distraction 402, 403, 405, 419
doctrine-followers (*dhammānusārins*)
157–8, 268, 744n, 748n
dogmatism 196, 654
doubt 122, 123, 447, 711–12, 750n; *see
also* fetters, second
Sangharakshita and 170, 173, 520, 522,
553, 728
Drama of Cosmic Enlightenment 741n
dreams 181, 184–5, 290, 662, 681
Sangharakshita's 685, 691
Dubash, D. 737n
duḥkha (Pāli *dukkha*) *see* suffering
duties 90–1, 155, 172, 317, 475, 545,
600, 624, 696, 699
to our friends 698–702
dysentery, case of 432–44

eating 13, 60, 221–2, 240, 316, 318, 747n
ecumenism 297, 509, 546, 609–10, 717
FWBO and 470, 713–14; *see also* FWBO
and Eastern Buddhism; Buddhist
tradition, FWBO and
not eclecticism 376–7; *see also* spiritual,
principles
and synthesis 297, 550, 678
effort 65, 84, 88, 107, 193, 210, 285,
314, 409, 498, 504, 688, 735; *see
also* energy; vigour; *vīrya*
four right efforts 369, 689
ego and ego-identity 129–30, 283–4,
574–5, 657, 735–6; *see also* self
egolessness 284, 705
Eight Important Rules (*garudhammas*)
422–31, 644
elements 282–3
six, *see* six element practice
elephants 162, 683, 744n
blind men and 719, 769n
Elliott, J. 495
emotion
perfect, *see* Perfect Emotion

positive, as stage of path 731, 733–5, 736
emotional
'centre' 194, 198, 203
equivalents, and understanding 194
emotions
and feelings (*vedanā*) 36–7, 121, 200,
267–8
higher, spiritual or supra-personal
202–4, 228–30
and higher evolution 146
negative 5–6, 11, 13, 27, 200–2
positive 11, 13, 25–6, 155, 160, 358,
553–4
and sex 574–6, 578, 582
emptiness, *see* śūnyatā; the Void
energies
emotional 6, 149, 192–4, 588
blocked, distorted or repressed 77–8,
120, 196, 198–200, 202, 267–8
coarse and refining 197, 202–4, 268,
621
Tantric symbols and 684
unification of 63, 65, 120, 149, 499; *see
also* concentration; integration
energy
effect of communication on 196, 199,
200, 202
misuse of as third precept 574
spiritual (*vīrya*) 6, 32–3, 52, 71, 102–3,
104, 151, 290, 294, 366, 428–9, 515,
622, 703; *see also* effort
ambition and complacency 398–9, 407
bodhisattva of, *see* Vajrapāṇi 292
FWBO as current of 350, 392
and sex 574–5
and vision 159
English Sangha Association 473
English Sangha Trust xx, xxi, 172,
494, 519, 545; *see also* Hampstead
Buddhist Vihara
Biddulph Old Hall retreat centre 495,
499, 761n
conflict with London Buddhist Society,
see under London Buddhist Society
enjoyment 45, 118, 204, 221, 576, 590,
620
Enlightenment 21, 46, 85–8, 91, 101,
110, 127, 156, 260, 291, 310,
321, 482, 489; *see also* awakening;
Buddhahood; Nirvāṇa
assurance of (*vyākaraṇa*) 217
for the benefit of all beings 282; *see also*
bodhicitta
beyond the rational/cognitive
(*atakkāvacara*) 8–9, 64, 303

and communication or teaching 277, 437; *see also* Buddha, teaching
as conquest of Māra 396
as experience 72–4, 79, 81–2, 85
personal (*pratyekabuddhayāna*) 255, 310
and *rūpaloka* 402
seed of 66, 324–5; *see also* Buddha-nature; immanence
seven limbs or factors of (*bodhyaṅgas*) 31–5, 42, 369, 739n
upekṣā synonymous with 35
will to 517; *see also* bodhicitta
entreaty and supplication 275–7, 279–80
environmental awareness 733
equanimity 150, 155; *see also* tranquillity (*upekṣā*)
Esperanto 298, 749n
Essen 563, 727, 764n
The Essential Sangharakshita 722, 730, 769n
eternity, and time 88, 147
ethics 30, 51, 60, 76, 129, 148, 185, 439, 510, 631, 678, 696, 703, 707, 722–6, 744n; *see also* morality; precepts
and confession, *see* confession
imagination and 724–5
spirit and letter of 480–1
European Buddhist Union Congress 460, 469, 470, 610, 669–70, 765n
evil 260, 262, 263–4
good and 72, 129
Evil One, *see* Māra
Evola, J. 316–17, 751n
evolution 4, 8, 21, 29, 31, 75, 108, 145, 463, 550, 752n
higher 96, 114–16, 134, 146–7, 395, 410, 515, 762n
lower and higher distinguished 115, 146, 395
existence
conditioned
or mundane 21, 46–7, 63, 105, 134, 156, 359, 402–3, 468; *see also* saṃsāra
planes of, *see* planes, of conditioned existence
three characteristics of 126, 445–6, 481, 510
as wheel, *see* wheel of life
experience
craving for 79–80, 82–4
direct xix, 52, 156, 158–9, 480, 654, 680, 750n
and Enlightenment 72–4, 76, 79–86
illumined 156, 477, 492, 499, 681, 683

religious 301–4, 475, 760n
relying/drawing on own 655, 667
as symbolic 682–3
versus letter of practice 480–1
'ex-Untouchables'
FWBO and 591–2, 596; *see also under* India
Sangharakshita's work with xix–xx, 171, 527, 549–50, 708
eye
of Dharma or Truth (*dharmacakṣus*) 446–7, 655, 725
divine (*divyacakṣu*) 109, 725
spiritual 161

A Face Revealed 466, 760n
faculties
imaginative 724–5, 745n; *see also* imagination
rational or thinking 146, 205, 453; *see also* mind, rational; thinking
spiritual, *see* spiritual, faculties
faith-followers (*saddhānusārins*) 157–8, 268, 747n, 748n
faith (*śraddhā*) 110, 203, 413, 477, 478, 622, 733–5, 751n
and devotion 6, 45, 58, 203–5, 232, 507; *see also* devotion; puja
families 48, 188–9, 195, 317, 358, 397–8, 462, 576, 580–1, 592, 686, 695
and spiritual community 390, 442–3, 464, 556, 607, 608
fear 5, 261, 263–4, 293, 399, 407, 699, 724
of God 263, 343, 345, 346, 361
feelings (*vedanā*) 35–7, 73, 78, 401; *see also* sensation
and emotions 36–7, 121, 200, 267–8
mindfulness or awareness of 121, 676–7, 732
'Female Will' 427–8
feminism and Feminism 425, 426, 533, 603, 611, 638–9, 640, 641, 765n
Feminization, Democratization and Integration 612–13
festivals 76, 89, 222, 229, 391, 478, 488
Buddha Day (Vaiśākha or Wesak) 394–6, 409–10, 478, 488–90
Dharma, or Dharmacakra Day 395, 410, 418
Parinirvāṇa Day 455, 457–8
Sangha Day 395
fetters (*saṃyojanas*)
first 710–11; *see also* views, false, of self
as 'habit' xix, 47–8, 50, 740n
second 711, 712; *see also* doubt
as vagueness xix, 47, 49–50, 740n
third (attachment to observances) 208

fetters (*saṃyojanas*), third (*cont.*)
　'as going through the motions' 711–12
　as superficiality xix, 47, 49–50, 76,
　　208, 740n
　three xix, 47–51, 134, 710–12, 740n
fidelity 579–80, 668
Finland xvi, xviii, xxi, xxiv, 390, 746n
The First Man-Made Man 710, 768n
Flaubert, G. 335, 753n
Foote, G. W. 344, 752n, 754n
force 339, 361; *see also* power
　impersonal (or supra-individual) xx, 151
　　of *bodhicitta* 285
forces
　of Māra 405, 410
　spiritual 222, 291
form, *see rūpa*
　world of, *see* worlds, of form
Foster Damon, S. 427–8, 758n
four limitless states (*brahma vihāras*) 155,
　743n
Four Noble Truths 417, 510, 653–4, 707
four reliances 668, 718–20, 768n
four right efforts 369, 689
Francis Xavier, Saint 297, 749n
freedom 25, 45–7, 51–2, 102, 264, 674,
　707, 709–10, 712
　of expression 326–30, 346–7
　friendship and 700
　liberation, by wisdom/of heart 156,
　　743n
　taste of 41, 45–7, 50–1, 707
Freethinker magazine 344, 754n
friendliness 129, 155, 308, 315, 324, 403,
　610, 651; *see also mettā*
friends 317, 696, 698–702; *see also*
　spiritual, friends
friendship 583–4, 585, 637–8, 698, 700,
　703, 712; *see also* spiritual, friendship
　fierce 431, 758n
　and sexual relationships 576, 577,
　　578–80, 637
Friends of the Western Buddhist Order,
　see FWBO
Fromm, E. 207, 209–10, 212, 214–15,
　550, 745n
FWBO (Friends of the Western Buddhist
　Order) xiv, 143–4, 350–2, 362,
　363, 370, 379, 392, 455, 506, 554,
　598, 668; *see also* Triratna Buddhist
　Community
　activities 94, 139, 177, 186, 221, 376,
　　390, 419, 461–2, 465–7, 469, 620–1,
　　662
　Buddha Śākyamuni vital to 690, 717

criticism of 664–5
early days 375, 461, 463, 465, 514–17,
　520–1, 550, 577, 586–7, 686, 727–30
and Eastern Buddhism 371, 374, 376–7;
　see also under Buddhist tradition
emphases of 376, 597–9, 669, 687,
　713–14; *see also* arts; ecumenism;
　Going for Refuge; right livelihood;
　spiritual friendship; Western Buddhist
　Order, a unified Order
expansion of 515, 524–7, 551–2, 554–7,
　596–7, 600, 617, 619, 627, 645, 729;
　see also under India
financial matters 465, 609, 760n
founding of 173–5, 350–1, 378, 382,
　468–9, 518–20, 547–9, 661–2,
　727–8, 770n
　anniversary (FWBO Day) 466, 625,
　　722, 727
Friends 178–9, 186, 189, 391, 392, 516,
　525, 593; *see also* Mitras
harmony in 617, 625, 668
institutions 463–4, 466, 469, 554, 597,
　609, 690
　centres, *see* centres, FWBO
　communities, *see* communities,
　　residential
　'co-ops' *see* right livelihood, businesses
a 'movement' not a society/organization
　xxiii, 350, 380, 382–3, 386, 390,
　549, 661, 663, 669
name change xiv, 661
neither monastic nor lay 176–7, 187,
　464, 468–9, 667; *see also* lifestyle,
　and commitment
and new society, *see* society, new
Order Members, *see* ordination, Order
　Members
publications 525, 562, 592; *see also*
　Buddhayan; *Dakini*; *Dharma Life*;
　FWBO News; *Golden Drum*;
　Windhorse Publications
relationship to WBO 177, 179, 380, 386,
　390, 392, 522, 555, 616, 661–2, 668–9
retreats, *see* retreats
Sangharakshita and, *see under*
　Sangharakshita
single-sex activities, *see under* single-sex
social and medical projects 591, 592,
　593, 596
sources of inspiration 70, 190, 266,
　370–1; *see also* Refuge Tree
survival of 586, 601–3, 616, 688–90
and teamwork 139, 186, 189; *see also*
　right livelihood, team-based

and wider Buddhist World 599
women's wing 631, 636, 645–6; see also
retreat centres, women's
FWBO Newsletter 501–2, 502, 565,
758n, 761n

Gampopa 309, 310, 321, 371; see also
The Jewel Ornament of Liberation
Gaṇakamoggallāna Sutta 360, 755n
garudhammas, eight 638
Gautama (Pāli *Gotama*) 19, 70, 98, 107,
109, 358, 365, 384, 415–16, 435; see
also Buddha
Gay News 326–8, 330–1, 335, 336,
341–2, 346–7
Gelugpa tradition 713
generosity 63, 169, 185, 256, 257, 319,
385, 507, 698; see also *dāna*; giving;
precepts, second
Germany 469, 563, 695, 727, 729, 764n;
see also Berlin; Essen
Ginsberg, A. 626, 766n
Girimānanda Sutta 755n
giving 169, 223–4, 243, 291, 476, 734;
see also generosity
God 106–7, 108, 147, 253, 300, 305,
331, 338, 362, 463, 572, 753n
blasphemy and 327, 329–31, 334–6, 345
creator 335, 337, 493, 512, 742n, 749n,
753n
as a power 151, 335, 339–40, 345–6, 361
goddess 239, 588
earth 15, 738n
of poetry 151
gods 28, 107, 239, 248, 250, 293, 492,
701, 745n; see also Brahmā; *devas*
the Buddha and the 323, 397, 411, 412,
492
false, see idols
realm or world of 165, 166, 248, 323, 402
Goethe, J. W. von 57, 90, 370–1, 463,
729, 740n, 741n
going for refuge, to nature or gods 247–8
Going for Refuge to the Three Jewels
67–70, 175, 258, 310, 383–90, 431,
467–9, 475, 599
as basis of WBO 523–4, 662, 667–9, 689
and *bodhicitta* 599
centrality of 469, 597, 599, 609–10,
613, 628, 649, 665, 669
and confession 260–1
defines a Buddhist 383–6, 467–8, 475,
662
devaluation of 387–8
effective 226, 257, 430–1, 616, 641; see
also ordination

levels of 430, 673, 758n
precepts and 68, 135, 175–6, 256–7,
468; see also Refuges and Precepts
real 616; see also Stream Entry,
irreversibility
ritual 214–15; see also Refuges and
Precepts, 'taking'
section in puja 247, 252–8, 260
going forth 132–3, 318, 365, 397–8,
430–1, 442; see also homeless, life;
renunciation
women and 421–2, 426–31, 643–4
Golden Drum magazine 501, 565, 566
Gott, W. J. 327, 328, 752n
Govinda, Lama 246, 288, 560–4, 741n,
747n, 763n, 764n
gratitude (*kataññutā*) 722, 725, 769n
Gray, T. 41–2
greed 261, 308, 715, 719, 723, 724; see
also craving
opposite of, see detachment
the group
going forth from or overcoming xxii,
398, 406–7
and the individual xix, xxi, 48, 179,
195, 295–6, 347, 352–63, 398
positive 195, 197, 272, 392
and the spiritual, community 179, 197,
224, 272, 300, 350, 355, 392, 442
Guhyaloka retreat centre 618, 765n
guilt 5, 200, 262, 267, 275, 343, 345,
346, 361, 509, 538, 540, 587
culture 375
Guṇabhadri 631
Guṇavati 764n
gurus 59, 83–4, 147, 290, 375–6, 609,
615, 666–7

habit 23, 58, 202, 307; see also *under*
fetters, first
Hakuin 266, 283, 651
Hampstead Buddhist Vihara 172, 218, 489,
494–5, 518, 520, 530, 543, 546, 547,
552, 583, 605
happiness 3, 11, 20, 25, 34, 147, 163–4,
321, 440, 590, 696–7, 736; see also joy
desire for others' 102, 265–7, 269,
701–2, 733, 735
as a *dhyāna* factor 149–50
Hardy, T. 343, 754n
harmony xxiii, 224, 395, 617, 668; see
also speech, harmonious
Harris, T. 495
hatred 5, 32, 122, 123, 153–4, 257, 261,
308, 639, 701, 715, 718–19, 723–4;
see also anger; animosity; aversion

heart 193-4, 209
  liberation of the (*ceto-vimutti*) 155-6
  to place the (*śraddhā*) 203; *see also* faith
Heart Sūtra 280, 294, 748n
heavenly world, *see also* gods, realm of
heavens 25, 28, 30, 57, 311, 320, 497
hell, realms 28, 166, 271, 321, 457
helping other people/friends 119, 286,
  325, 698; *see also* altruistic activity
heroism 293, 397, 633-4
hierarchy
  of being or existence 505-7
  of consciousness, *see under* consciousness
  or power structure, ecclesiastical 355,
    508, 613, 667
  spiritual 272-3, 483-4, 506-7, 613, 617
  of symbolism 683
Hīnayāna 217-18, 254-5, 284, 318-19,
  720; *see also* Theravāda; *yānas*
  and Mahāyāna 217, 246, 254-5, 285-6,
    306-7, 319, 716-17
hindrances, five 122-4, 575, 588, 658
Hinduism 158, 238-9, 289, 353, 509,
  663, 664, 671; *see also* caste system
  ritual 211, 234-5, 237, 239-40, 696
Hindus 305, 347, 353, 664
  attitude to the Buddha 253
  and Maha Bodhi Society 174
Hipkin, J. 495
homeless
  life 41, 132, 421-2, 435, 491, 568-9;
    see also going forth
  ones 624; *see also anagārikas*
  wanderers ((*parivrājakas*)) 453, 512
homosexuality 331, 582-5
Hookham, M. 495
House of Commons 326
Huineng (Wei Lang) 170, 266, 715-16
humanism 251, 509
human realm or society 28, 166, 271,
  321-3, 402
humiliation 429
Humphreys, C. ('Toby') xxi, 534, 541-4,
  546, 757n, 762n
hungry ghosts (*pretas*) 28, 166, 321
Huxley, A. 362, 755n

ideal
  natural 103-5, 110
  spiritual 99-100, 179, 246-7, 309-12,
    318, 320, 684, 734
idols 612-14, 765n
ignorance 29, 35, 37, 46, 108, 261, 313,
  401, 483, 719; *see also* delusion
  overcoming/transforming 18, 257, 292,
    306, 403-4

Il Convento, Tuscany xvi, xviii, 556-8
illumination 156, 307, 477, 492, 499, 681
imagination xxiii, 88, 146, 160, 161, 181,
  264, 625, 724-6, 745n
immanence 689; *see also* Buddha-nature
  and transcendence 325, 655-7
immortality, nectar of (*amṛta*) 413
impermanence (*anitya*) 29, 167, 241, 364,
  404, 445-8, 454, 481, 703
incense 217, 221, 235-7, 239-41, 243-4
India 113, 187-8, 367, 374, 380, 527
  FWBO in 174-5, 390, 562, 591-4,
    596-7, 623, 645, 663-4, 669, 718,
    744n, 770n; *see also* TBMSG
  Aid For India (later Karuna Trust) 556
  Sangharakshita and, *see under*
    Sangharakshita
  WBO in, *see under* Order Members;
    ordination; Triratna Bauddha
    Mahasangha
individual 176, 619, 649
  and altruistic aspects of spiritual life
    255, 271
  and *bodhicitta* 285
  Buddhist 53, 95, 301, 315, 468-9, 478,
    802
  'fall' of in Blake 427-8
  Friends, Mitras and Order Members
    becoming 179
  and the group xix, xxi, 48, 179, 195,
    295-6, 347, 352-63, 398
  and higher evolution 146
  and individualist, distinction 363
  and spiritual, community 134-5, 362,
    386
  statistical 354-5, 357
  true xvii, xix, xxii, 43, 47, 48, 50, 51,
    94, 105, 352, 354-5, 358-9, 363
individualism, spiritual 217, 406-7; *see*
  also self-regard
  and altruism 318-19
individuality, true xix, xxi-xxii, 32,
  183-4, 224, 355, 635
Inquisitions 342, 361, 755n
insight (*vipaśyanā*) 46-7, 50-1, 64,
  126-7, 156, 193, 653, 703, 716; *see*
  also vision, clear; wisdom
  attachment and 539-40
  and *dhyānas*, or higher states 64, 588
  and faith 203, 204
  fetters and, *see* fetters
  hindrances and 122, 588
  initial, *see* path of Vision
  into impermanence 404, 405, 445-6,
    447, 448

transcendental 257; *see also* Stream Entry
inspiration 150, 151–2, 266, 325, 370–1,
    379, 431, 668
Refuge Tree and 714–17, 720–1
insubstantiality, *see anātman*; *śūnyatā*
integration 34, 46, 63, 150–1, 320, 466,
    731–3, 736, 766n; *see also* energies,
    unification of
'Democratization and Feminization' of
    Buddhism 612–13
'horizontal' and 'vertical' 120–2, 124, 150
ritual and 212, 214, 227, 241
interdependence 27, 278
intoxicants, abstention from 256, 258,
    317, 498
intuition 40, 146, 170, 202, 584–5, 656,
    745n
Ireland, J. 495
irreversibility 163; *see also* Stream Entry;
    path, transcendental
Islam 270, 296, 346–7, 351, 509, 688
Istanbul 627
Italy 544, 561–2, 564

Jainism 296, 355, 369
Jambudvīpa 297
James, W. 475, 760n
Jamyang Khyentse Rimpoche 455–6, 765n
Japan 89, 170, 209, 372, 374–6, 510,
    522, 542, 570, 679, 714, 756n
Japanese Buddhism, *see* Buddhism,
    Japanese
Jaspers, K. 354, 755n
Jayacitta 764n
Jayaprabha 764n
Jenkins, O. 495
Jerome, Saint xvi
The Jewel Ornament of Liberation 309,
    310, 319, 321, 371, 377, 744n, 750n,
    752n, 756n; *see also* Gampopa
Jinananda 737n
Jinaratana 562, 764n
jinas 253, 407, 415
Jinists 407, 409
Jivaka 456, 710, 760n, 768n
Jiyu-Kennett Rōshi 375–6, 756n
Johnson, S. 724, 769n
joy (*pramuditā*) 6, 13, 34, 64, 149, 164,
    267, 734; *see also* delight; happiness
joy, sympathetic (*muditā*) 155, 734–5
Judaism 296, 346, 509
Jung, C. G. 15, 207, 550, 683, 754n

Kagyupa Tradition 372, 713
Kalimpong 171–3, 196, 210, 236, 251,
    380, 456, 529, 546, 679, 713,

720, 747n, 763n, 766n; *see also*
    Sangharakshita, and India; Triyana
    Vardhana Vihara
kalyāṇa 440, 704; *see also* beauty
kalyāṇa mitratā, *see* spiritual friendship
Kalyanaprabha 631
Kalyanavaca 766n
Kamalashila 625
kāmaloka, *see* world of sensuous desire
Kangyur 372, 509
Kapilavastu 365, 420–1
Kapleau, P. 611
Karaṇīyamettā Sutta 102, 741n
Sangharakshita's commentary on, *see*
    Living with Kindness
karma 28, 209, 263, 292, 403, 650, 747n
    and rebirth 510, 512
karma-formations 35
Kashyap, Bhikkhu 549
Kāśyapa Mātaṅga 485
Keats, J. 448, 682, 767n
Kennedy, P. 710, 768n
Kevaddha Sutta 329, 752n
Khantipālo, Bhikkhu (Laurence Mills)
    545, 763n
Khuddaka Nikāya 309, 750n, 752n
killing 322, 400, 658, 719; *see also*
    precepts, first
kindness 436–7, 439, 444, 507, 736; *see
    also* mettā
Kirkup, J. 327, 328, 331, 341, 342–3
kleśas (Pāli *kilesas*) 401–3, 405
knowledge 101, 103, 104, 483
    of the destruction of the 'biases' (*āsravas*)
        30, 46, 314
    self- 90, 199, 677
    or thought, conceptual 14, 56, 73, 653
    virtue and 192–3, 745n
    and vision, of things as they really are
        (*yathābhūtajñānadarśana*) 46–7, 50
Koṇḍañña 446–7
Kovida 466, 760n
Kulananda 532, 534, 765n
Kulanandi 764n
Kusinārā or Kuśinagara 305, 427, 449,
    451–3, 491, 717–18

ladder or stairway 15, 30, 167, 321, 738n
laity and monks, *see* monks, and laity
lakṣaṇas, *see* existence, conditioned, three
    characteristics of
Lakshmi 253
Lalitavistara Sūtra 16, 738n, 741n
language, or terms
    Buddhist 47, 134, 386, 413, 446, 510,
        658

mettā (Sanskrit *maitrī*) *(cont.)*
  distinguished from *pema* 701
mettā bhāvanā 13, 153–5, 268, 284, 376,
  404, 461, 510, 639, 701, 728
Middle Way 19, 295, 518, 542, 546
middle way or path 72, 222, 417, 477,
  479, 481, 496–8, 518, 540, 542, 546
Milarepa 266, 367–8, 372, 377, 571, 651,
  678, 723, 756n, 769n
mind 20–1, 710, 750n
  absolute and relative 21, 25
  depths and heights 657–8
  'Eastern' and 'Western' 83, 373
  illumined, *see* illumination
  intellectual, emotional and volitional
    aspects 649–50
  'One' 21, 505
  rational 8–9, 11, 14–15, 49, 159; *see*
    also faculties, rational
  reactive and creative 21–38, 164, 179
  symbols of 26–31
mindfulness 12, 120–1, 477–8, 625–6,
    629; *see also* awareness; recollection
  of the body 32, 34, 36, 121, 369, 451,
    498, 731
  of breathing (*ānāpānasati*) 123, 150,
    376, 405, 461, 481, 510, 728
  and ethical precepts 256, 309
  four dimensions of 731–3
  four foundations of (*satipaṭṭhānas*) 42,
    369, 451
  and overcoming the *kleśas* 403, 405
  Sangharakshita and 553, 629
  Satipaṭṭhāna Sutta 739n
  three kinds of 121
Mindfulness and Money 765n
mitra, meaning 733
Mitra Ceremony 391
Mitras 97, 178–9, 186, 189, 391–2, 457,
    458, 525, 593, 602, 618, 636, 686
monastic
  code or rules 309, 317–19, 389, 752n;
    see also prātimokṣa; Vinaya
  community 135–6, 187, 318
  formalism 70, 523, 665, 763n
monasticism 118, 317–18, 388–9, 470,
    598, 665, 667, 692; *see also* lifestyle,
    and commitment
  and celibacy/chastity 570, 571, 590
  Western Buddhist Order and 176–7,
    187, 464, 468–9, 641, 662, 667
  'monks' 523, 524, 556, 665
  women and 641–2, 645
money 169, 182, 186, 187, 236, 275,
    465, 604, 607, 636, 698, 747n, 765n

monks 70, 135, 317–18, 388–9, 420, 469,
    475–6, 491; *see also bhikkhus*
  and chastity 318, 569, 570, 571
  and laity 68, 388, 464, 470, 475,
    512–13, 568, 570–1, 600
  novice *śrāmaṇeras* 258, 747n
  and precepts 68; *see also* monastic,
    code
  sick 161, 432–44, 744n
  and women 425, 570, 644–5
moon, full or new 39, 317, 395, 415, 456,
    478, 488
morality 208, 305–25, 480, 531, 750n,
    754n; *see also* ethics
  Buddhaghosa's three kinds of 324–5
  mundane and transcendental 313–14, 320
  natural, and conventional 262
  nature of 307–9
  and the Noble Eightfold Path 306, 314,
    498
  as a *pāramitā* 291, 307, 385
  and threefold path or trainings 306–7,
    498, 656
  three grades of 315–16
mountains
  in Kalimpong 171, 196
  as metaphor 167, 247, 260
Moving Against the Stream 675, 745n,
    746n, 760n, 761n, 762n, 763n, 766n,
    767n, 770n
Mozart, W. A. 204, 371
Mucalinda 15, 738n
mudrās 211, 212, 249–50, 293
Murasaki Shikibu 634
Murry, J. Middleton 754n
music 34, 195–6, 204, 227–9, 238, 371,
    466–7, 621, 692, 735, 747n
myths 15–16, 75, 76, 161, 165, 212,
    214, 355, 492, 679, 738n; *see also*
    archetypes; non-rational

Nagabodhi xv, 96, 501, 518, 532, 545,
    565, 567, 591, 595, 606, 699
Nāgārjuna 723, 726, 769n
nāgas 151
Nagpur 708
Nalanda 171
Nanda 588
National Secular Society 329–30
nature 33, 64, 146–7, 184, 195, 196, 240,
    395, 452
  worship of, *see* animism
Newman, Cardinal 340, 754n
New Mexico 627
New Zealand 93–6, 97, 390, 627, 651,
    729, 770n; *see also* Auckland
Nichiren Buddhism 143, 660

nidānas
cyclic 404, 757n; *see also under*
conditionality
positive 45–6
Nietzsche, F. 370
Nigantha Nātaputta 369, 756n
Nin, A. 634
nirmāṇakāya 226; *see also trikāya*
Nirvāṇa (Pāli *nibbāna*) 41, 63, 86,
116, 403, 413, 510; *see also*
Enlightenment; the Unconditioned
giving up or postponing 276–7, 278, 283
and *saṃsāra* 36, 63, 277, 293, 312, 313
sphere of (*nirvāṇadhātu*) 656
'without remainder' 403; *see also*
parinirvāṇa
Nityabandhu 685
noble and ignoble quest 312
Noble Eightfold Path 30, 186, 193–4,
306, 314, 369, 385, 408, 417,
465, 498, 510, 689, 707, 715, 719,
761n; *see also* path, of vision and
transformation
stages as 'Perfect' rather than 'right' 193,
194, 498, 761n
noble ones (*āryas* or *ārya-pudgalas*) 47,
160, 266, 314; *see also* Āryasaṅgha
non-duality, door to 726; *see also* self,
and other
non-rational or irrational 9, 11, 192, 207;
see also myths
non-returners 42, 254, 422, 450
nun, French (Ani-La) 250, 747n
nuns 70, 135, 317, 318, 425–8, 469,
491, 568, 633; *see also bhikkhunīs*,
ordination of women
Nyingma
Institute 765n
tradition 372, 376, 713, 767n

offerings 217, 221, 227–9, 234–44, 249,
453, 680; *see also* worship
once-returners 42, 254, 422, 450
One Mind 21, 60, 505
Order Members 174–9, 186, 188, 189,
390–1, 443, 522–3, 551, 621, 690;
see also dhammacāris/dhammacārinīs;
ordination; Western Buddhist Order
'Fifteen points for Old - and New' 624,
766n
and FWBO/Triratna activities 177, 390,
522–5, 555–7, 597, 601–2, 617–19,
635–6, 688, 690, 764n
in India 527, 591–2, 593, 597, 664, 718
precepts, *see* precepts, ten; precepts, and
Going for Refuge

Sangharakshita's relationship with 516,
526, 666–7, 686; *see also* disciples,
Sangharakshita's
as *upāsakas/upāsikās*, in early WBO xiv,
94, 521, 523
Order of Buddhist Contemplatives 375–6,
756n
ordination 68, 70, 135, 386, 420; *see also*
commitment, to the Three Jewels;
Going for Refuge, effective
in F/WBO and TBM 175–80, 454–5,
469–70, 503, 636, 641–2, 645,
667–8, 690, 770n
asking for 276, 391
ceremonies 175–6, 454–5
conducted by Order Members 175,
557, 660
in India 558; *see also* Order Members,
in India
in New Zealand 94–5, 770n
preceptors, *see* preceptors
retreats 556, 557, 558; *see also* Il
Convento
training/preparing for 179, 430, 645,
686, 770n
lay 68; *see also upāsakas/upāsikās*
monastic 68, 70, 317, 523, 667
reasons for wanting 426–30
Sangharakshita's 171, 305, 427, 460,
749n
at the time of the Buddha 420–1, 447–8,
454
of women 421–3, 425–7, 641–3; *see*
also nuns
in F/WBO and TBM, *see* Western
Buddhist Order, a unified order
other people, awareness of 723–6, 732–3
other people/friends
helping 119, 286, 325, 698; *see also*
altruistic activity
treating like self 698–9, 700, 704–5,
724–5, 735–6; *see also* non-duality
other power 688–9
Ouspensky, P. D. 198, 745n

Padmaloka Retreat Centre 2, 420, 432,
472, 562, 628, 770n
Padmapāṇi 292
Padmasambhava 288, 293–4, 455, 485,
714–15, 768n
paganism 248; *see also* animism
Pāli canon 207–8, 315, 332, 379, 417,
488, 642, 690, 716–17, 719–20;
see also Tipiṭaka, and individual
Nikāyas
Pañcavaggi Sutta 364, 755n

poisons, three 26–7, 603; *see also* mental
    states, unskilful; three roots of,
    unskilfulness
'political correctness' 641; *see also*
    pseudo-liberalism
political language 690
politics 7, 46, 147, 179, 182–3, 197, 300,
    359, 361, 382, 532, 533, 611, 623,
    688
Poona 562, 664
Pope, A. 143, 743n
Popper, K. 532, 762n
power 424, 609; *see also* force
    God as a 151, 335, 339–40, 345–6, 361
    mode and love mode 700–2, 705, 767n
    'other' 688–9
    Sangharakshita and 686
    spiritual community and 185, 686; *see*
      also authority
    structures 185, 248, 299–301, 353, 355
Prajñāpāramitā, mantra 287, 294
Prajñāpāramitā, texts, *see* Perfection of
    Wisdom, literature
praśrabdhi, see under tranquillity
prātimokṣa (Pāli *pātimokkha*) 317–18,
    756n; *see also* monastic code
pratyekabuddhayāna 255, 310
preceptors, in WBO/TBM
    private 175, 689, 770n
    public 176, 615–16, 623, 661, 667–9,
      689, 765n, 770n
precepts 118, 208, 309; *see also* ethics
    bodhisattva 68
    of celibacy (*anagārika*) 176, 316, 537,
      587
    eight 317, 319, 536
    five (*pañca-śīla*) 255–8, 317, 319, 478,
      567, 747n
      canonical sources 258, 747n
      compared to ten 257–8
      'Tantric' version 574
    and Going for Refuge 68, 135, 175–6,
      256–7, 468
    monks 68; *see also* monastic code
    novice or *śrāmaṇera* 258, 747n
    negative and positive formulations 256,
      480–1
    and Refuges, *see* Refuges, and Precepts
    speech, *see* speech, precepts
    ten 175–6, 255–6, 469, 537, 642,
      669, 690, 723, 747n; *see also* skilful
      actions, ten
      first 256, 723–4; *see also* abortion;
        killing; *mettā*; reverence, for life;
        vegetarianism

    second 256, 658, 724; *see also*
      generosity
    third, *see* contentment; sexual
      misconduct, abstention from
    fourth, *see* speech, truthful (abstaining
      from false)
    fifth, *see* intoxicants, abstention from;
      mindfulness
    fifth to seventh (of ten), *see* speech,
      precepts
    eighth, *see* covetousness
    ninth, *see* hatred
    tenth, *see* ignorance, transforming;
      views, false, abstention from
Precious Garland (*Ratnamāla*) 723, 769n
The Priceless Jewel xiv, 326, 752n
pride 261, 266, 415, 428, 559
prīti, see rapture
projection, pseudo-spiritual 82, 83–4,
    340, 573, 576–7, 686
protection 89, 102, 152, 253, 287, 352,
    696
protectors
    Buddhas and bodhisattvas as 253, 263,
      292
    of the Dharma, *see dharmapālas*
Protestantism 75–6, 82, 206, 207–8,
    215, 228, 379, 533, 670; *see also*
    Christianity
pṛthaḡlanas (Pāli *puthujjanas*) 160, 314;
    see also worldlings
pseudo-liberalism 521, 603, 610–11;
    see also Democratization; 'political
    correctness'; views, false, modern
psychic forces, integration of 293
psychic powers, *see* supernormal, powers
psychoanalysis 207, 497
psychological
    analysis in early Buddhism 678
    approach to Dharma 546, 549–50,
      657–8
    distinguished from spiritual 128–9, 674,
      680
    or pseudo-spiritual, projection 82, 83–4,
      340, 573, 576–7, 686
    type 157; *see also* temperament
psychology 200, 492, 497, 550; *see also*
    conditioning, psychological
    and interpretation of Buddhist cosmology
      28
    of ritual 205–15
puja 12, 184, 197–8, 213, 248–9, 375,
    391, 650, 685, 711; *see also* ritual;
    worship
    approaching 220–30

puja (*cont.*)
books, FWBO/Triratna 218, 746n
bowls 210, 239
Buddha in 216, 223–4, 239; *see also*
worship
call and response 226, 287
as collective practice 204, 212, 223, 225,
228, 243, 285
cosmic 225–6, 246
cultural roots 237–8
music in 227–9
practising alone 224–5
Sevenfold xviii, 178, 204, 213, 218, 376,
457, 510, 621, 746n
origins 216–19, 235
stages 218
sixfold 218
Sūtra of Golden Light 219
Threefold or Short xviii, 224, 293, 746n
Pundarika (Archway) Centre 525, 536,
770n
Pure Land, *see* Sukhāvatī
sūtras 741n, 759n
tradition 688
purification 256–7, 689
humiliation and 429
purifications (*visuddhis*), seven 30–1, 306,
313, 750n
purity 72, 123, 668, 682
of mind 657, 724
path of, *see* Visuddhimagga

*The Rainbow Road from Tooting
Broadway to Kalimpong* 749n, 756n,
762n, 764n
Rājagṛha (Pāli *Rājagaha*) (or Rajgir) 171,
332, 360
rapture (*prīti*) 33–4, 45–6, 149, 164, 320
Rathavinīta Sutta 306, 749n, 750n
rationalism 206–7, 679, 745n
rationalizations 25, 136, 160, 167, 578,
603
Ratnasambhava 730
reality 17, 21, 64, 65, 115, 126, 156,
505–7
archetypal, *see* sambhogakāya
beyond the rational mind 8–9, 680–1
orders of 492; *see also* realms
realization 116, 446, 653–4, 720
behind/beyond words and concepts 175,
418, 653, 680
realms, *see also* planes; worlds
human, or human society 28, 166, 271,
321–3, 402
'spiritual' 673–7
transcendental 468

in wheel of life
individual, *see* animal; *asura;* god; hell;
human; hungry ghost
six 27–8, 30, 165–6
rebirth 29, 35–6, 58, 252–4, 282, 388,
401, 403, 428, 449–50, 573, 629
karma and 265, 510, 512
morality and 257, 311, 320, 321, 323
previous life or existence 17, 29, 164,
249, 573
Sangharakshita and 628–9, 692
spiritual 134, 176, 384
receptivity 275–80, 385, 507, 688, 703
Rechung Rimpoche 713
recollection 64, 120, 498; *see also*
awareness; mindfulness
recollections (*anussatis*), ten 306
reflection 23, 150, 157, 404, 423, 603,
649, 690
Refuge
definition of 384–5, 468
family and friends as 442–3, 699
Going for, *see* Going for Refuge...
subjective, and objective 450
'in yourself' 451
Refuges
and Precepts, 'taking' 311, 454, 478; *see
also* Going for Refuge..., ritual
or reciting as a formality 69, 257,
387–8, 662
three, *see* Three Jewels
Refuge Tree 87, 668, 688, 713–21
rejoicing in merit 218, 264–9, 278, 703,
734
relationships 83, 182, 577–8, 695–705
heterosexual 581–3
homosexual 582–3
lesbian 637–8
Platonic 584
sexual 538–9, 569, 573, 575–80, 582,
584, 597, 637, 697
religion 270–1
art as 75, 204
'brotherhood is' 700
Buddhism as 76, 108, 142, 296, 298,
301–4, 463, 509
comparative 302, 511; *see also*
Buddhism, and Christianity
conditioning effect, *see* conditioning,
religious
ethnic 295–6, 353
and faith 203
interfaith dialogue 508, 660
non-theistic 108, 296, 463, 492, 509

seen as experience 74–6, 85, 301–4, 475, 760n
as theological monarchism 335, 338, 346–7
universal 295–6, 297
religious tolerance and intolerance 345, 513, 670–1
remorse, non- (*avippaṭisāra*) 320
renunciation 133, 316, 750n; *see also* going forth
responsibility xxii, 134, 147, 263, 358, 441, 444
and citizenship 624, 635
for the environment 733
in FWBO xxiii, 391, 516, 523, 555–6, 617, 635–6, 640, 689
Sangharakshita and, handing on 516, 525, 557, 600–3, 615, 618, 660–1, 671, 686, 691
restlessness and worry 122–3, 477
retreat or meditation centres
Biddulph, of English Sangha Trust 495, 499, 761n
FWBO 117, 177, 478, 524, 593, 728; *see also* Bhaja; Guhyaloka; Padmaloka
women's 557, 645–6; *see also* Taraloka; Tiratanaloka
non-FWBO 608
retreats 117, 139, 184–5, 202, 478, 580–1
FWBO 177–8, 390–1, 503, 521, 593, 639, 663, 770n
early 174, 462, 464, 515, 557, 662, 728
rainy season 171, 416–17, 422, 423, 447, 450
reverence 56–7, 58, 155, 217, 224, 246, 248, 385, 452, 478; *see also* devotion
for life 468, 636; *see also* precepts, first
Rewata Dhamma 765n
right livelihood 33, 117, 174, 176, 376, 391, 465, 498, 596, 608
businesses/co-ops, team-based 178, 186–9, 351, 465–7, 524, 554, 596–7, 598, 604, 616, 662, 705, 715, 760n
as 'Perfect Livelihood' 193, 314, 498
rites and rituals, attachment to, *see* fetters, third
ritual 51, 75, 76, 119, 123, 148, 205–15, 678, 679, 680; *see also* puja
devaluation of 119, 206–8, 214
difficulty with 206, 213, 215, 221–3, 250–1
Hindu, *see under* Hinduism
neurotic 207, 210
preparation for 210–11, 232, 233
prostration in 214, 249–51

Theravāda, or Hīnayāna and 208–9, 214, 218
Rossetti, C. 635
Rousseau, J. J. 745n
Rousseauism 195, 197, 745n
rūpa 401, 681–2
Buddha, *see* Buddha images
and *śūnyatā* 681–2
Rupachitta 631
rūpaloka, see worlds, of form

Sabbāsava Sutta 755n
Saccasaṃyutta 417, 758n
Saddharma Puṇḍarīka Sūtra, see White Lotus Sūtra
Śākyamuni 246, 293, 690; *see also* Buddha
mantra 242, 287, 289
Sāleyyaka Sutta 258, 747n
Sallekha Sutta 657–8, 767n
salutation 245–51, 260
Samacitta 722–3
samādhi xx, 34, 46, 63–4, 306, 320, 480–1; *see also* absorption; *dhyāna*; meditation
Perfect 193, 498
Sāmagāma Sutta 369, 756n
sambhogakāya 225–6, 437, 759n; *see also trikāya*
saṃgraha-vastus 699–700
saṃjñā, see perception
saṃsāra 5, 64, 208, 272, 401; *see also* the conditioned; existence, conditioned
saṃskāras, see volitions
Saṃyutta Nikāya 87, 123, 275, 307, 417, 478, 703, 741n, 743n, 748n, 749n, 755n, 757n, 758n, 761n, 768n
San Francisco
FWBO centre 607
Zen Center 609
Saṅgārava Sutta 123, 743n
sangha 68, 90, 332, 468, 651, 662; *see also* spiritual community
ārya, see Āryasaṅgha
beginnings of in Britain 475–6
diverse nature of in WBO 390
early, as monks and nuns 491
F/WBO, *see* FWBO, Western Buddhist Order
Going for Refuge to 67, 175, 385–6, 468, 482, 650–1
Sangha Day 395
Sangharakshita xxiii, 169–73, 460, 463, 562, 675, 685–6, 727, 735
biography, *see Bringing Buddhism to the West*; Sangharakshita, memoirs

Sangharakshita (*cont.*)
  as channel/impersonal force xx, 687,
    691–2
  criticism of 664–5
  and death 628–9, 651–2, 661, 671–2
  early connections with Dharma/
    Buddhism 170, 541, 715
  friendships 353, 517, 542, 560, 562,
    563, 583–4, 663, 670, 685, 692,
    737n, 762n
  and FWBO 514–17, 520, 551–4, 557–8,
    562–3, 577, 586, 595, 598, 601,
    616–18, 626–8, 649, 651, 660–9,
    686–7, 692, 736; *see also* FWBO,
    founding
    handing on responsibility for 516, 525,
      557, 600–3, 615, 618, 660–1, 671,
      686, 691
    sabbatical from 514–16, 525, 552
  and India, *see also under* 'ex-
    Untouchables'; Kalimpong; Triyana
    Vardhana Vihara
    experiences in 170–1, 305, 353,
      380–2, 388, 460, 549, 687, 746n,
      764n
    pilgrimages 717–18
    relationship with 173, 518, 519, 527,
      542, 545, 558, 562, 594, 596
  lectures 94–6, 172, 174, 463, 495, 515,
    517, 529, 530, 542, 547, 558, 619,
    662, 671, 687, 728
    made into books xiv, 719–20, 726,
      730, 762n, 769n; *see also* Spoken
      Word Project
  library 616
  memoirs 380, 526, 529–30, 552, 563,
    585, 675–7, 747n
  ordination of 171, 305, 427, 460, 749n
  at Padmaloka 2, 472
  personal practice 170, 220–1, 237,
    552–3, 569, 673–7, 679–80, 685,
    690–1, 714–15, 720
  and poetry 553, 554, 569, 626, 635,
    735
  preceptor (U Chandramani) 305, 427,
    749n
  referred to as 'Bhante' 215, 514, 518,
    591, 595, 732
  return to England xx, 172, 494, 495,
    518–20, 542, 545–7, 664
  seminars xiv, xv, 525, 536, 619, 692,
    699, 722, 723, 737n, 744n, 756n
  and sex 583–5
  at Taraloka 694

teachers 171, 172, 173, 460, 519, 549,
  666, 668, 680, 685, 690, 691, 720;
  see also Chattrul Sangye Dorje;
  Dhardo Rimpoche; Jamyang Khyentse
  Rimpoche; Kasyap (Bhikkhu)
teachings, essence of 730–1
travels 94–5, 97, 531, 562, 606, 607,
  609, 627, 651, 729, 754n, 765n,
  766n
way of operating 548–50, 554, 558,
  584–5, 595, 616–17, 618, 619, 625,
  661–2, 664, 667, 669, 687, 692, 716,
  735, 736
wearing robes 665–6
writing/literary work 171, 404, 495,
  517, 518, 525, 526–7, 532, 558,
  603, 617, 619, 627, 663, 673–7,
  692, 722–3, 729–30; *see also The
  Buddhist*; *Maha Bodhi* journal;
  Sangharakshita, memoirs; *Stepping-
  Stones*
Śāntaraksita 485, 715
Śāntideva 204, 216, 246; *see also
  Bodhicaryāvatāra*
Sānzàng 372, 509
Śāriputra 163
Sarnath 171, 717–18
Sarvamitra xvi–xvii, xxi, xxii, xxiv
Sarvāstivāda 445, 510, 716
Satipaṭṭhāna Sutta 739n
satsaṅgh 119
Sayadaw, Mahasi 741n
scapegoats 340–1
Schopenhauer, A. 370, 729
Schumacher, E. F. 533–4, 762n
science 113, 159, 292, 390, 663
scientific approach to Buddhism 387, 492;
  see also psychological, approach
secularism 70, 75, 183, 228, 299–301,
  329–30, 342, 351, 371, 600, 607,
  664, 679
self 364, 497, 735–6, 755n; *see also* ego
  development 364; *see also* spiritual,
    development
  'no-' 121; *see also anātman*
  and other, *see also* other people
    treating friends like ourselves 698–9,
      700, 704–5, 724–5, 735–6
self-affirmation and self-denial 496–9
self-awareness, *see* self-consciousness
self-confidence 415, 492, 635
self-conquest or control 194–5, 333–4
self-consciousness or awareness xxii, 32,
  115–16, 121, 145–6, 354, 358, 363,

575, 731–2; *see also* individuality, true
selfishness 183, 284, 701, 704–5, 735
self-knowledge 90, 199–200, 677
selflessness 403, 404–5, 446, 734, 735; *see also anātman*
self-love 154
self-preoccupation 266, 477
self-regard 324–5; *see also* individualism, spiritual
self-reliance (*attadīpā*) 451
self-surrender 218, 283–4
self-transcendence 497–9, 505
sensation (*vedanā*) 29, 32, 34, 122, 148, 402, 451; *see also* feelings
sense-consciousness 115–16, 148, 225
sense-organs, six 22, 29, 35, 86, 159, 755n
sensuous experience (*kāma*) 122, 306, 313
  plane or world of (*kāmaloka*) *see* world, of sensuous desire
Sevenfold Puja, *see* puja, Sevenfold
sex 78, 122, 199, 338, 537–40
  change of 710
  communication and 575, 579, 584–5
  and the spiritual life, interview with Sangharakshita 567–90
sexual abstinence 747n; *see also* celibacy
sexual desire 572–3, 588
sexuality, *see* bisexuality; relationships, heterosexual, homosexual and lesbian; transsexuality
sexual misconduct
  abstention from (3rd precept) 130, 256, 308, 316–17, 498, 567–8, 574, 586
  adultery, incest and promiscuity 202, 323, 567–8
sexual relationships, *see under* relationships
Shakespeare, W. 686
shame
  culture 375–6
  or regret (*hrī*) 262
Shelley, P. B. 343, 370, 448, 754n
Shin Buddhism 372, 486, 510
Shinran 688, 717
shrines 210–11, 226, 232–3, 239, 243–4, 249, 457
Siddhārtha 132–3, 397–400, 738n; *see also* Buddha
Sigāla 695–6, 698
Sigālovāda Sutta 317, 695–9, 702, 751n
śīla (Pāli *sīla*) *see* ethics, morality
silence 118, 162, 202, 294, 320, 383, 418, 510
single-sex

activities 521, 522, 636; *see also under* communities, residential
  'principle' 598, 608
Sinhadevi 631, 633
six element practice 404–5, 448
skandhaka (Pāli *khandhaka*) 318
skandhas (Pāli *khandhas*) 401, 403, 755n
skilful (*kuśala*)
  actions, ten (*kusala dhammas*) 258, 308, 309, 316, 317, 319, 321–3; *see also* precepts, ten
  meaning of term 129, 308, 674
  mental states, *see under* mental states
  sloth and torpor 122, 123
Sobhana 631
social service 139, 148, 478, 596, 651; *see also* altruistic activity
society
  degeneration and disintegration of 321–3, 621
  integration of Buddhism into Western 459–70, 522, 605, 613, 679
  new 169–80, 185–6, 379, 623
  precariousness of 269–72
Socrates 192, 745n
Sogyal Rimpoche 629, 765n, 766n
soul 58, 192, 509, 674, 711
  immortal (*ātman*) 512; *see also anātman*
space (*ākāśa*) 282–3
  and time 88, 160, 246, 457
speech 200–2, 209, 258, 333, 569
  harmonious 131, 309, 468, 498, 625
  harsh 130, 256, 308, 698
  helpful 131, 257, 468, 498
  keeping our word 699
  kindly or affectionate 131, 308, 436–7, 498, 698, 700, 705
  lord of, *see* Mañjughoṣa
  precepts 256, 257, 258, 308–9, 468, 625
  ritual 213
  truthful (abstaining from false) 131, 256, 257, 258, 308, 468, 480, 498, 676–7
  useless xix, 130, 200, 256, 316, 755n
Spinoza, B. 448–9, 745n
spiral path, *see* path, spiral
spiritual
  altruism and individualism 318–19
  attainment 80–1, 82, 284, 318, 666–7
    ten stages of, *see bhūmis*
  communities, residential, *see* communities, residential
  community 40–1, 43, 44, 128–40, 269, 272, 296, 298, 387, 419, 663; *see also* sangha

spiritual, community (*cont.*)
  and *bodhicitta* 285–6
  care for sick in, *see* case of dysentery
  and confession/ethics 260, 264, 268, 325
  and death 457–8
  and the group 179–80, 197, 224, 272, 300, 350, 355, 392, 442
  individuals and 134–5, 362, 386
  meditation and puja/ritual in 94, 212, 223, 225, 228, 243
  and ordination 135–6
  and power 185, 686; *see also* authority
  precariousness of 269–70
  not a religious organization 386–8
  and transcendental community 134; *see also* Āryasaṅgha
  transforming world into 183, 185–6; *see also* society, new
  WBO as 386–7, 390, 443–4, 469, 662
death 731, 735–6
development 45–6, 96, 136, 179, 364, 430, 521, 571, 582, 586–7; *see also* development, personal
Feminism and 638–9
likened to a house 65
likened to a plant 64–6, 87–8, 167, 293, 325, 486, 507, 515, 516; *see also* parables, of herbs
sex and 578–80, 582, 586–7
stages of 30–1, 45, 64–6, 85, 310–11, 313, 730–6; *see also* path, stages of
'subjective and objective' refuges 451
discipline 243, 267, 314, 574, 589, 620; *see also* spiritual, practice, regular
faculties (*indriyas*), five 42, 369, 477–9, 761n
friends 262, 263, 371, 437, 506, 578, 666, 703, 705; *see also* friends
feedback or criticism from 431, 758n
friendship (*kalyāṇa mitratā*) 67, 119, 385–6, 439–40, 444, 583–4, 637–8, 703–5; *see also* friendship
  FWBO/WBO and 71, 178, 180, 390, 443, 602, 604, 608, 609, 615–16, 663, 688, 690, 728
'horizontal' and 'vertical' 609
near enemy of 651
'whole of spiritual life' 703–4
hierarchy, *see* hierarchy, spiritual
indigestion 279
life 21, 24, 44, 67, 116–17, 407, 413, 674, 682; *see also* brahmacarya
and breakthroughs 4–8, 10–11, 13, 16–18

as growth 4, 37, 49, 64–5, 81–2, 86–9, 109, 145–7, 370, 379
metaphors of ascent and descent 656–8
maturity, five things conducive to 703
practice 130
  caution regarding 37; *see also* meditation, caution regarding
  direct and indirect methods 94, 116–20, 123, 148, 461–2, 466
  as purification, *see* purification
  regular and sustained 12–13, 60, 221–2, 311, 489, 510; *see also* spiritual, discipline
  and temperament, *see* doctrine-followers, faith-followers, temperament
principles 379, 486
rebirth 134, 176, 384
Sangharakshita's use of term 128–9, 131, 674, 677
teachers 277, 279, 317, 369, 398, 478, 503, 508, 598, 668, 705, 720–1; *see also* Buddhist teachers
  on Refuge Tree 713–17, 720–1
teaching, requesting 275–7, 279–80
treasures (*ariyadhanas*) 306
warriors 407, 409
Spoken Word Project xiv, 729, 737n
śraddhā, *see* faith
śrāvakayāna 255, 310
Sri Lanka 143, 209, 372, 679; *see also* Ceylon
status, socio-religious 315, 319, 642; *see also* lifestyle
Stepping-Stones 139, 529–30, 762n
Stream Entrants xix, 42, 47, 50, 254, 426, 435, 447, 450, 569, 651
  FWBO and 586, 616
Stream Entry 257, 271, 285–6, 422, 446, 450
  and *bodhicitta* 285–6
study 118, 184, 186, 188, 193, 230, 377, 508–13, 663, 685, 690
  as discussion 37, 299, 301, 361, 418, 462, 478, 495, 508, 703
  groups 178, 390, 391, 478
stupas (*caityas*) 226, 249
Subhadda 453–5
Subhuti 534, 544, 557, 617, 729, 770n
  books xx, 544, 557, 619, 621, 623, 640–1, 737n, 762–3n, 766n
subject–object duality or polarity 21, 101, 116, 255, 325; *see also* non-duality; self and other
Sudata 501

time (cont.)
  puja and 219, 225, 226, 229
  sense 9–10, 16–17
  and space 88, 160, 246, 457
  two kinds of 9–10, 11, 16
Tipiṭaka 372, 509; see also Pāli canon
Tiratanaloka retreat centre for women
    770n
titans, see asuras
tolerance 330, 360, 671; see also patience
Trailokya (later Triratna) Bauddha
    Mahasangha Sahayak Gana, see
    TBMSG
tranquillity
  or equanimity (upekṣā) 31, 34–5, 150,
    155, 257, 403–4, 405
  or tension release (praśrabdhi) 34, 45,
    46
transcendence
  and immanence 325, 655–7
  self- 497–9, 505
the transcendental (lokuttara) 170, 313,
    468, 619, 656
  distinguished from 'spiritual' 131, 674
transcendental consciousness 18, 115,
    116, 355, 358, 413
transference of merits 218, 281, 283–4
transsexuality 710
tree
  bodhi 15–16, 87, 109, 161, 167, 396,
    400, 405, 410, 482
  cosmic 30
  or plant, FWBO as 515, 516
trees
  sāl 449, 451–2, 458
  wish-fulfilling 165, 235
  worship of, see animism
trikāya 226, 759n; see also Buddha,
    historical; sambhogakāya;
    dharmakāya
Triratna (formerly Trailokya) Bauddha
    Mahasangha 764n, 770n; see also
    Order Members, in India
Triratna Buddhist Community xiv, xxi,
    760n; see also FWBO
Triratna Buddhist Order xiv, xxi; see also
    Western Buddhist Order
The Triratna Story 760n, 765n
triyāna, see yānas, three
Triyana Vardhana Vihara 142, 171–3,
    450, 456, 542, 710, 768n
truth 159, 364–5, 410, 446–7, 492, 655,
    676; see also speech, truthful
Tsongkhapa 713, 750n
Turner, J. M. W. 685, 767n

Udāna 39–40, 42, 44, 377, 383, 435, 588,
    702, 707, 719, 738n, 740n, 742n,
    756n, 759n, 764n, 768n, 769n
udānas 383, 411–12, 447, 756n
Uddaka Rāmaputta 398–9, 413–14
the Unconditioned 21, 25, 42, 46, 126–7,
    156, 248, 325, 481; see also the
    Absolute; Nirvāṇa
  and the conditioned 11, 312–13, 619,
    677
the unconscious 49, 150, 207, 212, 214,
    291, 497, 658
understanding 56–7, 192–4, 211, 483,
    653–5, 670
United States (USA) 374, 597, 729, 770n
  Buddhism in 606–11, 628, 765n
  FWBO in 524, 607, 627, 628, 651, 729
unskilful (akuśala), meaning of term 129,
    308
unskilfulness, three roots of 27, 32, 401,
    674, 723
'Untouchables' 707–8; see also 'ex-
    Untouchables'
Upaka 414–15
upāsakas/upāsikās 68, 317, 475, 548; see
    also lay disciples
  in early WBO xiv, 94, 521, 523
upekṣā, see equanimity; tranquillity
Uposatha Sutta 39, 707, 740n, 768n

vagueness, second fetter as, see fetters,
    second
Vaiśālī 421, 424
vajra 292, 294, 751n
Vajrabodhi xviii, 746n
Vajracchedikā Prajñāpāramitā Sūtrā, see
    Diamond Sūtrā
Vajrapāṇi 287, 292
Vajrapushpa 631
Vajrasara 647, 685
Vajrasattva, mantra 455–7
Vajrayāna 243, 291, 320, 378, 571;
    see also Tantric Buddhism; Tibetan
    Buddhism; yānas
Vammika Sutta 719, 769n
vedanā, see feelings; sensation
vegetarianism 60, 174, 481, 605
Vidyadevi xiii, xv, 615, 722–3, 730,
    737n
view, right or Perfect 158–60, 168, 193,
    309, 498, 614, 625, 653–5; see also
    Perfect Vision
views, or speculative opinions 306, 313,
    750n
  debating, see debate

false or wrong (*micchā-diṭṭhis*) 46,
158–60, 167, 332–3, 360, 522, 540,
654–5, 702, 716, 742n
abstention from 256–8, 308
modern 653; *see also* pseudo-liberalism
of self/fixed personality 364, 710,
755n; *see also ātman;* fetters, first
vigour (*vīrya*) 291, 385, 477, 478; *see also*
effort; energy
viharas 478, 591, 593; *see also*
Hampstead Buddhist Vihara
Dharmodaya 251
Sangharakshita's, *see* Triyana Vardhana
Vihara
women's 645–6
vijñāna 302, 401, 718; *see also*
consciousness
Vimalakīrti 571
Vimalakīrti-nirdeśa 534, 726
Vinaya 318, 366, 455, 568, 706, 751n;
see also monastic code
Eight Important Rules (*garudhammas*)
for women 422–31, 644
Vinaya Piṭaka 109, 162, 163, 421–3, 434,
447
vipaśyanā (Pāli *vipassanā*) *see* insight;
meditation, *vipassanā*
Viriya, Sāmaṇera 494–5, 761n
vīrya 32, 477; *see also* effort; energy
Vishvapani xv, 647, 653
vision
clear 126, 462, 716; *see also* insight
of human existence 157–68, 179
path of, *see under* path
perfect, *see* Perfect Vision
visualization of Buddhas and Bodhisattvas
127, 216, 224–5, 288, 290–1, 294,
454, 683, 715, 741n
Visuddhimagga 306, 312, 749n,
750n, 751n, 752n, 764n; *see also*
Buddhaghosa
the Void 17, 21, 66, 170, 505; *see also*
śūnyatā
volitions (*saṃskāras*) 34, 35, 146, 308,
401
morality and 309, 311–12, 313–14, 315
as 'moving centres' 194, 204
Voltaire 382, 756n
vows
bodhisattva or great (*praṇidhāna*) 14,
217, 278, 318, 751n
and monastic formalism 523

Walshe, M. 473, 495, 759n
Walshe, R. 495
war 201, 270, 272, 342, 361, 616

Western Buddhist Order WBO xiv, 70–1,
175–6, 389–90, 506, 525, 548; *see
also* Triratna Buddhist Order
authority/leadership in 615, 660, 667,
690; *see also* responsibility in FWBO
in broader context of history 554
and celibacy 587–90
chapters 556, 690
College of Public Preceptors 615–16,
623, 661, 667–9, 689, 765n
conventions and Order weekends 420,
432, 562, 718, 758n
founding of 174, 469, 662–3; *see also*
FWBO, founding of
in India 744n; *see also under* Order
Members; ordination
neither monastic nor lay 176–7, 187,
464, 468–9, 641, 662, 667
newsletter (*Shabda*) 686, 688
in New Zealand 94–5
ordination into, *see* ordination
Refuge Tree of, *see* Refuge Tree
relationship to FWBO 177, 179, 380,
386, 390, 392, 522, 555, 616, 661–2,
668–9
Sangharakshita and, *see* Sangharakshita,
and FWBO
ten precepts of, *see* precepts, ten
a unified order 469–70, 521, 636, 641–2
based on Going for Refuge 523–4,
662, 669, 689–90
wheel
of the Dharma 218, 410, 417, 447
of life 5, 12, 26–30, 165–7, 401, 573
and spiral path, intersection of 35–7
*White Lotus Sūtra (Saddharma Puṇḍarīka
Sūtra)* 87, 143, 246, 255, 367, 466,
509, 716, 741n, 747n, 756n
Whitman, W. 169, 744n
will (*cetanā*), and wilfulness 649–51
will, 'Female' 427–8
Willis, Lord 327, 330
Windhorse Publications xv, 326, 737n,
740n, 741n, 743n, 745n, 746n, 747n,
748n, 758n, 759n, 760n, 763n, 765n,
766n, 766n; *see also* Spoken Word
Project
Windhorse Trading (later
Windhorse:Evolution) 465, 760n
wisdom (*jñāna* (Pāli *ñāṇa*)) 718, 743n
five Buddhas and 126–7
wisdom (*prajñā* (Pāli *paññā*)) 32, 37, 257,
313, 315, 324, 477, 478, 481, 674,
750n

A GUIDE TO THE COMPLETE
WORKS OF SANGHARAKSHITA

Gathered together in these twenty-seven volumes are talks and stories, commentaries on the Buddhist scriptures, poems, memoirs, reviews, and other writings. The genres are many, and the subject matter covered is wide, but it all has – its whole purpose is to convey – that taste of freedom which the Buddha declared to be the hallmark of his Dharma. Another traditional description of the Buddha's Dharma is that it is *ehipassiko*, 'come and see'. Sangharakshita calls to us, his readers, to come and see how the Dharma can fundamentally change the way we see things, change the way we live for the better, and change the society we belong to, wherever in the world we live.

Sangharakshita's very first published piece, *The Unity of Buddhism* (found in volume 7 of this collection), appeared in 1944 when he was eighteen years old, and it introduced themes that continued to resound throughout his work: the basis of Buddhist ethics, the compassion of the bodhisattva, and the transcendental unity of Buddhism. Over the course of the following seven decades not only did numerous other works flow from his pen; he gave hundreds of talks (some now lost). In gathering all we could find of this vast output, we have sought to arrange it in a way that brings a sense of coherence, communicating something essential about Sangharakshita, his life and teaching. Recalling the three 'baskets' among which an early tradition divided the Buddha's teachings, we have divided Sangharakshita's creative output into six 'baskets' or groups: foundation texts; works originating in India; teachings originally given in the West; commentaries on the Buddhist scriptures; personal writings; and poetry, aphorisms, and works on the arts. The 27th volume, a concordance, brings together all the terms and themes of the whole collection. If you want to find a particular story or teaching, look at a traditional term from different points of view or in different contexts, or track down one of the thousands of canonical references to be found in these volumes, the concordance will be your guide.

1. FOUNDATION

What is the foundation of a Buddhist life? How do we understand and then follow the Buddha's path of Ethics, Meditation, and Wisdom? What is really meant by 'Going for Refuge to the Three Jewels', described by Sangharakshita as the essential act of a Buddhist life? And what is the Bodhisattva ideal, which he has called 'one of the sublimest ideals mankind has ever seen'? In the 'Foundation' group you will find teachings on all these themes. It includes the author's *magnum opus, A Survey of Buddhism*, a collection of teachings on *The Purpose and Practice of Buddhist Meditation*, and the anthology, *The Essential Sangharakshita*, an eminently helpful distillation of the entire corpus.

2. INDIA

From 1950 to 1964 Sangharakshita, based in Kalimpong in the eastern Himalayas, poured his energy into trying to revive Buddhism in the land of its birth and to revitalize and bring reform to the existing Asian Buddhist world. The articles and book reviews from this period are gathered in volumes 7 and 8, as well as his biographical sketch of the great Sinhalese Dharmaduta, Anagārika Dharmapala. In 1954 Sangharakshita took on the editing of the *Maha Bodhi*, a journal for which he wrote a monthly editorial, and which, under his editorship, published the work of many of the leading Buddhist writers of the time. It was also during these years in India that a vital connection was forged with Dr B. R. Ambedkar, renowned Indian statesman and leader of the Buddhist mass conversion of 1956. Sangharakshita became closely involved with the new Buddhists and, after Dr Ambedkar's untimely death, visited them regularly on extensive teaching tours.

From 1979, when an Indian wing of the Triratna Buddhist Community was founded (then known as TBMSG), Sangharakshita returned several times to undertake further teaching tours. The talks from these tours are collected in volumes 9 and 10 along with a unique work on Ambedkar and his life which draws out the significance of his conversion to Buddhism.

3. THE WEST

Sangharakshita founded the Triratna Buddhist Community (then called the Friends of the Western Buddhist Order) on 6 April 1967. On 7 April the following year he performed the first ordinations of men and women within the Triratna Buddhist Order (then the Western Buddhist Order). At that time Buddhism was not widely known in the West and for the following two decades or so he taught intensively, finding new ways to communicate the ancient truths of Buddhism, drawing on the whole Buddhist tradition to do so, as well as making connections with what was best in existing Western culture. Sometimes his sword flashed as he critiqued ideas and views inimical to the Dharma. It is these teachings and writings that are gathered together in this third group.

4. COMMENTARY

Throughout Sangharakshita's works are threaded references to the Buddhist canon of literature – Pāli, Mahāyāna, and Vajrayāna – from which he drew his inspiration. In the early days of the new movement he often taught by means of seminars in which, prompted by the questions of his students, he sought to pass on the inspiration and wisdom of the Buddhist tradition. Each seminar was based around a different text, the seminars were recorded and transcribed, and in due course many of the transcriptions were edited and turned into books, all carefully checked by Sangharakshita. The commentaries compiled in this way constitute the fourth group. In some ways this is the heart of the collection. Sangharakshita often told the story of how it was that, reading two *sūtras* at the age of sixteen or seventeen, he realized that he was a Buddhist, and he has never tired of showing others how they too could see and realize the value of the '*sūtra*-treasure'.

5. MEMOIRS

Who is Sangharakshita? What sort of life did he live? Whom did he meet? What did he feel? Why did he found a new Buddhist movement? In these volumes of memoirs and letters Sangharakshita shares with his readers much about himself and his life as he himself has experienced it, giving us a sense of its breadth and depth, humour and pathos.

6. POETRY, APHORISMS, AND THE ARTS

Sangharakshita describes reading *Paradise Lost* at the age of twelve as one of the greatest poetic experiences of his life. His realization of the value of the higher arts to spiritual development is one of his distinctive contributions to our understanding of what Buddhist life is, and he has expressed it in a number of essays and articles. Throughout his life he has written poetry which he says can be regarded as a kind of spiritual autobiography. It is here, perhaps, that we come closest to the heart of Sangharakshita. He has also written a few short stories and composed some startling aphorisms. Through book reviews he has engaged with the experiences, ideas, and opinions of modern writers. All these are collected in this sixth group.

In the preface to *A Survey of Buddhism* (volume 1 in this collection), Sangharakshita wrote of his approach to the Buddha's teachings:

> Why did the Buddha (or Nāgārjuna, or Buddhaghosa) teach this particular doctrine? What bearing does it have on the spiritual life? How does it help the individual Buddhist actually to follow the spiritual path?... I found myself asking such questions again and again, for only in this way, I found, could I make sense – spiritual sense – of Buddhism.

Although this collection contains so many words, they are all intent, directly or indirectly, on these same questions. And all these words are not in the end about their writer, but about his great subject, the Buddha and his teaching, and about you, the reader, for whose benefit they are solely intended. These pages are full of the reverence that Sangharakshita has always felt, which is expressed in an early poem, 'Taking Refuge in the Buddha', whose refrain is 'My place is at thy feet'. He has devoted his life to communicating the Buddha's Dharma in its depth and in its breadth, to men and women from all backgrounds and walks of life, from all countries, of all races, of all ages. These collected works are the fruit of that devotion.

We are very pleased to be able to include some previously unpublished work in this collection, but most of what appears in these volumes has been published before. We have made very few changes, though we have added extra notes where we thought they would be useful. We have had the pleasure of researching the notes in the Sangharakshita Library at 'Adhisthana', Triratna's centre in Herefordshire, UK, which houses his own collection of books. It has been of great value to be able to search among the very copies of the *suttas*, *sūtras* and commentaries that have provided the basis of his teachings over the last seventy years.

The publication of these volumes owes much to the work of transcribers, editors, indexers, designers, and publishers over many years – those who brought out the original editions of many of the works included here, and those who have contributed in all sorts of ways to this *Complete Works* project, including all those who contributed to funds given in celebration of Sangharakshita's ninetieth birthday in August 2015, and to a further outpouring of generosity after Sangharakshita's death in October 2018. All these donors have made the publication of this series possible, and we are very grateful. Many thanks to everyone who has helped; may the merit gained in our acting thus go to the alleviation of the suffering of all beings.

Vidyadevi and Kalyanaprabha
Editors

THE COMPLETE WORKS OF SANGHARAKSHITA

WINDHORSE PUBLICATIONS

Windhorse Publications is a Buddhist charitable company based in the UK. We produce books of high quality that are accessible and relevant to all those interested in Buddhism, at whatever level of interest and commitment. We are the main publisher of Sangharakshita, the founder of the Triratna Buddhist Order and Community. Our books draw on the whole range of the Buddhist tradition, including translations of traditional texts, commentaries, books that make links with contemporary culture and ways of life, biographies of Buddhists, and works on meditation.

To subscribe to the *Complete Works of Sangharakshita,* please go to: windhorsepublications.com/sangharakshita-complete-works/

THE TRIRATNA BUDDHIST COMMUNITY

Windhorse Publications is a part of the Triratna Buddhist Community, an international movement with centres in Europe, India, North and South America and Australasia. At these centres, members of the Triratna Buddhist Order offer classes in meditation and Buddhism. Activities of the Triratna Community also include retreat centres, residential spiritual communities, ethical Right Livelihood businesses, and the Karuna Trust, a UK fundraising charity that supports social welfare projects in the slums and villages of India.

Through these and other activities, Triratna is developing a unique approach to Buddhism, not simply as a philosophy and a set of techniques, but as a creatively directed way of life for all people living in the conditions of the modern world.

For more information please visit thebuddhistcentre.com

SANGHARAKSHITA.ORG

You can find out more about Sangharakshita's life, teachings, and the Buddhist movement he founded on his official website: sangharakshita.org